The Faith of the Early Fathers

THE FAITH
of the
EARLY FATHERS

Volume Three

A source-book of theological and historical passages from the writings of Saint Augustine to the end of the Patristic Age

selected and translated

by

W. A. JURGENS

The Liturgical Press   *Collegeville, Minnesota*

Cover design by Janice St. Marie

Nihil obstat: Rev. Joseph C. Kremer, S.T.L., *Censor deputatus. Imprimatur*: ✝ George H. Speltz, D.D., Bishop of St. Cloud. January 25, 1979.

ISBN 0-8146-1021-8

Dedicated to the Memory

of

IGNATIUS EUGENE GOBLOWSKY

TABLE OF CONTENTS

FOREWORD

The first volume of *The Faith of the Early Fathers* appeared eight years ago. The excellent reception that it received is attested by the fact that it is about to be released again in its third edition. When volume one of the work, covering the patristic period up to about the end of the fourth century, was put to press in March 1970, I promised on its good reception to provide a second volume, which I supposed would suffice to cover the second half of the patristic age.

The pressure of other writing and translating has delayed the completion of the work, which at the same time has grown so that now not only a second but a third volume, the two to appear simultaneously, are necessary for the adequate treatment of the period.

Volume two covers the post-Nicene and Constantinopolitan eras, stopping short of St. Augustine. Besides a number of secondary lights its principal luminaries are the three Cappadocians (SS. Basil and the two Gregory's, of Nyssa and of Nazianz), St. John Chrysostom, St. Ambrose, and St. Jerome.

Volume three, which you have in hand, begins with St. Augustine and marches on through the rest of the patristic age, the end of which period is marked in the West by the death of St. Isidore of Seville († 636 A. D.) and in the East by the death of St. John Damascene († ca. 749 A. D.).

The format of volume three is precisely that of volumes one and two, which is explained at some length in the introduction to volume one. Each selection is numbered; and the numerical order of passages is the same as that established by M. J. Rouët de Journel in his *Enchiridion patristicum*. Passages not to be found in Rouët de Journel are given a number with an alphabetic postscript. The marginal numbers pertaining to each passage refer to the numbered theological propositions in the Doctrinal Index (pp. 359-386). With the numbered theological propositions in the Doctrinal Index are the reference numbers of all the passages which in some way pertain to the theological propositions. In this third volume the Scriptural, Doctrinal, and General Indices cover all three volumes. This is true also of volume two; and while the current third edition and earlier editions of volume one have their indices pertinent only to that one volume, it is already planned that when a fourth edition of volume one is required it too shall have the full indices covering all three volumes.

Properly used and with its mechanism understood *The Faith of the Early Fathers* will be of immense help to students, especially in their research and classroom papers and exercises in any area of theology and Christian antiquity. The seminarian and theological student who takes but a few minutes to understand the mechanics of the Doctrinal Index will benefit immeasurably thereby. Testimonials to the utility of the work have been received from all over the United States, from Africa, India, and Australia. Several priests have told me that they use *The Faith of the Early Fathers* to supplement the readings in their recitation of the Liturgy of the Hours. It is likewise a work much used by the laity in study clubs and for their private reading.

As with volume one and volume two, the source of the texts I translate in this volume three is regularly that which is currently regarded as the standard or best available edition. At the same time, however, and as a convenience, I refer also to the proper place in Migne's *Patrologiae cursus completus*.

In using *The Faith of the Early Fathers* in any of its three volumes it is important to remember that this is a work which presents a view of the faith in its formation and development. It is proper, therefore, that it includes the writings of heretics: and not every isolated statement in the texts presented is to be taken as a sound declaration of the Faith. Passages which contradict or seem to contradict the theological propositions of the Doctrinal Index are numbered there in parentheses.

Not the least of the lessons to be learned from a work of the present kind is how marvellously the Faith is a seamless robe. Cut it here, tear it there, excise a piece from it anywhere, and the whole of it unravels. It is not possible to deny any one dogma of the Faith without having ultimately to deny them all. If there is no original sin neither is there any redemption. If the Word did not become flesh, Scripture is not inspired and there was no death on the cross. If Christ be not Man, Mary is not the Mother of God. If God did not become Man, neither does man become God. If Christ be not God, we have been deceived and the Church is not infallible. *If Christ be not risen our faith is in vain and we are still in our sins.*

W. A. JURGENS

Cleveland, Ohio
October, 1978

INDEX OF SELECTIONS

TABLE OF ABBREVIATIONS

AND OF LATIN TERMS

A.D. = year or years [of the Lord].

ante = before.

apud = in, among, with.

aut = or [else].

ca. = circa = about.

Ch. = chapter.

Chs. = chapters.

CSEL = *Corpus scriptorum ecclesiasticorum latinorum*. Series of Latin texts of the Fathers, edited by the Wiener Akademie der Wissenschaften, 1866ff. Commonly called the *Vienna Corpus*.

CSCO = *Corpus scriptorum christianorum orientalium*. Series of the writings of the Fathers in the various oriental languages, each accompanied by a translation in a more commonly understood language. Publication began at Paris in 1903, and continues, now at Louvain. The corpus has seven sub-series: Syriac, Coptic, Arabic, Armenian, Georgian, and Ethiopic texts and translations; and *Subsidia*, embracing various monographs and linguistic treatises.

et postea = and afterwards.

fl. = *floruit* = flourished.

forte = perhaps.

GCS = *Die griechischen christlichen Schriftsteller der ersten [drei] Jahrhunderte*. Series of Greek texts of the Fathers, edited by the Preussische Akademie der Wissenschaften, 1897ff. Commonly called the *Berlin Corpus*.

inter = among, between

nisi forte = or maybe.

paulo post = soon after.

PG = Abbé J. P. Migne, *Patrologiae cursus completus: Series graeca*. 161 volumes, Paris, 1857–1866. Greek texts with Latin translation.

PL = Abbé J. P. Migne, *Patrologiae cursus completus: Series latina*. 221 volumes including 4 of indices, Paris, 1844–1855.

post = after.

postea = afterwards.

regn. = *regnavit* = reigned.

seu = or [also].

sive = or [also].

Vs. = verse.

VV. = verses.

The Faith of the Early Fathers

ST. AUGUSTINE OF HIPPO [*A. D.* 354–*A.D.* 430]

If we were faced with the unlikely proposition of having to destroy completely either the works of Augustine or the works of all the other Fathers and Writers, I have little doubt that all the others would have to be sacrificed. Augustine must remain. Of all the Fathers it is Augustine who is the most erudite, who has the most remarkable theological insights, and who is effectively the most prolific. If Origen or Didymus the Blind or some other Father or Writer wrote more than Augustine—a hypothesis by no means certain—it is now of little account, because their works have not survived.

Born at Tagaste in Numidia on Nov. 13, 354, Aurelius Augustinus was the son of a pagan father, Patrick, a civil official of Tagaste who embraced Christianity shortly before his death in 371, and the sainted Monica, daughter of a Christian family and herself a model of virtue.

In 371, at the age of seventeen, Augustine went to Carthage to pursue more advanced rhetorical studies. His pursuits there went somewhat beyond rhetoric and in 372 his son Adeodatus was born of a concubine.

Although he had been very early a catechumen Augustine's Baptism was postponed. In 374 he joined the Manichean sect, fleeing all the while from the Christ he could not escape. In 383 he finally met the Manichean teacher, Faustus of Milevis. His disillusionment at the ignorance of Faustus was complete, and he abandoned Manicheism.

Journeying to Italy in 383 he obtained a position as teacher of rhetoric in Milan. At Milan he was much impressed by the preaching of Ambrose. Marius Victorinus' Latin translations of various Neoplatonic writings were also a strong element in Augustine's gradual conversion. In the autumn of 386 he brought his mother Monica and his son Adeodatus to Cassiciacum near Milan, where he retired to prepare himself for Baptism, which he received in April of 387 at the hands of Ambrose. A few months later he set out again for Africa; and his mother, having had the joy of witnessing his long prayed for Baptism, died in the port city of Ostia.

For nearly three years Augustine lived a monastic life at Tagaste. It was during this time that Adeodatus died. In 391 Augustine was ordained to the priesthood by Bishop Valerius of Hippo. Shortly before his death in 395, Valerius, along with Megalius of Calama and Primas of Numidia, consecrated Augustine co-bishop of Hippo, to which see Augustine succeeded in full in that same year. If I do not err this is the first record of what might be termed a co-adjutor bishop with right of succession.

Augustine's writings are no less remarkable than his life. The surviving corpus of his letters is one of the most instructive known from antiquity; and the corpus of his sermons is the largest. His *Confessions*, the source of so much autobiographical information, is in a form quite unique in its time; and his *City of God*, which might be termed his major and typical writing, constitutes the earliest known theology of history. Again, his *Corrections* is perfectly unique, being a work written towards the end of his life, in which he pronounces judgment, generally quite severe, on the effectiveness individually of all his previous writings.

Of all the Fathers, none wrote so well or so much as Augustine; and in modern times none other has been so much written about. He was unique in his time, and none like him has since been seen.

LETTERS

The Maurist edition of Augustine's letters contains 270 numbered items, of which 53 are addressed to Augustine; and in addition, one other item (now listed as No. 171A) which the Maurists found too late for inclusion in its proper place. When Migne

reprinted the work of the Maurists he added two more letters (184A and 202A) which had been first published in the eighteenth century by the Abbot Gottfried Bessel. In preparing the Vienna Corpus edition Alois Goldbacher added Nos. 92A, 173A, and 185A. Germain Morin and Cyril Lambot have discovered a few more since Goldbacher's work was completed, so that the entire corpus of Augustine's correspondence now numbers 279 items.

Letter 211, addressed to certain religious women who were experiencing difficulties in their way of life, is commonly called the *Rule* of St. Augustine. While not to be regarded in itself as a religious rule, it has frequently been adapted and added to so as to constitute such.

The standard text of Augustine's letters superseding the Maurist editions and Migne is that of Alois Goldbacher in the Vienna Corpus, Vols. 34, 1 (1895—nos. 1-30); 34, 2 (1898—nos. 31-123); 44 (1904—nos. 124-184A); 57 (1911—nos. 185-270); 58 (1923—prefaces and indices).

LETTER OF AUGUSTINE TO JEROME. A. D. 394 *aut* 395.

1417

[28, 3, 3]

In reading certain writings attributed to you on the Epistles of the Apostle   25
Paul, wherein you were attempting to explain some difficulties in Galatians, I
came upon that passage where the Apostle Peter is saved from a dangerous
dissimulation. I must admit that I regretted very much that a lie should
be defended by a man such as yourself, or by someone else if the writing is not
really yours; and I must continue in this frame of mind until it is refuted—if
what disturbs me is capable of refutation. I think it is dangerous to believe
that anything in the Sacred Books is a lie (1). . . . For if we once admit in that
supreme monument of authority even one polite lie (2), no shred of those
books will remain. Whenever anyone finds anything therein that is difficult to
practice or hard to believe, he will refer to this most pernicious precedent
and explain it as the idea or practice of a lying author.

LETTER OF AUGUSTINE TO GENEROSUS. *ca. A. D.* 400.

1418

[53, 1, 2]

If the very order of episcopal succession is to be considered, how much more   432
surely, truly, and safely do we number them from Peter himself, to whom,
as to one representing the whole Church, the Lord said: "Upon this rock I will
build My Church, and the gates of hell shall not conquer it (3)." Peter was
succeeded by Linus, Linus by Clement, Clement by Anacletus, Anacletus by
Evaristus, Evaristus by Sixtus, Sixtus by Telesphorus, Telesphorus by
Hyginus, Hyginus by Anicetus, Anicetus by Pius, Pius by Soter, Soter by
Alexander, Alexander by Victor, Victor by Zephyrinus, Zephyrinus by
Callistus, Callistus by Urban, Urban by Pontianus, Pontianus by Anterus, Anterus
by Fabian, Fabian by Cornelius, Cornelius by Lucius, Lucius by Stephen,
Stephen by Sixtus, Sixtus by Dionysius, Dionysius by Felix, Felix by
Eutychian, Eutychian by Caius, Caius by Marcellus, Marcellus by Eusebius,
Eusebius by Melchiades, Melchiades by Sylvester, Sylvester by Mark, Mark by
Julius, Julius by Liberius, Liberius by Damasus, Damasus by Siricius,
Siricius by Anastasius. In this order of succession not a Donatist bishop is to be
found.

LETTER OF AUGUSTINE TO JANUARIUS (4). *ca A. D.* 400.

1419

[54, 1, 1]

   In the first place I want you to hold as basic to this discussion that our Lord   801
Jesus Christ, as He Himself said in the Gospel, subjected us to His yoke and
to His burden, which are light (5). He has, therefore, obliged the society
of His new people to the Sacraments, very few in number, very easy of
observance, and most sublime in meaning. Such, for example, is Baptism,   808
consecrated in the name of the Trinity; the Communion of His Body and
Blood (6); and whatever else is commended in the canonical Scriptures, except   794
those things which are read in the five books of Moses, which imposed on the old
people (7) a servitude in accord with their hearts and the prophetic times in
which they lived. But in regard to those observances which we carefully   100
attend and which the whole world keeps, and which derive not from
Scripture but from Tradition, we are given to understand that they are
recommended and ordained to be kept, either by the Apostles themselves or by   452
plenary councils, the authority of which is quite vital in the Church (8).

1419a

[54, 1, 3]

   When my mother, who had followed me to Milan, found that the Church   899
there did not fast on Saturday she began to be anxious and was uncertain
what she ought to do. At that time such things meant nothing to me, but for her
sake I consulted on this matter with Ambrose, that man of most blessed
memory. He replied that he could teach me nothing but what he did himself
since, if he knew anything better, he would be doing it. When I supposed that
he wanted to impose his views on us solely by his own authority and
without giving any reason for them, he continued and said to me: "When I am
in Rome, I fast on Saturday; but here I do not. If you do not want to scandalize
or be scandalized, follow the custom of whatever church you attend."
When I told this to my mother she was glad to accept it. I recall this advice again
and again and always esteem it as something given by a heavenly oracle.
I am often grieved and dismayed that the weak are so much disturbed by the
obstinate aggressiveness or superstitious fears of certain of the brethren who
stir up controversial questions and will accept nothing as proper except that
which is their own custom. These are things of a kind that are not prescribed   100
by the authority of Scripture nor by the Tradition of the universal Church, and   101
they serve no good purpose for the amending of one's life, but are insisted
upon simply because someone thinks up a reason for them or because
someone was accustomed to such in his own country or because on a
pilgrimage somewhere he saw them done and thought they must be more
correct because they were quite unlike his own customs.

1420

[54, 5, 7]

   It is crystal clear (9) that when the disciples first received the Body and Blood   876
of the Lord they were not fasting. [6, 8] On this score, then, is the whole
Church to be calumniated because she always receives fasting?

LETTER OF AUGUSTINE TO JEROME. paulo post A. D. 405.

1421

[82, 1, 3]

I have learned to hold those books alone of the Scriptures that are now   25
called canonical in such reverence and honor that I do most firmly believe that
none of their authors has erred in anything that he has written therein. If
I find anything in those writings which seems to be contrary to the truth, I   27
presume that either the codex is inaccurate, or the translator has not followed   28
what was said, or I have not properly understood it. . . . I think that you,
dear brother, must feel the same way. And I say, moreover, that I do not
think you would want your books to be read as if they were the books of
Prophets or Apostles, about whose writings, free of all error, it is not lawful
to doubt. Let us not even think such a thing, in view of your great humility and
your true opinion of yourself.

LETTER OF AUGUSTINE TO VINCENT THE ROGATIST (10). *ca. A. D. 408.*

1422

[93, 7, 23]

You seem to be saying something very perceptive when you derive the   421
name Catholic not from the communion of the whole world but from the
observance of all the divine precepts and of all the Sacraments, as if we relied
on the meaning of the name and not on the promises of God and on so
many and such clear pronouncements of truth itself to prove that the Church
is found among all nations. Yet it is a fact that the Church is called Catholic
because it truly embraces the whole of that truth, some particles of which
may be found even in various heresies.

LETTER OF AUGUSTINE TO BONIFACE, A BISHOP. A. D. 408.

1423

[98, 2]

It is this one Spirit who makes it possible for an infant to be regenerated   800
through the agency of another's will when that infant is brought to Baptism
(11); and it is through this one Spirit that the infant so presented is reborn. For
it is not written: "Unless a man be born again by the will of his parents"
or "by the faith of those presenting him or ministering to him", but: "Unless a   790
man be born again of water and the Holy Spirit (12)." The water, therefore,
manifesting exteriorly the sacrament of grace, and the Spirit effecting
interiorly the benefit of grace, both regenerate in one Christ that man who was
generated in one Adam.

1424

[98, 9]

Was not Christ immolated only once in His very Person? In the Sacrament,   895
nevertheless, He is immolated for the people not only on every Easter   890
Solemnity but on every day; and a man would not be lying if, when asked,
he were to reply that Christ is being immolated. For if Sacraments had not a   790
likeness to those things of which they are Sacraments, they would not be

Sacraments at all; and they generally take the names of those same things by   853
reason of this likeness. Just as the Sacrament of the Body of Christ, therefore,
is in a certain way the Body of Christ, and the Sacrament of the Blood of Christ
is the Blood of Christ, so too the Sacrament of faith is faith (13). To believe,
however, is nothing other than to have faith. That is why [at Baptism]   541
response is made that the little one believes, though he has as yet no awareness
of faith. Answer is made that he has faith because of the Sacrament of faith.

1425

[98, 10]
   Although the little one has not yet that faith which resides in the will of   541
believers, the Sacrament of that same faith already makes him one of the   542
faithful. For since response is made that they believe, they are called faithful,
not by any assent of the mind to the thing itself but by their receiving the
Sacrament of the thing itself.

LETTER OF AUGUSTINE TO DEOGRATIAS (14). *A. D.* 408 *aut* 409.

1426

[102, 12]
   From the beginning of the human race, therefore, whoever believed in   389
[Christ] and knew Him and lived justly and piously in accord with His
commands,—whenever and wherever they lived, undoubtedly they were
saved through Him.

1427

[102, 14]
   What will the pagans answer, if, apart from the depth of the wisdom and   204
knowledge of God, wherein, perhaps, some other divine purpose has long   704
lain hidden, and without prejudice even to other possible causes which
can be investigated by prudent men, in the discussion of this question, for the
sake of brevity, we say only this to them: that Christ willed to appear among
men and to preach His doctrine among them at a time and in a place when and
where He knew there would be those who would believe in Him (15)?

1428

[102, 15]
   Yet, from the beginning of the human race, sometimes obscurely and   204
sometimes openly,—whatever, as it seemed to His providence, was suited to
the times,—He never ceased to prophesy. Before He appeared in the flesh
there were men who believed in Him, from Adam to Moses, among the people
of Israel, by divine ordinance the prophetic race, and among other peoples
also. In the sacred books of the Hebrews there is mention of many from
the time of Abraham who were not of Abraham's stock nor of the Israelite
nation and who were not joined by any kind of alliance to the people of
Israel but who were participants in His worship. Why, then, should we not
believe that betimes there were other men, here and there among other
peoples, who worshipped Him, even if we find no mention of them in those
same sacred books? The salvation which belongs to this religion, the only   400

true religion through which alone true salvation is truthfully promised, was   416
never wanting to anyone who was worthy of it; and anyone to whom it was   417
wanting was not worthy of it (16). From the beginning of human propagation
to the end He is preached to the reward of some and to the judgment of
others.

LETTER OF AUGUSTINE TO CONSENTIUS. ca. A. D. 410.

1429

[120, 1, 3]

Far be it from God to hate in us that faculty by which He made us so much   552
more excellent than the other living creatures. Far be it, I say, that we should so   561
believe that we would neither accept nor seek a reason for our belief; for
if we had not rational souls we could not believe at all. In some points,   562
then, that pertain to the salvific doctrine, which we can not yet grasp by reason,
—though someday we shall,—let reason be preceded by faith, which
cleanses the heart, so that the heart may receive and retain the light of great
reason; and this too is reasonable. Therefore it is reasonable for the Prophet to
say: "Unless you believe you shall not understand (17)." In this passage   563
the Prophet undoubtedly made a distinction between believing and
understanding and advised us to believe first so that we might afterwards
understand what we believe. Hence it is reasonably demanded that faith
precede reason.

LETTER OF AUGUSTINE TO VOLUSIAN. A. D. 412.

1430

[137, 2, 8]

The very greatness of His power, which feels no narrowness in narrow   781
places, made the Virgin's womb fertile not from without but by an intrinsic   782
childbirth (18). That power took to itself a rational soul and with it also a human   312
body, and chose to better the lot of all mankind without being impaired in any
way itself, deigning to take the name of humanity from man while granting
to man a share in divinity. That same power which afterwards brought
the body of the young man through closed doors (19), brought the body of the
infant forth from the inviolate virginal womb of the Mother. If you seek out   320
the reason for this it will no longer be marvelous. If you demand a comparable
example it will no longer be unique. Let us grant that God can do something
which, we confess, we cannot fathom. In such matters the whole explanation
of what is done is to be found in the power of the one doing it.

1431

[137, 3, 11]

There are some who demand an explanation of how God is mingled with   320
man so as to become the one person of Christ, when this is a perfectly unique   324
occurrence. As if they themselves could explain something that happens
every day, how the soul is mingled with the body so as to form the one person
of a man! Just as the soul employs the body in the unity of a person to form
a man, so too God makes use of man in the unity of a person to form Christ.

LETTER OF AUGUSTINE TO MARCELLINUS THE TRIBUNE AND LEGATE. A. D. 412.

1432

[138, 1, 6]

God had no need of those [Old Testament] sacrifices, nor does He ever need   790
any. Rather, they are signs of divinely bestowed favor, intended either to
endow the mind with virtues or to assist in the attaining of eternal salvation.
The purpose of their celebration is the exercise of devotion useful not to
God but to us. [7] It would take too long to discuss adequately the variety of
signs which, when they pertain to divine things, are called Sacraments.

LETTER OF AUGUSTINE TO THE CATECHUMEN HONORATUS (20). A. D. 412

1433

[140, 3, 9]

This is the grace of the New Testament, which lay hidden in the Old, though   740
there was no end of its being prophesied and foretold in veiled figures so that   755
the soul might recognize its God and, by God's grace, be reborn to Him.
This is truly a spiritual birth, and therefore it is not of blood nor of the will of
man nor of the will of the flesh, but of God (21). [4, 10] This is called adoption.
For we were something before we became sons of God, and we received
a benefit by which we became what we were not. One who is adopted is not
yet, before he is adopted, the son of him by whom he is adopted; nevertheless,
he is at that prior time one who can be adopted. And from this begetting   340
by grace we distinguish that Son, who, when He was Son of God, came
that He might become the son of man; and He thereby enabled us, who
were sons of man, to become sons of God (22).

LETTER OF AUGUSTINE TO MACEDONIUS THE IMPERIAL VICAR OF AFRICA. ca. A. D. 413.

1434

[153, 3, 6]

After they have been released from your severe sentence we separate from   904
association at the altar those whose crimes are public, so that by repenting   923
and by punishing themselves they may be able to placate Him for whom, by
their sinning, they showed their contempt (23).

1435

[153, 3, 7]

Iniquity, however, sometimes makes such progress in men that even after   904
they have done penance and after their reconciliation to the altar they   906
commit the same or more grievous sins; and still God makes His sun to rise
even on such men and bestows His most lavish gifts of life and health on
them no less than He did before. And although that place of penance in the   907
Church (24) is not granted them, God will not be unmindful of His patience in
their regard. . . . If, therefore, it be a careful and salubrious provision
that the place of that most humble penance in the Church is granted only once,
lest that medicine, by becoming too common should thereby become less

useful to the sick, which now is the more healthful as it is the more respected,—
who, on that account, would dare to say to God: "Why do You pardon this
man a second time when after his first penance he is caught again in the
snares of his iniquities?"

LETTER OF AUGUSTINE TO THE SICILIAN LAYMAN HILARY. A. D. 414.

1436

[157, 2, 10]
   Neither is freedom of will taken away because help is given. Rather, help is   700
given because freedom is not taken away. Anyone who says to God: "Be my
help (25)," admits that he wants to do what God commands; and such a
one asks the assistance of Him who commands, so that he may be able to do
what is commanded.

1436a

[157, 4, 31]
   Among those things which He commanded them to leave, even a wife is   975
mentioned; yet human law does not allow a wife to be sold, nor does the law of   976
Christ allow her to be dismissed except for fornication (26). What then do
these precepts mean—they cannot be contradictory—except that an
emergency may sometimes arise when either a wife or Christ has to be
dismissed, such as would be the case—passing over other instances—when a
Christian husband has become unacceptable to a wife and she gives him the
choice of separation from her or from Christ? . . . When either one of the
pair is an unbeliever the advice of the Apostle is our guide: . . . (27).
If the unbeliever refuses to remain with a believing spouse, let the believer
recognize that he is free; let him not regard himself as in servitude so as to give
up even the faith rather than to lose an unbelieving spouse.

LETTER OF AUGUSTINE TO JEROME (28). A. D. 415.

1438

[166, 2, 4]
   Although it is difficult to convince those who are slow of understanding   501
that the soul is incorporeal, I profess that I am convinced of it. . . . The soul
extends through the whole body which it animates, not by spatial diffusion
but by a certain vital impetus. It is wholly present through every part of
the body, not less in smaller parts and more in larger parts, but in some places
more conscious and in other places less attentive, while wholly in all parts and
wholly in each part.

1439

[166, 7, 21]
   Anyone who would say that even infants who pass from this life without   831
participation in the Sacrament [of Baptism] shall be made alive in Christ   835
truly goes counter to the preaching of the Apostle and condemns the whole
Church, where there is great haste in baptizing infants because it is believed
without doubt that there is no other way at all in which they can be made alive
in Christ.

1440

[166, 8, 23]

The Blessed Cyprian (29) was not issuing some new decree but was keeping to the   835
most solid belief of the Church in order to correct some who thought that infants
ought not be baptized before the eighth day after their birth, when he said that it was
not the flesh but the soul that was [in danger of] being lost; and he agreed with
certain of his fellow bishops that a child is able to be duly baptized as soon as he is
born (30).

1441

[166, 8, 24]

Let each one think what he likes contrary to any of Cyprian's opinions but let no   618
one hold any opinion contrary to the manifest belief of the Apostle. . . . [25]   506
A reason must be sought and given why souls, if they are newly created for each
one being born, are damned if the infants die without Christ's Sacrament (31). That
they are damned if they so depart the body is the testimony both of Holy Scripture
and of Holy Church.

LETTER OF AUGUSTINE TO JEROME (32). *A. D.* 415.

1442

[167, 2, 4]

The Stoics alone dared to argue the equality of all sins, against every experience   634
of the human race. In following that opinion of theirs Jovinian showed himself a Stoic,
though he was an Epicurean in grasping after and defending pleasures. You
refuted him brilliantly from the Holy Scriptures (33).

LETTER OF AUGUSTINE AND COLLEAGUES TO INNOCENT OF ROME.
A. D. 416.

1443

[177, 7]

Let [Pelagius] openly profess that grace which Christian doctrine proves and   726
preaches as the property of Christians, which is not nature but that by which nature
is saved and assisted, not by a teaching resounding in the ears or by some visible   682
assistance, as if it were somehow planted and irrigated from without, but by the
interior ministering of the Spirit and by His hidden mercy, as God, who gives the
increase (34), is accustomed to act. If by some faulty reasoning that by which we are   680
created is called the grace of God, so that our being something, and that something not
merely like a cadaver which is not alive, nor a tree which has no consciousness, nor
a beast which has no understanding, but men, so that we exist and have life and
awareness and understanding, and are able to give thanks to our Creator for this
great favor—if this might rightly be called grace in the sense that it is not granted   711
on account of the merits of any previous actions, but is given gratuitously by
the goodness of God, then there is still another grace by which, predestined, we are   204
called, justified, and glorified.

LETTER OF AUGUSTINE TO BONIFACE, VICAR OF AFRICA (35). *ca. A. D.* 417.

1444

[185, 11, 49]
  When He said: "Whoever sins against the Holy Spirit and whoever says a word   903
against the Holy Spirit (36)", He did not mean for every sin against the Holy
Spirit in word or in deed to be understood, but some certain and particular sin. And this
sin is hardness of heart persisted in to the end of this life. by which a man refuses to
accept the remission of sins in the unity of the body of Christ, that body which is
vivified by the Holy Spirit.

LETTER OF AUGUSTINE TO PAULINUS OF NOLA. A. D. 417.

1445

[186, 3, 7]
  If anyone says that faith merits the grace of doing good works, we cannot deny it;   758
rather we admit it most readily. This is the faith we wish they might have, the faith by   568
which they might obtain that love which alone truly does good works, those   592
brothers of ours who glory so much in their works! Love, however, is so much the
gift of God that it is called God (37).

1446

[186, 3, 10]
  Let no one say to himself: "If [justification] is from faith, how is it freely given (38):   758
If faith merits it, why is it not rather paid than given?" Let the faithful man not   773
say such a thing; for, if he says: "I have faith, therefore I merit justification," he
will be answered: "What have you that you did not receive (39)?" If, therefore, faith
entreats and receives justification, according as God has apportioned to each in the
measure of his faith (40), nothing of human merit precedes the grace of God, but
grace itself merits increase, and the increase merits perfection, with the will accompanying   772
but not leading, following along but not going in advance.

LETTER OF AUGUSTINE TO OPTATUS OF MAURETANIA TINGITANA. A. D. 418.

1447

[190, 3, 9]
  With a brevity that is the more concise as his authority is the greater, the Blessed   204
Apostle tells why even those are created whom the Creator knows will belong not to   208
grace but to damnation. . . . Yet it would seem unjust that vessels of wrath be made
for perdition (41), if the whole of creation had not, from Adam, been condemned
in aggregate (42). That they become in birth vessels of wrath is due to a penalty
deserved; but that in a rebirth they become vessels of mercy is due to grace
undeserved.

1448

[190, 4, 14]
  Those who assert that souls are propagated from the one that God gave the   501
first man, and say that they derive from parents,—if they follow the opinion of   508

Tertullian (43), they certainly maintain that souls are not spirits but bodies, and
that they take their origins from corporeal seed. What more perverted a notion could be
expressed? But it is not surprising that Tertullian could dream up such an idea, since he
even thought that God the Creator could not exist except as a body (44).

LETTER OF AUGUSTINE TO SIXTUS (45). A. D. 418.

1449

[194, 3, 6]

What merits of his own has the saved to boast of when, if he were dealt with   773
according to his merits, he would be nothing if not damned? Have the just then   770
no merits at all? Of course they do, for they are the just. But they had no merits by   776
which they were made just.

1450

[194, 3, 9]

Certainly they can say that forgiveness of sins is a grace which is given with no   656
antecedent merits. For what good merits can sinners have? Yet even the very remission   653
of sins is not without some merit, if faith asks and obtains it. For there is some   758
merit even in faith, the faith by which that man said: "Lord, be merciful to me,
a sinner (46)''; and he went down justified by the merit of humble faith, because he
that humbles himself shall be exalted (47). It remains, then, that faith itself, from   568
which all justice takes its beginnings, ... is to be attributed not to the human free 728
will which those men extol, nor to any antecedent merits, since whatever good merits
there are begin in faith, which we acknowledge as a gratuitous gift of God.

1451

[194, 4, 16]

If we say that prayer is antecedent to merit, productive of it so that grace may   711
follow,—well, it is true that prayer, by asking and obtaining, clearly shows that
whatever it does ask and obtain is a gift of God; for a man would not ask for
something if he thought that having it was already within his own power. Lest we
should think that the merits of prayer are antecedent [to grace],—in which event
grace were not gratuitously given and would not be grace at all since it were
given as something owed to us,—even prayer itself is counted among the gifts of
grace.

1452

[194, 5, 19]

What merit, then, does a man have before grace, by which he might receive   711
grace, when our every good merit is produced in us only by grace, and, when   770
God, crowning our merits, crowns nothing else but His own gifts to us?

1453

[194, 5, 20]

After he had said: "The wages of sin is death (48)'', who would not have   771
agreed that it would have been most consistent and logical for him to have added:

"And the wages of justice is eternal life"? And it is true; because just as death is paid out as the wages deserved by sin, so too eternal life is the wage deserved by justice.

1454

[194, 6, 27]

Every sinner is inexcusable, be he a sinner by original guilt (49) or by an additional guilt of his own will, whether he knows or not, whether he judges or not; for ignorance itself in those who do not want to know is without doubt a sin, and in those who are unable to know it is the penalty of sin. In neither case, then, is there a just excuse; but in both cases there is just condemnation. 636

LETTER OF AUGUSTINE TO VALENTINE (50). A. D. 427.

1455

[215, 4]

As strongly as we could we urged them, your brothers and ours, to persevere in the sound Catholic faith, which neither denies free will, whether to pursue a wicked life or a good one; nor attributes to it such efficacy that it can do anything at all without God's grace, whether to be converted from evil to good, or to persevere and advance in good, or to attain the eternal good, where there is no longer any fear of falling away. 650

LETTER OF AUGUSTINE TO VITALIS, LAYMAN OF CARTHAGE. ca. A. D. 427.

1456

[217, 5, 16]

Since by Christ's favor we are Catholic Christians: 507

1. We know that children not yet born have done nothing good or evil in their own life, nor have they any merits from some prior life, which no individuals can have as their own, until they come into the miseries of this life; that, being born carnally 615 according to Adam, at birth they first contract the contagion of that ancient death; nor are they freed from the penalty of eternal death, which just condemnation 618 derives from one and is passed on to all, unless through grace they be reborn in Christ.

2. We know that the grace of God is given neither to children nor to adults 711 according to our merits.

3. We know that in adults it is given for individual acts. 650

4. We know it is not given to all men, and, in the case of those to whom it is given, not only is it not given in accord with the merits of good works, not even is it given in accord with the merits of the will of those to whom it is given,—which is obvious in the case of infants.

5. We know that God's mercy is gratuitously given to those to whom it is given at all.

6. We know that it is by a just judgment that it is not given to those to whom it is not 720 given at all.

7. We know that we shall all stand before the tribunal of Christ, so that each may 1020 receive in accord with those things he did in the body, whether good or evil (51), and not according to what he might have done had he lived longer.

8. We know that even infants will receive either good or evil according to what

they did in the body. They did these things, however, not of themselves, but
through those by whose answering for them they too are said to renounce the
devil and to believe in God. . . . They are judged according to what they have done
in the body, . . . when they believed or did not believe through the mouths and
hearts of those who carried them, when they were baptized or were not baptized,
when they ate the flesh of Christ or did not eat it, when they drank His Blood or
did not drink it—it is according to these things which they did in the body that they
are judged, and not according to what they might have done had they lived longer
in this world.

9. We know that the dead who die in the Lord are happy (52), and what they
might have done had they lived a longer time is of no concern to them.

10. We know that those who in their own heart believe in the Lord do this of their
own will and free choice.

11. We know that we, who already believe, act in upright faith when we pray for   713
those who do not want to believe, that they may will to believe.

12. We know that when some of these believe, we ought to give thanks uprightly
and sincerely to God, as we are accustomed to do, on their behalf, as for benefits
received.

1457

[217, 6, 19]

Just as that saying: "all shall be made alive in Christ (53)", when so many are   201
punished with eternal death, means that of all those who receive eternal life, none
receive it except in Christ, so too the saying: "God wills that all men be saved (54)",
when there are so many whom He does not will to be saved, means that of all
those who are saved, none would be saved unless He willed it; and if there be any
other way in which to understand these words of the Apostle, it cannot contradict
the very evident truth by which we see that so many men are not saved because
God does not will it, even if men do.

1458

[217, 6, 25]

It is clear from those twelve statements (55) which, you cannot deny, belong   692
to the Catholic faith, that, taken not only all together but even individually, their   684
effect is to make plain that we confess that the willing actions of men are preceded
by the grace of God, and these actions are prepared by grace rather than being
productive of merits in view of which grace were given.   711

LETTER OF AUGUSTINE TO PASCENTIUS, THE ARIAN TAX-COLLECTOR. ca. A. D. (?)

1459

[238, 2, 14]

It is our faith to believe and profess that the Father and the Son and the Holy   281
Spirit are one God; but we do not call Him Father who is the Son, nor do we call   270
Him Son who is the Father, nor do we designate Him either Father or Son who
is the Spirit of the Father and of the Son. For by these appellations that is signified
by which they are related one to another, and not their substance itself, which is one.

1460

[238, 2, 24]

   If the Son of God has been born of the Father, the Father has now ceased to   256
beget; and if He has ceased, He began. If, however, He began to beget, there
was a time when He was without the Son. But He was never without the Son, because   261
His Son is His Wisdom, which is the brightness (56) of eternal light. Therefore
the Father is always begetting and the Son is always being born.

1. Augustine is taking issue with Jerome over the latter's *Commentaries on the Epistle to the Galatians* 2:11-14, wherein Jerome defends the Apostle Peter's dissimulation, and says that Paul saw that Peter had acted rightly, but said that he had not acted rightly, in order to appease those who objected. The present letter went astray and did not reach Jerome until long after it had been given public circulation in Africa, word of it reaching Jerome first through rumor. Jerome was rather angry about it and Augustine had to soothe the lion's temper in later letters. See Augustine's letters nos. 40 and 82 to Jerome, treating of the same problem as the present letter no. 28.
2. *officioso aliquo mendacio*.
3. Matt. 16:18. Augustine's reading is: *et portae inferorum non vincent eam*.
4. In his *Corrections* 2, 46 Augustine reckons letters 54 and 55 as "two books entitled *Answer to the Inquiries of Januarius*." He says of these two books that they contain many disputed points about the sacraments.
5. See Matt. 11:30.
6. *communicatio corporis et sanguinis ipsius*.
7. *populi veteris*, as opposed to *novi populi* mentioned immediately above.
8. *vel ab ipsis apostolis vel plenariis conciliis quorum est in ecclesia saluberrima auctoritas*.
9. *Liquido apparet*.
10. The Rogatists were a Donatist sect in Mauretania of no great consequence, followers of Rogatus of Cartenna, to whose see and schism Vincent succeeded.
11. *cum offertur consecrandus*. We have specified "infant" though the Latin simply presents the subject through the verb endings of *possit* and *offertur*. It is clear that an infant is meant, however, for the discussion has been about the effectiveness of the parents' will in respect to one who has no awareness of what is being done.
12. John 3:5.
13. *Sicut ergo secundum quemdam modum sacramentum corporis Christi corpus Christi est, sacramentum sanguinis Christi sanguis Christi est, ita sacramentum fidei fides est*.
14. Augustine mentions the present letter in his *Corrections* 2, 57, referring to it as "a rather short book in explanation of six questions raised by the pagans."
15. See also § 1985 below.
16. In his *Corrections* 2, 57 Augustine calls attention to this passage and, as if to guard against a Pelagian interpretation, says: "I did not mean this as if anyone were worthy according to his own merits." See also § 1986 below.
17. Is. 7:9 in the Septuagint reading.
18. *uterum virginalem non adventitio sed indigena puerperio fecundavit*.
19. John 20:19, 26.
20. The present letter is treated in the *Corrections* 2, 62, where Augustine calls it "one book to Honoratus, on Grace in the New Testament."
21. See John 1:13.
22. See John 1:12.
23. *Quosdam, quorum crimina manifesta sunt, a vestra severitate liberatos a societate tamen removemus altaris, ut paenitendo placare possint quem peccando contempserant, seque ipsos puniendo*.
24. *in ecclesia locus ille paenitentiae*. It is my impression that the term *locus paenitentiae* and its Greek equivalent is of such frequent occurrence in Christian writings of the earliest centuries that we can scarcely doubt that it is a *terminus technicus*. Its precise origins and implications are yet to be investigated, but I suspect that *locus* hides a great deal more than is revealed by the usual contextual translation *opportunity*.
25. Ps. 26[27]:9.
26. Matt. 5:32.
27. In the portion omitted Augustine quotes 1 Cor. 7:15.
28. Letters 166 and 167 are books sent to Jerome at Bethlehem. As books they are treated in Augustine's *Corrections* 2, 71, where they are listed as "Two Books to the Priest Jerome: One on the Origin of the Soul and the Other on a Passage from James."
29. See §§ 585 and 586 above in volume 1.
30. *et mox natum rite baptizari posse*. Sister Wilfred Parsons in her excellent five volume translation of Augustine's Letters in the *Fathers of the Church* series renders *rite* as *validly*, which, I suspect, is an anachronism. I think that it means simply *in the usual way*, or *in the ordinary course of events*, that is, *duly*. But the notion of *validly* cannot be dismissed entirely and the idea is certainly at least in the process of formation.
31. The state of infants who die without Baptism has long been one of the knottier problems of theology. If there were not a constant tradition in the Fathers that the Gospel message of "unless a man be born again *et reliqua*" is to be taken absolutely, it would be easy to say that Our Savior simply did not see fit to mention the obvious exceptions of

invincible ignorance and physical impossibility. But the tradition in fact is there; and it is likely enough to be found so constant as to constitute revelation. The Church has always admitted Baptism of desire as a rescuing factor, when the desire is a personal and conscious one on the part of the one desiring Baptism for himself, as in the case of a catechumen.

Some loose thinkers are content to apply Baptism of desire to an infant, who is incapable of knowing and desiring. That being pointed out, they will posit the desire in parents on behalf of children; but if in fact the parents do not desire or if they positively reject Baptism for their infant child, is the infant then to be damned because of the parents' ignorance or malice? Many today are content to ignore the problem as if it did not exist, or to treat it as a ridiculous scruple. We hear them quote the Scriptures, that God desires all men to be saved, as if that had any application here! Let us turn back to the notion of Baptism of desire, and I think we will find a solution apart from the generous but questionable notion of limbo, without condemning these infants outright as Augustine reluctantly does, and without doing violence either to Scripture or Tradition.

Saint Thomas notes that the Eucharist is absolutely necessary for salvation. If a man has never received the Eucharist, he cannot be saved. But Thomas then adds these distinctions: that if one is dying and has never received the Eucharist, his positive desire for it will suffice (the precise parallel of Baptism of desire); or in the case of infants or ignorant savages the desire on their behalf on the part of the Church herself will suffice. If this latter is true in regard to the Eucharist, why not in regard to Baptism? Tradition already admits Thomas' first Eucharistic distinction in regard also to Baptism: a desire on the part of the individual himself. Why not, then, his second distinction in regard to infants and the invincibly ignorant, a desire supplied by the desire of the Church herself? This obviates the necessary objection to a desire supplied by parents: they may not have such a desire. The Church always desires the welfare of mankind and it is impossible that she should not desire it.

32. See note 28 above.
33. The reference is to Jerome's *Adversus Iovinianum*, especially at 2, 21-34.
34. 1 Cor. 3:7.
35. In the *Corrections* 2, 74 the present letter is referred to as "One Book on the Correction of the Donatists."
36. Matt. 12:32.
37. See 1 John 4:8.
38. See Rom. 5:1 and 3:24.
39. 1 Cor. 4:7.
40. Rom. 12:3.
41. See Rom. 9:22.
42. *si non esset ipsa universa ex Adam massa damnata*.
43. See §§ 346, 349 and 355 above. There are other similar places in Tertullian.
44. See § 374 above. Augustine's quarrel with Tertullian on this point is largely a difficulty of terminology. The word body did not mean the same thing to Tertullian that it did to Augustine: and Tertullian defines that which exists as corporeal, that which is incorporeal being non-existent (§ 355 above).
45. Afterwards Pope Sixtus III (432-440 A. D.).
46. Luke 18:13.
47. Luke 18:14.
48. Rom. 6:23.
49. *reatu originis*: literally, *by guilt of origin*.
50. Valentine was the Abbot, or if that be an anachronism, the acknowledged leader of a community of monks at Hadrumetum. See also the introductory remarks on Augustine's *Grace and Free Choice*, pp. 154-155 below.
51. See Rom. 14:10 and 2 Cor. 5:10.
52. *felices*. The Apocalypse passage which the statement reflects (14:13) uses the term *beati*.
53. 1 Cor. 15:22.
54. 1 Tim. 2:4.
55. See § 1456 above.
56. *candor*.

EXPLANATIONS OF THE PSALMS [*inter A. D.* 392-418]

Augustine's *Enarrationes in psalmos* is a collection of sermons, some intended for reading, but most intended for preaching, the writing of which occupied Augustine's attention periodically throughout the larger part of his career, from the year 392 *A. D.* until the year 418 *A. D.* S. Zarb's assignment of dates to the writing of each section of the work is reprinted in Vol. 38 of the *Corpus Christianorum*, pp. xv-xviii.

Capelle, in his *Le texte du Psautier latin en Afrique (Collectanea Biblica Latina 4)*, Rome 1913, pp. 83-169, has shown that the version of the Psalms on which Augustine based his explanations was not of Italic but of African origin.

The *Enarrationes* is truly a work of monumental erudition—and of monumental proportion, as well. The Maurist reprint in Migne occupies the whole of two volumes, PL 36-37. That edition is now superseded, however, by the three volume edition of Eligius Dekkers and Iohannes Fraipont in the *Corpus Christianorum*, Vol. 38-40, each volume having appeared in 1956, and each volume covering fifty Psalms.

1461

[18, 1, 7]

"And there is no one who can hide himself from its heat (1)." But when the   724
Word too was made flesh and dwelt among us (2), taking our mortality,
He allowed no mortal man to excuse himself from the shadow of death; for the
heat of the Word penetrated even it.

1462

[29, 2, 1]

The Mediator between the Trinity and the weakness and wickedness of   387
men was made man, not wicked, but nevertheless weak. This was done so   348
that by what was not wicked, He might join you to God, so that by what
was weak, He might approach you: and thus, so that He might be Mediator
between man and God, the Word was made flesh (3), that is, the Word was
made man.

1463

[31, 2, 4]

What then? Is it that no works can precede faith, that is, that prior to faith   654
no works can be given a "well done"? For those very works, which are said
to have been done prior to faith, although they appear to men to be
praiseworthy, are really in vain. It seems to me that they are like the great
power of the swiftest runner, whose race, however, in on the wrong track.

1464

[33, 1, 10]

"And he was carried in his own hands (4)." But, brethren, how is it possible   852
for a man to do this? Who can understand it? Who is it that is carried in his
own hands? A man can be carried in the hands of another; but no one can be
carried in his own hands. How this should be understood literally of David,
we cannot discover; but we can discover how it is meant of Christ. For
Christ was carried in His own hands, when, referring to His own Body, He
said: "This is My Body (5)." For He carried that Body in His hands.

1465

[34, 2, 13]

"Attend to my judgment, my God and my Lord, in my cause (6)." Not to my   88
punishment, but to my cause. . . . For punishment is the same to good
men and to evil. Therefore it is the cause, not the punishment, that makes
martyrs. If punishment made martyrs, all the mines would be full of martyrs,
every chain would drag martyrs, all who die by the sword would be martyrs.

1466

[36, 2, 2]

You did not know that there is a day of the unjust, on which he will be   558
punished? But He that does know did not hide it from you. It is no small part of the
knowledge that is given to one who knows. He has eyes of knowledge;
yours are of belief. What God sees, you must believe.

1467

[37, 3]

"Lord, rebuke me not in Your indignation, nor correct me in Your anger   1000
(7)." . . . In this life may You cleanse me and make me such that I have no
need of the corrective fire, which is for those who are saved, but as if by
fire. . . . For it is said: "He shall be saved, but as if by fire (8)." And because it
is said that he shall be saved, little is thought of that fire. Yet plainly, though
we be saved by fire, that fire will be more severe than anything a man can
suffer in this life.

1468

[49, 2]

It is evident, therefore, that He called men gods because they were deified   754
by His grace, and not because they were born of His substance. For He
justifies, being just of Himself and not from another; and He deifies, being God
of Himself and not by participation in another. But He that justifies does   755
also deify, because by justifying He makes sons of God. For, "He has given
them the power to become sons of God (9)." If we are made sons of God, we
are also made gods; but this is by grace adopting, and not by nature begetting.

1469

[55, 19]

What are you going to give, that you did not receive from Him? For, "What   541
have you that you did not receive (10)?" Will you give from your heart? He gave
you faith, hope, and love: this you can offer, this you can sacrifice. But   544
plainly, everything else can be taken from you against your will by an enemy;
but this cannot be taken from you unless you are willing. Everything else
perishes, even against your will. You will to have gold; and gold perishes.   545
You will to have a home; and your home perishes. But no one's faith perishes
unless he spurns it.

1470

[56, 9]

When we wish to show that Christ was prophesied about, we set those   81
writings before the pagans. And if perhaps, hard to convince, they say that we   300
Christians composed them, so that together with the Gospel which we
preach we forged the Prophets through whom what we preach might seem to
have been prophesied, we prove to them that all these writings are from the
Jews, that the Jews have all of these writings. We draw codices from enemies
in order to refute other enemies. In what sort of reproach, then, are the
Jews? A Jew carries the codex, by which the Christian may believe. They have

become our librarians, just as servants are accustomed to carry codices behind
their masters; and the former faint by carrying them while the latter grow
strong by reading them.

1471

[63, 15]

When the earth quaked the Lord rose again. Such miracles were done   84
around the sepulchre that even the very soldiers who had come to guard it
became witnesses, if they wanted to tell the truth. But the same avarice which
made captive the disciple and companion of Christ (11) made captive also the
soldier who was on guard at the sepulchre. "We will give you money," they
said, "and you can say that while you were sleeping His disciples came
and took Him away (12)." Truly, "the examiners will not bear examinations
(13)." What is it that you have said, O unhappy cleverness? Have you so
abandoned the light of the counsel of piety that you plunge into the depths of
cunning and can say this: "Say that while you were sleeping His disciples came
and took Him away"? You bring forward sleeping witnesses! Truly, you
have yourself fallen asleep, who fail so greatly upon examination! If they were
asleep, what could they see? And if they saw nothing, how are they
witnesses?

1472

[67, 41]

Only those are to be called good works which are done for the love of God.   653
But it is necessary that faith be antecedent to them, so that they have their   595
origin in faith, and not that faith have its beginning from them. For nothing
is done for the love of God unless first there be belief in God.

1473

[70, 2, 1]

Grace is gratuitously given. For if it were not gratuitious, it would not be   711
grace. But if it is grace because it is gratuitous, nothing on your part precedes it
for the sake of which you might be receiving it. For if some good works
of yours preceded it, you were receiving a payment, not a gratuitous gift.
But the only payment that is owed us is punishment.

1474

[77, 32]

"God is of my heart; and my portion forever is God (14)." The heart was   593
made chaste; God is loved by it freely; it seeks no other reward. Whoever   585
seeks another reward from God and desires for that reason to serve God is
making that which he wants to receive more dear than Him from whom he
wants to receive it. What then? Is there no reward from God? None, except
Himself! The reward from God is God Himself. This the heart loves, this
it prizes. If it loves another, it will not be a chaste love. . . . [34] "It is good,"   581
he says, "to cling to God (15),"—but this only as in an approach to Him,
because the realization has not yet been achieved (16),—"to put my hope in
Him (17)"; so, although you have not yet clung to Him, put there your hope. If
you waver, get an anchor into the ground. If you cannot yet cling to His
actual presence, hold on to Him in hope.

1475

[73, 2]

   If we distinguish between the two Testaments, Old and New, there are not   790
the same Sacraments, not the same promises. . . . The Sacraments are   794
not the same, because there are some Sacraments giving salvation, others
promising a Savior. The Sacraments of the New Testament give salvation, the
Sacraments of the Old Testament promise a Savior.

1475a

[75, 1]

   But because Christ Himself is of the seed of David according to the flesh, and   284
God, blessed above all forever, He is our King and our God. He is our King
because He was born of the tribe of Juda according to the flesh, Christ, Lord
and Savior; but He is our God, who exists before Juda, and before the heavens
and the earth, through whom all things were made, both spiritual and
corporeal.

1476

[83, 11]

   "They will walk from powers to power (18)." . . . The four powers active   547
in our lives are described by many, and are found in the Scriptures. . . .
Those powers (19) are given us now by the grace of God in this vale of tears.
From these powers we will go to that other power. And what will that be
except the power of the contemplation of God alone?

1477

[83, 16]

   He bestowed forgiveness, the crown He will pay out. Of forgiveness He is   770
the donor; of the crown, He is the debtor. Why debtor? Did He receive   774
something? . . . The Lord made Himself a debtor not by receiving something
but by promising something. One does not say to Him: "Pay for what You
received," but, "Pay what You promised."

1478

[88, 2, 14]

   Let us love our Lord God, let us love His Church; Him as a Father, her as a   415
Mother; Him as a Master, her as His Handmaid; for we are the children of the
Handmaid herself. But this marriage is held together by a great love; no one
offends the one and gains favor with the other. No one can say: "Certainly I go
to idols, I consult demoniacs and fortune-tellers (20); but I do not abandon
the Church of God. I am a Catholic." While clinging to your Mother, you have
offended your Father (21). Another says likewise: "Far be it from me. I
consult no fortune-teller, I seek out no demoniac, I look to no sacrilegious
divinations, I do not go to the worship of idols, nor do I bow down to stones;
but I am in the party of Donatus." What does it profit you not to have offended
your Father, when He will vindicate your offended Mother? What does it
profit you to confess the Lord, to honor God, to preach Him, to acknowledge
His Son, to confess the Son seated at the right of the Father, if you blaspheme
His Church? . . . Cling, then, beloved, cling all with one mind to God our
Father and to the Church our Mother.

1479

[90, 2, 1]

Our Lord Jesus Christ is, as it were, a whole and perfect man, both head and   401
body. We recognize the Head in that Man who was born of the Virgin Mary,
suffered in the time of Pontius Pilate, was buried, rose again, ascended
into heaven, sits at the right of the Father, whence we await Him as Judge of
the living and the dead. He is the Head of the Church. The Body belonging to   400
this Head is the Church: not the local Church here, but both the local
Church and the Church throughout the whole world; not the Church which
belongs to the present time, but that which exists from the time of Abel himself
even to all those who will ever be born, even to the end, and who will
believe in Christ, the whole population of the saints who belong to but one city,   416
which city is the Body of Christ, and of which Body Christ is the Head.
There the angels too are our fellow citizens; but because we are yet on   480
pilgrimage, we labor; they, however, await our arrival in that city. And from   20
that city to which we journey, letters come to us: those letters are the Scriptures   22
which exhort us to live properly.

1479a

[98, 9]

"And adore the footstool of His feet, because it is holy (22)." . . . In   311
another place in the Scriptures it says: "The heavens are My throne, but the   851
earth is the footstool of My feet (23)." Is it the earth, then, that He commands
us to adore, since in this other place the earth is called the footstool of God's
feet? . . . I am put in jeopardy by such a dilemma (24): I am afraid to
adore the earth lest He that made heaven and earth condemn me; again, I am
afraid not to adore the footstool of my Lord's feet, because the Psalm does say
to me: "Adore the footstool of My feet." I ask what the footstool of His feet is;
and Scripture tells me: "The earth is the footstool of My feet." Perplexed,
I turn to Christ, because it is He whom I seek here; and I discover how the earth is
adored without impiety, how without impiety the footstool of His feet is
adored. For He received earth from earth; because flesh is from the earth, and
He took flesh from the flesh of Mary. He walked here in the same flesh, and
gave us the same flesh to be eaten unto salvation. But no one eats that flesh
unless first he adores it; and thus it is discovered how such a footstool of the
Lord's feet is adored; and not only do we not sin by adoring, we do sin
by not adoring.

1480

[98, 9]

"Unless he shall have eaten My flesh he shall not have eternal life (25)."   850
[Some] understood this foolishly, and thought of it carnally, and supposed that   857
the Lord was going to cut off some parts of His body to give them. . . .
But He instructed them and said to them: "It is the spirit that gives life; but the
flesh profits nothing: the words that I have spoken to you are spirit and life
(26). Understand spiritually what I said. You are not to eat this body which you
see, nor to drink that blood which will be poured out by those who will
crucify Me. I have commended to you a certain Sacrament; spiritually
understood, it will give you life. And even if it is necessary that this be
celebrated visibly, it must still be understood invisibly.

1480a

[101, 2, 3]

The remission of sins is their unbinding. What good would it have done
Lazarus when he came out of the tomb, if it had not been said: "Unbind him,
and let him go (27)"? . . . He came forth bound; not on his own feet,
therefore, but by some power leading him. Let this be in the heart of the
penitent: when you hear a man confessing his sins, he has already come to life
again; when you hear a man lay bare his conscience in confessing, he has
already come forth from the sepulchre; but he is not yet unbound. When is he
unbound? By whom is he unbound? "Whatever you loose on earth," He says,
"shall be loosed also in heaven (28)." Rightly is the loosing of sins able to
be given by the Church, but the dead man cannot be raised to life again except
by the Lord's calling him interiorly; for this latter is done by God in a more
interior way.

900
911
916

1481

[101, 2, 10]

Eternity itself is the substance of God, which has nothing that is changeable.
There is nothing there that is past, as if it were no longer; nothing there is
future, as if it not yet were. There is nothing there except "is".

156
150

1482

[102, 8]

Raise your hope to the good of all goods. He will be your good, by whom
you, in your kind, have been made good, and by whom all things, in their own
kind, have been made good. For God made all things very good (29).

581

1483

[102, 16]

He calls everywhere for correction, He calls everywhere for repentance, He
calls creatures to rewards, He calls by imparting a time for living, He calls by
the readings, He calls by the sermons, He calls by inmost reflection, He calls
by the scourge of rebuke, He calls by the mercy of consolation: "Patient
and filled with mercy (30)."

681

683

1484

[103, 1, 15]

The angels are spirits; but it is not because they are spirits that they are
angels. It is when they are sent, that they become angels. For angel is the
name of an office, not of a nature. If you ask the name of this nature, it is spirit;
if you ask the office, it is angel. By reason of what they are, they are spirits.
By reason of what they do, they are angels (31).

483

1485

[118, 17, 3]

The Lord teaches agreeableness by inspiring pleasure, He teaches discipline
by tempering grief, He teaches knowledge by insinuating cognition. There
are some things we learn only so that we may know them, other things

683
684

we learn so that we may also do them. When God teaches these things, He so teaches them that, by His opening the truth, we may know what is to be known; He so teaches that, by His inspiring agreeableness, we may do what is to be done.

1486

[118, 18, 3]
   Unless something be understood, no one is able to believe in God; but the   559
very faith by which a man believes is a restorative, so that he may understand   563
more fully. There are some things which we do not believe unless we
understand; and there are others which we do not understand unless we
believe. For if faith depends on hearing, and hearing on the word of Christ (32),
how is a man to believe in the faith that is being preached, if, to say nothing
of other things, he does not understand the language that is being spoken? But
again, unless there were some things which we cannot understand unless   562
we first believe, the prophet would not have said: "Unless you shall have
believed, you shall not understand (33)." Our intellect, therefore, is of profit for   565
our understanding what it may believe; and faith is of profit for our believing
what it may understand; and likewise the mind is of profit so that these same
things may be more and more understood in the intellect itself. But this
does not come about as if by our own natural powers, but through God,   555
helping and bestowing, just as it is by medicine and not by nature that a
diseased eye receives again the power to see.

1487

[127, 7]
   "Where their worm does not die and their fire is not extinguished (34)."   914
Men hear this; and because it is truly the future lot of the impious, they
are afraid and keep themselves from sin. They harbor fear; and through fear
they keep themselves from sin. Indeed, they do fear, but they do not love
justice. But since through fear they keep themselves from sin, a habit of
justice begins to grow, and what was difficult begins to be loved, and God
becomes agreeable (35); and now a man begins to live righteously, not because
he fears punishment but because he loves eternity.

1488

[130, 7]
   Illnesses of the body, for the most part, are caused by Satan's angels; but those angels   494
cannot do this unless they are permitted to. Even holy Job was tested thus.

1489

[134, 4]
   As if it were He alone who exists, He said: "I am who am"; and, "Tell the   140
children of Israel: 'He Who Is has sent me to you (36).'" He did not say: "The   141
Lord God, almighty, merciful, and just"; which, if He had said it, would
certainly be true. Rising to the heights of all that God could be named and
called, He answers that He is to be called Being Itself (37); and as if this were His
name, He says: "Tell them this: 'He Who Is sent me.'" For He exists in
such a way that in comparison to Him created things do not exist. Aside from

such comparison, they do exist, because they are from Him; but, compared to
Him, they do not exist, because really to exist is to be unchangeable, which
He alone is.

1490

[134, 10]
   We must hold and believe unshakably that whatever creatures there are   460
in the heavens, whatever on earth, whatever in the sea and in all the depths,
they have been created by God; because, as we have already said: "He
made all that He willed, in the heavens and on earth, in the sea and in all the
depths (38)." He was not compelled to make all that He made; rather,   463
"everything that He willed, He made." The cause of all that He made is His
will. You make a house; but, if you did not want to make it, you would remain
without a dwelling place. Necessity forces you to make a house, not free
will. . . . God created by reason of His goodness; He was in need of nothing
that He made; therefore, "everything whatsoever He willed, He made."

1491

[134, 11]
   This is to love freely, not as if in expectation of receiving a reward; for the   585
very highest reward will be yours, God Himself, whom you love freely. And   593
you ought to love in such a way that you do not stop desiring Him for
your reward, who alone can satisfy you, just as Philip desired when he said:
"Show us the Father, and it will be enough for us (39)."

 1. Ps. 18[19]:7.
 2. John 1:14.
 3. John 1:14.
 4. Possibly an alternate reading of 3 Kgs. 20:13.
 5. Matt. 26:26; Mark 14:22; Luke 22:19.
 6. Ps. 34[35]:23.
 7. Ps. 37[38]:2.
 8. 1 Cor. 3:15.
 9. John 1:12.
10. 1 Cor. 4:7.
11. Matt. 26:14-16.
12. See Matt. 28:13.
13. Ps. 63[64]:7.—*Defecerunt scrutantes scrutationes.*
14. Ps. 72[73]:26.
15. Ps. 72[73]:28.
16. *sed modo in peregrinatione, quia nondum venit res.*
17. Ps. 72[73]:28.
18. Ps. 83[84]:8.—*Ambulabunt a virtutibus in virtutem.*
19. Augustine specifies these powers or virtues as prudence, justice, temperance, and fortitude, commonly called the
    cardinal virtues since they are the hinges of all other virtues.
20. *arreptitios et sortilegos consulo.*
21. The correct reading is *"Tenens matrem, offendisti patrem."* The reading *"Tenens patrem, offendisti matrem"* is
    probably only a misprint without manuscript support at all.
22. Ps. 98[99]:9.
23. Is. 66:1.
24. *Anceps factus sum.*
25. See John 6:54-55.
26. John 6:64.
27. John 11:44.
28. Matt. 16:19.
29. Gen. 1:31.

30. Ps. 102[103]:8.
31. The reasoning of this passage depends upon the fact that the word *angelus* is a Latinization of the Greek word ἄγγελος, which means *messenger*, one who is sent.
32. Rom. 10:17.
33. Is. 7:9 in the Septuagint version.
34. Is. 66:24 and Mark 9:43.
35. *et dulcescit Deus*. Augustine does not mean, of course, that the unchangeable God becomes agreeable; but that God and the things of God and the contemplation of God become agreeable to men.
36. Ex. 3:14.
37. *ipsum esse se vocari respondit*.
38. Ps. 134[135]:6.
39. John 14:8.

SERMONS [*inter A. D.* 391-430]

Just as Chrysostom was the greatest preacher in the East, so too was Augustine in the West. For the student who would like to read Augustine's sermons in their entirety. however, there are several problems. Augustine left an enormous number of undoubtedly genuine sermons; and there is also an enormous number of questionable or clearly unauthentic sermons that have been at one time or another attributed to him. Father Hugh Pope (*Saint Augustine of Hippo*, New York, 1937, p. 179) estimated that the extant sermons "of one sort or another" attributed to Augustine must exceed 1000; and his figure is undoubtedly rather conservative. Yet, the number of sermons that Augustine actually delivered must far exceed the number extant, genuine and spurious.

Even though it was not usual in Augustine's time and place for a simple priest, as distinguished from a bishop, to preach, Augustine, because of the inadequacy of his bishop, Valerius, who spoke but little Latin, was designated to preach from the time of his first receiving priestly orders in 391. We know that from that time until his death forty years later he preached regularly on Sundays and feast days, and frequently throughout the week. If he preached only twice a week on the average, that would amount to about 4000 sermons. There are indications, in fact, that he preached much oftener even than that; and had all his sermons been recorded, the figure might well run to seven or eight thousand.

Some of Augustine's sermons are found as "books" among his numerous writings. Also, there are three large collections which tradition sets apart as special collections of sermons: his *Enarrationes in psalmos*, his *In Iohannis evangelium tractatus*, and his *In epistulam Iohannis ad Parthos tractatus*. These we are treating as separate works, although they do really belong to any consideration of his sermons.

It is Augustine's other sermons that we are presently treating. The Maurist edition, commonly called the Vulgate, contains 363 sermons, divided into four classes: a) Homilies on Old and New Testament (1-183); b) Sermons on the Feasts of the temporal cycle (184-272); c) Sermons of the sanctoral cycle (273-340); d) Sermons on miscellaneous subjects and occasions (341-363). Following these are the sermons of dubious authenticity, numbered from 364 to 395; and then another whole series of fragmentary and clearly unauthentic sermons, numbered from 1 to 317. All the above is as in the fifth volume of the original Maurist edition, and is reprinted in Migne, PL 38-39.

Over the years numerous supplementary collections of sermons attributed to Augustine were published: 25 by Michael Denis in 1792 (Migne, PL 46, 813-940); 4 by Francis Fontani in 1793 (Migne, PL 47, 1113-1140); 10 by Octavius Frangipani in 1819 (Migne, PL 46, 939-1004). Too late for Migne are the 164 published by Armand Caillau and the 201 by Angelo Cardinal Mai, the larger part of which are regarded as spurious. And in still more recent years additional sermons have been published by Germain Morin and several other great patristic scholars of our own times.

What is needed now is a critical edition of all the sermons of Augustine, taking account of all the post-Maurist findings. Until such is available, there is an excellent if necessarily cumbersome summation of all these findings in Adalbert Hamman's *Supplementum* to the Migne Patrology, Vol. 2, pp. 397-1360.

In volume 41 (1961) of the *Corpus Christianorum* is the start of a new critical edition, Cyril Lambot's texts for the first fifty sermons of the Vulgate numbering, all and only the sermons on Old Testament texts, along with nine others more recently discovered. And Lambot had already published in 1950 in the series *Stromata* his critical edition of eighteen various sermons of Augustine, *Sancti Aurelii Augustini sermones selecti duodeviginti*, representing the Vulgate numbers 14-15, 24, 60, 101, 104, 166, 177, 184, 221, 254, 261, 298, 302, 339, 355-356, and 358.

In our translations below we will depend on Lambot's texts where available; otherwise, upon the Migne reprint of the Maurist edition. We will, however, cite no sermon that is now commonly regarded as unauthentic or of questionable authenticity.

1492

[3]

Sara said: "Cast out the bondwoman and her son; for the son of a bondwoman   415
shall not be heir with my son Isaac (1)." And the Church says: "Cast out
heresies and their children; for heretics shall not be heirs with Catholics." But why
shall they not be heirs? Are they not born of Abraham's seed? And have they not   830
the Church's Baptism? They do have Baptism; and it would make the seed of Abraham
an heir, if pride did not exclude them from inheritance. By the same word, by the
same Sacrament you were born, but you will not come to the same inheritance of   417
eternal life, unless you return to the Catholic Church.

1493

[7, 7]

Already, then, an angel, and the Lord through an angel, told Moses, when he was   140
asking the Lord's name: "I am who am. Tell the sons of Israel this: 'He Who Is   155
sent me to you (2).'" Being is a name of unchangeableness. For everything that
is changed ceases to be what it was and begins to be what it was not. Being is. True
being, pure being, genuine being is had only by Him who does not change (3).

1494

[20, 2]

If you want God to forgive, you must confess (4). Sin cannot go unpunished. It   910
were unseemly, improper, and unjust for sin to go unpunished. Since, therefore, sin   923
must not go unpunished, let it be punished by you, lest you be punished for it.   919
Let your sin have you for its judge, not its patron. Go up and take the bench
against yourself, and put your guilt before yourself. Do not put it behind you, or God
will put it in front of you.

1495

[26, 8]

Notice how closely reasoned is that which they want to say. "By the very fact,"   725
[the Pelagianist] says, "that I defend man's free choice, and just because I say
that free choice is sufficient that I may be righteous, I do not thereby say that this is

without the grace of God." See how the ears of the pious perk up! As soon as
a pious man hears that, he begins to offer congratulations. "Thanks be to God!
He does not defend free choice without the grace of God. For there is free choice,
but it avails nothing without the grace of God. If, then, they do not defend free
choice without God's grace, what evil are they speaking?" Show us, then, O learned
teacher, what you mean by grace. He replies: "When I say 'free choice of man',
notice that I say 'of man'." So what? "Who created man? God. Who gave him free
choice? God. If, then, God created man, and God gave him free choice, to whose
grace is owed whatever man can do of free choice, if not to His who created him
with free choice?" And that is what they call very sharp reasoning!

1496

[27, 6]
    When we shall have come into His sight, we shall behold the equity of God's   720
justice. Then no one will say: "Why did He help this one, and not that one? Why   711
was this man led by God's direction to be baptized, while that man, though he lived
properly as a catechumen, was killed in a sudden disaster, and was not baptized?" . . .   205
Look for deserts, and you will find none except punishment. Look for grace: "O,   209
sublimity of riches (5)!" Peter denies, the thief believes. "O, sublimity of riches!"

1497

[38, 10]
    There is kingdom against kingdom, there are earthquakes, there are grievous   15
calamities, scandals in abundance, love has grown cold, and there is wickedness
aplenty. Read all these things; they have been predicted. Read, and see that all you
see has been predicted; and believe, when you count up how many have already come to
pass, that you will see those predictions too that have not yet come to pass.

1498

[43, 1]
    The beginning of a good life, to which also life eternal is owed, is correct faith.   567
Faith, however, is believing what you do not yet see; to which faith the reward   771
is seeing what you believe. Let us not fail in the time for faith, therefore, as in a time
for sowing, and let us not fail even to the end; but let us persevere, until we can reap
what we have sown.

1499

[43, 7]
    How do we differ? You said: "Let me understand, so that I may believe." I said: 562
"Believe, so that you may understand." A controversy has been born. Let us come
before a judge; let the Prophet judge; indeed, let God judge through the
Prophet. Let us both be silent. What both of us said has been heard. "Let me understand,"
you say, "so that I may believe." "Believe," I say, "so that you may understand." Let
the Prophet respond: "Unless you shall have believed, you shall not understand (6)."

1500

[47, 21]
    "I, the Lord," He says, "will be their God, and My servant David a prince in   387
their midst (7)." Why, "in their midst?" Because, "the Word was made flesh, and dwelt

among us (8)." A Prince in their midst. Hence also, "a Mediator of God and men (9)," because He is God with the Father, and because He is Man with men. Not a Mediator-Man apart from the Godhead. Not a Mediator-God apart from humanity. Behold the Mediator. Divinity without humanity is no mediator, humanity without divinity is no mediator. But between divinity alone and humanity alone, the Mediator is the human divinity and the divine humanity of Christ.

1501

[71, 7]

Some are of a mind that the only ones who sin against the Holy Spirit are those   903
who, after they have been washed in the bath of rebirth in the Church and have
accepted the Holy Spirit, have afterwards plunged themselves, as if ungrateful for so
great a gift of the Savior, into some death-dealing sin (10): such are either adultery,   902
or murder, or apostasy itself, either from the Christian name altogether, or from the
Catholic Church. But how this meaning could be shown, I do not know, since in   901
the Church there is no denial of a place of repentance for any crime whatsoever.

1502

[87, 6]

In that pay, then, we shall all be equal, the first like the last and the last like   771
the first. Because that denarius (11) is eternal life, and in eternal life all will be equal.   1046
For although they will shine, some more and some less, by a diversity of merit, what
pertains to eternal life will be given equally to all.

1503

[90, 8]

I do not exhort you to have faith, but love. For you cannot have love without   595
faith; I mean the love of God and neighbor. Whence can it come without faith?   598
How can he love God, who does not believe in God?

1504

[99, 6]

O you who say you have not committed many sins: why have you not? by whose   681
guidance? . . . Your God says this to you: "I guided you to Me. I kept you for Me. That
you might not commit adultery, no enticer was there; and that no enticer was there was My
doing. Place and time were lacking; and that they were lacking was My doing. An enticer
was there, place was not lacking, and time was not lacking; but so that you might not
consent, I alarmed you. Acknowledge, therefore, His grace, to which you owe also what
you have not done. Another owes Me for what was done, and you have seen him forgiven.
You owe it to Me what you did not do." There is no sin which a man commits that
another man may not also commit, if He by whom man was made be lacking as Guide.

1505

[117, 5]

If we speak of God, what wonder is it if you do not comprehend? For if you   173
comprehend, He is not God. Let there be a pious confession of ignorance rather than a rash
profession of knowledge. That one's mind only touch God a little is great happiness; to
comprehend Him is utterly impossible.

1507

[131, 10]
   [On this matter of the Pelagians] two Councils have already been sent to the   435
Apostolic See; and from there rescripts too have come (12). The matter is at an end;   451
would that the error too might sometime be at an end (13)!

1508

[141, 2]
   It occurred to Paul that someone might ask him: "Whence do these impious men   131
hold back the truth (14)? Has God ever spoken to any of them? Did they receive the   134
Law, as the nation of Israelites did through Moses? Whence, then, do they hold back the
truth, even in their very iniquity?" Listen to what follows, and he will show you.
"Because what is known of God," he says, "has been manifested to them: for God has
manifested it to them (15)." Did He manifest it to those to whom He did not give the Law?
Hear how He manifested it. "For His invisible attributes are clearly perceived, being
understood through the things that have been made (16)." Ask the world, the beauty of the
heavens, the splendor and arrangement of the stars; the sun that suffices for the day; the
moon, the comfort of the night; ask the earth, fruitful in herbs and trees, full of animals,
adorned with men; ask the sea, filled with so many swimming creatures of every kind; ask
the air, replete with so many flying creatures. Ask them all, and see if they do not, as if in
a language of their own, answer you: "God made us." Noble philosophers too have sought
these things, and have recognized the Artisan by the art.

1509

[151, 7]
   What good, then, am I doing, in that I do not consent to wicked concupiscence?   658
I do good, and I do not perfect the good; and my enemy, concupiscence, does evil, and it
does not perfect the evil. How do I do good, and not perfect the good? I do good, when I
do not consent to wicked concupiscence; but I do not perfect the good, so as to be entirely
without concupiscence. Again, therefore, how does my enemy do evil, and yet not perfect
the evil? He does evil, because he moves me to evil desire; but he does not perfect the evil,
because he does not drag me to the evil. And the whole life of the saints is involved in that
war.

1510

[156, 11]
   Someone says to me: "Since we are acted upon, it is not we who act." I answer,   700
"No, you both act and are acted upon; and if you are acted upon by the good, you act   690
properly. For the spirit of God who moves you, by so moving, is your Helper. The very
term helper makes it clear that you yourself are doing something."

1511

[158, 2]
   God is made a debtor not by receiving something from us but by promising us what   774
He is pleased to promise. For sometimes we say to a man: "You owe me because I gave
you something"; and other times we say: "You owe me because you promised me
something." . . . In that way, then, we can make a demand of our Lord and say, "Pay
what You promised because we did what You commmanded." And you can do this
because, by your labors, you helped.

1512

[158, 8]

What about hope? Will there be hope in heaven? There will no longer be hope, when   586
the reality will be present. For hope itself is necessary on our pilgrimage, by which hope we
are consoled on the way. For a wayfarer, when he expends himself in walking, can tolerate
that labor, because he hopes for his goal. Take away his hope of achievement, and
immediately his strength for walking is broken. So too the hope which we have now
belongs to the righteousness of our pilgrimage.

1513

[159, 1]

There is an ecclesiastical discipline, as the faithful know, when the names of the   833
martyrs are read aloud in that place at the altar of God (17), where prayer is not   1001
offered for them. Prayer, however, is offered for other dead who are remembered.   122
For it is wrong to pray for a martyr, to whose prayers we ought ourselves be
commended.

1514

[161, 8]

"Do not fear those who can kill the body and then can do nothing more; but fear   914
Him who has the power to kill both body and soul in the Gehenna of fire: so I tell you, fear
Him (18)." If, then, the Lord inspired fear, and inspired it strongly, and doubled it by
repeating the threat, I ask you, is it wrong of you to fear? I would not say that. Fear
openly, there is nothing better for you than fear; there is nothing you ought to fear more.

1515

[169, 13]

"He was handed over for our offenses, and He rose again for our justification (19)."   690
What does this mean, "for our justification"? So that He might justify us; so that He   760
might make us just. You will be a work of God, not only because you are a man, but also
because you are just. For it is better that you be just than that you be a man. If God made
you a man, and you made yourself just, something you were doing would be better than
what God did. But God made you without any cooperation on your part. For you did not
lend your consent so that God could make you. How could you have consented, when you
did not exist? But He who made you without your consent does not justify you without
your consent. He made you without your knowledge, but He does not justify you without
your willing it.

1516

[172, 2]

But by the prayers of the Holy Church, and by the salvific sacrifice, and by the alms   897
which are given for their spirits, there is no doubt that the dead are aided, that the Lord   1001
might deal more mercifully with them than their sins would deserve. For the whole Church
observes this practice which was handed down by the Fathers: that it prays for those who
have died in the communion of the Body and Blood of Christ, when they are
commemorated in their own place in the sacrifice itself; and the sacrifice is offered also in
memory of them, on their behalf. If, then, works of mercy are celebrated for the sake of
those who are being remembered, who would hestitate to recommend them, on whose
behalf prayers to God are not offered in vain? It is not at all to be doubted that such prayers

are of profit to the dead; but for such of them as lived before their death in a way that
makes it possible for these things to be useful to them after death.

1517

[174, 2]

   If man had not been lost, the Son of Man would not have come. Man, therefore,   360
was lost; the God-Man came, and man was found. Man was lost by free will; the   362
God-Man came by a freeing grace. . . . Never was the kindness of grace and the
liberality of God's omnipotence more evident than in the Man who was Mediator of
God and men, the Man, Christ Jesus (20). . . . We know and we hold that the
Mediator of God and men, the Man, Christ Jesus, insofar as He was man, was of the   313
same nature as we are. For our flesh is not of one nature and His flesh of another, nor
our soul of one nature and His soul of another. He took this nature which He judged   312
needed to be saved. In nature He had nothing less; but in guilt, He had nothing.

1518

[186, 1]

   Let us rejoice, brethren; let the nations exult and be glad. It was not the visible sun,   781
but its invisible Creator who consecrated this day for us, when the Virgin Mother,   782
fertile of womb and integral in her virginity, brought Him forth (21), made visible for   783
us, by whom, when He was invisible, she too was created. A Virgin conceiving, a
Virgin bearing, a Virgin pregnant, a Virgin bringing forth, a Virgin perpetual. Why
do you wonder at this, O man? It was fitting for God to be born thus, when He deigned   324
to become man. . . . The same One who is God is Man, not by a confusion of nature   302
but by a unity of person. Finally, He that is the Son of God by being generated and   256
who is coeternal always with the Father,—that same One begins to be Son of Man   311
from the Virgin. And so too humanity is added to the Son's divinity; and yet, no
quaternity of Persons results, but the Trinity remains.

1519

[227]

   I am mindful of my promise. For I promised you, who have now been baptized, a   851
sermon in which I would explain the Sacrament of the Lord's Table, which you now   873
look upon and of which you last night were made participants. You ought to know   860
what you have received, what you are going to receive, and what you ought to receive
daily. That Bread which you see on the altar, having been sanctified by the word of
God, is the Body of Christ. That chalice, or rather, what is in that chalice, having   849
been sanctified by the word of God, is the Blood of Christ. Through that bread
and wine the Lord Christ willed to commend His Body and Blood, which He poured
out for us unto the forgiveness of sins. If you have received worthily, you are what   880
you have received. For the Apostle says: "Because the Bread is one, we, though
many, are one body (22)." Thus he explained the Sacrament of the Lord's Table:
"Because the Bread is one, we, though many, are one body." Thus, by that Bread, you
are taught how you must love unity. For is that bread made of but one grain of
wheat? Were there not in fact many grains? But before they became bread, they were
separate; by water they were joined together, and that was after a certain *contritio* (23).

1520

[234, 2]

   The Lord Jesus wanted those whose eyes were held lest they should recognize   810

Him (24), to recognize Him in the breaking of the bread. The faithful know what
I am saying. They know Christ in the breaking of the bread. For not all bread,
but only that which receives the blessing of Christ, becomes Christ's body.

864
856

1520a

[242, 5]

If we were to tell those pagan philosophers that our bodies are going to be victorious
on a new earth and not in heaven, we would be speaking boldly and rashly, yes, even
against the faith. For we ought to believe that we are going to have such bodies that we
shall be wherever we wish whenever we wish.

1044

1521

[259, 2]

The eighth day signifies the new life at the end of the world; the seventh day, the
future rest of the saints on this earth. For the Lord will reign on earth with His saints, as the
Scriptures say, and here He will have His Church, into which no wicked person will enter,
separated and cleansed from every contagion of iniquity (25).

1016

1522

[264, 6]

The flesh will rise again, but what will it become? It is changed, and it becomes
itself a celestial and angelic body. Do angels have flesh? But there is this difference,
that that flesh will rise, that flesh which was buried, that flesh which dies; that
which is seen, which is felt, which needs to eat and drink if it is to continue; which
grows ill, which suffers pain; that same body has to rise again, unto everlasting punishment
in the case of the wicked, but to undergo a transformation in the case of the good.

1011
483
1013
1044

1523

[267, 4]

What the soul is to man's body, the Holy Spirit is to the Body of Christ, which
is the Church. The Holy Spirit does in the whole Church what the soul does in
all the members of one body. But see what you must beware of, see what you must take
note of, see what you must fear. It happens that in the human body,—or rather,
off the body,—some member, whether hand, finger, or foot, may be cut away.
And if a member be cut off, does the soul go with it? When the member was in the
body, it lived; and off, its life is lost. So too, a Christian man is Catholic while he lives
in the body; cut off, he is made a heretic; the Spirit does not follow an amputated
member.

413

415

1523a

[268, 2]

"One body," says the Apostle Paul: "One body and one spirit (26)." Take note
of our own members. The body is make up of many members, and one spirit enlivens them
all. . . . The duties of the members are divided, but one spirit connects them all. . . .
What our spirit, that is, our soul, is to our members, the Holy Spirit is to the members of
Christ, the Body of Christ, which is the Church.

413

1524

[272]

What you see is the bread and the chalice; that is what your own eyes report to you.   860
But what your faith obliges you to accept is that the bread is the Body of Christ   851
and the chalice the Blood of Christ. This has been said very briefly, which may
perhaps be sufficient for faith; yet faith does desire instruction. . . . How is the bread
His Body? And the chalice, or what is in the chalice, how is it His Blood? Those   790
elements, brethren, are called Sacraments, because in them one thing is seen, but
another is understood. What is seen is the corporeal species; but what is understood
is the spiritual fruit. If, then, you wish to understand the Body of Christ, hear the
Apostle speaking to the faithful: "You, however, are the Body of Christ and His   878
members (27)." If, therefore, you are the Body of Christ and His members, your
mystery is presented at the table of the Lord: you receive your mystery. To that which
you are, you answer: "Amen"; and by answering, you subscribe to it. For you
hear: "The Body of Christ!" and you answer: "Amen!" Be a member of Christ's
Body, so that your "Amen" may be the truth.

1525

[294, 2]

"An infant," [the Pelagians] say, "even if he be not baptized, by merit of innocence,   618
since he has no sin at all, neither his own nor original sin, contracted neither on   619
his own nor from Adam,—it is necessary," they say, "that he have salvation and   831
eternal life, even if he be not baptized; but for this reason he is to be baptized, so that
he may also enter into the kingdom of God, that is, into the kingdom of heaven
(28)." . . . Is there eternal life, then, outside the kingdom of heaven? [3] First,
turn your ears away from this error, eradicate it from your minds. This is something
new in the Church, previously unheard of: that there is eternal life outside the kingdom
of heaven, that there is eternal salvation outside the kingdom of God. First, brother,
see whether you ought not perhaps agree with us, that whoever does not belong to
the kingdom of God, undoubtedly belongs to damnation. The Lord, who will come
and who will judge the living and the dead, just as the Gospel says, will make a division
in two parts, on the right and on the left. To those on the left He will say: "Go into   1034
eternal fire, which was prepared for the Devil and his angels (29)"; and to those   1033
on the right He will say: "Come, blessed of My Father, receive the kingdom which
was prepared for you from the foundation of the world (30)." To one group He
designates a kingdom, to the other, damnation in company with the Devil. There is no
one left for a middle place, where you may try to place infants. Judgment will be
made of the living and of the dead. Some will be on the right hand, others will
be on the left hand: another hand I never knew.

1526

[295, 2]

Before His suffering the Lord Jesus Christ, as you know, chose His disciples, whom   430
He called Apostles. Among these Apostles almost everywhere Peter alone merited to
represent the whole Church. For the sake of his representing the whole Church,
which he alone could do, he merited to hear: "I will give you the keys of the kingdom
of Heaven (31)." For it was not one man, but the unity of the Church, which   900
received those keys. In that way, therefore, Peter's own excellence is foretold, because
he acted the part of the unity and totality of the Church herself, when to him it was
said, "I hand over to you," what was in fact handed over to all (32).

1527

[344, 4]

Your silver redeems you from the barbarians, your money redeems you from the
first death; the blood of your Lord redeems you from the second death. He had
the blood by which He might redeem us; and He took that blood for this purpose: so
that He might have that which He could pour out for our redemption. The blood
of your Lord, if you will it, is given for you; but if you do not want this to be so, it is
not given for you. But perhaps you are saying: "My God had the blood by which He
could redeem me; but already when He suffered, He gave it all; what does He have
left that He can give also for me?" This is the great thing about it, that what He gave
once, He gave for all. The blood of Christ is salvation to those who want it, and
torment to those who do not.

374

386
388

1528

[349, 1]

There are two kinds of love, divine and human. And of human love, there is that
which is licit and that which is illicit. . . . [2] That is a licit human love by which
a wife is held dear; illicit, by which a whore or someone else's wife is held dear. . . .
Have, then, a love that is licit. It is human; but, as I said, it is licit. It is licit, indeed,
not only in such a way that it is permitted, but it is licit in such a way that, were it
lacking, its absence would be reprehensible. It is licit for you, with a human love,
to love your spouses, to love your children, to love your friends, to love your
fellow citizens. For all those names have the bond of necessity, and the glue,
as it were, of love. But you see that even the impious, that is, the pagans, the Jews,
and the heretics, are capable of that love.

593
594

651
653
654

1532

[352, 8]

It but remains for me to speak briefly about the third kind of penance (33), so
that, by God's help, I may accomplish what I proposed and promised to do. It is the
more grave and more baleful penance, in which those who, in the Church, are
properly called penitents, are even removed from participating in the Sacrament of the
Altar, lest by receiving unworthily, they eat and drink to their own judgment (34).
That penance, then, is a baleful one. There is a grave wound: perhaps adultery
was committed, perhaps homicide, perhaps some sacrilege; a grave matter, a grave
wound, lethal, death-dealing; but there is an All-powerful Physician. . . . Beloved,
no one proposes this kind of penance for himself; no one prepares himself for this
kind of penance; but if perhaps it should come to that, let no one despair.

904

875

902

901

1533

[352, 9]

There have been those who would say that no penance is available for certain
sins; and they have been excluded from the Church and have been made heretics.
Holy Mother Church is not rendered powerless by any kind of sin (35).

901

1. Gen. 21:10.
2. Ex. 3:14.
3. *Esse est. Verum esse, sincerum esse, germanum esse non habet nisi qui non mutatur.*
4. *Tamen si vis ut ille ignoscat, tu agnosce.*
5. Rom. 11:33.
6. Is. 7:9 in the Septuagint.

7. Ezech. 34:24.

8. John 1:14.

9. 1 Tim. 2:5.

10. *mortifero aliquo peccato.*

11. Matt. 20:2.

12. The two councils were held at Carthage and Milevis respectively, their proceedings being found in the corpus of Augustine's letters, nos. 175 and 176. The rescripts from Rome, from Pope Innocent I, are likewise found in the same corpus, letters nos. 181 and 182.

13. *Causa finita est: utinam aliquando finiatur error!*

14. See Rom. 1:18.

15. Rom. 1:19.

16. Rom. 1:20.

17. *cum martyres eo loco recitantur ad altare Dei.*

18. Luke 12:4-5. See also Matt. 10:28.

19. Rom. 4:25.

20. 1 Tim. 2:5.

21. *quando eum . . . visceribus fecundis et genitalibus integris virgo mater effudit.*

22. 1 Cor. 10:17.

23. This passage really defies translation, since *contritio* means both *contrition* and *grinding*, and both meanings are implied. After contrition we are baptized, and in the water are made one. After grinding the wheat into flour, water is added, and in the loaf becomes one.

24. Luke 24:16.

25. Augustine later retracted the Millenarianist views of the earlier years of his conversion. See § 1769 below.

26. Eph. 4:4.

27. See 1 Cor. 12:27.

28. Many of Augustine's sermons come to us not by his own writing of them, but by their having been taken down in shorthand while he preached. We have translated this initial sentence rather literally; and it certainly bears the marks of the shorthand secretary.

29. Matt. 25:41.

30. Matt. 25:34.

31. Matt. 16:19.

32. *quod omnibus traditum est.*

33. The three kinds of repentance which Augustine describes are *baptism*, which obtains forgiveness of all sins; *prayer*, which obtains forgiveness of venial sins; and, what he now describes, the humility of formally ordered *penance*, by which forgiveness of grave sins is obtained. See also § 1536 below.

34. See 1 Cor. 11:29.

35. *In quibuscumque peccatis non perdit viscera pia mater ecclesia.* A rather strange idiom is involved here, by which *viscera* can mean *power* and *wealth*. Otherwise, the passage might be translated literally: "Pious Mother Church does not lose her guts with any kind of sins whatsoever."

SERMON TO CATECHUMENS, ON THE CREED [*forte ca. A. D.* 395]

The Benedictine edition offered four sermons under the heading *Sermones de symbolo ad catechumenos*, PL 40, 627-668 in Migne's reprint. The Benedictine editors had already recognized that the last three of these were not authentic (they are to be attributed to Augustine's disciple, Quodvultdeus); and the first was somewhat under a cloud by association.

The genuinity of the first of the four, however, that which concerns us here, was satisfactorily demonstrated nearly forty years ago by A. Sizoo in his article *De echtheid van Augustinus' sermo de symbolo ad catechumenos* in the *Gereformeerd Theologisch Tijdschrift*, Vol. 41 (1940), pp. 286-300. The Maurist text in Migne (PL 40, 627-636) is now replaced by the recent edition of R. Vander Plaetse in the *Corpus Christianorum*, Vol. 46 (1969), pp. 185-199.

1535

[6, 14]

This Church is holy, the one Church, the true Church, the Catholic Church, fighting as she does against all heresies. She can fight, but she cannot be

418
401

beaten. All heresies are expelled from her, like the useless loppings pruned
from a vine. She remains fixed in her root, in her vine, in her love. The gates of
hell shall not conquer her (1).

1536

[7, 15]

Let no one say: "I did that; perhaps I will not be forgiven." Because you did   836
it? How great is the sin you committed? Tell me what you have done,   658
something serious, something horrible, something terrifying even to think   811
about. Whatever you might have done, did you kill Christ? There is nothing
worse than having done that, because there is nothing better than Christ.
How great a wrong is it to kill Christ? But the Jews killed Him; and afterwards
many of them believed in Him and drank His Blood: and the sin which they had
committed was forgiven them. When you shall have been baptized, keep to
a good life in the commandments of God, so that you may preserve your
Baptism to the very end. I do not tell you that you will live here without sin, but   633
they are venial sins which this life is never without (2). Baptism was instituted
for all sins; for light sins, without which we cannot live, prayer was instituted.
What does the prayer say? "Forgive us our debts as we too forgive our
debtors (3)." We are cleansed only once by Baptism; by prayer we are cleansed   875
daily. But do not commit those sins on account of which you would have to
be separated from the Body of Christ; perish the thought! For those whom you   902
see doing penance have committed crimes, either adultery or some other   904
enormities: that is why they are doing penance. If their sins were light, daily   928
prayer would suffice to blot them out. [8, 16] In the Church, therefore, there are
three ways in which sins are forgiven: in Baptism, in prayer, and in the   929
greater humility of penance; yet, God does not forgive sins except to the   831
baptized.

1. Matt. 16:18.
2. *sed sunt venialia, sine quibus vita non est.*
3. Matt. 6:12.

ORDER [A. D. 386]

It was in 386 that Augustine was converted. And to that same year belong his works
entitled *Soliloquia, De beata vita, Contra academicos*, and *De ordine*. All were written
while he waited and prepared for his Baptism, which would not take place until the
Easter season in the Spring of 387. The *De beata vita* was the first completed,
sandwiched in, as it were, between the first and second books of the *Contra
academicos*; and the *Soliloquia* was never finished at all. The four works, written all
together in a very short period of time, have much in common: all are of a philosophical
bent, all rush forth from Augustine's pen amid the freshest tears of his gratitude to God
for the grace of enlightenment and conversion; and, concomitant with this latter point,
all bear a strong stylistic similarity to his *Confessions*, though they have not the maturity
that another fifteen years will give to the last named work.

The order with which *De ordine* is concerned is the dispensation of divine providence,
with particular attention to the problem of evil and how evil is to be reconciled to an
all-governing providence.

In his *Corrections* 1, 3, Augustine showed considerable dissatisfaction with many of

the approaches he had taken in the *De ordine*, which same might be said of all his earliest writings, when he still took a perhaps too pedantically philosophical approach to theological problems, while allowing the Platonic and Pythagorean too intimate a hold on his thought. Yet, many of the things which he later "retracted" and regretted are of no great moment, and the universal judgment that Augustine judged his own writings too harshly is quite valid.

The Maurist text in Migne PL 32, 977-1020 is superseded by Pius Knöll's edition in the Vienna Corpus, CSEL, Vol. 63 (1922), pp. 121-187. The more recent edition of William M. Green in the series *Stromata*, Vol. 2 (1955), pp. 99-148 is of excellent merit but cannot really be said to have dislodged Knöll from the position of standard text.

1537

[2, 12, 35]

That which is rational in us saw that vocables, that is, certain meaningful   524
sounds, had to be attached to things, if men, unable to read each other's minds, were, by using the meaning of these sounds more or less an an interpreter, to have any intercourse among themselves. . . . But they could not hear the words of the absent. Reason, therefore, when it had noted and distinguished all the sounds of mouth and tongue, invented letters.

THE MORALITY OF THE CATHOLIC CHURCH [*A. D.* 388]

The *De moribus ecclesiae catholicae* with its companion work, *De moribus Manichaeorum*,—or if one prefer, these two parts of a single work,—belong to the year 388 A. D. In his *Corrections* 1, 6 Augustine himself seems to have regarded the two books as two distinct works, though this itself is not so clearly the case as to be beyond dispute. That, however, is purely an inconsequential matter of mechanics; for the writings have but a single purpose, to confound "the boasting of the Manicheans about their false and deceptive continence or abstinence" (*Corrections* 1, 6, 1).

The Maurist text in Migne PL 32, 1309-1378 is still the standard while we await the completion of the series of Augustine's writings in the Vienna Corpus or in the *Corpus Christianorum*.

1538

[1, 25, 46]

What further need have I to argue about moral conduct? If God is man's   592
greatest good, which you cannot deny, it clearly follows, since to seek the   593
greatest good is to live well, that to live well is nothing else but to love
God with all one's heart, all one's soul, and all one's mind. From this comes the
fact that such a love must be preserved pure and intact, which is the task of
temperance; that it must not be broken by any sort of troubles, which pertains
to fortitude; that it must serve no other, which belongs to justice; that it must
be vigilant in its examination of things, lest deception and guile gradually
steal in, which is the part of prudence.

GENESIS DEFENDED AGAINST THE MANICHEANS [*A. D.* 389]

In his solitude at Tagaste and with the regrets over his Manichean years still fresh upon him, Augustine wrote his *De Genesi contra Manichaeos* in 389 A. D. Its purpose is to defend the first three chapters of Genesis against the attacks of the Manicheans, whose direct dualism found the narratives of the creation and fall particularly unacceptable.

The Maurist text in Migne PL 34, 173-220 remains at present the standard edition.

1539

[1, 3, 6]

That light (1), however, does not nourish the eyes of irrational birds, but the pure hearts of those men who believe in God and turn from the love of visible and temporal things to the fulfilling of His precepts. All men can do this if they will, because that light illuminates every man coming into this world (2).

724

1540

[1, 6, 10]

God is quite rightly believed to have created all things from nothing (3), because even if all things formed have been made from matter at hand (4), that matter itself was created entirely out of nothing (5). For one must not be like those men who do not believe the omnipotent God was able to make something out of nothing, when they give thought to the fact that builders and artisans of any kind can build nothing unless they have something out of which to build.

461

1541

[1, 7, 11]

That shapeless matter (6), therefore, which God made out of nothing, was called at first heaven and earth; and it was said: "In the beginning God made heaven and earth" (7), not because this already was, but because this was able to be; for it is also written that heaven was made afterwards. Just as if taking thought about the seed of a tree, we say that the roots and the trunk and the branches and the fruit and the leaves are there, not because they are there already, but because that is, whence they shall be; so too it was said: "In the beginning God made heaven and earth," speaking, as it were, of the seed of heaven and earth, since, as yet disorganized, it would be the matter of heaven and earth. And because it was certain whence heaven and earth would come to be, that matter itself was already called heaven and earth.

470

1542

[1, 14, 20]

"And evening was made, and morning was made (8) . . . .". From this we are to understand that these terms are used for the distinctions themselves of works done in a certain period of time (9): evening on account of the conclusion of work completed, and morning on account of the beginning of work to be done, from a likening of it to works done by men, because for the most part they begin in the morning and they cease in the evening. For it is customary for the divine writings to transfer the words used in human transactions to things divine.

470

1543

[2, 12, 17]

And if the visible woman was actually (10) made by the Lord God in the beginning   510
from the body of the man, it was not done thus without a purpose, so as to hint at some
secret. Was there a lack of slime from which woman might be formed? Or, if He willed,
could God not withdraw a rib without pain from a waking man? If those things were said
figuratively, or even if they were done figuratively, it is not pointless that these things are
said or done in this way; but plainly they are mysteries and sacraments, intended either to
indicate in this way our tenuous condition, or if there be some better explanation, they are
to be interpreted and understood in accord with sound faith (11).

1544

[2, 20, 30]

The man who has cultivated that remote land (12) and who has gotten his bread   1000
by his very great labor is able to suffer this labor to the end of this life. After this life,
however, it is not necessary that he suffer. But the man who perhaps has not cultivated the
land and has allowed it to be overrun with brambles has in this life the curse of his land on
all his works, and after this life he will have either purgatorial fire or eternal punishment
(13).

1. See John 1:9.
2. Augustine notes in his *Corrections* that this passage is not to be understood in a Pelagian sense; that is, as if men could
   fulfill God's commands by their own strength of will and without the help of God's grace. See § 1968 below.
3. *omnia de nihilo fecisse*.
4. *etiamsi omnia formata de ista materia facta sunt*.
5. *de omnino nihilo facta est*.
6. *Informis ergo illa materia*. I have avoided saying "that formless or unformed matter", so as not to give a handle to a
   hylomorphic interpretation which could only be read into and not out of the passage.
7. Gen. 1:1.
8. Gen. 1:19.
9. *in ipsa quidem mora temporis*.
10. *secundum historiam*.
11. This final sentence is rather anacoluthic, but its meaning is plain enough: Possibly Scripture only describes God's
    shaping of man from slime and His shaping of woman from a rib taken from the man while God had cast him into a deep
    sleep, in a figurative way; or, if God actually proceeded in this fashion, His actions were still figures of some higher
    truth. Perhaps the point of the figure is to show the fragile character of man's existence. If someone can think of a better
    explanation, accept that one; only be certain that it is not in conflict with sound Catholic doctrine.
12. See Gen. 3:17.
13. *habebit vel ignem purgationis vel poenam aeternam*.

FREE CHOICE [*inter A. D.* 388-395]

The first book of the *De libero arbitrio* and possibly part of the second book were
written at Rome in 388; and the rest of the second book and all of the third and final
were written at Hippo in the year 395 A. D.

Augustine wrote his *Free Choice* to combat the errors of Manicheism. Little did he
then suppose that his anti-Manichean polemic would afterwards be turned against him by
Pelagius, who quoted the *De libero arbitrio* as evidence against its own author!
Augustine, in writing his *Corrections* 1, 8, found it necessary to point out at
considerable length that in any of the passages in *Free Choice* in which he speaks of
man's ability to turn his will to what is good, if he did not specify that man required
grace to make his choice, it was only because grace was not then under attack. He quite
rightly denies that in attacking Pelagianism he has changed his earlier opinions as

expressed in *Free Choice*, insisting that his manner of expression never was intended to espouse such opinions as are now held by Pelagius, but which, at the time of his own writing, were unheard of.

Migne's Maurist reprint of the text in PL 32, 1221-1303 is now superseded by the edition of William M. Green in the Vienna Corpus, CSEL Vol. 74 (1956).

1545

[2, 6, 14]

Augustine: But I ask you, if you should find that there is nothing superior to our   136
own reason except that which is eternal and unchangeable, would you hesitate to call that God? . . .

Evodius: I would openly acknowledge that that to which it is agreed there exists nothing superior is God.

Augustine: Agreed! It will be enough, then, for me to show that something of this sort exists; and either you will acknowledge that this is God, or, if there is something superior thereto, you will admit that the latter is God.

1546

[2, 20, 54]

Augustine: Every good is from God. There is no nature, therefore, which is not   630
from God. That movement, however, of turning away from God is what we   631
acknowledged was sin, because it is a defective movement and every defect is from nothing. See whence it comes, and you may be certain that it does not come from God. Nevertheless, because it is voluntary, this very defect lies within our power.

1547

[3, 4, 11]

Augustine: Just as you do not, by your memory of them, compel past events to   190
have happened, neither does God, by His foreknowledge, compel future events to take place. And just as you remember certain things which you have done, but have not done all   193
that you remember, so too God foreknows all the things of which He is the Author, but He is not Himself the Author of all that He foreknows. He is not the evil author of what He is the Just Avenger.

THE TRUE RELIGION [*ca. A. D.* 390]

One of Augustine's earlier anti-Manichean writings, the *De vera religione* was written at Tagaste about the year 390. It contrasts the monism of the belief in one true God who is good with the dualism of the Manicheans, which amounts virtually to a belief in two gods, one of good and one of evil. The work is treated in the *Corrections* 1, 12.

The text in Migne, PL 34, 121-172, is superseded by two excellent critical editions of recent years: that of William M. Green, published in 1961 in Vol. 77 of the Vienna Corpus (CSEL); and in 1962, that of K. D. Daur in Vol. 32, pp. 187-260, of the *Corpus Christianorum*. The passages below are translated from Daur's edition.

1548

[7, 12]

We must hold to the Christian religion and to communication in her Church which is   421
Catholic, and which is called Catholic not only by her own members but even by all her
enemies. For when heretics or the adherents of schisms talk about her, not among
themselves but with strangers, willy-nilly (1) they call her nothing else but Catholic. For
they will not be understood unless they distinguish her by this name which the whole
world employs in her regard.

1549

[14, 27]

If that defect, however, which is called sin, should, like a fever, take hold against   631
one's will, the penalty consequent upon sinning, which is called damnation, would
rightly seem to be unjust. Indeed, sin is so voluntary an evil that what is not
voluntary is certainly not a sin (2).   636

1550

[18, 36]

Even if the world was made from some shapeless matter (3), this matter itself was   461
made entirely out of nothing. . . . Thus all that does exist, insofar as it exists, and all that
does not yet exist, insofar as it is able to exist, is from God. This can be said in another
way: all that is shaped, insofar as it is shaped, and all that is not yet shaped, insofar as it
can be shaped, is from God.

1551

[25, 46]

The first decision to be made is whether we should prefer to believe those who call   157
us to the worship of many gods, or those who call us to the one God. Who can   564
doubt that it is preferable to follow those who call us to one, especially when those
worshippers of many agree that this one God is the ruler of all others? And certainly, rank
begins at one (4). Those, therefore, are to be followed first who say that there is only one
supreme God, the true God, who alone is to be worshipped. If truth does not shine forth
with them, then a change is to be made (5).

1. *Velint nolint.*
2. I think no one will quarrel with this statement. Augustine, nevertheless, though it necessary, lest there be any
   misunderstanding possible, to defend it in his *Corrections* 1, 12, 5 (see § 1969 below).
3. *Quapropter etiam si de aliqua informi materia factus est mundus.* In Augustine's theological pre-history, God may first
   have created shapeless matter,—better, I think, to avoid the term formless matter, lest one become involved in a
   discussion of hylomorphism, which is hardly what Augustine had in mind,—and then from this shapeless matter which
   He had made out of nothing, He shaped the world and all that is in it. In no way, then, does Augustine involve himself
   in a denial of *creatio ex nihilo*. Indeed, of the formless matter itself Augustine says expressly: *haec ipsa facta est omnino
   de nihilo.*
4. *Et certe ab uno numerus incipit.*
5. In his *Corrections* 1, 12, 6 (see § 1970 below) Augustine explains and defends this passage, apparently fearing lest
   anyone take the hypothetical doubt, which is no more than a manner of expression, as a real doubt.

EIGHTY-THREE DIVERSE QUESTIONS [*inter A. D.* 389/396]

Augustine's work entitled *De diversis quaestionibus octoginta tribus* is treated in the *Corrections* 1, 25. From the time of his conversion and his return to Africa, whenever questioned on some point of religion, it was Augustine's custom to dictate a reply. The number of these replies grew and there was no order or arrangement about them. But when Augustine was made a bishop, as he himself states, he ordered that they be collected and set down all in one book; and each section was to be numbered for easy reference. The *Eighty-three Diverse Questions*, then, can be dated as having been written intermittently between 389 and 396 A. D.

The Maurist edition in Migne Pl 40, 11-110 is still the standard.

1552

[35, 2]

But what else is it to live happily, except to know that one has something eternally? For that only is eternal of which it is rightly believed that it cannot be lost by him that loves it: that very thing, then, to have which is nothing else but to know it. . . . For whatever is had in the mind is had by knowing; and there is no good perfectly known that is not perfectly loved.

1043
1041

1553

[46, 2]

Individual creatures, therefore, are created according to fit reasons. But where must it be judged that these reasons reside, except in the mind itself of the Creator? For He did not contemplate something located outside Himself as a model by which He might fashion that which He fashioned; to think that would be sacrilege. But if the reasons for all things created and about to be created are contained in the mind of God, and if in the divine mind there can be nothing that is not eternal and unchangeable,—and Plato calls these principal reasons of things ideas,—they are not only ideas but they are real, because they are eternal and at the same time they remain unchangeable. It is by participation in these that it comes about that a thing is whatever it is in whatever way it is.

464

1554

[48]

There are three kinds of credible things. First there are those things which are always believed and never understood. An example of such is all history, concerned as it is with temporal events and human affairs. Second, there are those things which first are understood, so that they can be believed. Of this class are all human reasonings, whether about numbers or about any kind of systematic instructions (1). The third class is of those things which are believed first and understood afterwards. Of such kind as this are the aspects of divine things which cannot be understood except by those who are pure in heart.

562

1555

[60]

When God is said not to know something (2), either it is said in reference to what He does not approve, that is, of something He does not acknowledge in discipline or in doctrines, as when it is said: "I do not know you" (3); or in reference to that which it is useless to know and from which He draws an advantage for those who do not know. It is well accepted, therefore, that when it is said that the Father alone knows, it was so stated

351

because it is He that makes the Son know; and when it is said that the Son does not know, it is so stated because He makes men not to know, that is, He does not avail them of a knowledge which it were useless for them to have.

1556

[68, 5]

And since no one is able to will unless he is incited and called, either intrinsically   682
where no man sees, or extrinsically by the sound of a word or by some visible signs,   692
it is shown that it is God who operates even the will itself in us (4). For to that supper   680
which, in the Gospel, the Lord says has been prepared (5), not all those who were   693
called were willing to come, nor would those who came have been able to come if they had not been called. Therefore those who came must not attribute it to themselves; for, having been called, they came; and those who willed not to come must not attribute it to others but to themselves alone, because they were called, and in free will they could have come.

1. *vel de numeris, vel de quibuslibet disciplinis.*
2. See Matt. 24:36.
3. Matt. 25:12.
4. Phil. 2:13.
5. See Luke 14:16-24.

THE ADVANTAGE OF BELIEVING [A. D. 391 aut 392]

Written most probably in the year 391 or 392 and certainly while he was a priest at Hippo, *De utilitate credendi ad Honoratum* is one of the earliest of Augustine's anti-Manichean works. The Honoratus to whom it was dedicated, as Augustine himself tells us in his *Corrections* 1, 13, 1, was a friend of Augustine still caught in the entangling snares of Manicheism. Honoratus was in the habit of sneering at Catholicism on the grounds that it ordered men to believe but did not then give them any solid reasons for their belief.

The Migne reprint of the Maurist text (PL 42, 65-92) is now superseded by the edition of J. Zycha in the Vienna Corpus, Vol. 25, 1 (1891), pp. 1-48.

1557

[16, 34]

If the providence of God does not govern human affairs there is no point in   132
troubling oneself about religion. But if both the outward appearance of all things,
which surely must be believed to emanate from some font of truest beauty, and   16
some, I know not what to call it except an inward consciousness, exhorts, in public   133
and in private as it were, certain better souls to seek God and to serve Him, we must
not give up hope that the same God Himself has established some authority by   11
which, when we rely on it as on a sure step, we may be lifted up to God.

THE TWO SOULS [A. D. 391 aut 392]

Shortly after writing *The Advantage of Believing*, and most probably in 391 or 392, Augustine wrote another and a more directly anti-Manichean work, *De duabus animabus contra Manichaeos*. The rationale of the title *The Two Souls* is to be found in the

Manichean teaching which credits man with two souls, a good one from God, and an evil one from the Darkness coeternal with God.

Augustine treats his *The Two Souls* in *Corrections* 1, 14, where he points out certain of his remarks that he regretted as being capable of erroneous and Pelagian interpretation. In *Corrections* 1, 14, 4 (see § 1973 below) he defends the definition of sin which is given in *The Two Souls* 11, 15, our § 1558 immediately below.

The Maurist text in Migne 42, 93-112, is superseded by J. Zycha's Vienna Corpus edition, CSEL Vol. 25, 1 (1891).

1558

[11, 15]

Before proceeding further, let us also define sin, which, as every mind reads divinely   636
written in itself, cannot exist apart from will. Sin, therefore, is the will to sustain or follow after what justice forbids, and from which the will is free to abstain (1). If, of course, it were not free, it would not be will; but I have preferred to define it rather more roughly than with any great precision (2).

1. See *Corrections* 1, 14, 4; in § 1973 below.
2. *Sed malui grossius quam scrupulosius definire.*

AGAINST FORTUNATUS THE MANICHEAN [*A. D.* 392]

At Hippo there was a Manichean priest named Fortunatus, who had made many converts to his sect and had in consequence of so large a following a rather comfortable living. Augustine, who thought little enough of comfortable livings, entered into a public debate with him on the twenty-eighth and twenty-ninth of August in the year 392—(the error of certain translations which give the date as the fifth of September undoubtedly originates in the fact that August 28 is the fifth Kalends of September). In his *Corrections* 1, 15, 1 Augustine recalls that on the second day of the debate Fortunatus admitted that he was himself somewhat short on arguments; and, though he did not become a Catholic, he did have sufficient grace to leave Hippo.

The proceedings of the debate were taken down by shorthand stenographers and were afterwards published by Augustine as a book, the title of which is usually given as *Acta seu disputatio contra Fortunatum Manichaeum*.

The Maurist text in Migne, PL 42, 111-130, is superseded by the edition of J. Zycha in the Vienna Corpus, Vol. 25, 1 (1891).

1559

[13]

Augustine: I say that the soul is made by God, just as all things else which are made   506
by God; and among the things which Almighty God made, the principal place was given to the soul (1). And if you ask me what God made the soul out of, just remember that you already agreed with me that God is almighty.

1560

[17]

Augustine: I now ask you, therefore, in reference to that passage which has been   636
read (2): how do we have sins, if a contrary nature compels us to do what we do? For if

someone is compelled by necessity to do something, he does not sin; anyone who sins, sins
by free choice.

1. In the *Corrections* 1, 15, 2 Augustine quotes the whole of this sentence and remarks that in so stating, he intended that it
   be understood in general about the souls of all rational creatures, though now he finds it either quite impossible or at least
   extremely difficult to discover in the Scriptures any mention at all of the souls of angels.
2. Fortunatus had just read aloud Eph. 2:1-18, as if in support of his own position.

FAITH AND THE CREED [*A. D.* 393]

Augustine, a priest only two years, was commissioned to address the Council of
Hippo, scheduled to meet in October, 393 A. D., on the subject of the creed. When
prevailed upon later to publish his address he very probably made some revisions, at least
of a literary kind; but the treatise we have under the title *De fide et symbolo* is at least in
substance his address to the Council of Hippo. And I think I still hear in its halting lines
some of the self-conscious embarrassment that the young man felt in delivering an
address on the faith to which he was so lately come, when his audience consisted of his
superiors, bishops grown old in that faith.
The text in Migne (PL 40, 181-196) is superseded by the edition of J. Zycha in Vol.
41 (1900) of the Vienna Corpus.

1561

[9, 19]
The subject of the Holy Spirit, however, has not yet been sufficiently nor so diligently　267
treated by the great and learned commentators on the Sacred Scriptures, that we can easily
understand what is proper to Him, in view of which property we can call Him neither
Father nor Son, but Holy Spirit only, except that they declare He is the Gift of God, so we
may believe that God does not give a Gift inferior to Himself.　　　　　　　　　　278

1562

[10, 21]
We believe also in the holy Church, that is, the Catholic Church; for heretics　　421
and schismatics call their own congregations churches. But heretics violate the
faith itself by a false opinion about God; schismatics, however, withdraw from
fraternal love by hostile separations, although they believe the same things we do.　415
Consequently, neither heretics nor schismatics belong to the Catholic Church; not heretics,
because the Church loves God; and not schismatics, because the Church loves neighbor.

1563

[10, 23]
And while man consists of these three elements: spirit, soul, and body,—which　500
sometimes are reckoned as two, for often soul is included in the designation of spirit (for　504
it is that certain rational part, which beasts do not have, that is called spirit),—our chief
element is the spirit.

UNFINISHED BOOK ON THE LITERAL INTERPRETATION OF GENESIS
[*ca. A. D.* 393 *aut* 394]

Augustine's *De Genesi ad litteram imperfectus liber* is treated in his *Corrections* 1, 17, where he says that it must be judged against his later and more mature finished work, the *De Genesi ad litteram*.

The titles of Augustine's works can in several instances be confusing. His first writing on Genesis was the *De Genesi contra Manichaeos*, already treated above with §§ 1539-1544, in which in two books he interpreted the first three chapters of Genesis in an allegorical fashion. This work was written in 389 A. D. While engaged in that writing, he conceived the idea of writing also a literal interpretation of Genesis. This he first undertook about the year 393 or 394; and he found it so exhausting a work that without finishing even its first book he laid the work aside. In later years, between 401 and 415 A. D., he began anew and wrote a finished work with the same title, the *De Genesi ad litteram*, in twelve books.

When writing his *Corrections* Augustine came upon his first and unfinished *De Genesi ad litteram*. Of a mind at first to destroy the unfinished work, he finally decided rather to preserve it as a record of his earlier thinking that might be compared with his more mature judgments in the twelve book work of the same title.

The Maurist edition reprinted in Migne PL 34, 219-246 was superseded already in 1894 by J. Zycha's edition in the Vienna Corpus, CSEL Vol. 28, part 1.

1564

[1]
Catholic discipline demands that this Trinity be called One God, and that it be   460
believed that He made and created all things that exist, insofar as they do exist.   461
This means that every creature, whether intellectual or corporeal,—or, to say it more
briefly in the words themselves of the divine Scriptures: whether invisible or
visible,—is not born of God but is made out of nothing by God. And there is   467
nothing in such a creature so formed that can pertain to the Trinity, except that   468
which the Trinity formed. On that account it is not allowed that any creature whatsoever
be said or believed to be either consubstantial or coeternal with God.

THE LORD'S SERMON ON THE MOUNT IN MATTHEW [*inter A. D.* 392/396]

Between the years 392 and 396 Augustine wrote intermittently at a work in two books entitled *De sermone Domini in monte secundum Matthaeum*. He treats of the work at greater length than is usual in his *Corrections* 1, 18.

The Maurist edition reprinted in Migne PL 34, 1229-1308 was superseded in 1967 by Almut Mutzenbecher's edition in the *Corpus Christianorum*, Vol. 35.

1565

[1, 12, 34]
There are three elements by which the process of sinning is completed: suggestion,   630
delectation, and consent. Suggestion can take place through the memory or   636
through the bodily senses, as when we see, or hear, or smell, or taste, or touch   632
something. And if there be a delight in enjoying this experience, if the delight is illicit, it
must be restrained (1). . . . If, however, consent is made to it, there will be a full sin,
known by God in our heart, even if, by deed, it remains unknown to men.

1. *Quo si frui delectaverit, delectatio illicita refrenanda est*.

AGAINST ADIMANT, A DISCIPLE OF MANI [ca. A. D. 394]

The *Contra Adimantum Manichaei discipulum* was written between 393 and 396 A. D., perhaps in 394. Its purpose, as given in the *Corrections* 1, 21, 1, was to refute certain writings of the Manichean Adimant, who had published his arguments that the Old Testament books are in opposition to those of the New.

The Maurist text in Migne, PL 42, 129-172 has yielded its place of standard edition to the text established by J. Zycha in 1891 in the Vienna Corpus, Vol. 25, 1.

1566

[12, 3]

In view of what is written, that the blood of a beast is its soul (1),—except that, as I   853 noted above, it is not my business to be concerned about the soul of a beast,—I can regard even that precept (2) as given by way of being a sign. For the Lord did not hestitate to say: "This is My Body" (3), when He wanted to give a sign of His body.

1567

[17, 2]

This is the clearest and most obvious difference between the two Testaments: fear and   50 love. Fear belongs to the old man, love to the new. Both Testaments, however, are proclaimed and united by the most merciful plan (4) of the One God.

1. See Lev. 17:10 and 17:14.
2. Lev. 17:10, like Gen. 9:4, forbids that the blood of an animal be eaten: "because the soul of the flesh is in the blood" (Lev. 17:11).
3. Matt. 26:26; Mark 14:22; Luke 22:19.
4. *misericordissima dispensatione*.

EXPLANATION OF THE EPISTLE TO THE GALATIANS [ca. A. D. 394]

In his *Corrections* 1, 23 Augustine recalls that, having completed his *Explanation of Certain Passages from the Apostle's Epistle to the Romans*, he then wrote a single book explaining not just selected passages but the whole of the Epistle to the Galatians. We can date this *Epistulae ad Galatas expositio* as having been written *ca.* A. D. 394.

The Maurist text, reprinted in Migne PL 35, 210-2148, is superseded by that of J. Divjak in Vol. 84, pp. 53-141, of the Vienna Corpus (CSEL) edition, 1971.

1568

[49]

Of necessity we act according to that which delights us the more. For example, the   702 shape of a beautiful woman comes to mind, and moves one to the delight of fornication   684 (1). But if that inner and unalloyed beauty apparent in chastity delights us more,   696 through the grace which is in the faith of Christ, we will live according to this and according to this will we act. And thus, not by sin reigning in us to the obeying of its desires, but by justice reigning in us through love, we will do with great delight whatever we know will be pleasing to God.

1. *Quod enim amplius nos delectat, secundum id operemur necesse est: ut verbi gratia occurrit forma speciosae feminae et movet ad delectationem fornicationis.*

VARIOUS QUESTIONS TO SIMPLICIAN [*ca. A.D.* 396]

The two books *De diversis quaestionibus ad Simplicianum* were written most probably in the year 396. Augustine says himself in his *Corrections* 2, 27 that this work is the first he wrote after his being made a bishop (395 A. D.). The Simplician to whom it is addressed was the successor of Ambrose in the See of Milan in 397 A. D.; but Augustine was well-acquainted with Simplician earlier, and there is nothing in the present work to suggest that Simplician is already a bishop.

The work deals with the interpretation of various passages of the Scriptures, concerning which Simplician had sent questions to Augustine.

The Maurist edition in Migne PL 40, 101-148 has recently been superseded by the edition of Almut Mutzenbecher in the *Corpus Christianorum*, Vol. 44 (1970).

1569

[1, 2, 2]

In many passages [Paul] often bears witness to this, putting the grace of faith before   656
works, not as if he wanted to put an end to works, but so as to show that works are the
consequences rather than the precedents of grace. Thus, no man is to suppose that he has   650
received grace because he has done good works but rather that he would not have been able
to do those good works if he had not, through faith, received grace.

1570

[1, 2, 6]

Is it to be said that there could have been no election if there had not been some   206
difference existing even in the mother's womb, either of faith or of works of some kind of
merits? But it is said: "That the purpose of God according to election might remain (1)."
. . . If we read, "When they had not yet been born and had done neither good nor evil,
that the purpose of God according to election might remain (2)," it would mean that they
have done no good nor evil, so that there could be no election based on the deeds of him
who had done good works. . . . The purpose of God according to election, therefore,
does not stand firm, except by His purpose to elect; that is, God does not find good works
in men for the sake of which He chooses them, and whereby His purpose of justification
stands firm of itself. Rather, because His purpose of justifying those who believe remains,
He consequently finds good works which He can then choose for the kingdom of heaven.
For if there were no election, there would be no elect; and it could not rightly be said:
"Who will make accusation against God's elect (3)?" Election, however, does not precede
justification, but justification precedes election. For no one is chosen unless he is already
quite different from him that is rejected. With this in mind, I do not see how it could be
written: "God chose us before the foundation of the world (4)," except in view of
foreknowledge.

1571

[1, 2, 10]

No one, therefore, who is not called believes; but not everyone believes who is   656
called. For many are called, but few are chosen (5): the chosen, certainly, are those
who were not contemptuous of Him who called them, but believed in Him and
followed Him, who believed in Him without doubt because they willed to do so. What   700
is to be said of what follows: "Therefore it is not of him who wills nor of him who runs,   690
but of God who has mercy (6)?" Does it not mean that we cannot even will unless we be
called, and that our willing avails nothing unless God assists us to perform it? It is a matter,

therefore, of willing and of running. For it would not be said in vain: "And on earth peace to men of good will (7)"; and: "Run in such wise that you may attain (8)." But it is not of him that wills nor of him that runs, but of God who has mercy, that we obtain what we will. Esau, then, did not will and did not run; but if he had willed and had run, he would have obtained the help of God, who by calling him would have given him both to will and to run, if he had not become reprobate by his having held that call in contempt.

1572

[1, 2, 12]

    In another place [Paul] says: "In fear and trembling work out your salvation. For 684 it is God who works in you both the will and the work for His own good pleasure (9)." There he shows that the good will itself is produced in us by the working of God. If he had said only: "It is not of him who wills nor of him who runs, but of God who has mercy (10)," because the will of man does not alone suffice for us to live justly 650 and righteously, unless we be aided by God's mercy, he could also have put it this way: "It is not of God, therefore, who has mercy, but of the man who wills it," 700 because the mercy alone of God does not suffice, unless the consent of our will be added. It is clear that we will in vain, unless God have mercy; but I do not know how it might be said that God has mercy in vain, unless we will. For if God does have mercy, we do also will; for the fact that we will pertains to that same mercy. For 696 it is God who works in us both the will and the performance, for His good will (11). If we ask whether a good will be the gift of God, it were remarkable if anyone would dare answer in the negative. But because good will does not precede the call, 692 whereas the call does precede a good will, that we do have a good will is rightly attributed to God, and that we are called cannot be attributed to ourselves. The saying therefore, that "it is not of him who wills nor of him that runs, but of God who has mercy (12)," cannot be taken to mean that without God's help we cannot achieve what we will, but rather that without His call we cannot even will.

1573

[1, 2, 13]

    But if that call is efficacious of good will, in such a way that everyone who is 696 called follows that call, how will it be true that "many are called, but few are chosen (13)"? But if this is true, and consequently not everyone who is called obeys 700 the call, since it is in the power of his will not to obey, it can rightly be said that it is not of God who has mercy, but of the man who wills and runs, because the mercy of God's calling him does not suffice unless it be followed by the obedience of him that is called. Or is it perhaps that those who are called in this way and do not 704 consent might be able to direct their wills to faith if they were called in some other way, so that it were still true that many are called but few are chosen, if many are called in one way, but not all are affected in the same way, and only those follow the call who are found fit to receive it? And thus it would be no less true that it is not of him who wills and of him who runs, but of God who has mercy (14): of God, who called in a way that was apt to those who followed His call. Certainly His call comes also to others; but because it were such that they could not be moved by it, nor were they apt to its reception, they can be said to have been called but not chosen. And again it would not be true that it is not of God who has mercy, but of man who wills and who runs. For the effect of God's mercy cannot be in the power of man, so that God would be merciful in vain if man willed not to have it; because, if God willed to be merciful even to those, He were able to issue a call that were apt to them, so that they would be moved and would understand and would follow His call. It is true, therefore, that many are called, but few are chosen. There are the chosen, who are called aptly (15); and there are those who neither correspond (16) to the call nor obey it, those who are not chosen, because they did not follow, even though they were called. And again it is true that it is not of him who is willing and who runs, but of God who has mercy, because, even if He calls many, it is on those whom He calls in such a way that they are apt to His call, so that they may follow it, that He has mercy.

1574

[1, 2, 14]

Since, therefore, men are moved to faith, one in this way and another in another way,   704
and the same thing said in one way may move them while said in another way it may not move them, and one man may be moved while another man is not moved, would anyone dare to affirm that God has no way of calling by which even Esau might have applied his mind and yoked his will to the faith in which Jacob was justified?

1575

[1, 2, 21]

We are commanded to live righteously, and the reward is set before us of our   771
meriting to live happily in eternity. But who is able to live righteously and do good   776
works (17) unless he has been justified by faith?

1576

[1, 2, 22]

Do we not see that many of our faithful people, walking in the way of God, cannot   684
be compared for natural ability (18), I will not say with certain heretics, but even with comic actors? Do we not see some of either sex living blamelessly in conjugal chastity, but who are either heretics or pagans, or who are in the true Church but are so luke-warm in the true faith, that we marvel to see them surpassed not just in patience and temperance, but even in faith, hope, and love, by whores and actors suddenly converted? It remains, therefore, that wills may choose. But the will itself, unless something happen which pleases and invites the mind (19), is not able to be moved in any way. That this should happen is not in man's power.

1. Rom. 9:11.
2. Augustine has expressed an uncertainty whether the line *ut secundum electionem propositum Dei maneret* belongs with what precedes or with what follows it in the Scriptures (Rom. 9:11). He has decided to connect it with the passage preceding, and the *that* or *so that* will then have the force of *whereby*; that is, they have done neither good nor evil *whereby* the election of God might stand.
3. Rom. 8:33.
4. Eph. 1:4.
5. Matt. 20:16.
6. Rom. 9:16.
7. Luke 2:14.
8. 1 Cor. 9:24.
9. Phil. 2:12-13. The phrase "for His own good pleasure" is *pro bona voluntate*. The line has a certain flavor in Latin, and especially in a context of Augustine's discussion of will, free will, and grace, which must be lost in English. Translated quite literally the Scripture passage would read: "For it is God who works in you both to will and to work, for good will." The good will is God's on account of which He so works in us. But I am not certain that it does not have overtones and secondary meanings in Augustine's mind, of God's producing a good will in us; and sometimes, as in the present instance, he seems to take the passage as if its primary meaning were that God works in us both the will to have a good will and also the actual production of that good will. This last, of course, is undoubtedly true; but that is not necessarily the meaning of the Scriptural passage which he so frequently cites.
10. Rom. 9:16.
11. *Deus enim est qui operatur in nobis et velle et operari pro bona voluntate.* Phil. 2:13. The quote is the same as above, at note 9.

12. Rom. 9:16.
13. Matt. 22:14.
14. Rom. 9:16.
15. *congruenter*.
16. *congruebant*.
17. *et bene operari*.
18. *ex nulla parte ingenio comparari*.
19. *animum*.

CHRISTIAN COMBAT [*A. D.* 396 *aut* 397]

Augustine's *De agone christiano* was written possibly in 396 but more probably in 397 A. D. In his *Corrections* 2, 29 he indicates that he wrote the work to expound in simple language the rule of faith and the precepts for living, for the sake of those faithful who were not capable of grasping the same notions when expressed in loftier theological language.

The Maurist text in Migne PL 40, 289-310 is superseded by the edition of J. Zycha in the Vienna Corpus, Vol. 41 (1900).

1577

[11, 12]

Are there any foolish people who say that the Wisdom of God could not otherwise   361
liberate men than by accepting manhood and being born of a woman, and by suffering all   261
things at the hands of sinners? We reply to them: He could have done anything;
but if He had done otherwise, He would still have displeased your stupidity. . . . We
have been shown to what fragility man has been reduced by his own fault, and from
what fragility he is delivered by divine assistance.

1578

[22, 24]

Let us not listen to those who say that our Lord had just such a body as was apparent   311
in the dove which John the Baptist saw descending from the sky (1) and hovering over the
Lord as a sign of the Holy Spirit. . . . Where we read that the Holy Spirit appeared   314
to John in the form of a dove, there too we read that Christ was born of a woman. We
ought not believe one part of the Gospel and disbelieve another. . . . But the
reason why the Holy Spirit was not born of a dove, as Christ was born of a woman, is that
the Holy Spirit did not come to liberate doves, but to signify for men innocence and
spiritual love, which He symbolized in a visible way in the form of a dove. Our Lord
Jesus Christ, however, who came to liberate mankind, in which both males and
females are destined to salvation, was not averse to males, for He took the form of a
male, nor to females, for of a female He was born. Besides, there is a great mystery (2)
here: that just as death comes to us through a woman, Life is born to us through a   784
woman; that the devil, defeated, would be tormented by each nature, feminine and
masculine, since he had taken delight in the defection of both.

1578a

[22, 24]

We do not mean to suggest that only the Lord Jesus Christ had a true body, and that   311
the Holy Spirit [when, at Christ's baptism in the Jordan, He appeared in the form of a   781
dove] took on a mere appearance in the eyes of men. We believe that both those

bodies were real. Just as it was impossible that the Son of God should deceive men, so too, it were unworthy of the Holy Spirit to deceive men. For it was not difficult for Almighty God, who formed the whole of creation out of nothing, to shape the real body of a dove without the agency of other doves, just as it was not difficult for Him to form a real body in Mary's womb without human seed.

1579

[31, 33]

Let us not listen to those who deny that the Church of God is able to forgive all sins. They are wretched indeed, because they do not recognize in Peter the rock (3) and they refuse to believe that the keys of the kingdom of heaven, lost from their own hands, have been given to the Church. These are the people who condemn as adulteresses widows who marry, and boast that theirs is a purity superior to the teaching of the Apostles!

900

1. *de caelo*.
2. *magnum sacramentum*.
3. *in Petro petram non intellegunt*.

AGAINST THE LETTER OF MANI CALLED "THE FOUNDATION" [*A. D.* 397]

The *Letter of Mani Called "The Foundation"* is not extant, except for the few quotes from it which Augustine offers. Apparently it was a treatise by Mani which served as a kind of catechism of Manicheism.

In the *Contra epistulam Manichaei quam vocant fundamenti*, written in 397 A. D., Augustine deals only with the beginning of the *Letter of Mani*. He made some notes on other parts of it, as he states in the *Corrections* 2, 28, with the idea of eventually writing a refutation of the whole work. Unfortunately he never did write the fuller work; if he had, we might now be able to reconstruct the whole of the *Letter of Mani*.

The Maurist text in Migne, PL 42, 173-206, has yielded its position of standard edition to the edition of J. Zycha in the Vienna Corpus, CSEL, Vol. 25, 1 (1891).

1580

[4, 5]

In the Catholic Church, not to speak of that purest wisdom, to the knowledge of which a few spiritual men attain in this life, in such a way that, in its least part only, for they are but men, they know it without any doubting, while the rest of the multitude finds its greatest safety not in lively understanding but in the simplicity of believing,— not to speak, I say, of that wisdom which you do not believe is present in the Catholic Church, there are many other things which, most properly, can keep me in her bosom. The unanimity (1) of peoples and nations keeps me here. Her authority, inaugurated in miracles, nourished by hope, augmented by love, and confirmed by her age, keeps me here. The succession of priests, from the very see of the Apostle Peter, to whom our Lord, after His resurrection, gave the charge of feeding His sheep, up to the present episcopate, keeps me here. And at last, the very name of Catholic, which, not without reason, belongs to this Church alone, in the face of so many heretics, so much so that, although all heretics want to be called Catholic, when a stranger inquires where the Catholic Church meets (2), none of the heretics would dare to point out his own basilica or house (3).

418

421
422

1581

[5, 6]

If you should find someone who does not yet believe in the Gospel, what would   450
you answer him when he says: "I do not believe"? Indeed, I would not believe in   100
the Gospel myself if the authority of the Catholic Church did not influence me to do
so (4).

1. *consensio*.
2. *ubi ad Catholicam conveniatur*.
3. *nullus haereticorum vel basilicam suam vel domum audeat ostendere*.
4. *Ego vero evangelio non crederem, nisi me catholicae ecclesiae commoveret auctoritas*.

CHRISTIAN INSTRUCTION [*A. D.* 397 *et* 426]

Augustine's *De doctrina christiana* is in four books. The first two books and most of
the third were completed by April of 397, and not much earlier than that. The work then
lay unfinished until Augustine had already begun writing his *Corrections*. When he
came to treat the work in his *Corrections*, he found it still unfinished; and before going
on with the *Corrections*, he completed it by finishing off book three and adding book
four, almost certainly in the year 427 A. D.

Apparently the work had been published earlier in what Augustine afterwards
regarded as an unfinished state; for in the *Corrections* 2, 30 Augustine corrects three
statements which he had made in book two of the work; and if it had not already been
published, he would undoubtedly simply have changed the passages rather than publish
a correction of them. In 2, 8, 13 he had said that the book of Wisdom was written most
assuredly by the author of Ecclesiasticus, Jesus (the son of) Sirach. He has now learned
that ben Sirach is almost certainly not the author of Wisdom.

Also in 2, 8, 13, he had said that the authority of the Old Testament rests in the
forty-four books thereof, which he enumerated. He is sorry now that he put it that way
without making it clear that he was using the term Old Testament as it is generally used
in the Church, whereas Paul seems to apply that term only to the covenant made on
Mount Sinai (Gal. 4:24). And a third point: he regrets that his memory deceived him
when he said (in 2, 28, 43) that Ambrose had settled a historical problem and had
demonstrated that Plato and Jeremias were contemporaries. He now suggests that readers
can check for themselves what Ambrose did actually say, in his *De philosophia* and in
his *De sacramentis*. The last remark, moreover, provides a valuable attestation to the
long disputed but now generally acknowledged authenticity of Ambrose's *De
sacramentis*.

The Maurist text in Migne PL 34, 15-122 has now been entirely superseded by the
edition of Joseph Martin in the *Corpus Christianorum*, Vol. 32 (1967), pp. 1-167.

1582

[1, 5, 5]

Thus there are Father and Son and Holy Spirit, and each of these individually is   282
God, and at the same time all are one God; and each of these individually is the full
substance of God, and at the same time all are one substance. The Father is neither   281
the Son nor the Holy Spirit; the Son is neither the Father nor the Holy Spirit;
the Holy Spirit is neither the Father nor the Son. The Father is the Father only, and
the Son is the Son only, and the Holy Spirit is the Holy Spirit only. The three have the
same eternity, the same unchangeableness, the same majesty, the same power. In the   279
Father there is unity, in the Son equality, and in the Holy Spirit the harmony of

unity and equality; and these three are all one because of the Father, all equal because of
the Son, all connected because of the Holy Spirit.

1583

[1, 22, 21]
    For this rule of love is divinely established. "Love your neighbor as yourself,"   594
He says; but "God with your whole heart, with your whole soul, with your whole mind   598
(1)," so that you will devote all your thoughts and all your life and all your intellect
to Him from whom you have those very things which you devote to Him.

1584

[2, 8, 12]
    With the canonical Scriptures, however, [the intelligent investigator] will follow   40
the authority of the greater part of the Catholic Churches (2), among which surely
are those which deserved to have Apostolic sees and to receive Epistles. He will keep to
this method, therefore, with the canonical Scriptures, preferring those which are
accepted by all Catholic Churches to those which some do not accept. With those,
however, which are not accepted by all, he will prefer those which the greater number
and more eminent Churches accept, to those which fewer Churches of lesser authority
hold (3).

1585

[2, 8, 13]
    The whole canon of the Scriptures, however, in which we say that that consideration   41
(4) is to be applied, is contained in these books: the five of Moses, namely, Genesis,
Exodus, Leviticus, Numbers, and Deuteronomy; and one book of Jesus Nave,
one of Judges; one little book which is called Ruth, which seems rather to pertain to the
beginning of Kingdoms; then the four of Kingdoms; and the two of Paralipomenon,
which do not follow the former, but are, as it were, joined to them side by side
and proceed along with them. These are the Historical Books, which contain a connected
account of the times and have an orderly arrangement. But there are others too, of a
different order, which neither belong to this order nor are they connected among
themselves, such as Job and Tobias and Esther and Judith and the two books of
Maccabees; and the two of Esdras, which seem rather to follow that orderly history up
to its termination in Kingdoms or Paralipomenon. Then there are the Prophets, in
which there is one book of the Psalms of David; and three of Solomon: Proverbs,
Canticle of Canticles, and Ecclesiastes. But as to those two books, one of which is
entitled Wisdom and the other of which is entitled Ecclesiasticus, and which are called
"of Solomon" because of a certain similarity to his books, it is held most certainly that
they were written by Jesus Sirach (5). They must, however, be accounted among
the Prophetic Books, because of the authority that is deservedly accredited to them.
The rest are the books of those who are properly termed Prophets: the individual books of
the twelve prophets, which are connected among themselves and are reckoned as
one, because they have never been separated, of which Prophets these are the names:
Osee, Joel, Amos, Abdias, Jonas, Micheas, Nahum, Habacuc, Sophonias, Aggeus,
Zacharias, and Malachias. Then there are the volumes of the four Major Prophets
(6): Isaias, Jeremias, Daniel, and Ezechiel. With these forty-four books the authority
of the Old Testament is concluded (7). That of the New is in the Gospel of four   42
books: according to Matthew, according to Mark, according to Luke, and according to
John; in the fourteen Epistles of the Apostle Paul: to the Romans, in two to the

Corinthians, to the Galatians, to the Ephesians, to the Philippians, in two to the
Thessalonians, to the Colossians, in two to Timothy, to Titus, to Philemon, to the
Hebrews; in two of Peter, in three of John; in one of Jude and in one of James; in the
Acts of the Apostles in one book, and in the Apocalypse of John in one book. [2, 9, 14]
In all these books those who fear God and are meek in their piety seek the will of God.

1586

[3, 10, 16]

I define love (8) as a movement of the mind (9) directed to the enjoyment of God for   593
his own sake, and self and neighbor for the sake of God. Lust (10), however, is a   594
movement of the mind directed to the enjoyment of self and neighbor and whosesoever   630
body, not for the sake of God.

1587

[3, 16, 24]

If a preceptive statement [in the Scriptures] forbids either vice or crime, or commands   850
what is either useful or beneficial, it is not figurative. If, however, it seems to command
vice or crime, or forbid what is either useful or beneficial, it is figurative. ''Unless,''
He says, ''you eat the flesh of the Son of Man and drink His blood, you shall not
have life in you (11).'' It seems to command crime or vice; therefore it is a figure,
prescribing that there be communication in the Lord's passion and a grateful and   849
salutary treasured remembrance that His flesh was crucified and wounded for us (12).

1588

[3, 27, 38]

When from the same words of Scripture not just one but two or more interpretations   30
are possible, even if the meaning intended by him who wrote it is unknown, there
is no danger, so long as one of them can be shown from other passages of the Holy
Scriptures to be in accord with the truth. But one who searches the divine sayings should   20
strive to arrive at the meaning intended by the author through whom the Holy Spirit
brought that Scripture into being.

1. Lev. 19:18; Deut. 6:5; Matt. 22:37-39.
2. *ecclesiarum catholicarum quam plurium auctoritatem sequatur*. It is apparent, moreover, from what follows, that
   Augustine sees this authority as obtaining a superiority not only through numbers but also through the comparative
   dignities of the individual Churches in question.
3. This rule is set down also in Can. 38 of the Council of Hippo of 393 A. D.; and in Can. 47 of the Council of Carthage of
   397 A. D.
4. He refers to the rule or method espoused in § 1584 immediately above.
5. As I noted in the introduction to the *Christian Instruction* Augustine retracted this statement in his *Corrections* 2, 30,
   where he says that he now knows it is quite improbable that Ben Sirach wrote the book of Wisdom.
6. *Deinde quattuor prophetae sunt maiorum voluminum.*
7. In his *Corrections* Augustine needlessly expressed some regret over this statement, as indicated above in the brief
   introduction to the present writing.
8. *caritatem.*
9. *animi.*
10. *cupiditatem.*
11. John 6:54.
12. *figura ergo est, praecipiens passioni domini esse communicandum et suauiter atque utiliter recondendum in memoria,*
    quod pro nobis caro eius crucifixa et uulnerata sit.

RUDIMENTARY CATECHESIS [*ca. A. D.* 400]

Undoubtedly the most commonly read of Augustine's works are his *Confessions* and his *City of God*. None could dispute that fact. If his third most popular work were to be asked for, most would reply, I think, that it is his *De catechizandis rudibus*. His friend, Deogratias, a deacon of the Church at Carthage, had asked Augustine for something that would be useful in instructing candidates to the catechumenate. The present work, in one book, is Augustine's response. It is not unlikely that this deacon Deogratias is the same person to whom, as a priest of Carthage a few years later, Letter 102 in the Augustinian corpus is addressed.

The *De catechizandis rudibus* is to be dated about 400 A. D., quite possibly belonging to that very year.

In his *Corrections* 2, 40 Augustine has but little to say of the work, but does note that in section 18, 30, where he stated: "The angel who, with the other spirits who were his satellites, forsook obedience to God through pride and became the devil, did not injure God in any way, but only himself; for God knows how to deal with souls that forsake Him"; he ought rather have said ". . . spirits that forsake Him", since he was speaking of angels.

The Maurist edition in Migne PL 40, 309-348 has lately been superseded by the edition of J. B. Bauer in the *Corpus Christianorum*, Vol. 46 (1969), pp. 121-178.

1589

[4, 7]

But what better reason is there for the coming of Christ, than that God might show   372
His love among us, and how very great that love is (1); for, when we were still his
enemies, Christ died for us (2)? But this was done also, since the end of the   596
commandment and the fullness of the law is love (3), so that we might love one another
and lay down our life for the brethren just as He laid down His life for us (4); and in
regard to God Himself, if before it were tedious to love Him, now at least it will
not be tedious; because God first loved us (5) and did not spare His only Son, but
delivered Him up for us (6). For there is no greater invitation to being loved than to offer
one's own love first. . . . [8] The Lord Jesus Christ, the God-man, is both a   373
manifestation of divine love in us and an example of human humility among us, so that
our great pride (7) might be healed by an even greater contrary medicine. For a proud
man is a great misery; but a humble God is a greater mercy.

1590

[5, 9]

It is certainly a very rare occurrence, nay, I should say that it never happens, that   760
anyone comes to us wishing to become a Christian, who has not already been struck
by some kind of a fear of God. For if it is in expectation of some preferential treatment
from men, whom he thinks he can please in no other way, or to avoid some
discriminatory treatment from men whose displeasure or hostility he dreads, that he
wishes to become a Christian, he wishes more to feign being one than really to be one.

1. *commendans eam vehementer.*
2. See Rom. 5:6-9.
3. 1 Tim. 1:5 and Rom. 13:10.
4. 1 John 3:16.
5. 1 John 4:10.
6. Rom. 8:32.
7. *magnus tumor noster.*

CONFESSIONS [*A. D.* 400]

When Augustine wrote the thirteen books of his *Confessiones*, about the year 400 and rather probably in that very year, he invented a new kind of literature. Nothing like it, either in form or in content, had ever been done before. And I am not certain that there has been anything quite like it since. In a sense his work is an autobiography; and yet the details of the author's life are not really of primary concern. It is all addressed to God, and it is as much a lengthy prayer as it is an autobiography. The first ten books of the work are about Augustine himself; the last three are about Sacred Scripture.

In the *Corrections* 2, 32, 1, Augustine says: "The thirteen books of my *Confessions* praise the righteous and good God for my actions, good and evil, and lift up the understanding and affection of men to Him." It is not certain, therefore, whether Augustine intended the term *Confessions* in the sense of confessions of faults or in the sense of confessions of faith.

The work is read in every language and has taken its place among the handful of Christian classics that are universally known and loved. Only God Himself can know how many souls have turned to Him through His having given them the grace to read Augustine's *Confessions*.

The Maurist text in Migne, PL 32, 659-868, has yielded its place as standard edition to that of P. Knöll in the Vienna Corpus, CSEL, Vol. 33 (1896).

1591

[1, 1, 1]

Man, who is but a portion of Your creation, wishes to praise You. You excite him so that he may find pleasure in praising You, because You made us for Yourself, and our hearts are restless until they rest in You.   1040

1591a

[1, 6, 10]

Was ever artisan equipped for creating himself? Or is there any other channel through which being and life might flow into us, except that we are made by You, O Lord, for whom being and living are not two different things, because infinite existence and infinite life are the same? For You are infinite and You do not change. Today does not pass away in You; and yet in You it does pass away, because all those things that do pass away are in You, and they could not have even any being that passes away if You did not hold them in existence.   140

1592

[2, 7, 15]

I count up Your graces and Your mercies, because You have melted my sins away as if they were ice. And whatever evils I have not done, that too I reckon as Your grace. For what might I not have done when I loved vice for its own sake? I acknowledge that all things have been forgiven me, both the evils I did of my own free will (1), and those which, by Your guidance, I did not actually do. Is there any man who, considering his own weakness, would dare to attribute his chastity and innocence to his own powers, and thereby love You less, as if Your mercy, by which You forgive the sins of those whom You have converted to Yourself, were less necessary to him?   681

657

1593

[7, 10, 16]

I found myself far from You in a region of dissension (2); and it was as if I heard Your   877
voice from on high: "I am the food of adults; grow, and you shall eat Me. You will   878
not then change Me into yourself, like the food of your flesh, but you shall be changed   16
into Me." And I came to know that You corrected man for his wickedness and
You made my soul shrivel up like a moth (3); and I said: "Is truth nothing at all, then,
because it has no extension in space, either finite or infinite?" And You called out
from afar: "I am who am (4)." And I heard as one hears in his heart, and there was   130
no longer any grounds in me for doubt. I would more easily have doubted my own   560
existence than I would have doubted that truth is that which is clearly seen,
being understood through the things that are made (5).

1594

[8, 8, 20]

If I tore my hair, if I beat my forehead, if I locked my fingers and clasped my knee, I   702
did it because I willed to do it. But I might have willed and not have done it, if
there had been no mobility in my limbs. I did so many things where the will to do them
was not the same thing as the ability to do them; and yet I did not do what would
have pleased me incomparably more to do, a thing which I could have done as soon as I
willed to do it, if as soon as I willed to do it I had willed wholeheartedly to do it. For in
that matter the power and the will were the same, to will it was indeed to do it;
and yet it was not done.

1595

[10, 43, 68]

Christ was shown to holy men of old, that they might be saved by faith in His   389
passion to come, just as we are saved by faith in His passion already past. Inasmuch as   387
He is a man, He is Mediator; inasmuch as He is the Word, He is not something in
between, because He is equal to God, God with God, and together one God. [69]   372
How much You have loved us, good Father, You that spared not Your only Son, but
delivered Him up for the sake of impious men (6)! How You have loved us! For us,
He decided not to cling to His equality with You, but was made obedient even to
death on the cross (7), He alone who was free among the dead, having the power to lay   350
down His life as well as that of taking it up again (8). For us He was to You both Victor   382
and Victim, and Victor because He was Victim. For us He was to You both Priest
and Sacrifice, and Priest because He was Sacrifice. From slaves He made us Your
sons, by His being a slave to You, who was born of You.

1596

[11, 4, 6]

Behold, there are the heavens and the earth; and they cry aloud that they were made,   137
for they change and vary. For if anything was not made and yet exists, there is   460
never anything in it that was not there before, which were to change and vary. They cry
aloud, too, that they did not make themselves: "We exist, because we were made; but
we did not exist before we began to exist, so that we might have given existence
to ourselves!" And their very presence is the voice with which they speak. You,
Lord, You that are beautiful made them, for they are beautiful; You that are good, for   179
they are good; You that are, for they are. But they are not beautiful, they are not   177
                                                                                              140

good, they are not in existence the same as You, their Creator; for compared to
You they are not beautiful, they are not good, and they are not.

1. *quae mea sponte feci mala.*
2. *in regione dissimilitudinis.*
3. Ps. 38[39]:12.
4. Ex. 3:14.
5. Rom. 1:20.
6. Rom. 8:32.
7. Phil. 2:6-8.
8. Ps. 87[88]:6.

AGAINST FAUSTUS THE MANICHEAN [*ca. A. D.* 400]

When Augustine was himself a hearer of Manicheism, as he recalls in his *Confessions*,
as often as he raised any objection or point of inquiry, he was told that he must wait
for the arrival of Faustus of Milevis, who would answer all his difficulties with an amazing
clarity. Finally Faustus, the great teacher, arrived; and Augustine found him as ignorant
as all the rest. Faustus remained a sore point with Augustine all his life, probably
in part because of his own chagrin at having been so gullible as to allow himself to have
been taken in for so long.

Of all his anti-Manichean writings, it is the *Contra Faustum Manichaeum*, in
thirty-three books and belonging quite possibly to the year 400, which may be regarded as
the major work. But for all his personal feeling in the matter, Augustine is always a
gentleman even in his polemical writings, and he does not cease to be a gentleman even in
his treatment of Faustus. Augustine is no more capable of losing his temper than
Jerome is of keeping his.

The Migne reprint of the Maurist edition, PL 42, 207-518, is superseded by J. Zycha's
edition, constituting the principal content of CSEL, Vol. 25, 1 (1891).

1597

[11, 5]

If something in the Scriptures seems to be absurd, it is not permissible to say: "The   25
author of this book does not keep to the truth." Rather, "Either the codex is faulty, or the   28
translator erred, or you have not understood it." . . . In that canonical collection of   61
sacred writings (1), whatever is shown, by the confirmation of the canon itself, to have
been said in his writings by even one Prophet or Evangelist, it is not permissible to doubt
that it is true. Otherwise there will be no page left to curb the infirmity of human
ignorance, if the most wholesome authority of those books is either wholly abolished
through contempt or is subjected to interminable confusion.

1598

[17, 3]

Tell us straight out that you do not believe in the Gospel of Christ; for you believe   566
what you want in the Gospel and disbelieve what you want. You believe in yourself
rather than in the Gospel.

1599

[18, 4]

The things in the Law and in the Prophets which Christians do not observe are   51
those which did but signify the things they do observe. They were but figures of things   52

to come, which figures, now that the things themselves have been revealed and made
present by Christ, must be removed, so that in the very fact of their removal the
Law and the Prophets may be fulfilled.

1600

[18, 6]
   In regard to the sacrifices of animals, who among us does not know that they were   51
enjoined more because they suited a perverse people than because God had any
desire for such sacrifices? But even in these sacrifices there were figures of ours;   300
for our being cleansed and God's being propitiated are as naught to us if there be no   892
blood. Christ, by whose blood we are redeemed and cleansed, is the truth of those
figures.

1601

[19, 11]
   There is no religion, true or false, in whose name men can gather, except they be   790
united under a bond of signs or visible Sacraments. The force of these Sacraments
can scarcely be told, and to hold them in contempt is sacrilegious.

1602

[19, 13]
   Thus those first Sacraments, which were observed and celebrated in obedience to   51
the law, were by way of prior announcements of Christ who was to come. And when   52
Christ, by His coming, had fulfilled them, they were taken away, and they were taken
away because they were fulfilled; for He came not to destroy the law but to fulfill it (2).
And now that the justice of faith has been revealed and the yoke of slavery (3), which had
suitably been given to a hard and carnal people, has been taken away from the sons of God
called to liberty (4), other Sacraments have been instituted, greater in strength, more
beneficial in their use, easier of performance, and fewer in number.

1603

[20, 21]
   A Christian people celebrates together in religious solemnity the memorials of   121
the martyrs, both to encourage their being imitated and so that it can share in their   122
merits and be aided by their prayers. But it is done in such a way that our altars are
not set up to any one of the martyrs,—although in their memory,—but to God
Himself, the God of those martyrs. Who, indeed, of the presiding priests
assisting at the altar in the places of the saints (5) ever said "We offer to you, Peter,
or Paul, or Cyprian"? What is offered is offered to God, who crowned the
martyrs. . . . That worship, which the Greeks call λατρεία and for which there is   1
in Latin no single term (6), and which is expressive of the subjection owed to
Divinity alone, we neither accord nor teach that it should be accorded to any save
to the one God.

1604

[20, 21]
   In the Psalms these words are sung: "A sacrifice of praise will glorify Me, and the   892
path is there, where I will show him My salvation" (7). Before the coming of Christ,
the Flesh and Blood of this sacrifice (8) is promised by victims offered as likenesses

thereto; in the Passion of Christ it is rendered in very truth; after Christ's Ascension it is   891
celebrated by sacramental memorial (9).   849

1605

[22, 27]
   Sin, therefore, is anything done, said, or desired against the eternal law. Truly,   630
the eternal law is the divine reason or will of God, commanding that natural order be
preserved and forbidding its breach. You ask what, then, in man, is this natural order. For
man consists of soul and body, but so do the beasts. There is no doubt that in the natural
order the soul is superior to the body. But in the soul of man there is reason, which is not
present in the beast. Therefore, just as the soul is superior to the body, so too in the soul
itself reason is superior, by the law of nature, to those other parts which the beasts also
have.

1606

[28, 2]
   Just as I believe that that book is of Mani, because it has been kept and handed down   64
by his disciples in a sure succession of your leaders (10) from the very time at which Mani
lived in the flesh up to your own times, so also do I ask you to believe that this book is of
Matthew, which has been handed down in the Church in a sure and connected succession
from the time when Matthew himself lived in the flesh, in an uninterrupted sequence of
time, even to the present.

1607

[33, 6]
   What writings can ever have any weight of authority if the evangelical and apostolic   40
writings have no authority? How can we ever be certain about the authenticity of any book,
if we doubt the apostolic origins of those writings which the Church, propagated by the
Apostles themselves and held in such great esteem among all peoples, claims and holds as
writings of the Apostles? And would it be regarded as certain that the Apostles wrote these
books, if, long after the existence of the Apostles, they were brought forward by heretics,
who are called by the names of their own founders and who are inimical to the Church?

1. *In illa canonica eminentia sacrarum litterarum.*
2. Matt. 5:17.
3. Gal. 5:1.
4. Gal. 5:13.
5. *Quis enim antistitum in locis sanctorum assistens altari.*
6. It is true that Latin was deficient in terms sufficient for the necessary distinctions in the theology of worship. But
   theologians have supplied for this deficiency by borrowing the terms from Greek and using them as Latin terms. *Latria* is
   the worship given God only. *Dulia* is the worship (veneration) given the saints. The special worship (veneration) given
   the Blessed Mother is called *hyperdulia*, as being something above *dulia* but still a species distinct from *latria*. We can
   see, then, that Latin has only one term, *cultus*, not distinguishing the three kinds thereby. English distinguishes *worship*
   (properly divine *cultus*) and *veneration* (sanctoral *cultus*); but it also uses the term *worship* generically as *veneration* and
   even *reverence*, in speaking of the *worship* of saints and of the Blessed Mother.
7. Ps. 49[50]:23.
8. *I. e.*, the sacrifice of Christ.
9. *per sacramentum memoriae.*
10. *praepositorum vestrorum* can be translated *your leaders*, or, just as easily, *your forebears*. Etymologically it speaks of
    those who are positioned ahead, but gives no indication of whether the aheadness is to be taken in regard to time or in
    regard to dignity.

THE HARMONY OF THE EVANGELISTS [ca. A. D. 400]

The *De consensu evangelistarum libri quattuor* was begun about 400 A. D. It is not a harmony of the Gospels such as Tatian's was, but is rather a treatise showing, passage by passage and in a very complete and thorough manner, that the Evangelists are not in disagreement with each other in their separate accounts. Augustine discusses this work, giving the reason for its having been written and offering three minor emendations, in his *Corrections* 2, 42.

The Maurist text in Migne PL 34, 1041-1230 is superseded by the Vienna Corpus edition of F. Weihrich in CSEL, Vol. 43 (1904).

1608

[1, 3, 6]

Since Matthew centers his purpose around the person of the King, while Luke is concerned with the person of the Priest, certainly they both bring into great prominence the humanity of Christ. For it is in His humanity that Christ is made both King and Priest. God gave Him the throne of His father David, so that His kingdom would have no end (1), and so that He, the Mediator of God and men, the Man Jesus Christ (2), might intercede for us.

382

387

1609

[1, 35, 54]

Since the Evangelists wrote what Christ stated and declared, it ought by no means be said that He wrote nothing Himself, when in fact His members accomplished that which they had knowledge of by the statements of the Head. For whatever He willed that we should read of His deeds and sayings, He commanded to be written by those Evangelists, as if they were His own hands.

21

1610

[2, 1, 2]

Matthew, therefore, follows out the human generation of Christ, noting His ancestors from Abraham onwards, carrying them on to Joseph, the husband of Mary, of whom Jesus was born (3). For in this way it was not allowed that He should be thought of as apart from the marriage of Mary, although she bore Christ not from intercourse in that marriage but as a virgin (4). By this example it is strongly intimated to the married faithful that even when continence is observed by their common consent, their marriage can still perdure and still be called a marriage, not by a physical joining of the sexes but by the maintaining of the affections of the mind.

973

781

1610a

[2, 12, 28]

And as much as it pertains to the highest morality to avoid falsehood, so much the more ought we be guided by so eminent an authority as that of the Evangelists; and we ought not suppose that they are falsehoods when we come upon varied accounts in the Evangelists, the variations of which narrative are only such as we might find in any authors. And at the same time we should understand that in what pertains more closely to the teachings of the faith (5), it is not so much the truth of words as the truth of facts that is to be sought and embraced; for when authors do not use the same manner of expression, so long as there is no discrepancy in their facts and opinions, we accept them as abiding in the same truth.

26

1611

[2, 12, 29]

There is a useful principle and one especially worthy of being kept in mind, when we   26
are speaking of the agreement of the Evangelists: It is no falsehood when one of them says
something different from what was really said by the person about whom he is writing, so
long as he makes explicit the meaning intended by that person, even as is done by the one
who reports his words precisely. By this principle we learn the salutary lesson that what we
are to seek is nothing other than the meaning intended by the person speaking (6).

1612

[2, 21, 51]

What difference does it make in what order anyone places an account, whether he   25
inserts it in its proper order (7), or whether he recalls what was previously omitted,
or whether he states earlier what was really done later, so long as he does not thereby
contradict either himself or another writer, in the narration either of the same events   24
or of others? For since it is in no one's power, however well and faithfully he knows his
facts, to determine the order in which he will remember them,—for whether one thing
comes into a man's mind before or after another depends not upon our will, but is simply
as it occurs (8),—it is probable enough that each of the Evangelists believed he ought to
proceed with his narrative in the same order in which God had willed to suggest to his
memory the events he was narrating, at least in those matters the order of which, whether it
were this or whether it were that, in no way diminished the authority and truth of the
gospel.

1. Luke 1:32.
2. 1 Tim. 2:5.
3. Matt. 1:16.
4. *quod non ex eius concubitu, sed virgo peperit Christum*.
5. *ad doctrinam fidelem*.
6. *nihil aliud esse quaerendum quam quid velit qui loquitur*.
7. *ex ordine*. Contrary to what one might expect, in Latin *ex ordine* is synonymous with *in ordinem*. To be out of its proper
   order would be *extra ordinem* or *nullo ordine*.
8. *sed ut datur*.

FAITH IN THINGS UNSEEN [*A. D.* 400 *aut postea*]

The *De fide rerum quae non videntur*, or perhaps better, *De fide rerum invisibilium*,
was written not before the year 400. Erasmus regarded it as a spurious work, and at one
time it was assigned to Hugh of St. Victor. The Maurist editors, however, were able to
show that at least one manuscript of the work, specifically attributing it to Augustine, is
actually older than Hugh himself. Moreover, it had undoubtedly escaped Erasmus that
Augustine claimed authorship of the work for himself in his Letter 231 to Darius, in
which he said that he was sending Darius, among else, his work on *Faith in Things
Unseen*.

The omission of the present work from Augustine's *Corrections*, the principal reason
for Erasmus' having pronounced against its authenticity, is easily explained: the work is
a sermon, and Augustine of set purpose excluded sermons from his *Corrections*. Its
authenticity has long been given universal acceptance.

The Maurist text in Migne PL 40, 171-180 has been superseded by the edition of M. P.
J. van den Hout in the *Corpus Christianorum*, Vol. 46 (1969), pp. 1-19.

1613

[1, 1]

    There are some who think the Christian religion is more to be laughed at than   551
supported, because in this religion it is not the thing that is seen that is declared,   561
but faith in things which are not seen is demanded of men. We certainly cannot,   564
for the purpose of refuting those who regard themselves as prudent when they refuse to
believe anything they cannot see, present to human eyes the divine truths which we believe;
but we can demonstrate to human minds that even those things which are not seen ought to
be believed.

1614

[4, 7]

    "Listen to me," the Church says to you. "Listen to me, whom you see, even   412
if you do not want to see. For those who were believers in those days in the land
of Judea learned of the marvelous birth of Christ of a Virgin, and of His Passion,   781
Resurrection, and Ascension, and being present there, they learned firsthand of all
His divine words and works. These things you have not seen, for which reason
you refuse to believe in them. Look, therefore, at these things, pay heed to these
things, think about these things which you do behold, which are not narrated to you
as past events, nor foretold to you as future events, but are demonstrated to you   85
as present events. Or does it seem to you to be vain and of no consequence, and do
you think it a small thing and no divine miracle that all mankind hastens to the name of
one Crucified Man?"

1615

[7, 10]

    How would the Crucified have been able to accomplish so much, if He had not   15
been God who became Man, even if no such things had been foretold by the   81
prophets? Since, however, such a great sacrament of piety did have its heralds and
prophets going before, by whose divine words it was foretold, and since it did
happen just as it was foretold, who is there who is so demented that He would say   63
that the Apostles lied about Christ, and preached that He had come just as the prophets
preached before hand that He would come, prophets who were not silent either about future
truths concerning the Apostles themselves?

AGAINST THE LETTER OF PARMENIAN [*ca. A. D.* 400]

    We gave the briefest of summations of Donatism when introducing Optatus of
Milevis, Vol. 2, pp. 139-140 above. And when treating Cyprian of Carthage (Vol. 1,
pp. 216-241) and others of his time we saw the tenacity with which the African Church
clung to its custom of re-baptizing converts from heresy. Donatism having begun in a
quarrel over the appointment of a bishop, the Donatists holding that his consecration was
invalid because of the alleged unworthiness and apostasy of his consecrators, and with the
predisposition of the African Church to re-baptism, it should be no surprise to find the
Donatists now practicing re-baptism.
    In a certain sense Donatism itself had its origins in a reduction of the practice of
re-baptism, which can hardly have died out entirely in the fifty years or so between
Stephen's pronouncement of his *nihil innovetur nisi quod traditum est* and the advent of
Donatus, to simple theory, and applying it then to the Sacrament of Orders. Then, with
its application to Orders, it is re-applied to Baptism from whence it came, and the

African custom so dear to Cyprian, if ever it had begun to die out, was strengthened anew.

If one holds that the Sacraments, as channels of grace, depend for their efficacy upon the dispositions of their ministers, re-baptism is perfectly logical—and the result is perfectly disastrous, for no one then can ever be confident of the Sacraments he receives. Every Baptism becomes questionable, every marriage, every ordination.

Parmenian had succeeded Donatus the Great as schismatic bishop of Carthage. That he was a capable leader can be presumed from the fact that the Donatists so soon came to be called Parmenianists. Optatus of Milevis had already written his *Contra Parmenianum*, published in six books in 365 and with a seventh added, in 385. Now, about the year 400, Augustine wrote his *Contra epistulam Parmeniani*. The letter which Augustine undertook to refute was one which Parmenian had addressed to Tychonius, another Donatist bishop. Augustine, in his *Corrections* 2, 43, says that in the three books of his *Contra epistulam Parmeniani* he did consider and resolve an important question: whether by participation in the Sacraments, and in view of sacramental unity, evil persons contaminate the good; and if not why not. He says that he discussed this problem in the interest of the whole Church spread abroad throughout the world, because evil persons were acting falsely in this matter and were causing a schism.

The Maurist text in Migne, PL 43, 33-108, was superseded already in 1908 by M. Petschenig's edition in the Vienna Corpus, CSEL, Vol. 51.

1616

[2, 10, 22]

We advise that this must be understood in nearly all such questions, because, of course, all the Sacraments, while they are injurious to those who administer them unworthily, are beneficial to those who receive them worthily, which is the case, too, with the word of God.

804
805

1617

[2, 13, 28]

Both of these, Baptism and Orders, are Sacraments, and each is given to a man by a certain sacred rite (1), the one, when he is baptized, and the other, when he is ordained. In the Catholic Church, therefore, it is not permitted to repeat either of these Sacraments. For if even their leaders (2), when they come over to us from among the schismatics, are received for the good of peace and to rectify the error of schism, and even if it is seen that it is feasible for them to carry on in the same offices which they had before, they are not ordained again, but, just as with their Baptism, so too their ordination remains whole; because the defect was in their separation which is corrected by the peace that comes of unity, and not in the Sacraments, which, everywhere they are found, are the same.

820
950
799

1618

[2, 13, 29]

If a layman, compelled by some necessity, has baptized some persons who are dying,—for, since he received Baptism himself, he has come to know how it must be given,—I do not know whether anyone can piously say that it must be repeated. For, if there were no compelling necessity, it would be usurpation of another's office; but if necessity urge that it be done, then there is no fault or, at most, a venial one (3). But if, in the absence of necessity, there is a usurpation, and Baptism is given by anyone who wishes to whomsoever he will, what has been given cannot be said not to have been given; but it can rightly be said that it was illicitly given (4).

829

1620

[2, 13, 30]

If we are doing evil, let them explain how the baptized cannot lose the Sacrament while the ordained can lose the Sacrament; for they say: "If one withdraws from the Church he certainly does not lose his Baptism; but he does lose the right to give it." If both are Sacraments, which no one doubts, why is the one lost and not the other? Actually, it is no injury to either Sacrament.   798

1. *quadam consecratione.*
2. *praepositi.*
3. *aut nullum aut veniale delictum est.*
4. *quod datum fuerit non potest dici non datum, quamvis recte dici possit illicite datum.* I do not think I know any earlier passage in which such a clear distinction is made between what is invalid and what is illicit; nor do I know of anyone earlier than Augustine who can use the word *illicite* so easily and effortlessly in a context in which its being a *terminus technicus* is so obvious.

BAPTISM [*A. D.* 400]

Among Augustine's several writings against Donatism the *De baptismo contra Donatistas*, in seven books from the year 400 A. D., may well be regarded as his major work. The Donatists, for their practice of re-baptism, appealed to the authority of Cyprian of Carthage. Augustine argued that the authority of Cyprian himself, in his letters and in his conduct, which demonstrate his perfect allegiance to unity in the Church, so far from supporting the Donatists, refutes them. It seems to me that on the particular point of re-baptism Augustine is able to claim the authority of Cyprian for the Catholic position only through doing some violence to the obvious meaning of certain of the texts he quotes. Cyprian did, of course, insist that he did not support re-baptism; but only because he denied that the baptism conferred by a heretic was a Baptism at all. But this much at least of Augustine's approach is quite laudable: while he cannot consistently agree with Cyprian's views on re-baptism, he can and does defend him as a Catholic bishop. The *De baptismo contra Donatistas* is treated in the *Corrections* 2, 44.

Books six and seven of *Baptism* respond, paragraph by paragraph, to the signed statements made by each of the Cyprianic bishops present in the Seventh Council of Carthage, of A. D. 256 (pp. 240-241 above in Vol. 1).

The Maurist edition reprinted in Migne (PL 43, 107-244) is superseded by M. Petschenig's critical edition of 1908 in the Vienna Corpus, CSEL, Vol. 51.

1621

[1, 12, 18]

The solution in the case of one who approached Baptism deceitfully (1) was that he is not to be baptized again, but will be cleansed by a pious conversion itself (2) and by a truthful confession (3), which were impossible without Baptism, so that what was given him before will now be enabled to initiate his salvation, when his dissimulation (4) is replaced by a truthful confession. So too, the man who, as an enemy of the peace and love of Christ, received the Baptism of Christ in some heresy or schism, which Baptism those heretics or schismatics did not lose when they separated themselves from the Church, although his sins are not remitted by this wicked sacrilege, when he has corrected himself and has come to the unity and society of the Church, he is not to be baptized again, because it is preserved and at hand for him through that very reconciliation and peace, and in unity that Sacrament begins to be of avail for the remission of his sins, to which it was of no avail when he received it in schism.   803

    830

    799
    797

1622

[1, 12, 20]

That sins once forgiven do return when there is no fraternal love is taught most clearly by the Lord in the Gospel about that servant whom, when He found him owing Him ten thousand talents, at his entreaties He forgave all (5). But when that man would not have mercy on his fellow servant who owed him a hundred denarii, the Lord ordered him to pay all that He had forgiven him. . . . Thus the grace of Baptism does not prevent Him from forgiving all the sins even if the one in whom they are forgiven perseveres in cherishing a hatred of his brother. . . . But then he immediately begins to be guilty again, not only for what follows, but even for the days, hours, and moments of the past, all those things forgiven now returning to him. This is so often what happens even in the Church.

931

836

1623

[2, 7, 12]

Do not raise against us the authority of Cyprian as favoring the repetition of Baptism, but join us in Cyprian's example for the preservation of unity. For this question of Baptism had not yet been completely worked out, but still the Church kept the most wholesome practice of correcting what was wrong, not repeating what was given; healing what was wounded in heretics and schismatics, not curing what was already sound. I believe that this practice comes from apostolic tradition, just as so many other practices not found in their writings nor in the councils of their successors, but which, because they are kept by the whole Church everywhere, are believed to have been commended and handed down by the Apostles themselves.

107

799
830
102

1624

[3, 10, 13]

It is one thing not to have something, and another to have it not by right or to usurp it illicitly. It is not that they are not the Sacraments of Christ and of the Church because they are used illicitly, and this not by heretics only, but by all the wicked and impious. Such persons ought to be corrected and punished, but the Sacraments should be acknowledged and revered.

804
805

1625

[3, 13, 18]

Although among heretics and schismatics there be the same Baptism of Christ, the remission of sins, nevertheless, is not operative there, because of the very rottenness of discord and wickedness of dissension. If, however, the same Baptism then begins to be of avail for the remission of sins when they have come to the peace of the Church, so that their sins having been truly forgiven they are not retained, neither is that Baptism to be disapproved as something alien or different, so that another Baptism were given (6); rather, it is the one and the same Baptism which outside the Church works death because of discord, and inside the Church works salvation because of peace.

830

797

1626

[3, 15, 20]

On this account if Marcion consecrated Baptism with the Gospel words, "In the name of the Father, and of the Son, and of the Holy Spirit (7)," the Sacrament was complete, although his faith expressed under those same words, since his opinion was other

830

than is taught by Catholic truth, was not complete but was contaminated by the falsity of fables.

1627

[3, 16, 21]

    The imposition of the hand, however, is not unrepeatable like Baptism. For what else is the imposition of hands but a prayer over the man?

792
799
924

1628

[4, 10, 16]

    Insofar as I can judge, it is already as clear as crystal (8) that in this question of Baptism what is to be considered is not who confers but what is conferred; not who receives but what is received; not who has it but what he has.

803
829

1629

[4, 21, 28]

    I do not hesitate to put the Catholic catechumen, burning with divine love, before a baptized heretic. Even within the Catholic Church herself we put the good catechumen ahead of the wicked baptized person. Nor do we thereby do any injury to the Sacrament of Baptism, which the former has not yet received, while the latter has it already. Nor do we think that the catechumen's Sacrament (9) is to be preferred to the Sacrament of Baptism, just because we recognize that a specified catechumen may be better and more faithful than a specified baptized person. The centurion Cornelius, not yet baptized, was better than Simon (10), already baptized. For Cornelius, even before his Baptism, was filled up with the Holy Spirit, while Simon, even after his Baptism, was puffed up with an unclean spirit.

832

1630

[4, 22, 29]

    That the place of Baptism is sometimes supplied by suffering is supported by a substantial argument which the same Blessed Cyprian draws from the circumstance of the thief, to whom, although not baptized, it was said: "Today you shall be with Me in paradise (11)." Considering this over and over again, I find that not only suffering for the name of Christ can supply for that which is lacking by way of Baptism, but even faith and conversion of heart (12), if, perhaps, because of the circumstances of the time (13), recourse cannot be had to the celebration of the Mystery of Baptism.

833
832

1631

[4, 24, 31]

    What the universal Church holds, not as instituted by councils but as something always held, is most correctly believed to have been handed down by apostolic authority.

100

1632

[4, 24, 31]

    Since others respond for children, so that the celebration of the Sacrament may be complete for them, it is certainly availing to them for their consecration, because they themselves are not able to respond. But if someone were to respond on behalf of a person who could make himself make answer, it would not likewise be of avail.

835
806

1633

[5, 8, 9]

Just as Judas to whom the Lord handed a morsel, furnished in himself a place for the devil, 855
not by receiving something wicked but by receiving it wickedly, so too anyone who 875
receives the Sacrament of the Lord (14) unworthily does not, because he himself is wicked,
cause the Sacrament to be wicked, or bring it about that he receives nothing because
he does not receive it unto salvation. For it was the Body of the Lord and the Blood of the
Lord even in those to whom the Apostle said: ''Whoever eats and drinks unworthily, eats
and drinks judgment to himself (15).''

1634

[5, 10, 12]

I ask, then, if the Baptism of John remitted sins, what more could the Baptism of Christ 821
do for those whom the Apostle Paul wanted to be baptized with the Baptism of Christ after
they had received the Baptism of John (16)?

1635

[5, 20, 28]

If what is said in the Gospel, ''God does not hear a sinner (17)'', is applicable to 804
this, so that the Sacraments cannot be celebrated by a sinner, how then does He
hear a murderer praying over the baptismal water, or over the oil, or over the Eucharist, 808
or over the heads of those on whom his hand is imposed? But all of these things are
done, and are valid even when done by murderers, that is, by those who hate their
brothers, even within the Church herself.

1636

[5, 23, 33]

Wicked sons do not have the Holy Spirit in the same way as do beloved sons, 830
and yet they do have Baptism; so too, heretics do not have the Church as Catholics
have, but they do have Baptism.

1637

[6, 9, 14]

If the one and true Baptism did not exist except in the Church, surely it would not 830
exist in those who depart from her unity. But it does exist in these; for upon returning
they do not receive it again, for the very reason that on leaving they did not lose it. . . .
When men come to Catholic peace, what was in them but did not profit them when 797
they were outside the Church, then begins to profit them.

1638

[6, 25, 47]

God is present in His own Gospel words, without which words the Baptism of 801
Christ were unable to be consecrated; and He Himself sanctifies His Sacrament, so 802
that the Sacrament may be availing unto salvation for the man who receives it, 797
either before He is baptized, or while he is being baptized, or afterwards, whenever
he turns in truth to God, which Sacrament, if he does not turn to God, will be availing
to his destruction. Is there anyone who does not know that it is not the Baptism of 826

Christ if the Gospel words, in which the sign consists (18), should be lacking there? But it is easier to find heretics who do not baptize at all, than to find any who baptize without those words.

1639

[7, 53, 102]

Were I perhaps to be seated in a council in which a question were raised on points   829
such as these, and were someone to urge me to tell him what I think, without   830
reference to the previously expressed opinions of others whose views I might wish
to follow, and if I were influenced by the same sentiments which led me to assert
what I said before, I could not doubt that all those have Baptism who received it
anywhere and from whomever, so long as it was consecrated with the Gospel words
and they received it without simulation on their own part (19) and with some
degree of faith, although it would not be availing to them for their spiritual salvation   806
if they were to be lacking in that charity by which they might be implanted in the
Catholic Church.

1. *fictus* = feigned. Augustine's description of such a hypothetical case makes it clear that it is not the sacramental rite that is feigned, but the recipient's dispositions to sorrow and contrition. This makes the recipient unworthy to receive the graces of the Sacrament, but does not prevent him from receiving the Sacrament itself. Similarly, when a heretic or schismatic is baptized, that person truly receives the Sacrament, but the effects of the Sacrament do not then take place: his personal sins are not forgiven, original sin is not forgiven, he does not receive sanctifying grace, nor does he receive sacramental grace. But when he is converted to the peace and unity of the one true Church and is filled with charity, then these sacramental effects revive.
2. *ipsa pia correctione*.
3. *veraci confessione*.
4. *fictio*.
5. Matt. 18:23ff.
6. The numerous manuscripts and editions display considerable variation in the number and arrangement of the negatives in the present structure. We have accepted the reading: "*. . . ut vere dimissa non retineatur, neque ut ille baptismus quasi alienus aut alius improbetur, ut alter tradatur, ...*"
7. Matt. 28:19.
8. *iam claret et liquet*.
9. The Council of Carthage of 397 A. D. mentions the Catechumen's sacrament as the sacrament of salt; and it is mentioned elsewhere also in Augustine. The rites of Baptism were then, as now again in the restored liturgy, given in stages. The tasting of salt, symbolizing purity and incorruption, is what was termed the Catechumen's sacrament.
10. Simon Magus is meant. See Acts 8:13, 18-19.
11. Luke 23:43. In the *Corrections* 2, 44 Augustine regrets having used the good thief as an example in this instance: for he now recalls that we have no certainty at all that the thief was not in fact baptized. Augustine's regret, of course, is solely over the example used; for he has no doubts at all about the efficacy of so-called Baptism of blood.
12. It is this latter, of course,—faith and conversion of heart,—that Dismas had and which Gestas lacked. Both suffered, and neither were martyrs.
13. *in angustiis temporum*.
14. *dominicum sacramentum*.
15. 1 Cor. 11:29.
16. See Acts 19:4-5.
17. John 9:31.
18. *quibus symbolum constat*.
19. See § 1621 and its note 1 above. In that place Augustine admits that Baptism received in a *fictio* is a valid Baptism, though its effects do not follow immediately but only revive if and when the recipient is converted to proper dispositions. It is clear in that instance that when speaking of a *fictio* he refers to the condition of one who is baptized with no intention of renouncing his former sinful ways. In the present instance, where he speaks of a *simulatio* on the part of the apparent recipient as preventing the reception of the Sacrament at all, it is in a context which makes it clear that he is referring to the case of one who is acting a role in a theater production, and only plays at being baptized. In the further knotty problem of one who, while acting a role of being baptized in a play, is suddenly overcome by a religious impulse and, filled with love, desires truly to be baptized—the problem of whether or not he actually receives a Sacrament Augustine can only refer to the judgment of Divine Wisdom.

THE ADVANTAGE OF MARRIAGE [*A. D.* 401]

Augustine wrote the treatise *De bono coniugali* in the year 401 A. D. In his *Corrections* 2, 48 he noted the circumstances which prompted his writing the work. The heresy of Jovinian which equated the merit of the state of consecrated virginity with that of marriage was so influential in Rome that even monks and nuns were abandoning their vows and hastening to marry. He says also that the proponents of this poisonous notion were boasting that no one could answer Jovinian without censuring marriage. Augustine did what was claimed to be impossible: he elevated the state of virginity by praising marriage. And if so many in our age pretend that his praise of marriage is really damnation by faint praise, is it not really that they have adulterated the purer ideals of an age that was closer to the Source of Truth and to Truth Himself? The hardness of our hearts precludes self-sacrifice and pride promotes the self-deception that we continue to follow ideals that we have in truth abandoned, the while we make virtue of our mediocrity. Jovinianism is now reborn and is stronger in our times than it was in Augustine's.

The Maurist text in Migne (PL 40, 373-396) is superseded by the edition of J. Zycha (1900) in Vol. 41 of the Vienna Corpus.

1640

[3, 3]
Since in the Gospel the Lord confirmed that marriage is a virtuous estate, not only when He forbade the dismissal of a wife except for cause of fornication (1), but also when, as invited guest, He came to the wedding (2), it will be worthwhile to inquire why it is a virtuous estate. It seems to me that this is the case not only because of the procreation of children, but also because of the natural companionship of the two sexes (3). . . . . Marriage has also this advantage, that carnal or youthful incontinence, even if it is defiling, is turned to the honorable task of propagating offspring, so that marital intercourse makes something good out of an evil appetite.

968
972

1641

[17, 19]
[In the Old Testament] the work of piety itself was to propagate children even carnally, because the begetting of that people was an announcement of future events and pertained to the prophetic order of events. [20] While, therefore, it was permitted that one man have several wives, it was not similarly permitted that one woman have several husbands, not even for the sake of offspring, if, perhaps, she was able to bear while her husband was not able to beget.

978

1642

[24, 32]
Among all nations and all men, therefore, the advantage of marriage is for the sake of begetting offspring and in the fidelity of chastity. In the case of the people of God, however, there is also the holiness of the Sacrament (4), on which account a woman is not permitted, even when she leaves with a repudiation (5), to marry another while her husband yet lives, not even for the sake of bearing children. Although this is the only reason why marriage takes place, even if this for which marriage takes place does not follow, the marriage bond is loosed only by the death of a spouse. It is just as if an ordination of the clergy took place in order to gather the people together, and the people did not in fact assemble in a congregation;

968

950
798

still, the Sacrament of ordination would remain in those ordained; and if, perhaps, someone is removed from office because of some fault, he will not lack the Sacrament of the Lord once it has been imposed, though now it remains to his judgment.

1. Matt. 19:9.
2. John 2:2.
3. *sed propter ipsam etiam naturalem in diverso sexu societatem.*
4. For Augustine Christian marriage is called a Sacrament in view of its indissolubility; this indissoluble bond is a Sacrament or sign of the union of Christ with His Church.
5. *etiam repudio discedentem.* Some conclude from such passages as the present one that only the wife was forbidden to remarry, and not the husband. But it is false to conclude from this frequent silence that the husband was permitted to remarry. See, in fact, § 1861 below, where Augustine, makes it clear that the man too, who dismisses his wife for any reason, adultery or not, cannot remarry. He does, however recognize a difference in the degree of guilt of the man who remarries after divorcing a wife for adultery, and the man who so remarries after divorcing a wife for cause other than adultery.

HOLY VIRGINITY [*A. D.* 401]

When the followers of Jovinian, who denied the superiority of virginity to marriage as estates, declared that no one could refute Jovinian without joining with the Manicheans in disparaging marriage, Augustine accepted the challenge and wrote *The Advantage of Marriage (De bono coniugali)*. That, of course, countered but half the problem; and he continued his refutation of Jovinian with *De sancta virginitate*. Jovinian had finally come to deny the virginity of Mary *in partu*; and Augustine waxes especially eloquent in defending Mary's perpetual virginity.

The Maurist text in Migne (PL 40, 397-428) is superseded by the edition of J. Zycha (1900) in the Vienna Corpus, Vol. 41.

1643

[4, 4]

In being born of a Virgin who chose to remain a Virgin even before she knew who   783
was to be born of her, Christ wanted to approve virginity rather than to impose it. And   785
He wanted virginity to be of free choice even in that woman in whom He took
upon Himself the form of a slave.

1644

[6, 6]

That one woman is both Mother and Virgin, not in spirit only but even in body.   311
In spirit she is Mother, not of our Head, who is our Savior Himself,—of whom,
rather, it was she who was born spiritually, since all who believe in Him, including
even herself, are rightly called children of the bridegroom (1),—but plainly she is   784
[in spirit] Mother of us who are His members, because by love she has cooperated so that
the faithful, who are the members of that Head, might be born in the Church. In body,
indeed, she is Mother of that very Head.

1. Matt. 9:15.

AGAINST THE LETTERS OF PETILIAN THE DONATIST, BISHOP OF CIRTA
[A. D. 401-403]

Augustine's *Contra litteras Petiliani Donatistae Cirtensis episcopi* is in three parts, written separately between the years 401 and 403. The first part is more truly a letter; the second and third really two books. The three were joined in a single work by Augustine himself, as he explains in his *Corrections* 2, 51.

Petilian had written a letter against the Catholic Church. When only the first short part of the letter had come into Augustine's hands, Augustine replied to that part in a letter addressed to Catholics everywhere. This letter became book one of the present work.

Later the whole of Petilian's letter found its way into Augustine's possession, who then undertook to reply to it point by point and at some length. This book, written in the fashion of a face to face disputation with Petilian, became book two of the present work.

While Augustine was yet writing this lengthier reply, his first answer was found by Petilian, who became quite angry and wrote a nasty and vituperative response to Augustine, very personal and not at all to the point.

To Petilian's rejoinder vile Augustine then addressed his response courteous, advancing no new arguments in support of his own position, but only pointing out the deficiencies and irrelevancies of Petilian's second letter. Nothing fans the flames of a man's already enkindled anger so much as a polite rejoinder and a logical reply. And this became book three of the present work.

The text in Migne (PL 43, 245-388) is superseded by M. Petschenig's edition of 1909 in the Vienna Corpus, CSEL, Vol. 52.

1645

[2, 35, 82]

When, therefore, it becomes clear to you that neither he that administered Baptism   804
nor he that received it did so with a pure conscience, do you judge that he must   807
be baptized again? Certainly you would not say this, nor would you do it. The purity of
Baptism, then, is entirely distinct from purity or impurity of conscience, whether of the one
giving or of the one receiving.

1646

[2, 72, 162]

Since the opportunity presents itself, I must not pass it by: It is certain that the ancient   795
people of God had circumcision instead of Baptism. I ask you, then, if the Pharisees,
against whom those words you quote were spoken, had made some proselyte, and if he, by
imitating them, became, as it is written, twice as much more a child of hell as they
themselves, and if he were then to be converted and should desire to imitate Simeon or
Zacharias or Nathanael, would it be necessary for him to be circumcised again by them?

1647

[2, 104, 239]

The Sacrament of Chrism . . . is a sacrosanct one in that class of visible signs,   840
like Baptism itself. But it can be present in the worst of men, who waste their   790
lives in the works of the flesh and who are not about to possess the kingdom of   820
heaven. . . . Distinguish the visible holy Sacrament, which can be present both   807
in good men and in the wicked,—unto a reward in the former and unto judgment in the
latter,—distinguish it from the invisible anointing of love, which belongs only to the good.

THE TRINITY [*inter A. D.* 400-416]

Augustine was occupied off and on for seventeen years, 400 to 416 A. D., in writing his *De Trinitate libri quindecim*. In his *Corrections* 2, 41, he explains that it was against his better judgment and only because of the pressure brought to bear by importunate friends that he released the *De Trinitate* to be published when he did, and before he had been able to find time to make the more thorough final revision that he would have preferred to make. Yet, in the *Corrections* he has very little to correct in the work, and less still that is of any consequence; for in his extended apology for having said originally that he had never heard of a four-footed bird he only adds several blunders to what had otherwise most probably have passed unnoticed.

The Maurist text in Migne has very recently been superseded by the edition of W. J. Mountain and Fr. Glorie (1968) in the *Corpus Christianorum*, Vols. 50 and 50A (books 1-12 in Vol. 50, pp. 1-380; books 13-15 in Vol. 50A, pp. 381-535).

1649

[1, 1, 2]

The divine Scriptures rarely posit things which are properly said of God but which   140
are not found in any creature; and such is the case, too, with what was said to Moses: "I
am who am," and "He Who Is sent me to you (1)." For since to be is posited
in some way even of body and soul, Scripture would not have stated it as it did unless it
intended it to be understood in some special way.

1650

[1, 4, 7]

All the Catholic interpreters of the divine books of the Old and New Testaments   230
whom I have been able to read, who wrote before me about the Trinity, which is God,
intended to teach in accord with the Scriptures that the Father and the Son and the   238
Holy Spirit are of one and the same substance constituting a divine unity with an
inseparable equality; and therefore there are not three gods but one God, although
the Father begot the Son, and therefore He that is the Father is not the Son; and
the Son is begotten by the Father, and therefore He that is the Son is not the Father;
and the Holy Spirit is neither the Father nor the Son, but only the Spirit of the Father   270
and of the Son, Himself, too, coequal to the Father and to the Son, and belonging   268
to the unity of the Trinity.

1651

[1, 13, 28]

But if it were not the very same one who is Son of Man on account of the form of   333
a slave which He took, and who is Son of God on account of the form of God in which   334
He is, the Apostle Paul would not have said about the princes of this world: "If
they had known, they would never have crucified the Lord of glory (2)." For He was
crucified in the form of a slave; and yet it was the Lord of glory who was crucified. For
such was that assumption that made God man and man God.

1652

[3, 4, 10]

Paul was able to preach the Lord Jesus Christ by means of signs, in one way by his   851
letters, in another way by the Sacrament of Christ's Body and Blood; for when we

speak of the Body of Christ and of His Blood, certainly we do not mean Paul's
speaking, nor his parchments nor his ink, nor the meaning of the sounds issuing
from his tongue, nor the signs of letters written on skins. By the Body and Blood of
Christ we refer only to that which has been received from the fruits of the earth   864
and has been consecrated by the mystical prayer, and has been ritually taken for   877
our spiritual health in memory of what the Lord suffered for us.   849

1653

[3, 11, 21]
    The substance, or, it might better be said, the essence of God, wherein we understand   170
in our limited measure and in however small a degree the Father and the Son and the
Holy Spirit, since it is in no way changeable, is in no way able to be visible in   236
itself. [22] Hence it is clear that all those things which were seen by the Fathers, when
God was presented to them according to His dispensation suitable to the times,
were done by a creature. And if the way in which God did this through the ministry
of angels is hidden from us, we still say that they were done by angels, not from
our own reasoning (3), lest to someone we seem more wise; but we are wise in
moderation (4).

1654

[4, 13, 16]
    The spirit of the Mediator has shown how it was no punishment of sin that brought   350
Him to the death of the flesh; for He did not abandon it unwillingly, but because He   345
willed, when He willed, and how He willed.   387

1655

[4, 13, 17]
    By His death He offered for us the only real sacrifice (5), and He washed away,   380
abolished, and extinguished whatever guilt there was whereby the Principalities   374
and Powers lawfully detained us for the suffering of punishments; and by His
Resurrection, having predestined us to a new life, He called us; and having called us, He
justified us; and having justified us, He glorified us (6). . . . And inasmuch as the
Lord, in His sufferings, yielded to the devil, the devil thought himself superior to the
Lord. For what is written in the Psalm is to be understood of the Lord: "You have
made Him a little less than the angels (7)," so that when the Innocent One Himself
would be put to death by the evil one, acting against us as if by a just right, the Innocent
One would then overcome him by a more just right, and thus would make captive the
captivity that was brought about by sin (8), and would liberate us from a captivity
that, by reason of sin, was a just one, by deleting the promissory note of death and by
redeeming sinners, who were to be justified by the unjust shedding of His just blood.

1656

[4, 20, 27]
    But if it is said that the Son is sent by the Father in this sense, that one is the Father   290
and another is the Son, this manner of expression in no way hinders our belief that   256
the Son is equal to the Father, consubstantial and coeternal with Him; and still   258
the Son is sent by the Father. Not that one is greater and the other less, but that one   257
is the Father and the other is the Son. One is the Begetter and the other the Begotten. One 259
is the by-whom He is sent, the other is the who-is-sent by whom.

1657

[4, 20, 28]

The Father, when He is known by anyone in time, is not termed sent; for there is no   250
one by whom He is, or from whom He proceeds. Wisdom surely declares: "I have come
forth from the mouth of the Most High (9)." And of the Holy Spirit it is said, "He   269
proceeds from the Father (10)." But the Father is from no one.

1658

[5, 1, 2]

What, therefore, we do not find in our better part [which is our mind], we ought   178
not look for in that which is far better than the better part of ourselves. And thus
we may understand, if we are able and insofar as we are able, that God is good without
quality, great without quantity, Creator without lack, Presider without local place (11);
Container of all things, Himself without limit (12); wholly everywhere without
spatial limitation (13), eternal without time; Maker of changeable things, who is Himself
without any change; and in no way acted upon from without (14). Anyone who thinks
in this way of God, although he will still not be able to discover fully what God is
(15), will thereby piously avoid, insofar as it is possible, thinking anything about
Him that He is not.

1659

[5, 3, 4]

Among the many points which the Arians are accustomed to dispute against the   292
Catholic faith, they themselves seem to think the following contrivance a most clever
argument. They say that whatever is said or understood of God is said not according
to accidents but according to substance. Consequently, to be unbegotten pertains to the
Father according to substance and to be begotten pertains to the Son according
to substance. But to be unbegotten is different from being begotten. The substance of the
Father, therefore, is different from the substance of the Son. To this we answer that if
whatever is said about God is said of His substance, then the saying, "I and the Father
are one (16)" applies likewise to His substance. The Father and the Son, therefore,
are of one substance. Or if these words do not refer to substance, then something is said
of God which does not refer to His substance, and consequently we are not obliged to
understand the terms unbegotten and begotten as referring to substance.

1660

[5, 5, 6]

In created and changeable things what is not said according to substance can only   151
be said as according to accident. . . . In God, however, certainly there is nothing
that is said according to accident, because in Him there is nothing that is changeable;
but neither is everything that is said of Him said according to substance. Nor is it   281
in regard to accident that He is said to be in relation to something, as the Father to the
Son, and the Son to the Father; for the one is always Father and the other is always Son,
and this is not because the Father, from whom the Son is born, never ceases to be
the Father because the Son never ceases to be the Son, but because the Son was always
born and never began to be the Son. . . . Consequently, although being the Father
differs from being the Son, there is still not a diversity of substance, because their
being called Father and Son does not refer to their substance, but to their relationship;
nor is their relationship an accident, because it is not changeable.

1661

[5, 13, 14]

When we say that the Father is the Principle (17) and the Son is the Principle, we are   283
not saying that the creature has two Principles; for both Father and Son are at the
same time the one Principle for a creature, just as they are the one Creator and the one
God.

1662

[5, 14, 15]

If, therefore, that which is given has for its principle the one by whom it is given,   273
because it did not receive from anywhere else that which proceeds from the giver, then it
must be confessed that the Father and the Son are the Principle of the Holy Spirit,
not two Principles, but just as Father and Son are one God and, relative to a creature,
one Creator and one Lord, so too, relative to the Holy Spirit, they are one Principle,
while relative to a creature, Father and Son and Holy Spirit are one Principle,   283
even as they are one Creator and one Lord.   467

1663

[5, 16, 17]

Whatever God begins to be called temporally, and which He was not previously   155
called, is manifestly said of Him in a relative way; such things, however, are not
said of God according to accident, as if something new had acceded to Him, but plainly
according to an accident of the creature with whom, in a manner of speaking, God has
entered into a relationship. And when a righteous man begins to be a friend of God, it is
the man himself who is changed; but perish the thought that God should love anyone
temporally, as if in Him, for whom past ages are not past and future ages already
exist, there were now a new love which was not in Him before.

1664

[6, 4, 6]

With the human soul, to be is not the same as to be strong, or prudent, or righteous,   150
or temperate; for the soul is able to exist while having none of these virtues. With
God, however, to be is to be strong, to be righteous, to be wise, and to be whatever else
you can say of that simple multiplicity or multiple simplicity by which His substance
is signified.

1665

[6, 5, 7]

[With the Father and the Son] the Holy Spirit, too, exists in this same unity of   279
substance and equality. For whether He be the unity of the Father and the Son,
or their holiness, or their love, or their unity because He is their love, or their love
because He is their holiness, it is clear that He is not one of the two, since it is by Him that
the two are joined, by Him that the Begotten is loved by the Begetter, and in turn
loves Him who begot Him.

1666

[6, 7, 8]

Certainly it is said in many ways that God is great, good, wise, blessed, true, and   150

whatever else He can be called that is not unworthy of Him. But His greatness is the same
as His wisdom, for He is great not in bulk but in power; and His goodness is the
same as His wisdom and greatness, and His truth is the same as all of these qualities; and
in Him it is not one thing to be blessed, and another to be great, or wise, or true, or
good, or to be all that He is.

1667

[6, 7, 9]

   Nor because He is a Trinity is He to be thought of as triplex; otherwise the Father   280
alone or the Son alone would be less than the Father and the Son together. Although it is
really not to be discovered how anyone could speak of either the Father alone or the
Son alone, when the Father is with the Son and the Son is with the Father always and
inseparably; not that both are the Father or that both are the Son, but because they
are always in each other, and neither of them is ever alone.

1668

[7, 4, 8]

   What we, in accord with our custom, have said about persons, must be understood   238
as applying to what the Greeks according to their custom say of substances. For they say
that there are in God three substances and one essence, whereas we say there are
three persons, and one essence or substance.

1669

[7, 5, 10]

   Things that are changeable and not simple are properly called substances. . . .   150
But it is wrong to say that God subsists and is the subject of His own goodness and that   151
goodness is not a substance, or rather, not an essence; and that God Himself is
not His own goodness, but that His goodness is in Him as in a subject. It is clear,
therefore, that God is improperly called a substance, by which term we are to understand
the more commonly used term, essence, the term that is truly and properly applied
to Him, and in such a way that perhaps God alone ought to be called an essence. For
God is truly alone, because He is unchangeable; and He declared His own name to   140
His servant Moses, when He said: "I am who am," and: "He Who Is has sent me
to you (18)."

1670

[8, Pref., 1]

   We said elsewhere that in the Trinity the things that are spoken of in reference to the   281
relationship of one to another are properly spoken of as belonging to the individual   278
persons distinctly, as the Father, and the Son, and,—the Gift of both,—the Holy
Spirit; for the Father is not the Trinity, nor is the Son the Trinity, nor is the Gift the
Trinity. But when they are spoken of individually in respect to themselves, they are not
spoken of as three in the plural number, but as one, the Trinity itself. Thus the
Father is God, the Son is God, the Holy Spirit is God; and the Father is good, the Son is   266
good, and the Holy Spirit is good; and the Father is almighty, the Son is almighty,
and the Holy Spirit is almighty. Neither, however, are there three gods, three goods,
three almighties, but one God, one good, one almighty, the Trinity itself. And so
too with whatever else is said, not in reference to the relationship of one to another,
but which is said of them individually in respect to themselves. For these things are said   150

according to essence, because with them, to be is the same as to be great, to be good, to be wise, and whatever else there is that is said of each Person in respect to Himself or of the Trinity itself. They are called three persons or three substances, therefore, not as if some diversity of essence might be understood, but so that when someone asks, "Three what?" or "What three?," we may be able to answer with some one word. And so sure is the equality in this Trinity, that not only is the Father not greater than the Son, in what touches upon divinity, but neither can the Father and the Son together be anything greater than the Holy Spirit, nor can any one whichsoever of the persons be anything less than the Trinity itself.   280

1671

[8, 3, 4]
This is good and that is good. Take hold of this and take hold of that, and see good   180
itself, if you can. In the same way, you will see God, who is good not by some other good, but who is the good of every good. For in all these goods, either those which I have mentioned, or others which might be perceived or known about, we could not say that one is better than another, when we judge correctly, unless there were impressed upon us the notion of good itself, against which we test a thing and compare one thing to another. Thus God is to be loved, not as this or that good, but as good itself.   593

1672

[9, 1, 1]
That purpose is right, which proceeds from faith. For a sure faith is in some   565
way the beginning of knowledge; but a sure knowledge will not be achieved except after this life, when we shall see face to face (19). . . . As to the immediate question,   239
therefore, let us believe that Father and Son and Holy Spirit are one God, the Creator and   237
Ruler of all creation; that the Father is not the Son, that the Holy Spirit is neither the Father nor the Son, but that there is a Trinity of persons related one to another, and a   281
Unity of equal essence. This same, however, let us strive to understand, while praying assistance from Him whom we wish to understand.

1673

[12, 6, 6]
For God said: "Let us make man to our image and likeness (20)." But shortly   512
afterwards it was said: "And God made man to the image of God (21)." Certainly *our*,   233
which is a plural number, would not have been used correctly if man were made to the image of one Person, whether the Father, or the Son, or the Holy Spirit. But he was made to the image of the Trinity, for which reason it was said: "to *our* image." Again however, lest it be supposed that in the Trinity we ought to believe in three gods when the same Trinity is but one God, it says: "And God did make man to the image of God," which is the same as if it had been said, "to His own image."

1674

[13, 8, 11]
Since, therefore, all men will to be happy (22), if they will truly, assuredly they will   1043
also to be immortal. For not otherwise could they be happy. Therefore, whether they be questioned about immortality or about happiness, all respond that they will it.

1675

[13, 14, 18]
What is the justice, therefore, by which the devil is conquered? What indeed, if not the   374
justice of Jesus Christ? And how is the devil conquered? Because, though he found
in Christ nothing worthy of death, he slew Him anyway; and certainly it is just that
the debtors whom the devil held should be set free, since they believed in Christ who,
though He had no debt, was slain by the devil (23). That is how we are said to be
justified in the blood of Christ (24). It was thus that for the remission of sins His innocent   383
blood was shed. . . . Would the devil have been conquered by that most equitable
right, if Christ had willed to contend with him by power and not by justice? But He held
back what He might have done, so that He might first do what it was fitting for Him
to do. That is why it was necessary for Him to be both Man and God. For unless He   363
were Man, He could not be killed; and unless He were God, it would not be believed
that He did not will what He might have done, but that He was not able to do what
He would have willed: we would not have thought that He preferred justice to power, but
that He lacked the power. But now He suffered human things for us, because He was
a Man; but if He had not willed it, He would also have been able not to suffer these
things, because He was also God. . . . [13, 15, 19] In this redemption the blood of   384
Christ was given as the price for us; but when he received the price the devil (25) was
not enriched but bound, so that we might be loosed from his obligations.

1676

[15, 13, 22]
But the knowledge that God has is also His wisdom; and His wisdom is His essence or   150
substance; for in the wonderful simplicity of His nature, to be wise is not something
else than to be; rather, to be wise is the same as to be.

1677

[15, 14, 23]
The Word, therefore, the only-begotten Son of God the Father, is in all things like   257
the Father and equal to the Father, God of God, Light of Light, Wisdom of Wisdom,   282
Essence of Essence. He is wholly what the Father is, but not Father; for the one
is Son, the other is Father. And therefore He knows all that the Father knows; but for
Him, to know is from the Father, just as to be is from the Father. For in this case, to know
and to be is one. And therefore, for the Father, just as to be is not from the Son, neither
is to know from the Son. Hence, just as if uttering Himself, the Father begot the   265
Word, equal to Himself in all respects. For He would not have uttered Himself wholly
and perfectly, if in His Word there was something less or something more than in
Himself.

1678

[15, 17, 29]
And yet it is not without reason (26) that in this Trinity only the Word of God is called   260
Son, only the Gift of God the Holy Spirit, and only He of whom the Word is begotten   278
and from whom principally the Holy Spirit proceeds is called God the Father. I   274
have added the term ''principally (27),'' because the Holy Spirit is found to proceed   273
also from the Son. But this too the Father gave the Son, not as if the Son did not already
exist and have it, but because whatever the Father gives the Son, He gives by begetting.
He so begot Him, then, that the Gift might proceed jointly from Him, and so that
the Holy Spirit would be the Spirit of both.

1679

[15, 18, 31]
"The love of God is poured into our hearts by the Holy Spirit who is given to us   591
(28)." [32] Nothing is more excellent than this gift of God. It alone is what makes
the division between the sons of the eternal kingdom and the sons of eternal perdition.
Other gifts too are given by the Holy Spirit, but without love they are productive
of nothing. . . . Certainly there can be faith without love, but such faith can profit   545
nothing.

1680

[15, 26, 46]
The Lord Jesus Himself has not only, as God, given the Holy Spirit, but also, as Man,   341
He has received Him. That is why He is said to be "full of grace (29) and of the Holy
Spirit (30)." And it is written more plainly of Him in the Acts of the Apostles,
"because God anointed Him with the Holy Spirit (31)." He was not anointed as if with
a visible oil, but with the gift of grace, which is signified by the visible anointing with
which the Church anoints the baptized. Neither was Christ anointed by the Holy
Spirit when, at His baptism, the Holy Spirit descended upon Him as a dove (32); for in
this He deigned to prefigure His Body, that is, His Church, in which the baptized
receive the Holy Spirit in a special way. But it is to be understood that He was anointed
in that mystical and invisible anointing when the Word of God was made flesh (33),
that is, when a human nature, without any preceding merits of good works, was joined   324
to the Divine Word in the womb of the Virgin, in such a way as to become one   329
person with the Divine Word. That is why we confess that He was born of the Holy   781
Spirit and of the Virgin Mary; for it were very foolish of us to believe that He received the
Holy Spirit when He was already thirty years of age (34).

1681

[15, 26, 47]
For if whatever the Son has, He has from the Father, certainly He has it from the   273
Father that the Holy Spirit proceeds from Him. . . . For the Father alone is not from   250
another, for which reason He alone is called unbegotten, not, indeed, in the Scriptures,
but in the practice of theologians (35), and of those who employ such terms as they
are able in a matter so great. The Son, however, is born of the Father; and the Holy Spirit   274
proceeds principally from the Father, and since the Father gives [to the Son all that
He has] without any interval of time, the Holy Spirit proceeds jointly from both   276
Father and Son. He would be called Son of the Father and of the Son if, which is   275
abhorrent to everyone of sound mind, they had both begotten Him. The Spirit was not
begotten by each, however, but proceeds from each and from both.

1681a

[15, 27, 48]
From Him from whom the Son has it that He is God (for He is God of God),—   276
from Him He certainly has it that the Holy Spirit also proceeds from Him; and therefore   275
the Holy Spirit has it from the Father Himself that He proceeds also from the Son   273
just as He proceeds from the Father. Here too it is in some way understood, insofar as it
can be understood by such as we are, why the Holy Spirit is not said to be born, but
rather to proceed: because if He Himself were also called the Son, He would certainly
be called the Son of both, which is most absurd; for a son is never of two, except father
and mother. Perish the thought, then, that we should ever suspect such a thing between
God the Father and God the Son (36).

1682

[15, 28, 51]

O Lord our God, we believe in You, Father and Son and Holy Spirit. For the Truth   234
would not say: "Go, baptize all nations in the name of the Father and of the Son and   237
of the Holy Spirit (37)," unless You were a Trinity. Nor would You command us,
O Lord God, to be baptized in the name of anyone who is not the Lord God. Nor
would it be said by the divine voice: "Hear, O Israel, the Lord your God is one God
(38)," unless You were a Trinity in such a way that You are the one Lord God. And if
You Yourself were God the Father as well as the Son, Your Word, Jesus Christ, and
Your Gift, the Holy Spirit, we would not read in the Books of Truth: "God sent His   290
Son (39)." Nor would You, O Only-begotten, say of the Holy Spirit: "Whom the   291
Father will send in My name (40)"; and: "Whom I will send you from the Father (41)."

 1. Ex. 3:14.
 2. 1 Cor. 2:8.
 3. *non ex nostro sensu*.
 4. See Rom. 12:3.
 5. *uno verissimo sacrificio*.
 6. See Rom. 8:30.
 7. Ps. 8:6.
 8. Eph. 4:8.
 9. Sir. 24:5.
10. John 15:16.
11. *sine situ praesidentem*.
12. *sine habitu omnia continentem*.
13. *sine loco ubique totum*.
14. *nihilque patientem*: literally, "and suffering nothing."
15. *etsi nondum potest omni modo invenire quid sit*.
16. John 10:30.
17. *principium*.
18. Ex. 3:14.
19. 1 Cor. 13:12.
20. Gen. 1:26.
21. Gen. 1:27.
22. *beati*.
23. To say that the devil slew Christ—and if it is a little less apparent in the locution of Augustine's Latin than it is in my
    English, it is present in the Latin nonetheless surely—is, it strikes me, offensive at least to pious ears; and I take it as a
    certainty that my own ears are not a whit more pious than the average ear. The viewpoint is much akin to that of Origen
    and some others of the Fathers, and which Augustine will declare quite directly a few lines below: that our debt which
    Christ paid for us was paid out to the devil. Such a view is quite unsatisfactory. See above, § 508, in Vol. 1.
24. Rom. 5:9.
25. See note 23 above.
26. *non frustra*.
27. *principaliter*.
28. Rom. 5:5.
29. John 1:14.
30. Luke 4:1.
31. Acts 10:38.
32. Matt. 3:16.
33. John 1:14.
34. See Luke 3:21-23.
35. *in consuetudine disputantium*.
36. Augustine quotes this entire passage from himself, as he himself indicates. He wrote it first in a Sermon on the Gospel of
    John, 99, 8-9, § 1840 below.
37. Matt. 28:19.
38. Deut. 6:4.
39. Gal. 4:4; John 3:17.
40. John 14:26.
41. John 15:26.

THE LITERAL INTERPRETATION OF GENESIS [*inter A. D.* 401-415]

After writing an interpretation of the first three books of Genesis according to the allegorical method, his *De Genesi contra Manichaeos* (§§ 1539-1544 above), Augustine decided to write also a literal interpretation of Genesis. He was not at all satisfied with his initial progress and at first abandoned the work after writing only one book. Later he put a hasty conclusion to it and published it as the *De Genesi ad litteram opus imperfectum* (§ 1564 above).

But if he abandoned his initial attempt at a literal interpretation of Genesis, he did not abandon the idea itself, and finally produced such a work in twelve books. In his *Corrections* 2, 50, relating the circumstances of his *De Genesi ad litteram libri duodecim*, Augustine remarks that he wrote this work at the same time as his work on *The Trinity*, beginning it after the latter and completing it before. We may consider that it was written in the years 401 to 415 A. D.

Augustine says also that in his twelve-book literal interpretation of Genesis he has asked more questions than he has answered, and even of the few that are answered, fewer still, he says, are answered definitively.

The Maurist text in Migne PL 34, 245-486, has long since been superseded by the edition of J. Zycha in the *Vienna Corpus*, CSEL, Vol. 28, part 1 (1894).

1683

[1, 18, 37]

If we read even in the divine Scriptures about hidden things and things most removed   470
from our eyes, it will be possible, saving always the faith which fills us, to formulate
various opinions about these matters. Let us, then, not be too hasty in accepting
any such opinion which, were the truth to be sought more carefully, might afterwards be
found unsound, and lest we might be found in error by our attempting to establish
what is but our own view and not that of the divine Scriptures, as if we would wish our
view to be that of the Scriptures, whereas we ought to wish that the view taken by
the Scriptures should become our own.

1684

[1, 19, 39]

It not infrequently happens that something about the earth, about the sky, about   470
other elements of this world, about the motion and rotation or even the magnitude and
distances of the stars, about definite eclipses of the sun and moon, about the passage of
years and seasons, about the nature of animals, of fruits, of stones and of other
such things, may be known with the greatest certainty, by reasoning or by experience,
even by one who is not a Christian. It is too disgraceful and ruinous, however, and
greatly to be avoided, that he should hear a Christian speaking so idiotically on these
matters, and as if in accord with Christian writings, that he might say that he could
scarcely keep from laughing when he saw how totally in error they are (1).

1685

[1, 20, 40]

In view of this (2) and keeping it in mind constantly while dealing with the Book of   470
Genesis, I have, insofar as I was able, explained in detail and set forth for consideration
the meanings of obscure passages, taking care not to affirm rashly some one meaning
to the prejudice of another and perhaps better explanation.

1686

[1, 21, 41]

Someone will say: "Why do you harp so much on this theme, why do you insist on   470
belaboring the subject (3)? Why, when almost everything about these questions is
obscure? Affirm something at least, since you have maintained that much about them
can be understood!" I will tell him that if I have ground fine his bread will be all the
better (4). I have learned not to pursue a man too closely, but to reply in accord
with the faith. Answer must be made to men who try to calumniate the books of our
salvation, so that we can show that our writings are not contrary to whatever they might
be able to demonstrate about the nature of things from truthful documents; and so that we
can either show by some eloquence, or may believe without hesitation, that whatever
they might advance from any of their own books is most false, if it is contrary to
our writings, that is, to the Catholic faith.

1687

[2, 9, 20]

With the Scriptures it is a matter of treating about the faith. For that reason, as I have   22
noted repeatedly, if anyone, not understanding the mode of divine eloquence, should   27
find something about these matters [about the physical universe] in our books, or hear   470
of the same from those books, of such a kind that it seems to be at variance with
the perceptions of his own rational faculties, let him believe that these other things are
in no way necessary to the admonitions or accounts or predictions of the Scriptures. In
short, it must be said that our authors knew the truth about the nature of the skies; but it
was not the intention of the Spirit of God, who spoke through them, to teach men
anything that would not be of use to them for their salvation.

1688

[4, 12, 22]

It is also possible to understand that God rested from the creating of different   530
kinds of creatures, insofar as He created no kinds additional to those He had already
created; but thereafter and even until now He worked the management of those kinds
already created. It is not, at any rate, that on the seventh day His power to govern
the heavens and the earth and all that He had created would cease; otherwise, everything
would immediately vanish.

1688a

[4, 12, 23]

Hence also what the Lord says, "My Father is working even until now (5)," is   530
illustrative of His work, by which He maintains and governs all creation. It could be
understood in a different way if He had said, "My Father is working even now,"
whereby it would not be necessary for us to understand a continuation of work; but it
must be understood differently, since what He does say is, "even until now," whereby
it is apparent that He has been working at all times ever since He first did the work of
creation.

1689

[4, 22, 39]

And it is undoubtedly because other creatures, which are made beneath the angelic   470
rank, are not made without His knowledge, that the same day is everywhere

repeated, so that in its repetition there may be just as many days as there are classes of
created things to be distinguished, in a series of completions determined in six
groupings. Thus, on the evening of the first day there is already the self-knowledge, that
it is not itself what God is; but on the morning after the aforesaid evening, on which
the first day is concluded and the second begins, there is its periodic return, in which
that which was created turns to the praise of its Creator, and perceives from the Word of
God the knowledge of creation made after itself, that is, of the firmament. . . .
Then comes the evening of that day, when the firmament knows itself, not in the
Word of God as before, but in its own nature; which knowledge, because it is lesser,
is rightly indicated by the name of evening (6).

1690

[4, 27, 44]
    Let us believe that those seven days exhibit a certain variance from others which,   470
when it is a question of days in which the term of one day is from the rising of the
sun until its setting, constitute a week, by the occurrence and recurrence of which
the seasons carry on, so that we will not hestitate in the least to say that these have a
similarity to the others, but in much they are unlike.

1692

[4, 33, 52]
    What the Scriptures tell of the Creator, that He completed His works in six days, is not   470
at variance with what is written elsewhere, that He created everything at once (7).
And consequently, He that made all things at once also made those six or seven days,
or rather, He made all at once one day repeated six or seven times.

1693

[5, 16, 34]
    He that created is closer to us than are many of the things that He created. "For in Him   130
we live and move and have our existence (8)." . . . From this it follows that it is more
difficult to discover those created things, than it is to discover Him by whom they
were made; moreover, the incomparable happiness experienced by a pious mind in
knowing Him in however small a way, is more excellent than that of understanding
all things else.

1694

[5, 20, 40]
    There are those who consider that only the world itself was made by God, and that   530
other things come into being through the world itself, just as He ordained and
commanded, but without God's doing the work Himself (9). The statement of the Lord,
however, is proposed against them: "My Father is working even until now (10)." . . .
Thus, let us believe or, if we are able, let us even understand that God is working
even to the present in such a way that if He were to withdraw His operation from the
things He created, they would fall apart.

1695

[5, 33, 45]
    Just as all those things, which, through the seasons, develop in the tree, were already   470
present but invisible in its seed, so too is it to be understood of the world: that when

God created all things at once, it had in it all things which were made by Him when day was made; not only the skies with the sun and moon and stars, the splendor of which remains in their circular motion (11), and the earth and the depths, which undergo a kind of irregular motion (12), and the lower regions which constitute another part of the world; but even those things which water and earth produces potentially and causally, before they make their appearance in the course of time. We recognize these things already in those works which God is working even to the present time.

1696

[6, 13, 23]

But how did God make Adam from the slime of the earth? Was Adam suddenly of   509
mature age, that is, a youthful adult (13), or was he formed even as men are now,
in the womb of their mothers? For it was not another who did this, but He who said:
"Before I formed you in the womb, I knew you (14)." Thus, all that was peculiar to
Adam was that he was not born of parents, but was made from the earth; in such a way,
however, that in the effecting of this and as he advanced in age, he passed through those
same stages that we see attributed to the nature of humankind. Or, in fact, is this
not to be demanded? But in whichever way He did it, God did what was fitting for
Him, in His wisdom and omnipotence, to be able to do and actually to do.

1697

[6, 13, 24]

[In regard to the miracles recounted in the Scriptures], these events, when they   12
take place, do not take place contrary to nature, except in man's view,—for we
have come to recognize the course of nature as being otherwise;—but not for God, for
whom whatever He does is natural.

1698

[6, 24, 35]

"How then," they will ask, "are we said to be renewed, if we do not receive what the   750
first man lost, in which man all die (15)?" Plainly, we receive this in a certain   611
way, and again in a certain way we do not receive it. Certainly we do not receive the
immortality of a spiritual body, which man never had; but we do receive righteousness,   520
from which man fell away by sin. We will be restored, therefore, from the long   610
duration of sin, not to the pristine living body (16) in which Adam was, but to a better,   1044
that is, to a spiritual body, when we are made equal to God's angels (17), suited to a
heavenly dwelling place, where we shall have no need of victuals that perish. We shall be
renewed, therefore, in the spirit of our mind (18), in accord with the image of Him
who created us, which Adam lost by sinning.

1699

[6, 25, 36]

For Adam, before he sinned, can be said to have had a body that was in one way   522
mortal, but in another way immortal. His body was mortal, because it was able to die;
but it was immortal because it was also able not to die. It is one thing not to be able to die,
like certain immortal natures God created; but it is another thing to be able not to
die (19) which is the way in which the first man was created immortal. This was
provided him by the tree of life, and not by the constitution of his own nature. When he   611
sinned he was separated from that tree, so that he was able to die, who, if he had

not sinned, had been able not to die. He was mortal, therefore, by the condition of his
living body (20), but immortal by the kindness of the Creator.

1700

[7, 28, 43]
   Now, however, about the soul, which God breathed into man by blowing on his   501
face, I affirm nothing, except that it is not the substance of God; and it is incorporeal,   506
which is to say, it is not a body, but a spirit; not begotten of the substance of God, nor
proceeding from the substance of God, but created by God; nor was it so created that
any other nature of body or irrational soul might be changed into its nature; and
consequently it was created out of nothing, and is immortal according to a certain mode   502
of life, which it can in no way lose; but in accord with a certain mutability, by which it is
able to become better or worse, it can also rightly be understood to be mortal; for
He alone has true immortality, of whom the words were properly spoken: "Who alone
has immortality (21)."

1701

[8, 12, 26]
   Just as air, in the presence of light, is not made bright, but does become bright,—   750
because if it were made bright, as opposed to becoming bright, it would remain
bright even in the absence of light,—so too man is illuminated in the presence of God
Himself, but in God's absence he is immediately darkened. Man is separated from God
not by a spatial interval, however, but by an aversion of the will.   761

1702

[9, 15, 26]
   Woman's nature was created; and although it was created from that of the man which   510
already existed, it was not created by some movement of natures already existing. The   462
angels, however, are utterly incapable of creating a nature; for of any kind of nature,   467
there is only one Creator, who is God, the Trinity, I mean, the Father and the Son
and the Holy Spirit.

1705

[10, 23, 39]
   The custom of Mother Church (22) in baptizing infants is certainly not to be scorned,   102
nor is it to be regarded in any way as superfluous, nor is it to be believed that its   835
tradition is anything except Apostolic. The age of infancy also has a great weight of
witness; for it was the infant age that first merited to pour out its blood for Christ (23).

1706

[11, 1, 3]
   "They were both naked (24)." It is true. The bodies of the two human beings   521
residing in paradise were entirely naked. "And they were not ashamed (25)." Why,
indeed, should they have been ashamed, when they were unaware of any law in their
members struggling against the law of their minds (26)? That penalty of sin came to them   610
after they had perpetrated their transgression, when, in disobedience, they had
taken what was forbidden them; and they were justly punished for what they had done.
But it was before this that they were naked, as it says, and were not ashamed. There was

no inclination in their bodies to cause any shame; and they took no thought of covering themselves, because they were aware of nothing that needed to be restrained.

1707

[11, 9, 12]

God knew in advance that an evil will was going to take hold of our first parents. 191
But because He knew, and because His foreknowledge cannot err, it does not follow
that the evil will was His rather than theirs. Why then did He create them, when He 192
knew what their future would be? Because just as He foresaw what evils they would 193
do, He also foresaw what good He would Himself draw from their evil deeds. . . .
[11, 10, 13] "But," someone will say, "He could have changed their will to good, 696
because He is almighty." Certainly He could have done so. Why, then, did He not?
Because He did not will to do it. And why He did not will to do it is His business.

1708

[11, 14, 18]

Some say the devil fell from his place on high because he was envious of man, 491
who was made in the image of God. Certainly, however, envy does not precede pride,
but follows it; for envy is not the cause of one's being proud, but pride is the cause
of one's being envious.

1. *toto caelo errare conspiciens risum tenere vix possit.*
2. The reference is to the matter of § 1684 immediately above.
3. *Quid tu tanta tritura dissertationis huius, quid granorum exuisti, quid eventilasti?* We have substituted equivalent expressions for Augustine's very mixed metaphor: What grain have you gotten by so great a threshing of this subject matter? Why do you discuss it?
4. *Cui respondeo, ad eum ipsum me suaviter cibum pervenisse.* I must confess that I am not entirely certain of this apparently idiomatic expression; but I take it to be Augustine's denial that he has ground his grain too fine or belabored his point; and he says that, in view of the gravity and complexity of the subject, he has really presented solid material in a most palatable fashion.
5. John 5:17.
6. That is to say, it is vespertinal knowledge, as opposed to matutinal; or, so to say, *post factum* knowledge as opposed to *ante factum*.
7. Sir. 18:1.
8. Acts 17:28.
9. *Deum autem ipsum nihil operari.* Apparently, then, the theory of evolution is not really a new idea in modern times.
10. John 5:17.
11. *eorum species manet motu rotabili.*
12. *quae velut inconstantes motus patiuntur.* I wonder if Augustine's *inconstantes* do not concern the problem of eccentric motion which was such a bane to pre-Copernican astronomy? In the present work he says himself that he mostly asks questions rather than answering them; so he can scarcely object to my doing the same.
13. *hoc est virili atque iuvenali.*
14. Jer. 1:5.
15. Rom. 5:12.
16. *non in pristinum corpus animale.*
17. Matt. 22:30.
18. Eph. 4:23.
19. The negative is so placed in the thesis and in the antithesis that it is clear that Augustine is contrasting an incapacity of dying to a capacity of not dying.
20. *condicione corporis animalis.*
21. 1 Tim. 6:16.
22. *matris ecclesiae.*
23. See Matt. 2:16.
24. Gen. 2:25.
25. *Ibid.*
26. See Rom. 7:23.

A DEBATE WITH FELIX THE MANICHEAN [*A. D.* 404]

Augustine's *De actis cum Felice Manichaeo* is, like his *Against Fortunatus the Manichean*, the record of a debate. In the *Corrections* 2, 34 Augustine recalls that a certain Felix, a Manichean preacher, came to Hippo ''to sow this very error.'' The debate was held in the church at Hippo on two days, December 7th and 12th, in the year 404 A. D. The proceedings were taken down by shorthand stenographers.

The Migne reprint of the Maurist text (PL 42, 519-552) is now superseded by J. Zycha's edition in the Vienna Corpus, CSEL, Vol. 25, 2 (1892).

1709

[1, 10]
You have stated that Mani taught you the beginning, the middle, and the end, and   22
how and why the world was made, and about the course of the sun and the moon and
about other things which you have mentioned. Nowhere in the Gospel do we read
that the Lord said: ''I am sending you a Paraclete who will teach you about the course
of the sun and the moon.'' For He wanted to make Christians, not mathematicians.

1710

[2, 4]
''Either make the tree good and its fruit good, or make the tree bad and its fruit bad''   700
(1). When He says *either make* this, *or make* that, He refers to power, not nature.
For no one except God is able to make a tree, but everyone has the power in his will to
choose what is good and to be a good tree, or to choose what is evil and be a bad tree.

1711

[2, 18]
All things that come into existence and which someone makes are either from oneself,   461
or out of something, or out of nothing. A man, since he is not almighty, makes a
son from himself; or, as an artisan, he makes things out of something else, such as a
coffer from wood, or a vessel from silver. For he can make a vessel, but he cannot make
the silver; he can make a coffer, but he cannot make the wood. No man, then, can
make something come into existence from out of nothing, out of that which does not   158
already exist. But God, because He is almighty, not only begets His Son from Himself,   462
but also makes the world out of nothing, and from its slime He shapes man; and by
these three capabilities He shows how powerful He is in all that He does.

1. Matt. 12:33.

THE NATURE OF THE GOOD [*A. D.* 405]

Another of Augustine's anti-Manichean writings, the *De natura boni* was written most probably in the year 405 A. D. In it Augustine argues against Manichean dualism by showing, as he tells us in his *Corrections* 2, 35, that all natures, spiritual or corporeal, come from God, who is unchangeable by nature and the highest good; and therefore all natures, insofar as they are natures, are good. He discusses also the origins of evil.

The Maurist text in Migne PL 42, 551-572 has yielded its place as standard to the edition of J. Zycha in the Vienna Corpus, CSEL, Vol. 25, 2 (1892).

1712

[22]

God cannot be said to have measure, lest it should seem that He is spoken of as   153
limited. Nor yet is he without measure, by whom measure is bestowed on all things, so
that in some measure they may exist. Nor again can He be said to be measured,
as if He received measure from someone else. Perhaps we can say something, however,
by calling Him the highest measure; but only if, in calling Him the highest measure,
we mean the highest good.

AGAINST THE GRAMMARIAN CRESCONIUS OF THE DONATIST PARTY
[ca. A. D. 406]

When a certain Cresconius, a grammarian and a layman of the Donatist sect, happened
upon a copy of the first book of Augustine's *Against the Letters of Petilian*, he wrote a
reply thereto addressed to Augustine. The present work, *Contra Cresconium grammaticum
partis Donati*, in four books written about 406 A. D., is Augustine's counter-reply
to Cresconius. It is treated in the *Corrections* 2, 52.

The Migne reprint of the Maurist text in PL 43, 455-594 is superseded since 1909
by M. Petschenig's edition in the Vienna Corpus, CSEL, Vol. 52.

1713

[1, 30, 35]

If by his entreaties a man obtains from the king forgiveness for his error and release   798
from military service, the royal brand on that man is not to be changed or removed   804
because a deserter has impressed the same character in gathering accomplices
around himself (1). Nor are the signs on the sheep to be changed when they are gathered
into the Lord's flock, because a runaway slave impressed the Lord's sign on them.

1. *quia eumdem characterem quo sibi satellites congregaret, desertor infixit.*

BRIEF ON THE CONFERENCE WITH THE DONATISTS [A. D. 411]

In 411 A. D. a conference of Catholic and Donatist bishops was held at Carthage,
called by order of the Emperor Honorius and presided over by his representative, Count
Marcellinus. It was hoped that the conference could achieve a reconciliation that would
end the schism. The conference did not in fact end the schism immediately and abruptly; but
from that time Donatism began its sharp decline from which it never recovered.

Soon after the conference Augustine drew up a brief or epitome of the proceedings,
which he published under the title *Breviculus collationis cum Donatistis*. The work is
treated in the *Corrections* 2, 65. The Maurist text in Migne PL 43, 613-650 has been
superseded since 1910 by M. Petschenig's edition in the Vienna Corpus, CSEL, Vol. 53.

1714

[3, 10, 20]

Catholics refute their calumny about two churches, proving again and again more   413
clearly what they declare, that is, that being now a Church mixed with evil members, it   414
does not on that account call itself a Church foreign to the kingdom of God, where
there will not be this mixture containing evil members; but the same Church, one and   419

holy, is now in one condition and then it will be in another. Now it is mixed and   420
has evil members, then it will not have such. Now it is mortal because it is made up of
mortal men; then it will be immortal, because there will be nothing corporeal in
it, nothing that can die.

FORGIVENESS AND THE JUST DESERTS OF SINS, AND THE BAPTISM OF INFANTS [*A. D.* 412]

After 411 A. D. Donatism was effectively a dead issue: and that largely through
Augustine's efforts. Nor had Manicheism any longer its earlier vigor. But still Augustine
could have no rest. Just when Donatism was gasping out its final breaths Pelagius (see
Vol. 2, pp. 214-216) landed in Africa, and there was a new war to be waged.

The earliest of Augustine's anti-Pelagian writings, his *De peccatorum meritis et
remissione et de baptismo parvulorum* in three books, was written in 412, addressed to
Marcellinus, a tribune at Carthage, in response to the latter's queries. The third of the
three books, as Augustine himself states in his *Corrections* 2, 59, is actually a letter to
Marcellinus which was joined to the preceding two books because of its similar subject
matter. In the first two books Pelagius is not named, because Augustine still had hopes
of regaining him. By the time he wrote the third book, in form a letter to Marcellinus,
he had read Pelagius' exposition of the Pauline Epistles, drawing new arguments against
original sin from Rom. 5:12 and other places, and Augustine saw the futility of that
hope of conversion; and knowing no other reason to protect him, in the third book he
named Pelagius straight out as the heretic whom he was refuting.

The Maurist text, reprinted in Migne PL 44, 109-200, was superseded in 1913 by the
edition of C. F. Urba and J. Zycha in the Vienna Corpus, CSEL, Vol. 60.

1715

[1, 9, 10]
Christ's saints imitate Him in order to pursue justice. Whence also the same   750
Apostle says: "Be imitators of me, even as I am of Christ (1)." But besides this   373
imitation, His grace also works within us our illumination and justification, by that
work of which His same preacher says: "Neither is he that plants anything, nor
he that waters, but He that gives the increase, God (2)." For by this grace baptized   836
infants too are ingrafted into His body, infants who certainly are not yet able   374
to imitate anyone. Christ, in whom all are made alive, besides offering Himself   835
as an example of righteousness for those who would imitate Him, gives also the
most hidden grace of His Spirit to believers, grace which He secretly infuses even
into infants. In a similar way Adam, in whom all die (3), besides being an example   614
for imitation to those who wilfully transgress the commandment of the Lord, by the
hidden depravity of his own carnal concupiscence, depraved in his own person all
those who come from his stock. . . . "Through one man," the Apostle says, "sin   611
entered the world, through sin death (4)." And this refers not to imitation but to   615
propagation.

1716

[1, 20, 27]
Will anyone dare to say that this statement, ["Unless you eat My flesh and drink
My blood you shall not have life in you (5)"], does not pertain to infants, and that   870
without participating in his Body and Blood they can have life in themselves, on the   874
grounds that He does not say: "*Whoever* does not eat," as when He says about   831
Baptism: "*Whoever* is not reborn (6)," but says instead: "If *you* do not eat (7)," as if He

were speaking to those who could hear and understand Him, which, of course, infants cannot do? But anyone who says this is not attentive of the fact that unless the statement embrace all, so that without the Body and Blood of the Son of Man they cannot have life, it is in vain even for those of more advanced years to be concerned about it.

1717

[1, 24, 34]

It is an excellent thing that the Punic Christians (8) call Baptism itself nothing else but *salvation*, and the Sacrament of Christ's Body nothing else but *life*. Whence does this derive, except from an ancient and, as I suppose, apostolic tradition, by which the Churches of Christ hold inherently that without Baptism and participation at the table of the Lord it is impossible for any man to attain either to the kingdom of God or to salvation and life eternal? This is the witness of Scripture too.

831
870

1718

[2, 3, 3]

They think they are quite sharp when they say (9)—as if any of us were ignorant of it!—that "if we do not will it, we do not sin; nor would God charge a man to do what were impossible to human volition." But what they do not see is that to overcome some things, whether they are things that it is evil to desire or things that it is evil to avoid, is sometimes a work requiring great strength and the total energy of the will; and He foresaw that we would not in every instance employ these energies perfectly (10).

727
636
652
657

1719

[2, 5, 5]

For sinning we have no help from God; but we cannot do what is just or fulfill the precept of justice altogether unless we are helped by God. For just as the bodily eye is not helped by the light to turn away, closed or averted, from that same light, but is helped by it so that it can see, which it cannot do at all unless it is helped, so too God, who is the light of the interior man, helps the gaze of our mind so that we can do something that is good, not according to our own but according to His righteousness.

655
650

1720

[2, 6, 7]

Those who maintain that a man can exist in this life without sin must not be immediately contradicted with an incautious rashness; for if we deny such a possibility we derogate both from the free choice of man, who in his will desires it, and from the power or mercy of God, who by His help effects it. But it is one thing to ask whether a man can so exist, and another to ask whether anyone does so exist. . . . If I were to be asked whether a man can be without sin in this life I would admit the possibility (11), through the grace of God and the man's own free choice, not doubting at the same time that even his own free choice pertains to the grace of God, that is, to God's gifts, not only for the fact that it exists, but also for the fact that it is good, that is, that it is directed toward keeping God's commands. And thus the grace of God not only points out what ought to be done, but even helps by making it possible to do what it points out. . . . I cannot doubt that God has given no impossible command to man, and that with God to aid and help, nothing is impossible by the doing of which His command is fulfilled. And in this way a man, helped by God, can, if he will, be without sin. [7, 8] But ask me the second question,

658

683
684

652

whether or not there really is such a sinless man, and I will say that I believe
there is not.

1721

[2, 11, 6]

    It was in view of that righteousness by which he saw what his own righteousness   346
was (12), that Job blamed himself and melted away and regarded himself as dust and
ashes (13). In his mind's eye he saw the righteousness of Christ, in whose divinity
not alone, but neither in whose soul nor in whose flesh could there possibly be
any sin.

1722

[2, 17, 26]

    If, with divine grace assisting the human will, a man is able to be without sin in   658
this life, I can tell you very easily and most truthfully why such does not happen: 700
men do not will it. But if you ask me why they do not will it, we are drawn into
a more lengthy statement. But without prejudice to a more diligent inquiry, I can
say this much briefly. Men do not will to do what is right either because what is
right is hidden from them or because it is unpleasing to them. . . . But it is the   702
work of God's grace, which assists men's wills, to make known that which was   683
hidden and to make agreeable that which was unpleasant. That men are not so   684
assisted has likewise its cause in themselves and not in God, whether they are
predestined to be damned on account of the wickedness of their pride or whether,   210
if they are children of mercy, they are to be judged and disciplined for
that same pride.

1723

[2, 18, 28]

    Let us take care not to defend grace in such a way that we would seem to take   700
away free choice; nor again can we insist so strongly on free choice that we could be
judged, in our proud impiety, ungrateful for the grace of God.

1724

[2, 19, 32]

    Insofar as it is granted us, let us be wise; and let us understand, if we can, that   683
the good God sometimes withholds even from His saints either the sure knowledge or   684
the triumphant delight of some righteous work, so that they may know that the light   702
which illuminates their darkness and the agreeableness by which their land yields
its fruit is not from themselves but from Him. [33] But when we beseech Him for His   712
help for the doing and perfecting of righteousness, what else are we praying for,
except that He may open up what was hidden and make agreeable that which was
not pleasant?

1725

[2, 27, 43]

    If anyone wonders why children born of the baptized should themselves be   835
baptized, let him attend briefly to this. . . . The Sacrament of Baptism is most   836
assuredly the Sacrament of regeneration. But just as the man who never lived cannot

die, and one who has not died cannot rise again, so too one who was never born
cannot be reborn. From this we conclude that no one who has not been born in his
parent is able to be reborn. . . . Unless we voluntarily depart from the rule of
the Christian faith it must be admitted that inasmuch as infants are, by the Sacrament
of Baptism, conformed to the death of Christ, they are also freed from the serpent's
venomous bite. This bite, however, they did not receive in their own proper life,   614
but in him who first suffered that wound.

1726

[2, 28, 46]
   In this law of concupiscence which is not yet done away with but still remains, its   836
guilt is taken away and will not exist, since there is a full remission of sins in Baptism.
Indeed, if a man departs this life immediately after his Baptism there is nothing at
all to which he can be held liable, since everything that bound him has been loosed.

1727

[2, 34, 55]
   Just as those first humans, though they afterwards lived righteously, whence they   389
are rightly believed to have been freed, through the Blood of the Lord, from   612
ultimate punishment, did not, however, deserve to be recalled to paradise in
this life, so too the flesh of sin, even if a man live righteously in it after his sins
have been forgiven, does not deserve to be exempted immediately from the death which
it drew from the progeny of sin.

1728

[3, 7, 14]
   In Adam all sinned when, by that power innate in his nature, by which he was   615
able to beget them, all were as yet the one Adam.   614

1. 1 Cor. 11:1.
2. 1 Cor. 3:7.
3. Rom 5:12.
4. Rom 5:12.
5. See John 6:54.
6. John 3:5.
7. John 6:54.
8. *Punici Christiani*; that is, the Christians in and around Carthage.
9. *acute autem sibi videntur dicere*.
10. *qua nos non perfecte in omnibus adhibituros praevidit*.
11. *confitebor posse*.
12. *secundum illam iustitiam qua se noverat iustum*. He saw that his own righteous was nothing. Some manuscripts have
    . . . *se noverat iniustum*. The latter is certainly the correct meaning, but the former is just as certainly the correct
    reading. *Iniustum* was introduced into the text by a dull-witted scribe who did not understand Augustine's ready use of
    antiphrasis, found often enough in Saint Paul, and which is all the more appropriate in the context of a discussion of
    Job, whose wife was so enamored of antiphrasis that she regularly urged Job: "Bless God and die!" when what the
    clever woman really meant was: "Curse God so that He will kill you!"
13. Job. 42:5-6.

THE SPIRIT AND THE LETTER [*A. D.* 412]

   Augustine treats his *De spiritu et littera ad Marcellinum* in the *Corrections* 2, 63. He
   notes that when he sent his *Forgiveness and the Just Deserts of Sins, and the Baptism of*

Infants to Marcellinus the latter was considerably disturbed at Augustine's having stated that in this life a man could be without sin, but that in fact such is never the case. Marcellinus wanted to know how Augustine could be so bold as to say that something could happen when there is no precedent whatever for it. The present work, treating in detail the statement of the Apostle in 2 Cor. 3:6, that the letter kills but the Spirit gives life, is Augustine's response to Marcellinus' inquiry; and at the same time it is another of Augustine's several responses to the error of Pelagianism.

The text in Migne PL 44, 201-246 is superseded by the 1913 edition of C. F. Urba and J. Zycha in the Vienna Corpus, CSEL, Vol. 60.

1729

[3, 5]

If the way of truth is hidden from a man, free choice avails him nothing except for sinning; and even after what he must do and what he must try to do begins not to be hidden, unless it delights him and is loved by him, he does not do it, does not accept it, and does not live well.

654

1730

[9, 15]

His words are: "The righteousness of God is manifested (1)." He does not say, the righteousness of man, or the righteousness of one's own will, but the righteousness of God: not the righteousness by which God Himself is righteous, but that with which He clothes a man when He justifies (2) the impious man.

750

1731

[19, 32]

Without the assistance of the Spirit, the [Law] is undoubtedly the letter that kills. But when the life-giving Spirit is present, He makes that to be loved as something written internally, which the Law caused to be feared as something written externally.

655

1732

[27, 47]

Nor should it be disturbing that the Apostle speaks of the Gentiles as doing the things that are of the law (3) naturally, and not by the Spirit of God, not by faith, and not by grace. For the Spirit of grace does this, in order to restore in us the image of God in which we were naturally created (4).

750

512

1733

[27, 48]

If, however, those who do naturally the things that are of the law (5) are not yet to be included in the number of those whom the grace of Christ justifies, but rather among the number of the impious who do not worship the true God truly and rightly, some of whose actions, however, since they are, insofar as we read or know or hear, done according to the rule of righteousness, we not only cannot blame but neither can we rightly and deservedly praise, although if the motivations of these actions were to be discussed they would hardly be found to be deserving of the praise and defense which are due to righteous conduct,—[28, 48] nevertheless, since the image of God has not, even until now, been so completely

651

erased in the human soul by the stain of earthly affections that nothing even of its barest
outlines remains, whence it can rightly be said that man, even in the very impiety
of his life, knows and does something of the law,—if this is what is meant when
it is said that the Gentiles who do not have the law, (the law of God, that is),
do naturally the things that are of the law, . . . the wide difference which   658
separates the Old Testament from the New is not disturbed. . . . For just as a   633
righteous man is not kept from eternal life by certain venial sins (6), which are   650
always a part of this life (7), so too some good works are of no avail for the
advancement of an impious man to eternal salvation; for it would be most difficult
to find the life of anyone, even the worst of sinners, without some good works.

1734

[31, 54]

See, now, whether anyone believes if he does not will to, or if anyone who wills to   553
believe does not. But if that is absurd,—for what is it to believe, except to agree that
what is said is true? and consent is certainly a matter of the will,—then certainly
faith is in our power. Yet, it is just as the Apostle says: "There is no power except from
God (8)." What is the reason, then, why it cannot be said to us also in this matter:
"What do you have that has not been given you (9)?" For although it is God who gives
us even to believe, nowhere do we read in the Holy Scriptures that there is no volition   656
except from God. And rightly is it not written, because it is not true. Otherwise,   638
God would be the author, perish the thought, even of sins, if there were no volition
except from Him; because the will to evil is already a sin, even if its being carried into   632
action is lacking, that is, even in the absence of the power to do it.

1735

[33, 58]

God, however, "wills all men to be saved and to come to a knowledge of the   201
truth (10)"; but not in such a way that He would take away their free choice, for the good   700
or evil use of which it is most just that they be judged. This being the case, unbelievers   209
certainly act contrary to God's will when they do not believe His gospel; but they
do not thereby overcome His will, but only defraud themselves of the great, yes, the
highest, good, while involving themselves in the evils of punishments, about to
experience, as they are, the power to punish that belongs to Him whose mercy in His gifts
they have despised.

1736

[34, 60]

God acts on us by the persuasions of our perceptions, that we may will and believe,   684
either extrinsically through the gospel exhortations, where even the commandments of   680
the law do something, if they warn a man about his weakness so that he flies to
the grace that justifies through believing; or extrinsically, where, though no man has in   682
his power what shall come into his mind, to consent thereto or dissent therefrom   700
belongs to his own will. When God acts in these ways with the rational soul, so that   656
it may believe in Him,—for there would be no ability at all in free choice to believe, if
there were no persuasion or summons to someone in whom to believe,—certainly
it is likewise God who works in man the will to believe, and in all things anticipates us
with His mercy. But to consent to God's summons or to dissent from it, as I said before,
belongs to our own will.

1737

[35, 63]

See, then, how it is that perfect righteousness in men is unexampled, but yet is not   658
impossible. For it might be, if so great a will were applied as is necessary for so
great an accomplishment. There would, however, be so great a will, if nothing of the
things necessary for righteousness were hidden from us; and if they so delighted the
mind that no matter what other hindrance there might be from pleasure or pain, that   702
pleasure would prevail. That such is not the case belongs not to impossibility but to the
judgment of God.

1. Rom. 3:21.
2. The terms herein which we translate *righteousness, righteous*, and *justifies*, are *iustitia, iustus*, and *iustificat*.
3. See Rom. 2:14.
4. Gen. 1:27.
5. Rom. 2:14.
6. *quaedam peccata venialia*.
7. *sine quibus haec vita non dicitur*.
8. Rom. 13:1.
9. 1 Cor. 4:7.
10. 1 Tim. 2:4.

FAITH AND WORKS [*A. D.* 413]

Augustine's treatise *De fide et operibus* was written most probably in 413 A. D.
It is usually categorized as one of his dogmatic writings; but if it is a work of considerable
interest to the dogmatist it is at least equally so to the moral theologian.

The Maurist text reprinted in Migne (PL 40, 197-230) is superseded by J. Zycha's
edition (1900) in the Vienna Corpus, CSEL, Vol. 41.

1737a

[1, 1]

Certain persons of lesser discernment think that everyone should be admitted to the   1000
font of rebirth which is in Christ Jesus our Lord, even those who, known for their   807
crimes and most flagrant vices, do not wish to change their wicked and shameful life,   975
but declare even by a public profession that they intend to persevere in their wickedness.
For example, if someone is attached to a whore, [they say] he need not be instructed
beforehand to give her up, so that he then may come to Baptism, but even while
remaining with her and admitting and even professing that he intends to remain with her,
he ought not be prevented from becoming a member of Christ, although he continues to
be the member of a whore (1); rather, he may afterwards be taught how evil this is,
and when already baptized he may be instructed on changing to better habits. . . .
[2] Those who are moved to argue in this fashion seem to be impelled to do
so because, if Baptism is denied such persons, it would have to be denied also to men
who have dismissed their wives and married others, or to women who have dismissed
their husbands and married others; for the Lord Christ bears witness beyond any
doubt (2) that these are not marriages but adulteries (3). . . . They judge that unless
they be baptized, they will be lost forever; if, however, they be baptized, even
persevering in these evils, they will be saved through fire (4).
[2, 3] In answer to these persons I would say, first of all, that in reading the
testimonies of Sacred Scripture which indicate that there is presently, or foretell that
there will be in the future, a mingling of good and evil persons in the Church, anyone
who understands these testimonies in such a way that he supposes the diligence and

severity of discipline ought to be relaxed altogether and be omitted is not taught by those
same writings but is deceived by his own conjecture. The fact that Moses, the servant of
God, bore most patiently that mixture of good and evil among the chosen people
(5) did not prevent him from punishing many, even with the sword. . . . . In our
times, when the sword has ceased to be visible in the discipline of the Church, what must
be done is pointed out by degradations and excommunications.

1. *membrum meretricis*. See 1 Cor. 6:13. *Membrum virile* is a classical usage which Augustine undoubtedly knew; but I
   doubt there is any deliberate *double entendre* in the Latin; and if there is, it is equally present in Paul's Greek.
2. Mark 10:11-12; Luke 16:18; Matt. 19:9. See also 1 Cor. 7:10-11.
3. Augustine is not accusing the hypothetical adversary of self-interest, but of a kind of misguided zeal in pity for those
   involved in invalid marriages. They expect that these persons would refuse the Sacrament rather than abandon their
   adulterous unions, and will therefore be lost forever; but they also expect that if these persons are baptized, even if they
   do not afterwards amend their lives, Baptism will obtain for them their being committed to purgatory, out of which they
   will finally be saved.
4. *salvos per ignem futuros*. The underlying notion is evidently that of purgatory. Not only the concept but even the term
   purgatorium itself is known to Augustine. See § 1920 below.
5. *illam primi populi permixtionem*.

THE CITY OF GOD [*inter A. D.* 413-426]

Augustine's *De civitate Dei*, a lengthy work in twenty-two books, is undoubtedly the
most popular of his writings other than his *Confessions*, if by most popular one may be
permitted to mean that which is most widely read. It is at the same time one of his most
profound works and is the vehicle for the exposition of many of his most excellent
insights.

As Augustine himself states in his *Corrections* 2, 69, the work was occasioned by the
consternation and popular anti-Christian feeling that was consequent upon the sack of
Rome by Alaric in 410 A. D. Augustine began writing his *City of God* in 413 A. D.,
and continued with it intermittently until it was finally completed in 426 A. D. *The City
of God* can easily be regarded as the first work ever written in the genre of theology of
history.

The Maurist edition in Migne, PL 41, was superseded at the turn of the century by the
edition of E. Hoffmann in the *Vienna Corpus*, CSEL, Vol. 40, part 1 (1899), embracing
books 1-13, and CSEL, Vol. 40, part 2 (1900), embracing books 14-22. Another critical
edition appeared twenty years ago, but it is doubtful that it can be said to have replaced
the Hoffmann in its position of standard edition: that of Bernard Dombart and Alphonsus
Kalb in the *Corpus Christianorum*, Vol. 47 (1955) containing books 1-10, and Vol. 48
(1955) with books 11-22.

Our translations are based on the Hoffmann text; and in the few instances
(§ § 1756-1758) where the chapter numbers differ in Migne and in Hoffmann, the Hoffmann
number is given first with Migne's number following in parentheses.

1738

[1, 13]

The bodies of the dead, nevertheless, are not to be despised and thrown aside,   123
and least of all, those of the righteous and faithful, which were used in a chaste
manner by the Spirit as the organs and vessels for all good works. For if the dress or the
ring or anything of the sort belonging to parents is the more dear to their offspring as their
affection for them was the greater, certainly then the bodies themselves are not to be
scorned, which are much closer and more intimately joined to us than anything we wear.

1739

[4, 20]

But how do the pagans know what faith is, the first and greatest duty of which   550
is that the true God be believed in? But why did virtue not suffice? Is faith, too,
not included therein?

1740

[5, 9, 4]

One who has not a foreknowledge of all future events is certainly not God.   191
For which reason, too, our wills have just as much power as God willed and   703
foreknew they should have; and, therefore, whatever power they have, they
have most assuredly; and whatever they are going to do, they are most certainly going to
do, because He whose foreknowledge cannot fail foreknew what they would have the
power to do and what they would do.

1741

[5, 10, 1]

Even though God can neither die nor be in error, He is rightly called almighty.   158
For almighty is posited by reason of doing what one wills, not by reason of
suffering what one does not will; if such a thing could befall God, He would not be
almighty at all. Hence there are some things He cannot do, for the very reason that He is
almighty.

1742

[5, 10, 2]

It does not follow, because God foreknew what would in the future be in our will,   191
that there is nothing in the power of our will. For it is not the case that He who foreknew   192
this, foreknew nothing. But if He who foreknew what would in the future be in our
will did not, therefore, foreknow nothing, but something, there is something in the
power of our will. We are, therefore, in no way compelled, if we retain the
foreknowledge of God, to discard our choice of will, or, if we retain choice of will,
to deny—which were shocking—God's foreknowledge of future events. Rather,
we embrace both, and both do we faithfully and truthfully confess. . . . Man,   193
therefore, does not sin because God foreknew that he would sin. Nor can it be doubted
that it is man himself who sins, when he does sin, because He whose foreknowledge
cannot err foreknew that it was not fate, nor fortune, nor something else, but
man himself who was going to sin.

1743

[10, 3, 2]

God himself is the source of our happiness, Himself the end of our desire. Choosing   1040
Him, or rather, rechoosing (1) Him, since we had lost Him by passing Him by   1
(2),—rechoosing Him, therefore, from which word also we have the term religion (3),
we tend to Him by love, so that we may rest in Him and find our happiness when
we have attained our end in Him.

1744

[10, 5]

The fact that our fathers of old offered sacrifices with beasts for victims, which   892

the presdent-day people of God read about but do not do, is to be understood in no
way but this: that those things signified the things that we do in order to draw
near to God and to recommend to our neighbor the same purpose. A visible   897
sacrifice, therefore, is the sacrament, that is to say, the sacred sign (4), of an invisible   790
sacrifice.

1745

[10, 20]
   Christ is both the Priest, offering Himself, and Himself the Victim. He willed that   382
the sacramental sign of this should be the daily sacrifice of the Church (5), who,   891
since the Church is His body and He the Head, learns to offer herself through Him.

1746

[11, 2]
   Since the mind itself, in which reason and intelligence are naturally present,   11
is prevented by certain dark vices of longstanding not only from abiding in and   563
enjoying His unchangeable light but even from enduring it, until that mind has been
day by day renewed and healed and made capable of such great happiness, it has
first to be imbued with faith and to be purified by it. And so that it might walk more   80
confidently to truth, the Truth itself, God, the Son of God, having taken up humanity
without destroying His divinity (6), established and founded this same faith, so that
there might be a path for man to man's God through the God-man (7). For this is the
Mediator of God and man, the Man Christ Jesus (8). For it is as Man that He is the
Mediator and the Way. . . . But the only way that is most secure against all error
is for the same person to be both God and Man: God, the end to whom we go, and
Man, the way by which we go (9).

1747

[11, 6]
   And if the sacred and utterly truthful Scriptures say that "in the beginning   468
God created the heavens and the earth (10)," so that nothing is to be understood
as having been created prior thereto,—for if He had made something before He created
all the rest, it would be this which would be said to have been created in the
beginning,—then beyond any doubt the world was not created in time but along
with time.

1748

[11, 10, 1]
   The Trinity is One God, and nonetheless simple for being a Trinity. . . . It is   150
said to be simple because it is what it has, with the exception of whatever is said   281
relatively of one Person to another. For certainly the Father has the Son, but is not
Himself the Son; and the Son has the Father, but neither is He Himself the Father.

1749

[11, 13]
   It will readily occur to anyone that the happiness which an intellectual nature   1040
desires as its legitimate object is effected by the combination of two things, that   1043
is, both that it enjoy without any interruption the unchangeable good, which is God,

and that it be certain beyond any doubt and beyond any possibility of error that
it is to remain eternally in that same enjoyment.

1750

[11, 24]

Though the Father is spirit and the Son is spirit, and though the Father is holy and   277
the Son is holy, yet [it is the third Person] who is properly called Holy Spirit, as being   268
their substantial holiness and consubstantial with the two.

1751

[11, 24]

But in that place where it is said: "God saw that it is good (11)," it is sufficiently   463
indicated that God created what He did create, not because of any necessity nor to
supply for any need of His own, but solely by reason of goodness, that is, because   465
He is good (12).

1752

[11, 29]

Those holy angels came to a knowledge of God not through audible words, but   172
by the presence itself of unchangeable Truth, that is, His Onlybegotten Word,   238
and the Word Himself and the Father and their Holy Spirit; and they know that this
Trinity is inseparable, that the individual Persons in it are its substance, and that
all constitute not three gods but One God,—all this they know in such a way that
they understand it better than we are understood by ourselves.

1753

[12, 6]

Thus the truest cause of the happiness of the good angels is that they cleave to   1041
Him who exists supreme. But if we seek the cause of the misery of the bad angels,   491
it occurs to us not unreasonably, that they are miserable because they have turned
away from Him who exists supreme, and have turned to themselves, who do not
exist supreme. . . . For if the will abandons what is superior and turns to what is   630
inferior, it is made evil not because that to which it turns is evil, but because the
turning itself is wicked. Therefore it is not an inferior thing that has made the will
evil, but it is itself that has made it so by wickedly and inordinately desiring an
inferior thing. For if two men, alike in physical and moral constitution, behold   695
the beauty of one and the same corporeal thing, by which sight one of them is   701
moved to an illicit enjoyment while the other perseveres in the modest restraint of
his will, what are we to think is the reason that in one there is an evil will while
in the other there is not? . . . If both were tempted by the same temptation, and
one yielded and consented to it, while the other remained as he was before, is it not evident
that the reason is simply that one did not will to fall away from chastity, but the other did
will it? What else can there be but their own will, when [we have posited that] the
physical and moral constitution of both is the same?

1754

[12, 7]

Let no one, therefore, seek the efficient cause of an evil will; it is not efficient   631
but deficient, because the will in this case is not an effecting of something but a

defecting. To defect from that which supremely exists to that which has less of being (13) is to begin to have an evil will. But to try to find the causes of those defections, since, as I said, they are not efficient but deficient, is as if someone tried to see darkness or to hear silence.

1755

[12, 9, 2]

This too must be discussed: if the good angels themselves made their own will good   486
did they do it with some kind of a will, or without a will? If without a will, certainly   490
they did not do it. But if with some kind of a will, was it an evil will or a good will? If it was an evil will, how could an evil will possibly be effectual of a good will? If a good will, they already had a good will. And who made that good will if not He that created them with that good will, that is, with the chaste love in which they   489
would cleave to Him, giving them at one and the same time their nature and endowing   740
it with grace?

1756

[12, 14(13), 1]

How can that be true happiness which has no assurance of lasting in eternity, while   1043
the soul either in ignorance of the truth does not know what misery is approaching, or is, in its happiness, unhappily terrified?

1757

[12, 17(16)]

I confess that I am ignorant of what ages may have passed before the human race   468
was instituted; yet I do not doubt that there is no creature whatever who is coeternal with the Creator.

1758

[12, 18(17), 2]

We are not permitted to believe that God is affected in one way when He rests   155
and in another way when He works; for it ought not be said that He is affected at all, as if there were something in His nature which previously was not there. Indeed, one who is affected is acted upon from without (14), and everything that is acted upon in any way from without is changeable (15). . . . But if earlier He rested, and afterwards He worked,—I do not know how this can be understood by a man,—undoubtedly that which is expressed by earlier and afterwards is in reference to those things which earlier did not exist and afterwards came into existence.

1759

[13, 7]

Those who, though they have not received the washing of regeneration, die for the   833
confession of Christ,—it avails them just as much for the forgiveness of their sins as if they had been washed in the sacred font of Baptism. For He that said: "If anyone is not reborn of water and the Spirit, he will not enter the kingdom of heaven (16)," made an exception for them in that other statement in which He says no less generally: "Whoever confesses Me before men, I too will confess him before My Father, who is in heaven (17)."

1760

[13, 15]

It is agreed among Christians holding truly to the Catholic faith that even the death   522
of our body is not inflicted on us by the law of nature, in which God made no death for   611
man, but that it is inflicted as the deserts of sin.

1760a

[13, 18]

If the angels can do [such marvels], . . . why may we not believe that the spirits   1044
of the saints, perfected and made blessed as a divine reward, can without difficulty carry
their own bodies where they will and hold them where they will?

1761

[14, 4, 1]

Man was made righteous so that he might live not according to himself but according   630
to Him who made him; that is, that he might do the will of Him who made him rather than
his own will. Not so to live as he was made to live,—that is a lie. He wills to be happy, but
does not by his manner of living make his being happy possible. What is there that is more
a lie than such a will as that? It can truly be said that every sin is a lie.

1762

[14, 26]

Certainly in paradise man lived as he willed to live as long as he willed what God had   525
commanded. He lived in the enjoyment of God, from which good he was good. He lived
without any want, and had it in his power so to live forever. Food was there, lest he
hunger; drink, lest he thirst; the tree of life, lest old age waste him. There was no
corruption in his body or from his body to produce anything unpleasant to any of his
senses. He feared no disease from within nor any blow from without. In his flesh there was
health supreme, and in his soul total tranquillity. Just as in paradise there was no
excessive heat nor chill, so too in its inhabitants there was no encroachment on good will
whether through cupidity or through fear.

1763

[14, 28]

Two loves, therefore, have made two cities. There is an earthly city made by the   593
love of self even to the point of contempt for God, and a heavenly city made by   630
the love of God even to the point of contempt for self. The earthly city glories in self,
while the heavenly glories in God. The earthly city seeks glory from men; but
conscience bears witness to the fact that God is the greatest glory of the heavenly city.

1764

[15, 6]

The Holy Spirit works within so that a medicine externally applied may be of some   682
value. Otherwise, even if God Himself, using creatures subject to Him, in some   680
human form exhort the human senses, whether those of the body or those which we
have very like them in sleep, if He does not rule and guide the mind by His interior
grace, no preaching of the truth will profit a man.

1765

[16, 2, 1]

While the hot restlessness (18) of heretics stirs up questions about many things   105
belonging to the Catholic faith, in order to provide a defense against these heretics we are
obliged to study the points questioned more diligently, to understand them more clearly,
and to preach them more forcefully; and thus the question raised by the adversary becomes
the occasion of instruction.

1766

[17, 6, 2]

"And the Lord will seek a man for Himself (19)," signifies either David, or the   21
Mediator Himself of the New Testament, who was figured in the chrism with which   387
David himself and his offspring were anointed. But God does not seek for Himself a man,
as if He did not know where that man was to be found. Through a man, He speaks in the
manner of men; and speaking in that sense, He seeks us.

1767

[18, 38]

In the history of the Kings of Juda and of the Kings of Israel, which recounts   24
their deeds and which we believe belongs to the same Canonical Scriptures (20), many
things are told which are not explained there in detail, and are stated to be found in other
books which were written by the prophets, and sometimes they are not silent even about the
names of these prophets (21); and yet these other books are not found in the Canon which
the people of God received. The reason for this, I confess, escapes me, unless it be, as I
suppose, that even those men to whom certainly the Holy Spirit revealed those things
which ought to be held in the authority of religion, might as men write some things by
historical diligence, and as prophets other things by divine inspiration (22): and so distinct
are these two groups that it is judged that the former are to be attributed to themselves, but
the latter to God speaking through them. Thus, the former pertain to an abundance of
knowledge and the latter to the authority of religion, in which authority the Canon is
guarded (23).

1768

[20, 6, 2]

Just as there are two regenerations, of which I have already spoken above, one   836
according to faith, which is accomplished now and through Baptism; and the   1011
other according to the flesh, which is to be accomplished in the incorruption and
immortality of the flesh, through the great and final judgment (24), so too are there
two resurrections: a first one, which takes place now and is of souls, and which
does not permit them to fall into a second death; and the second resurrection, which
takes place not now, but is to be at the end of time (25), and which is not of souls   1020
but of bodies, and which, through the last judgment (26), will send some to the
second death and others to that life in which there is no death.

1769

[20, 7, 1]

The same Evangelist John has spoken of these two resurrections in his book which   1016
is called the Apocalypse, but in such a way that some of us have not understood the   1017

first of the two, and thereby have turned it into some ridiculous fancies. For the Apostle John says in the aforementioned book:

"And I saw an angel coming down from heaven, having in his hand the key to the abyss and a great chain. And he captured the dragon, the ancient serpent, who is the devil and Satan, and he bound him for a thousand years; and he sent him into the abyss, and he closed it and sealed it over him so that he could lead no more peoples astray until the thousand years should be finished; and after this it is necesssary that he be loosed for a short time. And I saw seats, and they sat upon them, and judgment was given them; and souls beheaded on account of witness to Jesus and on account of the word of God, and who did not adore the beast nor his image, and who did not accept his mark on their foreheads or on their hands; and they came to life and reigned with Christ for a thousand years. The rest of the dead did not come to life until the thousand years were finished. This is the first resurrection. Blessed and holy is he that has part in the first resurrection: in these the second death has no power; but they will be priests of God and Christ, and will reign with Him for a thousand years (27)."

Those who, because of this passage in this book, have suspected that the first resurrection is future and bodily, have been influenced, especially, among other things, by the number of a thousand years, to suppose that it were fitting that among the saints there should be during that time a kind of sabbatism, a holy vacation as it were after the labors of the six thousand years since man was created. . . . This opinion would be somewhat tolerable, if the delights of that sabbath to be enjoyed by the saints were, through the presence of the Lord, of a spiritual kind. For we too were at one time of this opinion (28).

1770

[20, 9, 2]

Neither are the souls of the pious dead separated from the Church which even now   122
is the kingdom of Christ. Otherwise there would be no remembrance of them at the
altar of God in the communication of the Body of Christ.

1771

[20, 19, 4]

Christ will not come to judge the living and the dead unless His adversary, the   1010
Antichrist, shall have come first, to seduce the dead in soul; although their being
seduced by the Antichrist pertains already to the hidden judgment of God.

1772

[21, 3, 1]

The soul is so connected to this body that it submits to the greatest pains and departs;   990
for the very structure of our members and vital parts is so infirm that it is unable to
sustain that force which is brought to bear by great and extreme pain. But in the life
to come (29) the soul will be connected in such a way to the body that the bond between
them will be dissolved by no length of time nor broken by any pain. . . . Death   1034
will be eternal when the soul will not be able to possess God and live, nor to die   1031
and escape the pains of the body. The first death drives the soul from the body
against her will; the second death holds the soul in the body against her will.

1773

[21, 8, 2]

We are accustomed to say that all portents are contrary to nature; but they are not.   12
For how is that contrary to nature which happens by the will of God, since the will of so

great a Creator is certainly the nature of every created thing? A portent, therefore, does not happen contrary to nature, but contrary to what we know about nature. . . . [5] Just as it was not impossible for God to create whatever He willed, so too it is not impossible for Him to change, into whatever He wills, the natures which He created.

1774

[21, 10, 1]
    Why can we not say that even incorporeal spirits are able to be afflicted in some   1032
real ways, however remarkable, with the punishment of corporeal fire, if the spirits   1033
of men, certainly themselves incorporeal, are able now to be contained in corporeal members, and in the future will be able to be bound indissolubly to the bonds of their own bodies? . . . [2] Gehenna, the which is called also a slough of fire and brimstone (30), will be a corporeal fire and it will torture the bodies of the damned, either of both men and of demons, the solid bodies of men and the ethereal (31) bodies of demons; or the bodies of men only, with their spirits, while of the demons, their spirits without bodies shall so cleave to the corporeal fires as to feel their punishment but not so as to give them life (32). But there will be one fire for both, as Truth   483
itself has declared (33).

1775

[21, 11]
    Sins which are punished by an extremely lengthy period of penalties are committed   1034
in an extremely short time (34); nor is there anyone who would suppose that the punishments should be as quickly over as the offenses were quickly performed, whether murder or adultery or sacrilege or any other crime whatsoever that is to be measured, not by how long it took to do it, but by the magnitude of its wickedness and impiety.

1776

[21, 13]
    Temporal punishments are suffered by some in this life only, by some after   1000
death, by some both here and hereafter; but all of them before that last and strictest   1002
judgment (35). But not all who suffer temporal punishments after death will come to eternal punishments, which are to follow after that judgment.

1777

[21, 15]
    He that is by nature the only Son of God, in His mercy to us, was made Son of Man,   340
so that we, by nature sons of man, might through Him by grace become sons of   755
God. . . . For just as we, by the sinning of one man, have fallen into this so deplorable   376
an evil, so too through justification wrought by one Man, the same who is God, we shall come to that good so sublime.

1778

[21, 16]
    Let it not be supposed that there are any future purgatorial punishments, except   1002
before that last and tremendous judgment. Yet it must not in any way be denied   1035
that even the eternal fire itself will be, because of the diversity of the deserts of the wicked, lighter for some and more severe for others, whether its own vigor and heat

will be varied according to the punishment deserved, or whether it will be equally
hot, but will not be felt with equal noisomeness.

1779

[21, 23]

How can eternal punishment be taken to mean a fire of long duration, and eternal   1034
life be believed to be without end, when in the very same place and in one and the same   1043
sentence Christ spoke of both together: "Those shall go into eternal punishment, but the
righteous into life eternal (36)?" If both are eternal, certainly it must be understood either
that both are of long duration but with an end, or both are perpetual and without end. For
they are related as being equal: on the one hand, eternal punishment, and on the other,
eternal life. But to say in this one and the same sense, eternal life will be without end and
eternal punishment will have an end, is quite absurd.

1780

[21, 24, 2]

The prayer either of the Church herself or of pious individuals is heard on behalf   1000
of certain of the dead; but it is heard for those who, having been regenerated in Christ,   1001
did not for the rest of their life in the body do such wickedness that they might be
judged unworthy of such mercy, nor who yet lived so well that it might be supposed
they have no need of such mercy (37).

1780a

[21, 25, 2]

"One bread and one body, we are many (38)." He, then, that is in the unity of   875
Christ's body, that is, in the structured Christian membership (39), the Sacrament of   854
which body the faithful, communicating at the altar, are accustomed to receive, the same is
truly said to eat the Body of Christ and to drink the Blood of Christ. And consequently
heretics and schismatics, separated from the unity of this body, are able to receive the same
Sacrament, but with no benefit to themselves,—indeed, more to their own harm, in that
rather than being liberated more slowly they are judged the more severely. For they are not
in the bond of peace, which is expressed by that sacrament.

1781

[21, 27, 4]

The daily prayer, which Jesus Himself taught and for which reason it is called   929
the Lord's Prayer, certainly takes away daily sins, when we say daily: "Forgive us
our debts (40)."

1782

[22, 1, 2]

He is God, who in the beginning created the world, full of all visible goods and   480
intelligible things, among which He created nothing better than spirits, to whom He   482
gave intelligence, and made them fit and capable to contemplate Him. . . . He   486
bestowed free choice on that same intellectual nature, such that if it were to will to
desert God,—its own happiness, to be sure,—misery would immediately follow.

1783

[22, 5]

It is unbelievable that Christ should have risen in the flesh and with flesh should   85
have ascended into heaven. It is unbelievable that the world should have believed so
unbelievable a thing. It is unbelievable that a very few men of the lowest class, ignoble and
ignorant as they were, should have been able actually to persuade the world and even its
learned men of so unbelievable a thing. . . . But if they do not believe that these miracles
were wrought by the Apostles of Christ so that they might be believed when they preached
the Resurrection and Ascension of Christ, this one grand miracle is enough for us, that the
whole world has believed without any miracles.

1784

[22, 8, 1]

"Why," they ask, "do those miracles not happen now, which you maintain did   13
happen formerly?" Certainly I might say that it was necessary, before the world
believed, so that it might believe. Moreover, anyone who demands prodigies today
so that he may believe is himself a great prodigy, since, though he is in a believing   85
world, he does not believe. But they say this because they do not believe that those
miracles were done then either. How is it, then, that Christ is everywhere celebrated   82
with such firm belief in His bodily Ascension into heaven? . . . For we are not able   391
to deny that many miracles were wrought which attest to that one grand and salubrious
miracle by which Christ ascended into heaven in the flesh in which He rose from the
dead. In those most trustworthy books everything is written, both the things that   63
were done, and that for the sake of belief in which they were done.

1785

[22, 20, 1]

Perish the thought that the omnipotence of the Creator were unable, for the raising   1011
of our bodies and for the restoring of them to life, to recall all parts, which were
consumed by beasts or by fire, or which disintegrated into dust or ashes, or were
melted away into a fluid, or were evaporated away in vapors. . . . [3] If it is contended   1013
that each shall arise with the stature of body in which he died, we shall not obstinately   1044
dispute this, so long as there shall be no deformity, no infirmity, no dullness and
no corruption.

1786

[22, 29, 1]

"Now we see obscurely by a mirror, but then face to face (41)." Thus do the holy   172
angels see already, who are also called our angels. . . . Just as they see, so too shall   1041
we see; but we do not yet see thus. That is why the Apostle says what I repeated
just above, "Now we see obscurely by a mirror, but then face to face." This vision is
reserved as a reward, certainly, for our faith; and of it also the Apostle John speaks: "When
He shall have appeared," he says, "we shall be like Him, because we shall see Him as He
is (42)." But the face of God is to be understood as His manifestation, not such a member
as we have in our body and which we designate by that name.

[2] Therefore when I am asked how the saints will comport themselves in that spiritual   171
body, I do not say what I already see, but I say what I believe, in accord with what I read
in the Psalm: "I believed; therefore I have spoken (43)." I say, then: In the body itself they
shall see God; but whether they shall see Him by means of the body, as we now see the

sun, the moon, the stars, the sea, and the land, and whatever is in them, that is no small
question.

1787

[22, 29, 6]

Even by means of our bodies we shall attentively behold the incorporeal God ruling   171
all things. Therefore, either God will be seen through our eyes, then possessing something
like the great excellence of the mind by which even an incorporeal nature may be
discerned, of which hypothesis it is either difficult or downright impossible to show any
other examples in the witness of the divine Scriptures; or, what is more easy to understand,
God will be so known and conspicuous to us that He will be seen by the spirit by
individuals among us in other individuals among us, He will be seen by one person in
another, He will be seen in Himself, He will be seen in the new heavens and in the new
earth, and in every creature which shall then exist.

1788

[22, 30, 1]

How great will be that happiness, where there will be no evil, where no good will   1041
remain hidden, where there will be leisure for the praises of God, who shall be all   1044
in all! . . . What power of movement such bodies will have there, I have not the
rashness to boldly define, because I have not the ability to conceive of it. Nevertheless,
I will say that both in motion and at rest, in their appearance they shall be handsome,
in that place where anything that is not handsome will not be. Certainly the body shall
immediately be wherever the spirit wills it to be; nor will the spirit will anything
which were unbecoming either to the spirit or to the body. . . . There the reward   1040
of virtue shall be God Himself, the Author of virtue; and He promised Himself, than
whom there can be nothing better or greater. . . . For thus too is that to be rightly
understood which the Apostle says: "That God may be all in all (44)." He Himself
will be the end of our desires. He shall be seen without end. He shall be loved without   1043
surfeit. He shall be praised without weariness. . . . [5] There we shall rest and
we shall behold, we shall behold and we shall love, we shall love and we shall praise.
This is what shall be in the end without end.

1. *religentes.*
2. *neglegentes.*
3. Many of the ancients derived the term *religio* etymologically from *religo* = to bind again. Augustine, however, began by
   contrasting not *ligantes* and *religantes*, but *eligentes* (those choosing) with *religentes*, which must be taken as formed not
   from *re* + *ligare* (to bind again) but from *re* + *eligere* (to choose again), *religentes* therefore meaning "those choosing
   again." This also is the manner in which Cicero derived the term *religio*. See § 635 above, where Lactantius rejects this
   etymology in favor of *religo*, from *religare*. Note that *religare* (*re* + *ligare*) and *religere* (*re* + *eligere*) both form their
   first person singular indicative active as *religo*; only in the former the *e* is short, whereas in the latter the *e* is long. In
   both cases the stress is on the antepenultimate syllable.
4. *sacramentum, id est, sacrum signum.*
5. *Cuius rei sacramentum cotidianum esse voluit ecclesiae sacrificium.* I am inclined to punctuate after sacramentum;
   but it is really of little consequence whether *cotidianum* modify *sacrificium* or *sacramentum*.
6. *homine assumpto, non Deo consumpto.*
7. *ut ad hominis Deum iter esset homini per hominem Deum.*
8. 1 Tim. 2:5.
9. *quo itur, Deus, qua itur, homo.*
10. Gen. 1:1.
11. Gen. 1:10.
12. *satis significatur Deum nulla necessitate, nulla suae cuiusquam utilitatis indigentia, sed sola bonitate fecisse quod
    factum est, id est, quia bonum est.*
13. *Deficere namque ab eo quod summe est, ad id quod minus est.*

14. This is still my tired old circumlocution for "suffers"; but I know none better. The Latin reads: *"Patitur quippe qui afficitur."*
15. Literally: "and everything that suffers something is mutable."
16. John 3:5.
17. Matt. 10:32.
18. Reading *calida inquietudine*; the reading *callida inquietudine* would be a cunning restlessness. I have proceeded on the supposition that the restless stirrings of heretics are more hot than cunning; but I do not know what Augustine thought.
19. 1 Sam 13:14.
20. By the term history of the kings of Juda and of the kings of Israel it is clear that Augustine means the First and Second Books of Paralipomenon, otherwise called First and Second Chronicles.
21. See 1 Par. 29:29 and 2 Par. 9:29.
22. *inspiratione divina.*
23. *custoditur canon.*
24. *per iudicium magnum atque novissimum.*
25. *in saeculi fine.*
26. *per ultimum iudicium.*
27. Apoc. 20:1-6. In regard to the misunderstandings of this passage and the ridiculous fancies to which Augustine refers, see the places noted under *Chiliasm* in the general index to the present work.
28. See § 1521 above.
29. *tunc autem.*
30. Apoc. 20:10.
31. *aëria.*
32. *aut tantum hominum corpora cum spiritibus, daemones autem spiritus sine corporibus, haerentes sumendo poenam, non impertiendo vitam corporalibus ignibus.* Possibly this last remark is intended to combat an Origenist notion that in hell the demons invest the flames after the manner in which a soul invests a body.
33. See Matt. 25:41.
34. Augustine has been speaking of the punishments which the civil law decrees; for example, in a scourging, he says, for kissing another man's wife, the pain of the scourging lasts considerably longer than did the pleasure of the kiss.
35. *ante iudicium illud severissimum novissimumque.*
36. Matt. 25:46.
37. Augustine has been explaining why the Church prays for her own in this life and after death, but for the wicked angels she prays not at all, and for heretics and other wicked persons, she prays while they yet live, but not after they have died. See the Code of Canon Law, C. 2262, 2, 2.
38. 1 Cor. 10:17.
39. *in christianorum compage membrorum.*
40. Matt. 6:12.
41. 1 Cor. 13:12.
42. 1 John 3:2.
43. Ps. 115[116]:10.
44. 1 Cor. 15:28.

THE ADVANTAGE OF WIDOWHOOD [*ca. A. D.* 414]

Erasmus questioned the authenticity of the treatise *De bono viduitatis*. Few if any would question it today. The absence of any mention of the work in Augustine's *Corrections* is insufficient argument against genuinity, especially since it is written in epistolary form and the *Corrections* was not concerned with letters. The supposed inconsistency of his views in chapter 11 with the Acts of the Fourth Council of Carthage to which he subscribed in 398 A. D. is not substantial. The work is attested very early as a genuine work of Augustine, and the style and content are his.

The work is generally dated in 414 A. D. It is addressed to Juliana, a widow whose daughter took the veil and vow of virignity at Carthage in 413 A. D.; and it treats of the excellence of widowhood, its superiority to the married state and the advantages of widowhood over marriage.

The Benedictine text reprinted in Migne PL 40, 429-450, is superseded as standard text by that of J. Zycha in the Vienna Corpus, CSEL, Vol. 41, pp. 303-343.

1789

[9, 12]

If modesty (1) is preserved in the marriage bond, certainly damnation is not to be 982
feared. But in virginal continence and in that of widowhood the excellence of a more 983
ample offering (2) is longed for. When this has been sought and chosen and consecrated 984
in the obligation of a vow (3) it is damnable not only to enter upon a marriage but,
although one does not actually marry, even to desire to marry.

1790

[12, 15]

Men often raise the question of third and fourth and even more marriages. To answer 979
briefly, I would say that I have not the audacity to condemn any number of marriages nor
to minimize the shame of their frequency.

1. *pudicitia*.
2. *excellentia muneris amplioris*.
3. *voti debito oblata*.

NATURE AND GRACE [*A. D.* 415]

The *De natura et gratia ad Timasium et Iacobum contra Pelagium*, dating from the
year 415, is treated in Augustine's *Corrections* 2, 68. It was written in refutation of
Pelagius' work entitled *De natura* at the request of two young Pelagians who were
beginning to see the light, Timasius and James. They continued to correspond with
Augustine and may be counted among his converts.

In the *Corrections* Augustine notes that Pelagius had quoted certain remarks as being
those of Pope Sixtus (or Xystus); and supposing them to be authentic, Augustine
defended the remarks, only to discover later that they belonged not to Sixtus of Rome
but to a Pythagorean philosopher. In point of fact the remarks are of that half-mystical
sort which may be true or false according to how one understands them. The remarks in
question are three in number, and all are in 64, 77: "God has given men freedom of will
so that by purity and sinlessness of life they may become like God"; and "A pure mind
is a holy temple for God, and a heart clean and sinless is His best altar"; and further,
"A man chaste and sinless has received from God the power to become a son of God."
Pagan in origin, the statements could as easily have come from the Gospels. Pelagius
gave them a Pelagian interpretation; Augustine explained them in accord with the true
faith. And if later, when he found that they were not the literary property of Sixtus of
Rome, Augustine had to apologize about them, his apology is not for his interpretation
of them, which remains orthodox, but for his having accepted them as authentic.

The text in Migne PL 44, 247-290 was superseded in 1913 by the edition of C. F.
Urba and J. Zycha in the Vienna Corpus, CSEL, Vol. 60.

1791

[4, 4]

This grace of Christ, however, without which neither infants nor those of more 650
mature age are able to be saved, is not given in view of merits; rather it is given 711
gratuitously, which, indeed, is why it is called grace (1). "They are," he says,
"justified freely by His blood (2)." Those, therefore, who are not liberated through 724
that blood, either because they have not yet been able to hear, or because they have
not willed to obey, or even because they did not, when, because of their youth,

they were unable to hear, receive the bath of regeneration which they were able to receive and through which they could be saved, are justly condemned, because they are not without sin, either that which they originally bore (3), or which they have added by their own wicked practices. "For all have sinned," whether in Adam or whether in themselves, "and need the glory of God (4)."

614

1792

[26, 29]

God Himself, since, through the Mediator of God and men, the man Jesus Christ (5), He spiritually heals the sick or gives life to the dead, that is, He justifies the impious; and since He leads him to perfect health, that is, to a perfect life and righteousness, does not forsake if He is not forsaken, so that life may always be lived piously and justly. For just as the eye of the body, even when fully healthy, cannot see unless it is aided by the brightening quality of light (6), so too a man, even most perfectly justified, unless he be divinely aided by the eternal light of righteousness, is unable to be upright in his conduct (7).

721
387

659

1793

[31, 35]

We too work, but as fellow-workers with Him who does the work, because His mercy anticipates us (8). He anticipates us, however, that we may be healed; and He will also follow after us so that, having been healed, we may grow. He anticipates us, that we may be called; and He will follow after us, that we may be glorified. He anticipates us, that we may live piously; and He will follow after, so that we may live always with Him, because without Him we are able to do nothing (9).

692
691
690

1794

[36, 42]

Having excepted the Holy Virgin Mary, concerning whom, on account of the honor of the Lord, I wish to have absolutely no question when treating of sins,—for how do we know what abundance of grace for the total overcoming of sin was conferred upon her, who merited to conceive and bear Him in whom there was no sin?— so, I say, with the exception of the Virgin, if we could have gathered together all those holy men and women (10), when they were living here, and had asked them whether they were without sin, what do we suppose would have been their answer? Would it be what Pelagius says, or would it be what the Apostle John says? I ask you, however excellent might their holiness have been when in the body, if they had been so questioned, would they not have declared in a single voice: "If we say we have no sin, we deceive ourselves, and the truth is not in us (11)!"?

785
786

658

1795

[43, 50]

God, therefore, does not command what is impossible, but in commanding He also admonishes you to do what you are able, and to ask His help for what you are unable to do. We should already see, then, whence comes the possibility and whence the impossibility. Pelagius says: "What is possible by nature comes not from a man's willing it." I say: "Certainly a man is not righteous by his will if he can be by nature; but with a remedy (12) he will be able to do what, by reason of his defect, he is unable to do."

652
712

1796

[53, 62]

"I see another law in my members, warring against the law of my mind, and making 712
me a prisoner to the law of sin that is in my members (13)." See what damage
disobedience of will has inflicted on man's nature. Let him be allowed to pray,
that he may be healed (14)! Why does he need to presume so much on the capability
of his nature? It is wounded, hurt, damaged, destroyed (15). What it needs is not
false defense but true confession (16).

1797

[57, 67]

A man is under the law when, without yet being free and removed from a will 915
toward sinning, he takes care to abstain from sinful deeds not out of love for righteousness
but because of his fear of the punishments which the law threatens. For in his very
will he is guilty, insofar as he would prefer, if it were possible, that what he fears
did not exist, so that he might do freely what secretly he desires.

1798

[70, 84]

Love begun is righteousness begun. Love advanced is righteousness advanced. 592
Great love is great righteousness. Perfect love is perfect righteousness; and this last
love is "love from a pure heart, and from a good conscience, and from faith
unfeigned (17)."

1. That is to say, *gratia* is given *gratis*. Grace is a gift; being truly a gift, it is free.
2. Again, the *freely* is *gratis*. See Rom. 3:24-25.
3. *quod originaliter traxerunt*.
4. Rom. 2:23.
5. 1 Tim. 2:5.
6. *nisi candore lucis adiutus*.
7. *recte non potest vivere*.
8. *quia misericordia praevenit nos*. See Ps. 58[59]:10. Augustine's notion of antecedent or prevenient grace is growing.
9. John 15:5.
10. Pelagius, in his *De natura*, had enumerated a considerable list of persons, mostly of the Old Testament, who were,
    according to him, without sin. The final entry on his list is the Mother of the Lord. His basis for considering that all
    these people were without sin in this life was that in one connexion or another each of them is mentioned in the
    Scriptures as being holy or righteous.
11. 1 John 1:8.
12. *medicina*.
13. Rom. 7:23.
14. *Orare sinatur ut sanetur*.
15. *Vulnerata, sauciata, vexata, perdita est*.
16. *Vera confessione, non falsa defensione opus habet*; that is: there is nothing to be gained by falsely arguing in behalf of
    capabilities that our nature does not have. What we need to do is openly admit our inability and pray to God for His
    strengthening grace.
17. 1 Tim. 1:5.

THE PERFECTION OF MAN'S RIGHTEOUSNESS [*A. D.* 415]

Augustine's *De perfectione iustitiae hominis*, belonging to the year 415, is not
mentioned at all in the *Corrections*. The reason is obvious enough when we recall that
the work is called also by another title, *Ad episcopos Eutropium et Paulum epistula*, by
which it is made clear that the book is in reality a letter; and Augustine of set purpose
excluded his letters from discussion in his *Corrections*.

The bishops Eutropius and Paul had given Augustine a copy of a document containing various theses or propositions drawn up by the Pelagian Caelestius. The present work is Augustine's refutation of these propositions, written as a letter to Eutropius and Paul.

The Migne text in PL 44, 291-318 has been superseded since 1902 by the edition of C. F. Urba and J. Zycha in the Vienna Corpus, CSEL, Vol. 42.

1799

[8, 19]

"Let us, therefore, as many as are perfect, understand this (1)'': (that is to say, as   546
many of us as are running perfectly now, let us be aware of this)—that we have not yet
been perfected as much as we shall be perfected in that place to which, until now, we
have been running as perfectly as we can (2); so that, "when that which is perfect
has come, that which is perfect only in part may be destroyed (3)''; (that is, so that it
may not be perfect only in part, but wholly so)—because to faith and hope the very
thing itself shall succeed, not just to be believed in and hoped for, but to be seen and to   591
be grasped. Love, however, which is the greatest of these three, will not cease (4).
Rather, it will be increased and fulfilled when it has gazed upon what it believed
and when it has attained that for which it had hoped.

1800

[15, 33]

However great may be a man's righteousness, he must take thought lest something   762
in him which he himself did not see be found to be deserving of blame when the righteous
King shall sit upon His throne, He whose knowledge our transgressions cannot
escape, not even those of which it is said: "Who knows his transgressions? (5).''

1801

[21, 44]

If, aside from our Head, the Savior of His body, they assert that there either have   658
been or are in this life any righteous men without any sin,—either by not consenting
to the body's desires, or because that must not be accounted as sin which is such that
God does not impute it to them because of their piety (although it is one thing for a man
to be so blessed as to be without sin and another for him to be so blessed that God does
not impute sin to him {6})—I do not care to argue the point at any length. I know that
some do hold this view, whose opinions in this matter, though I cannot defend them,   712
I do not dare to condemn. But this, quite plainly, I do not hesitate to say: If anyone
denies that we must pray: "Lead us not into temptation'' (and they deny it who
contend that God's grace is not a necessary help to a man for the avoidance of sin,
and that after receiving only the law, the human will suffices), he should be removed
from the ears of all and be anathematized by every mouth.

1. See Phil. 3:15-16.
2. *Quotquot ergo perfecti, hoc sapiamus; id est, quotquot perfecti currimus, hoc sapiamus, quod nondum perfecti sumus, ut illic perficiamur, quo perfecte adhuc currimus.* The reader will notice that I have somewhat paraphrased this in translating, in the interests of a clarity only partially achieved, and which probably could not be wholly achieved without scrapping Augustine's text in this instance entirely, and rewriting it. On the other hand, I have no assurance that I have grasped him perfectly either, and if I go too far from his text I may do him another disservice.
3. 1 Cor. 13:10.
4. 1 Cor. 13:13.
5. Ps. 18[19]:13.
6. Ps. 31[32]:2.

TO OROSIUS AGAINST THE PRISCILLIANISTS AND ORIGENISTS [*ca. A. D.* 415]

The Orosius for whom Augustine wrote his *Ad Orosium presbyterum contra Priscillianistas et Origenistas liber unus* about the year 415 A. D. is the same Paulus Orosius (*q. v.*) who was for a long time an intimate friend and follower of Augustine, and who wrote the *Liber apologeticus* quoted below at § 2020.

The present work, which Augustine treats in his *Corrections* 2, 70, deals with various errors of the Origenists and of the Priscillianists, the latter comprising a sect which was rather widespread in parts of Spain for about two hundred years but which seems never to have spread outside Spain. It was a curious mixture of Manicheism, various sorts of gnosticism and other heresies, intermingled with astrology and mythology. Priscillian, the Bishop of Avila, from whom, though he was not its founder, the heresy takes its name, was charged with being a magician, and was executed at Treves in 385 A. D., by the order of Maximus the Usurper, at that time recognized as legitimate emperor in Gaul. St. Martin of Tours had tried to save Priscillian's life, but to no avail.

The Maurist text in Migne, PL 42, 669-678, is still the standard edition.

1802

[6, 7]

"These will go into eternal fire; the just, however, into eternal life (1)." In both instances the Greek has αἰώνιον (2). If mercy calls us to believe that the future punishment of the impious will not be punishment without end, what are we to believe about the reward of the righteous, when eternity is specified in both clauses in the same passage, in the same sentence, and with the same word? Or are we to say that even the just are going to fall away from that holiness and eternal life, into the uncleanness of sins and into death? Far be it from the soundness of Christian faith. Both, for the reason that they are without end, are called eternal, that is, αἰώνιον.

1034
1043

1042

1803

[8, 9]

The reasons for all the things He would make but had not yet made were able to be in the wisdom of God. For all things were made by the same Agent, and that same Agent was not made, because that same Agent is the Word, of Whom it is said: "Through Him all things were made (3)." God, therefore, knew everything He made before He made it. For we cannot say that He made things He did not know and that He would not have known them unless He had made them.

189
464

1804

[9, 12]

Just as in the Gospel, although everything that is said is truly said, it is not be believed that everything said is said truly; for much is truly born witness to in the gospel writings that was falsely and impiously said by the Jews: so too in this Book of Job, where the statements of many persons are related in the narrative, consideration must be made not only of what is said but also of who said it. . . . When we are inquiring, and we want something to be proved to us by the testimony of the holy sayings, it is not necessary for us to believe a thing just because it is written in a Gospel, if perhaps the Evangelist is recording the statement of someone who did not have the faith.

26

1805

[11, 14]

Certainly the Apostle says: "whether Thrones, whether Dominations, whether   488
Principalities, whether Powers (4)." And therefore I do most firmly believe that   480
in the heavenly splendors there are Thrones, Dominations, Principalities, and Powers,
and I believe with an unhesitating faith that they somehow differ among themselves.
But you may ridicule me for this, if you wish, whom you regard as a great teacher: what
they are and how they are different from each other I do not know.

1. Matt. 25:46. The Vulgate, however, speaks of *supplicium aeternum* where Augustine writes *ambustionem aeternam*. A good many witnesses to the pre-Hieronymian Latin read *ignem*. Cyprian, along with Augustine, knew the reading *ambustionem*. Fulgentius writes *combustionem*, which is found also in Augustine in other places where he quotes the same passage.
2. The point Augustine is making is that both heaven and hell are termed eternal in this passage of the Scriptures, and with the support also of the authoritative Greek text.
3. John 1:3. There is something of a rhetorical device in the Latin which I do not capture in English: *"Omnia enim* per ipsam *facta sunt, non et* ipsa *facta est, quia et* ipsa *est* Verbum de quo dicitur: *'Omnia* per ipsum *facta sunt.'"*
4. Col. 1:16.

HOMILIES ON THE GOSPEL OF JOHN [*A. D.* 416 *et* 417]

Augustine's collection of one hundred and twenty-four *In Ioannis evangelium tractatus* belongs to the years 416 and 417. For Augustine, a *tractatus* in a sermon or homily. He himself speaks of *tractatus populares quos Graeci homilias vocant*—the *popular treatises which the Greeks call homilies*; so he remarks, at any rate, in his *Letter 224* to Quodvultdeus. We are justified, then, in translating *tractatus* as *homilies*, as well from Augustine's own linguistic usage as from the fact that the style of these treatises or tracts makes it clear that they were actually preached. And because they are homilies or sermons, the collection finds no place in Augustine's *Corrections*, from which the genres of Letters and Sermons are of set purpose excluded.

The Maurist text in Migne, PL 35, 1379–1976, has been superseded in its position of standard by the edition of Radbod Willems in the *Corpus Christianorum*, Vol. 36 (1954).

1806

[3, 4]

You are not much different from cattle, except that you have intelligence; so do not   512
glory in anything else. Do you claim to be strong? You will be beaten by beasts. Do
you claim speed? Flies are faster. Do you claim beauty? What great beauty there is in a
peafowl's feathers! How are you better, then, than these? By the image of God.
And where is God's image? In your mind, in your intellect!

1807

[3, 9]

What is grace? Something given *gratis*. What is given *gratis*? That which is   711
bestowed rather than paid as owed. If it is owed, it is wages paid, not a gift
graciously given. If it was truly owed, you have been good; but if, as is the case,
you have been evil, but you did believe in Him who justifies the impious (1):—
and what is meant by "He justifies the impious?" That He makes the impious pious—
think what was rightly threatened you by the law, and what you have obtained by grace!

But since you have gotten that grace of faith, you shall be just by faith; for the
just man lives by faith (2). And by living faith you shall deserve well of God;
and when you shall have deserved well of God by living by faith, as reward you   771
shall receive immortality and eternal life. And that is grace. Because of what merit,
then, do you receive eternal life? Because of grace.

1808

[4, 10]
   For not in iniquity was Christ conceived, because He was not conceived of   344
mortality. He whom the Virgin conceived, He whom the Virgin bore,—neither   781
did His Mother give Him growth in her womb in sins, because she conceived by   782
faith and got Him by faith. Therefore, "Behold the Lamb of God (3)!" He is not a   313
sprout from Adam; His flesh only did He take from Adam; sin He did not take.

1809

[5, 1]
   No one has anything of his own except falsehood and sin. If any man has anything   651
of truth and justice, it is from that fountain for which we ought to thirst in this desert,
so that bedewed, as it were, by certain droplets thereof, and consoled betimes in this
pilgrimage, lest we fall by the wayside, we might come at last to His rest and be
satisfied.

1810

[5, 18]
   "Although He Himself did not baptize, but His disciples (4)." Himself, yet not   802
Himself; He, by power, they, by ministry. They performed the service of baptizing;
the power of baptizing remained in Christ. His disciples, therefore, baptized, and
Judas was still among His disciples. Those, therefore, whom Judas baptized were not   804
baptized again; but those whom John baptized, were they not baptized again?
Certainly again, yet not in a repeated Baptism. For those whom John baptized,   821
John baptized; but those whom Judas baptized, Christ baptized. So too, then, those
whom a drunkard baptized, those whom a murderer baptized, those whom an
adulterer baptized, if the Baptism was of Christ, Christ baptized.

1811

[7, 4]
   It is necessary, therefore, that He baptize, who is the only Son, not the adopted   340
son, of God. Adopted sons are the ministers of the only Son. The only Son has
power, adopted sons have ministry.

1812

[9, 2]
   Having been invited, the Lord came to the marriage in order to affirm conjugal   972
chastity and to show that marriage is a Sacrament. Moreover, the bridegroom at   983
that marriage to whom it was said, "You have kept the good wine until now (5),"
is a figure of the person of the Lord. For Christ has kept the good wine, that is, His
gospel, until now.

1813

[9, 10]

In that very beginning Adam and Eve were the parents of all peoples, not of the   511
Jews only; and whatever was represented in Adam about Christ certainly pertained
to all peoples, whose salvation is in Christ.

1814

[9, 10]

Now we are permitted to seek Christ everywhere. . . . Adam sleeps that Eve   801
may be formed; Christ dies that the Church may be formed. Eve is formed from the side of
the sleeping Adam; the side of the dead Christ is pierced by the lance, so that the
Sacraments (6) may flow out, of which the Church is formed. Is there anyone to whom it is
not obvious that future events are represented (7) by the things done then, since the Apostle
says that Adam himself was the figure of Him that was to come? "He is," he says, "the
figure of Him who is to come (8)."

1815

[11, 3]

All catechumens are such [as was Nicodemus, who believed in Jesus but was   810
not yet reborn, so that Jesus did not trust Himself to him]. They already believe
in the name of Christ, but Jesus does not trust Himself to them. Listen, beloved
brethren, and understand (9). If we should say to a catechumen: "Do you believe in
Christ," he will answer, "I do believe," and he will sign himself. He already   125
carries the cross of Christ on his forehead, and he is not ashamed of the cross
of the Lord.—See, he believed in his name (10)! Let us ask him: Do you eat of the   851
flesh of the Son of Man and drink the blood of the Son of Man? He does not know
what we are talking about, because Jesus has not entrusted Himself to him (11).

1816

[14, 7]

In the way that you speak a word that you have in your heart and it is with   265
you, . . . that is how God issued the Word, that is to say, how He begot the Son.
And you, indeed, beget a word too in your heart, without temporal preparation (12);   256
God begot the Son outside of time (13), the Son through whom He created all times.   284

1817

[15, 4]

What is the Baptism of Christ? "The washing with water, in the word (14)."   791
Take away water and it is not Baptism. Take away the word and it is not Baptism.   822

1818

[23, 6]

Let Christ lift you up by what is man, lead you by what is God-man, and guide   314
you on to what is God. The whole preaching and dispensation of Christ is this, brethren,   375
and nothing else: that your souls may be raised again, and that your bodies too may be
raised again. For each of them had died, the body of infirmity, the soul of iniquity.
Because each was dead, let each rise again. Each what? Soul and body. By what
means shall the soul rise again, if not Christ God? By what means shall the body rise

again, if not Christ Man? For in Christ too was a human soul, a complete soul;   312
not the irrational part only of the soul, but the rational part too, which is
called the mind.

1819

[24, 1]

Certainly the miracles done by our Lord Jesus Christ are divine works, and they   82
prompt the human mind to an understanding of God by means of visible things. But   13
because God is not of such substance as can be seen with the eyes, and because His
miracles by which He rules the whole world and governs the whole of creation are so
consistently unappreciated that hardly anyone takes the trouble to consider the marvelous
and stupendous works of God in every grain of seed, God has, in His mercy, reserved to
Himself certain works outside the accustomed order and course of nature which He
performs at an opportune time so that those who do not appreciate His daily works may be
amazed at seeing what is not greater but only less frequent. For the governing of the whole
world is a greater miracle than the feeding of five thousand men with five loaves of bread.
Yet no one marvels at it; but men do marvel at the latter, not because it is greater, but
because it is rare. . . . [2] Yet it is not enough to observe these things in the miracles of
Christ. Let us ask the miracles themselves what they tell us of Christ; for if they be
understood, they have a tongue of their own. For because Christ Himself is the Word of
God, even the deed of the Word is word for us.

1820

[25, 12]

"Jesus answered and said to them: 'This is the work of God, that you might believe   855
in Him whom He sent (15).'" This is, then, to eat "the food which does not
perish, but which remains unto eternal life (16)." To what end do you prepare teeth and
belly? Believe, and you have already eaten.

1821

[26, 2]

"Do not be murmuring to each other; no one is able to come to Me unless the   650
Father who sent Me draw him (17)." A great attestation of grace! No one comes   684
unless he is drawn. He draws one, and another He does not draw. Do not try to judge   720
why He draws one and does not draw another, if you do not wish to err. Accept
it at once, and understand. You are not yet drawn? Pray that you may be drawn.   712
What are you saying about this, brethren? "If we are drawn to Christ, we believe   700
against our will; it is a matter of force being applied, not of the will being moved!"
A man is able to come into the Church unwillingly, he is able to approach the
altar unwillingly, he is able to receive the Sacrament unwillingly; but he is not able
to believe except willingly. If we believed with the body, men might be made to
believe against their will. But to believe is not something done with the body.   553

1822

[26, 4]

So that no one may ask: "How do I believe willingly, if I am drawn," I tell you: 684
It is not so much that you are drawn by will as by pleasure. . . . Moreover, if it   702
was right of the poet to say, "Everyone is drawn by his own pleasure (18)";—not by
necessity, but by pleasure; not by obligation, but by delight;—how much more   16

surely ought we say that a man is drawn to Christ, when he delights in truth, when
he delights in righteousness, when he delights in eternal life, all of which Christ
is? . . . Give me a man who loves, and he will feel what I say. Give me a man
who yearns, a man who hungers, a man who travels in this wilderness, and thirsts
and sighs for the fountain of his eternal fatherland; give me such a man, and he
will know what I am talking about. But if I speak to a cold man he will not know
what I am saying.

1823

[26, 7]

    See how the Father draws us. He gives us pleasure by teaching us, not by   700
imposing a necessity. See how He draws us: "they shall all be taught by God (19.)"   702

1824

[26, 13]

    "My flesh," He says, "is for the life of the world (20)." Believers know the Body   850
of Christ if they do not neglect to be the Body of Christ. They can become the   878
Body of Christ if they will to live by the spirit of Christ. None lives by the spirit
of Christ except the Body of Christ. . . . The Body of Christ cannot live except   880
by the spirit of Christ. That is why the Apostle Paul, explaining this Bread, says: "One
Bread and one Body, we are many (21)." O Sacrament of piety! O sign of unity! O Bread
of love! Anyone who wants to live has both where to live and whence to live. Let him draw
near, let him believe; let him be embodied, that he may be made to live.

1825

[36, 1]

    In the four Gospels, or rather, in the four books of the one gospel, the holy Apostle   60
John, who, in spiritual understanding, is not undeservedly likened to an eagle, elevated   67
his preaching to a higher and much more sublime level than did the other three. For the
other three Evangelists walked on earth with the Lord as a man; they say but little of His
divinity. But John, as if he disdained to walk on earth, just as in the very beginning of his
discourse he thunders over us, raises himself up . . . and goes directly to Him through
whom all things were made, when he says: "In the beginning was the Word, and the Word
was with God; and the Word was God. In the beginning, with God, He was. All things
were made through Him, and nothing that was made was made without Him (22)."

1826

[40, 9]

    What does He promise believers, brethren? "And you shall know the truth (23)."   562
Why? Did they not come to know it when the Lord was speaking? If they did not know,
how did they believe? They did not believe because they knew, but they believed so   557
that they might know. For we believe so that we may know, we do not know that we may
believe. . . . For what is faith, except to believe what you do not see? Faith,
therefore, is to believe what you do not see, truth is to see what you have believed.

1827

[44, 13]

    "But we know that God does not hear sinners; but if any man is a worshipper of   713

God and does His will, that man God will hear (24)." He still speaks as one only
anointed (25). For God does listen to sinners too. If God did not listen to sinners,
it would have been all in vain for the publican to cast down his eyes to the ground
and strike his breast saying: "Lord, be merciful to me, a sinner (26)." And that
confession merited justification, just as the blind man merited enlightenment (27).   760

1828

[49, 2]
Everyone who sins dies. Every man fears the death of the flesh, few the death of the   639
soul. In regard to the death of the flesh, which without a doubt must someday come,
all guard against its coming: that is the reason for their labors. Man, destined to die,
labors to avert his dying; and yet man, destined to live in eternity, does not labor
to avoid sinning.

1829

[49, 10]
All souls, when they go forth from the world, have their own different kinds of   996
receptions. The good have joy; the wicked, torments. But after the resurrection has   1012
come to pass, both the joy of the good will be greater and the torments of the wicked
more severe, when they will be tortured along with their body. . . . The rest which is
given immediately after death is received by everyone when he dies, if he is worthy of
it. . . . Some are already in that rest for a long time, others not so long; some for fewer
years, others not for so short a time. But when they awake from this sleep, all will receive
at once what was promised.

1829a

[51, 4]
But what was it to the Lord to be King of Israel? What great thing was it for the   375
King of Ages to be a king of men? For Christ's being King of Israel was not for the
purpose of exacting tribute, or of furnishing an army with weapons in order visibly
to conquer enemies. He was King of Israel in order to rule minds, that He might
counsel them unto eternity, that He might lead those who believed in Him, who
hoped in Him and who loved Him, into His heavenly kingdom.

1830

[53, 6]
"They were not able to believe (28)," because Isaias the Prophet foretold   703
this disbelief; and the Prophet foretold it, because God foreknew that this would be   723
the case. But if you ask me how it was that they could not, I will quickly answer:
"Because they did not will to." For God, from whom future things cannot be hidden,
certainly foresaw their wicked will, and He foretold it through the Prophet. "But,"
you say, "the Prophet gives another reason, not their will." What reason does
the Prophet give? That "God gave them a spirit of stupor (29), eyes that could not   722
see, and ears that could not hear, and He blinded their eyes and hardened their
hearts (30)." I answer too, that this is what their will deserved. For God so blinded
and so hardened by abandoning them, by not helping them; what He can do in
His hidden judgment cannot be unjust.

1831

[67, 2]

The denarius which the householder orders to be given to all of those who   1046
worked in his vineyard, with no distinction between those who labored less and
those who labored more, is given equally to all (31). By that denarius it is
certainly eternal life that is signified, in which no one lives longer than anyone
else, since in eternity life has no diversity in its measure. But the many mansions
(32) signify different worths of merits in the one eternal life.

1832

[74, 1]

There is the Apostolic declaration: "No one says: 'Jesus is Lord!' unless   650
in the Holy Spirit (33)." And who says "Jesus is Lord!" except one who loves Him, if he
says it in the way the Apostle wanted to be understood? For many say it in words, but deny
it in their heart and in their deeds. . . . No one, therefore, says: "Jesus is Lord!" with his
mind, his voice, his actions, his heart, his mouth, his works, no one thus says "Jesus is
Lord!" unless in the Holy Spirit.

1833

[79, 1]

This is praiseworthy faith indeed: when what is believed is not seen. For what   567
great thing is it to believe what is seen, as is indicated by that statement of the
Lord Himself, when, reproving a disciple, He said: "Because you have seen, you
have believed; blessed are those who have not seen and have believed (34)"?

1834

[80, 3]

"You are already clean because of the word that I have spoken to you (35)."   791
Why does He not say: "You are clean because of the Baptism with which you have
been washed," instead of: "because of the word that I have spoken to you," except
that in the water too it is the word that cleanses? The word advances to the element
of water, and it becomes a Sacrament, itself too, as it were, a visible word. For
certainly when He washed the feet of the disciples He said this also: "He that has   809
washed has no need to wash, except his feet, and he is entirely clean (36)." Whence   800
has water so great a power that it can touch the body and cleanse the heart, unless
by the action of the word; and not that it is spoken, but that it is believed? For
also in the word itself, the fleeting sound is one thing, the abiding power another.

1835

[81, 3]

Lest anyone suppose that the branch can by itself bear at least some small amount   650
of fruit, since He had said, "He bears much fruit (37)," He did not add that
without Me you can do little, but, "Without Me you can do nothing (38)." Whether,
therefore, it be a question of little or of much, without Him it cannot be done, without
whom nothing can be done.

1836

[82, 4]

What he says also about the Father, "I abide in His love (39)," is to be understood   340
of that love with which the Father loved Him. But is that love with which the Father   341
loves the Son to be understood as referable to grace, just as that with which the Son
loves us, since we are sons by grace and not by nature, whereas the Onlybegotten
is Son by nature and not by grace? Or is this too in the Son Himself to be referred to
His humanity? Certainly it is. For by saying, "Just as the Father loved Me, I too
have loved you (40)," He points to the grace He had as Mediator. But Christ   387
Jesus is Mediator of God and of men, not in that He is God but in that He is Man (41).
And certainly it is in reference to His being Man that we read: "And Jesus advanced
in wisdom and age and grace before God and men (42)."

1837

[86, 2]

If He had chosen us on the grounds that He foreknew that we would be good, He   204
would also at the same time have foreknown that we would not have been about to
choose Him first. For we could not possibly in any other way be good; unless
perhaps he is to be called good who never chose the good. What, then, did He chose
in those who were not good? For they were not chosen because they were good, who
would not have been good unless they were chosen. "Otherwise grace is grace no   711
longer (43)," if we insist that merits preceded it.

1838

[96, 3]

Even if the Sacraments of the faithful are not exhibited to catechumens it is not   810
because the catechumens cannot bear them; but they are honorably hidden from
them so that they may desire them all the more ardently.

1839

[99, 7]

Why, then, should we not believe that the Holy Spirit proceeds also from the   273
Son, when He is the Spirit also of the Son? For if the Holy Spirit did not proceed from
Him, when He showed Himself to His disciples after His resurrection He would not have
breathed on them, saying: "Receive the Holy Spirit (44)." For what else did He signify by
that breathing upon them, except that the Holy Spirit proceeds also from Him?

1840

[99, 8]

*This passage is given above at § 1681a, where Augustine
quotes himself in his* De Trinitate.

1841

[106, 4]

The name "God", which is spoken by every creature and by all peoples, even   2
before they believed in Christ, could not have been unknown in every way. Such is   135

the energy of true divinity that it cannot be utterly and entirely hidden from any
rational creature which makes use of its reason. For with the exception of a few in
whom nature is just too depraved the whole human race confesses that God is the
Author of this world. In this regard, at least, that God made this world that is
visible in the sky and on earth, He was known to all nations even before they were
imbued with the faith of Christ.

131

1842
[108, 5]

"That they may also be sanctified in the truth (45)." And what else is "in the
truth" except "in Me", since the truth is the Word that in the beginning is God?
In which also the Son of Man Himself was sanctified from the beginning of His
creation, when the Word was made flesh; for the Word and man were made one
person. Then, therefore, did He sanctify Himself in Himself, that is, the man
himself in the Word Himself; for the Word and the man is one Christ, sanctifying
humanity in the Word.

341
329

324

1843
[110, 7]

Since we know that the Creator of all goods granted no grace for the reparation
of the wicked angels, should it not rather be our understanding that their guilt
was judged to be all the more damnable as their nature was the more sublime?

491
371
482

1844
[118, 5]

What is the sign of Christ, as everyone knows, if not the cross of Christ? For
unless that sign be applied, whether to the foreheads of believers, whether to the
very water out of which they are regenerated, whether to the oil by which they are
anointed with chrism, or whether to the Sacrifice by which they are nourished,
none of these is properly administered.

125
808
842
890

1845
[124, 5]

A man is compelled to endure [this miserable life] even when his sins are forgiven,
because the first sin was the cause of his falling into such misery. For the penalty
is more protracted than the guilt, lest the guilt be thought of as being small, if
the penalty were to end with it. And this is why, either to demonstrate the
misery he deserves, or for the amendment of his disgraceful life, or for the exercise
of needful patience, a man is detained temporally in punishment even when by his
guilt he is no longer held liable to eternal damnation.

922

1. Rom. 4:5.
2. Rom. 1:17 and Hab. 2:4.
3. John 1:29.
4. John 4:2.
5. John 2:10.
6. *sacramenta*; which should here be taken, no doubt, in the broader meaning of *mysteries*.
7. *figurata sunt*.

8. Rom. 5:14.

9. *Intendat et intellegat caritas vestra*: literally, "May your charity listen and understand."

10. Probably these sermons were taken down in shorthand while Augustine preached. It appears not unlikely that at this point one of the catechumens, wrapt in attention to Augustine's words and oblivious to everything about him, made the sign of the cross on his forehead. Augustine saw it, called attention to it, and used it to illustrate his point.

11. If my hypothesis is correct, that this is a fortuitous example occasioned by a pious catechumen's having blessed himself (note 10 above), the statement, "*He* does not know what we are talking about—*nescit quid dicimus*," is not to be taken literally. Augustine would not have spoken so readily of eating and drinking the flesh and blood of Christ in the presence of one so utterly uninitiate that he knew nothing of it. He means only that the catechumen has never experienced the reception of the Sacrament.

12. *ex tempore*.

13. *sine tempore*.

14. Eph. 5:26.

15. John 6:29.

16. John 6:27.

17. John 6:43-44.

18. Virgil, *Eclogues* 2, 64.

19. Is. 54:13.

20. John 6:52.

21. 1 Cor. 10:17.

22. John 1:1-3.

23. John 8:32.

24. John 9:31.

25. *Adhuc inunctus loquitur*. This was the man speaking, to whom the Lord had restored sight. The Lord had anointed his eyes with mud, and had told him to go and wash it off in the pool of Siloe. When he went there and washed, he saw. Augustine has been playing upon the notion that when anointed, he is on the brink of restoration; when washed, he sees. Augustine speaks of two classes of Pharisees, some anointed, some not yet anointed; *i. e.*, some almost convinced, some still far from the truth. The anointing is God's call; the washing is acceptance of the call and Baptism. The point of the present remark is that the man is wrong when he says that God does not hear sinners; with such an opinion, the man speaks as one who is not yet washed, but only anointed. He has good will and is coming close; but he has not yet arrived.

26. Luke 18:13.

27. *illuminationem*. There is still an overtone here about the washing of the man's eyes; for illumination is one of the terms for Baptism. See § 407 above, with its note 2.

28. John 12:39 in reference to Is. 6:10.

29. *spiritum compunctionis*. Both Augustine and the Vulgate so read at Rom. 11:8, but the Greek term which this translates can mean either *remorse* or *stupor*. Certainly Augustine understood *compunctionis* in the latter sense, though I doubt that any dictionary would accord it that meaning. We must suppose, however, that Augustine knew his language better than do the modern compilers of dictionaries.

30. Rom. 11:8; John 12:40; Is. 6:9-10.

31. Matt. 20:9.

32. John 14:2.

33. 1 Cor. 12:3.

34. John 20:29.

35. John 15:3.

36. John 13:10.

37. John 15:5.

38. *Ibid*.

39. John 15:10.

40. John 15:9.

41. 1 Tim. 2:5.

42. Luke 2:52.

43. Rom. 11:6.

44. John 20:22.

45. John 17:19.

HOMILIES ON THE EPISTLE OF JOHN TO THE PARTHIANS [A. D. 416]

Augustine's ten homilies *In epistulam Ioannis ad Parthos* belong to the year 416 A. D. The Epistle that Augustine designates *ad Parthos* is the canonical First Epistle of John; and his terming it *ad Parthos*, presumably meaning *to the Parthians*, is one of the patristic world's minor but nonetheless exciting mysteries. The title cannot be traced with any certitude to anyone earlier than Augustine. The Venerable Bede says that Athanasius knew this address; but there is nothing extant today in Athanasius to show that Bede was correct. After Augustine's time, the address is found often enough.

St. John is known to have been accorded the title "the virgin"; and Gieseler has suggested the hypothesis that πρὸς πάρϑους is a corruption of τοῦ παρϑένου,—that is, that Greek manuscripts of the Epistle once read τοῦ παρϑένου in the heading, which was corrupted to πρὸς πάρϑους and then translated *ad Parthos*. This hypothesis has gained considerable acceptance, and, so far as I can see, there is only one difficulty about it: no one has ever seen a Greek manuscript of the First Epistle of John having either τοῦ παρϑένου or πρὸς πάρϑους in its heading. That being the only difficulty with this hypothesis, anyone who can strain gnats and swallow camels should have no problem with Gieseler. If there are comparatively recent Greek manuscripts of the *Second* Epistle of John with the reading πρὸς πάρϑους, it only adds another problem while contributing nothing to a solution.

The Maurist text in Migne PL 35, 1977-2062, remains at present the standard text.

1846

[1, 6]

So long as he is in the flesh, a man is not able to be without sins, at least the lesser   658
ones (1); but do not make light even of those sins called lesser. If you make light of   633
them when you weigh them, be terrified when you count them. Many lesser ones   635
make one big one; many drops fill a river; many grains make a lump. And what
hope is there? Before all, confession; lest anyone suppose himself just, and in the   916
eyes of God, who sees things as they are, a man who did not exist and who now does
exist is lifting up his neck in pride—before all, therefore, there is confession; then   912
there is love (2); for what is it that is said about love (3)? "Love covers over
a multitude of sins (4)."

1847

[3, 5]

"And you shall have anointing by the Holy One so that you may be manifest to   842
yourselves (5)." The spiritual anointing is the Holy Spirit Himself, the Sacrament of   790
whose coming is in a visible anointing (6).

1848

[4, 7]

"And everyone who has this hope in Him makes himself chaste even as He is   700
chaste (7)." See how, lest he take away free choice, he says, "he makes himself   690
chaste." Who makes us chaste, if not God? But if you are not willing, God does not
make you chaste. Therefore, because you join your will to God, you make yourself

chaste. You make yourself chaste not by yourself but by Him who comes to indwell within you (8).

1848a

[7, 7]

Such is the force of love that, as you can see, it alone separates, it alone distinguishes   597
the actions of men. [7, 8] We said this is the case where the actions are similar.
Where they are different we can find a man made savage by love and another made gentle
by iniquity. A father beats a boy, and a seducer of boys caresses. If you but name the two
actions, who would not choose the caresses and decline the blows? But if you take note of
the persons whose actions they are, it is love that beats the boy and iniquity that caresses
him. See then what we are insisting upon: that the deeds of men are discerned only by
reason of love. . . . A short precept, therefore, is given you: Love, and do what you will.
If you are silent, be silent for love; or if you cry out, cry out for love. If you chastise,
chastise for love; if you spare, spare for love.

1849

[8, 1]

Works of mercy, sentiments of love, the holiness of piety, the integrity of chastity,   547
the modesty of sobriety, are always to be fostered . . . because all these virtues that I have
named are interior. But who could name them all? It is as if there were an army of an
emperor seated interiorly in your mind. And just as an emperor through his army does
whatever he pleases, so too the Lord Jesus Christ, when He begins through faith to dwell in
our interior man, that is, in our mind (9), uses those virtues as His ministers.

1. *levia peccata*.
2. *dilectio*.
3. *de caritate*.
4. 1 Peter 4:8. Whereas the Vulgate has "*caritas operit . . .*", Augustine reads "*caritas coöperit . . . .*"
5. See 1 John 2:20.
6. *Unctio spiritualis ipse Spiritus Sanctus est, cuius sacramentum est in unctione visibili.*
7. 1 John 3:3. Augustine reads: "*Et omnis qui habet spem hanc in ipso, castificat semetipsum, sicut et ipse castus est.*"
8. *ut inhabitet te*.
9. See Eph. 3:17.

THE PROCEEDINGS IN REGARD TO PELAGIUS [*A. D.* 417]

The *De gestis Pelagii ad Aurelium episcopum*, addressed to Aurelius, the Bishop of
Carthage, was written in 417. It is a digest and commentary on the minutes of Pelagius'
trial for heresy at Diospolis in 415, a trial at which the judges were fourteen bishops
convoked by John of Jerusalem. The trial at Diospolis, at which Pelagius was
exonerated, is one of history's minor engimas. Jerome, as might be anticipated, came
down very hard on the whole proceeding and referred to it as "that miserable synod."
Augustine, always kind, always the gentleman, takes the approach that if the bishops
exonerated Pelagius it can only be because Pelagius disavowed the opinions attributed to
him. In his *Corrections* 2, 73 Augustine says that he wrote the *De gestis Pelagii* so
that none could say that Pelagius' teachings were vindicated by the action of the bishops
or that his exoneration showed that the bishops shared his views; rather, he wanted it

made perfectly clear that if Pelagius had not condemned the views attributed to him he would not himself have avoided condemnation.

As is so often the case, what is almost certainly the truth may be found in a middle course. The bishops were not the reprobates that Jerome saw them to be, nor however, were they the excellent judges that a cursory glance at Augustine seems to make them—though in this connexion it must also be noted that Augustine was in no way deceived, and if he calls them pious judges and Christian judges and Catholic judges, he knew well that they were gullible judges and had been deceived by Pelagius; and he calls them judges of too little discretion.

When Pope Innocent read the minutes of the trial he said in some amazement that he could not refuse the judges either blame or praise. He saw very well that they were praiseworthy for having kept the faith, and that at the same time they were worthy of blame for having allowed themselves to be hoodwinked by Pelagius, who managed to convince them of his orthodoxy while retracting nothing.

The text in Migne PL 44, 319-360 was superseded in 1902 by the edition of C. F. Urba and J. Zycha in the Vienna Corpus, CSEL, Vol. 42.

1850

[1, 3]

We are reminded that there are two classes of aids. Of one sort are those without   693
which we could not accomplish that to which they lend their aid. No one, for example, can sail without a ship. No one can speak without a voice. No one can walk without feet. No one can gaze intently at a thing without light. And there are many other such examples. And to this class also we can ascribe the fact that no one can live righteously without God's grace. Of another sort, however, are the aids by which we are helped, when, even without them, we might in some other way accomplish that to which they were assisting us. Such are those which I have already mentioned: flails for threshing grain, a pedagogue to lead a boy to school, a remedy produced by human art for restoring health, and other such things.

1851

[14, 33]

Since Pelagius does not say: "God gives grace to whomever He will"; but, "God   711
gives all these graces to the man who has shown himself worthy to receive them,"   726
I could not help being suspicious upon reading such words. For the very name of   728
grace [*gratia*] and the thing signified by that name is taken away, if it is not given gratuitously [*gratis*], but he that is worthy receives it. Does anyone, perhaps, say that I do the Apostle an injury because I do not say that he was worthy of grace? On the contrary, I should certainly do him an injury and prepare a punishment for myself if I did not believe what he himself declares. Has he not pointedly defended that grace so that by the very name that is given it, it might be shown that it is given gratuitously? For he says expressly: "But if by grace, it is no more by works; otherwise grace is grace no more (1)."

1. Rom. 11:6.

THE GRACE OF CHRIST AND ORIGINAL SIN [*A. D.* 418]

In the *Corrections* 2, 76, Augustine says that it was after—and the implication is that it was immediately after or very soon after—the condemnation of the Pelagian heresy by Zosimus of Rome that he wrote his two books *De gratia Christi et de peccato originali*

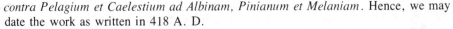

contra Pelagium et Caelestium ad Albinam, Pinianum et Melaniam. Hence, we may date the work as written in 418 A. D.

Melania, granddaughter of Melania the elder, was the wife of Pinian; and Albina was her mother. The three had fled Rome before the advancing barbarians, coming to Africa in 410. The present work is in response to their queries.

Zosimus very nearly made the same mistake that had been made at Diospolis with John of Jerusalem and the other thirteen bishops. First he saw little to quarrel with in the statements of Pelagius, and was minded to temporize. When the fuller implications of Pelagianism were pointed out to him, however, he condemned that heresy immediately.

The first book of *The Grace of Christ and Original Sin* deals with the matter of the first part of the title, and the second with the latter part; and this in such a way that they might easily have been regarded as two distinct works, except that it is clear in the *Corrections* that Augustine himself considered that they constituted but a single work in two books.

The text in Migne PL 44, 359-410, reprinting that of the Maurists, was superseded alreay in 1902 by the edition of C. F. Urba and J. Zycha in the Vienna Corpus, CSEL, Vol. 42.

1852

[1, 12, 13]

This grace, however, by which strength is made perfect in weakness (1), leads   683
the predestined and those called according to the [divine] purpose (2) to the highest   684
perfection and glorification. By this grace it is effected not only that we recognize
what we ought to do, but also that we do what we so recognize; not only that we
believe the things we ought to love, but that we love what we have so believed.

1853

[1, 24, 25]

God converted [King Assuerus] and turned the latter's indignation into gentleness   682
(3). But who cannot see that it is a much greater thing to convert and change   683
indignation completely into gentleness than it is to incline a heart toward something,   684
when that heart is not already occupied by either affection, but is in the middle,
between the two? Let them read and understand, let them ponder and confess that it is not
by law and doctrine sounding from without, but by an internal, secret, wonderful and
indescribable power that God works in men's hearts not only true revelations but even good
dispositions of will.

1854

[1, 25, 26]

God has not only given us the ability and His help in exercising it, but He also works   690
in us "to will and to do (4)," not because we do not will, or because we do not do, but   700
because without His help we neither will nor do anything good.

1855

[1, 29, 30]

Likewise in another place in that same book [the *De libero arbitrio*], Pelagius   727
says: "So that through grace men may more easily accomplish what they are commanded   650
to do through free choice." Take away the "more easily" and its meaning will not only be
complete but sound, if it be regarded as saying simply this: "So that through grace men

may accomplish what they are commanded to do through free choice.'' The addition of the words ''more easily,'' however, suggests a possibility of accomplishing good works even without the grace of God. But such a meaning is disallowed by Him who says: ''Without Me you can do nothing (5).''

1856

[1, 47, 52]

But because that question which discusses the choice of the will and the grace   700
of God has such difficulty in its distinctions that when free choice is defended it seems   725
to be a denial of God's grace and when God's grace is asserted free choice may seem to be taken away, Pelagius is able so to involve himself in the concealments of this obscurity that he can even declare that he agrees with these things that we have quoted from the writings of Saint Ambrose.

1857

[2, 24, 28]

In what concerns these two men (6), by one of whom we are sold under sin, by the   376
other of whom we are redeemed from sins, by one of whom we are precipitated into death, by the other of whom we are liberated unto life, because the one ruined us in himself by doing his own will and not that of Him by whom he was made, while the other has saved us in Himself by not doing His own will but that of Him by whom He was sent (7),—in what concerns these two men, therefore, the Christian faith   387
properly consists. ''For there is one God, and one Mediator of God and men, the man Christ Jesus (8)''; because ''there is no other name under heaven given to men, in which it is necessary for us to be saved (9)''; and in Him God gave assurance (10) to all men in respect to their faith, by raising Him from the dead (11). Without that faith, therefore,—that is, without faith in the one Mediator of God   569
and of men, the man Christ Jesus,—without faith, I say, in His Resurrection, by which God gave assurance to all (12), and in which certainly no one could believe without His Incarnation and death; without this faith, then, in the Incarnation, death, and Resurrection of Christ, Christian truth does not hesitate to say that the righteous of ancient times (13), so that they might be righteous, could not possibly have been cleansed   389
of their sins and justified by the grace of God. . . . For by this same faith in the Mediator were their hearts cleansed, and love was poured out in them by the Holy Spirit (14) who breathes where He will (15), not in consequence of merits but even producing these very merits. For the grace of God would not be grace in any   711
way unless it were gratuitous in every way.

1. 2 Cor. 12:9.
2. Rom. 8:28.
3. Esther 15:11.
4. Phil. 2:13.
5. John 15:5.
6. The two men are Adam and Christ.
7. John 4:34; 5:30.
8. 1 Tim. 2:5.
9. Acts 4:12.
10. *definivit*.
11. Acts 17:31.
12. *quam Deus omnibus definivit*.
13. *antiquos iustos*. It is clear in the context that Augustine refers to the saints of the old Testament era. In fact, *antiquus* is
    a very frequent word in Augustine's usage, when referring to anything of the Old Testament.
14. See Rom. 5:5.
15. John 3:8.

DISCOURSE TO THE PEOPLE OF THE CHURCH AT CAESAREA [*A. D.* 418]

Augustine's *Sermo ad Caesariensis ecclesiae plebem Emerito praesente habitus* was delivered on September 18, 418, in the midst of a debate scheduled for September 18 to September 20. The Caesarea in question was neither that of Palestine nor that of Cappadocia, but the obscure Caesarea in Mauretania. Emeritus was the Donatist Bishop of the place.

Augustine himself gives us the historical setting of this discourse in his *Corrections* 2, 77. He had gone to Caesarea in Mauretania to settle some disputes, and there met Emeritus, with whom he arranged to have a public debate in the church at Caesarea. The stenographic records of this debate are the substance of Augustine's *Gesta cum Emerito Donatista liber unus*. At one point in the debate, when Emeritus could find no reply to make and sat in embarassed silence, Augustine kept the floor and delivered the present *Sermo*. The principal theme of the *Discourse* is the utter necessity of a reconciliation between the Catholics and the Donatists.

The Maurist text in Migne PL 43, 689-698, is superseded by M. Petschenig's edition of 1910 in the *Vienna Corpus*, Vol. 53.

1858

[6]

A man cannot have salvation, except in the Catholic Church. Outside the Catholic   417
Church he can have everything except salvation. He can have honor, he can have   803
Sacraments, he can sing alleluia, he can answer amen, he can possess the gospel,
he can have and preach faith in the name of the Father and of the Son and of the Holy
Spirit; but never except in the Catholic Church will he be able to find salvation.

AGAINST A DISCOURSE OF THE ARIANS [*A. D.* 418]

Sometime in the year 418 copies of an anonymous sermon betokening an Arian theology of the Trinity were being circulated in Hippo.

Augustine has preserved this Arian sermon for posterity by his happy manner of refuting it: he numbered the topical divisions of the Arian sermon and then attached to it his point by point refutation, publishing the whole as his *Contra sermonem Arianorum liber unus*. The work belongs to the year 418 A. D., and is treated in the *Corrections* 2, 78.

The Maurist text in Migne PL 42, 677-708, remains at present the standard edition.

1859

[8]

The Son is said to have been crucified and buried, although He did not endure   347
this in His divinity itself, in which He is the Onlybegotten, coeternal with the Father,   256
but in the infirmity of His human nature. . . . The Blessed Apostle shows (1) that this   324
unity of person of Christ Jesus our Lord involves each nature, the divine, of   334
course, and the human, so harmoniously that whatever is named peculiar to the one is
imparted also the other (2), both the divine to the human, and the human to the divine.

1860

[16]

In man there is something that is similar to that Trinity which is God, though   233
in no way comparable in degree of excellence. . . . It is said: "in Our image (3)." This is
most rightly understood in reference to the personality of the Trinity itself (4). We think of
those three elements in the mind (5) of man: memory, intelligence, and will; everything we
do is accomplished by these three.

1. Phil. 2:5-8.
2. *ut quaelibet earum vocabulum etiam alteri impertiat.*
3. Gen. 1:26.
4. *Quod ex persona ipsius Trinitatis rectissime accipitur.* Augustine is suggesting that the way in which we are created in
   God's image is this: just as He has Three Persons and is a Triune God, so too in man, in his mind or soul, there are three
   elements that enter into everything he does: memory, intelligence, and will.
5. *anima.*

PATIENCE [*ca. A. D.* 417]

Augustine's *De patientia* is usually dated with no great claim for accuracy as having
been written before 418 A. D., and perhaps about 417.

Erasmus was of a mind that *Patience* is not an authentic work of Augustine at all,
basing his opinion on certain peculiarities of style, largely the occasional uses of
assonance and rhymed endings in the work. The passage usually noted as an example is
from chapter 12: "*Cautior fuit iste in doloribus, quam ille in nemoribus: ille victus et in
deliciis, iste vicit in poenis; consensit ille oblectamentis, non cessit iste tormentis.*"

I think no one today doubts the authenticity of the *De patientia*. That the work is not
mentioned in the *Corrections* is not to be wondered at; for it is a sermon, and sermons as
such are not included in the *Corrections*. Much more important is the positive fact that
Augustine does refer to the work as his own, in the *Letter to Darius* 231, 7. The latter
fact would seem to be conclusive enough; though I suppose it might be argued that he
mentions therein such a work, which is not necessarily this work. I would, however, say
this also: while admitting that it is rather rude to deny a man's major, I do not
understand why it seems always to have been taken for granted that Erasmus had a
well-founded point in his objection by reason of style. In truth, the assonances in the *De
patientia* are not entirely unparalleled throughout the rest of Augustine's writings. They
are perhaps a bit more striking in the present work—some might even say strident,—but
certainly they are not foreign to Augustine's style. We have already quoted his jibe at
Julian in the *Opus imperfectum* 4, 50: "*In disputatione loquacissimus, in contentione
calumniosissimus, in professione fallacissimus.*" A man capable of giving us a line like
that is certainly capable also of the one noted above which disturbed Erasmus so much.

The Maurist edition in Migne PL 40, 611-626 is superseded by that of J. Zycha in the
Vienna Corpus, CSEL, Vol. 41 (1900).

1860a

[26, 23]

If anyone, not having love,—which belongs to the unity of spirit and the bond of   598
peace by which the Catholic Church is gathered and joined together,—is involved in
some schism, but rather than deny Christ he suffers tribulations . . . for fear of hell
and eternal fire, this is certainly not blameworthy; on the contrary, he exhibits a
patience that is laudable. . . . When the Apostle says: "If I give my body to be
burned, but have not love, it profits me nothing (1), it should be understood that he

means it would profit him nothing in respect to gaining the kingdom of heaven,
but not in respect to his undergoing a more tolerable punishment in the last judgment.   1035
[27, 24] It can rightly be asked whether this patience too is the gift of God, or whether
it is to be attributed to the powers of the human will; the patience, I mean, by
which someone who is separated from the Church suffers temporal pains for fear
of eternal pains, not for the sake of the error which separated him from the Church, but for
the sake of the truth of the Sacrament or word (2) which has remained with him. . . . It
cannot be denied that it is good that a man believe he will be punished with eternal
punishment if he deny Christ, and for that belief endure and make light of any kind of
human punishment. [27, 25] Hence, just as it is not to be denied that this is a gift of God,
so too it is to be understood that some gifts are possessed by the sons of that Jerusalem
which is our free mother above, gifts which are in some way hereditary, in which we are
heirs of God and joint heirs with Christ (3); while other gifts can be received even by the
sons of concubines, to which carnal Jews and schismatics and heretics are compared.

1. 1 Cor. 13:3.
2. *sed pro veritate sacramenti seu verbi*.
3. Rom. 8:17.

ADULTEROUS MARRIAGES [*A. D.* 419 *aut* 420]

Augustine's treatise *De coniugiis adulterinis*, also called *De incompetentibus nuptiis*,
was written near the end of the year 419 or perhaps early in 420. In his *Corrections* 2,
83 he judges that he did not reach a perfect solution to the problems of adulterous
marriages, but thinks that he did succeed at least in clarifying many of the obscurities
surrounding the problem.
    The Maurist text reprinted in Migne (PL 40, 451-486) has been superseded by the
edition of J. Zycha (1900) in the Vienna Corpus, Vol. 41.

1861

[1, 9, 9]
    Neither can it rightly be held that a husband who dismisses his wife because of   974
fornication and marries another does not commit adultery. For there is also adultery   975
on the part of those who, after the repudiation of their former wives because of
fornication, marry others. This adultery, nevertheless, is certainly less serious than
that of men who dismiss their wives for reasons other than fornication and take other
wives. . . . Therefore, when we say: "Whoever marries a woman dismissed by her
husband for reason other than fornication commits adultery," undoubtedly we
speak the truth. But we do not thereby acquit of this crime the man who marries a
woman who was dismissed because of fornication. We do not doubt in the least that
both are adulterers. We do indeed pronounce him an adulterer who dismisses his
wife for cause other than fornication and marries another, nor do we thereby defend
from the taint of this sin the man who dismisses his wife because of fornication
and marries another. We recognize that both are adulterers, though the sin of one is
more grave than that of the other. No one is so unreasonable as to say that a man   634
who marries a woman whose husband has dismissed her because of fornication is
not an adulterer, while maintaining that a man who marries a woman dismissed
without the ground of fornication is an adulterer. Both of these men are guilty of adultery.

1862

[1, 26, 33]

    In regard to catechumens, therefore, who are at the end of this life, whether they   831
are stricken by disease or from some other circumstance, and who though they are still   834
alive, cannot request Baptism for themselves or answer questions, since their
disposition of will toward the Christian faith is already known, let them be baptized
in the way in which infants are baptized, of whose will in this matter there is no
evidence. We ought not condemn those, however, who act more reservedly in this
matter than seems to us to be the way in which they ought to act. . . . There are   807
men who think that in these matters as well as in others what we read that the Lord
said must be observed, to wit: "Do not give what is holy to dogs, neither cast your
pearls before swine (1)." In deference, then, to these words of the Savior they
do not have the boldness to baptize those who are unable to answer for themselves,
lest perhaps they act contrary to the choice of such a person's will. This cannot be
applied to children, however, in whom there is as yet no use of reason. But not only   835
is it incredible that a catechumen would not wish to be baptized at the end of this
life, but even if his will is unknown (2), it were much more satisfactory to give what
he does not want than to deny him what he does want. In a case where his willing
or not willing is not clear, it is easier to believe that, were he able, he would more
likely prefer to say that he wished to receive those Sacraments without which he
already believed that it were not proper for him to go forth from the body.

1863

[2, 4, 4]

    "Therefore, while her husband is alive, she will be called an adulteress if she be   974
found with another man. But if her husband shall have died, she has   975
been set free from the law, so that she is not an adulteress if she has been with
another man (3)." These words of the Apostle, so often repeated, so often inculcated, are
true, living, sound, and clear. A woman begins to be the wife of no later husband unless
she has ceased to be the wife of a former one. She will cease to be the wife of a former
one, however, if that husband should die, not if he commit fornication. A spouse (4),
therefore, is lawfully dismissed for cause of fornication; but the bond of chastity (5)
remains. That is why a man is guilty of adultery if he marries a woman who has been
dismissed even for this very reason of fornication.

1864

[2, 16, 16]

    I realize what the incontinent can say: . . . that if a man, accusing his wife of   836
adultery, kills her, this sin, since it is finished and does not perdure in him, if it   928
is committed by a catechumen, is absolved in Baptism; and, if it is done by one who is   906
baptized, it is healed by Penance and reconciliation. Are we supposed to declare,   974
then, that adultery, committed without doubt if another wife is taken while the adulterous
spouse still lives, is not adultery?

1. Matt. 7:6.
2. *si voluntas eius incerta est*. It is clear from the context that the lack of certitude about his will is on the part of others, not
   the catechumen himself.
3. Rom. 7:2-3.
4. *coniux*.
5. *vinculum pudoris*.

QUESTIONS ON THE HEPTATEUCH [*A. D.* 419]

While engaged in writing his seven books on peculiar idioms in the heptateuch, the *Locutionum in heptateuchum libri septem*, that is, in the year 419 A. D., Augustine wrote also the present related work of seven books on various problems in the heptateuch, the *Quaestionum in heptateuchum libri septem*. The former is treated in *Corrections* 2, 80, the latter in 2, 81.

The Maurist text, in Migne PL 34, 547-824, was superseded already in 1895 by J. Zycha's *Vienna Corpus* edition in CSEL, Vol. 28, part 2. We have employed Zycha's text as basis of our translations below, in spite of the appearance in 1958 of I. Fraipont's edition in the *Corpus Christianorum*, Vol. 33, pp. 1-377.

1865

[2, 21]

Within corporeal things through all the elements of the world there are certain hidden   470
seminal reasons (1) by which, temporal and causal opportunity presenting itself,   480
various kinds burst forth, distinguished by their own styles and purposes. And just
as the angels who make them are not called creators of living things, so too the farmers
who plant seeds of trees or whatever in the ground are not called creators of growing
things, although they know how to furnish the visible opportunities and causes so
that these things spring up. But what the farmers do visibly, the angels do invisibly;
God, however, is the one and only Creator, who implanted the causes themselves   462
and the seminal reasons in things.

1866

[3, 57]

By those sacrifices of the Old Law, this one Sacrifice is signified, in which there   892
is a true remission of sins; but not only is no one forbidden to take as food the   897
Blood of this Sacrifice, rather, all who wish to possess life are exhorted to drink   870
thereof.

---

1. *seminariae rationes*.

MARRIAGE AND CONCUPISCENCE [*A. D.* 419-420]

With the condemnation of Pelagianism by Pope Zosimus early in the year 418, to which all bishops were expected to subscribe, Pelagius himself disappears from history. But not so his doctrine. Julian, Bishop of Eclanum in Apulia, headed a party of eighteen bishops who refused to subscribe to the condemnation of Pelagius, and he now became leader of the proponents of Pelagianism. Deposed by Zosimus and exiled by the civil authority, he began a kind of wandering existence in the East that would last the rest of his life.

The *De nuptiis et concupiscentia ad Valerium comitem* is the first of Augustine's four writings against Julian of Eclanum. In two books, the first book was published in 419. Answer was made to it by Julian in four books. The Count Valerius at Ravenna, who had already inspired the first book, sent extracts from Julian's answer to Augustine for rebuttal, who then added the second book to the work. Augustine afterwards provided a fuller rebuttal in his *Against Julian* (§§ 1898-1912 below).

The text in Migne, PL 44, 413-474, was superseded in 1902 by the Vienna Corpus edition of C. F. Urba and J. Zycha, CSEL, Vol. 42.

1867

[1, 10, 11]

Certainly it is not fecundity only, the fruit of which is in offspring, not chastity
(1) only, the bond of which is in fidelity (2), but a certain sacramental bond
of marriage (3) that is recommended to the faithful who are married, when the Apostle
says: "Men, love your wives, as also Christ loved the Church (4)." Undoubtedly the
substance of the Sacrament (5) is of this bond, so that when man and woman have
been joined in marriage they must continue inseparably as long as they live, nor is it
allowed for one spouse to be separated from the other except for cause of fornication (6).
For this is preserved in the case of Christ and the Church, so that, as a living one
with a living one, there is no divorce, no separation forever. So perfect is the observance
of this bond . . . in the Church of Christ by all married believers, who are
undoubtedly members of Christ, that, although women marry and men take wives
for the purpose of procreating children, one is never permitted to put away even
an unfruitful wife for the purpose of getting another to bear children. If anyone does
this, in the law of the gospel he is guilty of adultery, just as a woman is if she marries
another. But this is not the case in the law of this world, wherein even without
crime a divorce is granted whenever the parties want to join in marriage with others, a
concession which, the Lord bears witness, even the holy Moses granted to the Israelites
only because of the hardness of their hearts (7). . . . Thus, between the living
spouses there remains a certain conjugal bond (8), which neither separation nor union
with another (9) can take away. It remains, however, for the injury of crime, and not
for the bond of covenant. So it is with the soul of an apostate. Even though its faith is
cast aside in withdrawing, as it were, from its marriage with Christ, it does not
lose the Sacrament of its faith, which it received in the bath of regeneration. . . .
The apostate retains the Sacrament even after his apostasy; but now it is for the
aggravation of his punishment and not for his meriting a reward.

968

972
974

981

978

798

1868

[1, 11, 12]

That the nuptial bond should be broken between those who, by mutual consent,
agree to abstain perpetually from the use of carnal concupiscence—perish the
thought! On the contrary, it will be made the stronger by reason of the pledges they have
entered into between themselves, which will have to be kept by a special endearment and
concord, not by the voluptuous joinings of bodies but by the voluntary affections of souls.
For it was not deceitfully that the angel said to Joseph, "Fear not to take Mary, your wife
(10)." She is called a wife from the first plighting of their troth, although he neither had
nor ever would have any carnal knowledge of her (11).

973

1869

[1, 17, 19]

In marriage, however, let the blessings of marriage (12) be loved: offspring, fidelity,
and the sacramental bond (13). Offspring, not so much because it may be born, but
because it can be reborn; for it is born to punishment unless it be reborn to life.
Fidelity, but not such as even the unbelievers have among themselves, ardent
as they are for the flesh. . . . The sacramental bond, which they lose neither
through separation nor through adultery,—this the spouses should guard chastely
and harmoniously.

968

975

1870

[1, 18, 20]

It is because of concupiscence that even in the righteous and legitimate marriage   615
of the children of God, not children of God but children of the world are begotten;
because they too who beget, even if they themselves are already regenerate, beget
not as children of God, but as still being children of the world.

1871

[1, 23, 25]

Concupiscence, which is atoned for (14) only by the Sacrament of regeneration,   614
does most certainly, by generation, pass on the bond of sin to the progeny, if they are   617
not loosed from it by the same regeneration. For concupiscence itself is certainly no   615
longer a sin in the regenerate, when they do not consent to illicit deeds and when
their members are not applied by the ruling mind (15) to the performance of such
deeds. . . . But because the guilt (16) of concupiscence is prevalent in man who was
born, that is called sin, in a certain manner of speaking, which was made by sin and which,
if it conquers, produces sin. This guilt, however, through the remission of all sins, is not
allowed to prevail in the man who is reborn, if he does not obey it when in some way it
commands him to perform evil works.

1872

[1, 24, 27]

Licit and honest cohabitation itself cannot be effected without the ardor of lust,   617
so as to accomplish that which belongs to reason and not to lust. . . . This
concupiscence of the flesh is the daughter of sin, as it were, and, as often as it consents
to shameful deeds, it is the mother of more sins. Whatever offspring is born of
this concupiscence of the flesh is bound by original sin (17), unless it be reborn in   614
Him whom the Virgin conceived without that concupiscence; for which reason, when
He deigned to be born in the flesh, He alone was born without sin.   344

1873

[1, 26, 29]

Just as in the case of those sins which cannot themselves be permanent, because   640
they pass away as soon as they are committed, but their guilt remains, and if not remitted,
will remain in eternity, so too with concupiscence: when remitted, guilt is taken   617
away. For not to have sin means not to be guilty of sin. If anyone, for example,
committed adultery, even if he never does it again, he is guilty of adultery until it be
remitted by the forgiveness (18) of the guilt thereof. He has the sin, therefore,
although that which he committed no longer exists because it passed away along
with the passing of the time at which he committed it.

1874

[1, 37, 38]

By the same bath of regeneration and by the word of sanctification absolutely all   836
the evils of a man, when he is regenerate, are cleansed and healed, not only all the
sins which are remitted in Baptism, but even those which are committed later
by human ignorance or weakness; not that Baptism can be repeated as often as sin
is committed, but because it is by virtue of that Baptism which is given only once,
that, not only before but even afterwards, forgiveness for sins of whatever sort may be

sought and obtained by the faithful (19). For of what avail would repentance be,   901
either before Baptism, if Baptism did not follow, or after Baptism, if Baptism did
not precede?

1875

[2, 11, 24]

From the time that circumcision was instituted among the people of God, which   795
then was a sign of the righteousness of faith, it availed as a sign of the purgation even
in infants of the original and ancient sin, just as Baptism, from the time at which
it was instituted, began to be of avail for the renewal (20) of mankind.

1876

[2, 26, 43]

Marriage is not the cause of the sin which comes with being born and is expiated   983
in being reborn; rather, the willful sin of the first man is the cause of original   614
sin (21). . . . [27, 44] Why, then, does [Julian] ask us: "Whence is it that sin is   616
found in an infant: through will, or through marriage, or through his parents?" . . .
[27, 45] For all this the Apostle has an answer. He accuses neither the will of the
infant, which is not yet matured in him for sinning; nor marriage as such, which   972
has not only its institution from God, but a blessing as well; nor parents as such,
who are licitly and legitimately joined together for the procreation of children. Rather,
he says: "Through one man sin came into this world, and through sin death; and
thus it passed through into all men, for in him all have sinned (22)."

1877

[2, 28, 48]

"If sin," [Julian] says, "is from the will, the will is evil because it does sin; but if   614
it is from nature, nature is evil." I quickly respond: "Sin is from the will." He   616
asks, perhaps, "And original sin too?" And I answer: "Absolutely original sin too.
Because this too was sown by the will of the first man, so that it existed in him and passed
on to all."

1. *pudicitia.*
2. *cuius vinculum est fides.*
3. *quoddam sacramentum nuptiarum.*
4. Eph. 5:25.
5. *sacramenti res.*
6. Matt. 5:32.
7. Matt. 19:8-9.
8. *Ita manet inter viventes quiddam coniugale.*
9. *cum altero copulatio.*
10. Matt. 1:20.
11. *Coniux vocatur ex prima desponsationis fide, quam concubitu nec cognoverat nec fuerat cogniturus.*
12. *bona nuptialia.*
13. *proles, fides, sacramentum.*
14. *expiatur.*
15. *a regina mente.*
16. *reatus.*
17. *originali est obligata peccato.*
18. *indulgentia.* In classical usage *indulgentia* meant kindness or tenderness—such as might prompt an over-indulgent
    grandmother. In post-classical usage it came to mean remission of punishment or forgiveness. The full expression in
    Augustine is: *reus est adulterii, reatus ipsius indulgentia remittatur;* and the translation in *The Nicene and Post-Nicene
    Fathers* will not do at all: "he is held to be guilty of adultery until the indulgence in guilt be itself remitted." *Indulgentia*
    must be taken as an ablative and not as a nominative if the statement is to make sense at all. Indulgence in guilt really

defies logic; for one does not indulge in guilt (even if one allow this transferred meaning which the verb *indulgeo* sometimes has, of indulging in something); rather, one is rendered guilty by indulging in sin.

19. Again the translation in *The Nicene and Post-Nicene Fathers* defies both logic and the text. In that series the passage is translated: "but that by its one only ministration it comes to pass that pardon is secured to the faithful of all their sins both before and after their regeneration." The Latin is clear enough: "*sed quia ipso quod semel datur fit, ut non solum antea, verum etiam postea quorumlibet peccatorum venia fidelibus impetretur.*"

20. *innovationem*. In reference to the meaning of this term and its verb *innovare*, see our footnote no. 1 on pp. 243-244 in Vol. 1. Augustine provides an example of the usage we indicated in that place, when we were discussing the classic *nihil innovetur nisi quod traditum est*.

21. *voluntarium peccatum hominis primi originalis est causa peccati*.

22. The Latin here reads precisely as the Vulgate text (Rom. 5:12): *. . . in quo omnes peccaverunt*. Even if the passage should read *because* rather than *in him* (or *in whom*), it is necessary to translate it in the way that Augustine understood it; and in what immediately follows upon the present passage, Augustine takes to task those who do not think with the Church, but suggest that the passage in Rom. 5:12 does not mean that in Adam we all sinned, but rather that those who choose to sin find in Adam a ready example. Augustine is often taken as the originator of the *in whom* interpretation of *in quo*. But we have already seen it in the Ambrosiaster (*q.v.*). Moreover, Jerome must have so understood it when he wrote *in quo* in his Vulgate translation of the ἐφ' ᾧ that stands in the Greek. Furthermore, since Augustine consciously avoided using the Vulgate, the *in quo* that is consistent in his quotations of the passage suggests that it was to be found in one or more of the pre-Vulgate Latin translations that go by the generic name of *Vetus itala*.

THE SOUL AND ITS ORIGIN [*A. D.* 419-420]

A certain Vincent Victor of Caesarea in Mauretania, a convert to Catholicism from the Rogatist sect of Donatism, while visiting in the home of a certain Spanish priest named Peter, came upon a short work of Augustine—probably it was Augustine's *Letter to Marcellinus*, no. 143 in the corpus, written about 412 A. D., or else, which is less probable, his *Letter to Optatus*, no. 190, dating from 418 A. D.—in which Augustine is uncertain whether the souls of men are transmitted along with their bodies, coming ultimately from Adam, or whether each is separately and directly created by God, while at the same time he asserts unhesitatingly that the soul is incorporeal.

Vincent Victor was very dissatisfied with these statements and wrote a refutation of Augustine in two books, addressed to Peter. Victor's work was apparently an incredible mishmash of Manicheism, Origenism, and Pelagianism, the product of a very young mind filled much more with confidence than with wisdom.

When a copy of Victor's work came into Augustine's hands, probably near the end of the year 419, through the good offices of an orthodox monk named Renatus, Augustine immediately undertook to defend himself and to refute Vincent Victor in the four books of the present work, *De anima et eius origine*, which may conveniently be dated in 419 and 420.

The first of these four books is addressed to Renatus, the second to Peter, and the third and fourth to Vincent Victor. Augustine notes in his *Corrections* 2, 82 that he treated Victor as gently as possible,—a fact to which the tenor of the work itself bears witness,—and received in fact the young man's grateful retraction.

The Maurist text reprinted in Migne PL 44, 475-548 was superseded in 1913 by the Vienna Corpus edition of C. F. Urba and J. Zycha in CSEL, Vol. 60, where the title of the work is given as *De natura et origine animae*.

1878

[1, 9, 11]

Let no one promise infants who have not been baptized a sort of middle place of rest	618
and happiness, such as he pleases and wherever he pleases, between damnation	831
and the kingdom of heaven. This is what the Pelagian heresy promised them (1).	619
	1037

1879

[2, 3, 6]

Whence, I pray you, do you believe that the soul came,—I do not say your soul or mine, but the first one given to that first man? If made out of nothing and breathed into him by God, then what you believe is what I too believe.

506

1880

[2, 4, 8]

That which Vincent Victor believes with perfect propriety and great soundness of view, that souls are judged when they go forth from their bodies and before they come to that judgment in which they must be judged when their bodies are restored to them and they are glorified or tormented in that very same flesh in which they lived here;—is it really a fact that you did not know this? For who ever had his mind so obstinately set against the Gospel that he never heard of this, or having heard it did not believe it, when that passage was set forth about the poor man who after death was carried away to the bosom of Abraham, and the rich man who was tormented in hell (2)?

995

1013
1020

1881

[3, 9, 12]

If you wish to be Catholic, do not believe, do not say, do not teach that infants who are overtaken by death before they can be baptized are able to come to a forgiveness of original sins (3).

831

1882

[4, 11, 16]

I simply hold what I see the Apostle taught most clearly: from one man all men born of Adam go into condemnation (4) unless they be reborn in Christ, accordingly as He, the most merciful bestower of graces, predestined to eternal life those whom He ordained to be reborn before they die in the body, who also is the most just awarder of punishment to those whom He predestined to eternal death, not only because of the sins which they add of their own willingness, but also because of original sin (5) even if, being infants, they add nothing of their own. This is my definition in that question, so that the hidden works of God may keep their own secret, without damage to my faith (6).

831

203
210

618
205

---

1. The notion is clearly that of limbo, a rather popular idea which, however, has never enjoyed any great repute among theologians. I think it is not generally pointed out that it finds its origins among the Pelagians.
2. *in inferno*. See Luke 16:19-24.
3. *pervenire posse ad originalium indulgentiam peccatorum*.
4. See Rom. 5:18.
5. *propter originale peccatum*.
6. *salva fide mea*.

AGAINST TWO LETTERS OF THE PELAGIANS [*A. D.* 420]

When the Count Valerius of Ravenna sent Alypius, a friend of Augustine, to Africa with Julian's reply to the first book of Augustine's *Marriage and Concupiscence*, Alypius brought along also two letters forwarded by Pope Boniface. The two letters, which had lately come into the hands of Boniface, were ascribed one to Julian and the

other to eighteen Pelagian bishops including Julian. The letters were in the nature not only of attacks on the faith, but also constituted personal attacks on Augustine. Boniface sent them along, of course, in a kindly spirit, so that Augustine could see what was being said. And Augustine, believing that to ignore the attacks of heretics could only be productive of great harm among the faithful, undertook to provide a rebuttal to the two letters in the four books of his *Contra duas epistulas Pelagianorum, ad Bonifatium Romanae ecclesiae episcopum*, written most probably in 420 A. D. Only be it noted that the *ad Bonifatium* in this title is the address of Augustine's reply and not of the *epistulas Pelagianorum*.

Augustine speaks very briefly of the present work in his *Corrections* 2, 87.

The Maurist text in Migne PL 44, 549-638 is superseded by the 1913 edition of C. F. Urba and J. Zycha in the Vienna Corpus, CSEL, Vol. 60.

1883

[1, 2, 5]

Who of us would say that by the sin of the first man free will perished from the human race? Certainly freedom perished through sin, but it was that freedom which was had in paradise, of having full righteousness with immortality; and it is on that account that human nature has need of divine grace.

613
612
650

1884

[1, 7, 12]

We say that both before the Law and in the time of the Old Testament men were freed from their sins . . . through the blood of the Redeemer Himself, who is the one Mediator of God and men, the Man Christ Jesus (1). But these enemies of God's grace, which is given to small and great through Jesus Christ our Lord, say that the ancient men of God were of perfect righteousness, and that it is not to be believed that they needed the Incarnation, Passion, and Resurrection of Christ, by faith in whom they have been saved.

389
387

569

1885

[1, 9, 15]

It is one thing to do good with the will of doing good, and quite another to be inclined by the will toward the doing of evil, so that one would actually do it if one could possibly be allowed to do it without punishment. For assuredly in this latter circumstance one sins inwardly in the will itself, who refrains from sinning not by will but by fear.

632
915

1886

[1, 13, 26]

We say that Baptism grants forgiveness (2) of all sins, and takes away crimes, not "shaving them off," nor in such a way that "the roots of all sins are retained in the evil flesh, like the hairs shaved from the head, whence the sins may grow again to be cut down again (3)."

751

1887

[1, 13, 27]

Although concupiscence is called sin, it is not called such because it is in itself

617

sin, but because it is the result of sin, just as a writing is said to be someone's hand because the hand wrote it.

1888

[1, 14, 28]

　Many of the baptized faithful are without crime; but I would not say that anyone in this life is without sin, however much the Pelagians are inflated and burst asunder by their madness against us because of our saying this. It is not because some sins remain which are not remitted in Baptism, but because we who remain in the infirmity of this life do not cease to commit daily those sins which, for those who pray faithfully and who do works of mercy, are daily remitted.

658
727

929
811

1889

[1, 18, 36]

　No one is forced by God's power unwillingly either into evil or to good; but when God forsakes a man, that man deservedly goes into evil, and when God helps him, without deserving it he is converted to good. For a man is not good if he is unwilling; but by the grace of God he is helped even to be willing; because it is not vainly written: "For it is God who, for His good pleasure, works in you both the will and the performance (4)"; and: "The will is prepared by the Lord (5)."

638
721
711

1890

[1, 19, 37]

　"No one can come to Me unless the Father who sent Me draw him (6)." He does not say, "unless He lead him", whereby we might in some way have understood that the man's will came first. For who is drawn, if he was already willing? And yet, no man comes unless he is willing. He is drawn in wondrous ways, therefore, to will, by Him who knows how to work within the very hearts of men, not in such a way that men who are unwilling should believe (which is impossible), but that men should be made willing from their having been unwilling.

650

700
696

1891

[1, 21, 39]

　You that are enemies to this grace will not have it that it should be believed that the ancients were saved by the same grace of Jesus Christ, but you make a distinction of times as Pelagius did, in whose books this is read. And you say that before the Law men were saved by nature, afterwards by the Law, and finally through Jesus Christ, as if men of two earlier periods, that is to say, before the Law and under the Law, the blood of Christ was not necessary, thus making void what is said: "For there is one God and one Mediator of God and of men, the man Christ Jesus (7)."

389
387
727

1892

[2, 3, 5]

　Caelestius' booklet was called Catholic, because this too pertains to a Catholic mind: that if someone perhaps thinks otherwise than the truth demands, he does not define it with utmost certainty but, when it is detected and demonstrated, he rejects it (8). For it was not to heretics but to Catholics that the Apostle was speaking when he said: "Let us, therefore, as many of us as are perfect, be of this mind; and if in anything you be

435
451

minded otherwise, that too God will reveal to you (9).'' This was thought to have been done in the case of Caelestius, when he responded that he agreed with the letters of Pope Innocent of blessed memory, in which all doubt in this matter was taken away.

1893

[2, 9, 21]

God does many good things in a man which the man does not do; but a man does none   690
which God does not cause him to do. . . . For if without God we can do nothing, certainly we can neither initiate nor perfect anything: because, for us to begin, it is said, ''His mercy shall anticipate me (10)''; and for us to perfect anything, it is said: ''His mercy shall follow me (11).''

1894

[4, 10, 27]

Now let us see the third point which, in the Pelagians, is no less shocking to Christ's   727
every member and to His whole body. They contend that in this life there are or have been righteous men having no sin at all. By this presumption they most clearly   658
contradict the Lord's Prayer, in which all the members of Christ cry aloud with true heart these words to be said each day (12): ''Forgive us our debts (13).''

1. 1 Tim. 2:5.
2. *indulgentiam*.
3. The quoted phrases are supposed opinions that Julian falsely attributed to Augustine.
4. Phil. 2:13. See also § 1572 above, with its note 9.
5. Prov. 8:35 in the Septuagint.
6. John 6:44.
7. 1 Tim. 2:5.
8. Caelestius, when charged with heresy, had presented a *libellus* or booklet to Pope Zosimus, in which he not only declared his faith but listed points on which he was still in doubt and about which he wished Zosimus to instruct him. Among these latter matters was the existence of original sin. Pope Zosimus said that his booklet was Catholic, meaning that his humble attitude of submission to magisterial authority was a properly Catholic attitude. In Caelestius, as a matter of fact, it was a feigned attitude; and he gave it out that Zosimus had declared the booklet, with its doubts and heresies, of Catholic content.
9. Phil. 3:15.
10. Ps. 58[59]:11, which reads: *''Misericordia eius praevenit me''*; that is, ''His mercy shall anticipate [*or* come before] me.'' The editors of *The Nicene and Post-Nicene Fathers* lost the sense entirely in accepting the translation, ''His mercy prevents me.''
11. Ps. 22[23]:6.
12. *cotidianis vocibus*: literally, *with daily words* or *with daily voices*.
13. Matt. 6:12.

AGAINST AN ADVERSARY OF THE LAW AND THE PROPHETS [*A. D.* 420]

At Carthage in 419 or 420 A. D. there were public readings to interested groups from a book written by an unknown heretic, a Marcionite or else one of very similar tendencies; *i. e.*, someone who attributed the Old Testament writings not to the authorship of God but to a wickedly deceptive demon.

Some zealous Christians obtained a copy of the book and sent it to Augustine for refutation. Augustine's reply was his *Contra adversarium legis et prophetarum libri duo*, which belong most probably to the early months of 420 A. D. The work is treated in Augustine's *Corrections* 2, 84.

The Maurist text in Migne PL 42, 604-666, is still the standard edition.

1895

[1, 17, 35]

Just as the one true God is the Creator of both temporal and eternal good things,   50
so too is He the Author of both Testaments, because the New is prefigured (1) in the
Old, and the Old is unveiled (2) in the New.

1896

[1, 20, 39]

That adversary actually uses testimonies from the apocryphal books which were   40
written under the names of the Apostles Andrew and John! If these books had really
been written by them, they would have been received by the Church, which has
continued from those times through the most certain successions of bishops to our own
times without a break.

1897

[2, 7, 26]

But what is the end of the Law? To this question it is not I, but the Apostle himself   51
who answers. "The end of the law," he says, "is Christ, unto justice for every
believer (3)." Christ is the end that perfects, not the end that destroys (4). For that
is called the end for the sake of which everything is done that is done in reference to   52
something else. . . . Just as the knowledge that we now have will be "put away,"
as the Apostle says, when we have that knowledge which he calls "face to face (5),"
so too it is necessary that the things given in shadows to the Jews in the Old Testament
be put away by the revelation of the New Testament.

1. *figuratum*.
2. *revelatum*.
3. Rom. 10:4.
4. *Finis perficiens, non interficiens*.
5. See 1 Cor. 13:11-12.

AGAINST JULIAN, DEFENDER OF THE PELAGIAN HERESY [*ca. A. D.* 421]

The *Contra Iulianum haeresis Pelagianae defensorem libri sex* is the earlier of
Augustine's two works specifically against Julian of Eclanum, and both entitled *Contra
Iulianum*. It must not be confused with the second work, the unfinished *Contra
secundam Iuliani responsionem imperfectum opus sex libros complectens*, commonly
called the *Opus imperfectum*, which Augustine was writing when he died (§§ 2007-2013
below).

When Julian replied to the first book of Augustine's *Marriage and Concupiscence*
with a personal attack against Augustine in the *Four Books to Turbantius*, Augustine
responded immediately with the second book of his *Marriage and Concupiscence*,
though at that time he had seen only excerpts from Julian's work. Now having read the
whole of the *Four Books to Turbantius*, he replied in a fuller manner in the six books of
the present work *Against Julian, Defender of the Pelagian Heresy*.

Though it is out of place to mention it here, we will, for greater clarity, only note that
Julian then countered Augustine's *Against Julian, Defender of the Pelagian Heresy* with
his own *Eight Books to Florus*; and it was as a response to the *Eight Books to Florus*
that Augustine was writing the *Opus imperfectum* when overtaken by death.

The present work of Augustine is treated in his *Corrections* 2, 88.

The Maurist text in Migne PL 44, 641-874 is still the standard.

[1, 6, 21-22]
  See St. John Chrysostom, § 1145a, *above*.

[1, 6, 26]
  See St. John Chrysostom, § 1145b, *above*.

1898

[1, 7, 30]
  You are convicted on every side. The numerous testimonies in regard to original   106
sin, testimonies of the saints, are clearer than daylight. Look what an assembly it is into
which I have brought you. Here is Ambrose of Milan. . . . Here too is John of
Constantinople (1). . . . Here is Basil. . . . Here are others too, whose general
agreement is so great that it ought to move you. This is not, as you write with an evil pen,
"a conspiracy of the lost." They were famous in the Catholic Church for their pursuit of
sound doctrine. Armed and girded with spiritual weapons, they waged strenuous wars
against the heretics; and when they had faithfully completed the labors appointed them (2),
they fell asleep in the lap of peace. . . . [31] . . . See where I have brought you: the
assembly of those saints is no common rabble (3). They are not only sons but also fathers
of the Church (4).

1899

[2, 10, 33]
  Holy and blessed priests, widely reknowned for their diligence in divine eloquence,   614
Irenaeus, Cyprian, Reticius, Olympius, Hilary, Ambrose, Gregory, Innocent, John,   106
Basil (5),—and whether you like it or not, I will add the presbyter Jerome, while omitting
those who are still alive,—have pronounced against you their opinion about original
sin in the guilty succession of all men, whence no one is exempted (6) except Him   344
that the Virgin conceived without the law of sin warring against the law of the mind (7).   781
[34] . . . What they found in the Church, they kept; what they learned, they taught; what   100
they received from the fathers, they handed on to the sons. We were never involved
with you before these judges; but our case has been tried before them. Neither
we nor you were known to them; we but recite their judgments delivered in our
favor against you.

1900

[2, 10, 37]
  These men are bishops, learned, grave, holy, and most zealous defenders of the truth   106
against garrulous vanities, in whose reason, erudition, and freedom, three qualities you
demand in a judge, you can find nothing to despise. . . . With such planters, waterers,
builders, shepherds, and fosterers the holy Church grew after the time of the Apostles.

1901

[3, 18, 35]
  God is good, God is just. He is able to deliver some men without good merits,   209
because He is good. He is able to condemn no man without evil deserts, because He   618
is just. An infant of eight days has no evil deserts from sins of his own. Why would he be
condemned if he were not circumcised (8), unless he contracted sin from his origin?

1902
[4, 3, 16]

But you, most bitter enemies of grace that you are, oppose us with examples of   727
impious men, "who," you say, "though strangers to faith, abound in virtues in   650
which, without the help of grace, there is only the good of nature, granted that it is
enslaved by superstitions. Such men," you say, "by the powers alone of their
innate liberty, are frequently found to be merciful and modest and chaste and sober."
But when you say this, only see: you have already taken away what you should
attribute to the grace of God: namely, the effectiveness of will. . . . How much   654
better, if it pleases you to praise the impious so much that you say they abound even
in true virtues,—as if you did not hear the Scriptures saying: "Whoever says the
impious man is righteous, cursed shall he be among the people and hated among
the tribes (9),"—how much better, I say, if you were to confess that even these
virtues that you find in them are the gifts of God.

1903
[4, 3, 17]

But perish the thought that there is any true virtue in anyone who is not just. And   650
perish the thought that anyone is truly just unless he lives by faith; for, "He that is   654
just lives by faith (10)." Who, then, of those, who wish to have it that they are
Christians, except the Pelagians alone, or, perhaps, even you alone among the
Pelagians, has ever called the unbeliever just, has ever called the impious man just, has
ever called a man in bondage to the devil just?

1903a
[4, 3, 19]

For all men would not, by a natural instinct, wish to be immortal and happy unless   370
they were able to attain it. But this highest good cannot come to men except through   383
Christ and Him crucified, by whose death death is conquered, by whose wounds our
nature is healed.

1904
[4, 3, 21]

You certainly know that virtues must be distinguished from vices not by their   654
functions but by their ends. The function is that which is to be done; but the end is   540
that on account of which it is to be done. When a man does something in which he
seems not to sin, if he does not do it on account of that on account of which he ought
to do it, he is convicted of sinning. Taking no heed of this, you separated the ends
from the functions and said that the functions, apart from the ends, are to be called   630
virtues. . . . Whatever a man does that seems to be good, and does not do it on account
of that on account of which true wisdom directs that it ought to be done, although
it seem good by reason of its function, it is not right in view of its end, and it is a sin (11).

1905
[4, 3, 25]

Their thoughts will defend these unbelievers on the day of judgment, so that they   651
will be punished more tolerably, because in some way they did naturally the things that   654
are of the law, having the work of the law written in their hearts (12) to this extent,
that they did not do to others what they would not wish to endure. But even in this they

were sinners, because, being men without faith, they did not refer their works to that end to which they ought to have referred them.

1906

[4, 8, 44]

"No one is able to come to Me, unless it be given him by My Father (13)." All   201
who are saved, therefore, and who come to a recognition of the truth (14), are saved by His willing it, and they come to the truth by His willing it. For even those who, like infants, have not yet the use of willing choice, are regenerated by Him by whose creating of them they were generated; and those who already use their choice of will are not able to will except by the will and by the assistance of Him by whom the will is prepared (15).

1907

[5, 3, 12]

When, therefore, a man is said to be given up to his desires, he thereby becomes   722
guilty, because, deserted by God, he yields and consents to his desires, and is conquered, seized, bound, and possessed by them. For by whatever a man is overcome, to this also he is forfeit as a slave (16); and the consequent sin becomes his punishment for the preceding sin. . . . We could recount many other (17) examples which clearly show that perversity of heart comes from a hidden judgment of God, with the result that the refusal to hear the truth leads to commission of sin, and that sin itself is also punishment for the preceding sin.

1908

[5, 11, 44]

Who can doubt that infants who are not baptized, and who have only original sin   618
unaggravated by any personal sins of their own, will be given the lightest condemnation of all (18)? Although I am not able to define the kind and degree of their punishment, I still do not dare to say that it were better for them never to have existed at all than to exist there.

1909

[5, 11, 45]

It is not to be supposed that the servants of God, before circumcision was given them,—   793
since, indeed, faith in a Mediator who was to come in the flesh did exist among them,—did not help their children by any sacrament of His, although for some necessary reason Scripture wished to conceal what that sacrament was. For we read even of their sacrifices, in which certainly that Blood is typified (19) which alone takes away the sin of the world.

1910

[6, 13, 40]

You state that I said grace does not make a man entirely new. I do not say that;   751
so listen carefully to what I do say: Grace makes a man utterly new, since it leads him even to immortality of body and full happiness. Now, it even renews (20) a man perfectly, to the extent that it achieves his deliverance from absolutely all sins, but not to such an extent as if it were to achieve his deliverance from all evils and from every corruption of mortality, by which the body is now a burden to the soul.

1911

[6, 16, 49]

But you, who think that if concupiscence were evil it would be absent in one who is baptized,—you are much mistaken. Every sin is absent in the baptized, but not every evil. It can be expressed more clearly thus: All guilt of all evils, but not all evils themselves, are absent from the baptized.

617

1912

[6, 19, 60]

I did say, to be sure: "Just as sins which pass away in their action, remain in their guilt, so too, contrariwise, it is possible that concupiscence remains in act and passes away in guilt (21)." . . . I spoke of the concupiscence which is in the members and makes war against the law of the mind (22), even though its guilt has passed away in the remission of all sins; just as, on the contrary, when a sacrifice is made to idols, if it is not afterwards repeated, it passes away in respect to its action, but remains in respect to its guilt, unless it is remitted through forgiveness (23).

640

1. John Chrysostom.
2. *perfuncti fideliter suae dispensationis laboribus.*
3. *multitudo popularis.*
4. If I do not err, this is the first recorded usage of the full and specific expression *patres ecclesiae*.
5. These are to be identified as Irenaeus of Lyons, Cyprian of Carthage, Reticius of Autun; Olympius, a bishop of Spain, who wrote against the Priscillianists; Hilary of Poitiers, Ambrose of Milan, Gregory of Nazianz, and Basil the Great.
6. *unde nemo eruit.*
7. Rom. 7:23.
8. He says circumcised because he has been speaking of Isaac, who was circumcised on the eighth day as a sign of the Baptism that would be. In speaking of circumcision, then, he refers by type or analogy to Baptism.
9. Prov. 24:24.
10. Rom. 1:17.
11. *etsi officio videatur bonum, ipso non recto fine peccatum est.*
12. Rom. 2:14-15.
13. John 6:66.
14. 1 Tim. 2:4.
15. See Prov. 8:35 in the Septuagint.
16. 2 Peter 2:19.
17. We have omitted the several examples he did give.
18. *in damnatione omnium levissima futuros.*
19. *figurabatur.*
20. *innovat.* In regard to the use of this interesting term, see note 1 to § 601a above in Vol. 1, the present passage being confirmatory of our linguistic conclusions in that place.
21. This is by no means a direct quote, but the substance still of Augustine's *Marriage and Concupiscence* 1, 26, 29: § 1873 above.
22. Rom. 7:23.
23. *per indulgentiam.*

THE ENCHIRIDION OF FAITH, HOPE, AND LOVE [A. D. 421]

Augustine entitles this work, written in 421 A. D., *De fide, spe, caritate liber unus*; but he also knows it as an *enchiridion*, the title which it is most often given. In his *Corrections* 2, 89, he says hardly more of it than: "I wrote also a book on faith, hope, and love, when the person to whom I addressed it [Lawrence] had asked me if he could have a work of mine to keep at hand, of the kind the Greeks call an enchiridion. In this work I have covered with sufficient diligence, I think, how God is to be worshipped, which divine Scripture defines as man's true wisdom."

The term *enchiridion* is the Greek equivalent of *handbook* or *manual*. The Lawrence for whom it was written was a Roman layman. The full title of the work in Latin is usually given as *Enchiridion ad Laurentium de fide, spe, et caritate liber unus*.

The Maurist text in Migne PL 40, 231-290, is now superseded by the edition of E. Evans in the *Corpus Christianorum*, Vol. 46 (1969), pp. 49-114.

1913

[2, 7]

Faith believes, hope and love pray. But without faith, the other two cannot exist; so faith also prays. That is why it is written: "How will they call upon Him in whom they have not believed (1)?" [8] What can be hoped for that is not believed? Yet, something can be believed that is not hoped for. For who of the faithful does not believe in the punishments of the impious? Yet, he does not hope for those punishments.   582

1914

[9, 32]

If no Christian will dare to say, "It is a question of man's willing, not of God's showing mercy," lest he quite openly contradict the Apostle, it but remains that the proper understanding of the saying: "It is not a matter of willing nor of running, but of God's being merciful (2)," is that the whole is attributed to God, who both prepares man's good will to help, and helps it when it has been prepared. For man's good will precedes many of God's good gifts, but not all of them; and it must itself be counted among those which it does not precede. For each of the following is to be found in the Holy Scriptures (3): "His mercy shall come before me (4)," and "His mercy shall follow me (5)." It comes before one who does not will, so that he may will; and it follows one who wills, so that his willing may not be in vain.   650 692 691

1915

[10, 33]

"For we have been by nature sons of wrath, just like the rest (6)." Since men were under this wrath because of original sin (7), so much the more grave and pernicious as were the sins added to it greater and more numerous (8), there was need of a mediator, that is, a reconciler, who would appease this wrath by the oblation of the singular sacrifice of which all the sacrifices of the Law and of the Prophets were but shadows.   363 380

1916

[13, 41]

Begotten or conceived (9), therefore, without any pleasure of carnal concupiscence, and, therefore with no original inheritance of sin (10), joined and formed by the grace of God in a marvelous and inexpressible way in a unity of person with the Word, the Father's onlybegotten Son not by grace but by nature, He Himself could commit no sin. But because of the likeness of the flesh of sin (11) in which He came, He was Himself called sin (12), who was to be sacrificed for a washing away of sin. . . . The Apostle says that God, to whom we needed to be reconciled, "for our sake made Him who knew no sin," that is, Christ, "to be sin (13)," that is, a sacrifice for sin, by means of which we are enabled to be reconciled. He, therefore, became sin, that we might become justice; not our justice, but God's; not justice in us, but in Him; just as the sin He became was not His own but ours.   344 346 340 324 345 383

1917

[16, 61]

Christ did not die for the angels. Yet, whatever was done to redeem and liberate 370
mankind from evil through His death was done also for the angels, since they too 371
are somehow affected by a return to grace after the enmity which sins had made
between men and the holy angels; and from the redemption itself of mankind the
damages done by the fall of the angels are repaired.

1918

[17, 64]

With the exception of the gift of Baptism, which is given against original sin, so 836
that what was brought by generation might be taken away by regeneration,—though 615
it also takes away actual sins (14), such as have ever been committed in thought, word,
or deed (15),—except, therefore, for this great indulgence whereby man's restoration
begins and in which all his guilt, both original and actual, is removed (16), the rest
of our life from the age of the use of reason, however much that life may abound 658
in righteousness, is always in need of the forgiveness of sins. . . . From the fact, 633
however, that every crime is a sin, it does not follow that every sin is a crime. Certainly
we say that the lives of holy men, though they lived in this mortal body, can be
found to have been without crime; but the Apostle says plainly: "If we say we have
no sin we deceive ourselves, and the truth is not in us (17)."

1919

[17, 65]

Yet those who do penance in accord with the kind of sin they have committed 901
are not to despair of receiving God's mercy in the Holy Church, for the remission of their
crimes, however serious. In the penitential action, however, where the crime committed
was such that he who committed it is separated from the body of Christ, it is not so much 911
the length of time as the depth of sorrow that is to be considered.

1920

[18, 69]

That there should be some such fire even after this life is not incredible, and it can 1000
be inquired into and either be discovered or left hidden whether some of the faithful may be
saved, some more slowly and some more quickly in the greater or lesser degree in which
they loved the good things that perish,—through a certain purgatorial fire (18).

1921

[19, 71]

For the daily sins of the brief and trivial kind without which this life cannot be 929
lived, the daily prayer of the faithful makes satisfaction. The faithful can say: "Our 658
Father, who art in heaven (19)"; for to such a Father they are already reborn of 811
water and the Spirit (20). This prayer takes away completely our lesser and daily sins.

1922

[23, 84]

A Christian ought in no way doubt that the flesh of all men who have been born 1012
and who will be born, and who have died and who will die, will rise again.

1922a

[23, 86]

Accordingly, it can be investigated and disputed most meticulously among the   1012
most learned men,—though I know not whether man can find an answer:—when it is that a
human being in the womb begins to live, and whether there is also a certain kind of hidden
life there which is not yet apparent in the movements of the living being. It seems very rash
to deny that those fetuses (21) ever lived, that are cut away and ejected limb by limb from
the wombs of the pregnant, lest the mothers perish too, if the fetuses be left there dead. But
from whatever time a man begins to live, from that time on certainly he is able to die; and I
am not able to discover any reason for denying that the resurrection of the dead pertains to
anyone who has died, no matter where his death occurred.

1923

[23, 89]

If a statue of some kind of soluble metal should either be melted by fire, or   1013
pounded into powder, or squeezed into a lump, and an artisan wished to make it over from
that same quantity of metal, whichever particles of metal were restored to whichever part of
the statue would be of no consequence to its integrity, so long as the restored statue took
up the whole of that material of which it was originally composed. So too, God, the
wonderful and inexpressible Artisan, will, with a wonderful and inexpressible speed, restore
our flesh from the whole of the material of which it was constituted, and it will make no
difference to its reconstruction whether hairs go back to hairs and nails go back to nails, or
whatever of these had perished be changed to flesh and be assigned to other parts of the
body, while the providence of the Artisan will take care that nothing unseemly result.

1924

[23, 93]

Surely the lightest punishment of all will be given those who, besides the sin   618
which they brought with them originally, have added no other; and among the rest   1035
who have added other sins, damnation there will be so much the more tolerable as
their wickedness here was the less serious.

1925

[24, 95]

What is hidden now will not be hidden then, when of two infants one will be taken   205
for mercy and the other left for judgment, and he that is taken will know what would
have been his due through judgment, if mercy had not intervened: why this one
rather than the other was taken up, when the situation of both was the same; why
powerful works (22) were not done among some, when, if they had been done, those
men would have done penance, while they were worked among others who were not
going to believe anyway. For this our Lord says most plainly: "Woe to you, Corozain!
Woe to you, Bethsaida! because if the powerful works done in you had been done in
Tyre and Sidon, they would long since have done penance in sackcloth and ashes (23)."   695
Certainly there was no injustice in God's not willing them to be saved, when they
were able to be saved if He had willed it (24).

1926

[25, 98]

Who would be so impious and so foolish as to say that God could not have converted   696 to good the wicked wills of men, those which He willed, when He willed, and where He willed? But when He does this, He does it through mercy.

1927

[27, 103]

When we hear and read in the sacred writings that God wills all men to be saved, while we are certain that not all men are saved, we must not on that account disparage in any way the almightiest (25) will of God. Rather, what is written, ''Who wills all men to be saved (26),'' we ought to understand as meaning that no man is saved except him whom He wills to be saved, and not that there is no man whom He does not will to be saved, but that no man is saved except him whom He wills to be saved; and therefore His willing it is to be sought in prayer, because if He wills it, so it must be. . . . Otherwise, ''He wills all men to be saved'' is said not as meaning that there is no man whom He does not will to be saved,—He who willed not to work powerful miracles among those of whom it is said that they would have done penance if He had worked those miracles,—but in such a way that by ''all men'' we are to understand every kind of man, by whatever groupings they be classified: kings and private persons, noblemen and base-born, the high and the humble, the learned and the untutored, those of sound body and the weak; the quick, the slow-witted, and the simple; the rich, the poor, and the middle class; husbands and wives; infants, children, adolescents, young people, middle-aged, and the old; people of every language, people of every custom, people in all the arts, people in all the professions, constituted in a numberless variety of wills and consciences, and according to whatever other differences can be found among men.

201

1928

[28, 104]

God would have been willing to maintain even the first man in that state of salvation in which he had been created and, at a fitting time after that man had begotten children, to lead him, without the intervention of death, to a better state, where not only would that man not commit sin, but he would not even have a desire to sin,—if God had foreseen in him a steadfast will to continue, as he was made, without sin. But because God foresaw that that man would make a wicked use of free choice, that is, that he would sin, God rather prepared His own will so that He would do well by that man even when that man did evil; and thus the good will of the Almighty would not be forestalled by the evil will of man, but would nevertheless be fulfilled.

522

191

1929

[28, 108)

When Adam was made, being a righteous man, he had no need of a Mediator. But when sins separated the human race far from God, it was necessary for us to be reconciled to God, even for the sake of the resurrection of the flesh to life eternal, through that Mediator who alone was born, lived, and was slain without sin. This was necessary so that human pride could be convicted and healed by the humility of God; and so that man might be shown how far he had departed from God, when through God made flesh he was called back; and so that to contumacious man a model of obedience might be provided by the God-man; and so that with the Onlybegotten taking the form of a slave, which form had no antecedent merit, a source of grace might be opened and the resurrection of the flesh, promised to the redeemed, might

360
363
387
344

373
375

be demonstrated in advance by the Redeemer Himself; and so that the Devil might be
conquered by that very nature which he rejoiced in having deceived.

1930

[29, 109]
   The time which interposes between the death of a man and the final resurrection   996
holds souls in hidden retreats, accordingly as each is deserving of rest or of hardship,
in view of what it merited when it was living in the flesh. [110] Nor can it be denied   1000
that the souls of the dead find relief through the piety of their friends and relatives who   1001
are still alive (27), when the Sacrifice of the Mediator is offered for them, or when   897
alms are given in the church. But these things are of profit to those who, when they   387
were alive, merited that they might afterwards be able to be helped by these things.
For there is a certain manner of living, neither so good that there is no need of these helps
after death, nor yet so wicked that these helps are of no avail after death. There is, indeed,
a manner of living so good that these helps are not needed, and again a manner so evil that
these helps are of no avail, once a man has passed from this life.

1931

[29, 111]
   After the resurrection, however, when the universal and final judgment has been   1042
made, two cities will have their boundaries: one, of course, of Christ, and the other   1043
of the Devil; one of the good, the other of the wicked; yet both made up of angels
and of men. For the one group there will be no will to sin, and for the other, no
power to do so; nor will there be any possibility of dying. The former will be living
truly and happily in eternal life; the latter will be enduring unhappily in eternal death   1034
without the power to die; for both shall be without end. Among the former one man
will be more pre-eminent in happiness than another; and among the latter the   1046
abiding misery of one man will be more tolerable than that of another.   1035

1932

[29, 112]
   In vain, therefore, do some men, indeed, very many, because of human sentiment,   1034
bewail the eternal punishment of the damned and their perpetual, unending torments,
without really believing that it shall be so. . . . But let them suppose, if it pleases
them, that the punishments of the damned are, at certain periods of time, somewhat   1036
mitigated. For even thus it can be understood that they remain in the wrath of God (28),   1031
that is, in damnation itself,—for it is this that is called the wrath of God, not some
disturbance in the divine mind:—that in His wrath, that is, by their abiding in
His wrath, He does not shut up His mercies; yet, He does not put an end to their
eternal punishment, but only applies or interposes some relief to their torments.

1933

[31, 117]
   Now as to love, which the Apostle says is greater than the other two, that is, than   591
faith and hope (29), so much the better is he in whom it is found. For when it is
asked whether someone is a good man, it is not asked what he believes or what
he hopes for, but what he loves. For if someone loves rightly, without a doubt he   592
believes and hopes rightly. But someone who does not love believes in vain even if what   585
he believes is true; and he hopes in vain, even if what he hopes for is rightly taught

as pertaining to true happiness—unless he believes and hopes for this also, that through prayer it may be given him to love. . . . This, however, is the faith of Christ which the Apostle commends, which works through love (30); and for whatever it does not yet have in love, it asks and receives, seeks and finds, knocks so that it will be opened to it (31). Faith asks and obtains what the law commands. For without the Gift of God, that is, without the Holy Spirit, through whom love is poured out into our hearts (32), the law could command but could not help. Moreover, the law could make a man a transgressor, who could not excuse himself on grounds of ignorance. Where there is no love of God, carnal desire does reign.

655

1. Rom. 10:14.
2. Rom. 9:16.
3. *in sanctis eloquiis.*
4. Ps. 58[59]:11.
5. Ps. 22[23]:6.
6. Eph. 2:3.
7. *per originale peccatum.*
8. Elsewhere Augustine seems to make concupiscence an actual part of original sin, rather than a result thereof; and in such a view, since practice in sinning will increase the concupiscible appetite, the present statement is perfectly logical.
9. *seminatus sive conceptus.*
10. *et ideo nullum peccatum originaliter trahens.*
11. Rom. 8:3.
12. 2 Cor. 5:21.
13. 2 Cor. 5:21. In the part omitted Augustine has explained that *"Is qui non noverat peccatum pro nobis peccatum fecit"* is a faulty manuscript reading of the Scripture, which correctly reads: *"Eum qui non noverat peccatum pro nobis peccatum fecit."* The difference between *is* and *eum* here is tremendous, a whole theology hanging thereupon. The incorrect reading could only be translated: *"He who knew no sin committed sin on our behalf."*
14. *activa . . . peccata.*
15. *quaecumque corde ore opere commissa invenerit.*
16. *omnis reatus et ingeneratus et additus.*
17. 1 John 1:8.
18. *per ignem quemdam purgatorium.*
19. Matt. 6:9.
20. John 3:5.
21. *puerperia.*
22. *virtutes* = miracles.
23. Matt. 11:21.
24. We have followed the reading: *"Nec utique Deus iniuste noluit salvos fieri, cum possent salvi esse si vellet."* This seems to be the reading attested by the better part of the manuscript evidence, though the reading *". . . si vellent—(if they had willed it),"* is also well-attested. The original Maurist edition read *vellet;* but many of those who otherwise reprinted it, including the Abbé Migne, changed this reading to *vellent. Vellet* is the reading known to Peter Lombard; and it was favored by several editors besides the Maurists, notably Antonius Arnaldus (Paris, 1648), J. B. Faure (Rome 1755), and Otto Scheel (Tübingen 1903). The most recent editor, E. Evans in the *Corpus Christianorum*, Vol. 46 (1969), p. 99, reads *vellent,* with *vellet* in the apparatus. *Vellent* is perhaps less startling at first; but I think Augustine would not have said it in that way, lest it give a handle to Pelagianism; I have preferred *vellet* because it seems to me that it is better suited to Augustine's theology; and in any case, it does seem to have the better manuscript evidence. Otto Scheel has remarked that this passage is one of the very few in Augustine wherein a variant manuscript reading is of any theological consequence.
25. *omnipotentissimae.*
26. 1 Tim. 2:4.
27. *pietate suorum viventium.*
28. John 3:36.
29. 1 Cor. 13:13.
30. Gal. 5:6.
31. Matt. 7:7.
32. Rom. 5:5.

THE CARE THAT SHOULD BE TAKEN OF THE DEAD [*A. D.* 421]

Augustine's treatise *De cura pro mortuis gerenda*, written in 421 A. D., was in reply, as Augustine remarks in his *Corrections* 2, 90, to a question posed to him by Paulinus of Nola.

A noble lady named Flora had asked Paulinus to bury her son Cynegius in the pilgrimage church of St. Felix. After Paulinus had complied with her request, she began to have some doubts about the matter, and returned to ask him whether being buried at the shrine of the saint would be of any advantage to her son. Paulinus replied without hesitation that it would; but on more careful consideration of the matter he too began to have some doubts, and wrote to Augustine for his views. Augustine's reply agreed with what Paulinus himself had suggested: the place of burial is of no consequence in itself; but solicitude for it on the part of the loved ones left behind shows a certain faith which will also prompt them to pray for him; and such prayers will profit him if he had sufficient merit in his own life to make those prayers of any avail to him now. In other words, those prayers will profit him, unless he was so wicked that he is already damned. Furthermore, proximity to a place of pilgrimage will probably prompt visitors who see his grave to pray for him.

The Maurist text in Migne (PL 40, 591-610) is now superseded by J. Zycha's edition in Vol. 41 (1900) of the Vienna Corpus.

1934

[1, 3]

We read in the books of the Maccabees (1) that sacrifice was offered for the dead. But even if it were found nowhere in the Old Testament writings, the authority of the universal Church which is clear on this point is of no small weight, where in the prayers of the priest poured forth to the Lord God at His altar the commendation of the dead has its place.

1001

1934a

[2, 4]

A cheap funeral or none at all is of no disadvantage to a good man.

991

1935

[15, 18]

The spirits of the dead are able to know some things which happen here, which it is necessary for them to know. And those for whom it is necessary that something be known, not only the present or the past but even the future,—they know these things by the revealing Spirit of God, just as not all men but the Prophets, while they lived, knew not all things but those only which the providence of God judged ought to be revealed to them.

122

1. See 2 Macc. 12:43.

GRACE AND FREE CHOICE [*A. D.* 426 *aut* 427]

In 418 A. D. Augustine had written a letter to Sixtus, afterwards Pope Sixtus III, on the errors of Pelagianism. In this letter Augustine had declared: "When God crowns our merits, He is crowning nothing else but His own gifts to us" (see § 1452 above).

About the year 426 a copy of the letter came into the hands of Florus, a monk of the community at Hadrumetum (the present day city of Sousse in Tunisia). When, unknown to Valentine, the superior at Hadrumetum, the letter was read to uninstructed and less discerning members of the community, it caused a great stir. Some denied that it could be an authentic writing of Augustine; others were content to object that their personal efforts toward virtue were certainly their own.

Valentine then sought to restore peace by seeking an explanation from Augustine himself. While providing explanations both orally and by letter (see § 1455 above), Augustine at the same time set about writing his *De gratia et libero arbitrio ad Valentinum et cum illo monachos* or *Grace and Free Choice*. The work may be dated in 426 or 427.

The Maurist text, reprinted in Migne PL 44, 881-912, remains at present the standard edition.

1936

[5, 12]

Lest it might be supposed that the will itself were able to do anything good without the grace of God, when Paul said: "His grace in me has not been empty, but I have labored more than all of them," he immediately added a further remark and said: "Not I, however, but the grace of God that is with me" (1); that is to say, "I am not alone, but the grace of God is with me"; and accordingly, it is not the grace alone of God, nor Paul alone, but the grace of God along with him. It was by God's grace alone, however, that Paul was called upon from heaven, and was converted by so great and efficacious a call (2); for Paul's deserts were great, but they were evil.

650

690

656

1937

[6, 14]

"There remains," he says, "a crown of justice for me, which the Lord, the just Judge, will give me on that day" (3). To whom would the just Judge give a crown, if the merciful Father had not given His grace? And how could that crown be one of justice, if grace, which makes the impious just, had not gone before?

650

771

1938

[7, 16]

"I have fought the good fight," he says, "I have finished the race, I have kept the faith" (4). First of all, those good works, if they had not been preceded by good thoughts, would be nothing at all. Note, then, what he says about those very thoughts. Writing to the Corinthians, he says: "Not as if we have strength of ourselves to think anything, as from ourselves; but our sufficiency is from God" (5).

650

692

1939

[13, 25]

Could nature itself be grace? Yet the Pelagians have dared to say even this, that grace is the nature in which we have been created, so that we have a rational mind by which we are able to understand, and we are made in the image of God, so that we have dominion over the fish of the sea and the birds of the sky and over all the beasts that crawl on the land. But this is not the grace which the Apostle commends through faith in Jesus Christ. For it is certain that we have this nature in common with the impious and the

710

726

unbelieving. But grace through faith in Jesus Christ is found only in those who have that very faith.

1940

[14, 29]

    If faith pertains only to free choice and is not given by God, why, in regard to those who do not want to believe, do we pray that they may come to believe? It would be utterly useless for us to do this if we were not entirely correct in our belief that even wills that are perverse and hostile to faith can be converted to belief by God Almighty.

656
713
696

1941

[16, 32]

    It is certain that we do keep the commandments, if we will to do so; but because the will is prepared by the Lord (6), we must ask Him to give our wills such a strength as will suffice for putting our will into action. It is certain that in willing anything, it is we that do the willing; but it is He that enables us to will what is good. . . . It is certain that in doing anything, it is we that act; but it is He that enables us to act, by His bestowing efficacious powers upon our will.

712
655
690

1942

[17, 33]

    However small and imperfect it may have been, love was not absent in Peter when he said to the Lord: "I will lay down my life for You" (7); for he thought he was able to do what he knew he willed to do. And who was it who began to impart to him that initial love, if not He that prepares our will and, by His coöperation, perfects in us the operation He begins? For He that first effects in us the power to will is the same who coöperates in bringing to perfection that which we will (8). . . . God, then, gives us the power to will, without our coöperation; but when we will, and will in such a way that we act, He coöperates with us; but without His effecting in us the power to will and without His coöperating with us when we will, we would be able to do no good works of piety.

692
691

1943

[18, 37]

    All these precepts concerning charity, which is love,—precepts whose nature and importance is such that whatever a man supposed he was doing well, if he did it without charity, he would not be doing well at all,—all these precepts of love would be given to men to no purpose at all if men did not have free choice of will.

598
653

1. 1 Cor. 15:10.
2. See Acts 9:1ff.
3. 2 Tim. 4:8.
4. 2 Tim. 4:7.
5. 2 Cor. 3:5
6. Prov. 8:35 in the Septuagint: ἑτοιμάζεται θέλησις παρὰ κυρίου—praeparatur voluntas a Domino.
7. John 13:37.
8. Phil. 1:6.

ADMONITION AND GRACE [*A. D.* 426 *aut* 427]

Like the *De gratia et libero arbitrio*, Augustine addressed also his *De correptione et gratia* to Valentine and his monks at Hadrumetum: so he stated in the final entry in his *Corrections* (2, 93). He had heard that someone in Valentine's community said that a man should not be admonished or rebuked for not keeping the commandments, but only that prayer should be offered for his amendment.

Even in those days there were foolish monks who thought they should be allowed to do whatever they wanted to, and that it was wrong for a superior to rebuke them;—no one asked whether a superior should not then have the same rights, and if rebuking their faults pleasured his will, what then?—he should only pray for them. They would have thought it very hard of him, no doubt, were he to have replied: "But if rebuking you is the thing I want to be free to do, why do you rebuke me for rebuking you? That is very wrong of you, and you should only pray for me!"

The Migne reprint of the Maurist edition in PL 44, 915-946 remains at present the standard edition.

1944

[6, 9]

But if someone already regenerate and justified should, of his own will, relapse into   761
his evil life, certainly that man cannot say: "I have not received"; because he lost
the grace he received from God and by his own free choice went to evil.

1945

[7, 11]

If, as truth itself has said, no one is loosed from the condemnation which was made   568
through Adam, except through the faith of Jesus Christ; and if not even they will free
themselves from this condemnation who are able to say that they did not hear the
gospel of Christ, while faith depends upon hearing (1), how much the less will they
free themselves who want to say: "We did not receive perseverance!"? The excuse
would seem more just of those who say: "We did not receive hearing," than of
those who say: "We did not receive perseverance," because reply can be made: 670
"Man, in what you heard and kept, in that much you could have persevered if
you had willed"; but in no way can it be said: "That which you did not hear, you
might have believed if you had willed."

1946

[7, 12]

Consequently both those who have not heard the gospel and those who, having   204
heard it, and having been changed for the better, did not receive perseverance, as
well as those who, having heard the gospel, did not will to come to Christ,—that is,
who did not will to believe in Him, since He Himself said: "No one comes to Me
unless to do so has been given him by My Father (2),"—and those also who, because   618
of their tender age, were not able to believe, but who might have been absolved from
the original offense (3) by the sole washing of regeneration, but who, not having
received it, perished in death (4): none of these are separated from that lump (5)   208
which is known to be damned, as all are going, by reason of one (6), into condemnation.

1947

[7, 13]

Whoever they be who are separated from the original damnation by the largesse of   202
divine grace, there is no doubt that hearing the gospel is also procured for them, and
when they hear, they believe; and they persevere to the end in the faith which operates
through love (7); and being admonished, if sometimes they stray, they amend their   673
ways; and some of them, even if they are not admonished by men, return to the path
which they left; and others of them, having received grace at whatever age, are
removed from the dangers of this life by the swiftness of death.

1948

[7, 14]

For whosoever they are that are chosen, without doubt they too are called. But not   206
all who are called are consequently chosen. These, therefore, are chosen, as has
often been stated, who are called according to God's purpose, who also are predestined   703
and foreknown (8). If any of these perishes, God is mistaken; but none of them
perishes because God does not err.

1949

[7, 16]

God knows who are his (9). The faith of these, which works through love (10),   694
assuredly either does not fail at all, or, if for some it does fail, it is restored to them
before this life is finished, and when the iniquity which intervened has been blotted
out, perseverance is granted them even to the end. But those who are not going to   208
persevere, and who thus are going to fall away from Christian faith and conduct (11) so
that the end of this life shall find them in such a state, certainly are not to be reckoned
in the number of the elect, even at a time when they are living piously and well.
For they are not separated from that mass of perdition (12) by the foreknowledge and
predestination of God. And therefore neither are they called according to God's   206
purpose (13); and consequently neither are they chosen. Rather, they are called with
those of whom it is said: "Many are called," and not among those of whom it is
said: "but few are chosen (14)." . . . [8, 17] If you ask me why God did not give   205
perseverance to those to whom He gave that love by which they might live in a
Christian manner, I can only answer that I do not know.

1950

[10, 27]

Certain angels, the leader of whom is he that is called the devil, have by their own   486
free choice been made outcasts from the Lord God. While fleeing His goodness, in   491
which they had been blessed, they could not likewise escape His judgment, through
which they have been made most wretched. Others, however, through the same free   490
will stood fast in the truth, and merited to know the most certain truth that they   1043
themselves would never fall.

1951

[10, 28]

But because Adam was, of his free choice, untrue to God, he experienced the just   614
judgment of God, so that he was condemned with his whole progeny which, since
as yet it was all still in him, sinned along with him. For as many of this progeny as are 203

delivered by the grace of God are certainly delivered from a condemnation in which
they were already bound. And even if no one were delivered from it, no one could
justly blame God's just judgment. That in comparison, therefore, to those who perish,   207
few are delivered, while in absolute numbers it is many who are delivered, is
effected by grace; it is gratuitously effected; and gracious thanks must be given because
it is effected (15), lest anyone be praised as if for merits of his own; but every mouth
be stopped (16), and whoever glories, let him glory in the Lord (17).

1952

[11, 29]

What then? Did Adam not have God's grace? Yes, he had it in great degree, but of   694
a different kind. He was the possessor of good things, which he received from the   525
largesse of his Creator; for he had not gotten those good things, in which he suffered
no evil at all, by his own merits. But saints in this life, to whom this grace of deliverance
belongs, are in the midst of evils out of which they cry aloud to the Lord: "Deliver
us from evil! (18)." In the midst of those good things Adam had no need of the death
of Christ; but the saints in the midst of evils are absolved from guilt, both hereditary
and personal, by the Blood of the Lamb. Adam had no need of that assistance which   521
they implore when they say: "I see another law in my members, waging war against the
law of my mind, and making me prisoner to the law of sin that is in my members.
Wretched man that I am, who will deliver me from the body of this death? The grace of
God through Jesus Christ our Lord! (19)." But Adam, tempted and disturbed in no such
conflict of himself against himself, enjoyed peace with himself in that place of happiness
(20).

1953

[11, 30]

God, therefore, took upon Himself our nature (21), that is, the rational soul and   312
flesh of the man Christ, in an undertaking that was singularly marvelous or marvelously   320
singular, so that, with no preceding merits of its own righteousness, it would be the
Son of God from the very beginning when it began to be Man, so that the Man and
the Word that is without beginning would be one person (22). . . . It was in no way   343
to be feared that the human nature taken up in that indescribable manner into a unity
of person by God the Word (23) would sin by the free choice of its will, since that   324
taking up itself was such that the nature of man so taken up by God would admit in
itself no movement of an evil will.

1954

[11, 31]

The first man did not have that grace by which he would never will to be evil; but   694
surely he had that in which, if he willed to remain, he would never be evil, and   700
without which, even by free choice, he could not be good, but which, nevertheless,
by free choice, he could forsake. Neither, then, did God will him to be without His   650
grace, which He left within that man's free choice. Free choice, therefore, suffices for
evil, but is too little for good, unless it be assisted by good that is almighty. If man   721
had not forsaken that assistance by his free choice, he would have been good always;   693
but he did forsake it and he was forsaken. For such was the nature of this assistance
that he could forsake it if he so willed and he could remain in it if he so willed; but it was
not such that it would bring it about that he would so will.

1955

[11, 32]

    God, therefore, gave man a good will, because He made him in that will when He   693
made him upright. He gave man assistance without which man could not continue in that   694
will even if he would; but that he would, God left to his free choice. Man was able,   700
therefore, to continue if he would, because the assistance was not lacking whereby he   670
was able, and without which he would not be able, to persevere in holding to the good
that he might will. But because he willed not to continue, certainly the blame is his
whose merit it would have been if he had willed to continue. It was the same with   491
the holy angels, who themselves, when others were falling by free choice, by the   490
same free choice stood firm; and they merited by this continuance to receive a due
reward (24), to wit, such a fullness of happiness as includes the utter certainty of
remaining in it always. . . . By this grace of God there is in us, in receiving good and   684
in perseveringly holding to it, not only the ability to do what we will, but even to will   695
to do what we are able. This was not the case with the first man; for the former of
these things was in him, but the latter was not.

1956

[12, 33]

    We must consider diligently and carefully how these pairs differ among themselves: 695
to be able not to sin, and not to be able to sin; to be able not to die, and not to be able   522
to die; to be able not to forsake good, and not to be able to forsake good. For the first man
was able not to sin, able not to die, able not to forsake good. . . . The first   1042
freedom of will, therefore, was to be able not to sin; but the last will be much greater,
not to be able to sin. The first immortality was to be able not to die; the last will be   670
much greater, not to be able to die. The first power of perseverance was to be able
not to forsake good; the last will be the happiness of perseverance, not to be able   671
to forsake good. But if the last blessings will be preferable and better, were the
first ones on that account not blessings at all or but trifling ones?

1957

[12, 34]

    The aids themselves, moreover, must be distinguished. The assistance without   693
which something does not come to pass is one thing, and the assistance by which
something does come to pass is another. For without food we cannot live; and yet, although
food be at hand, it does not cause a man to live if he should will to die. The assistance of
food, therefore, is that without which it does not come to pass that we live, not that by
which it does come to pass that we live. But indeed, when the happiness which a man does
not have is given him, he immediately becomes happy. For this is an assistance not only
without which a thing does not come to pass but also by which that does come to pass for
the sake of which it was given. On this account that assistance is both by the which a thing
comes to pass and without the which it does not come to pass; because both propositions
are true: if happiness be given a man, he immediately becomes happy; and if it is never
given him, he will never be happy.

1958

[12, 38]

    And thus God willed that His saints should not, in respect even to perseverance in   672
good, glory in their own strength, but in Himself, who gives them not only such
assistance as He gave the first man, without which they could not persevere even

if they willed to, but He also works in them the will to persevere. . . . Aid, therefore,   696
is brought to the weakness of the human will, so that it might be affected firmly
and invincibly by divine grace; and thus, although weak, it will not fail nor be overcome
by any adversity (25).

1959

[13, 39]
    I say this (26) about those who are predestined in the kingdom of God, whose   206
number is so certain that no one can be added to them nor be taken away from them;   207
not of those who, when He had announced and had spoken, were multiplied beyond
number (27). For they can be said to have been called but not chosen, because they
were not called according to purpose (28).

1960

[13, 42]
    But those who do not belong to this number of the predestined . . . are judged   207
most justly according to their deserts. For either they lie under sin which they contracted   615
originally by their generation and go forth with that hereditary debt which was not
forgiven by regeneration, or they have added others besides through free choice: choice,
I say, and free; but not freed (29). . . . Or they receive God's grace, but they are   721
temporal (30) and do not persevere; they abandon it and are abandoned. For by free   672
will, since they have not received the gift of perseverance, they are sent away in
God's just and hidden judgment.

1961

[14, 43]
    Thus to will or not to will is in the power of him that wills or does not will, in such   700
wise that it does not thwart the divine will nor overcome the divine power. For
even in respect to those who do what He wills them not to do, He does what He wills
to do.

1962

[14, 44]
    And what is written, that "He wills all men to be saved (31)", while in fact not   201
all are saved, can certainly be understood in many ways, as we have noted in others of
our works (32). Here I will note but one way (33). The saying, "He wills all men
to be saved," is to be understood in reference to all the predestined; because every kind
of man is among them.

1963

[14, 45]
    It is not to be doubted, therefore, that human wills are unable to resist the will of   696
God, who "did all things whatsoever He willed, in heaven and on earth (34)," and
who "did even those things that are to come (35)," so as to prevent His doing what
He wills, when, even with the very wills of men, He does what He wills and when He
wills it, . . . having, without doubt, the almightiest power (36) of bending human
hearts as He pleases.

1964

[15, 47]

It can also be understood that "God wills all men to be saved (37)" in the sense that   201
He makes us to will it; just as it is said that "He sent the Spirit of His Son crying: Abba,
Father (38)!" when it is meant that the Spirit of His Son makes us cry, "Abba, Father!"

1. Rom. 10:17.
2. John 6:66.
3. *originalis noxa: i.e.,* original sin.
4. Logically, by reason of its grammatical construction, the passage should mean that because they did not receive Baptism
   they perished in death, that is, in spiritual death, meaning their souls were lost. But in fact Augustine probably means
   that they were not baptized because they died too soon to have had opportunity.
5. *conspersione.* A *conspersio* is a mass of dough. This is equivalent to the *massa* of the Ambrosiaster and to Augustine's
   massa damnata.
6. *I.e.,* Adam.
7. Gal. 5:6.
8. Rom. 8:28.
9. 2 Tim. 2:19.
10. Gal. 5:6.
11. *a fide Christiana et conversatione lapsuri sunt.*
12. *a massa illa perditionis.*
13. Rom. 8:28.
14. Matt. 20:16.
15. English cannot capture fully the wordplay of the Latin: *gratia fit, gratis fit, gratiae sunt agendae quia fit.*
16. Rom. 3:19.
17. 1 Cor. 1:31, quoting Jer. 9:24.
18. Matt. 6:13.
19. Rom. 7:23-25.
20. *in illo beatitudinis loco.*
21. *Deus ergo naturam nostram . . . suscepit.*
22. The "it" in this passage is the human nature that God took upon Himself. I am not entirely comfortable using a neuter
    pronoun here; but if "he" be used, it would tend to make it appear that the Word was simply superimposed upon an
    existing man. The Latin seems not to share the clumsiness that is inevitable in English: ". . . *ut nullis iustitiae suae
    precedentibus meritis Filius Dei sic esset ab initio quo esse homo coepisset, ut ipse et Verbum quod sine initio est una
    persona esset."*
23. *a Verbo Deo.*
24. *debitam mercedem.*
25. This is said not of the will in the generality of men, but of the will of those predestined to salvation.
26. See the final sentence in § 1958 immediately above, which is the antecedent of "this".
27. Ps. 39[40]:6. There is certainly a verbal reference here to the Psalm verse; but there is no similarity of context. The
    Psalm speaks of God's wonderful mercies when it says in the most literal of translations: "I have announced and have
    spoken: They have been multiplied beyond number."
28. The purpose referred to is God's purpose of salvation. Rom. 8:28.
29. *arbitrium, inquam, liberum, sed non liberatum.* We have free choice, but that free choice is not freed from responsibility
    and accountability.
30. *sed temporales sunt.* They are temporal creatures, temporally minded, destined not to live in eternity but to die in
    eternity.
31. 1 Tim. 2:4.
32. See §§ 1457, 1735, 1906, and 1927 above; and § 1964 below.
33. In § 1964 below he does in fact state another way.
34. Ps. 134[135]:6.
35. See Is. 45:11 in the Septuagint.
36. *omnipotentissimam potestatem.* Here only the language is bent a little along with hearts. Clement of Rome knew how to
    bend the knees of the heart. See § 27 above in Vol. 1, with its note.
37. 1 Tim. 2:4.
38. Gal. 4:6.

CORRECTIONS [*A. D.* 426 *aut* 427]

This work was never translated into English in its entirety until comparatively modern times. English speaking authors usually avoid the problem of what the title means by the simple expedient of referring to it by its Latin title, *Retractationes*. When it is mentioned in English and in the English translations now available it is invariably referred to either as *Retractations* or *Retractions*. The first is an affront to English and the second is incorrect. Actually Augustine had very little to retract, and the meaning of *Retractationes* is *Reconsiderations, Revisions, Second Thoughts* or, as I have called it, *Corrections*.

With the *Corrections*, Augustine again invented a new literary genre: a summation and criticism of his own writings. He had originally intended to include in his review his books, letters, and sermons. But when he had completed the review of his books in 426 or 427, he was persuaded to publish the work as it then stood, intending to write later a similar review of his letters and sermons. The latter laudable intention, most unfortunately, was never brought to fruition. If Augustine had succeeded in writing such a review of his letters and sermons, it would undoubtedly be of immense value in finding the solution to many a knotty problem of authenticity, especially in regard to the sermons.

There are several systems of numbering the chapters to the present work. We have followed that of Pius Knöll, whose critical edition in the Vienna Corpus, CSEL, Vol. 36 (1902), has superseded the Maurist edition, reprinted in Migne, PL 32, 583-656.

1965

[1, 1, 3]

Without doubt, therefore, the original direction of the happiness of the soul is   506
God Himself, who certainly did not beget it from Himself, but created it from no other thing, as He created the body from the earth. For what touches on its origin and how it comes to be in the body, whether it is from that man who was first created, when man was made into a living soul (1), or whether in a like fashion individual souls are created for individual men, I did not know then (2), nor do I know now.

1966

[1, 8, 6]

See how long it was before the Pelagian heresy came into existence that we argued as   650
if we were already disputing against them (3)! For while all good things, that is, the great, the intermediate, and the least, were said to come from God, the free choice of will is certainly found among the intermediate goods, because we can use it wrongly. . . . And because all good, as was said, the great, the intermediate, and the least are from God, it follows that even the good use of free will, which is virtue and enumerated among the great goods, is from God (4).

1967

[1, 8, 6]

The ignorance and difficulty from which every man suffers from the beginning of   612
his birth belong to the misery of just condemnation; nor is anyone freed from this evil except by the grace of God. Since they deny original sin, the Pelagians will not have   619
it that this misery comes from a just condemnation; although, even if ignorance and difficulty belong to man's primordial state, God is not to be blamed for it but praised.

1968

[1, 9, 2]

Just because I said: "This light, however, does not nourish the eyes of irrational
birds, but the pure hearts of those men who believe in God and turn from the love of
visible and temporal things to the fulfilling of His precepts; all men can do this if they
will (5)," the new Pelagian heretics are not to suppose that it was said in agreement
with them. For it is quite true that all men can do this if they will; but the will is
prepared by the Lord (6), and is strengthened so much by the gift of love that they
are thereby enabled. This was not stated here at that time (7), because it was not then
pertinent to the question under discussion.

724
656

1969

[1, 12, 5]

It is not absurd to call voluntary even that which in infants, who have not yet
the use of choice of will, is called original sin; for, contracted from the first evil
will of man, it has become in a certain sense hereditary. What I said, therefore,
is not false: "Sin is so voluntary an evil that what is not voluntary is certainly not a
sin (8)."

616

1970

[1, 12, 6]

Again in another place I said: "Those are to be followed first who say that there is
only one supreme God, the true God, who alone is to be worshipped. If truth does not
shine forth with them, then a change is to be made (9)." This can appear to have been said
as if I had doubted the truth of this religion; but I spoke in a way adapted to him to whom
I was writing (10); for I said: "If truth does not shine forth with them," never
doubting that with them it would shine forth.

560

1971

[1, 13, 2]

"Then I shall know, even as I have been known (11)." Those who have discovered
this must themselves be said to be in possession of the happiness to which the way of
faith which we hold, leads, and to which we desire to arrive by believing. But who
those perfectly happy men are who are already in possession of that to which this way
leads is a great question. Certainly there is no question that the holy angels are there;
but it can rightly be asked whether it can be said that holy men now dead are already in
possession of it. For they certainly have already gone forth from the corruptible body by
which the soul is weighed down; but they too still await the redemption of the body (12),
and their flesh rests in hope (13), not yet shining in the incorruption that is to come. But
this is not the place to debate whether they still lack anything that is needed for the
contemplation of truth with the eyes of the heart, as it is said, "face to face (14)."

1041

490
996

1972

[1, 14, 2]

Likewise, because I said: "Sin, of course, can never exist except in the will (15),"
the Pelagians can suppose that it was said to their advantage, because infants, whom
they deny have the original sin which is remitted them in baptism, have not yet the
use of free choice. Indeed, as if sin, which we say they derive originally from Adam,
that is, by being implicated in his guilt and for this reason held liable to punishment,

616

could ever exist except from the will, by which will it was committed when
transgression was made of the divine command! . . . . The guilt of concupiscence   617
is remitted in Baptism, but a weakness remains; and against this weakness, until it is
healed, every faithful person who makes good progress struggles most assiduously.
But sin, which never exists except in the will, is to be understood especially as that
which is followed by a just condemnation: for this is what "through one man entered
into the world (16)."

1973

[1, 14, 4]
   Likewise, the definition of sin in which we said: "Sin is the will to sustain or   636
follow after what justice forbids, and from which it is free to abstain (17)," is true because
it defines only what is sin and not also what is the punishment of sin. For when sin is said
in such a sense that it is the same as the punishment of sin, how much has the will,
dominated by passion, in its power, except perhaps, if it be pious, to pray for help? For it
is free insofar as it has been freed, and to this extent it is called will.

1974

[1, 22, 2]
   It is not grace if any merits precede it; for then what is given is given not as gratuitous   711
but as owed, it is paid out for merits rather than bestowed (18).

1. Gen. 2:7; 1 Cor. 15:45.
2. The discussion is of Augustine's *Contra academicos*, known also as the *De academicis libri tres*. Hence, the *tunc* or *then* refers to the time at which the *Contra academicos* was being written, that is, 386 A. D. The first possibility which Augustine describes is simply traducianism, which has been condemned numerous times, and to which the theological note attaches of being *proximate to heresy*, since direct creation of the soul is termed *proximate to the faith* and *of Catholic faith*. It is not a problem, however, which has been much discussed in comparatively modern times; and I would suspect, subject always to the magisterial rulings of the Church, that spiritual traducianism as distinct from material traducianism could be explained in an acceptable manner in our times.
3. The incorrect number is Augustine's.
4. The passage is from the discussion of the *De libero arbitrio libri tres*.
5. See § 1539 above.
6. See Prov. 8:35 in the Septuagint version.
7. That is, when Augustine was writing the work now under discussion, his *Genesis Defended against the Manicheans*.
8. See § 1549 above.
9. See § 1551 above.
10. The *De vera religione*, from which the passage is taken, was written for a certain Romanianus.
11. 1 Cor. 13:12.
12. Rom. 8:23.
13. Ps. 15[16]:9.
14. See 1 Cor. 13:12. Passage § 1971 is from the discussion of *The Advantage of Believing*.
15. See § 1558 above.
16. Rom. 5:12.
17. See § 1558 above.
18. Passage § 1974 is from the discussion of the *Expositio quaerundam propositionum ex epistula apostoli ad Romanos*.

HERESIES [*A. D.* 428]

   With his *De haeresibus*, dedicated to the Carthaginian deacon Quodvultdeus,
Augustine follows in the tradition of St. Irenaeus, St. Epiphanius, and other great
authors of encyclopedic works on heresies. Augustine lists and describes the
characteristic doctrines of eighty-eight heresies and heretics, beginning with Simon
Magus and concluding with Pelagius.

On the heresies to which he is himself a contemporary,—and they are rather considerable in number,—Augustine is quite original in his treatment. For earlier heresies he depends very heavily, sometimes almost verbatim, on two sources: the *Epitome* of Epiphanius' *Panarion*, and not the *Panarion* itself, which *Epitome* is probably not authentic; and the catalogue of heresies compiled by Filaster of Brescia.

The Migne reprint of the Maurist edition, PL 42, 21-50, has now been superseded by the edition of Roel Vander Plaetse and C. Beukers in the *Corpus Christianorum*, Vol. 46 (1969), pp. 286-345.

1974a

[1]

The Simoniacs (1) are called so from Simon Magus, who, after he was baptized   711
by the Deacon Philip, as we read in the Acts of the Apostles, wanted to buy for a money price from the Apostles the faculty of conferring the Holy Spirit through the imposition of hands. By his magic deceptions he misled many. He taught also the detestable turpitude of making a promiscuous use of women. He held that God did not make the world, and he even denied the resurrection of the flesh. And he claimed that he himself was Christ; likewise he wanted people to believe that he was Jove, and that a certain whore named Helen, whom he made the companion of his crimes, was Minerva. He provided images of himself and of his whoreson disciples for adoration. These also he established at Rome by public authority as if they were the likenesses of gods. At Rome the Apostle Peter destroyed him by the true power of Almighty God (2).

1974b

[31]

The Adamites (3) are called thus after Adam, whose nakedness in paradise they   983
imitate, because it was prior to sin. Whence also they are opposed to marriage, because before Adam had sinned and before he was expelled from paradise, he did not know his wife. They believe, therefore, that there would have been no marriages if no one had sinned. Naked they gather together, men and women alike; naked they listen to the readings; naked they pray; naked they celebrate the sacraments; and that is why they reckon their own church as paradise.

1974c

[40]

The Apostolics (4), who most arrogantly call themselves by that name, do not   983
receive into their communion those who use their spouses and who possess things of their own. The Catholic Church too has such, both monks and most of her clerics. But these others are heretics, because they separate themselves from the Church and   415
judge that there is no hope to be had for those who use these things which they lack. They are similar to the Encratites (5); and they are also called Apotactites (6). But whatever else is peculiar to their heretical teaching, I do not know.

1974d

[56]

Heretics called Antidicomarites (7) are those who contradict the perpetual virginity   783
of Mary (8), and affirm that after Christ was born she was joined as one with her husband (9).

1974e

[63]

The Passalorhynchites (10) are so eager to keep silence (11) that they stick a   415
finger over their lips and up their nose (12) rather than ask for silence with a word, when
they judge they ought to keep silence; and hence the name by which they are called. For
in Greek a peg is called πάσσαλος, and the nose is ῥύγχος. But why those who made up
this name would want to call a finger a peg I do not know. The Greek word for finger is
δάκτυλος, and they might, therefore, much more appropriately, be called
Dactylorhynchites.

1974f

[65]

The Coluthians are called such after a certain Coluthus, who said that God did not   469
create evils, contrary to what is written: "I, God, creating evils (13)." [66] The Florinians
are called such after Florinus, who, in an opposite way, said that God did create evils,
contrary to what is written: "God made all things, and behold, they were very good (14)."
And consequently, although they stated contrary things, both were resisting the divine
statements. For God does create evil, by imposing most just punishments, which Coluthus
did not understand; but He does not create evil natures and substances insofar as they are
natures and substances, wherein Florinus erred.

1975

[82]

The Jovinianists too are among those whom I have known. This heresy had its   634
origins from a monk, a certain Jovinian, in our own time, when I was still a young man.
Like the Stoic philosophers, he said that all sins are equal. He said also that a man was
not able to sin after he had received the bath of rebirth; and that there is no profit in
fasting nor in abstaining from particular foods. He destroyed the virginity of Mary,
saying that it was lost by her parturition. He equated the merits of chaste spouses   782
and of the faithful with the virginity of consecrated women (15) and the continence   984
of the male sex in holy persons choosing a celibate life.

1976

[88]

The Pelagians went even farther, and say that in this world the life of the just   727
can be entirely without sin, and that in the midst of our mortality it is of these that   658
the Church of Christ is composed, so that it is entirely without stain and blemish (16),
as if it were not Christ's Church which, in every land on earth, cries out to God:
"Forgive us our debts (17)." They even deny that infants, born carnally according to   619
Adam, have contracted the contagion of ancient death by their first birth. For they
assert that infants are born without any bond of original sin, so that there is no
necessity of its being forgiven them in a second birth. They assert rather that infants
are baptized so that, having been adopted in a rebirth, they may be admitted to the
kingdom of God, thus translated from good to better, and not absolved by that rebirth
from some evil of ancient obligation. For even if infants be not baptized they promise   1037
them, outside the kingdom of God, to be sure, but nevertheless a certain life of their
own, eternal and blessed.

---

1. *Simoniani*; and so too, our term *simony*.
2. See the *Acts of Peter*, 8, 23-29. There is also considerable information on Simon Magus in the Clementine *Recognitions*.

3. *Adamiani*.
4. *Apostolici*.
5. In chapter 25 the *De haeresibus* states that the terms Tatianists and Encratites are synonymous.
6. The term means *persons specially appointed*, and in basic significance it is not much different from apostles. Epiphanius knows heretics called Apotactites.
7. *Antidicomaritae*.
8. *qui Mariae virginitati usque adeo contradicunt*.
9. *eam post Christum natum viro suo fuisse commixtam*.
10. *Passalorynchitae*.
11. *in tantum silentio student*.
12. *ut naribus et labiis suis digitum apponant*.
13. Is 45:7.
14. See Gen. 1:31.
15. *virginitatem etiam sanctimonialium*.
16. Eph. 5:27.
17. Matt. 6:12.

SERMON AGAINST THE JEWS [*post A. D.* 425]

The *Adverus Iudaeos*, since its command of ideas worked out at length in the *City of God* seems to indicate that the latter work had already been written, must be dated after 425 A. D. B. Blumenkranz has shown that the work is in fact a sermon; hence the absence of any mention of it in the *Corrections* is in no way surprising.

The Maurist text in Migne PL 42, 51-64 is still the standard.

1977

[9, 13]

" 'From the rising of the sun even to its setting My name is great among the   890
Gentiles, and in every place sacrifice is offered to My name, a clean oblation; for My   894
name is great among the Gentiles,' says the Lord Almighty (1)." What do you answer
to that? Open your eyes at last, then, any time, and see, from the rising of the sun to its
setting, the Sacrifice of Christians is offered, not in one place only, as was established
with you Jews, but everywhere; and not to just any god at all, but to Him who foretold
it, the God of Israel. . . . Not in one place, as was prescribed for you in the earthly   897
Jerusalem, but in every place, even in Jerusalem herself. Not according to the order of   893
Aaron, but according to the order of Melchisedech.

1. Mal. 1:11.

THE PREDESTINATION OF THE SAINTS [*A. D.* 428 *aut* 429]

Augustine's *De praedestinatione sanctorum liber ad Prosperum et Hilarium primus* was written later than the *Corrections*, in 428 or 429 A. D. It is in response to letters from Prosper of Aquitaine (§§ 2024-2025 below) and a certain Hilary (§§ 2021-2022 below), acquainting Augustine with an outbreak in Southern Gaul of that modified form of Pelagianism which was then called Massilianism (from its origin in Marseilles) and afterwards came to be known as semi-Pelagianism.

The Massilians or semi-Pelagians remained Pelagians to this extent, that they contended that the beginning of salvation and faith is in ourselves, and that it is in view of this antecedent merit that God's graces are bestowed. Augustine readily admits that early in his career and before his acceptance of the episcopate he believed this himself, but was afterwards convinced otherwise, upon pondering the Scripture passage: "But what have you that you did not receive?"

The Migne text in PL 44, 959-992 remains the standard edition.

1978

[2, 3]

There is no departure here from that opinion which Pelagius himself was obliged   728
to condemn in the episcopal trial in Palestine (1), as is testified to in the Acts of those   729
same proceedings (2): "The grace of God is given us according to our own merits."
[There is no departure here, I say, from this condemned opinion], if it is not by   656
God's grace that we begin to believe, but rather, that on account of our beginning to
believe, an increase is given us, so that we may believe more fully and more perfectly;
and thus, we first give God the beginning of our faith so that He may return to us both
its supplement and whatever else we might faithfully request.

1979

[2, 4]

The Apostle says: "It is given you on Christ's behalf not only to believe in Him   656
but also to suffer for Him (3)." He shows that both are God's gifts, because he said
that both were given. Neither does he say: "that you may believe in Him more fully and
more perfectly," but: "that you may believe in Him." Nor did he say that he had
himself obtained mercy to be more faithful, but to be faithful (4), because he knew
that he had not first given the beginning of his faith to God to have it returned by
Him with its increase. Rather, he knew that he had been made faithful by God, by
whom also he was made an Apostle. For the beginnings of his faith are written down
and are very well known by their being read in the ecclesiastical assembly (5).
For he was turned against the faith, which he was destroying, and was violently opposed   696
to it, when he was suddenly converted to it by a more powerful grace.

1980

[2, 5]

And, therefore, commending that grace which is given not according to any   656
merits but which itself produces all good merits, he says: "Not that we are sufficient
to think anything as if of ourselves, but our sufficiency is from God (6)." Let those
who think the beginning of our faith is of ourselves while the increase of that faith is   552
from God attend carefully to those words and weigh them well. For who is there   564
who cannot see that thinking is prior to believing? For no one believes something
unless he has first thought that it ought to be believed. Though it be ever so sudden,
ever so rapid, some thoughts do fly before the will to believe, and the will to
believe presently follows as if most closely joined to them. Yet, it is necessary that
everything that is believed should be believed after thought has come before; though
too, belief itself is nothing else but the thought with assent.

1981

[3, 7]

"But what do you have that you did not receive? And if you received it, why do   656
you glory as if you had not received it (7)?" It was chiefly by this testimony that I   729
myself too was converted, when I likewise erred, thinking that the faith by which we
believe in God is not a gift of God, but is in us from ourselves, and that through
it we obtain the gifts of God by which we are able to live temperately and
righteously and piously in this world.

1982

[5, 10]

To be able to have faith, just as to be able to have love, belongs to men by   710
nature; but actually to have faith, as also actually to have love, belongs to the
faithful by grace. That nature, therefore, in which the possibility of having faith is
given to us, does not distinguish one man from another; but faith itself distinguishes
the believer from the unbeliever. And consequently, where it is said: "For who   656
distinguishes you? And what have you that you did not receive (8)," anyone who
would dare to say: "I have faith from myself; therefore, I did not receive it," would
certainly contradict this most evident truth, not because to believe or not to believe
is not in the choice of the human will, but because in the elect "the will is prepared
by the Lord (9)."

1983

[8, 14]

Just as we speak correctly of some teacher of literature who is the only one in   201
the city, when we say of him: "He teaches literature here to everyone," not because
all learn, but because all who do learn literature there learn from him; so too we
rightly say: "God teaches all to come to Christ," not because all do come, but
because no one comes in any other way. . . . God teaches all these to come to
Christ (10); for He wills all these to be saved, and to come to a knowledge of the
truth (11).

1984

[8, 16]

Faith, therefore, both initial and perfected, is a gift of God. And let no one have   656
any doubt at all, unless he wishes to be in conflict with the plainest of the sacred   720
writings, that this gift is given to certain ones, while to certain others it is not
given. But why it is not given at all ought not disturb the believer, who believes
that it is undoubtedly most just that from one all go to condemnation, so that
even if not one were to be delivered therefrom, it would be no just cause for finding   614
fault with God.

1985

[9, 18]

What is more true than that Christ foreknew who was going to believe in Him,   203
and when, and in what places? But whether by Christ having been preached to   204
them, they themselves were going to have faith of themselves, or whether they would   703
receive it as a gift of God, that is, whether God only foreknew them or whether
He also predestined them, I did not then think it necessary to inquire or discuss.
What I said at that time: "Christ willed to appear among men and to preach His
doctrine among them, at a time and in a place when and where He knew there
would be those who would believe in Him (12)," can also be expressed thus: "Christ   400
willed to appear among men and to preach His doctrine among them, at a time
and in a place when and where He knew there would be those who had been
chosen in Him before the foundation of the world (13)."

1986

[10, 19]

Again, what I said: "The salvation that belongs to this religion was never   204

wanting to anyone who was worthy of it; and anyone to whom it was wanting was
not worthy of it (14)'';—if it be discussed and it be questioned whence anyone
can be worthy, there is no lack of those who will say, ''by the human will!'' But
we say, ''by divine grace and predestination.'' Furthermore, between grace and
predestination there is this difference only, that predestination is the preparation
for grace, while grace is already the gifting itself (15).

724

1987

[16, 32]

God calls the predestined with that calling which the Apostle pointed out when
he said that ''to those that are called, both Jews and Greeks'' he was himself to
preach ''Christ, the Power of God and the Wisdom of God (16).'' For he says:
''But to them that are called,'' in order to show that some are not called, and
knowing that there is a certain sure calling of those ''who have been called
according to purpose, whom He already foreknew and predestined to become
conformed to the image of His Son (17).''

206

261

1988

[17, 34]

The elect were chosen before the foundation of the world in that predestination
in which God foreknew what He Himself would do; but they were chosen out
of the world in that calling by which God fulfilled what He had Himself predestined.
For those whom He predestined, the same He also called, with that calling which is
according to His purpose. Not others, therefore, but those whom He predestined,
the same also did He call; not others, but those whom He called, the same did He
justify; not others, but those whom He predestined, whom He called, whom He
justified, the same did He glorify (18); to that end, assuredly, which has no end. . . .
By choosing them, therefore, He makes them rich in faith, and heirs of the
kingdom (19). Rightly, then, is He said to choose in them that for the making of
which in them He chose them.

203

206

1989

[18, 36]

''He knew,'' says the Pelagian, ''who would be holy and immaculate through
the choice of their free will, and on that account He chose them before the
foundation of the world in that same foreknowledge of His in which He foreknew
that they would be such. He chose them,'' he says, ''before they existed,
predestining sons whom He knew beforehand would be holy and immaculate;
certainly, then, He did not make them such, nor did He foresee that He would
make them such, but that they would be such.'' Let us, therefore, examine the
words of the Apostle . . .: ''. . . just as He chose us in Himself before the
foundation of the world, that we might be holy and immaculate (20).'' Not, therefore,
because [He foreknew that] we were going to be such, but so that we might be
such. Assuredly it is certain, assuredly it is manifest that we were going to be such,
because He Himself chose us, predestining us so that by His grace we might be
such. . . . ''So that He might show us the mystery of His will, according to His
good will (21).'' In this mystery of His will He put the riches of His grace according
to His good will, and not according to ours. Ours would not be able to be good
unless He, according to His good will, were to aid it so that it might be good.

728

204

205

1990

[19, 38]

It was not because we did believe, but so that we might believe, that He chose   204
us, so that we could not be said to have chosen him first, and, perish the thought,
the Scriptural saying be false: "You have not chosen Me, but I have chosen   206
you (22)." We are called, not because we believed, but so that we might believe;
and by that calling which is without repentance (23) it is effected and carried
through that we should believe.

1991

[19, 39]

God operates, therefore, in the hearts of men by that calling in accord with His   206
purpose, of which we have spoken at length, so that they should not hear the   696
gospel in vain, but having heard it, they should be converted and believe.

1. *in episcopali iudicio Palaestino*. See the introduction to *The Proceedings in regard to Pelagius*, pp. 126-127 above.
2. *eadem gesta*. The reference is to chapter 14 of *The Proceedings in regard to Pelagius*.
3. Phil. 1:29.
4. 1 Cor. 7:25.
5. *suntque ecclesiastica celebri lectione notissima*.
6. 2 Cor. 3:5.
7. 1 Cor. 4:7.
8. *Ibid., loc. cit.*
9. Prov. 8:35 in the Septuagint.
10. See John 6:45.
11. 1 Tim. 2:4.
12. *Letter of Augustine to Deogratias* 102, 14, written in 408 or 409 A. D. See § 1427 above.
13. Eph. 1:4.
14. *Letter of Augustine to Deogratias* 102, 15; § 1428 above.
15. *gratia vero iam ipsa donatio*.
16. 1 Cor. 1:23-24.
17. Rom. 8:28-29.
18. Rom. 8:30.
19. James 2:5.
20. Eph. 1:4.
21. Eph. 1:9.
22. John 15:16.
23. *quae sine paenitentia est*. See Rom. 9:29. Repentance here means revocation. God's predestining call is not subject to revocation. The Lord has spoken and He will not repent.

THE GIFT OF PERSEVERANCE [*A. D.* 428 *aut* 429]

The *De dono perseverantiae liber ad Prosperum et Hilarium secundus* is a
continuation of the preceding work, the *De praedestinatione sanctorum liber ad
Prosperum et Hilarium primus;* and nothing except tradition prevents their being treated
as two books of but a single work. Prosper of Aquitaine, writing to Hilary after
the death of Augustine, refers to this second book that Augustine had dedicated to them
simply as the second book of Augustine's *De praedestinatione sanctorum*; and from
Prosper's having considered that the two books constituted but a single work, we might
conclude that quite probably that was Augustine's view also.

In some manuscripts the title is given as *De* bono *perseverantiae* rather than *De* dono
perseverantiae; but in this context *bonum* and *donum* are synonymous anyway.

The Maurist text in Migne PL 45, 993-1034 remains at present the standard.

1992

[1, 1]

We assert, therefore, that perseverance, by which one perseveres in Christ even   672
to the end, is a gift of God. I say the end, however, meaning the point at which that   673
life is finished during the term of which there was always some danger that one might
fall. As long as a man is still alive, therefore, it is uncertain whether he has received this
gift. For if he fall before he has died, he is said not to have persevered; and most truly is it
said. . . . But lest anyone should object and say: "If someone, from the time that he
became a believer, lived, for example, ten years, and lapsed from the faith halfway through
that period, did he not persevere for five years?" I am not arguing about words. If it is
thought that this too should be called perseverance, which lasted but for a time, certainly it
is not to be said that that man had in any degree, since he did not persevere to the end, that
perseverance of which we are now treating, and by which one perseveres in Christ to the
end.

1993

[6, 10]

We are speaking of that perseverance by which one perseveres to the end. If this   673
is given, one does persevere to the end; and if one does not persevere to the end, it
was not given. . . . Since no one has perseverance to the end unless he does in fact
persevere to the end, many may have it, and none can lose it. It is not to be feared
that when a man has persevered to the end some evil will may arise in him so that he   672
does not persevere to the end. This gift of God, therefore, can be obtained by   713
supplication; but when it has been given, it cannot be lost by contumacy.

1994

[7, 15]

In this matter let the Church not look at all for laborious disputations, but attend   713
to her daily prayers. She prays that the incredulous may believe; and on that account
God converts them to the faith. She prays that believers may persevere; and on that
account God gives perseverance to the end. God foreknew that He would Himself   202
do this: for this is the very predestination of the saints whom "He chose in Christ
before the foundation of the world, so that they should be holy and unspotted before Him
in love, whom He predestined to the adoption of sons through Jesus Christ (1)."

1994a

[8, 19]

Are there, then, two natures of men? Perish the thought. If there were two natures,   711
there would be no grace; for none would be given a gratuitous liberation, if it were
but repaid as a debt of nature.

1995

[9, 21]

Of two infants, therefore, equally bound by original sin (2), why the one is taken   720
and the other left; and of two impious persons grown old, why the one is called in   205
such a way that He follows Him who calls, while the other either is not called or
is not called in that same way: these are inscrutable judgments of God. But when   672
it is a question of two pious men, why the one is given perseverance to the end,
and the other is not given it: these judgments of God are even more inscrutable.

1996

[9, 22]

Not to speak of how it is possible for God to convert the wills of men disinclined   696
and adverse to His faith, and to work in their hearts so that they yield to no adversities
nor are they overcome by any temptation so as to depart from Him, since He is able
to do that too of which the Apostle speaks, and He need not allow them to be tempted
beyond their endurance (3);—not to speak of those considerations, certainly God,   194
foreknowing that certain men would fall away, was able to take them from this life
before that would happen. Or are we to return to that point where we were still
arguing what a great absurdity it is to say that dead men are judged even for those
sins which God foreknew they would have committed if they had lived? That idea is so
abhorrent to Christian, yes, even to human sensibilities, that one is embarassed even to
refute it.

1997

[9, 23]

It is false, therefore, that the dead are judged also in regard to what they would   618
have done if the gospel had reached them while they were alive. And if this is false,
there is no reason why it might be said of infants who perish because they die
without Baptism that in their case it happens deservedly because God foreknew that if
they had lived and the gospel had been preached to them, they would have heard it
without belief. It remains, therefore, that they are held bound by original sin alone,
and for this alone they go to damnation; and we see that with others original sin is   204
remitted only through the gratuitous grace of God in regeneration.

1998

[11, 25]

What we see in the case of those whose deliverance is preceded by no good merits   204
of their own, and in those, whose damnation is preceded by original sin only, common
to both alike,—this we do not at all hesitate to say is the case also with adults, that
is, we do not think that grace is given to anyone because of his own merits, nor   209
do we suppose that anyone is punished except on his own deserts.

1999

[13, 33]

From the foregoing it is shown with sufficient clarity that the grace of God,   711
both for a beginning and for perseverance to the end, is given not according to our   672
merits, but according to His own most secret, more just, most wise, and most
beneficent will, because those whom He predestined, them also He called (4), with that
call of which it is said: "The gifts and the call of God are without repentance (5)."   206
This is the call to which no man, until he has departed from this world, can be said   673
by men, with certitude of affirmation, to pertain. . . . We will, therefore; but   690
God works in us to will also. We work, therefore; but God, in his good pleasure (6),
works in us to work also. It is advantageous to us both to say this and to believe it;
it is pious and it is true; and all is given to God, so that our confession is humble
and submissive.

2000

[14, 35]

This and nothing else is the predestination of the saints: God's foreknowledge,   202

to wit, and the preparation of His kindnesses, whereby anyone who is liberated is   208
liberated most certainly (7). But where are the others left by the just divine judgment,
except in the mass of perdition (8), where the men of Tyre and Sidon were left, who
had also been able to believe if only they had seen the miracles (9) of Christ? But
since it was not given them to believe, the means by which they might have believed
were denied them.

2001

[16, 39]

   There are some, moreover, who either pray not at all or pray coldly, because they   120
know from the Lord's having said it that God knows what is necessary for us even
before we ask it of Him. Must the truth of this statement be given up or is it to be
supposed that it should be deleted from the gospel on account of such people? On   204
the contrary, while it is a fact that God prepares some things to be given even to   713
those who do not pray, such as the beginning of faith, and other things not to be given
except to those who pray for them, such as perseverance to the end, certainly one who
thinks that he has this of himself does not pray to have it. We must beware, then, lest,
while we fear that exhortation may grow cool, prayer be extinguished and presumption (10)
advanced.

2002

[17, 41]

   See now how foreign to the truth it is to deny that perseverance to the end of this   672
life is a gift of God, since He Himself puts an end to this life when He wills, and if He   673
puts an end to it before an impending fall, He makes a man persevere to the end.
But more marvelous and more evident to the faithful is the largesse of God's goodness,   203
in His giving this grace even to infants in whom there is, at that age, no obedience
to which it might be given.

2003

[17, 42]

   Those who put only the beginning of faith and perseverance to the end in our   729
power in such a way that they suppose them not to be gifts of God, and think that
God does not operate in our thoughts and wills so that we may have and retain them,
do concede, nevertheless, that He Himself gives other gifts, if they be sought
from Him with the faith of the believer. Why do they not fear that the definition of
predestination will impede exhortation to these other things and preaching about these
other things (11)? Or do they perhaps say that these other things are not
predestined? Then either they are not given by God, or He did not know He was   202
going to give them. But if they are given, and He knew He was going to give
them, certainly He predestined them (12).

2004

[19, 50]

   Such great doctors as [Cyprian, Ambrose, Gregory of Nazianz], when they   106
say we have nothing of which we can boast as if it were from ourselves, which
God did not give us, and that even our very heart and our thoughts are not in our
power, and who attribute all to God, confessing that it is from Him that we   656
receive even our conversion to Him and its continuance, so that what is good   650

appears good even to us and we will it, so that we honor God and receive Christ,
so that from being indevout we are made devout and religious, so that we believe
in the Trinity and confess even vocally that we believe:—certainly these great
doctors attribute all things to the grace of God, they acknowledge them as God's
gifts, and bear witness that they are from Him and not from ourselves.

2005

[21, 55]

Let those, however, to whom, since they love me, I ought not be ungrateful, who   711
profess that they embrace, besides what comes into the present question, all my
views, as you write; let them see, I say, whether in the latter portions of the first
of the two books that I wrote to Simplician, the Bishop of Milan, at the beginning
of my own episcopate and before the Pelagian heresy made its appearance (13),
there remained anything by which it might be called into doubt that the grace of
God is not given in accord with merits, and whether from the things which I did   656
say there it does not shine forth as a consequence thereof, even if it was not
expressed, that even perseverance to the end is not given except by Him who has   672
predestined us to His kingdom and glory.

2006

[23, 64]

"God sent the Spirit of His Son into our hearts, crying: 'Abba, Father' (14)."   656
And what is this crying, except a making to cry, by that same figure of speech
whereby we call a day that makes us happy a happy day? . . . We understand,
therefore, that this too is itself the gift of God, that with a true heart and in a
spiritual manner we cry to God. Let them note, then, how they err who suppose that
our asking, our seeking, and our knocking is of ourselves and not something
given to us.

1. The quotation continues through Eph. 1:4-11.
2. *originali peccato*. By the time he wrote the second of the two books to Prosper and Hilary, Augustine was entirely comfortable with the term *peccatum originale*. The term is not entirely absent from his earlier writings, and the notion is always there; but formerly he was more likely to write *peccatum originis, damnatio originalis, originalis perditio, noxa originalis*, or the like; whereas now his more frequent and more usual term is *peccatum originale*.
3. 1 Cor. 10:13.
4. Rom. 8:30.
5. *paenitentia*, that is, *revocation*. See note 23 to § 1990 above.
6. *pro bona voluntate*. The entire sentence reads: *Nos ergo operamur, sed Deus in nobis operatur et operari pro bona voluntate*. See Phil. 2:13.
7. Augustine knows very well that foreknowledge of man's merits is not the cause of predestination. When he defines predestination as the foreknowledge and preparation of God's gifts whereby anyone who is liberated is liberated most certainly the foreknowledge of which he is speaking is not God's foreknowledge of a man's merits but His foreknowledge of a man's salvation through the gifts of efficacious grace that He will give him.
8. *in massa perditionis*.
9. *mira illa Christi signa*.
10. *elatio*.
11. That is to say, why are they not afraid that the idea of predestination will impede exhortation to *pray for* these other things and preaching about *the need to pray for* these other things.
12. This follows logically from Augustine's definition of predestination in § 2000 above. If predestination is God's foreknowledge of a man's salvation accompanied by the efficacious graces needed for that salvation, then certainly if God gives those graces and knew He was going to give them, He has predestined the man to whom they are given. For Augustine, predestination to damnation consists simply in God's not electing a man out of the lump of perdition.
13. The two books referred to constitute the work entitled *Various Questions to Simplician*, dating from about 397 A. D. See above, §§ 1569-1576.
14. Gal. 4:6.

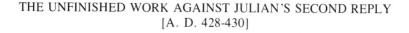

THE UNFINISHED WORK AGAINST JULIAN'S SECOND REPLY
[A. D. 428-430]

Augustine wrote his six books *Contra Iulianum (q. v.)* in 421 as a response to Julian's reply to the first book of his *Marriage and Concupiscence*. A second reply of Julian addressed to the second book of Augustine's *Marriage and Concupiscence*, Julian's *Eight Books to Florus* (§§ 1415-1416 above), called forth another *Contra Iulianum*, the present one, from Augustine. It is given the title *Contra secundam Iuliani responsionem imperfectum opus sex libros complectens*, but is usually called simply the *Opus imperfectum*, that is, *The Unfinished Work*.

The *Opus imperfectum* is written in the manner of a dialogue, Julian's part being supplied from the *Eight Books to Florus*, which Augustine refutes paragraph by paragraph. As a consequence, six books of the *Eight Books to Florus*, not extant as such, can be reconstructed from the present work of Augustine.

The first half of the *Opus imperfectum*, that is, books 1-3, was published in 1974 in the Vienna Corpus in the edition produced by Michaela Zelzer as a reworking of unpublished material of Ernest Kalinka: CSEL, Vol. 85, part 1. Until the second half, books 4 through six, appears, we shall have to continue to rely on the Maurist edition in Migne PL 45, 1049-1068, at least for these latter books. For our translations below we have used Zelzer's Kalinka for passages from books one and two; Migne's Maurist for passages from books four through six.

2007

[1, 48]

Augustine: Ambrose says (1): "Adam was brought into being, and in him we were all brought into being. Adam perished and in him all perished." "But by another's sins," you say, "they surely ought not perish." They are of another; but they are paternal; and therefore, by the law of semination and germination they are also ours. Who delivers from this perdition, except Him who comes seeking what [Adam] lost? In those, therefore, whom He liberates, we receive mercy; but in those whom He does not liberate, we recognize a judgment that is assuredly most hidden, but without any doubt most just.

614

615

370

205

2008

[2, 146]

Augustine: This is the hidden and frightful poison of your heresy, that you want the grace of Christ to be in His example, not in His gift; and you say that men are made just through imitating Him, and not through the ministering (2) of the Holy Spirit.

726

2009

[2, 165]

Augustine: You are the only authorities who suppose that justification is conferred by the remission alone of sins. Certainly God justifies the impious man not only by remitting the evil deeds which that man does, but also by granting love, so that the man may turn away from evil and may do good through the Holy Spirit.

751

542

2010

[4, 104]

Augustine: All who, not yet having been born, were able to do nothing good   616
and nothing evil by their own wills, were able to sin in the one in whom they
existed by reason of his seed, when he, by his own will, sinned that great sin;
and in himself he weakened, changed, and damaged human nature, except in that One   344
Man who was procreated certainly of that same seed but not in a seminal fashion.
Understand this if you can; and if you cannot, then believe.

2011

[5, 1]

Augustine: You are not considering in accord with the Christian faith what sort   523
of a man Adam was made, who gave names to all the different kinds of living animals,
which, as we read even in secular writings, betokened his most excellent wisdom. . . .
And what Christian would doubt that if the genius of those who, in this world crammed full
of errors and hardships, seem to be most clever, but whose souls are burdened with corruptible bodies,—if their genius were to be compared to the genius of Adam, it would be
outdistanced more than tortoises are outdistanced by the swiftness of birds?

2012

[5, 61]

Augustine: That good is so great that it was reserved as a reward for the saints.   1042
You have forgotten them, just as you have forgotten God. For then we shall not be
powerless to live, when we are granted an inability ever to abandon God, because we shall
not then be able to will such a thing. For the good will then be ours with certitude, when,
as is promised, we shall be always with God (3), in such a way that we will not will, nor
will we be able to will, to depart from Him.

2013

[6, 22]

Augustine: Indeed, the more superior is a rational nature, so much the worse is   491
its ruin; and the more unbelievable is its sin, so much the more damnable it is.
The angel, therefore, fell irreparably, because more is demanded of him to whom
more is given (4). . . . Adam, the first man, was of such an excellent nature,   610
because that nature was not yet weakened, that his sin was much greater by far than
are the sins of other men. Therefore his punishment too, which was the immediate   611
consequence of his sin, seemed much more severe. It had been in Adam's power
not to die; but now he was immediately bound by the necessity of dying, and
he was immediately sent away from the place of such great happiness; and he was   525
immediately barred from access to the tree of life. But when this was done, the
human race was still in his loins. . . . Thus all the sons of Adam were infected   614
through him with the contagion of sin and were subjected to the state of death.

1. See § 1306a above.
2. *sumministrationem*. This term might also be translated *aid* or *gift*.
3. 1 Thess. 4:16.
4. See Luke 12:48.

ST. INNOCENT I, POPE [*regn. A. D.* 401-417]

Nearly all the early catalogues indicate that Pope Innocent I began his pontificate on December 20, 401 A. D. Prosper of Aquitaine, however, would have it that his pontificate began in 402. Innocent died on March 12, 417, and must be reckoned as one of the greatest popes the Church had yet seen. He is of particular importance in respect to the development of the concept of the Roman Primacy.

During the sack of Rome by Alaric in 410 A. D. Innocent took refuge for a short time at Ravenna. Perhaps the most important single act of Innocent's pontificate was his condemnation of Pelagius and Caelestius when, in his Letter no. 30 to the Fathers of the Council of Milevis, he declared that these "founders of novelties . . . are to be deprived of ecclesiastical communion until they recover their senses."

LETTERS [*inter A. D.* 402-417]

If Innocent wrote anything other than his letters, it has not been preserved. The collection of his letters, however, is of very considerable importance. At least thirty-six letters attributed to Innocent are regarded as authentic. A few others, known to have been written by him, are not extant; and there are also a few extant that are not accounted as genuine.

The texts of Pope Innocent's letters are to be found in Migne, PL 20, 463-638.

LETTER OF POPE INNOCENT I TO VICTRICIUS, BISHOP OF ROUEN.
Feb. 15, 404 A. D. [Etsi tibi frater]

2014

[2, 3, 6]

If cases of greater importance are to be heard, they are, as the synod decrees and   433
as happy custom requires, after episcopal judgment, to be referred to the Apostolic See.

2014a

[2, 8, 11]

Those coming from the Novatianists or from the Montanists are to be received by   830
the imposition of the hand only, because although they were baptized by heretics,
they were, nevertheless, baptized in the name of Christ.

2015

[2, 13, 15]

Likewise, if those who have been wedded spiritually to Christ, and who merited to   902
receive the veil from a priest, afterwards either marry publicly or allow themselves   982
to be corrupted in secret, they are not to be admitted to the performance of penance
unless he to whom they joined themselves has departed from this world. For if the
practice is observed by all of regarding as adulteress a woman who marries a second   974
time while her husband yet lives, and permission to do penance is not granted her
until one of them is dead, how much more should this be observed in the case of a
woman who first joined herself to the Immortal Bridegroom, and afterwards changed
over to a human marriage!

LETTER OF POPE INNOCENT I TO EXSUPERIUS, BISHOP OF TOULOUSE.
Feb. 20, 405 A. D. [Consulenti tibi]

2015a

[6, 2, 5]

It has been asked what is to be done about those who, after Baptism, have given 899
themselves on every occasion to the pleasures of incontinence, and at the very end of
their lives ask for Penance and at the same time the reconciliation of Communion. . . .
[6] The former rule in their regard was more difficult, the recent more lenient, because
mercy has intervened. For the former custom held that Penance was to be granted but
Communion denied. For in times when there were cruel persecutions, lest the ease with
which Communion was granted might not restrain men, confident of reconciliation, from a
lapse, Communion was rightly denied; but Penance was granted, lest the whole be entirely
denied; and by reason of the times, forgiveness was made more difficult. But after our Lord
restored peace to His Churches, terror having now been removed, it was decided that
Communion should be given the dying, as a Viaticum for those about to set forth, both on
account of the mercy of the Lord and lest we seem to be following the harshness and rigor
of the Novatianist heretic in refusing forgiveness. With Penance, therefore, a last
Communion will be given, so that men of this sort or in their final extremities, our Savior
permitting, may be delivered from eternal ruin.

2015b

[6, 7, 13]

A short annotation shows what books are to be accepted as canonical. As you wished 41
to be informed specifically, they are as follows: The five books of Moses, that is,
Genesis, Exodus, Leviticus, Numbers, Deuteronomy; and Jesus Nave, one of Judges,
four of Kingdoms, and also Ruth, sixteen books of Prophets, five books of Solomon,
the Psalter. Likewise, of histories, one book of Job, one book of Tobias, one of Esther,
one of Judith, two of Maccabees, two of Esdras, two books of Paralipomenon. Likewise,
of the New Testament: four books of Gospels, fourteen Epistles of Paul, three 42
Epistles of John, two Epistles of Peter, the Epistle of Jude, the Epistle of James,
the Acts of the Apostles, the Apocalypse of John.

Others, however, which were written under the name of Matthias or of James the Less,
or under the name of Peter and of John, by a certain Leucius,—or under the name of
Andrew, by the philosophers Nexocharis and Leonidas,—or under the name of Thomas,
and such others as may be, are not only to be repudiated, but, as you know, are also to be
condemned.

LETTER OF POPE INNOCENT I TO RUFUS AND OTHER BISHOPS OF
MACEDONIA. *Dec. 13, 414 A. D.* [Magna me gratulatio]

2015c

[17, 5, 10]

Indeed, from the canon of Nicaea, Paulianists coming to the Church are to be 830
baptized, but not the Novatianists (1). . . . Clear reason declares what is distinct 826
in the two heresies themselves; for the Paulianists never baptize in the name of the
Father and of the Son and of the Holy Spirit, and the Novatianists do baptize in those
same tremendous and venerable names; neither among the Novatianists has any question
ever been raised about the unity of the divine power that belongs to Father, Son, and 257
Holy Spirit. 268

LETTER OF POPE INNOCENT I TO DECENTIUS, BISHOP OF GUBBIO.
March 19, 416 A. D. [Si instituta]

2015d

[25, 3, 6]

In regard to the confirming of infants (2), however, it is clear that it is not permitted   840
to be done by any other than the bishop. For the presbyters, granted they be   841
secondary priests, do not, however, possess the summit of the pontificate (3). This   842
pontifical power (4), however, by which they confirm (5) or confer the Spirit Paraclete,   843
is shown to belong only to bishops, not only by ecclesiastical custom but also by
that passage of the Acts of the Apostles which declares that Peter and John were directed to
give the Holy Spirit to persons already baptized (6). For it is permitted presbyters, when
they baptize either without a bishop or in the presence of a bishop, to anoint the baptized
with chrism, but with chrism which has been consecrated by a bishop; they are not
permitted, however, to sign the forehead with that same oil, which signing pertains to
bishops only, when they confer the Spirit Paraclete.

2015e

[25, 8, 11]

Truly, since Your Love has wished to take counsel in this matter just as in others,   940
my son Celestine, the deacon, has also added in his letter that Your Love has raised
a question concerning what was written in the Epistle of the Blessed Apostle James:
"If there is anyone sick among you, let him call in the presbyters and let them pray over
him, anointing him with oil in the name of the Lord; and the prayer of faith will save the
sufferer, and the Lord will raise him up, and if that man has committed sin, He will forgive
him (7)." There is no doubt that this is to be taken or understood in regard to the sick
faithful, who are able to be anointed with the holy oil of chrism, which, having been
confected by a bishop, is permitted not only to priests but also to all as Christians, for
anointing in case of their own necessity or in that of their people (8). The other question
submitted seems to be superfluous, as if to doubt that it is permissible for a bishop to do
what there is no doubt the presbyters may do. For it is stated in respect to presbyters,
because bishops, prevented by other occupations, are not able to go to all the sick.
Otherwise, if the bishop either is able or thinks someone worthy to be visited by himself,
he can without hestitation both bless and touch with the chrism, it being his task to confect
it. But it cannot be administered to penitents, because it is a kind of Sacrament. For how
should it be supposed that one kind of Sacrament could be granted to those, who are denied
the other Sacraments?

LETTER OF POPE INNOCENT I TO THE FATHERS OF THE COUNCIL
OF CARTHAGE. Jan. 27, 417 A. D. [In requirendis]

2015f

[29, 1]

In seeking the things of God, ... following the examples of ancient tradition, . . .   433
you have strengthened . . . the vigor of your religion with true reason, for you have   434
acknowledged that judgment is to be referred to us, and have shown that you know   435
what is owed to the Apostolic See, if all of us placed in this position are to desire to
follow the Apostle himself from whom the episcopate itself and the total authority of this
name have emerged. Following him, we know how to condemn evils just as well as we
know how to approve what is laudable. Or rather, guarding with your priestly office what

the Fathers instituted, you did not regard what they had decided, not by human but by divine judgments, as something to be trampled on. They did not regard anything as finished, even though it was the concern of distant and remote provinces, until it had come to the notice of this See, so that what was a just pronouncement might be confirmed by the total authority of this See, and thence other Churches,—just as all waters proceed from their own natal source and, through the various regions of the whole world, remain pure liquids of an incorrupted head,—might take up what they ought to teach, whom they ought to wash, whom the water worthy of clean bodies would shun as being soiled with a filth incapable of being cleansed.

LETTER OF POPE INNOCENT I TO THE FATHERS OF THE COUNCIL OF MILEVIS. Jan. 27, 417 A. D. [Inter caeteras Romanae]

2016

[30, 5]
    But that which Your Fraternity asserts the Pelagians preach, that even without the   619
grace of Baptism infants are able to be endowed with the rewards of eternal life, is quite   831
idiotic (9). For unless they shall have eaten the Flesh of the Son of Man and shall   870
have drunk His Blood, they shall not have life in them (10). But those who defend
this for them without rebirth seem to me to want to quash (11) Baptism itself, when
they preach that infants already have what is believed to be conferred on them only
through Baptism.

LETTER OF POPE INNOCENT I TO A CERTAIN PROBUS. Date unknown. [Conturbatio]

2017

[36]
    We have decided, with the support of the Catholic Faith, that the marriage which   977
was first strengthened by divine grace is to be upheld; and the arrangement with the
second woman, the first woman surviving and not dismissed by divorce, can by no   974
means be legitimate (12).

---

1. See Canons 8 and 19 of Nicaea, §§ 651n and 651y above in Volume 1. The Cathari of that Council's Canon 8 are the Novatianists.
2. *De consignandis vero infantibus.*
3. *Nam presbyteri, licet secundi sint sacerdotes, pontificatus tamen apicem non habent.*
4. *pontificium.*
5. *consignent.*
6. Acts 8:14-17.
7. James 5:14-15.
8. *Quod non est dubium de fidelibus aegrotantibus accipi vel intelligi debere, qui sancto oleo chrismatis perungi possunt, quod ad episcopo confectum, non solum sacerdotibus, sed et omnibus uti Christianis licet in sua aut in suorum necessitate ungendum.* At first reading it might appear that the Pope is stating that not only priests but any Christian can confer the Anointing of the Sick; but, of course, there is never any suggestion of such a thing anywhere else in all antiquity. More careful reading shows that Innocent is explaining that it is not only priests who may receive that sacrament, but anyone who is a Christian may do so. Apparently the bishop of Gubbio had asked two questions in regard to this Anointing. Innocent says his second question is rather silly; and it appears to us that both questions must have been quite inane. Of course it is dangerous to judge the character of what no longer exists and cannot be examined; and Decentius' letter is not extant: but from the answers given, it must be assumed that the questions were something like this: "In regard to the Anointing of the Sick: 1) since the Scripture says, 'if someone *among you* is sick, let him call in the presbyters,' are we to take the *among you* as meaning among the presbyters, so that only such may be anointed, or may the laity also receive this anointing; and, 2) since the Scripture says, 'let him call in *the presbyters*, and they will pray over him, anointing him in the name of the Lord,' does it mean to restrict this to presbyters only, or may this anointing be conferred also by the bishop?''

9. *perfatuum*.
10. John 6:54.
11. *cassare*.
12. This passage is Innocent's solution to a marriage case submitted by Probus. Fortunius, after his first wife, Ursa, was kidnapped by barbarians, married Restituta. But Ursa later escaped and came back. Innocent affirms that the bond of earlier marriage rendered the attempted second marriage invalid. Some have found in the statement: *"priore superstite nec divortio eiecta—the first woman surviving and not dismissed by divorce"*, a denial of the indissolubility of marriage, and an affirmation of the legitimacy of a second marriage after divorce. They are then obliged to assume that what the Pope is saying is, "if the man had gotten a divorce, his second marriage would be valid; but he did not get a divorce, so his first marriage remains." The first rule of all interpretation, and which is of special importance when dealing with documents of an age so far removed from our own, is to read only what the document says, and to refrain from reading more into it than is actually there. Those who view the Pope's statement as involving the acceptance of the notion of the acceptability of civil divorce read far more between the lines than is to be found in the lines themselves. They assume that unless divorce were acceptable, the statement would make no sense. Yet, if Probus' inquiry had brought up the question of divorce and had stated that after Ursa was kidnapped Fortunius did get a civil divorce before marrying Restituta, the supposedly enigmatic remark of Innocent would then become a perfectly logical one within the framework of what has always been supposed to have been Catholic practice from the beginning: civil divorce is of no consequence in the face of an ecclesiastically valid marriage. In this hypothesis, Innocent is only pointing out that the divorce is without effect: the woman was not dismissed by the divorce. It may be said that I have broken my own rule and have read what is not there: namely, the wording of Probus' inquiry, which is not extant. But not so. I only offer a hypothesis which makes Innocent's statement entirely orthodox. I still insist on reading no more than what he actually said: "the woman was not dismissed by divorce." What he did not say, and what the opponents of my view read into his remark is: "the woman was not rightly dismissed, because no divorce was gotten; if a divorce had been gotten, the marriage would have been dissolved." That he certainly did not say; and if some think that was what he meant to say, they must do one of two things: either produce evidence that that is what he meant, or prove that he cannot have meant something else. The first is in itself virtually impossible; and the second remains impossible so long as I am able to hypothesize that Probus may have asked whether, since Fortunius did obtain a civil divorce, that first marriage may not be reckoned as dissolved. And unless they produce Probus' letter, which none of us has ever seen, they cannot prove the unavailability of my hypothesis. Furthermore, § 2015 above demonstrates that Innocent would not countenance the second marriage of a woman while her first husband was still alive. Since § 2017 deals with the second marriage of a man, those who would hold that in § 2017 the Pope allows that a divorce can abrogate a legitimate marriage will be obliged to restrict this to the case of a man; they will be obliged to hold that Innocent allowed men to divorce and remarry, but not women. This latter, of course, cannot be dismissed out of hand, and we have seen that the Ambrosiaster is of such a view. But it still remains to be demonstrated that this view, which, under the influence of Roman civil law, regards only the woman's marriage as indissoluble and not that of the man, had any acceptance outside the Ambrosiaster, and, more to the point, that it was shared by Innocent.

ST. CELESTINE I, POPE [*regn. A. D.* 422-432]

Pope Celestine is of no small importance for his dealings with the Eastern patriarchs, especially in regard to Nestorius and the Council of Ephesus (431 A. D.). Except for a fragment of a sermon that appears in the corpus of his letters (no. 10), his letters are his only surviving writings. His pontificate is dated from Sept., 422 A. D. to his death in July of 432 A. D.

LETTERS [*inter A. D.* 422-432]

The corpus of Celestine's letters contains about twenty-seven items, of which sixteen are generally regarded as authentic. The usual source for the texts of his letters is Migne, PL 50, 417-558.

LETTER OF POPE CELESTINE I TO HIS LEGATES TO THE COUNCIL
OF EPHESUS. May 8, 431. [Cum Deo nostro]

2018

[17]

We enjoin upon you the necessary task of guarding the authority of the Apostolic   433
See. And if the instructions handed you have to mention this and if you have to be
present in the assembly, if it comes to controversy, it is not yours to join the fight, but
to judge of their opinions.

LETTER OF POPE CELESTINE I TO THE BISHOPS OF GAUL. 431 A. D.
[Apostolici verba]

2018a

[21, 2]

We kept Augustine always in our communion, a man of holy memory because of his   412
life and merits. Nor did ever so much as a rumor sully him with untoward suspicion. We
remember him as a man of such great knowledge that even my predecessors before me
accounted him among the best teachers.

MARIUS MERCATOR [*fl. ca. A. D. 431*]

In view of his relationship to Augustine, it is likely enough that Marius Mercator was
by birth an African. Later he lived at Rome, from whence, in 418, he sent Augustine
two treatises, not now extant, against the Pelagians. By 429 A. D. we find him living in
a Latin monastery in Thrace, where he wrote a number of works opposing Pelagianism
and Nestorianism, largely for the benefit of his fellow monks.

Besides composing numerous short writings of his own, he also translated a
considerable number of Nestorian works from Greek into Latin, in a slavishly literal
manner, so that his fellow monks could see the genuine heresy of the Nestorians.

ADMONITORY MEMORANDUM AGAINST THE HERESY OF PELAGIUS AND CAELESTIUS [*ca. A. D. 431*]

Marius Mercator's *Commonitorium adversum haeresim Pelagii et Caelestii vel etiam
scripta Iuliani*, the first of two *Commonitoria* against Pelagianism, was written not long
after Augustine's death, possibly already in 430, not later than 432, and most likely in
431 A. D. It offers a rather bitter critique of the views of Julian of Eclanum.

The writings of Mercator, along with other related documents, were assembled,
probably after 533 A. D., and probably by a Scythian monk in Constantinople or
Thrace, in a compilation called the *Collectio Palatina*, now residing in the Vatican
Library as the *Codex Vat. Palat. 234*. In this *Collectio Palatina* the first item is the
present *commonitorium*.

The *Collectio Palatina* has been published in an excellent edition by E. Schwartz, in
his *Acta conciliorum oecumenicorum*, Vol. I, part 5. Otherwise, the text can be gotten
from Migne, PL 48, 109-172, Migne's edition being largely a reprint of J. Garnier's
edition of 1673, with some attention given also to the edition of Stephen Baluze of 1684
and that of A. Gallandi of 1772, which latter was itself hardly more than a reprint of
Baluze.

2019

[5]

[Caelestius] has become so bold that openly and publicly he spreads his views abroad   619
among the people, in words much the same as these: Adam was created mortal and he   611
would have died whether he had sinned or not. The sin of Adam injured himself alone   614
and not the whole human race. When infants are born they are in the state in which Adam
was before the fall. Since not everyone belonging to the human race dies through Adam's   831
death, neither does everyone belonging to the human race rise up through Christ's   1012
resurrection. Infants have eternal life even if they are not baptized. These five headings   618
are productive of one most impious and abominable opinion: he adds, moreover, that a   727
man is able to be without sin, and can easily keep the commandments of God; that
before the coming of Christ there were men without sin, and that the Law, just like
the Gospel, does also obtain the kingdom of heaven.

PAULUS OROSIUS [fl. ca. A. D. 415]

Orosius is generally accounted a Spanish priest, though in fact his birthplace is most
likely to have been Bracara, now Braga, in Portugal. Fleeing before the Vandals, he
came in 414 A. D. to Hippo, where he presented to Augustine his *Commonitorium de
errore Priscillianistarum et Origenistarum*. He asked Augustine to use this outline of
errors in writing a major refutation. Augustine's response was his *Ad Orosium presbyter
contra Priscillianistas et Origenistas liber unus;* (above, §§ 1802-1805).

Augustine was much taken with the abilities of Orosius, and sent him to Bethlehem in
415 A. D. to consult with Jerome on the question of the origin of the soul, and likewise
to warn Jerome about Pelagius, who had lately gone to Palestine. At Bethlehem in that
same year Orosius wrote his *Liber apologeticus*.

Orosius had been less than a year in Palestine when he left, intending to return to
Spain. Arriving at the Island of Minorca, the reports of the wars and barbarian
atrocities in Spain frightened him off, and he went instead to Hippo and Augustine. At
Hippo he wrote his best-known work, the *Historiarum adversum paganos libri septem*.
After 418 A. D. we hear of him no more. Whether he died in Africa or did finally
return to Spain is not known.

Orosius' *Historiarum* was translated into Anglo-Saxon by King Alfred, and has been
published by H. Sweet in Vol. 79 of the *Publications of the Early English Text Society*.

APOLOGY [A. D. 415]

Upon his arrival at Bethlehem in 415 A. D., Orosius almost immediately became
deeply involved in the Pelagian controversy. He was summoned to the Council of
Jerusalem on July 30, 415, to inform the synodal fathers on the standing of Pelagius in
Africa, and what was being done about him there. The president of the Council was
John of Jerusalem, who had taken Pelagius under his wing and found no fault with him.
The information given by Orosius angered John, and heated words were exchanged in
the Council itself.

Soon after the Council, John accused Orosius of blasphemy, on the grounds that he
had said that not even with God's help, could a man remain without sin. Orosius, of
course, could not let that charge pass unnoticed, and he replied with his work entitled
Liber apologeticus, which he addressed to the *beatissimi sacerdotes* who had been in
attendance at the Council of Jerusalem.

The Migne edition, reprinting that of S. Haverkamp, is in PL 31, 1173-1212. The
better edition, however, is that of C. Zangmeister in Vol. 5 (1882) of the Vienna Corpus
(CSEL).

2020

[19]

My invariably constant and undoubted opinion is this: God supplies His help not   724
only in his own body, which is the Church, to which He affords His gifts of grace on
account of the faith of believers, but also to all peoples in this world, because of the
patience and eternal clemency which is His own; and not as you assert, [Pelagius],   726
with your disciple Caelestius,—for whom already in the African Council the inner
character of your impious teachings had been crushed,—that in natural good alone and in
free choice one grace is commonly bestowed on all; rather, that grace is supplied to each
and all individually, in season and out, every day, every minute, and at every smallest
moment of time.

HILARY [*fl. ca. A. D.* 428 / 429]

The Hilary with whom we are here concerned has sometimes been confused with St.
Hilary of Arles, who flourished at about the same time, and was Bishop of Arles. They
cannot, however, be identified. The Bishop of Arles was an opponent of St. Augustine's
doctrine of free will and predestination, while our present Hilary was its staunch
advocate.

Of this present Hilary, very little is known. He was at one time personally acquainted
with Augustine. He is considerably younger than Augustine. Possibly he is originally
from Africa, and was a pupil of Augustine. He is a layman. And when we first meet him
he is living in Southern Gaul, perhaps at Marseilles, with his parents.

We know that Hilary wrote at least two and probably more letters to Augustine. If he
wrote anything else, it is not recorded. And of his letters to Augustine, only one has
survived, no. 226 in the corpus of Augustine's letters.

LETTER OF A CERTAIN HILARY, A LAYMAN, TO AUGUSTINE
OF HIPPO [*A. D.* 428 *aut* 429].

The purpose of Hilary's letter to Augustine is to acquaint the latter with the doctrinal
situation in Marseilles and Southern Gaul, where Massilianism (so-called from its
origins at Marseilles) or Semi-Pelagianism was making great headway. He recounts
something of the arguments used by the Massilians, by which they claim to refute
various writings of Augustine. The reply called forth by Hilary's letter is Augustine's
The Predestination of the Saints (see above, §§ 1978-1991).

The text of the letter will be found wherever Augustine's letters are found. Currently
the best critical edition, superseding the Maurist text, is Goldbacher's edition in the
Corpus Vindobonensis, CSEL, Vol. 57 (1911).

2021

[226, 2]

[The Massilians] agree that in Adam all men perished, and that no one can be saved   729
from that death by his own choosing (1). But they assert that it is consistent with truth or
congruous with preaching, that, when the opportunity for obtaining salvation is announced
to men who are prostrate and never able to rise up by their own powers, they can be cured
of their illness by the merit of their having willed and believed, and that an increase of their
faith and their total cure follow as an effect. Otherwise, they agree that no one is able to
suffice for himself, either for the beginning of this work or for carrying it through to

completion. Neither do they think that the fact that everyone who is sick wills, with a terrified and suppliant will, to be made well, is to be ascribed as a reason for their being cured. As to the words, "Believe, and you shall be saved (2)," they assert that one of these is demanded, while the other is offered, in such a way that if that which is demanded is complied with, on that account will what is offered be given. They think it follows from this that faith must be exhibited by him, to whose nature it is granted by his Creator; and they think that no nature is so debased or destroyed that it ought not or cannot will to be healed; for which reason either it is healed of its illness, or, if it does not will it, it is punished by being left with it. [They think] it is not a denial of grace to say that grace is preceded by such a will as can only seek its physician but can do nothing by itself. . . . [3] But when they are asked why [the faith] is preached or not preached to some persons and in some places, or whether it will now be preached, though formerly almost all were without preaching, just as even now some peoples are without preaching, they reply that it is because of the divine foreknowledge, and that the truth was announced or will be announced at that time and in that place, when and where God foresaw that it would be believed.

2022

[226, 4]

Otherwise [the Massilians] contend that foreknowledge and predestination or purpose   729
amount to this, that God foreknew, or predestined, or purposed to choose those who were
going to believe; neither can it be said in regard to this belief, "What have you that you did
not receive (3)?" since this belief remains in the same nature which, though now vitiated,
was whole and perfect when it was given. . . . Hence the foreknowledge which [the
Massilians] accept is to be understood as a foreknowledge of a future faith; and they would
have it that the perseverance given to anyone is not a grace from which that person is not
able to stray, but a grace from which, by his own will, he is able to fall away and be
weakened.

1. *proprio arbitrio.*
2. Acts 16:31. See also Mark 16:16.
3. 1 Cor. 4:7.

PAULINUS OF MILAN [*fl. ca. A. D.* 380-420]

Paulinus was a cleric at Milan, a deacon; but, although Isidore of Seville calls him a priest, it remains doubtful that he ever advanced in orders beyond the diaconate. It was soon after 375 A. D. that he received his clerical training in Milan, and he served from that time on as secretary to St. Ambrose.

After Ambrose's death on April 4, 397 A. D., Paulinus went to Africa. There, under Augustine's influence, he wrote his *Life of Saint Ambrose*. His only other extant writing is his denunciation of Caelestius, addressed from Carthage to Pope Zosimus on November 8, 417: *Libellus adversus Caelestium Zosimo Papae oblatus*.

LIFE OF SAINT AMBROSE [*ca. A. D.* 420]

Ambrose had always been held in the greatest reverence by Augustine, who regarded him as the father of his conversion; and Augustine knew also of the great bond of friendship which had existed between Ambrose and Paulinus, and their long years of

association which gave Paulinus a better knowledge of Ambrose than anyone else could have. Consequently, upon meeting Paulinus in Africa, Augustine suggested to him that he ought to write an account of the life of Ambrose. Paulinus' protests of his own unworthiness and lack of ability are, of course, no more than the literary device that etiquette demanded. He performed the task quite ably.

The Migne reprint of the Maurist text of Paulinus' *Vita Sancti Ambrosii* is to be found in PL 14, 27-46. Suggestions as to better readings can be found in the dissertation on Paulinus' *Vita* by Sister Simplicia Kaniecka, published at The Catholic University of America, Washington, in 1928.

2023

[39]

[Ambrose] rejoiced also with those who rejoiced, and wept with those who wept (1).   921
For whenever anyone confessed his sins to him to receive a penance, he so wept that he forced the penitent too to weep. For he considered that he was himself in a state similar to that of the penitent. But when cases of crimes were confessed to him, he spoke of it to none but the Lord alone, with whom he interceded; and thus he left a good example to later priests, to be intercessors with God rather than accusers among men. For even according to the Apostle, love is to be confirmed in dealing with a person of this kind (2); for he has become his own accuser who does not wait for but anticipates the accuser; and thus, by confessing, he lightens his own sin, lest he have something of which the adversary might accuse him (3).

1. See Rom. 12:15.
2. See 2 Cor. 2:8.
3. The adversary who might accuse us, as well as the accuser whom we ought not wait for but rather anticipate by becoming our own accuser, is Satan. See Origen, *Homilies on Leviticus* 3, 4, § 494 in Volume 1 above.

ST. PROSPER OF AQUITAINE [† *post A. D.* 455]

Not much is known of St. Prosper of Aquitaine, and even of that little, most must be gleaned from his own writings. He was a monk at Marseilles, but not in clerical orders; a friend of Hilary who wrote letter no. 226 in the corpus of Augustine's letters; but unlike Hilary, he had no personal acquaintance with Augustine.

Soon after Augustine's death in August of 430, Prosper and Hilary went in person to Rome, where they asked Pope Celestine I to issue a formal condemnation of Semi-Pelagianism, then called Massilianism. Celestine did issue a letter to the bishops of Gaul (§ 2018a above), generally commending Augustine; but he did not condemn Semi-Pelagianism, and only enjoined a silence upon the disputed points.

Beginning in 432 A. D. Prosper himself commenced to drift away from the strictest interpretations of Augustinian theology. He no longer held a predestination to damnation that is prior to any foreknowledge of a man's deserts. He did continue to see, however, that the root of the Pelagian and Semi-Pelagian errors is in the teaching that is central to them: the thesis that grace is given men in accord with their merits.

When Leo the Great became Bishop of Rome in 440 A. D., Prosper came down again from Gaul and was given a post in the papal chancellery. According to Gennadius of Marseilles, it was Prosper who drafted certain letters of Pope Leo against Eutyches and Monophysitism. Prosper cannot be found alive after 455 A. D.

LETTER OF PROSPER OF AQUITAINE TO AUGUSTINE OF HIPPO
[*A. D.* 428 *aut* 429]

When Hilary wrote to Augustine his letter (no. 226) informing Augustine of the great inroads being made by Semi-Pelagianism or Massilianism, he said in the same letter that he would have a friend also write to Augustine, a friend who was better qualified to give Augustine an accurate description of the situation. The man referred to was undoubtedly Prosper of Aquitaine; and Prosper's letter to Augustine is preserved as no. 225 in the corpus of Augustine's letters. Prosper's letter no. 225 in conjunction with Hilary's letter no. 226 was conjointly responsible for calling forth Augustine's reply, his *The Predestination of the Saints* (see above, §§ 1978-1991).

Since the letter in question is preserved with the letters of Augustine, the best source of the text is Goldbacher's edition in the *Vienna Corpus*, CSEL Vol. 57 (1911), which has superseded the Maurist edition and Migne.

2024

[225, 4]

Indeed, some of these [Massilians] are so far from abandoning Pelagian paths that,   729
when they are obliged to confess the grace of Christ, which is antecedent to any human merits,—for, were it given in view of merit, it would not be right to call it grace,—they hold that the situation of every man is this: when man has no prior merits because he has no previous existence, the grace of the Creator makes him rational and gives him free choice, so that through his discernment of good and evil, he may be able to direct his own will to the knowledge of God and to obedience to His commands; and through the use of a natural faculty, by asking, by seeking, and by knocking, he is able to attain even to that grace by which we are reborn in Christ: and thus he can receive, he can find, and he can enter in, because, having made good use of a good gift of nature, he has merited, with the help of initial grace, to attain to the grace of salvation.

2025

[225, 5]

When we offer as objection to these arguments the countless multitude of infants,   619
who, except for original sin, under which all men alike are born into the condemnation of the first man, have as yet no will, no proper actions, and who, not without a judgment of God, are cut off and are to be carried away before any experience of this life gives them a discernment of good and evil, so that some, through rebirth, are enrolled among the heirs of the heavenly kingdom, while others, without Baptism, pass over among the debtors of eternal death: such are lost, they say, and such are saved, according to what the divine knowledge foresees they would have done in their adult years, if they had been preserved to a responsible age (1)!

1. *si ad activam servarentur aetatem.*

RESPONSES ON BEHALF OF AUGUSTINE TO THE ARTICLES OF OBJECTIONS RAISED BY HIS CALUMNIATORS IN GAUL [*A. D.* 431 *aut* 432]

Augustine was dead. He could no more speak for himself. So Prosper would speak for him. When the Massilians or Semi-Pelagians of Marseilles renewed their attacks on Augustine's doctrine of predestination Prosper answered in his stead, with his *Pro*

 *Augustino responsiones ad capitula obiectionum Gallorum calumniantium*, written in 431 or 432 A. D.

In PL 45 Migne reprints the Maurist edition. The best edition of the present work, however, is that which was first published at Paris in 1711, the work of J. B. Le Brun des Marettes and L. Mangeant. It was reprinted in 1774 and again in 1782; and although he had already reprinted the Maurist edition in PL 45, Migne also reprints the Mangeant edition in PL 51, 155-174. This latter seems to be still the standard.

2026

[*Resp. ad. Obi.* 3]

Just as good works are to be referred to Him that inspires them, God, so too evil   214
works are to be referred to those who are sinning. For sinners have not been abandoned   721
by God so that they might themselves abandon God; rather, they have abandoned and have
been abandoned and have been changed from good to evil by their own will; and
consequently, although they may have been reborn, although they may have been justified,
they are not, however, predestined by Him who foreknew what kind of persons they would
be.

2027

[*Resp. ad Obi.* 6]

Indeed, a man who has been justified, that is, who from impious has been made   773
pious, since he had no antecedent good merit, receives a gift, by which gift he may also   772
acquire merit. Thus, what was begun in him by Christ's grace can also be augmented
by the industry of his free choice; but never in the absence of God's help, without which
no one is able either to progress or to continue in doing good.

2028

[*Resp. ad Obi.* 7]

Since there can be no doubt that perseverance in good even to the end is a gift of   672
God,—which, it is clear, some, from the very fact that they have not persevered, never   673
had,—it is in no way a calumniation of God to say that these were not given what was
given to others; rather, it is to be confessed both that He gave mercifully what He did   720
give, and He withheld justly what He did not give, so that, although the cause of a man's
falling away originates in free choice, the cause of his standing firm does not
likewise have its origins in himself. If falling away is done by human effort, standing
firm is accomplished by means of a divine gift.

2030

[*Sent. super Cap.* 8]

Again, whoever says that God does not will all men to be saved, but only the certain   200
number of the predestined, is saying a harsher thing than ought to be said of the   201
inscrutable depth of the grace of God, who both wills that all should be saved and come
to a knowledge of the truth (1), and fulfills the proposal of His will in those whom,
when He foreknew them, He predestined, when He predestined them, He called, when
He called them, He justified, and, when He justified them, He glorified (2). . . .   215
And thus, those who are saved are saved because God willed them to be saved, and those
who perish do perish because they deserved to perish.

1. 1 Tim. 2:4.
2. Rom. 8:30.

RESPONSES ON BEHALF OF AUGUSTINE TO THE ARTICLES OF OBJECTIONS RAISED BY THE VINCENTIANISTS [*A. D.* 431 *aut* 432]

The present work, *Pro Augustino responsiones ad capitula obiectionum Vincentianarum*, is similar to the last in the time of its being written, in its purpose, form, and largely even in its content. The Vincentianists here is, as a term, somewhat overblown; for they are in fact none other than Vincent of Lerins personally. We shall meet him shortly, and find that he is quite important in the history of doctrine, and is generally rather highly respected; but he was, in fact, a Semi-Pelagian. The *Obiectiones* of Vincent, to which Prosper now offers the replies that Augustine would have given were he alive, is no longer extant.

The Maurist edition of the present work can be found reprinted in Migne, PL 45. The better edition, that of Mangeant, which still seems to be the standard, is reprinted in Migne, PL 51, 177-186.

2031

[*Resp. ad Obi.* 1]

The true and powerful and only remedy against the wound of original sin, by which sin   374
in Adam the nature of all men has been corrupted and has been given a death blow,
and whence the disease of concupiscence takes firm hold, is the death of the Son of God,
our Lord Jesus Christ, who, though He was free of the debt of death and alone was   345
without sin, died for sins and for debtors to death. In view of the magnitude and potency   383
of the price, and because it pertains to the universal condition of the human race, the   386
blood of Christ is the redemption of the whole world.

2032

[*Resp. ad Obi.* 10]

It is a detestable and abominable opinion that makes God the author of any kind of   638
evil will or evil action. His predestination is never outside His goodness, never outside
His justice. . . . Plainly He predestined His judgment, in which recompense will be
made to each one for what he has done, whether good or whether evil. But if it
were by God's will that men sin, there would be no future judgment at all.

2033

[*Resp. ad Obi.* 12]

These, however, of whom it is said: "They have gone forth from us, but they were   703
not of us. For if they had been of us, they would surely have remained with us (1),"   214
went forth voluntarily and voluntarily they fell. And because it was foreknown that they
would fall, they were not predestined. But they would have been predestined if they
were going to return and remain in holiness and truth. And consequently, God's
predestination is the cause of the standing firm of many, but for no one is it the
cause of their falling.

1. 1 John 2:19.

THE GRACE OF GOD AND FREE CHOICE: A BOOK AGAINST
THE CONFERENCE MASTER [*A. D.* 433 *aut* 434]

Prosper's *De gratia Dei et libero arbitrio liber contra Collatorem* was written after
the death of Pope Celestine I (July 31, 432), and probably in 433 or 434. The
Conference Master or *Collator* against whom Prosper is writing is clearly John
Cassian, the Abbot of the monastery at Marseilles, himself a Semi-Pelagian, and the
author of a work called the Conferences, in Latin, *Collationes*, (below, §§ 2050-2053).
Cassian is, in fact, largely because of book thirteen of his *Conferences*, generally
regarded as the father of Semi-Pelagianism.

The principal point of attack for Prosper is that same thirteenth book of the
Conferences, in which Cassian says that God's grace sometimes precedes and sometimes
follows man's will.

Like the previous two works, the present one also is found in two places in Migne; the
Maurist edition reprinted in PL 45; and better, the Mangeant edition in PL 51, 213-276,
this latter remaining even yet the standard text.

2034

[3, 1]

How is it that you do not perceive that you have fallen into that error, and, like it   711
or not, you are convicted of saying that the grace of God is given according to our merits,
when you affirm that there is something of the good works of men themselves that is
antecedent, on account of which they are given grace? For the faith of asking, the piety
of seeking, and the urgency of knocking cannot be unproductive of merit, especially   656
since they are all alike connected with the reward of receiving, of finding, and of
entering. Thus it is superfluous, nay, it is impious, to want a place for merits to exist
prior to grace, in such a way that what the Lord says were not entirely true: "No one
comes to Me, unless the Father who sent Me draw him (1)," which He could not say
at all if it were to be believed that there could be any sort of conversion of a man without   683
God's enlightening him, or if the will of man could in any way reach out to God without
God's grace.

2035

[7, 2]

Truth says: "No one comes to Me, unless the Father who sent Me draw him (2)."   684
If, then, no one comes unless he is drawn, all who come in whatever way are drawn.   680
The contemplation of the elements and the most orderly beauty of all that is in them surely
draws us to God. For his invisible attributes, from the creation of the world, are clearly
perceived by the intellect, through the things that were made (3). . . . And who can
perceive or tell through what sentiments the visitation of God can lead the human soul, so
that what it fled, it follows; what it hated, it loves; what it felt distasteful, it longs for; and
by a sudden and marvelous change, what was closed to it is opened; what was burdensome
is light; what was bitter is sweet; what was hidden is made clear?

2036

[9, 3]

For in that ruin of the universal fall neither the substance nor the will of human   612
nature has been snatched away; but it has been deprived of the light and glory of its   613
virtues by the deceit of the Envious One. But when it had lost that by which it would have
been able to achieve eternity and an incorruption of body and soul that could not be

lost, what did it have left except that which pertains to temporal life, the whole of which belongs to damnation and punishment? That is why those born in Adam need to be reborn in Christ, lest they be found in that generation which perishes.

2037

[13, 3]

And thus it is most clearly evident that in the souls of the impious no virtue dwells,   653
but all the works of those who have wisdom that is not spiritual but animal, not
heavenly but earthly, not Christian but diabolic, not from the Father of Lights
but from the Prince of Darkness, are impure and polluted, while even those things
that they would not have except by God's gift of them, they put at the disposal of him
who first drew away from God.

2038

[18, 3]

[We profess] that free choice, given to man naturally, can remain in nature, but   613
changed in quality and condition through the Mediator of God and men, the Man,   387
Christ Jesus (4), who turns the will itself aside from that which it was perversely   376
willing, and directs it to that which it would be good for it to will.

1. John 6:44.
2. John 6:44.
3. Rom. 1:20.
4. 1 Tim. 2:5.

EXPLANATION OF THE PSALMS [A. D. 433]

Prosper's *Expositio psalmorum*, written in 433 A. D., is a gleaning entirely or almost entirely from Augustine's *Enarrationes in psalmos*. In the form in which we have the work, it treats only of Psalms 100-150, however, whereas Augustine commented on the whole psalter of 150 Psalms. It has sometimes been remarked that Prosper's treatment of the first 99 Psalms is not extant, as if he had written such but it had not come down to us. More probably, since there is absolutely no trace at all of any such work of Prosper on Psalms 1-99, he only wrote of Psalms 100-150. It seems probable that he had no copy of the first two thirds of Augustine's work; for neither is anything from Augustine's explanations of the first 99 Psalms to be found in Prosper's *Liber sententiarum*, gleaned from the writings of Augustine.

The text in Migne, PL 51, 277-426, is now superseded by the edition of P. Callens in the *Corpus Christianorum*, Vol. 68A (1972), pp. 1-211.

2039

[Ps. 103(104):19]

"The sun has known its setting." Christ knew His suffering. The Passion of Christ   350
is Christ's setting. But does the sun so set that it rises not again? "Is he that sleeps not
allowed to rise up again (1)?" But what does "it has known its setting" mean, except that
it was acceptable to Him that He should die? For willingly He accepted cross and death.
And just as He takes no notice of what is not agreeable to Him, so too the things that are in
accord with His will He knows and acknowledges.

2040
[Ps. 132(133):2]

"Like ointment on the head, which ran down upon the beard, upon the beard of that   382
Aaron.*"* By the priest Aaron, that Priest is indicated who alone fulfills the sacrament
of the true High Priest (2), not with a victim of another kind, but in the oblation of His
own body and blood: same Priest, same Victim, Propitiator and Propitiation, the One
who effects all the mysteries for which He was announced. Who died, was buried,   391
and rose again, He ascended into heaven, exalting human nature above every other   291
name, and sending the Holy Spirit, whose unction would penetrate every Church (3).

1. Ps. 40[41]:9.
2. *veri pontificis sacramentum.*
3. *cuius unctio omnem ecclesiam penetraret.*

BOOK OF THESES GLEANED FROM THE WORKS OF ST. AUGUSTINE
[ca. A. D. 450]

About the year 450 A. D. Prosper compiled his *Sententiarum ex operibus S. Augustini
delibatarum liber.* It is a collection of 392 citations, mostly very short, taken directly
from Augustine's writings. There is no systematic order to the collection. Apparently
Prosper simply read through Augustine's writings, as complete as he could find them,
and copied down these 392 theses or theological propositions as he found them. Yet they
do constitute a satisfactory summation of Augustinian theology.

When the Council of Orange in 529 finally condemned Semi-Pelagianism, sixteen of
its twenty-five canons were taken in whole or in part from Prosper's *Liber sententiarum.*

The edition of Luke Mangeant in Migne, PL 51, 427-296 is now superseded by the
critical edition of M. Gastaldo in the *Corpus Christianorum*, Vol. 68A (1972), pp.
257-365.

2041
[106]

The life of every non-believer is sin, and nothing is good without the Highest Good.   654
Where knowledge of eternal and unchangeable Truth is lacking there is but false virtue
even with the best of conduct.

THE CALL OF ALL NATIONS [ca. A. D. 450]

The authenticity of the *(Duo libri) De vocatione omnium gentium* as a work of
Prosper of Aquitaine was first seriously questioned by P. Quesnel in the seventeenth
century. Quesnel attributed the work to Pope St. Leo the Great. In antiquity, though the
work is anonymous, it was generally attributed to Prosper, although a few manuscripts
had assigned it to St. Ambrose. Actually, of course, Ambrose does not come into it at
all, since he was dead before Pelagianism or Semi-Pelagianism had come to life. After
Quesnel, a number of authors accepted it as a work of Pope Leo; and some assigned it to
an otherwise unknown Prosper.

M. C. Coppuyns established the Prosperian (he of Aquitaine) authenticity of the work
in his article *"L'auteur du De vocatione omnium gentium,"* in the *Revue Bénédictine*,
Vol. 39 (1927), pp. 156-170, a view which he himself supplemented and strengthened

with further articles in Vol. 41 of the same Maredsous periodical. His findings are now generally accepted as conclusive.

Soon after Augustine's death Prosper himself began to have some doubts about the notion of a predestination to damnation. Perhaps Augustine had never said that predestination to eternal death was based on God's foreknowledge of the sinner; but it can easily be inferred from Augustine, whether or not he consciously implied it; and what is more to the present point: Prosper thought that such was Augustine's notion. Prosper soon found it indefensible, however; and by the time he wrote *The Call of All Nations*, in the period of comparative quiet between the two outbreaks of Semi-Pelagianism and when there was less urgency about the extirpation of heresy, he was trying to reconcile certain aspects of the Augustinian and Semi-Pelagian views to each other.

Prosper stresses God's universal salvific will much more than Augustine did; and he brings human freedom more to the fore than Augustine had. Like Augustine, he stresses very much the gratuitous quality of grace; it must not be made dependent upon any initial movements on the part of man. But in connexion with grace, Prosper speaks not of predestination but of election. And if it be said that it is the same thing but a different term, that is itself a very telling point: now Prosper did not even want to use the term predestination. For Prosper, election is the result of God's foreknowledge of the elect, and is the only answer to the mysterious question of why God chooses—elects or predestines—one person and not another. Prosper does not yet know of grace that is sufficient but not efficacious, which is given to all men so that they could, if they would cooperate and will to be saved, achieve an eternal reward.

The text established by Luke Mangeant, and reprinted in ML 51, 647-722, is generally regarded as the standard.

2042

[1, 7]

Although an attempt was made by some, by the natural light of reason, to resist   654
vices, it was but a sterile embellishment of their earthly lives, and did not bring them to true virtues and eternal happiness. For without worship of the true God, even what might seem to be virtue is sin; without God, no one is able to please God.

2043

[1, 8]

When the word of God, through the ministry of those who preach, falls upon the   680
ears of the flesh, the action of divine power is mixed with the sound of a human   682
voice, and He that inspires the preacher's office strengthens also the hearer's heart.

2044

[1, 17]

And if you direct the attention of your mind to those who, growing old in shameful   711
deeds and crimes, are renewed by Christ's sacrament of Baptism at the very end of   773
their life, and, without any good works to plead for them, are transferred to the assembly of the kingdom of heaven, how will you understand this divine judgment, unless you acknowledge that God's gifts are undoubtedly gratuitous? And just as there are no crimes so detestable that they can prevent the gift of grace, so too there can be no works so eminent that they are owed in condign judgment that which is given freely. Would it not be a debasement of redemption in Christ's blood, and would not God's mercy be made secondary to human works, if justification, which is through grace, were owed in view of preceding merits, so that it were not the gift of a Donor, but the wages of a laborer?

2045

[1, 24]

By these testimonies [of Scripture], I think it is abundantly demonstrated,—although   656
many other texts might also be assembled,—that faith, by which the impious man   711
is made just, cannot be had except as God's gift; and it is not to be attributed to preceding
merits, but is given so that it might itself be the source of merits, and, while it is itself
given unprayed for, the prayers it inspires obtain all other favors.

2046

[2, 17]

And if perhaps, just as we know that in former times some peoples were not admitted   724
to the assembly of the sons of God, in like manner even now in the most remote parts of
the world there are some nations on which the light of the Savior's grace does not yet
shine, still, we do not doubt that in God's hidden judgment a time of calling has been
appointed for them, when they too will hear and accept the Gospel they have not yet heard.
Nevertheless, that measure of general help, which is always provided for all men, is not
denied them from above (1).

2047

[2, 29]

Certainly God's manifold and indescribable goodness, as we have abundantly proved,   724
always provided and does yet provide for the totality of mankind, so that none of those
perishing can plead the excuse that he was excluded from the light of truth, and neither is
anyone free to boast of his own righteousness, since the former go down to punishment by
their own wickedness, and the latter go on to glory by the grace of God.

1. Prosper has not caught the notion of sufficient grace; in its fuller context it is clear that with this present line he is still
   talking only about the perception of God's existence through creation. Yet, using this notion as he does, it is not really
   a very great step to arrive at the idea of sufficient grace.

LEPORIUS [*fl. ca. A. D.* 426]

Leporius was a monk in Gaul, probably of the Diocese of Treves, when, because of
his heretical doctrines, he was obliged to leave his monastery to become a homeless
wanderer. His journeyings brought him to Africa where he met Augustine; and the great
doctor of Hippo cured his heretical tendencies.

DOCUMENT OF AMENDMENT [*ca. A. D.* 426]

At a Council of Carthage of uncertain date but probably about 426 A. D., Leporius
submitted a profession of his now reformed faith. This *Libellus emendationis* of
Leporius was then forwarded by the Fathers of Carthage, Bishops Aurelius, Augustine,
Florentius and Secundinus, to the Bishops of Gaul, along with a covering letter, the
Epistula episcoporum Africae ad episcopos Galliae (no. 219 in the collected letters of
Augustine), recommending the now orthodox and properly chastened Leporius.

From the *Libellus emendationis* or *Document of Amendment* it is evident that
Leporius' former errors were in the area of Christology, and that he actually held a kind
of Nestorianism in advance of Nestorius, believing that there were in Christ not just two
natures inseparably united in one person, but two distinct persons, a human and a

divine. According to Cassian and Gennadius, he also foreswore Pelagianism. Of no great importance in itself, Leporius' *Libellus emendationis*,—revised somewhat by Augustine, no doubt,—has achieved a certain prominence and celebrity as a monument of Christology.

The text of the *Libellus emendationis*, along with the letter to the Bishops of Gaul, is reprinted in Migne, PL 31, 1221-1232, from the edition of Andreas Gallandi. Both texts are found also in Mansi, Vol. 4, pp. 518-528. The letter to the bishops of Gaul would best be read in Goldbacher's edition of Augustine's letters in the Vienna Corpus, CSEL, Vol. 57 (1911). But we are presently concerned not with the letter but with the *Libellus*; and for that I am not aware of any edition more reliable than Migne's Gallandi.

2048

[3]

We confess, therefore, that our Lord and God, Jesus Christ, the only Son of God,   302
born of the Father before the ages, and in times most recent, made man of the Holy   311
Spirit and the Ever-Virgin Mary, was born God; and confessing each substance, we   783
accept, in the light of pious faith, that His humanity and His divinity are united   329
inseparably. And thus, from the time when He took flesh, we say that all that was of God passed into the Man, and all that was of man came into God; and that is what we mean when we say that the Word became flesh: not that by some conversion or change He began to be what He before was not, but that by the power of the divine economy   321
the Word of the Father, never departing from the Father, deigned to become really   320
man; and the Only-begotten was incarnate in that secret mystery which He understood (for it is ours to believe, His to understand).

2049

[6]

Our faith consists largely in this: that we believe that the only Son of God, not adoptive   340
but His own, not a phantasm but real, not temporary but eternal, suffered all things   383
for us according to the flesh. . . . [10] But so that I may leave no suspicion in anyone's   351
mind in regard to this matter, I did formerly say, or rather, I answered to objections and said that our Lord Jesus Christ, as Man, was without [certain] knowledge. But now I not only do not presume to say such, but I even anathematize my earlier opinion advanced in this matter; for it is not allowed to be said that, even as Man, the Lord was ignorant of the Prophets.

ST. JOHN CASSIAN [*ca. A. D.* 360 – *ca. A. D.* 435]

John Cassian is not a saint of the Church's universal calendar; but he is reckoned and revered as a saint in a good many local Churches of France. In spite of some evidence and arguments to the contrary, it remains most probable that Cassian was a native of Southern Gaul. Bardenhewer remarks that Ménager's suggestion that Scythopolis in Palestine was Cassian's birthplace "will hardly win many friends."

As a youth in company with an older friend Germanus, Cassian sojourned for a while in a monastery in Bethlehem. Later, about the year 385 A. D., his pursuit of asceticism took him to Egypt, where he spent seven years learning the science of asceticism from the monks and ascetics of monasticism's homeland. A second time he came to Egypt and spent another year in the deserts of Scete, which he later termed the habitat of the most perfect monks.

Journeying on to Constantinople he was ordained to the diaconate by John Chrysostom himself. In 405 A. D., with Chrysostom a second time in exile, Cassian, still in the company of Germanus, came to Rome; but after this, we hear of the faithful Germanus no more.

In 415 A. D., Cassian, now a priest, founded two monasteries at Marseilles, one for men and the other for women; and there, until his death about twenty years later, he ruled his monasteries as abbot.

It was in these monasteries at Marseilles and with Cassian as its father that Semi-Pelagianism was born. Originally the Semi-Pelagians were called Massilians after their origins at Marseilles; and if we fall into the very common error of regarding Semi-Pelagianism as no more than a kind of diluted Pelagianism we will never understand John Cassian. As a Semi-Pelagian, he held no brief at all with the Pelagians. The latter he condemned roundly. He regarded Pelagianism as the mother of Nestorianism, which he termed Pelagianism's "pupil and imitator," because, while Pelagianism taught that man could by his own efforts and without God's help achieve righteousness, Nestorianism taught that the Man Jesus, by the virtuous conduct of His life, came himself to deserve union with the Divine Majesty.

If the latter notion seems very similar to the rather common idea of our own times to the effect that Christ only came gradually to realize that he was God and perhaps was not fully aware of it until He was hanging on the cross—is this the same as saying that His divinity was only gradually actualized and that perhaps it was not fully actualized until He was hanging on the cross?—possibly it is because Nestorianism is not nearly so dead an issue as some suppose, and there is an effective revival of it among some "Catholic" theologians even today. Heresies never die; they just change their names. I cannot recall any modern heresy that is really new; nor do I know of any ancient heresy that has been slain outright. Catholic doctrine is so entirely cohesive that if only one thread of it is cut the whole unravels. Heresy, at least within a limited number of theological categories, seems to bear a similar stamp of cohesion, so that if a man fall into only one, he is soon forced to all, even the seemingly diametrically opposed.

The Semi-Pelagians roundly denied that they were Pelagians; but they still thought that *sometimes* God bestows His grace because, even before grace, man's natural goodness might bring him to turn first to God.

The Abbot St. John Cassian is best remembered for three great works: a) *De institutis coenobiorum;* b) *Collationes;* c) *De incarnatione Christi contra Nestorium*. We will concern ourselves only with the last two.

CONFERENCES [*inter A. D.* 420-428]

The *Collationes* is a quite lengthy work in three parts, the first part dating from 420 or soon thereafter, the second part from before 426, and the third part no later than 428 A. D. In the first part of the *Conferences*, embracing conferences 1-10, Cassian recalls his earliest days in Scete and the wisdom learned of the holy anchorites he knew there. The second part, conferences 11-17, recalls what he learned from the saintly monks introduced to him by a certain Bishop Archebius of Panephysis near Thennesus at the Tanitic mouth of the Nile. In the third part, conferences 18-24, we find him with various other monks and ascetics of Egypt.

It was in the thirteenth conference that Cassian threw down the gauntlet, so to speak, of his Semi-Pelagianism, with his speculation that grace sometimes precedes and sometimes follows the movements of man's good will, a notion to which Prosper of Aquitaine reacted with a violence that bordered on frenzy.

In its literary form the *Conferences* is very closely related to the various collections of sayings of the Fathers, such as the *Apophthegmata patrōn* and the *Verba seniorum*, and the various collections that go under much these same names. Incidentally, Cassian must have left something of his mark on the Egyptian ascetics; for I notice that the Ethiopic *Paternicon* speaks of an 'Abba Qesyânos, who can only be our Cassian.

The text given in Migne, PL 49, 477-1328, is a reprint of A. Gazet's Douai edition of 1616. It has, happily, been replaced by M. Petschenig's critical edition in the Vienna Corpus (CSEL), Vol. 13 (1886).

2050

[1, 7, 13]

Granted, we may maintain that some spiritual natures exist, such as the Angels, Archangels, and other powers, and, indeed, our own souls, or certainly, plain air; nevertheless, we ought not consider them in any way as incorporeal. For they have in their own way a body in which they subsist, granted it be much more tenuous than our own bodies, in accord with the Apostle's view when he says: "There are heavenly bodies and there are earthly bodies (1)", and again: "Sown an animal body, it rises a spiritual body (2)." From these passages it is clearly to be gathered that there is nothing incorporeal except God alone (3).

483
501

152

2051

[1, 7, 15]

No one doubts that unclean spirits can influence the character of our thoughts, but this is by affecting them from without by sensible influences, that is, either from our dispositions or from our words and from those pursuits to which they see we are inclined with a greater propensity. But they cannot approach at all to that which has not yet come forth from the inner recesses of our soul.

485

2052

[2, 13, 8]

When God sees in us the beginnings of a good will, He enlightens it at once and strengthens it and urges it on towards salvation, giving increase to that which either He Himself implanted or which He sees has arisen by our own efforts (4).

656
729

2053

[2, 13, 9]

Never does anyone enjoy health by his willing it, nor is he freed from illness and disease because he chooses and desires it. What good is it to desire the grace of health, unless God, who grants the very use of life, imparts also the vigor of its preservation? That it might be more evidently clear that even through natural goodness (5), which is bestowed by the munificence of the Creator (6), sometimes the first beginnings of a good will arise (7), which, however, unless they be directed by God, cannot achieve the full performance of virtues, the Apostle is witness, when he says: "Now, to will belongs to me; but I do not find the means to accomplish what is good (8)."

656
729

1. 1 Cor. 15:40.
2. 1 Cor. 15:44.
3. This passage is sometimes cited to show that Cassian denied that the soul is incorporeal. Verbally, of course, he does; but it ought to be clear that the term incorporeal does not mean the same thing to Cassian that it does to us when we state that the soul is incorporeal. Obviously his supposed denial of the incorporeality of the soul is no more than a confusion of terminology.
4. Here, of course, is Cassian's Semi-Pelagianism: that a good will can commence in us by our own efforts, before God gives grace.

5. *per naturae bonum.*
6. *quod beneficio creatoris indultum est.*
7. *nonnumquam bonarum voluntatum prodire principia.*
8. Rom. 7:18. Except for the passage from St. Paul, quoted somewhat out of context and somewhat beside the point, virtually the whole passage is a fine exposition of Semi-Pelagian thought. It might be well to note here that this particular doctrine, a good will on the part of man that is (sometimes) antecedent to grace, can appear very much to be only a diluted form of one of the key doctrines of Pelagianism; and that, of course, is why Cassian and his followers were called Semi-Pelagians, though they themselves condemned Pelagianism quite pointedly. They do have little else in common with the Pelagians and rightly resented being classed with such. And properly analyzed, even the admission of a sometimes antecedent good will is very different from the Pelagian notion of an invariable natural goodness which merits grace. Probably it would have been better all around if the term Massilianism had perdured in usage, rather than the quite misleading term Semi-Pelagianism. On the other hand, however, one could hardly hold the Semi-Pelagian position that some men sometimes anticipate God's grace and gain it by their own good will without being eventually forced to the Pelagian position that any man or man in the abstract can, by his own natural goodness, remain sinless even without God's grace, or, if you will, that the grace of God is no more than a man's own natural goodness.

THE INCARNATION OF CHRIST [*ca. A. D.* 429 / 430]

Since Cassian's seven books *De incarnatione Christi contra Nestorium*, written at the behest of the Roman Archdeacon who was later Pope St. Leo I, makes no mention of the Roman Synod which proceeded against Nestorius in August of 430 A. D., it must be concluded that the work was completed before that date. It cannot, however, have been written much before that time, and probably belongs either to the last months of 429 or to the first half of 430.

As we pointed out in our introduction to Cassian (pp. 197-198 above), he regarded Nestorianism as a logical derivation of Pelagianism. His Christological analyses in the *De incarnatione* constitute, though one of the earliest, yet one of the most lucid documents to come out of the Nestorian controversy. Few theologians have written so well of the two natures united in the one Person of Christ as did John Cassian.

The Gazet text reprinted in Migne PL 50, 9-272 has been superseded by that of M. Petschenig in the Vienna Corpus, CSEL, Vol. 17 (1888).

2054

[2, 2]

Now, heretic, you say, whoever you are who deny that God was born of the Virgin,   780
that Mary, the Mother of our Lord Jesus Christ, cannot be called Theotokos, that is, the   781
Mother of God, but Christotokos, that is, the Mother only of Christ, and not of God.
For no one, you say, gives birth to one older than herself. And of this utterly stupid
argument, wherein you suppose that the birth of God can be understood by a carnal
intellect and believe that the mystery of His Majesty can be resolved by human   320
reasoning, we will, if God permit, offer a refutation later on (1). In the meantime,
however, let us prove by divine testimonies both that Christ is God and that Mary is the
Mother of God.

2055

[4, 6]

[The Word of God Himself] said that the Son of Man was in heaven; and He stated   557
that the Son of Man had come down from heaven (2). What does it mean? What are you   558
muttering to yourself? Deny it, if you can. Do you ask a reason for what is said? I am
not about to give you one. God said it. God has spoken. For me, His word is the best
reason. I put aside arguments, I put aside discussions. The Person of the One Speaking

is sufficient to command my belief. I deem it not permissible to doubt the trustworthiness
of what is said; neither is it permissible to argue about it. What business have I to   554
question how what God said can be true, when I must not doubt the truth of what God
says?

2056

[5, 7]
"Through the blood of His cross," Paul says, "making peace for all things, whether   327
those in heaven or those on earth (3)." Certainly he made it perfectly clear that he   334
was speaking of Him whom he called the First-Born of the dead. For are all things
reconciled and brought to peace by the blood of the Word or the Spirit? Certainly
not; for no sort of suffering can befall a nature that cannot suffer, nor can any but a man
pour out his blood, nor any but a man die. And yet, the same [Person] who in the
following verses is said to be dead is announced in the prior verses as the Image of the   264
invisible God. How can this be? Because the Apostles took every possible precaution to
avoid the appearance of any kind of division in Christ, or that by any kind of erratic
interpretation the Son of God united in the Son of Man should begin to have two Persons
(4), and He that is in Himself but one [Person] should, through perverse and impious
opinions, be made into two [Persons] by us.

2057

[6, 22]
The Author of all the sacred writings so joins and incorporates the Lord's manhood   329
(5) in God that no one is able to sever Man from God in time, nor God from Man in the
Passion. For if you look to time, you will find the Son of Man always with the Son of
God; and if you look to His Passion, you will find the Son of God always with the Son
of Man. Christ, the Son of Man and the Son of God, is in Himself so united and indivisible
that, insofar as the language of Scripture is concerned, neither can the Man be separated
from God in time, nor can God be separated at all from Man in the Passion. . . . There
was not, therefore, before the Virgin gave birth, in the past the same eternity belonging   781
to the Man as belonged to God; but because in the womb of the Virgin God was united
to Man, it follows that when we use the name of Christ, it is quite impossible to speak
of one without the other.

1. Cassian returns to this matter in 4, 2 and again in 7, 2.
2. John 3:13 and 6:63.
3. Col. 1:20. A few lines above the present place, Cassian quoted the whole of Col. 1:12-20.
4. Here the term *persona* is expressed—*(duas habere personas)*. Elsewhere, where we have it in brackets, we have supplied
   it from the context.
5. *dominicum hominem*.

NESTORIUS, *post A. D.* 381–*ca. A. D.* 453

Nestorius was born after the year 381 of Persian parents. He came very early to
Germanicia in Syria Euphratensis, and from there to Antioch. His theological training
was in the School of Antioch, where he was possibly a student of Theodore of
Mopsuestia. He entered the monastery of St. Euprepius near Antioch, and there he was
ordained to the priesthood. His eloquence was considerable and his reputation as a
preacher prompted the Emperor Theodosius II (*regn. A. D.* 408-450), when Sisinnius of

Constantinople died in December of 427, to have Nestorius elevated to the episcopacy in the Patriarchal see. He was consecrated on April 10, 428.

The beginning of Nestorianism and of the theological quarrel that has left its very distinct mark on all subsequent Christianity even to our own time dates to as early as 429 A. D., when Nestorius preached that Mary should not be called the Theotokos or Mother of God, but the Christotokos, Mother of Christ. He was challenged by Eusebius, still a layman but afterwards Bishop of Dorylaeum, who posted on the doors of the Hagia Sophia a rebuttal accusing Nestorius of fostering the Adoptionism of Paul of Samosata. Eusebius sent copies of Nestorius' sermons to Pope Celestine and Nestorius sent Celestine an explanation of his teaching and of what he meant by Christotokos.

Shortly thereafter Cyril of Alexandria wrote twice to Nestorius warning him of the heretical implications of his position. By the middle of 430 A. D. Cyril sent an account of the dispute and a denunciation of Nestorius to Pope Celestine.

In a Roman Synod of August, 430 A. D., Nestorius was given ten days to retract, and Cyril was commissioned to obtain the retraction. In Alexandria Cyril called a Synod in November 430, at which Nestorius was condemned. Cyril then wrote his famous third letter to Nestorius, to which he attached twelve anathemas for Nestorius' signature. (The *Twelve Counter-Anathemas*, supposedly Nestorius' reply to Cyril, are not authentic, but were composed by Nestorians long after the Patriarch's death. See E. Schwartz, *"Die sogenannten Gegenanathematismen des Nestorius,"* in the *Sitzungsberichte der bayerischen Akademie der Wissenschaften, Phil.-hist. Klasse*, Munich 1922, pp. 1-29. In F. Loofs' *Nestoriana* these *Counter-Anathemas* are on pp. 203-224.)

Nestorius' reply was to counter-charge Cyril with being an Apollinarist; and he invited the Emperor to call a council to settle the matter. The Third Ecumenical Council met in Ephesus in June 431. Nestorius refused to attend when he learned that Cyril, as Celestine's legate, would preside. On June 22, 431, Nestorius was condemned for heresy.

Deposed by Theodosius, Nestorius was first returned to his monastery near Antioch; but in 436 A. D., at the insistence of John of Antioch, he was exiled to the Great Oasis in Libya. When Theodosius died in 450 Nestorius was still alive. He died probably soon thereafter. A fragment from Mar Shadost of Teheran in the Cambridge University's Ms. Oriental 1319 says that Nestorius lived for twenty-two years after the Council of Ephesus. That would place his death in 453 A. D.; and the statement cannot be far wrong. (See Luise Abramowski and Alan E. Goodman, *Nestorian Christological Texts*, 2 volumes, Cambridge 1972: Vol. 1 [Syriac text], p. 36, and Vol. 2 [English translation], p. 24.)

Nestorianism spread rapidly to the East, from Edessa to Persia; and with Persia as its center, by missionary expansion into Turkistan, Tibet, India, and China. It has declined since the fourteenth century, its main centers being now in Iran, Iraq, Syria, and the United States.

A. von Harnack, F. Loofs, J. Bethune-Baker, and Msgr. L. Duchesne, with other modern historians, have made a considerable attempt to rehabilitate the person of Nestorius and even his actual doctrine. Certainly not much of what passes as Nestorianism can be attributed directly to Nestorius, and is the product much more of later Nestorians and especially of Babai the Great, an important Nestorian theologian of the seventh century. Eusebius of Dorylaeum had accused Nestorius of being a proponent of the Adoptionism of Paul of Samosata. Adoptionism regarded Christ as a man who by His sufferings and virtues was given the dignity of a Son of God. Nestorius was never an Adoptionist. Perhaps something very much akin to Adoptionism and the Adoptionist mentality is perceptible in our own times in those modern theologians who wonder when Christ first became aware of His own Godhead!

Certainly a major part of the problem with Nestorius was one of terminology. We hold, of course, that Christ had two natures in one person; but Cyril himself was still

speaking of Christ as having one nature *(mia physis)*. Taken literally, that were Monophysitism; but for Cyril a nature implied a concretely subsisting subject, and was in fact a *hypostasis* or person. Nestorius defined nature in terms of *ousia* or substance, as we would; and though later Nestorianism speaks of two *hypostases* in Christ, Nestorius himself seems not to have equated *ousia* and *hypostasis*. Nestorius speaks of a *"prosōpon* of union," as resulting from the union of the divine and human *prosōpa*. It is clear enough that Nestorius could not grasp the notion of a *physis* or nature without its own subsistence. Consequently, each of the two natures in Christ is, for the Nestorian, an independently subsisting person; or at least it is if the Nestorian is a logical thinker. Nestorius distinguished the natures very well; but even with his *"prosōpon* of union" he was not able to succeed in investing those two natures with a single personality.

Theodosius II ordered the destruction of Nestorius' writings in 435 A. D., and very little has escaped the fire. F. Loofs published in 1905 a collection of the fragments of Nestorius' sermons, letters, and treatises, and this remains the standard edition, although it is decidedly incomplete and must be supplemented by a host of other fragments published since 1905 by P. Bedjan, A. E. Goodman, R. Hespel, J. Lebon, W. Lüdtke, G. Mercati, C. Martin, A. Sands, E. Schwartz, F. Nau, L. Abramowski and others.

SERMONS

F. Loofs' collection of the fragments of Nestorius entitled *Nestoriana: Die Fragmente des Nestorius, gesammelt, untersucht und herausgeben, mit Beiträgen von S. A. Cook und G. Kampffmeyer,* Halle 1905, includes in whole or in fragment thirty sermons, of which ten are complete or nearly complete. Nine of these, five Christological and four anti-Pelagian, are preserved in the Latin translation of Marius Mercator. Loofs and Haidacher have shown that a homily on Heb. 3:1 preserved under Chrysostom's name belongs properly to Nestorius (in Migne, PG 64, 479-492, and in Loofs, *Nestoriana*, pp. 230-242). F. Nau has likewise demonstrated that three sermons on the temptation of Christ, though attributed to Chrysostom, are in fact by Nestorius (in Migne, PG 61, 683-688, and F. Nau, *"Le texte grec de trois homélies de Nestorius,"* in the *Revue de l'Orient Chrétien,* Vol. 15 [1910], pp. 113-124, reprinted in Nau's *Le livre d'Heraclide de Damas, suivi du texte grec des trois homélies de Nestorius sur les temptations de Notre Seigneur,* Paris 1910, pp. 333-358). In 1953 C. Baur published three previously unpublished homilies from a manuscript attributing them to Chrysostom, one on Easter and two on the Ascension, which certainly belong not to Chrysostom but to the period of the Nestorian controversy, and the second of which may well be by Nestorius himself (C. Baur, *"Drei unedierte Festpredigten aus der Zeit der nestorianischen Streitigkeiten,"* in *Traditio,* Vol. 9 [1953], pp. 101-126).

2057a

[9: Loofs, p. 251]

Among ourselves there is frequent discussion, and they will ask, "Is Mary the   327
Theotókos, that is, the *Deipara* or Mother of God or is she rather the *Anthropotókos,* that is, Mother of Man?"

Does God have a Mother? A Greek who would introduce mothers of gods would be blameless. . . . A creature did not bring forth the Creator, but bore a Man, an instrument of divinity (1).

2057b

[12: Loofs, p. 281]

There is a division of the divinity and the humanity. Christ, inasmuch as He is Christ,   322 is undivided; the Son, inasmuch as He is the Son, is undivided. For we do not have two Christs, nor do we have two Sons. With us there is not a first Christ and a second, nor this Christ and another one, nor this Son now, and again another Son; rather, the same one is twofold (2), not by dignity but by nature.

2057c

[15: Loofs, p. 291]

The Word of God is the God of Christ. . . . For the same was both Infant and Master 327 (3) of the Infant (4). You have approved what I said; but do not clap your hands for it without examining it. For I said, "The same was Infant and Inhabitant (5) of the Infant."

1. θεότητος ὄργανον.
2. ἀλλ᾽ αὐτὸς ὁ εἷς ἐστι διπλοῦς.
3. δεσπότης.
4. If the London *Times* had carried this sermon it would, at this point have bracketed the word [*applause!*]; for the next sentence is: ἐπηνέσατε τὴν φωνήν, ἀλλὰ μηδὲ αὐτὴν ἀβασανίστως κροτεῖτε.
5. οἰκήτωρ. Had Greeks been in the habit of addressing mail to "Occupant," the envelope would have read οἰκήτωρ. Perhaps, then, the Master above is not the Divine Master as such, but the master of the house, which house is the infant.

THE BAZAAR OF HERACLIDES OF DAMASCUS [ca. A. D. 450]

The Bazaar of Heraclides of Damascus is the only treatise of Nestorius extant in its entirety. It is extant, however, not in its original Greek, but in a Syriac translation. It has been conjectured that the title in Greek may have been Ἐμπόριον, but Πραγματεία (Ἡρακλείδου) is much more likely. And if the latter is correct the title ought to be the *Treatise* or *Proceedings* of Heraclides. The Syriac will have fixed upon the notion of *Proceedings* or *Transactions* in calling it the *Tegurta* or *Bazaar* of Heraclides. The catalogue of Ebedjesu calls it simply the *Book of Heraclides*.

Heraclides of Damascus is the pseudonymn under which Nestorius wrote the *Bazaar* in his last years while in exile at the Great Oasis in the Libyan desert. In the *Bazaar* he severely criticizes Cyril of Alexandria and the decisions of the Council of Ephesus of 431 A. D., while maintaining that his own beliefs are identical to those of Pope Leo I and Flavian of Constantinople. The concluding lines contain a very moving plea for charity and forgiveness.

It is *The Bazaar of Heraclides*, unknown when Loofs published his *Nestoriana*, that prompted so many historians in the first quarter of the present century to revise their views of Nestorius in an attempt to find him orthodox. It is surely true that Nestorius was never fully a "Nestorian"; but his doctrines are not without problems even if we attribute the balder part of the heresy to developments among his later followers long after his death.

The Bazaar of Heraclides was discovered in Syriac translation in 1895 and was first published by P. Bedjan, *Nestorius: Le livre d'Héraclide de Damas*, Paris 1910. F. Nau's French translation appeared along with it, *Nestorius: Le livre d'Héraclide de Damas, traduit en français*, Paris 1910.

2057d

[1, 1, 76]

God is incarnate in Man in His own *prosōpon* (1), and He makes Man's *prosōpon* 327 His own *prosōpon*. The *prosōpon* of the Man cannot be accorded a secondary position, because the *prosōpon* of the Man is God's own, and because God gives His own *prosōpon* that [Christ] used, because He took it for Himself.

2057e

[1, 3]

    Certainly I said and I do affirm that the union is in the one *prosōpon* of Christ.   327
I necessarily pointed out that God the Word who is incarnate was also at the same time God
the Word in the Manhood, because Christ is incarnate in it. That is why when the Fathers
teach us who Christ is, a matter which they did discuss, they first decide the natures which
constitute Christ. But you, [Cyril], are doing the opposite. You want God the Word to be
the *prosōpon* of the union of the two natures. . . . From the combining in the union of
divinity and humanity there comes one Christ, but not God the Word, for the Word was
eternal. Christ, then, is the *prosōpon* of the union, and God the Word is not the *prosōpon* of
the union but of His own nature; and to say and understand this is not the same.

2057f

[2, 1]

    Essence is not to be thought of apart from *hypostasis*, as if the essences were   327
united in one essence, and there were then a *prosōpon* of one essence. The natures,
however, subsist in their own *prosōpa* and in their own natures and in the *prosōpon*
of the union. What pertains to the natural *prosōpon* of one, the same is used by the other,
by virtue of the union; and thus there is one *prosōpon* of two natures. The *prosōpon*
of one nature uses the *prosōpon* of the other.

2057g

[2, 1]

    Divinity uses the *prosōpon* of humanity and humanity uses the *prosōpon* of   327
divinity; and that is why we say there is one *prosōpon* of both (2).

1.   ܦܪܨܘܦܐ   is simply a transliteration of the Greek πρόσωπον.
2. If Cyril had seen this statement of Nestorius he would no doubt have protested: "But Nestorius' statement is utterly
illogical! A *prosōpon* is a person! When he says that in Christ the divine nature uses the *prosōpon* of the human nature
and the human nature uses the *prosōpon* of the divine nature, whatever he may mean by a person using a nature, he has
got two persons. And when he adds, 'this is why we say there is one person of both,' the emphasis ought to be placed on
say; for with Nestorius clearly there are still really two persons, but he finds it a convenience to *say* there is one." Later
Nestorians did in fact confess two persons as well as two natures. But with Nestorius himself, I am not sure that his
prosōpon of union cannot be understood as a valid explanation of the hypostatic union.

ST. CYRIL OF ALEXANDRIA [† 444]

    Cyril was the nephew of Theophilus, Patriarch of Alexandria. The latter died on
October 15, 412, and Cyril succeeded him in a not uncontested succession. The political
power favored Timothy, the Archdeacon of Alexandria; but it was Cyril who prevailed,
who was consecrated, and who obtained the patriarchal see.
    Theophilus had opposed John Chrysostom, and Cyril had assisted in Chrysostom's
deposition at the Synod of The Oak in 403 A. D. As Patriarch Cyril supported his late
uncle's prejudices. Not until 417, ten years after Chrysostom's death, did Cyril restore
his name to the diptychs. Besides his uncle's prejudices, Cyril shared also something of
his ruthlessness. His treatment of the Jews, of the Novatianists, and of all the several
heresies which had proponents at Alexandria was severe in the extreme. His methods
included expulsion and confiscation of property.
    When the celebrated, dignified, and honored lady Hypatia, a pagan teacher of

philosophy, was dragged to the steps of a church in Alexandria by a mob of Christians, and was there stripped naked and chopped to pieces with the sharp edges of roofing tiles, Cyril was accused of the murder. That he encouraged such an act of violence directly and was guilty in any legal sense is probably false. But that it would not have happened if he had not already shown a certain brutality and a considerable ruthlessness in dealing with the Jews and the Novatianists is surely true, and morally he must in some degree share in the guilt of this atrocity.

It is Cyril's fate that in history's memory he is inseparable from the Nestorian controversy. Here too had he shown a more temperate nature and as much kindness and consideration as is evident in Nestorius himself, the controversy might have been resolved without a perduring heresy and schism.

At Ephesus, however, Cyril presided, and Nestorius was condemned, deposed, and excommunicated already in the first session on June 22, 431 A. D. It would not be unfair to say that with Cyril, Nestorius stood condemned before ever the Council was called.

Cyril was a prolific writer and even though many of his works are lost, the collected edition still fills ten volumes in Migne, PG 68-77.

LETTERS

The letters of Cyril of Alexandria have a considerable importance for the general history of his times and especially for the Nestorian controversy.

Letter no. 39, the third of the so-called ecumenical letters, was addressed to John of Antioch in the spring of 433 A. D., to consolidate the newly established peace between the patriarchates of Antioch and Alexandria. The creed appended to the end of the letter was sent to Cyril by the Antiochian bishops for his subscription, and was probably drawn up by Theodoret of Cyr. It is better known as the *Creed of Union* or the *Creed of Ephesus*, and was given formal recognition at Chalcedon in 451 A. D.

The Migne edition contains eighty-eight items in the collection of Cyril's letters. Of these, however, seventeen are addressed to Cyril; and a few are spurious (PG 77, 401-981). E. Schwartz has published an additional five letters in Greek, of which four were previously unknown while one was extant only in a Latin version. Other letters are preserved in Syriac, Coptic and Armenian versions.

My citations below are from letters 1, 39, and 46. The best source for 1 and 46 is probably still Migne, PG 77. For letter 39, the so-called *Symbolum Ephesinum*, a better source than Migne is P. E. Pusey, *S. Cyrilli epistolae tres oecumenicae*, Oxford 1875, pp. 40-53, or E. Schwartz, *Acta conciliorum oecumenicorum*, Vol. 1, part 1, sect. 4, pp. 15-20. The letter has been published also in Ethiopic (A. Dillmann, *Chrestomathia Aethiopica*, Leipzig 1866, pp. 72-76).

LETTER OF CYRIL, BISHOP OF ALEXANDRIA, TO THE MONKS OF EGYPT.
inter A. D. 423 / 431.

2058

[1]

I have been amazed that some are utterly in doubt as to whether or not the Holy   780
Virgin is able to be called Mother of God (1). For if our Lord Jesus Christ is   781
God, how should the Holy Virgin who bore Him not be the Mother of God?

2059

[1]

But perhaps you will then inquire: "Tell me, then, was the Virgin the Mother of   779
His divinity?" And to this we will respond that His living and enhypostate (2)   302
Word is confessedly begotten of the very essence (3) of the God and Father and has His
subsistence (4) without a beginning in time, always co-existing with the Father who
begot Him, co-subsisting and co-discerned (5) in Him and with Him. And in these   311
last times of the age, when He was made flesh, that is, when He was united to a
body having a rational soul, He is said to have been born also in fleshly manner
of a woman.

THE CELEBRATED CREED OF UNION OR CREED OF EPHESUS: A LETTER OF CYRIL, BISHOP OF ALEXANDRIA, TO JOHN, BISHOP OF ANTIOCH. A. D. 433.

2060

[39]

We confess therefore that our Lord Jesus Christ is the Only-begotten Son of God,   302
perfect God and perfect Man, having a rational soul and a body; according to His   312
divinity, born of the Father before the ages, and in these last days, according   781
to His humanity, born of the Virgin Mary for us and for our salvation. According   311
to His divinity He is consubstantial with the Father, and according to His humanity   313
He is consubstantial with us. A union was made of the two natures, on which   323
account we confess one Christ, one Son, one Lord. In accord with this understanding   779
of the unconfused union we confess that the Holy Virgin is the Mother of God (6),   780
through God the Word's being incarnate and becoming Man, and, from this   329
conception, His joining to Himself the temple assumed from her. As to the   334
evangelical and apostolic sayings about the Lord, we know that theologians (7) make
some common, as if pertaining to the one Person (8), and divide some, as if
pertaining to two natures; and those that are divinely apt they concede to the divinity
of Christ, but the lowly they attribute to His humanity.

LETTER OF CYRIL, BISHOP OF ALEXANDRIA, TO SUCCENSUS. inter A. D. 433 / 435.

2061

[46, 2]

Those who are perverting the correct teachings (9) are again ignorant that in truth   321
there is one nature (10) of the Word incarnate. For if there is one Son, . . . according 324
to the assumption but endowed with an intellectual soul, and He became a Man born
of woman, He is not thereby to be divided into two persons and sons, but remains one,
except that He is not without flesh nor without a body, and has His own propriety
answering to the undivided unity. If it is stated thus, in no way whatever does it point
to a mingling or confounding or anything else of the sort at all; nor does such a
mingling follow at all from any kind of logical necessity. For even if we say the Only-
begotten Son of God, incarnate and made Man, is one, it does not follow from this that
there was any confounding as they suppose, nor that the nature of the Word has passed
over into the nature of the flesh; nor has the nature of the flesh passed over into
that of the Word; but since each remains and is recognized in the propriety of its

own nature, . . . it shows us one nature of the Son, except, as I said, that He is incarnate. For not in those things only that are by nature simple is *one* truly predicated, but also in those things that are united by synthesis, which is precisely the case with the man of soul and body.

500

2062

[46, 4]

Since divinely inspired Scripture (11) says that [Christ] suffered in the flesh it is better also for us to speak in this way than, for example, to say that He suffered in the nature of His humanity, even if this latter statement, if it is not spoken perversely by anyone, certainly does no violence to the expression of the mystery. For what else is the nature of humanity except flesh endowed with an intellectual soul, by which also we can speak of the Lord's having suffered in the flesh? They speak quite over-elaborately (12), therefore, who say that He suffered in the nature of His humanity, as if they were disjoining it from the Word and setting it apart in its own propriety, so that two [persons] might be understood when there is still but one, the Word of God the Father, incarnate and made Man.

323

500

1. θεοτόκος. The same term is used also in the next sentence.
2. ἐνυπόστατος.
3. ἐξ αὐτῆς τῆς οὐσίας.
4. τὴν ὕπαρξιν.
5. συνυπάρχων καὶ συννοούμενος.
6. θεοτόκον.
7. τοὺς θεολόγους ἄνδρας.
8. ἐφ' ἑνὸς προσώπου.
9. τὰ ὀρθά.
10. μία φύσις. Although Cyril says *one nature* it is clear that in the present context *one person* is what is meant.
11. τῆς . . . θεοπνεύστου γραφῆς.
12. περιεργότατα.

FESTAL LETTERS [*A. D.* 414-442]

Cyril continued the practice of his Alexandrian predecessors in issuing to all the churches of Egypt a Lenten pastoral, noting the date of Easter and the terms of Lent. The pastorals are sometimes of a moral and sometimes of a dogmatic character. Twenty-nine of Cyril's *Festal Letters* or *Lenten Pastorals* have been preserved for the years 414 to 442 A. D.

In the collected editions these pastoral letters have usually been called *Paschal Homilies*, and they form a collection apart from the general *Letters*. That the *Festal Letters* form a distinct collection separate from the *Letters* is a great convenience; but they are not homilies.

It is in *Festal Letter* 17 for the year 429 A. D. that Cyril first raises objections to Nestorius. This *Festal Letter* 17 is extant also in a Latin translation falsely attributed to Arnobius the Younger. Arnobius used the Latin translation, but there is no reason to suppose that he authored it.

The standard Greek text of the *Festal Letters* is still that of Migne, PG 77, 401-982. Appended to the Greek text of *Festal Letter* 17 Migne reprints Angelo Cardinal Mai's edition of the Latin translation under the name of Arnobius the Younger. A newer edition of this Latin version is that of J. Scharnagl, *S. Cyrilli XVII. homiliae sive epistulae paschalis interpretatio quae vulgo Arnobii iunioris dicitur latina*, Vienna 1909.

THE TENTH FESTAL LETTER [A. D. 422]

2063

[10, 2]

Sin, therefore, is condemned, put to death first by Christ and now about to be put to   374
death in us, when we receive (1) Him into our own souls by means of faith and the   750
communion of the Spirit, who renders us conformable to Christ, by means, of course,   285
of the quality of sanctification. For the Spirit of Christ our Savior is, as it were, His   754
form, a divine stamp that in some manner leaves its imprint on us.

THE SEVENTEENTH FESTAL LETTER [A. D. 429]

2064

[17, 2]

[Christ] was, as I said, God even in His humanity, allowing the nature He had like   322
ours to proceed according to its own laws, while preserving in the midst of this the purity
of His divinity. For in this way and not otherwise it would be perceived both that He   781
that was born was by nature God, and that what the Virgin Mother brought forth   779
would be called not simply flesh and blood, as is the case with us, of course, and our
mothers, but rather Lord and God clothed in our likeness.

---

1. εἰσοικίζωμεν. I should have liked to have translated this *when we enhouseled Him*, as a more literal translation of the
Greek and more expressive in English; but unfortunately the English term *housel* is long since archaic, no one has used it
for several generations past, and it with all its parts is now lost to the language.

TREASURY OF THE HOLY AND CONSUBSTANTIAL TRINITY [inter A. D. 423-425, nisi forte paulo post A. D. 412]

The date at which the *Thesaurus de sancta et consubstantiali Trinitate* was written has
been the subject of some dispute, and there is no general agreement in this matter even
yet. Certainly it predates the Nestorian controversy. G. Jouassard locates it between the
years 423 and 425 A. D., while J. Liébart and N. Charlier think it belongs to the
beginning of Cyril's episcopal career, which commenced in 412 A. D.

Cyril is known as the chief advocate among the Greek Fathers of what in the West
was later termed scholastic methodology. He employs proofs from the Fathers as an
adjunct to proofs from Scripture; and he likewise introduces into his proofs the proof
from reason. This had already been done by the Arians and Apollinarists and it may be
that Cyril is making a conscious effort to employ their own methodology against them.

Probably it is because of his contributions to methodology as well as the actual
content of his doctrine that the Sacred Congregation of Rites gave him the title of Doctor
of the Church on July 28, 1882.

In the *Thesaurus* Cyril borrows heavily from the third of Athanasius' *Discourses
Against the Arians*; and he also makes use of Didymus the Blind's *Contra Eunomium*, a
work which is no longer extant, unless it is to be identified as the *De dogmatibus et
contra Arianos* known to Jerome, and which is probably identical with the spurious
fourth and fifth books of St. Basil's *Contra Eunomium*.

The *Treasury* is in fact a *Summa Trinitatis*, comprising the Arian objections, their
refutation, and the lasting results of the Trinitarian controversies of the previous century.

The standard edition, Migne's reprint of J. Aubert's edition, is in PG 75, 9-656.

2065

[Thesis 4]

If the human mind issues the uttered word (1) from itself without dividing itself and   265
bears no suffering in itself because of this, but the word is to be seen in the mind and the
mind in the word, and each of them is vividly depicted by the other, and no one of any
wisdom would say that the mind had ever been without word, for if it have not
word it be no longer mind (2), then we are not calling *word* that only which is emitted
on the tongue but that too which is moved mentally in the mind. Thus no one would
say that God's own Word is not wholly in God, which Word has the whole image   260
totally of the Father and is observed in the Father by reason of the inalterable sameness   264
of essence (3).

2066

[Thesis 7]

If it is your opinion that God is composite because of His having nature and choice   151
or will, look at it this way: It belongs to the Father by nature (4) to beget, and it belongs   255
to Him to create by agency (5) through the Son, and there is not on this account a   284
composite, because what is produced is fruit of one nature. And the same reasoning
will prevail in regard to the good, the incorruptible, the invisible, and all suchlike
that belongs to the divine nature.

2067

[Thesis 11]

The nature of the Godhead, which is simple and not composite, is never to be divided   151
into two by the concepts of Father and Son, unless some difference be pleased to show   258
itself; I mean, of course, a difference conceived not in reference to essence but external   281
thereto, by which the underlying *prosōpon* of each is introduced in the subsisting and
particularized *hypostasis*, and into the unity of the Godhead, which unity is bound
together by identity of nature.

2068

[Thesis 12]

Again, the Son is not in the Father in the same way that we are. For in our case,   255
in God "we live and move and have our being (6)." The Son, however, in the Father
by nature, proceeding from the essence of the Father as if from some eternally living
fountain, is by nature life, which vivifies all. Not as we are is He vivified, by participation
in life; for that would not be life by nature.

2069

[Thesis 15]

God, who knows the things that belong to the future and not just events when they   189
happen, knew even before the foundation of the world the things that were going   191
to come to pass in the last times. Therefore, effecting such purposes as were befitting
Him, not when we were made did He first direct His will to us; but even before He
produced the earth and the ages, He had in Himself the knowledge of our affairs.   375
And in His foreknowledge He had already determined in regard to His own Son, that
we, being built up by Him (7), should rise up again in incorruption (8), who, through
transgression, had fallen victim to corruption. For He knew that we were going to be
corpses on account of sin.

2070

[Thesis 19]

And what, dear friend, will you say about John, who calls the Son *Word*, and   260
attributes to Him this title most authoritative and most indicative of His essence? For
he says: "In the beginning was the Word, and the Word was with God, and the Word
was God (9)." You see how this name is made to suggest the essence of the Son,
and how His being called Word betokens what He is by nature. . . . And even if
the divine Scripture calls the Son by many other names, in calling Him Word it
pronounces something that is wonderful and supernatural. Never does it join anything
else to this name, such as we see it doing with Paul, when it says, "Paul the Apostle
(10)." To suggest the essence of the Son it is sufficient to say *Word*.

2071

[Thesis 20]

The Word of God, as God, is ever Most High; as Man He is exalted. As God He is   322
in want of nothing; as Man He is said to receive. As God He is adored by all; now as   342
Man He accepts adoration. . . . He that subjects Himself to humanity certainly   341
cannot reasonably be blamed for not refusing to bear those things also that pertain to
humanity. And it is proper to man's nature to receive from God, in accord with the
famous saying: "What have you that you did not receive (11)?" As man, therefore,
He accepted by grace what as God He had by nature.

2072

[Thesis 22]

"But how," [the heretics] ask, "will the Son be like (12) the Father in respect to   351
essence, when He says that He knows not the day of the consummation of the age?" . . .   334
It is easy to see that as God He does know both the day and the hour even if,
referring to what is human in Himself, He can say that He does not know. For if He
clearly specifies all the things that are to happen before that day and hour, and says
"this will be, and that will happen, and then the end," it is clear that if He knows
the things that are to happen before that day, He knows also the day itself. For after
the things predicted by Him, He specifies that this is the end (13). What else, after
all, would the end be, except the last day, which, He says, in view of His Incarnation
(14), He does not know, thus preserving again in His humanity the rank befitting it?
For it is proper for humanity not to know the future.

2073

[Thesis 31]

Certainly it is possible to have varying opinions about something, without these   188
views being false or perverse. What, then, will hinder God Himself from knowing
perfectly what He is according to essence, and us, who are men, from knowing about   174
Him in a lesser degree and with notions that are by no means actually erroneous?   176

2074

[Thesis 31]

We see many names predicated of God, but none of them seems to indicate what   178
God is according to essence. Rather, they either show what He is not, or they indicate   174
some condition distinct from another. For example, *incorruptible* and *immortal* indicate
what He is not; but *Father* or *unbegotten*, that He is the begetter, which distinguishes

Him from the Son, and that He is not produced; but neither of these is indicative of essence, as I said before, but indicates something of what surrounds the essence.

2075

[Thesis 32]

If everything that has been created (15) has been brought over from not being to being, and if Christ, who is the Wisdom and Power of God the Father, were, as some would have it, of created nature, it would be necessary to agree that God was once without wisdom and power, and that this wisdom and power was produced only afterwards, being called into existence with the Son. For such is the nature of creatures. But to entertain such a notion about God is no less stupid than it is blasphemous.

461
251
261

2076

[Thesis 32]

How then is [the Son], who by His nature is God, to be ranked among creatures, or the Master of all to be classed with slaves? And if He is heir of all things (16), He is apart from all things, of which He is the heir. And if through Him God created the worlds (17), certainly He will not be one of the creatures, since He existed before the worlds. Indeed, no creature has his origin before the beginning of the world, but is created in time. To the Son alone does it pertain to exist timelessly with the Father.

251

468
256

2077

[Thesis 32]

As God, therefore, He abrogated the prior precept, and on His own authority promulgated a second. For this is evidently the significance of His statement, "But I tell you (18)." How, then, should He be made or created, who makes laws as one who is by nature God, and for that reason cannot be of later origin (19)?

80
340

2078

[Thesis 33]

Since the Son is a most exact Image of the Father, whoever receives Him has also the Father (20). So too, following along the same form of analogy, whoever receives the Image of the Son, that is, the Spirit, has the Son wholly through Him, and in the Son the Father. How, then, should the Holy Spirit be accounted among the creatures, when He is in every respect Image of the Son of God? . . . And if the Spirit is called Image of the Son, then He is God and not something else.

264

271
266

2079

[Thesis 34]

Since the Holy Spirit when He is in us effects our being conformed to God, and He actually proceeds from Father and Son, it is abundantly clear that He is of the divine essence, in it in essence and proceeding from it.

754
273
268

2080

[Thesis 34]

If in being sealed by the Holy Spirit we are reshaped to God, how should the Holy Spirit be creature, when through Him the image of the divine essence is stamped

750
267

on us, making us, making the seals of increated nature abide in us? For it is not, I suppose, after the fashion of a painter that the Holy Spirit depicts in us the divine essence, as if He Himself were foreign to it; nor is it in this way that He leads us to likeness with God. No, He who is God and who proceeds from God is invisibly impressed, after the fashion of a seal and as if in wax, on the hearts of those who receive Him through communion and likeness with Himself, painting a man's nature again in the beauty of the Archetype, and displaying the man anew according to the image of God.

285
752

1. τὸν προφορικὸν ἀπογεννᾷ λόγον.
2. If this seems somewhat gratuitous the problem is one of semantics. Remember that λόγος is both *word* and *reason*, and at various places in the passage it requires sometimes the one translation and sometimes the other. But I have consistently translated the term *word*; for were we to change English terms within the passage what seems now only vaguely gratuitous would cease to have any semblance of logic at all. What has happened, of course, is that whereas earlier Cyril was speaking of theλόγος προφορικὸς or uttered word, he suddenly and without an adjective uses only the term λόγος in speaking of the λόγος ἐνδιάθετος or internally conceived word.
3. διὰ τὸ τῆς οὐσίας ἀπαράλλακτον.
4. φυσικῶς.
5. δημιουργικῶς.
6. Acts 17:28.
7. See Eph. 2:20.
8. See 1 Cor. 15:53.
9. John 1:1.
10. 2 Cor. 1:1.
11. 1 Cor. 4:7.
12. ὅμοιος.
13. See Matt. 24:14.
14. οἰκονομικῶς. A literal but meaningless translation were "Which He says He does not know economically." In the classical language one who is *economical* is *acquainted with the management of a household*. In earlier Christian writings and in later too *the economy* is the *divine plan of salvation*. The central point of this plan, of course, is the Incarnation; and by Cyril's time the term *economy* can mean simply and straightforwardly the *Incarnation*. Hence the adverb οἰκονομικῶς = *economically* = *incarnationally*, i.e., *in view of the Incarnation*, or *in His humanity*.
15. τὸ ὡς ἐν ὑποστάσει πεποιημένον, i. e., brought into subsistence.
16. Heb. 1:2.
17. *Ibid.*
18. Matt. 5:22.
19. The point of this last line is that the Son is not contemporary with creatures but co-eternal with the Father. The Greek is διά τε τοῦτο πρόσφατος εἶναι μὴ δυνάμενος, which is clear enough, meaning literally, "and through this is not able to be recent." The term πρόσφατος = *recent* is a rather strange one, however, from πρὸς + φένω meaning more properly *newly slaughtered* and *fresh meat*. On this figure the passage might have been translated "on which account He is not to be regarded as something fresh from the butcher shop." Understand that there is no hint here of calvary. That is mere coincidence. This is simply an idiomatic figure, and if we wanted to transfer the Greek idiom to our own we might say, "on which account He is obviously no greenhorn." But however we put it, it still must mean that He is older than creation and co-ancient with God the Father.
20. Matt. 10:40.

DIALOGUES ON THE HOLY AND CONSUBSTANTIAL TRINITY [*ante A. D.* 426]

The seven *Dialogues on the Holy and Consubstantial Trinity* is the second of Cyril's specifically anti-Arian works and was written soon after the *Treasury of the Holy and Consubstantial Trinity*, but while Atticus of Constantinople was still alive: therefore, before October 10, 425. Like the *Treasury* the *Dialogues* too is dedicated to a certain Brother Nemesius. The first six of the dialogues are concerned with the divinity of the Son, the seventh with that of the Holy Spirit.

The text in Migne is still standard and is found in PG 75, 657-1124. A treatise of similar title, *De sancta et vivifica Trinitate*, found in Migne at PG 75, 1147-1190 is not authentic to Cyril but should be attributed to Theodoret of Cyr.

2081

[1]

We are created in God's image and likeness (1). But that is not the way it would be,   151
or indeed, much else would be needed; for we are myriads apart! We are not by nature   152
simple; but the divine nature, perfectly simple and incomposite, has in itself the   153
abundance of all perfection and is in need of nothing.

2082

[2]

When He enacted into law the rule of holy Baptism and laid the ancient foundation   238
of blameless faith for men of every nation under the sun, while ignoring and setting aside
these things, I mean the *incorruptible* and the *unbegotten* and the rest, did He not command
that Baptism be given "in the name of the Father and of the Son and of the Holy Spirit
(2)?" I think He deliberately passes by those things through which the Holy Trinity is
manifested only in the very least way, and chooses and sets forth publicly these other
names which prove to us in the most distinct fashion the proper subsistence of each of the
Persons named (3).

2083

[2]

A. A word is always from the mind and in the mind; and just as surely, the mind   265
is in the word. . . . For the mind is always the root and origin of the word, and
furthermore the word is the fruit and offspring of the mind. The mind, however, is never
without the word, even if it gives birth to the word; and the word, never without the quality
and appearance of the mind begetting it, as if this quality and appearance were its proper
nature,—the word, I say, having been chosen, goes forth, damaging in no way the mind
that has given it birth. . . .

B. But really, how should the force of both of the examples (4), since they pertain to us,
apply in the case of the Father and the Son?

A. Because the conveying of the word is from the mind to the outside, and because its
generation is without passion, and certainly because that which was born is not cut off but
still remains firmly in the mind that conceives it, and the mind conceiving it has it wholly
in itself, . . . it is clearly seen that the examples are applicable.

2084

[3]

B. "But if we grant," they say, "that there are three subsistences (5), then the   237
Godhead too, by any logical reasoning, would be understood to be triplex.

A. But the very words of the true mystagogy (6) taught us that this is not the way it
is. For we were baptized in Father and Son and Holy Spirit, and in no way at all did
we profess a faith in three gods, but in one Godhead, worshipped in the Trinity. How,   239
then, can you balk and try to submit to human reflection the things that are above mind
and reason, and which, I do suppose, ought, without curiosity and by faith alone,
be held in reverence?

2085

[4]

The significance that relative names have somehow between themselves is inferred   281
from both, each bearing (7) the knowledge of the other. If someone has learned which

hand is his right, He will absolutely and everywhere discover so much the more easily
which hand is his left (8); and certainly that even the reverse is true, each and everyone
will concede. Father, however, is a relative name, and in the same way, son too
is relative. . . . Anyone who denies the Father does also deny the Son; and "whoever
denies the Son, neither does he have the Father (9)." Both fairly and strongly, and
truly spoken! If the Father is not Father because He naturally begot, neither will anyone   252
concede that the Son remains. For the Son is the Son because He is begotten; and if
there is no Son, as one having been begotten, neither will there be a Father, according
to the conspicuous and logical reasoning of the mental faculties. For the Father is the
Father because He has begotten.

2087

[5]
   If we had not sinned [Christ] would not have become like us; and if He had not   342
become like us, neither would He have endured the cross; and if He had not died, neither
would He have had to be worshipped by ourselves and by the angels.

2088

[6]
   A saying of Paul instructed us that the Son, having become Man, both sanctifies   341
and is sanctified, by nature and in truth: "For both He that sanctifies," he says, "and   322
they who are sanctified are all from one. That is why He is not ashamed to call them
brothers, when He says, 'I will declare your name to My brothers' (10)." For
He Himself sanctifies, being holy in accord with His nature as God; and He is sanctified
with us, in accord with His humanity.

2089

[7]
   [Paul says:] "My little children, of whom I am again in travail, until Christ shall   285
have been formed in you (11)." He is formed in us by the Spirit, who regenerates us   752
to God through Himself. Since, therefore, we are formed to Christ, and He is signified
in us and His image beautifully worked in us by the Spirit in a likeness according to
nature, surely the Spirit is God, the Spirit who transforms to God, not as rendering   266
assistance through grace, but as dispensing participation in divine nature, by Himself,
to those who are worthy.

2090

[7]
   The nature that is simple and not composite is supreme (12), broadened by different   238
peculiarities of hypostases, of Persons and of names; and going into the Holy Trinity
(13), it still concurs in One by unity of nature and by an identity in every respect
unalterable (14). This nature is God by name and in fact; and all this in such a way   280
that the whole nature is understood in each, each having always His own peculiarity,
plainly by reason of hypostatic considerations. Each, therefore, remains what He is,
possessing through unity of nature with the others what is in His own nature. For the Father
is in the Son and in the Holy Spirit, and likewise the Son and the Spirit are in each other
(15).

1. Gen. 1:26.
2. Matt. 28:19.
3. τῶν σημαινομένων.
4. ἀμφοῖν τοῖν παραδειγμάτοιν is a splendid usage of the dual number.
5. τρεῖς εἶναι . . . τὰς ὑποστάσεις. We might also translate it *three Persons* or *three subsisting Persons*.
6. τῆς ἀληθοῦς μυσταγωγίας. A mystagogy is an initiation; the phrase means *of the true initiation* or, if you will, *of Baptism administered according to its correct form*.
7. συνωδίνοντα. The verb συνωδίνω in earlier Greek means *to share in an agony* or *to be in travail together*.
8. τὸ εὐώνυμον. Cyril uses the common euphemism for *left*, the term actually meaning *good-omened*. The word ἀριστερός, more proper for *left*, was an ill-omened word, like the Latin *sinistra* and the French *gauche*. The term got its sinister connotation from the habit of Greek augurs, looking North, of expecting trouble from the left, the West being always a place of wickedness, so much so that hell has its chimneys in Sicily. As to the *sinistra*, there is in Latin an adage to the effect that persons born left-handed are destined to be thieves. There are other reasons also why the left hand is held less honorable. Be that as it may, it appears that Cyril is engaging in a bit of sarcasm with his remarks on right and left; and his use of the euphemism *good-omened* for *left* heightens the sarcasm.
9. 1 John 2:23.
10. Heb. 2:11-12.
11. Gal. 4:19.
12. παντός ἐστιν ἐπέκεινα. Literally, *is on the yonder side of everything*.
13. καὶ εἰς ἁγίαν ἰοῦσα τριάδα. This is not a happy expression. It too easily lends itself to a visualizing of the Godhead as Three Persons coming together into a unity rather than a simple Three and One.
14. It would have been better to make it explicit that this identity is of nature.
15. ἐν ἀλλήλοιν is another beautiful use of the dual number.

WORSHIP AND ADORATION IN SPIRIT AND IN TRUTH
[*ante A. D.* 429 *et post A. D.* 412]

This lengthy work in seventeen books is in the form of a dialogue between Cyril and Palladius. It presents a typological or allegorical exegesis of various Pentateuch passages directed toward showing that the Law was abrogated in the letter but not in the spirit.

Categorically, therefore, *Worship and Adoration in Spirit and in Truth* belongs among Cyril's exegetical writings on the Old Testament. It is not a systematic exegesis, however, and only selects passages as they are useful to the purpose of the work. Book One deals with the fall of Adam and the task of mankind of freeing itself from Satan's bondage and of returning to obedience to God's laws. Books Two and Three show that this goal is reached only through the grace of Christ and not through the Mosaic Law. Books Four and Five show the need of man's own cooperation with grace; Book Six, the basis of salvation in faith and love; Books Seven and Eight, that love of neighbor is an inseparable concomitant of the love of God. Books Nine and Ten deal with the firmament and its construction; Eleven and Twelve, the priests and levites and their sacrificial duties; Fourteen to Sixteen, the obligations of the people in respect to ritual purity and holiness; and Seventeen, the final book, on the holy days and especially the Passover. Throughout, of course, the Jewish institutions are treated as types and foreshadowings of Christian fulfillment.

The standard edition is still that of Migne, PG 68, 133-1125.

2091

[1]

Since the nature of man is none too firm, nor has it sufficient strength to be able   658
to win out against vice, God gives it sufficiency and He assists in the struggle. Thus   683
it is seen that it had double grace to nourish it: for it is persuaded by admonitions and   684
discovers assistance, and it does better than the present and tyrannizing vice.

2092

[6]

But you, if some part of your body is suffering, and you really believe that saying   940
the words "Lord Sabaoth!" or some such appellation which divine Scripture attributes to
God in respect to His nature has the power to drive that evil from you, go ahead and
pronounce those words, making them a prayer for yourself. You will be doing better than
you would by just uttering those names, and you will be giving the glory to God and not to
impure spirits. I recall also the saying in the divinely inspired Scripture: "Is anyone among
you ill? Let him call in the presbyters of the Church and let them pray over him, anointing
him with oil in the name of the Lord. And the prayer of faith will save the sick man, and
the Lord will raise him up, and if he be in sins they shall be forgiven him (1)."

1. James 5:14-15.

POLISHED COMMENTS [*ante A. D.* 429]

The *Glaphyra* or *Polished Comments* is complementary to *Worship and Adoration in
Spirit and in Truth* and was written along with or soon after the latter. The subject
matter of the *Polished Comments* is similar to that of *Worship and Adoration*, but it
presents a more systematic treatment and is not in the dialogue form.

The *Polished Comments* consists of thirteen books: seven on Genesis, three on
Exodus, and one each on Leviticus, Numbers, and Deuteronomy. The division into
books, however, seems not to have originated with Cyril and is the work of a later
editor.

The standard edition is that in Migne PG 69, 9-678.

2093

[1, 2]

Although the intention of those who worship idols, of discerning perhaps who is   135
the maker of the universe, is corrupt and false, nevertheless, an innate and necessary law is
operative therein and spontaneous knowledge does stir up the need to conceive of
something more excellent and incomparably better than ourselves, which is God.

COMMENTARY ON THE PSALMS

That Cyril wrote an exegetical work on the Psalms is implied by Ephraim of Antioch,
through Photius, and by the unknown author of the *Doctrina patrum de incarnatione
Verbi* published by F. Diekamp in 1907. All that is extant of what is presumed to have
been a general commentary on all the Psalms is a very large number of fragments,
mostly from *catenae*.

The collected fragments of the *Commentary on the Psalms* are found in Migne, PG
69, 717-1273.

2094

[On Ps. 11(12):3]

When the divine Scripture presents sayings about God and remarks on corporeal   152
parts, do not let the mind of those hearing it harbor thoughts of tangible things, but from   175

those tangible things as if from things said figuratively let it ascend to the beauty of
things intellectual, and rather than figures and quantity and circumscription and shapes
and everything else that pertains to bodies, let it think on God, although He is above all
understanding. We were speaking of Him in a human way; for there was no other way
in which we could think about the things that are above us.

2095

[On Ps. 113B(115):16]
 Even if we make images of pious men it is not so that we might adore them as gods   124
but that when we see them we might be prompted to imitate them; and if we make images
of Christ, it is so that our minds might wing aloft in yearning for Him.

COMMENTARY ON ISAIAS [*ante A. D.* 429]

Cyril's *Commentary on Isaias* was written after his two works on the Pentateuch,
Worship and Adoration in Spirit and in Truth and *Polished Comments*, and before the
outbreak of the Nestorian controversy in 429 A. D. The work is in five books, a division
made by Cyril himself. The introduction has some valuable comments on the task of the
interpreter to explain first the literal and then the spiritual meaning of a passage.
 The standard edition is that of Migne, PG 70, 9-1450.

2096

[1, 4]
 Those who repudiate the history recounted in the divinely inspired Scriptures as   22
outmoded preclude the possibility of gaining a right understanding, according to the
sense intended (1), of what is written in them. For the spiritual (2) viewpoint is good
and useful; and by bringing better light to the eyes of the mind, it perfects the
understanding. When some historical deed is introduced to us in the Sacred Writings,   27
then it is seemly to seek out the usefulness of that history, so that on all sides the divinely
inspired Scripture is seen to benefit and assist us.

2096a

[3, 5]
 Christ reigned over this whole world beneath the heavens, and He tells us as much   334
when He says: "All power in heaven and on earth is given to Me (3)." And although as
God He exercised power over all things, by reason of His Incarnation (4) He speaks of
what as God He had, as given to Him. When therefore He was ruling, He ordained the holy
Apostles as princes over us; and the Apostles likewise commanded us with judgment, that
is, with justice.

2097

[4, 2]
 When God says to sinners, "You shall have help even yet (5)," He gives assurance   723
that even for those entangled in many and unavoidable sins, He will keep a remnant
of kindness and clemency; and He says that even those He will not prevent from being
saved if they will choose to return to better and more proper ways, in keeping with His
laws.

2098

[4, 2]

God is the beginning of the whole universe. He Himself is without beginning;   460
but everything has its origin from Him. He, however, is produced of none, but is He   140
who is and who will be. For this is the implication of His name (6).

2099

[4, 2]

Christ is formed in us, bringing into us by the Holy Spirit a certain divine form   750
through justification and sanctification. So it is, thus the imprint of the substance (7)   285
of God and Father is made conspicuous in our souls, conforming (8) us to Him, as I said,
by the Holy Spirit through sanctification.

1. καθ᾽ ὃν προσήκει τρόπον.
2. πνευματική. In regard to the senses of Scripture see above in Vol. I, § 469, note 30.
3. Matt. 28:18.
4. διὰ τὴν μετὰ σαρκὸς οἰκονομίαν.
5. Is. 44:2 in the Septuagint.
6. The name He spoke to Moses: I am who am.
7. ὁ χαρακτὴρ τῆς ὑποστάσεως.
8. ἀναμορφοῦντος.

COMMENTARY ON THE TWELVE MINOR PROPHETS [*ante A. D.* 429]

Cyril's *Commentary on the Minor Prophets* dates from about the same time as his *Commentary on Isaias*. It is in twelve books, one for each of the minor prophets. There is a prologue to each book and an introduction to the whole.

The Migne edition is in PG 71 and 72, 9-364; but the standard edition is P. E. Pusey's *Sancti patris nostri Cyrilli archiepiscopi Alexandrini in duodecim prophetas*, 2 volumes, Oxford 1868.

2100

[*Joel*, section 32]

The living water of holy Baptism is given to us as if in rain, and the Bread of Life   808
as if in wheat, and the Blood as if in wine. In addition to this there is also the use of   820
oil, reckoned as perfecting those who have been justified in Christ through holy   860
Baptism.   840
  846

COMMENTARY ON MATTHEW [*post A. D.* 428]

Leontius of Byzantium, Ephraim of Antioch, Facundus of Hermiane and others know a commentary by Cyril on the Gospel of Matthew. It is now extant, however, only in a small number of fragments gleaned from *catenae*. The fragments are of sufficient breadth, however, to make it clear that Cyril did write a full and complete commentary and not just on selected passages. The work seems to be later than the outbreak of the Nestorian controversy and is to be dated after 428 A. D.

The fragments of the *Commentary on Matthew* are in Migne, PG 72, 365-374. Preferable, however, is the more recent critical edition by J. Reuss in his *Matthäus-Kommentare aus der griechischen Kirche*, Vol. 61 in the series *Texte und Untersuchungen*, Berlin 1957, pp. 103-269.

2101

[On Matthew 26:27]

    He states demonstratively: "This is My Body," and "This is My Blood (1)," lest   852
you might suppose the things that are seen are a figure (2). Rather, by some secret of the   856
all-powerful God the things seen are transformed into (3) the Body and Blood of Christ, truly
offered in a sacrifice in which we, as participants, receive the life-giving and sanctifying   877
power of Christ (4).

1. Matt. 26:26-28.
2. τύπον.
3. μεταποιεῖσθαι εἰς.
4. δύναμιν τοῦ Χριστοῦ.

HOMILIES ON THE GOSPEL OF LUKE [A. D. 430 aut paulo postea]

    Often referred to as a commentary on the Gospel of Luke, Cyril's work in this regard
is actually a course of homilies. A mention of Cyril's *Twelve Anathemas* in homily 63
(Syriac) makes it evident that the work belongs to the end of the year 430 A. D. or
soon thereafter.

    Of the original Greek only three complete homilies and a quite substantial number of
fragments of others from *catenae* are preserved. The first of the three is *On the
Transfiguration of the Lord*, in Migne, PG 77, 1009-1060; and the second and third are
combined in the text tradition as if one, *On the Approach of the Lord*, PG 77,
1039-1050. The *catenae* fragments are in Migne PG 72, 475-950. Additional fragments
from the *Catena* of Nicetas of Heraclea have been published by J. Sickenberger in his
Fragmente der Homilien des Cyrill von Alexandrien zum Lukasevangelium, Vol. 34/1 in
the series *Texte und Untersuchungen*, Leipzig 1909, pp. 63-108.

    Although only three of Cyril's *Homilies on the Gospel of Luke* are complete in Greek,
a Syriac version dating from the sixth or seventh century has preserved entirely or
almost entirely at least 156 of these homilies.

    The Syriac version was first published by R. Payne Smith at Oxford in 1858 from
manuscripts in the British Museum. In 1874 W. Wright published from a Nitrian
manuscript some fragments supplementary to homilies 112-116. J. B. Chabot began a
new critical edition of the Syriac version, publishing the first part, homilies 1-80, in
1912 in the series *Corpus scriptorum christianorum orientalium*, Vol. 70/Syr. 27, with a
Latin translation by R. M. Tonneau following it in the same series after a delay of
forty-one years: CSCO 140/Syr. 70. Part two which presumably will complete the work
has not yet appeared.

    The sole passage which I will cite is from the Greek fragments, in Migne, PG 72,
921.

2103

[On Luke 22:42]

    Certainly Christ did not unwillingly endure the suffering, burdensome as it was even   350
otherwise, because of the ignominy of it and because of the pestiferousness of the
synagogue of the Jews. . . . But since He was not to refuse to undertake the suffering,
He chose it for Himself, the God and Father approving of it with Him. Thus with   349
the human nature there was the excitation of groaning; with the divine, however,   332
completely unbroken serenity. The thought of impending death disturbs Jesus; but the
power of the divinity immediately subdues the feeling aroused, and transforms it to
courage.

COMMENTARY ON JOHN [*ante A. D.* 429]

Since John is the theologian among the Evangelists it is not surprising that Cyril's *Commentary on John* is more theologically and polemically orientated than his other exegetical works. The *Commentary on John* denounces Arians and Eunomians; but while it inveighs against the Christology of the School of Antioch nowhere does it mention Nestorius or the term *Theotokos*, so that the presumption must be that the work was written before the year 429 A. D. G. Jouassard thinks it was begun in 425 and completed in 428; J. Lebon and N. Charlier think that it is the oldest of Cyril's exegetical writings. I am rather inclined to the latter view, if only because the commentary seems to be the work of a younger man in the flower of his brashness.

The *Commentary on John* is a very lengthy work in twelve books. Books seven and eight are extant only in a few *catenae* fragments, the authenticity of which is generally doubtful.

The text in Migne is in PG 73 and 74, 9-756; but a better edition is P. E. Pusey's *Sancti patris nostri Cyrilli archiepiscopi Alexandrini in Divi Iohannis evangelium*, 3 volumes, Oxford 1872.

2104

[1, 9 on John 1:9]

Our forefather Adam does not seem to have progressed gradually in wisdom as is the case with us, but immediately and from the very first days of his existence he is found perfected in intelligence, preserving in himself the enlightenment given him by God still unsullied and pure, and having the dignity of his nature still unadulterated.

523

2105

[1, 9 on John 1:9]

That it is utterly absurd to suppose that the soul existed before the body and to imagine that it is sent down into earthly bodies because of its prior sins we shall attempt to demonstrate to the best of our ability from the subjoined [twenty-four] arguments.

507

2106

[1, 9 on John 1:12]

Made partakers of God through the Spirit, we have been sealed unto likeness with Him, and we mount upwards to the exemplar of the image according to which also we were made, as the divine Scripture tells (1). For as soon as we have regained the ancient beauty of our nature and are conformed (2) to that divine nature, we will be superior to the evils attendant upon us from the transgression (3). Thereupon we mount up to supernatural dignity through Christ; not that we shall be indistinguishable from Him and Sons of God too, but we will be like Him in an imitative fashion through grace. For He is the true and subsisting Son of the Father; we, however, adoptive sons of God's love of mankind, receiving our portion in grace according to the saying, "I have spoken: you are gods all and sons of the Most High (4)." The creature, having been created a slave, is called to things supernatural by the mere will and pleasure of the Father; but the Son, who is both God and Lord, is not in these dignities by the will of the God and Father, nor is it solely by its being willed that He is possessed of being God and Son; rather, blazing up from the very essence (5) of the Father, His own proper essence is gotten naturally (6).

754
752

740
755
340

253

257

2107

[1, 9 on John 1:13]

  If the Spirit is not God by nature; if He is not peculiar Spirit of God Himself, and   267
does not on that account exist by nature (7) in Him, but is something other than God,   285
and is not far removed from being of the same nature as created things, how are we,   266
who are born through Him, said to be born of God (8)? For either we must confess
that the Evangelist is wholly false, or, if he is truthful, and it is as he says and not
otherwise, then the Spirit must be God and from God by nature (9). We that are made   754
worthy to participate in Him through faith in Christ are brought to perfection as
participants of the divine nature (10), and are said to be born of God, and on that account
are given the title gods, not flying up to the glory above us by grace alone, but as   753
already having God indwelling and taking lodging in us, according to what is set forth
in the Prophet: "I shall dwell among them and walk about in their midst (11)."

2108

[2, 1 on John 2:1]

  When the wedding was celebrated [at Cana] it is clear that it was entirely decorous: 972
for indeed, the Mother of the Savior was there; and, invited along with His disciples,
the Savior too was there, working miracles more than being entertained in feasting,
and especially that He might sanctify the very beginning of human generation, which
certainly is a matter concerning the flesh.

2109

[2, 1 on John 3:5]

  When Nicodemus did not understand how he was to do it, or even what being born   752
again from above was intended to signify, [the Lord] instructed him more clearly in   285
His teachings and declared to him in a plainer fashion the knowledge of the mystery. For
our Lord Jesus Christ was proclaiming that regeneration through the Spirit is from
above, which shows that the Spirit is of the essence that is the highest of all, and it is
through Him that we are made participants of the divine nature (12).

2110

[2, 1 on John 3:5]

  For the spirit of man is sanctified by the Spirit, when the body has been sanctified   800
by water. For just as water, when it is poured into cauldrons and set over a blazing fire,   285
draws power from the fire, so too by means of the operation of the Spirit the tangible
water is tranformed (13) to some divine and indescribable power, and it sanctifies those
in whom it would work rebirth.

2111

[4, 4 on John 6:70]

  "And we have believed and have known that You are the Holy Christ of God   565
(14)." . . . . They say that they both believe and know (15), applying both to the
same. For it is needful both to believe and to know (16). . . . And again it is well that
they do not say they first knew and then believed; but when they have entertained   562
faith, then in second place they bring in knowledge. For knowledge comes after faith
and not before it, according to what is written: "If you have not believed, neither
have you understood (17)." When we have first within us a kind of basis for the   563

augmentation of faith, then knowledge is built up little by little, and we are restored
to the measure of stature in Christ and are made a perfect man and spiritual (18).

2112

[6 on John 8:51]

All are revivified and all go back into life hereafter, believers and disbelievers alike.   1012
The resurrection is not at all selective, but is the same for all, in accord with the saying
that all must needs be restored to life.

2113

[9 on John 13:18]

All things considered, I think it must be clear that the Creator of the universe gave   505
to rational creatures their own proper reins of choice and permitted them to follow
whatever spontaneous inclinations each of them might wish, going whatever way
might seem best. . . . That is how the first man, Adam I mean, was made from the
beginning. . . . So He chose Judas and reckoned him among His holy disciples,   215
clearly having him as one of His closest followers in the beginning. But afterwards
little by little Satan tempted Judas and led him into sordid greed until, having fallen
victim to passion and having become a traitor on account of it, he finally despaired.
That was certainly no fault of Him who chose him.

2114

[9 on John 14:17]

That the Spirit is divine and not of an essence different (19) from that of the Father   268
and the Son I think no one of any wisdom will hold in doubt, and compelling reason will   267
convince us of it. For if someone says that He is not of the essence of God, how
should a creature be participant of God by receiving the Spirit? In what respect should   753
we be called and actually be temples of God, if we take the Spirit as creature or of   285
some other race, but not as one who is the [Spirit] of God? How are those who are,
in the words of the saints, "participants of the Spirit (20)" to be regarded as "sharers of
the divine nature (21)," if He is to be accounted among the creatures and not prior to
us and from the divine nature?

2115

[9 on John 14:20]

It is evident, I suppose, and perfectly plain to everyone, that it was for these reasons   376
most of all that the Only-begotten, God and subsisting of God according to nature,
became man: clearly it was so that He might condemn sin in the flesh; put Death to
death by His own death; make us sons of God, regenerated from our earthly condition   740
to a supernatural dignity in the Spirit. Undoubtedly and assuredly this was the very
way in which He would reconstitute and restore to its pristine condition the fallen race,
that is, the human race.

2116

[10, 2 on John 15:1]

The Savior Himself declares, "Whoever eats My Flesh and drinks My Blood abides   850
in Me and I in him (22)." By this statement it is to be seen that Christ does not say He
will be in us only after the fashion of some relation that is solely intellectual, but also
through a participation truly according to nature. Just as if someone were to entwine two   878

pieces of wax together and melt them with a fire, so that both are made one, so too through participation in the Body of Christ and in His Precious Blood, He is united in us and we too in Him. In no other way can that corruptible nature be vivified except by being united bodily to the Body of Him who is, by His very nature, life: that is, the Only-begotten.

2117

[10, 2 on John 15:12]

If the love of neighbor contains and accomplishes the fulfillment of all the commands   592
of our Savior, how should not the man who fulfills this commandment sincerely
and blamelessly be regarded as truly marvelous, since, as it is said, this is the head,
containing all the virtues in it? For the love of others is second to the love of God, and the   594
whole virtue of piety toward God is included in this one saying: ''Thou shalt love thy
neighbor as thyself (23).''

2118

[11, 9 on John 17:12]

We do not reckon that it was by a divine and invincible decree that the traitor among   636
the disciples became entangled in the hunter's snare and was caught in the diabolic   638
traps; for certainly he would be guiltless if the outcome was determined by decree from
on high. For who could withstand God's decree? But now condemned and abominable,
he were better off if he had never been born (24). Why? Because the wretch has been
convicted of what he did by his own will and not from any kind of necessity.

2119

[11, 9 on John 17:13]

The Godhead is not in a place, but is never absent at all from anything that exists;   154
for He fills all things and, since He goes through all things, is outside all things and
in all things.

2121

[12, 1 on John 20:23]

In what way, then, and by what reason does the Savior bestow upon His own disciples   900
the dignity which belongs to the divine nature alone? Certainly the Word, who is
in the Father, would not err in what is seemly, and what He does is right and proper.
He considered that those who already had in themselves the Divine and Lordly Spirit
ought to be lords also of forgiving the sins of some, and of retaining those of others if
they wished, the Holy Spirit indwelling in them forgiving or retaining according to
their own will, even though the matter is executed directly through men. Bearers of the
Spirit, they forgive sins or retain them, or so it seems to me, in two ways: for either
they call to Baptism those who are worthy, men already tested for the faith by the   836
sobriety and constancy of their lives, or they prohibit and exclude from divine grace
those who are not yet worthy; or in still another way they forgive and retain sins when   916
sons of the Church conquer their sins and, confessing them (25), reform their lives.

1. Gen. 1:26.
2. ἀναμορφωθέντες.
3. ἐκ παραβάσεως. The parábasis is Adam's fall.
4. Ps. 81[82]:6.
5. ἐξ αὐτῆς τῆς οὐσίας.

6. τὸ ἴδιον αὐτῆς ἀγαθὸν κατὰ φύσιν ἀπάφεται. Understand οὐσίας with αὐτῆς.
7. οὐσιωδῶς.
8. John 1:13.
9. κατὰ φύσιν.
10. 2 Peter 1:4.
11. Lev. 26:12; 2 Cor. 6:16.
12. 2 Peter 1:4.
13. μεταστοιχειοῦται.
14. John 6:69.
15. ἐγνωκέναι.
16. νοεῖν.
17. Is. 7:9 in the Septuagint.
18. Eph. 4:13.
19. ἑτεροούσιον.
20. Heb. 6:4.
21. 2 Peter 1:4.
22. John 6:56.
23. Gal. 5:14.
24. Matt. 26:24.
25. συγγινῶσκοντες.

COMMENTARY ON THE EPISTLE TO THE ROMANS

All that is left of Cyril's *Commentary on the Epistle to the Romans* is a substantial number of fragments gathered from *catenae*. What form the work was in originally is hardly even a subject for conjecture. Possibly it was a unified and systematic commentary like that on the Gospel of John; but a slightly educated guess will suspect that it was a course of homilies, like the so-called commentary on Luke.

The fragments of the work on Romans were first published by Cardinal Mai in his *Nova patrum bibliotheca*, Vol. 3/1, Rome 1845, pp. 1-47; and it is Mai's edition that is reprinted in Migne, PG 74, 773-856. The preferred edition is that of P. E. Pusey, in his edition of the *Commentary on John*, Vol. 3, Oxford 1872, pp. 173-248.

2122

[On Rom. 5:18 — Pusey, p. 186]

We became sinners through the disobedience of Adam in this way: he was created   614
in immortality and in life; and in the paradise of pleasure his manner was always and   522
entirely absorbed in the vision of God, his body in tranquillity and quiet, without   525
any shameful pleasure; for there was in him no uproar of untoward movements. But   521
when he fell into sin and became subject to corruption, then impure pleasures crept in   612
upon the nature of the flesh, and the law of the violent was brought forth in our members.
Our nature, therefore, contracted the illness of sin "through the disobedience of the
one," that is, of Adam; and thus "the many were made sinners (1)," not as if they had
sinned along with Adam, for they did not yet exist, but as having his nature, which
fell under the law of sin.

2123

[On Rom. 6:6 — Pusey, p. 192]

Even if in Christ the law of sin was not set in motion, it is because of its having been   343
quieted by the power and operation of the incarnate Word (2); but if the nature of the   313
flesh be considered in itself, that which is in Christ is not something different from
that which is found in us. We, therefore, were crucified with Him when His flesh was

crucified, because the whole nature was somehow contained in Him, just as in Adam, of   614
course, when he fell under the curse, the whole nature fell ill of the curse (3).

1. Rom. 5:19.
2. τοῦ οἰκονομοῦντος λόγου.
3. τὴν ἀράν. The term ἡ ἀρά originally meant a prayer, but usually a prayer for evil to befall another, *i. e.*, a curse. It
   means also the effect of such a curse, or ruin. *Ara* is the Greek goddess of destructive revenge, corresponding to the Latin
   Dira.

SCHOLIA ON THE INCARNATION OF THE ONLY-BEGOTTEN [*post A. D.* 431]

The term used for *Incarnation* in the title of this work is ἐνανθρώπησις and might
perhaps be rendered more literally as *enhominization* or *hominization*, except that this
English term has too many evolutionary overtones and, properly used, ought to imply
something that the Incarnation was not: a gradual process. *Scholia* are remarks or
comments.

The *Scholia on the Incarnation of the Only-begotten* was written after the Council of
Ephesus, after the year 431 A. D. The work begins with an explanation of Christ's
names, Emmanuel and Jesus; and it proceeds to an explanation of the union of the
human and the divine in the hypostatic union as being neither a purely external
conjunction or association nor yet an indistinguishable mixture resulting in some third
nature.

In the original Greek the work is extant only in a few fragments. The whole is extant
in a Latin translation associated with Marius Mercator, but which, as M. Richard has
shown, goes back to Cyril himself; or at any rate, Richard has shown that the translation
used by Leo the Great goes back to Cyril, and presumably there was in antiquity but one
Latin translation. The complete text is extant also in translations in Syriac and in
Armenian.

The Armenian version, in an edition with Armenian text and English translation, was
published by F. C. Conybeare, London 1907. The Greek fragments are found in Migne,
PG 75, 1369-1412; and the Latin translation in PL 48, 1005-1040. Both the Latin
translation and the Greek fragments are in P. E. Pusey's *S. Cyrilli Alexandrini epistolae
tres oecumenicae, etc.*, Oxford 1875, pp. 498-579. The Syriac version, if I do not err,
has never been published; but it was used in manuscript by Pusey in the preparation of
his edition mentioned immediately above.

The best edition at present is generally acknowledged to be that of E. Schwartz in his
Acta conciliorum oecumenicorum, Vol. 5/1, Latin version at pp. 184-215, Greek
fragments at pp. 219-231.

2124

[17]
He through whom God the Father made the world was truly made Man. It is not as   324
some think, that He was in man, so that He might be understood by us as a man having   321
God indwelling in Him. If those who believe this were correct in their assumption,
it must be seen that the remark of the Blessed Evangelist John were quite unnecessary,
where he says: "And the Word was made flesh (1)." For where would there have been
any necessity of an Incarnation (2)? Or why is God the Word called incarnate if He did
not become flesh? The force of [the term] Incarnation (3) signifies that He has been   313
made like to us, while yet He remained superior to us, superior indeed to the whole of
creation.

2125

[26]

The Word, then, was God, and He became also Man; and since He was born   779
according to the flesh for the sake of mankind, it is necessary that she who bore Him is the   780
Mother of God (4). For if she did not bear God, neither is He that was born of her to
be called God. If the divinely inspired Scriptures name Him God, as God having been
made Man and incarnate (5), He could not become Man in any other way than
through birth from a woman: how then should she who bore Him not be the Mother of
God (6)?

1. John 1:14.
2. Passage § 2124 is not extant in Greek; but the Latin text itself at this point employs the Greek term ἐνανϑρωπήσεως.
3. Vis ἐνανϑρωπήσεως. See note 2 immediately above.
4. ϑεοτόκος.
5. ὡς ϑεὸν ἐνανϑρωπήσαντα καὶ σεσαρκωμένον.
6. ϑεοτόκος.

MEMORIALS ON THE TRUE FAITH [A. D. 430]

Under this title three separate memorials are included, all belonging to the earlier days
of the Nestorian controversy. Cyril addressed the first to the Emperor Theodosius II. The
second and third memorials are addressed simply "to the royal Ladies," with no names
specified. It is generally assumed that John of Caesarea was correct when, about seventy
years after the memorials were written, he said that the first of the two to the imperial
ladies was addressed to the Emperor's two younger sisters, Arcadia and Marina, while
the second of the two was addressed to the Emperor's older sister Pulcheria Augusta,
and to his wife, Eudokia Augusta.

My citations below are both from the second of the three memorials, the first of the
two ταῖς βασιλίσσαις known also as the De recte fide ad dominas as distinguished
from the De recte fide ad augustas. The text of this memorial is in Migne, PG 76,
1201-1336 and in P. E. Pusey's De recte fide, etc., Oxford 1877, pp. 154ff. The
preferred edition is that of E. Schwartz in his Acta conciliorum oecumenicorum, Vol. 1,
part 1, section 5, pp. 62-118.

2126

[2(1), 3]

We believe in one God, Father almighty, Creator of all things visible and invisible;   460
and in one Lord Jesus Christ, His Son, begotten of Him according to nature before   255
all ages and time; for as to time He is co-unoriginate and coeternal with His own Father,   256
seated with Him in equal honor, and enjoying equality with Him in every respect,   257
for He is the stamp and splendor of His substance (1). And we believe in like manner   268
too of the Holy Spirit, not cataloging (2) Him as foreign to the divine nature; for He is by   269
nature of the Father, poured out upon creation through the Son; for thus the Holy   291
and Adorable Trinity is understood to be one and consubstantial (3) and in an identity   237
of glory.

2127

[2(1), 13]

If the world was to be saved in no other way except in blood and death accepted as   363
service rendered and in accord with the divine plan (4) "for the remission of past

sins in the forbearance of God (5)," and we have in fact been saved through Christ, how should the manner of the Incarnation not be necessary for the Word brought forth of God, that He might justify in His blood those who believe in Him, and that He might reconcile [us] to the Father, through the death of His own body, and so that we might have life together with Him (6)?

1. Heb. 1:3, wherein the term ὑπόστασις is used in the sense of substance or essence.
2. καταλογιζόμενοι.
3. ὁμοούσιος.
4. χρησίμως παραληφθέντι καὶ οἰκονομικῶς.
5. Rom. 3:25.
6. ἵνα καὶ συζήσωμεν αὐτῷ.

AGAINST THE BLASPHEMIES OF NESTORIUS [A. D. 430]

Cyril's *Five Books of Contradiction against the Blasphemies of Nestorius* was written in the Spring of 430. Cyril shows a certain deferential kindness in the work inasmuch at least as he never mentions Nestorius by name. Although Nestorius' name is in the title of the work as we now have it, it must be remembered that very often the titles of patristic writings have been supplied by later authors.

The work refutes selected passages from homilies of Nestorius. Book one concerns the Theotokos, refuting Nestorius' denial of the title. Books two through five challenge and refute passages in which Nestorius' defends a duality of persons in Christ.

The text in Migne is in PG 76, 9-248. P. E. Pusey's text is in his *Epistolae tres oecumenicae, etc.*, Oxford 1875, pp. 54-239. The preferred edition at the present time is that of E. Schwartz in his *Acta conciliorum oecumenicorum*, Vol. 1, part 1, section 6, pp. 13-106.

2128

[1, 1]
Let him in turn listen to us: The divinely inspired Scripture says that the Word of   311
God the Father was made flesh, that is, He was united unconfusedly and hypostatically   321
(1) to flesh; for the body united to Him, born of woman, was not foreign to Him, but   324
just as each of us has his own body proper to himself, so too the body of the Only-
begotten was proper to Him and not to another; for that is what it meant for Him to be
born according to the flesh (2). . . . But even otherwise for those on earth the fleshing   314
or incarnation of the Word (3) was most useful. For if He had not been born like us
according to flesh, if He had not communed on an equal basis in what pertains to us,
He would not have absolved the nature of man from the crimes contracted in Adam.

2129

[3, 1]
Why are you afraid to call [Christ] High Priest (4) in reference to mankind? For He   380
offers us in sacrifice in a sweet odor arising from the faith, and He offers Himself as a
most fragrant Victim to the Father on our behalf.

2130

[3, 3]
Christ speaks to us not as being still the naked Word, but as Man like us, and as still   334

understood to be one after the flesh has been united to Himself. . . . The proprieties of the Word become proper to humanity, and again the proprieties of humanity become proper to the Word Himself. For it is thus that Christ and Son and Lord is understood to be one.

2131

[4, 5]

"And he that eats Me," He says, "that person shall live (5)." But we eat, not   850
assimilating the divinity (6) — away with such a folly!—but the flesh proper to the   877
Word, which has become life-giving because it became His, who lives by the Father.   323

2132

[5, 6]

Thus even if the Father is said to effect the bestowing of life on the Divine Temple   283
(7), it is effected through the Son; and if the Son is seen to be operating, it is not apart
from the Father in the Spirit. For the nature of the Godhead is understood to be one in
three personal hypostases (8), and to have Its movement and operation,—intellectual,   238
of course, and becoming to God,—in all [Three] acting [concurrently] (9).

1. καθ᾽ ὑπόστασιν.
2. οὕτω γὰρ καὶ γεγέννηται κατὰ σάρκα, literally, *for thus too He was born according to the flesh*.
3. ἡ τοῦ λόγου σάρκωσις ἤγουν ἐνανθρώπησις.
4. ἀρχιερέα.
5. John 6:57.
6. οὐ τὴν θεότητα δαπανῶντες.
7. See John 2:19 and 1 Peter 1:21. The *Divine Temple* is Christ's incarnational body.
8. ἐν τρισὶν ὑποστάσεσιν ἰδικαῖς νοουμένη.
9. ἐφ᾽ ἅπασι τοῖς δρωμένοις. If my translation seems to do so much with so little, remember that Tertullian's wonderful line, "The blood of martyrs is the seed of Christians," is actually someone's marvelously expansive reflection (which I appropriated as common property in § 285, either from memory or from I do not remember whom) on a niggardly Tertullianic *"semen est sanguis Christianorum."*

THE TWELVE ANATHEMAS [*A. D.* 430]

When Cyril and Nestorius, accomplishing nothing by their mutual exchange of letters, both appealed to Pope Celestine, a synod was convened in Rome in August 430. The synod condemned Nestorius, and Celestine commissioned Cyril to inform Nestorius of that decision.

In conveying Celestine's message to Nestorius, Cyril formulated and appended to his letter (*Epistula* 17) the famous *Twelve Anathemas* which excited so much controversy because of their very strange terminology; and he threatened Nestorius with deposition and excommunication unless he would retract within ten days.

In immediate reaction to Cyril's *Twelve Anathemas* Andrew of Samosata leveled a charge of Apollinarism against Cyril, who defended himself in the first of three apologies for the twelve anathemas, entitled *Against the Oriental Bishops, an Explanation of the Twelve Chapters*. At the same time Theodoret of Cyr accused Cyril of Monophysitism, a charge to which Cyril was much more vulnerable than that of Apollinarism; and Cyril replied in his second apology, the *Letter to Euoptius against the Attack on the Twelve Chapters Made by Theodoret*. Both of these apologies belong to the earlier half of the year 431 A. D. Later in the year, in August or September, when

Theodosius II had imprisoned both Nestorius and Cyril, from his prison cell Cyril issued his third apology, the *Explanation Given at Ephesus of the Twelve Chapters*.

Cyril's third letter to Nestorius (*Ep.* 17) along with its *Twelve Anathemas* found its way into the Acts of the Council of Ephesus. But even at Ephesus a certain suspicion did attach to the wording of the *Anathemas*, and although included in the *Acta* they did not receive a formal note of ratification. Only at a later time did the mistaken notion prevail that the *Letter* with the *Twelve Anathemas* had received formal approval and adoption both at Ephesus in 431 and at Chalcedon in 451.

With so much controversy over the *Twelve Anathemas* there are an enormous number of places where the texts thereof may be found. In the recently published *Nestorian Christological Texts* (Vol. 1, Syriac texts, Vol. 2, English translation), by Luise Abramowski and Alan E. Goodman, Cambridge 1972, the *Twelve Anathemas* in Syriac are found no less than three times, along with Nestorian refutations. The first is in a work of Mar Shadost of Teheran (Tarihan); the second, an anonymous work originally in Greek but translated into Syriac; and third, in an anonymous work containing the *Twelve Anathemas* along with the so-called *Twelve Counter-Anathemas* falsely ascribed to Nestorius.

The standard text of the original Greek of the *Twelve Anathemas* is no longer that of Migne (PG 77, 105-122) nor that of Pusey (*S. Cyrilli epistolae tres oecumenicae, etc.*, Oxford 1875, pp. 12-39), but that in E. Schwartz, *Acta conciliorum oecumenicorum*, Vol. 1, part 1, sect. 1, pp. 33-42.

2132a

[1]

If anyone does not confess that the Emmanuel is in truth God, and that the Holy   780
Virgin is Mother of God (1), because she bore according to the flesh the Word of God   327
when He became flesh: let him be anathema.

2132b

[2]

If anyone does not confess that the Word of God the Father is united hypostatically   324
(2) to the flesh, and that Christ with His own flesh is one, that is to say, the same one is   327
God and Man at the same time: let him be anathema.

2132c

[3]

If anyone makes in the one Christ a division of hypostases after the union, connecting   324
them only in a conjunction which is according to dignity or even authority and power,
and not rather by a coming together which is according to a union of natures: let   327
him be anathema.

2132d

[4]

If anyone apportions between two Persons or even personalities (3) those words   324
contained in the Gospels and Apostolic writings, either those things said about Him by   334
the saints, or by Him about Himself, and applies some of them to the Man understood
as if He were on His own apart from the Word of God, and some, as if they were   327
befitting the divinity, to the Word alone of God the Father: let him be anathema.

2132e

[5]

    If anyone dare to say that Christ is a God-bearing Man, and not rather that He is God   340
in truth, as Son who is one and by nature, in that the Word became flesh (4) and shared   313
like us flesh and blood (5): let him be anathema.   327

2132f

[6]

    If anyone says that the Word of God the Father is the God or Master of Christ, and   322
does not rather confess that He is God and Man at the same time, in that the Word   324
was made flesh (6) according to Scripture: let him be anathema.   327

2132g

[7]

    If anyone says that Jesus was energized as a Man by the Word of God, and that He   323
attached the glory of the Only-begotten to Himself as if to another existing apart   324
from the Only-begotten: let him be anathema.   327

2132h

[8]

    If anyone dare to say that it is needful that the Man who was assumed be co-adored   323
with the Word of God, and is to be co-glorified and is to be co-titled God, as if He were   324
one in another—for it is necessary to understand that this is always what is proposed   342
by the syllable co-—and does not rather worship the Emmanuel in one reverence and   327
attach to Him one glorification, insofar as the Word became flesh (7): let him be
anathema.

2132j

[9]

    If anyone says that the one Lord Jesus Christ has been glorified by the Spirit, as if   324
through the Spirit He had made use of a power foreign to Himself, and from the Spirit   270
received the ability to work against unclean spirits, and to perform divine signs among
men, and does not rather say that the Spirit, through whom He did indeed work His   327
divine signs, is His own: let him be anathema.

2132k

[10]

    Divine Scripture says that Christ has been made our High Priest and the Apostle   323
of our confession (8), and that He offered Himself as an odor of sweetness to the God   324
and Father (9). If, therefore, anyone says that the Word Himself of God was not made   340
our High Priest and Apostle when He became flesh and Man like us, but that it was
another, apart from Him (10), who was man born of woman; or if anyone says He
offered Himself in sacrifice on His own behalf and not rather for us alone, for He had   345
no need of a sacrifice who knew no sin: let him be anathema.   327

2132m

[11]
   If anyone does not confess that the body of the Lord is life-giving and belongs   324
peculiarly to Him that is Word of God the Father, but that it belongs to someone other   334
than Him and is conjoined to Him according to dignity, or that it had only the divine
indwelling; and that it was not as we have said, life-giving, because it became the
peculiar possession of the Word, who is strong to give life to all: let him be anathema.   327

2132n

[12]
   If anyone does not confess that the Word of God suffered in the flesh, and was crucified   334
in the flesh, and tasted death in the flesh, and was made firstborn from the dead (11),
insofar as He is also, as God, life and bestower of life: let him be anathema.   327

1. ϑεοτόκον.
2. καϑ' ὑπόστασιν.
3. προσώποις δυσὶν ἤγουν ὑποστάσεσι.
4. John 1:14.
5. Heb. 2:14.
6. John 1:14.
7. John 1:14.
8. Heb. 3:1.
9. Eph. 5:2.
10. The *Him* is the Word.
11. Col. 1:18.

AGAINST THOSE WHO DO NOT WISH TO CONFESS THAT THE HOLY VIRGIN IS THE MOTHER OF GOD

   The Emperor Justinian I wrote a *Treatise against the Monophysites* about the year
542. In chapters thirteen and fourteen of that work he twice quotes from the *Against
Those Who Do not Wish to Confess that the Holy Virgin is the Mother of God*, and
attributes authorship of the work to Cyril.
   The *editio princeps* of this present work is quite late, being Cardinal Mai's edition of
1833 in his *Scriptorum veterum nova collectio*, Vol. 8, part 2, pp. 108-135, where only
the Greek is given. Mai published the text a second time along with a Latin translation
in 1844, in his *Nova patrum bibliotheca*, Vol. 2, pp. 75-104. Mai's second edition is
reprinted by Migne, PG 76, 255-292. The present standard edition, however, is that of
E. Schwartz in his *Acta conciliorum oecumenicorum*, Vol. 1, part 1, section 7, pp.
19-32.

2133

[4]
   Jesus did not first come into being as a simple man, before the union and communion   329
of God in Him; but the Word Himself, coming into the Blessed Virgin herself,   311
assumed for Himself His own Temple from the substance (1) of the Virgin, and came
forth from her a man in all that could be externally discerned, while interiorly He was
true God. Therefore He kept His Mother a Virgin even after her child-bearing, which   783
was done for none of the other saints.

1. ἐκ τῆς οὐσίας.

THAT CHRIST IS ONE

In dialogue form, the work entitled *That Christ is One* is a refutation of the idea that the Word of God was not in fact incarnate but was only conjoined to the man Jesus, so that there were a true and natural Son of God, and another person, an adopted son of God.

The work enjoyed a special celebrity in antiquity and deservedly so. It is much more refined and much clearer a presentation than most of Cyril's other dogmatic writings, and probably represents his more mature thoughts on the subject, being, no doubt, one of his last anti-Nestorian efforts.

The text in Migne, PG 75, 1253-1361, is superseded by that of P. E. Pusey, in his *De recta fide ad imperatorem, etc.*, Oxford 1877, pp. 334-424.

2134

[Pusey, Vol. 7, p. 364]

How, then, is Christ to be understood as one out of two (1), divinity and humanity?   324
In no other way, I suppose, than that by which things brought together in each other   329
may be in an inseparable union, and which, as I said, is beyond our understanding.   320
You want an example? Well, then, do we not say that a man like ourselves is one,   500
and that his nature is one, even though he is not of one kind, but is composed rather of
two, of soul, I mean, and of body? That surely is what we say!

1. Understand this as saying one *person* of two *natures*.

DEFENSE OF CHRISTIANITY AGAINST THE BOOKS OF THE IMPIOUS EMPEROR JULIAN [*A. D.* 433 / 441]

Letter 83 of Theodoret of Cyr knows that Cyril sent a copy of his apology against Julian to John of Antioch. John and Cyril were reconciled to each other in 433, and John died in 441; hence, the apology against Julian, or the *Defense of Christianity against the Books of the Impious Emperor Julian*, can be dated between those years.

Julian the Apostate had written in 363 A. D. a work of three books *Against the Galileans*. Julian's polemic is lost; but it can be reconstructed in part from Cyril's refutation of it. Unfortunately for such reconstruction, however, large parts of Cyril's work are lost too.

Of Cyril's work, books 1-10 are extant in the original Greek; and these ten books deal with book 1 of Julian's work. Greek and Syriac fragments are extant of books 11-20 of Cyril's work, and these fragments are sufficient to warrant the conclusion that books 11-20 dealt with book 2 of Julian's work. This is not sufficient to warrant a firm conclusion, however, that Cyril must have written also ten books, entirely lost, on Julian's book 3. There is a certain logical coziness to it: but no concrete evidence of such books remains, and it is always possible that Cyril ignored Julian's book 3.

The introduction to Cyril's work implies, as we might have guessed, that paganism was still a force to be reckoned with in Egypt. Cyril remarks too that Julian's accusations against Christianity were such as struck the popular fancy; and they remained popular, regarded by many as being unanswered or unanswerable.

The text of books 1-10 of Cyril's work is found in Migne, PG 76, 509-1058, reprinted from the collected edition of Aubert. At PG 76, 489-504 Migne reprints a portion of the preface to the separate edition of Cyril's work by E. Spanheim, Leizig 1676. The fragments of books 11-19 given in Migne at PG 76, 1057-1064 are reprinted from volume 2 of Cardinal Mai's *Nova patrum bibliotheca*, Rome 1844, pp. 488-491. Other fragments of books 11-20 are found in C. J. Neumann's *Iuliani Imperatoris librorum contra Christianos quae supersunt*, fascicle 3 of his *Scriptorum Graecorum qui Christianam impugnaverunt religionem quae supersunt*, Leipzig 1880, pp. 42-63: "*Cyrilli Alexandrini librorum contra Iulianum fragmenta syriaca, edidit E. Nestle,*" and pp. 64-87: "*Cyrilli Alexandrini librorum contra Iulianum 11-20 fragmenta graeca et syriaca latine reddita, disposuit C. J. Neumann.*" In regard to unpublished Greek fragments of Cyril's books 12-14 in a Venetian manuscript *(cod. Venet. Marc. 165)*, see F. Diekamp in the *Sitzungsberichte der königlichen preussischen Akademie der Wissenschaften*, Berlin 1901, p. 1051, note 1, as also his edition of the *Doctrina patrum de incarnatione Verbi*, Münster 1907, introduction, p. L. Further fragments are found in the series *Patrologia orientalis*, Vol. 14, fasc. 1, pp. 245-246; in R. Draguet's article, "*Pour l'édition du Philalèthe de Sévère d'Antioche,*" in the *Byzantinische Zeitschrift*, Vol. 30 (1929/30), pp. 278-279; and in L. Früchtel's article, "*Neue Zeugnisse zu Clemens Alexandrinus,*" in the *Zeitschrift für die neutestamentliche Wissenschaft und die Kunde der älteren Kirche*, Giessen, Vol. 36 (1937), pp. 88-90.

2135

[2]

    [Moses] says, "In the beginning God created the heavens and the earth (1)." For matter cannot be understood, as some would have it, as co-unoriginate and coeternal with God, and uncreated, . . . but, on the contrary, in time and in a beginning, God calls to origin, He sets the boundaries of creation, as if, in accord with His will, bringing that which does [now] exist into existence out of what did not [then] exist.

468

461

2136

[2]

    It is utterly inconsistent with this divine glory that others too should be thought to be able to create and to call things into existence when such things do not exist. For certainly it is not right to say that the properties and peculiarities of the divine and inexpressible nature are able to be naturally inherent in some created things by themselves. This pertains to the divine nature alone and belongs necessarily to the glory of Him who is supreme.

462

2137

[3]

    We say emphatically that the knowledge of God is disclosed to human nature, the Creator having invested that nature with the innate knowledge (2) of all that is useful and necessary for salvation. And it was ever seemly that that nature for which such wonderful things had been prepared should go straight to the truth, as [reasoning] from the origination of the world, from its order and beauty, and from its continuance in such, to recognize that the wisdom and power of Him who created [all this] and brought [it] into existence far surpasses every [created] mind.

135

131

2138

[8]

    When [the Word] took His most chaste body, animated by an intelligent soul, from the Holy Virgin, and came forth a Man, He did not cease to be God nor did He reject the dignity of His own preeminence; for in this, as I said, no change is known. . . . The

311

312

321

manner of the Incarnation (3) is marvelous and beyond mind and reason (4). Truly this   320
is a great and august mystery.

1. Gen. 1:1.
2. αὐτοφυᾶ τὴν εἴδησιν.
3. τῆς μετὰ σαρκὸς οἰκονομίας. I have pointed out before that the *economy* or the *divine economy* is God's plan of salvation. The *economy with the flesh*, therefore, is the *Incarnation*. By this time, in fact, the unadorned term οἰκονομία often means *Incarnation*.
4. ὑπὲρ νοῦν καὶ λόγον. This might also be rendered *beyond intelligence and understanding*, or *beyond understanding and description (speech)*.

AGAINST THE ANTHROPOMORPHITES

A work entitled *Against the Anthropomorphites* is not, in the form we have it, from the pen of Cyril. Nevertheless, most of that work is authentic to him.

Cyril wrote a work entitled *Responses to the Deacon Tiberion and His Associates*, giving answers to fifteen questions submitted to him, of which nearly two-thirds are on the Incarnation. To a similar group of nine or ten questions submitted to him by Egyptian monks Cyril addressed a similar work entitled *Explanation of Teachings* (Περὶ δογματῶν ἐπιλύσεως).

A later hand has combined these two works of responses so that they constitute chapters 1-23 of the *Against the Anthropomorphites*. The last five chapters of the work, 24-28, are drawn from a Christmas homily of St. Gregory of Nyssa. Prefixed to the work is a genuine letter of Cyril addressed to Bishop Kalosyrius of Arsinoë in Central Egypt. The preface and the first twenty-three chapters of the *Against the Anthropomorphites*, therefore, may be regarded as authentic Cyrilliana.

The title of the work, *Against the Anthropomorphites*, is drawn from a complaint of Cyril in the letter of Cyril to Kalosyrius to the effect that the monks of Kalosyrius' diocese are taking too anthropomorphic a view of God, casting Him in human form. They are arguing that since Scripture says man is created in God's image, and man has a body of flesh, God too must be corporeal. Apparently those monks had never heard of Barbara Celarent. A syllogism has sixty-four possible moods, only nineteen of which are valid. Their argument, reduced to syllogistic form, is in one of the forty-five invalid moods.

If the anthropomorphic problem of certain fifth century Egyptian monks seems to be incredibly naive, I think we must remember that even in our own times the preacher dare not overestimate the level of the faith of those whom Augustine called the *rudes*. As recently as January 10, 1911 six parishioners of St. Stanislaus Church in Cleveland addressed an allegation of complaint to Bishop Farrelly specifying that the Franciscan priests of their parish were ignorant of Church doctrine, or unable to express it properly, because those priests were preaching that "God is spirit, has no eyes, ears or mouth, therefore he can not hear, see or talk, but why do we see on the pictures, that God has ears, eyes, and mouth and the Holy scripture tells that God spoke to mankind often."

The text of the *Against the Anthropomorphites* is in Migne, PG 76, 1065-1132. P. E. Pusey's edition separates the work into its components in his *S. Cyrilli Alexandrini in Divi Ioannis evangelium*, Vol. 3, Oxford 1872, pp. 547-566, *De dogmatum solutione*; pp. 567-602, *Responsiones ad Tiberium*; and pp. 603-607, *Epistula ad Calosyrium*.

2139

[From the *Letter to Kalosyrius*]

I hear that they are saying that the mystical blessing does not avail unto sanctification,   865
if some of [the Eucharistic species] be left over to another day. They are utterly mad   864

who say these things; for Christ is not made different, nor is His holy body changed, but the power of the blessing and the life-giving grace is uninterrupted in Him.

2140

[16]

The Divine Scripture says that the judgment is to take place after the resurrection   1020
of the dead. But the resurrection is not to take place until Christ returns to us from
heaven in the glory of the Father with the holy angels. So too says the all-wise Paul,
"The Lord Himself shall descend from heaven with a shout of command, with the voice
of an Archangel, and with the trumpet of God (1). For the trumpet shall sound and
the dead in Christ shall be raised incorruptible (2)."

Since, therefore, the Judge of all has not yet descended from heaven, neither has   996
the resurrection of the dead taken place. How, then, should it not be thought incredible
that some recompense has already been made either for works of evil or for good works?
What is said by Christ, therefore, about the rich man and Lazarus (3), is elegantly
expressed in the manner of a parable. . . .

Since, therefore, Christ the Savior of all has not yet come down from heaven, neither
has the resurrection taken place, nor has compensatory action been visited upon any;
but it is as in a figure that the rich man is described by the parable as living in luxury
and as being without mercy, and the poor man as being in ill health, so that those who
possess the wealth of this world might know that if they do not wish to be liberal and
generous and social, and choose to come to assist the needs of the poor, they will be
overtaken by a terrible and inevitable punishment.

2141

[23]

They are utterly stupid who represent, I know not how, that Christ was able to err,   346
because of His having been made incarnationally (4) into a form like us. . . . And if
he wore the nature of man for this very reason, that just as that nature in Adam was
weakened, in Himself it might prove most powerful and superior to sin, why do they
waste their time vainly seeking what they cannot possibly find? . . . Just as in Adam   376
we were condemned because of his disobedience and his transgression of the command,
so too in Christ we have been justified because of His utter sinlessness and His perfect
obedience and blamelessness; and it is in Him that human nature has its boast.

1. 1 Thess. 4:16.
2. 1 Cor. 15:52.
3. Luke 16:19ff.
4. οἰκονομικῶς.

THE COUNCIL OF EPHESUS [A. D. 431]

The first and second ecumenical councils at Nicaea in 325 A. D. and at
Constantinople in 381 A. D. had defended the divinity of the Son and of the Holy Spirit
respectively, and their consubstantiality with the Father. Now as theological explanation
progressed in the area of Christology it became necessary to define more clearly the
relationship between the divine and human natures in Christ.

In this developing theology and as has already been explained in the course of our
presenting selections from the writings of those men who were intimately involved in the
problem, there was a decided clash between the Antiochian and Alexandrian schools of

theology, concretized in the persons of the patriarchs of Constantinople and Alexandria, the Antiochian Nestorius and the Alexandrian Cyril.

Nestorius failed to perceive a sufficiently intimate union between the natures of Christ; and although he does speak of one Person in Christ he did in effect hold that Christ, the Incarnate Word, is two Persons; for he clings to the Aristotelian notion that there can be no nature without a person. He therefore denied that Mary is the Theotokos or Mother of God, calling her only Christotokos or Mother of Christ. Cyril's terminology is also defective, and he can speak of Christ as having one nature; and if in this context by nature he meant person, he does nevertheless give a handle to Monophysitism.

The problem of Nestorius' theology and of his preaching was referred to Rome, where Nestorius was already suspect for having given refuge to the Pelagian Caelestius. With Roman decisions going against him, Nestorius invited Emperor Theodosius II to convoke the Third Ecumenical Council, which met at Ephesus at Pentecost in 431 A. D.

Nestorius arrived at Ephesus with sixteen of his suffragans, closely followed by Cyril with fifty of his bishops. John, the Patriarch of Antioch and a Nestorian sympathizer, deliberately postponed his own arrival. The three papal legates, Arcadius and Prospectus (bishops) and Philip (priest) were delayed by storms at sea. Cyril, under the impression that he himself was the papal representative, opened the council on June 22 over the protests of sixty-eight bishops. Nestorius refused to attend; and in the opening session one hundred and fifty-three bishops were present. Nestorius was deposed. Ultimately more than two hundred bishops signed to the deposition of Nestorius.

Four days after the first session John of Antioch arrived with his suffragan bishops from Syria. Forty-three strong, they protested the council's having proceeded without them and opened their own synod, at which they decreed the deposition of Cyril. At about the same time the papal legates arrived and agreed to recognize the sessions over which Cyril had presided. On July 17 the fifth session of Ephesus deposed and excommunicated John.

The emperor recognized and confirmed both assemblies, and imprisoned both Nestorius and Cyril. Later he invited representatives to his court at Chalcedon. When the representatives failed to agree the emperor reversed himself and condemned Nestorius but reinstated Cyril. Nestorius was sent back to his monastery in Antioch, while Cyril was permitted to return to Alexandria as patriarch. A partial union was achieved in 433 A. D. The last fifteen years of Nestorius' life were spent in exile in Arabia, Libya, and finally in the desert of Upper Egypt.

Nestorianism as a surviving theological system is far more the product of Nestorius' followers than of his own thought. With more charitable understanding and less prideful chicanery on both sides a lasting heresy might have been avoided.

CANONS [A. D. 431]

The Council of Ephesus wrote no new creed but reaffirmed the Creed of Nicaea. The acts of the council include the second and third letters of Cyril to Nestorius, the third with its famous twelve anathemas; a definition against the Messalians or Euchites or Adelphians, who were a fanatical spiritual sect and apparently the direct forbearers of the medieval Bogomili; and eight canons. Of the eight canons the first five are directed against Nestorius, numbers one and four referring also to the Pelagian Caelestius, to whom Nestorius had given refuge.

The text of the *Canons* of Ephesus can be found at the appropriate places in Mansi, Harduin, Hefele, and Hefele-Leclercq; but the source usually taken as standard is Eduard Schwartz, *Acta conciliorum oecumenicorum* 1, 1, 3, pp. 27 ff.

2141b

[Canon 1]

If the metropolitan of the eparchy, in apostasy against the holy and ecumenical   452
council, have been associated with the assembly of apostasy or if he afterwards so
associate himself with it, or if he have been or be now minded to the [views] of
Caelestius, he is unable to take any action whatever against the bishops of the eparchy,
nor henceforward participate at all in ecclesiastical communion; for he is straightaway
deposed by the council and rendered ineffective; and he is made subject to the bishops
of the eparchy and to the surrounding metropolitans who are minded to the [views] of
orthodoxy, to be deposed entirely even from the grade of episcopate (1).

2141c

[Canon 4]

If any of the clergy apostatize and dare either privately or publicly to accept the   452
[views] of Nestorius or the [views] of Caelestius, these too are deemed by the holy
council to be deposed.

1. εἰς τὸ πάντη καὶ τοῦ βαθμοῦ τῆς ἐπισκοπῆς ἐκβληθῆναι.

THEODORET OF CYR [ca. A. D. 393–ca. A. D. 466]

Theodoret was born at Antioch about the year 393. In 423, when only about thirty
years of age, he was, somewhat against his will, made Bishop of Cyr (Cyrus or Cyrrhos
or Κύρρος), a small town of Syria about two days journey from Antioch (two days by
donkey, not by automobile). There he governed his diocese very capably for more than
forty years.

Statements to the effect that Theodoret was a fellow student of Nestorius and John of
Antioch under the tutelage of Theodore of Mopsuestia may very well be true, but they
rest on little or no real evidence. He was nevertheless a product of the Antiochian
School of Theology and was indeed the last of the great theologians of Antioch.

Theodoret, with his Antiochian training, was convinced that Cyril of Alexandria's
theology was of Apollinarist tendency; and in 431 he wrote a no longer extant polemical
work entitled Refutation of the Twelve Anathemas of Cyril of Alexandria. At the Council
of Ephesus Theodoret sided with John of Antioch even after Nestorius had been
condemned. He then wrote a comprehensive work in five books against Cyril and
Ephesus.

Theodoret was a man of firm principle and great moral rectitude. Although the
so-called Creed of Union that Cyril accepted in 433 A. D. (see § 2060 above) was
probably composed by Theodoret himself in the autumn of 432, Theodoret refused to
accept the Union of Cyril and the Eastern Bishops under its original terms, and finally
joined it only when the demand for formal recognition of the condemnation of Nestorius
was dropped.

Now, however, Theodoret was very soon engaged in a struggle against
Monophysitism, the heresy of Eutyches, diametrically opposed to Nestorianism. In
capsule, if you will, Nestorianism holds that in Christ there is no true union of natures
and since the two hypostases remain, there are in Christ two persons. Monophysitism
holds that in the Incarnation the two natures are so inextricably interwoven that they
become one, and Christ has only one nature.

Cyril was succeeded in Alexandria by Dioscurus. If Cyril occasionally used a

monophysite terminology, he was orthodox in his thought. But Dioscurus was fully a
Monophysite.

At the Synod of Ephesus in 449 Dioscurus succeeded in deposing Theodoret and forced
him into exile. Theodoret appealed to Pope Leo I, and Leo declared the proceedings at
Ephesus in 449 null and void. It was Leo himself who tagged that infamous synod with
the name that has clung to it ever since, the *Latrocinium ephesinum*, the Ephesian
convocation of thieves, or *Robber Synod of Ephesus*. The Emperor Marcian returned
Theodoret to Cyr in 450 A. D.

When Theodoret appeared at the Council of Chalcedon in 451 there was, however,
considerable reluctance to seat him. Only when he agreed to anathematize Nestorius,
and "all who do not confess that the Blessed Virgin Mary is the Mother of God and who
divide into two the only Son, the Only-begotten." With that he was formally reinstated
as Bishop of Cyr, and was recognized by the Fathers of Chalcedon as an orthodox
teacher.

Theodoret was a man of high principle and there is no reason to suppose that he
anathematized Nestorius without first having been fully convinced of the latter's heresy.
In his *Compendium of Heretics' Fables*, written about 453 A. D., Nestorius has a place.
Long after Theodoret's death his writings against Cyril and Ephesus, along with some of
his letters of that period, were condemned in the Three Chapters of the Fifth Ecumenical
Council of Constantinople in 553. (See above in the introduction to Theodore of
Mopsuestia, p. 000).

Theodoret had an excellent knowledge of the classical Greek authors. His mother
tongue was Syriac, but his writings were in Greek of an excellent and simple style. In
450 A. D. he estimated that he had written thirty-five books. The larger part of his
writings are lost. The collected edition of his writings, edited by J. L. Schulze and J. A.
Nösselt, was printed at Halle in five volumes, 1769-1774. It is basically this edition, but
with numerous additions and exceptions, that is printed in Migne, PG 80-84.

LETTERS

The larger part even of Theodoret's letters has perished, and many of them,
apparently, have been lost in comparatively modern times. In the fourteenth century
Nicephorus Callistus had more than 500 of Theodoret's letters. We can lay our hands on
less than half that many, only 232. Of these, 147 were first published by J. Sirmond in
1642, and reprinted in Migne (PG 83, 1173-1409). J. Sakkelion published another
forty-seven (his edition has forty-eight, but one is repeated) at Athens in 1885, from a
Patmos manuscript of the eleventh or twelfth century, *Codex Patmensis 706*. A further
thirty-six letters are found in collections of conciliar acts, four in Greek and thirty-two in
a Latin version. There is also a *Letter to Abundius* in Migne, PG 83, 1492-1494; and a
Letter to John of Aegea, extant only in Syriac fragments.

The Patmos manuscript published by Sakkelion actually contains fifty-two letters; but
five of them (16, 21, 24, 25, 26) are identical to five already published in Migne (58,
23, 19, 20, 22).

The Patmos collection has been re-edited in the series *Sources chrétiennes*, Vol. 40,
Paris 1955. A second volume is planned for the same series, to contain the Sirmondian
collection found in Migne. The letters preserved in conciliar acts can be found in E.
Schwartz, *Acta conciliorum oecumenicorum*, I, 1, 4; I, 1, 7; and I, 5. Syriac fragments
of the letter to John of Aegea, edited by F. Nau, are in the *Patrologia orientalis* (PO),
Vol. 13, pp. 190-191. More recently discovered fragments are in the *Contra impium*

grammaticum 3, 18 and 3, 29 of Severus of Antioch, edited by J. Lebon in the series *Corpus scriptorum christianorum orientalium* (CSCO), Vols. 93/94 (1929; repr. 1952), p. 218; and 101/102 (1933; repr. 1952), pp. 174-175.
    I shall cite only Letter 89 from the Sirmondian collection, translating the text of Migne, PG 83, col. 1284.

LETTER OF THEODORET, BISHOP OF CYR, TO FLORENTIUS

2142

[89]
We are guarding the dogmatic teaching of the Apostles intact even to the present time.   102
. . . Handing this teaching down to us are not only the Apostles and the prophets,   106
but also those whose writings interpret their books, Ignatius, Eustathius, Athanasius,
Basil, Gregory, John, and the other lights of the ecumene, and before these the holy
Fathers gathered in Nicaea, whose confession of faith we guard inviolate as a
paternal inheritance.

THE CURE OF PAGAN MALADIES [*ante A. D.* 449]

Theodoret's work in full title *The Cure of Pagan Maladies or the Truth of the Gospels Proved from Greek Philosophy* was written before the year 449; for it is mentioned in his letter 113 of that year. R. P. Canivet, author of the latest critical edition, places it as early as 423, before Theodoret was made a bishop. The work is the last of the great apologies of Christianity and, extant in its entirety, is perhaps the best refutation of paganism that has come down to us.
    In twelve discourses Theodoret poses the fundamental questions of philosophy and religion, and gives the answers, side by side, that are provided by Christianity and by paganism. He quotes more than one hundred pagan authors in about 340 passages.
    The Migne edition, PG 83, 783-1152, is a reprint of the edition of T. Gaisford, Oxford 1839. There have been other critical editions also, notably that of J. Raeder in the series *Bibliotheca Teubneriana*, Leipzig 1904; but the most recent is that of R. P. Canivet, *Théodoret de Cyr, Thérapeutique des maladies hélleniques*, 2 volumes in the series *Sources chrétiennes*, Vols. 57/1 and 57/2, Paris 1958.

2143

[1]
I have heard you people say even this, that we produce no proof at all of our dogmas,   564
but that those whom we teach we only exhort to believe. If you speak against the
title of the faith you calumniate our teaching most baldly; for to our words we join
the testimony of our deeds. But you, on the contrary, you, as the proverb says, have
shown your true colors (1). . . . Who then will be so foolish or rather so very stupid   558
that he will doubt even the God of the universe who is teaching him and will not
believe His pronouncements, and will not accord to the God of the universe even as
much reverence as is bestowed on Pythagoras by those who have devoted themselves to
that man's teaching?

2144

[1]
Let none of you, my friends, speak against the faith. Even Aristotle called faith   560
the criterion of knowledge (2). Epicurus called it a preconception of the mind (3) and he   563

said that preconception, having gained knowledge, becomes comprehension (4).   552
According to our view, faith is voluntary assent of the soul, or contemplation of a thing   553
inscrutable; or it concerns that which is taken as certain, and it is such comprehension   554
of things invisible as is consistent with nature; or it is the disposition in which no doubt
is found in the souls of those who enjoy it. Faith, however, requires knowledge, just   559
as knowledge requires faith; for neither is there any faith without knowledge, nor
can there by any knowledge apart from faith. Faith is in command of knowledge, and   562
knowledge is attendant upon faith; impulse hinders knowledge, and action hastens
after impulse.

2145

[4]
    The God of the universe lacks nothing; but human skills are in want of this or   461
that. . . . The Creator of all is in need neither of instruments nor material. What
material and instrument, and even time and effort, and ability and diligence are to other
artisans, His will is to the God of the universe.

2146

[4]
    It is easy for God to be an Artisan both with what does not exist and with what   506
does exist. Indeed, He did this both in the past and, quite literally, He does it every day.
For He shapes the bodies of living things from existing bodies, and from what does not
exist He creates souls, not for all living creatures, but only for man.

2147

[5]
    It was very easy for God to give orders for the whole earth and the sea straightway   511
to be filled with inhabitants; but so that no one might suppose there were any difference
in the nature of men, He commanded that the myriads of tribes of men come from that
one couple. That too is why He did not form the woman in some other way but took   510
the means of her beginning from the man, lest she might think she had a nature other
than that of the man and go contrary to men.

2148

[8]
    The noble souls of the triumphant are sauntering around heaven, dancing in the   123
choruses of the bodiless; and not one tomb for each conceals their bodies, but cities and
villages divide them up and call them healers and preservers of souls and bodies, and
venerate them as guardians and protectors of cities; and when they intervene as
ambassadors before the Master of the universe the divine gifts are obtained through them;
and though the body has been divided, its grace has continued undivided. And that little
particle and smallest relic has the same power as the absolutely and utterly undivided
martyr.

1. A rather more literal translation were, "But you, by your feathers you have shown yourselves."
2. See § 418 with its note no. 8. Theodoret is not quoting Aristotle; he is quoting from Clement of Alexandria's *Stromateis* a
   line that is clearly Clement's own, but which follows immediately after Clement's purported quote from Aristotle.
3. πρόληψιν διανοίας.
4. κατάληψιν.

THE THEOLOGY OF THE TRINITY AND THE DIVINE
INCARNATION [*ante A. D.* 430]

That Theodoret wrote a work "on theology and the divine incarnation" has the best testimony possible, his own, in his letter 133. In one of his letters preserved only in Latin he refers to the same work as being "on the Trinity and Divine Dispensation." Severus of Antioch quotes the work and gives its title as *The Theology of the Trinity and the Divine Dispensation*. The term *dispensatio* and *dispensation* certainly represents the Greek *oikonomía*, which should be translated *Incarnation*.

The work is extant: but it has been preserved as two separate writings, both parts attributed to Cyril of Alexandria. It is found in Cyril's writings as *The Holy and Life-Giving Trinity* (PG 75, 1147-1190) and *The Incarnation of the Lord* (PG 75, 1419-1478: and here the Greek term rendered *Incarnation* is *enanthrópesis*; but as noted above, Severus of Antioch, using the term *dispensation*, can only have read *oikonomía*). Preservation of Theodoret's work under the name of Cyril is all the more remarkable inasmuch as the "Apollinarists" against whom the work is written are really none other than Cyril himself and the Fathers of the Council of Ephesus.

The work was first printed by Cardinal Mai under the name of Cyril, in Mai's *Scriptorum veterum nova collectio*, Vol. 8, pp. 27-1073, and in his *Nova patrum bibliotheca*, Vol. 2, pp. 1-74, reprinted in Migne, PG 75, 1147-1190 and 1419-1478. More recently discovered fragments have been published by E. Schwartz in the 1922 volume of the *Sitzungsberichte der bayerischen Akademie der Wissenschaften, phil.-hist. Klasse*, pp. 32-40; in his *Acta conciliorum oecumenicorum*, Vol. 1, 5, pp. 169-170; and by J. Lebon, in his article entitled "*Restitutions à Théodoret de Cyr*," in the *Revue d'Histoire Ecclesiastique*, Louvain, Vol. 26 (1930), pp. 524ff.

The passage below is translated from the text given in Migne, the second part of the work, PG 75, col. 1448.

2149

[18]

But Apollinaris, who values drivel more than truth, and who sets his homely prattle   312
before the pious dogmas, says God the Word put on (1) flesh and used it rather like
a veil (2); and that, having no need of a soul (3), He takes the place of a soul (4) in the   361
body. But, my dear, someone may say to Apollinaris that God the Word had no need
of a body either, for He had no lack at all. He was able even to carry out our salvation
by a simple command; but He wanted also to have some properly arranged communion
with us. To that end He assumed sinful nature (5) and justified that nature by His own   374
deeds. He set it free from the bitter tyrants, Sin and Devil and Death, and deemed   314
it worthy of heavenly thrones, and through that which He assumed He gave to all the   386
race a share in liberty.

1. ἀνειληφέναι.
2. τινὶ παραπετάσματι.
3. τοῦ δὲ νοῦ.
4. ἀντὶ νοῦ γενέσθαι.
5. φύσιν.

ERANISTÈS OR POLYMORPH: A DIALOGUE BETWEEN A BEGGAR AND
A TRUE BELIEVER [*ca. A. D.* 447 *et* 451]

Eranistés, meaning a beggar or more properly, a collector, is the title of Theodoret's principal dogmatic and Christological work. It is a treatise in dialogue form agaisnt the

Monophysites. *Eranistès* is the Monophysite, and his opponent in the dialogue is called *Orthódoxos*, which I will render *True Believer*, since history more or less reserves the term Orthodox for another context.

Eranistes is called also *Polýmorphos*, meaning a person of many faces. This Monophysite, then, is a many-faced beggar. In the introduction to the work Theodoret says that Monophysitism is simply a miscellany of manifold or polymorphic absurdities begged or collected from Simon Magus, Cerdo, Marcion, Valentine, bar-Daisan, Apollinaris, Arius, and Eunomius. The work was written about the year 447, but was enlarged after the Council of Chalcedon (451 A. D.), in which augmented form it incorporates also the twenty patristic passages which Pope Leo I had appended in 450 A. D. to his *Epistula dogmatica ad Flavianum* of 449 A. D., the celebrated *Tomus Leonis* (see §§ 2182-2183 below). It is in this latter and expanded form, dating from the year 451 or shortly thereafter, that *Eranistès* is now extant. It was undoubtedly Theodoret himself who expanded the work.

Eranistès is especially valuable for its inclusion of 238 passages quoted from eighty-eight patristic sources. It has been shown, however, that the work leans very heavily in its form and arrangement and even in its content upon a comprehensive *florilegium* which the bishops of Antioch had long ago drawn up to use against Cyril at Ephesus. It is nevertheless a work of great originality.

The text in Migne, PG 83, 27-336, has recently been superseded by the excellent critical edition of Gerard H. Ettlinger, New York, Oxford University Press, 1975.

2150

[1]

True Believer: We, however, using pious reasoning and believing the divine   170
affirmations which distinctly declare that "no one has ever seen God (1),"—we
say that those who have seen have not seen the divine nature (2), but certain visions
accommodated to their capacity.

Beggar: We say that too.

True Believer: That too is what we may understand about the angels when we hear that   172
"daily they see the face (3) of your Father (4)." For they do not see the divine essence,
that which is not circumscribed, which is not comprehended, which is not understood, but
which is able to control the universe; rather, they see a certain glory accommodated to their
nature (5).

2151

[2]

Beggar: You have opportunely introduced a word about the divine mysteries, for directly
I will prove to you that the body of the Master (6) is changed into another nature (7). Do
but answer my questions!

True Believer: I will answer.

Beggar: What do you call the gift that is presented, prior to the priestly invocation (8)?   863

True Believer: It is not proper to divulge this; for it is probable that some of the   810
uninitiate are present.

Beggar: You can answer it enigmatically.

True Believer: Food from certain seeds.

Beggar: And how do we call the other token (9)?

True Believer: It is a common name, signifying a species of beverage.   856

Beggar: And after the consecration (10) how do you address them?

True Believer: Body of Christ and Blood of Christ.   851

Beggar: And do you believe you receive the Body of Christ and His Blood?

True Believer: That is what I do believe.

Beggar: Well then, just as the tokens of the Body and Blood of the Master are one thing before the priestly invocation, and after this epiclesis are changed and become something else, so too after the assumption [of flesh] the body of the Master is changed into the divine essence (11).

True Believer: You are hoist with your own petard! For after the consecration the mystical tokens do not retire from their own nature (12); for they remain with their former essence and outward appearance and shape (13), and they are visible and tangible just as they were before. They are understood, however, to be what they have become; and by faith they are believed; and they are adored as that which they are believed to be.

1. John 1:18.
2. τὴν θείαν φύσιν.
3. τὸ πρόσωπον.
4. Matt. 18:10.
5. τῇ αὐτῶν φύσει.
6. τοῦ δεσποτικοῦ σώματος.
7. τὴν εἰς ἑτέραν φύσιν μεταβολήν.
8. πρὸ τῆς ἱερατικῆς ἐπικλήσεως. Literally, *before the priestly epiclesis.* The πρὸ here is temporal. The True Believer is asked what we call the bread and wine before it has been consecrated; and he shows as a by-the-way in his question that he regards the epiclesis or invocation as consecratory. As the dialogue continues it is interesting to see that the arcane discipline prevents the True Believer from speaking openly of the tokens or symbols of the Body and Blood of Christ before the consecration as bread and wine. Yet he can speak openly of the Eucharist as Body and Blood of Christ!
9. τὸ δὲ ἕτερον σύμβολον.
10. τὸν ἁγιασμόν.
11. τὴν οὐσίαν τὴν θείαν.
12. οὐδὲ γὰρ μετὰ τὸν ἁγιασμὸν μυστικὰ σύμβολα τῆς οἰκείας ἐξίσταται φύσεως. The mystical tokens or signs or symbols are the bread and wine.
13. μένει γὰρ ἐπὶ τῆς προτέρας οὐσίας καὶ τοῦ σχήματος καὶ τοῦ εἴδους. The "they," of course, is τὰ μυστικὰ σύμβολα of the previous clause; remember that in Greek a nominative neuter plural subject regularly takes a singular verb. I am convinced that my translation is correct, but I am not entirely certain of what Theodoret means in this instance by οὐσία; and I have perforce translated it as *essence* as synonymous with *substance.* If it is clearly a verbal denial of transubstantiation, we must remember that that terminology will not be determined until long after Theodoret's time; and no matter his explanation, he does very clearly affirm at least a belief in the real presence. That is all that might be expected at so early a period.

It might have been argued that though he says that the former essence or substance remains, it is not certain that he does not in this place intend σχῆμα and εἶδος, the *outward appearance* and *shape* (or *species*), as qualifiers to what he means by οὐσία rather than as being a second and third thing that remain. Possibly it were not necessary to take the καὶ . . . καὶ as mere consecutives, but as specifying limits to the οὐσία thus: "For the mystical tokens remain by their former substance, both as to outward appearance and as to shape." But if we do that to try to force a modern orthodoxy upon Theodoret or the True Believer, we destroy the effectiveness of His argument against Eranistes the Beggar, who said that the flesh assumed by Christ is transformed into the Divine Essence, and who demonstrates a transubstantiational understanding of the Eucharistic transformation in establishing a parallel. Since Theodoret denies the parallelism of Eranistes' argument, it is necessary to accept that Theodoret is really saying that after the consecratory epiclesis, when the bread and wine has really become what it is believed to be, the Body of Christ, the substance of bread remains. If that is really what Theodoret means, then he is an impanationist and a very good Lutheran.

COMPENDIUM OF HERETICS' FABLES [*ca. A. D.* 453]

Theodoret's *Compendium (or Epitome) of Heretics' Fables,* a history of heresies, was written about the year 453 A. D. It is in five books, the first four describing all heresies from Simon Magus to Eutyches, and including Nestorius. The fifth book provides in twenty-nine chapters a systematic presentation of the Church's teaching. This last book is quite unique.

Theodoret himself mentions among his sources Justin the Martyr, Irenaeus, Clement

of Alexandria, Origen, Eusebius of Caesarea, Eusebius of Emesa, Adamantius, Rhodo, Titus of Bostra, Diodore of Tarsus, George of Laodicea, and others. It is clear that he relies mainly on book one of Irenaeus' *Adversus haereses*, Eusebius' *History of the Church*, and the tenth book of the *Philosophoumena*, which he ascribes not to Hippolytus but to Origen. It is remarkable that Theodoret seems not to be acquainted with the *Panarion* of Epiphanius.

The text of the *Compendium of Heretics' Fables* in Migne, PG 83, 335-556, is still the standard.

2152

[1, 20]

[Tatian] also put together the Gospel called the *Diatessaron*, pruning away the genealogies and the other [parts] which show that the Lord was born of the seed of David according to the flesh. And it found use not only among the members of his own sect but even with those who are followers of the Apostolic teachings, and who, unable to perceive the villany of the compilation, in their simplicity use it as a concise Bible (1). And I myself have discovered more than two hundred books of this kind held in honor in our own churches; and I have gathered them all together and sequestered them and have introduced in their place the Gospels of the four Evangelists.

61
69

2153

[5, 19]

Thus completing the sacrament of Baptism (2), we receive the hope of resurrection and expect the resurrection of bodies. The term itself makes this clear. For ἀνάστασις (resurrection) means *standing up alive again* (3). It is the body that is corrupted and dissolved and changed into a mound of earth. . . . Rightly, then, is its restoration among the living (4) called resurrection. For, indeed, there is no resurrection of the immortal soul; it is but given a way back into the body.

1011

2154

[5, 21]

The Munificent Giver promised that He would give not a perishable nor a transitory enjoyment of good things but an eternal one. For, unlike that of Cerinthus and of those whose views are similar to his, the kingdom of our God and Savior is not to be of this earth, nor circumscribed by a specific time. Those men create for themselves in imagination a period of a thousand years, and luxury that will pass, and other pleasures, and, along with them, sacrifices and Jewish solemnities. As for ourselves, we await the life that knows no growing old.

1043
1017

2155

[5, 25]

If marriage were evil, God the Master would not have made laws concerning it from the beginning, nor would He have called being fruitful with children a blessing. Indeed, for this reason He did not forbid the ancients to have many wives: so that the race of men might be increased. . . . The Lord Himself not only did not prohibit marriage, but was even a guest at a marriage, and presented at the wedding a gift of wine that had seen no cultivation. He so confirmed the law of marriage that by another law He forbids the action of a man who wants to dissolve his marriage apart from

983
972
978

974

fornication. "For anyone," He says, "who dismisses his wife except by reason
of fornication, makes her commit adultery (5)."

1. In regard to the *Diatessaron* see the introduction to Tatian on pp. 65-66 of Vol. 1 of the present work.
2. οὕτω τελοῦντες τὸ μυστήριον τοῦ βαπτίσματος.
3. ἡ ἄνωθεν στάσις. The term ἡ στάσις means a *standing posture*. The adverb ἄνωθεν means *from heaven* or *on high*; but it is used also as an indeclinable noun, οἱ ἄνωθεν being *those who are alive*. Here I suppose ἄνωθεν is an adverb, best translated by an adverbial prepositional phrase: standing up *among the living*. In compounds the force of ἀνα is simply *up*; and the root sense of ἀνάστασις is a *standing up*.
4. ἡ ἄνωθεν σύστασις. The *systasis* of our dust to its former condition as a living body is called *anastasis*.
5. Matt. 5:32.

QUESTIONS ON THE OCTATEUCH [*post A. D.* 453]

The *Questions on the Octateuch* is not a complete commentary but, as its title might imply, deals with selected passages. The Octateuch is the five books of Moses, along with Josue, Judges, and Ruth. The work was written by Theodoret after the year 453 A. D., and is dedicated to Hypatius, "the dearest of his sons."
The text in Migne, PG 80, 75-528, is still the standard for reference.

2156

[On Gen. 1]
We learn that the divine nature (1) alone is not circumscribed, which also, to be sure,   154
is increate, without beginning, and eternal. It is quite clear that things which have a
beginning of existence have existence that is circumscribed. Although we affirm that   483
the nature (2) of the angels is bodiless, still we say that their subsistence (3) is   484
circumscribed. . . . But I suppose no one will deny that the angels have their   492
essence (4) circumscribed, since Christ the Master said that each man has been   493
committed to the charge of one of the angels.

2157

[On Num. 10:6-7]
"Sound the trumpet at the time of the new moon, on the auspicious day of your   810
festival (5)." By these words we too are taught that every assembly of the people is called
together by trumpet signal, and not by openly significant commands (6). For because of the
uninitiate we discourse obscurely about the divine mysteries. When the uninitiate are not
present we teach the initiate in a more open manner.

1. τὴν θείαν φύσιν.
2. τὴν φύσιν.
3. τὴν ὑπόστασιν. Perhaps hypostasis might be translated here as *personal existence*.
4. τὴν οὐσίαν.
5. Ps. 80[81]:4.
6. καὶ οὐ σημασίαις.

INTERPRETATION OF THE PSALMS [*inter A. D.* 441 / 449]

Theodoret's *Interpretation of the Psalms*, written between the years 441 and 449, is a continuous commentary on the whole of the Psalter, line by line. In his preface to the work Theodoret says that he has read several commentaries on the Psalms, some of which are too prone to allegorical interpretation, and others which interpret even

Messianic prophecies as pertaining to prior events. In writing his own commentary he has regarded it as his duty, he says, to avoid both extremes. "Whatever refers to history I shall explain as historical event; but the prophecies about Christ the Lord, about the Church among the gentiles, about the gospel and about the preaching of the Apostles will not be explained as referring to certain other things, as is customary with the Jews."

Besides the original Greek, the entire work is extant also in an Old Slavonic version which, however, has not yet been published.

The standard edition is still that in Migne, PG 80, 857-1998, with some fragmentary additions in PG 84, 19-32.

2158

[Preface]

Some say that not all the Psalms are by David, but that some are by others. . . .   20
About this I make no very strong affirmation. What difference does it make to me   23
whether all of them or some of them [are David's], when it is clear in any case
that all are written under the operation of the Divine Spirit?

2159

[On Ps. 31(32):10]

For all men, even if they are adorned with deeds of virtue, are in need of divine   659
grace. The Apostle too, on this account, cries out: "By grace you have been saved
through faith; and this is not of yourselves but it is a gift of God (1)."

1. Eph. 2:8.

INTERPRETATION OF THE CANTICLE OF CANTICLES

Theodoret's *Interpretation of the Canticle of Canticles* is a continuous commentary, and is the earliest of his exegetical writings. In the introduction to the work Theodoret reminds us that the Canticle of Canticles is a spiritual book, and he rejects the view that its subject matter is the mutual love of man and woman. As to Theodore of Mopsuestia's idea that the Canticle of Canticles is Solomon's reply to the critics of his marriage to the Egyptian princess—that explanation, says Theodoret, would be out of place even in the mouth of a crazy woman. The Mopsuestian's view seems never to have had any substantial following and has in fact been condemned by the Second Council (Fifth Ecumenical) of Constantinople in 553 A. D. Christ is the Spouse, and His Bride is the Church.

The standard text is in Migne, PG 81, 27-214.

2160

[On Cant. 3:4]

As to essence (1), the Bridegroom is incomprehensible even to the holy angels; and   173
they, therefore, gave no answer to my inquiry, teaching me in silence that He,   493
being the increate, can never be comprehended by creatures. I departed from
them, to seek Him whom I desired.

1. τὴν οὐσίαν.

INTERPRETATION OF DANIEL

Theodoret's *Interpretation of Daniel*, a continuous commentary, is his earliest commentary on any of the prophets. It does not include Susanna or Bel and the Dragon.

Prolegomena for a new edition were published by L. Canet already in 1914; but such an edition has not appeared. The text in Migne, PG 81, 1255-1546 is still the standard.

2161

[On Dan. 10:13]

We are taught that each one of us is entrusted to the care of an individual angel 492
to guard and protect us, and to deliver us from the snares of evil demons. Archangels 494
are entrusted with the tasks of guarding nations, as the Blessed Moses taught
(1), and with those remarks the Blessed Daniel is in accord; for he himself speaks of "the
chief of the Kingdom of the Persians," and a little later of "the chief of the Greeks,"
while he calls Michael the chief of Israel (2).

1. See Deut. 32:8 in the Septuagint.
2. Dan. 10:13, 20.

INTERPRETATION OF THE FOURTEEN EPISTLES OF PAUL

Theodoret's commentary on the fourteen Pauline Epistles is all that survives of any commentaries that he may otherwise have written on New Testament books.

Of an anonymous Oxford edition of 1852 only part one appeared, covering the Epistles to the Romans, Corinthians, and Galatians. The text in Migne is still standard (PG 82, 35-878).

2162

[On Rom. 8:30]

"Those whom He predestined, those also did He call; and those whom He called, 213
those also did He justify; and those whom He justified, those also did He glorify (1)."
Those whose resolve He foreknew, He predestined from the beginning. Predestining
them, He did also call them. Calling them, He justified them by Baptism; and justifying
them, He glorified them, calling them sons and bestowing on them the grace of the
Holy Spirit. But no one would say that His foreknowledge is the cause of this: for His 190
foreknowledge does not accomplish such things as these. Rather, God, since He is God, 191
does see from afar those things that are going to be. . . . The God of the universe,
since He is God, sees all things from afar. Assuredly this imposes no necessity on 192
anyone of practicing virtue, nor on anyone of doing evil. For if a man be compelled to 214
either course, it is not right that he be either praised and crowned, or condemned to
punishment. If God is just, as just He be, He encourages to those things that are good,
and dissuades from the contrary; and He praises those who do good, and punishes
those who voluntarily embrace evil.

2163

[On Eph. 2:8]

"For by grace you have been saved through faith (2)." The grace of God deems 656
us worthy of these good things. And all we bring to it is our faith. But even in this the 758

divine grace has become our co-worker. For [Paul] adds, "And this is not of yourselves,   759
but it is a gift of God; not of works, lest anyone should boast (3)." It is not of our own
accord that we have believed, but we have come to belief after having been called;
and when we had come to believe, He did not require of us purity of life, but approving
mere faith, He bestowed on us forgiveness of sins.

2164

[On Phil. 1:1]
   [Paul] yokes together bishops and deacons, making no mention of presbyters (4);   441
certainly it was not possible that many bishops should be shepherds in one city, so it is   953
clear that he calls the presbyters bishops. Indeed, in the same Epistle he called the
Blessed Epaphroditus their apostle: "Your apostle," he says, "and the co-worker of my
necessity (5)." Clearly, therefore, Epaphroditus, since Paul gives him the title
of apostle, has been entrusted with the episcopal office (6).

2165

[On 1 Tim. 3:1]
   At that time they called the same persons presbyters and bishops; and those we now   441
call bishops they designated apostles. In the course of time, however, they abandoned   953
the name of apostle to those who truly were Apostles; and the title of bishop they
accorded to those who had of old been called apostles. Thus Epaphroditus was apostle
of the Philippians: "Your apostle," he says, "and the co-worker of my necessity (7)."
Thus in Crete Titus and in Asia Timothy were apostles. Thus too the apostles and the
presbyters wrote from Jerusalem to those in Antioch (8).

1. Rom. 8:30.
2. Eph. 2:8.
3. Eph. 2:8-9.
4. Tit. 1:7.
5. Phil. 2:25.
6. τὴν ἐπισκοπὴν οἰκονομίαν.
7. Phil. 2:25.
8. This pericope of Theodoret and the previous are sometimes taken as if Theodoret were denying the proposition that
   bishops constitute an order superior to priests. I fail to see it. He is simply explaining a confusing change of terminology.
   He says that what we call bishops were once called apostles; and what we call priests were once called either presbyters or
   bishops. He does not say that the office of priest and bishop were the same, but that the term priest (presbyter) and the
   term bishop were synonymous at a time when what we now call bishops were known as apostles.

SOCRATES SCHOLASTIKOS [ca. A. D. 380 – post A. D. 439]

   Socrates has the cognomen Scholastikos, a term which in its root meaning implies
both laziness and longwindedness, and therefore means a scholar in general and a lawyer
in particular. He was a lawyer.
   Nothing of much value is known of Socrates' life. He was born about the year 380 at
Constantinople, where he was educated by the pagan grammarians Helladius and
Ammonius or Ammoun, who had lately fled Egypt in consequence of the disturbances
following upon the cleansing of the Mithreum and the destruction of the Serapeum by
Theophilus, Bishop of Alexandria and uncle of Cyril who succeeded him.
   Socrates' History of the Church is his solitary claim to fame, and the claim is a solid
one.

HISTORY OF THE CHURCH [*A. D.* 439 *aut paulo postea*]

Socrates is the best equipped of the continuators of Eusebius Pamphili of Caesarea. It is interesting to observe that were we deprived of just a few early Church historians, mainly Eusebius, Philostorgius, Socrates, Sozomen and Theodoret, we would for the most part lack a solid and continuous history of the Church's first four hundred years. It will be objected, no doubt, that that history could be mostly reconstructed from a multitude of other sources, and that is no doubt true. But at the same time, some of it would be lost entirely, much of it would be the subject of less certain conjecture, and an enormous amount that we now take as fact would remain somewhat under a cloud of uncertainty.

Socrates' *History of the Church* in seven books was written at the request of a certain Theodore, probably a monk or a cleric, whereas Socrates himself was a layman. The history is professedly a continuation of Eusebius' *History of the Church*, which work concluded in 323 A. D. or just prior to the Council of Nicaea in 325 A. D. Socrates backtracks a few years to 305 A. D. and the abdication of Diocletian, because of things that Eusebius had omitted, and because, in matters concerning Constantine and Arius, Socrates found that "Eusebius was more intent on the rhetorical polish of his composition and on the praises of the emperor than he was on an accurate statement of the facts" (Socrates 1, 1).

Socrates' history covers the years 305-439 A. D.: from the first year of the 271st Olympiad, in which Constantine was proclaimed emperor, to the second year of the 305th Olympiad, the seventeenth consulate of the Emperor Theodosius II. The text as we have it represents Socrates' own second edition of the work, in which books 1 and 2 were severely revised. Socrates himself remarks at the beginning of the second book that the first two books have been thoroughly revised because in the first edition he had erred in relying too heavily upon Rufinus, who went egregiously astray in respect to the chronology of the period covered therein, and especially though not exclusively in reference to the order of events in the life of Athanasius. The rest of the work was revised only haphazardly. Book 6, chapter 11, recounting a disagreement between Chrysostom and Severian of Gabala, is extant in two recensions. Undoubtedly the two recensions represent Socrates' first and second editions.

His *History of the Church* shows that Socrates was a very competent historian. He is genuinely objective; and he knows how to correlate secular and ecclesiastical history. If there is a fault in his work it is the layman's fault of a lack of theological discernment and the inability even to discover the importance of theology. But he is objective, and his objectivity prompts him to an attitude of considerable sympathy for the Novatianists, so much so that Nicephorus Callistus, Cardinal Baronius, and the Jesuit Philip Labbè have suggested that Socrates was himself a Novatianist, a view which a more careful reading of his work makes untenable. Nor is there any reason to suppose, as some have, that he was in his earlier life a Novatianist, though a Catholic when he wrote his history.

The text of the second edition of Socrates' *History of the Church* is entirely extant in the original Greek and in an Armenian version of the seventh century, the latter published in 1897 by Ter-Mosesean. The edition in Migne, PG 67, 29-872, is a reprint of W. Reading's reworking of H. Valesius' edition. R. Hussey's Oxford edition in three volumes (1853, reprinted in 1878 and again in 1893) has no reason to be preferred over Migne. A new edition is much needed and was planned long ago by J. Bidez for inclusion in the series *Die griechischen christlichen Schriftsteller der ersten Jahrhunderte*, called the Berlin Corpus or GCS. Bidez' edition was not forthcoming; and an edition for the GCS is presently being edited by R. Hanslik. Presumably it will replace Migne and the Oxford edition when it appears.

2165a

[5, 19]

At this time it was resolved to abolish the [office of] the presbyter penitentiary (1) in the churches, for the following reason. When the Novatianists separated themselves from the Church (2) because they did not want to communicate with those who had lapsed during the persecution in the time of Decius (3), the bishops added to the ecclesiastical institutes the presbyter in charge of repentance (4), so that those who had sinned after Baptism might confess their sins (5) before this appointed presbyter. This rule (6) prevails until the present time among all the other sects (7). Only those minded to the homoousios, and the Novatianists, like-minded with them according to faith, have set aside the [office of the] presbyter penitentiary. Indeed, the Novatianists never admitted its addition in the beginning. The [homoousians], now prevailing in the Churches, after long retaining [this office], abrogated it in the time of Bishop Nectarius (8) because of a certain incident that took place in a church.

A certain woman of the nobility came to the presbyter penitentiary and confessed in succession (9) the sins which she had committed after Baptism. The presbyter instructed the woman to fast and to pray ceaselessly, so that with her confession she might also have some works to show, worthy of repentance. In the course of time the woman denounced herself [as guilty of] another lapse. For she related that a deacon of the church had had sexual traffic with her.

With this statement preparations were made to expel the deacon from the church, but the people started a commotion; for not only were they offended because of what had happened but also because the deed had brought infamy and outrage upon the Church. When priestly men began to be disparaged as a result of this, a certain Eudaemon, a presbyter of the church and an Alexandrian by birth, convinced Bishop Nectarius to abolish [the office of] the presbyter penitentiary, and to leave each person to his own conscience in the matter of participating in the Mysteries (10); for only in this way could the Church be safeguarded against defamation.

Having heard this from Eudaemon I have not hesitated to commit it to writing in the present work. For, as I have often said, I have made every effort to ascertain the events from each of those best acquainted with them, and to investigate them thoroughly, lest I might write something that is not true. So I said to the Presbyter Eudaemon (11): "Whether your advice, O Presbyter, has been of profit to the Church or not, God only knows; but I see that it provides an excuse for not rebuking one another's sins and for not keeping the precept of the Apostle which declares: 'Have no fellowship with the unfruitful works of darkness, but rather rebuke them (12).''

On this matter I have said enough.

1. The term is ὁ ἐπὶ τῆς μετανοίας πρεσβύτερος, *the presbyter in charge of repentance*. It seems, however, to be a technical term, and I will render it *presbyter penitentiary*.
2. Some have thought that Socrates was a Novatianist; and he does frequently show a certain sympathy to them. But the phrasing of the present statement is not that which could be chosen by their fellow-sectarian. That he was in fact a Novatianist is untenable.
3. Decius was emperor from 250 to 253 A. D.
4. οἱ ἐπίσκοποι τῷ ἐκκλησιαστικῷ κανόνι τὸν πρεσβύτερον τὸν ἐπὶ τῆς μετανοίας προσέθεσαν.
5. ἐξομολογῶνται τὰ ἁμαρτήματα.
6. οὗτος ὁ κανών.
7. ἐν ταῖς ἄλλαις αἱρέσεσι.
8. Nectarius succeeded Gregory of Nazianz as Bishop of Constantinople in 381 A. D., remaining there until his death in 397 A. D.
9. κατὰ μέρος is *in turn* or *in succession*, and I suppose it means that the woman confessed her specific sins; that is, she did not make simply a generic confession.
10. That is, in deciding whether to receive the Eucharist.
11. πρὸς τὸν Εὐδαίμονα πρότερον. The word πρότερον here is of uncertain meaning. I suspect that it is a colloquial usage meaning πρεσβύτερος, just as in Latin the term *senior* sometimes translates πρεσβύτερος even when the Greek term means *priest* or *bishop*, and not just when it means *elder* or *older*.

12. Eph. 5:11. In note 2 above I gave reason for the impossibility of Socrates' having been a Novatianist. An even better argument is found in the present statement of Socrates to Eudaemon, in which Socrates evidently regrets the abolition of sacramental confession. No Novatianist could so state his conviction; for Novatianists did not admit restoration to the Church at all after public lapse, and negated the Church's power to forgive; or perhaps more precisely, if they did not deny the Church's power to forgive they denied at least the wisdom of her doing so and did not themselves practice it.

SALAMAN HERMES SOZOMEN SCHOLASTIKOS [† *post A. D.* 439]

Sozomen was born at Bethelia near Gaza in southern Palestine, of a pious Christian family. Little enough is known of his life. After traveling to Italy he settled at Constantinople where, like Socrates, he practiced law. No date can be assigned to his birth. As to his death we can say only that he was alive in 439 A. D., and if he has not died since then he must still be alive.

HISTORY OF THE CHURCH [*inter A. D.* 439 / 450]

Sozomen wrote two histories of the Church. The first, which covered the period from the Ascension of our Savior to the fall of Licinius in 323 A. D., is not extant at all. The second covered from the years 323 to 439 A. D., ending like that of Socrates with the seventeenth consulate of Theodosius II. It is this latter work which now concerns us; and it is extant almost in its entirety, lacking only the last few chapters of the ninth and final book, a portion covering fourteen years. Thus the work as we have it covers the period from 323 to 425 A. D. The work addresses itself to Theodosius II, who died in 450 A. D., and states that it covers the period to his seventeenth consulate: hence it must have been written after 439 A. D. and before 450 A. D.

The sources employed by Sozomen are numerous and broad; and not the least of them is Socrates. Sozomen's use of the latter is such as would now be called plagiarism; but theft of literary property was not a developed concept in antiquity.

Photius preferred the style of Sozomen to that of Socrates. It is true that he has a more pleasant manner than Socrates. He is easier to read and holds one's attention longer; but his historical sense and critical judgment is inferior to that of Socrates. Sozomen is more inclined to repeat mere gossip; but even gossip can be extremely valuable when it has aged for more than fifteen hundred years.

The text in Migne, PG 67, 844-1630 and that of R. Hussey's Oxford edition of 1860 are both superseded by the edition of Bidez and Hansen in the series *Die griechischen christlichen Schriftsteller der ersten Jahrhunderte*, Vol. 50, Berlin 1960. Joseph Bidez began preparing the edition in 1902. At his death it was brought to completion by Günther Christian Hansen and was finally published in 1960.

Passage § 2165b is Sozomen's account of the same incident told about by Socrates in passage § 2165a. Here the accounts seem to be quite independent of each other. One suspects immediately that Socrates' account is historically the more reliable. Yet the account of Sozomen, with all its digressions and gossipy details, provides much more of the material from which a liturgical and sacramental history can be written.

2165b

[7, 16, 1]

About this time Nectarius, in charge of the Church of Constantinople, first abolished   917
the office of the presbyter imposing penances. His example was followed by bishops everywhere. As to the nature and origin of the office, and the cause of its being abolished, some have said one thing and others another. I shall tell what I think about it.

[2] Because to be entirely without sin belongs more to divine than to human nature, God has decreed that pardon is to be extended to those who repent even after many transgressions. Since in asking pardon it is necessary to confess the sin, it seems likely that from the very beginning priests (1) saw that it was burdensome for the people to confess their sins in public and with the whole church as witness. So they appointed a presbyter who could conduct himself with the utmost self-control and prudence to be in charge of this. [3] It was to him that the penitents went to confess their transgressions. His was the task of assessing the penalty that had to be exacted for each sin and, when satisfaction had been made, of absolving them.

[4] This never was required by the Novatians, who do not believe in penance; but it has prevailed even to the present time among all other heretics, and is diligently observed in the Western Churches, especially in that of Rome. [5] There a special place is set aside for those who are in penance, where they stand mourning and weeping as it were, until the completion of the Divine Liturgy, not being privileged to participate with the initiate, the while they throw themselves prostrate on the ground, with groaning and lamentation.

[6] The bishop conducts the ceremony, faces them weeping, and likewise prostrates himself on the pavement, while the whole church bursts into tears and weeps aloud. After this the bishop is the first to stand up and he raises up the others who are prostrate. He prays on behalf of the repentant sinners and then dismisses them.

[7] Each of the penitents then submits to voluntary suffering either by fastings or abstentions from bathing or from a sufficiency of food, or by other prescribed means, for a time appointed for him by the bishop. When the time arrives for him to be released from punishment his sin is forgiven and he attends church with the people. The priests of Rome have carefully observed these usages from the beginning until our own times.

[8] In the Church of Constantinople a presbyter was appointed to have charge of the penitents until a woman of the nobility gave a deposition that when she, because of her sins, presented herself before this presbyter to fast and to beseech God, and when she tarried in the church for this purpose, an attempt to rape her had been made by a man who was a deacon (2).

[9] Inasmuch as the people learned of this, there was great distress because of the disgrace to the Church; and sacred things were much calumniated. After hesitating as to what must be done Nectarius finally decided to depose the deacon; and at the advice of certain persons who urged that each individual should be able to examine his own conscience and confidently communicate in the Mysteries, he abolished the office of the presbyter penitentiary.

[10] From that time until the present this order has prevailed over the most ancient usage; and, it seems to me, great laxity of principle has been substituted for the severity and rigor of antiquity. Under the ancient system, I think, offences were of less frequent occurrence; for people were deterred from sinning by reason of their dread of confessing their sins and of exposing them to the scrutiny of a severe judge.

[11] It was for this same reason, I think, that the Emperor Theodosius, always zealous in promoting the honor of the Church, enacted the law (3) forbidding women, unless they had had children and were over sixty years of age, to be accepted into the diaconate, in accord with the precept of the Apostle [Paul] (4), and decreeing that women who shaved their heads were to be expelled from the churches, while the bishops who admitted such women were to be deposed from the episcopate.

908

957

---

1. ἱερεῦσιν.
2. ἐκπεπορνεῦσθαι παρὰ ἀνδρὸς διακόνου κατεμήνυσεν. It is not entirely clear to me whether the deacon did actually rape her or only attempted to do so.
3. *Cod. Theod.* 16, 2, 27; changed in Justinian's *Novell.* 123, 13.
4. See 1 Tim. 5:9.

MACARIUS THE MAGNESIAN [*fl. ca. A. D.* 400]

The Fathers of the Egyptian desert claim two Macarii: Macarius the Egyptian, known also as the Elder and the Great, who was from Upper Egypt and who spent sixty years in the desert at Scete; and Marcarius the Alexandrian, called the Town Man to distinguish him from the other Egyptian Macarius. He the Great was born about the year 300 and died about 389. The Town Man was born a few years before him and died a few years after him, attaining almost to the age of 100.

The present Macarius, called Magnes or the Magnesian, is a third Macarius. Photius says that at the Synod of The Oak (403 A. D.) Macarius, Bishop of Magnesia, was the accuser of Heraclides, whom Chrysostom had consecrated Bishop of Ephesus. Presumably Macarius the Magnesian, author of the *Answer-book or rather the Only-begotten Christ Himself to the Pagans*, is to be identified with Photius' Macarius, Bishop of Magnesia.

ANSWER-BOOK OR RATHER THE ONLY-BEGOTTEN CHRIST HIMSELF TO THE PAGANS [*ca. A. D.* 400]

The *Answer-book* or, as it is usually called, the *Apocriticus* is a Christian apology presented in dialogue form, representing a fictitious debate of five days' duration between Macarius and "the Philosopher." As an apology the work is of no special merit; but its singular importance is in its accurate presentation of the pagan objections. Duchesne was of a mind that the pagan position is supplied from the treatise of the Neoplatonist Hierocles, the governor of Bithynia who wrote an anti-Christian work representing Apollonius of Tyana as a magician whose works were superior to those of Jesus, and who instigated the persecution in the time of Diocletian. J. A. Wagenmann first, followed by H. Hauschildt and Adolf von Harnack, however, identified the Philosopher with Porphyry, and reckoned that the objections are from Porphyry's lost work in fifteen books *Against the Christians*.

It is probable that the identification of the Philosopher with Porphyry is correct; but unfortunately Macarius seems to have used not the lost original work of Porphyry but an anonymous epitome of it, also lost.

The *Answer-book* can be dated only ca. 400 A. D., or between 390 and 410 A. D. If T. W. Crafer dated the work a hundred years earlier it is because he supposed that the text represented not a fictitious but a real debate, and that the dispute was not with Porphyry's book, but with Porphyry in person.

Macarius' *Answer-book* is extant only in a somewhat fragmentary state; and there is no presently known manuscript of it at all. The *Editio princeps* by C. Blondel, finished at Blondel's death by his friend P. Foucart, was published at Paris in 1876 under the title Μακαρίου Μάγνητος Ἀποκριτικὸς ἢ Μονογενής. *Macarii Magnetis quae supersunt ex inedito codice*, from a fifteenth century manuscript discovered at Athens in 1867. The manuscript disappeared after Blondel's work was published. Even in the state in which Blondel saw it, the manuscript was mutilated at both ends. It began in the midst of book 2, chapter 7 and ended in the midst of book 4, chapter 30.

In the sixteenth century the Jesuit F. Torres, engaged in his Eucharistic controversy with the Lutherans and knowing a manuscript of Macarius at Venice, quoted not only from books 2, 3, and 4, now known in Blondel's edition, but also from a lost book 5. The Venetian manuscript is not now known. It may be concluded, however, that the work consisted of just five books, one for each day of the disputation.

In the ninth century Nicephorus, Patriarch of Constantinople, quoting variously from the *Answer-book*, included a passage from the otherwise unknown book 1.

Of the five books of the *Apocriticus*, therefore, we have only book three complete, with the greater part of books two and four, and but minor fragments of books one and five.

The passage below is translated from the edition of Blondel and Foucart, Paris 1876, p. 105.

2166

[3, 23]

[Christ] took the bread and the cup, each in similar fashion, and said: "This is My   851
Body and this My Blood (1)." Not a figure of His body nor a figure of His blood (2), as some persons of petrified mind are wont to rhapsodize, but in truth the Body and the Blood of Christ, seeing that His body is from the earth, and the bread and the wine are likewise from the earth.

1. Matt. 26:26, 28.
2. οὐ γὰρ τύπος σώματος οὐδὲ τύπος αἵματος.

SYNOPSIS OF SACRED SCRIPTURE [*ca. A. D.* 490 / 500]

A work entitled *Synopsis of Sacred Scripture* is preserved in the tradition of the writings of St. Athanasius. Its lack of authenticity was perceived already by the Maurist editors. Call it pseudo-Athanasian or call it anonymous; but it cannot be of Athanasius for the telling and obvious reason that the canon which it displays is not the canon expressly proclaimed by Athanasius in his thirty-ninth *Festal Letter* (see above in Volume 1, § 791).

Dating from the closing years of the fifth century, the *Synopsis of Sacred Scripture* is referred to with some frequency, for the sake of its scriptural canon. The work is, however, considerably more than a mere canonical list. It provides the opening line of each book of Scripture and a substantial digest of the content of each book.

The text in Migne, where it appears among the *dubia* of St. Athanasius, PG 28, 283-438, is still standard.

2167

[1]

All divinely inspired Scripture belongs to us Christians (1). The books are not   20
undefined but defined, and have canonical status. The books of the Old Testament are these: Genesis, . . . Exodus, . . . Leviticus, . . . Numbers, . . . Deuteronomy, . . .   41
Jesus, Son of Nave, . . . Judges, . . . Ruth, . . . First and Second Kingdoms, . . .
Third and Fourth Kingdoms, . . . First and Second Paralipomenon, . . . First and Second Esdras, . . . the Davidic Psalter, . . . the Proverbs of Solomon, . . . Ecclesiastes, . . . Canticle of Canticles, . . . Job, . . . the Twelve Prophets in one book: . . . Osee, . . . Amos, . . . Micheas, . . . Joel, . . . Abdias, . . . Jonas, . . . Nahum, . . . Habacuc, . . . Sophonias, . . . Aggeus, . . . Zacharias, . . . Malachias. . . . These are the Twelve Prophets in one book, besides which there are four others: . . . Isaias, . . . Jeremias, . . . Ezechiel, . . . Daniel. . . .

[2] The canonical books of the Old Testament are therefore twenty-two in number, equal in number to the letters of the Hebrew alphabet. Besides these there are also other books of the same Old Testament, which are not canonical, and which are read only to the catechumens. These are the Wisdom of Solomon, . . . the Wisdom of Jesus, Son of Sirach, . . . Esther, . . . Judith, . . . Tobias. . . . These are not canonical.

[3] So much then for the books of the Old Testament, both the canonical and the non-canonical.

Of the New Testament the defined and canonical books are these: . . . Matthew, . . .   42 Mark, . . . Luke, . . . John, . . . Acts of the Apostles. . . . The Catholic Epistles of various Apostles are seven in number, enumerated in one book: one of James, . . . two of Peter, . . . three of John, . . . one of Jude. . . . Of the Apostle Paul there are fourteen Epistles enumerated in one book: . . . first, to the Romans, . . . two to the Corinthians, . . . fourth, to the Galatians, . . . fifth, to the Ephesians, . . . sixth, to the Philippians, . . . seventh, to the Colossians, . . . two to the Thessalonians, . . . tenth, to the Hebrews, . . . two to Timothy, . . . thirteenth, to Titus, . . . fourteenth, to Philemon, ... Besides these there is also the Apocalypse of John the Theologian. . . . [4] These are the canonical books of the New Testament. . . .

1. Πᾶσα γραφὴ ἡμῶν χριστιανῶν θεόπνευστος. This is the opening line of the work.

THE WISDOM OF THE ELDERS OF ETHIOPIA [*saec.* 6 / 7 *et postea*]

The monachism of Egypt, embracing all manner of variations from the well-organized monastery to the solitary ascetical life of the hermit in his cave, has bequeathed to us a new literary genre which we can call *apophthegmata*, or *sayings*.

An anonymous collection of the *Sayings of the Fathers*, the *Apophthegmata patrōn*, was compiled in Greek perhaps about the end of the fifth century from undetermined sources; and with its maxims of the great Desert Fathers and its anecdotes about them it provides a marvelous view of the spirit and style of the monks and solitaries of Egypt. There was old black Moses, the butt of all the monastic jokes because he was a man of color. When a poor brother was caught stealing, they sent up the mountain to tell Moses to come down to the church, where a trial was to be held. He did not come. So they sent a second time and ordered him to come. Moses got a reed basket and filled it with rocks, tied a rope to it and the other end of the rope around his waist. Down the mountain road he came, dragging the basket of rocks behind him. When he came to the church they said to him, "You're a fool, Moses; why are you dragging those rocks?" "I have come here today," said Moses, "to judge one of my brothers; and yet, I am dragging my own sins along behind me, where I cannot see them." There was no trial.

Before the *Apophthegmata patrōn* was written down in Greek it must have existed, perhaps in written fragments in various languages, and surely in an oral tradition in Coptic. And the organized Greek collection of Apophthegmata was quickly translated and retranslated into a host of other patristic languages, copied, reorganized, added to, deleted from, until there were many such collections in several languages.

One of the more interesting of these collections is found in Ge'ez or Ethiopic. The recent critical edition of the Ethiopic by Victor Arras gives the work the title *Paternicon aethiopice*, or *The Ethiopic Paternicon*. I call it *The Wisdom of the Elders of Ethiopia*. They are both good titles; but the work itself proclaims its own title as *maṣeḥaf : zénáhome : la' abbawe : wanagaromu : zajesamaje : gannata ::* or *The Book of the History of the Fathers and of Their Words, Which is Called the Paradise*. We might also, therefore, call it simply *Gannat* or *The Paradise*.

The *Gannat* consists of 450 paragraphs (283 in its own less than convenient numbering system), the content of most of which can be found in other collections in other languages, such as the Greek *Apophthegmata patrōn* (Cotelier's edition in Migne, PG 65); *The Spiritual Meadow* of John Moschus (Migne, PG 87/3); the Latin collections of *Verba seniorum* of Pelagius and John (Migne, PL 73, 855-1022), of Paschasius (Migne, PL 73, 1025-1062), of Martin of Dumio (Migne, PL 74, 381-394), of the Pseudo-Rufinus (Migne, PL 73, 739-810); the two volume Syriac collection of E. A. Wallis Budge entitled *The Paradise or Garden of the Holy Fathers*, and numerous additional items in the periodical literature.

Paragraphs of the *Gannat* which have not yet been found elsewhere are nos. 102, 105-107, 110, 119-120, 129-130, 134-142, 145-146, 149-150, 152-153, 157-164, 166, 168-185, 187-191, 193-196, 199-200, 203-206, 208, 219-220, 222, 279-282, 286-289, 292-293, 298, 300, 302, 309, 312, 315-323, 329, 348, 350-351, 353-374, 386, 414, 424-425, 428, 431, 436-440, 443-444, 449-450. That is an apparent total of 114 selections; but since no. 187 simply repeats no. 157, it is 113 different selections, which may contain items peculiar to the Ethiopic. It is likely, however, that a good many of these may yet be found elsewhere when a more diligent search of other likely sources, including Coptic and Armenian collections, is made.

Since little or no literature went from an Ethiopic original into other patristic tongues, when an anecdote is found both in Ethiopic and in another language, and with no indications to the contrary, the presumption will be that the Ethiopic is not the original. Aside from the presumption of Greek or Coptic originals, internal indications will sometimes show which came first. For example in no. 35 of the *Gannat* (29 in the Ethiopic numbering in *Ms. Zotenberg* 125) the Abba Paul beheld Satan shooting arrows at a certain elder who was being tempted. In the *Verba seniorum* of Pelagius and John (both of whom later became Popes, Pelagius I [*regn.* 556-561] and John III [*regn.* 561-574]) the same anecdote is told (5, 4); but it is not Satan or demons, but a group of little black Ethiopians who are shooting the arrows. Obviously an Ethiop would have had reason to change the text, Ethiopians to Satan, whereas a Greek or Copt or a Syrian would have had no reason to change Satan to Ethiopians. A non-Ethiopian might envision demons as little black Ethiopians; an Ethiopian would not. So whatever the original language of the anecdote, it was not Ethiopian.

When the apophthegmata began to be translated into Ethiopic, and when the translations perhaps began to be augmented by local anecdotes in Ethiopia cannot be determined. As early as the sixth and seventh centuries certainly seems likely enough. Nor can it be determined when the *Gannat* took the form in which we have it today.

The critical edition of Victor Arras, which is also the *editio princeps*, is based on seven manuscripts of the fifteenth to the eighteenth centuries: *Zotenberg* 125, *Abbadie* 75, and *Oriental* 762, 764-767. The oldest and best of these is *Zotenberg* 125, of the fifteenth century.

Arras' edition, on which my translations are based, is published in two volumes, Ethiopic with Latin translation, in the series CSCO, the Ethiopic text in Vol. 277/Eth. 53 and Arras' Latin translation thereof in Vol. 278/Eth. 54, Louvain 1967. In the numbering of the selections below, the first number is that of Arras' system, while the second and parenthetic number is that of *Ms. Zotenberg* 125.

2167a

[15 (11)]

Abbâ Reslâwos visited the dwelling of Abbâ Esjâs in the desert and found him eating.   86
Esjâs had taken water and salt and had put them in a bowl. When the elder came in,   760
Esjâs hid the dish under some palm leaves. And the elder said to him, "What are you eating?"

Esjâs said to him, "Forgive me, Abbâ, but I went to cut palm leaves, but it was so hot I came back to the house. And I was so thirsty for water that I could not even swallow my bread because my throat was so dry. And I put some water on the salt so that I might eat my food. I beseech you, Abbâ, forgive me!"

But the elder cried out, "Come here! Look at Esjâs! See how even in the desert he is eating gravy!"

And to Esjâs he said, "If you crave to eat gravy, go into the land of Egypt (1)!"

2167b

[29 (23)]

A saying about a certain monk. On a journey and while walking down the road he   984
saw some virgin anchoresses, so he turned aside from the road. But the Emma (2) of
the ladies' convent shouted across to him, "You there! If you were a real monk you
wouldn't even have noticed that we are women!"

2167c

[71 (64)]

About discretion and patience. They told how some men, having heard of Abbâ   415
Agâton's reputation, came to him with the intention of testing his discretion and patience,
to see if he could be made angry.

They said to him, "Are you Agâton? We have heard what a great fornicator you are!"

He gave thanks and said to them, "That is quite correct, that's just what I am!"

Again they said, "Are you the Agâton who is such a slanderer and calumniator of
men?"

"Yes," he said, "that's who I am!"

Then they said to him, "Are you not Agâton the heretic?"

At this he answered and said, "No, I am not! A heretic I have never been!" And was he
angry!

So they inquired further and said to him, "Tell us why you willingly bore what we said
at first, but our last remark you will not tolerate at all?"

He replied, "I took what you said first, because it was good for me to do so; but were I
to declare myself a heretic, I would be separating myself from the Lord!"

Hearing this statement, they marveled at him and went away edified.

2167d

[78 (71)]

A truly great man came, a man from Rome who had lived in the palace of the   86
Neguś. He went to live at Scete near the church; and with him one of his servants who
waited on him. When the priest of Scete saw the infirmity of that man's body, and knowing
that he had come from such a delicate nurturing, he asked the Lord to console him and to
provide for him. The man would go to the church at the time for prayer, and then he would
return to his dwelling. He remained thus in Scete for twenty-five years. He possessed
knowledge, and his reputation was spreading abroad.

One of the elders of Egypt heard the Roman's fame, and he wanted to see him; for he
expected he would find in him a great ascetic and that he would learn from him something
useful in his own struggle. When he entered the Roman's house he asked for a blessing;
then they prayed and sat down.

The Egyptian saw the old Roman clothed in soft garments, a sheep skin spread out
beneath him, and a little cushion for his head; and he saw that his feet were clean and that
he wore shoes. Seeing him thus the Egyptian looked askance at him, because to live in
such a way was not the custom of that place where asceticism was practiced; and yet
knowledge had been given him and his fame had spread abroad.

The Roman understood that the Egyptian elder looked down on him; but he said to his
servant: "Go, my son, and prepare a feast for us, for the sake of our good Abbâ."

The servant took a few vegetables and prepared them, and when it was evening they ate. There was also a little something to drink, which the Roman kept at hand for the sake of his bodily infirmity; and they drank.

When it was time for sleep they recited twelve psalms and slept; and they did likewise through the night. At dawn the Egyptian arose and said to the Roman, "Pray for me"; and he went away having profited nothing by the experience.

After the Egyptian had gone a little while the Roman wanted to offer him something advantageous, so he sent his servant after him, and again he welcomed him with joy and asked him: "From what province are you, and from what city?"

"I never lived in a city," the Egyptian answered.

Again the Roman asked him, "What kind of work did you do where you lived?"

He answered, "I was a herdsman in the fields."

The elder asked him, "Where did you sleep and what did you use for a blanket?"

The Egyptian replied, "I slept in the desert; no use for a blanket there."

Again the Roman asked him, "But how, then, did you sleep?"

"I slept on the bare ground," he replied.

The Roman asked, "What did you eat and drink?"

"In the desert," the Egyptian replied, "what would I find to eat and drink?"

Still the Roman questioned him, "What was your way of living like?"

The Egyptian answered, "I ate a little bread and fish, and I drank water from the river."

The elder said to him, "That was a difficult way and laborious." And then he said to him, "Was there a bath in your village where you could wash?"

The Egyptian replied, "Of course not! When I wanted to wash I went down to the river."

All this the elder asked him, and he understood that the Egyptian's life had been a difficult one before he became a monk. Wanting him to understand also, he began to tell him what his own life had been like, and what had been his own manner of living when he was still in the world. He said to the Egyptian, "I, this poor man you see before you, I am from the great city of Rome, and from among the great ones of the palace of the Neguś."

The Egyptian, hearing him begin to speak, was filled with compunction and listened attentively to what he had to say.

The elder continued, "I left Rome and came to this desert. I left the palace behind, and I despised that great wealth and joy. I rejected it all, glad to have only this little dwelling of mine. I, the poor man you see before you, had golden beds and most excellent coverings of great worth; and in place of those I am thankful for this couch and this skin. Once my fine clothes were of great worth; and in place of them I am thankful for this linen garment which you see. In place of my many different foods, God Himself nourishes me with these few vegetables and a single cup of wine to drink. There were many servants waiting on me then; and in exchange for them God has sent me this one old man to take compassion on me and to attend me. For the bath which I enjoyed, it is enough for me to wash my feet and put shoes on them because of my infirmity. In place of music and songs, I recite twelve psalms by day and by night. For these former joys and great honors, I am glad now to have this little prayer at its proper time. So I ask you now, Abbâ, please do not be scandalized at my weakness."

When the Egyptian heard these words he was gripped in his heart by remorse; and he said, "Woe is me, for that I lived in the world in difficult circumstances, in many afflictions and sorrows; and see, now that I have come over to prayer, the refreshing leisure I had not before I do now have. You, however, you came from refreshing leisure and great honors into difficulties, and from wealth into poverty and labor."

Having found great advantage the Egyptian departed from him, being now his love. To the Roman, however, was given spiritual grace; and the grace in him was filled with the good odor of the Holy Spirit.

2167e

[102 (ex 92)]

They told about a monk who dwelt on the mountain and spent his days there. Two   1035
young men were with him, his disciples, one of whom was lazy about spending time   494
in prayer, nor was there any zeal in that young man's soul to make his ministry   492
pleasing to the Lord.   1032

The elder who was his teacher frequently admonished the young man and instructed him to be diligent about praying; and he taught him and said to him: "My son, know that there is nothing worse for a monk than to abandon his prayers; and there is nothing that Satan, the adversary, wants more than for us to stop praying. Beware, my son, lest Satan prove too strong for you in this struggle."

The elder exhorted the monk and rebuked him; but he could not reform him nor convert him from his laziness and indolence. While things were at such a pass, the brother died.

The elder wanted to know what had happened with his disciple and whither he had gone; so he remained in his dwelling as a solitary and afflicted his soul with fasting and prayer and lengthy vigils. When he had prolonged his labors he asked the Lord to show him what he wanted to know; and the Lord sent him a dream. Asleep, the elder saw in his dream one of the angels.

The angel took him by the hand and led him into the mansion of the just and into the dwelling place of the saints. The elder marveled at the peace and joy of those residing in these rooms; and the angel said to him, "These are the ones who pleased the Lord with their works; as Christ said in the Gospel, 'In My Father's house are many mansions (3)!'"

Then the angel led the elder into another place where sinners suffered punishment. There, where the elder saw various torments and where there was loud thunder, fear gripped him because of the horror of this terrifying sight.

The angel, however, said to him, "Fear not and be comforted! You are going to learn about him for whom you afflicted yourself in penance!" So the elder's heart was comforted and his soul was buoyed up.

Then he saw a huge cauldron like a broad ark and there was a blazing fire in it and its flames were boiling up. There were men standing in the cauldron; and some were in flames up to their neck, some up to their chest, some up to the lower part of their belly, and others up to their knees. When he saw them he marveled at them; and then he saw his lazy disciple standing at prayer in the midst of the fire, with flames up to his belly button (4).

The elder said to him, "I was your teacher, and didn't I threaten you with this? I warned you but you weren't afraid! O, my son, how it grieves me to see what has befallen you!"

The elder wept; but his disciple said to him, "Abbâ, don't be weeping like that, because I can tell you something really true that will cheer you up: I am standing on a bishop's (5) shoulders!"

When the elder's dream was finished he awoke from sleep and praised the Lord mightily.

2167f

[239 (174)]

Abbâ Peter said: when I was living in the Jordan monastery one of the brothers   392
died and there was an elder who didn't know about it. And when the horn was sounded   1011
for them to gather and they had come from the caves, the elder saw in the church (6) the one who had died and it grieved him that he had not visited him before he went forth from the world; and he went up to him and said to him, "Arise, O my brother, so that we might give each other the kiss of peace."

And the dead one got up and embraced the elder. And the elder said to him, "Peace to thee, O my son; and now do thou sleep in peace until Christ our Lord comes and bids thee arise."

1. ሖር ፡ ብሐሬ ፡ ግብጽ ። = ḥor : beḥéra : gebṣ :: = go into the land of Egypt. This does not, however, indicate an extra-Egyptian origin, nor a change by the translating Ethiop. For the Desert Fathers the land of Egypt was the bright lights and loose living of the big city, Alexandria.
2. እም ፡ = 'emma = mother. As a title it is the female counterpart of 'abbá; but in the present instance the lady seems in fact to be the superioress, whereas these titles usually seem to be entirely honorary and reverential. It would be a mistake to think of the 'abbá and the 'emma as abbot and abbess.
3. John 14:2.
4. ኅንብርቱ ። = ḥenbertu = his belly button.
5. ኤጲስ ፡ ቆጶስ ፡ = 'épis : qopos : = bishop. This almost incredible form is the standard Ge'ez term for bishop, and not just an idiosyncrasy of the Mss. of the Gannat. Since the Ethiopic turns the Greek loan word into two words, one might at least have expected 'épi : s(e)qopos. But 'épis : qopos is consistent in the language. As for the story itself, I am confident that I have heard a variation with the same punch line at a clerical gathering within the last six months. And I am certain that the man who told it did not read Ge'ez.
6. ቤተ ፡ ክርስቲያን ፡ = béta : krestijan : = church. Literally, Christian house. The term is standard.

ST. VINCENT OF LERINS [† ante A. D. 450]

Vincent of Lerins was canonized, so to speak, by Cardinal Baronius, who entered his name into the Roman Martyrology that he had been commissioned to prepare. Tillemont expressed some doubts as to whether or not the Cardinal had had sufficient grounds to do that; but, of course, Tillemont was questioning only the Cardinal's historical evidence and not the sanctity itself of St. Vincent.

Vincent was a priest and monk at Lerins, the island monastery near Nice. He is known as the author of three works: a) the Obiectiones, an anti-Augustinian work, now lost, but against which Prosper of Aquitaine wrote one of his Pro Augustino responsiones (see above, §§ 2031-2033); b) the Commonitoria, with which we shall deal directly; and c), if the manuscript attribution is correct, a florilegium of passages from Augustine's works dealing with the Trinity and the Incarnation, designed largely for use against Nestorius, and entitled Excerpta sanctae memoriae Vincentii Lirinensis insulae presbyteri ex universo beatae recordationis Augustini episcopi in unum collecta, discovered only in our own times and first published by J. Madoz at Madrid in 1940. It is reprinted in Hamman's Supplementum to the Migne Patrology, Vol. 3, 23-44.

It is not entirely incredible that Vincent should have made such a use of Augustine as is exhibited in the Excerpta. If he appears through his Obiectiones and his Commonitoria as Augustine's opponent in respect to the latter's doctrine on grace, and in general as a Semi-Pelagian, nevertheless, he did hold Augustine in such reverence that in writing against his doctrine, he never — at least in the Commonitoria; for we have not the precise text of his Obiectiones, but only their substance through Prosper,—names Augustine as the author of the doctrines against which he argues.

THE NOTEBOOKS [ca. A. D. 434]

Vincent's Commonitoria, which we can translate Notebooks in this instance, has not come down to us in its entirety, and it is not entirely certain why it has not. Certainly the Commonitoria was written originally in two books, and the second is lost. Gennadius says that before Vincent had an opportunity to publish the work, the second book was stolen; and he being too tired and worn out and disheartened to rewrite the second book entirely, he only made an outline of it from memory, which was published along with the first book. Gennadius' explanation, however, does not fit the work as we have it today. To the first book a recapitulation is always attached, and the recapitulation does seem to be Vincent's own; but it is a summation not just of a lost second book, but also of the first book to which it is attached; and it seems to have been made while the second book still existed. Moreover, it is in any case doubtful that any part of the work was published in Vincent's own lifetime. It appears that at least early on in the writing of the *Commonitoria*, he intended the work only for his own use and reflection.

We noted that in the *Commonitoria* Vincent never names Augustine, though he does write (at no great length) against the novelty that is Augustine's theory of grace. But he never names himself either. The author calls himself Peregrinus, that is, a pilgrim. But it cannot be doubted that Vincent is the Peregrinus. R. M. J. Poirel argued in 1895 that Peregrinus was not Vincent, but Marius Mercator. His arguments were not convincing, and it may be said that Vincent's authorship of the work is virtually unchallenged.

Very little of Vincent's Semi-Pelagianism comes through in the *Notebooks*; and if we knew nothing of him except what can be gotten from the *Notebooks*, he would probably escape that label entirely. But knowing from Prosper of Aquitaine the content of Vincent's *Obiectiones*, there are a few places in the *Notebooks* where we need read only a little between the lines to see him as Augustine's opponent. But putting that aside, Vincent shows himself also as a man of such remarkable perception that there is a certain timelessness to his writing. What he has to say of preserving the faith and of keeping to the rule of faith fits any period and all times, and might have been written yesterday.

Vincent develops the notion that our faith is based on the authority of divine Law, which must be understood and interpreted in the light of the Tradition of the Church. And this Tradition, if it need be discovered, is *quod ubique, quod semper, quod ab omnibus creditum est:* what has been believed in the Church everywhere, always, and by all. Vincent's doctrinal principle does not exclude progress and development; but it does exclude change. For Vincent, progress is a developmental growth of doctrine in its own sphere; change, however, implies a transformation into something different.

In his encyclical *Pascendi gregis* against modernism, Pope Saint Pius X refers favorably to St. Vincent; and so also does the Second Vatican Council in its *Dogmatic Constitution on the Catholic Faith*.

The text of Stephen Baluze reprinted in Migne, PL 50, 637-686, has been supplanted by that of G. Rauschen in fasc. 5 of the series *Florilegium patristicum*, Bonn 1906. Rauschen is the first since Baluze to actually examine the four extant manuscripts of the work.

2168

[2, 1]

With great zeal and closest attention, therefore, I frequently inquired of many men,   100
eminent for their holiness and doctrine, how I might, in a concise and, so to speak,
general and ordinary way, distinguish the truth of the Catholic faith from the falsehood
of heretical depravity. I received almost always the same answer from all of them, that
if I or anyone else wanted to expose the frauds and escape the snares of the heretics
who rise up, and to remain intact and sound in a sound faith, it would be necessary,
with the help of the Lord, to fortify that faith in a twofold manner: first, of course,
by the authority of the divine law; and then, by the Tradition of the Catholic Church.   101
[2] Here, perhaps, someone may ask: "If the canon of the Scriptures be perfect, and
in itself more than suffices for everything, why is it necessary that the authority of
ecclesiastical interpretation be joined to it?" Because, quite plainly, Sacred Scripture,
by reason of its own depth, is not accepted by everyone as having one and the same
meaning. The same passage is interpreted in one way by some, in another by others,
so that it can almost appear as if there are as many opinions as there are men. Novatian
explains a passage in one way, Sabellius in another, Donatus in another; Arius,
Eunomius, Macedonius in another; Photinus, Apollinaris, Priscillian in another;
Jovinian, Pelagius, Caelestius in another; and afterwards in still another, Nestorius.
And thus, because of so many distortions of such various errors, it is highly necessary

that the line of prophetic and apostolic interpretation be directed in accord with the norm
of the ecclesiastical and Catholic meaning. [3] In the Catholic Church herself every   106
care must be taken that we may hold fast to that which has been believed everywhere,
always, and by all (1). For this is, then, truly and properly Catholic. That is what the
force and meaning of the name itself declares, a name that embraces all almost
universally (2). This general rule will be correctly applied if we pursue universality,
antiquity, and agreement. And we follow universality in this way, if we confess
this one faith to be true, which is confessed by the whole Church throughout the whole
world; antiquity, however, if we in no way depart from those interpretations which, it
is clear, our holy predecessors and fathers solemnized; and likewise agreement, if,
in this very antiquity, we adopt the definitions and theses of all or certainly of almost
all priests and teachers.

2169

[9, 14]

To announce, therefore, to Catholic Christians something other than that which they   104
have received has never been permitted, is nowhere permitted, and never will be
permitted. And to anathematize those who announce anything other than that which
has been received once and for all has never been unnecessary, is nowhere
unnecessary, and never will be unnecessary.

2170

[13, 19]

One and the same Christ is God and Man; the same, increate and created; the same,   324
unchangeable and not subject to suffering, the same, transformed and having suffered;   334
the same, both equal to and less than the Father; the same, begotten of the Father
before the ages, the same, born of a Mother in time: perfect God, perfect man; in   311
God, the highest divinity, in Man, full humanity. Full humanity, I say, since, while   312
He has both soul and flesh, it is true flesh, ours, from His Mother, and a soul endowed
with intelligence, possessing mind and reason. In Christ, therefore, there is Word,
soul and flesh; but the whole of this is one Christ, one Son of God, and our one Savior
and Redeemer. He is one, however, not by a corruptible—I do not know what to call   321
it—confusion of divinity and humanity, but by a certain integral and special unity of
Person. For that conjunction neither converted nor changed one into the other,—which
is the characteristic error of the Arians,—but instead united both in one and in such
a way that while in Christ the singularity of one and the same Person always remains,   329
the peculiarity of each nature also remains forever.

2171

[15, 20]

This unity of Person in Christ, therefore, was formed and completed, certainly   329
not after the virginal birth, but in the very womb of the Virgin. [21] We must take the
utmost of precautions so that we may confess a Christ who is not merely one, but who has
always been one, because it is an intolerable blasphemy if, although you concede
that He is now one, you contend that earlier He was not one but two; one, of course,
after the time of His Baptism, but two at the time of His birth. We cannot avoid
this enormous sacrilege in any other way at all, except by our confessing that Man is
united to God, and this in a unity of Person, not from His Ascension or Resurrection or
Baptism, but already in His Mother, already in her womb, and finally, already in the
virginal conception itself. On account of this unity of Person the attribution to Man of   781

the things proper to God and the ascription to God of what is proper to the flesh is made
indifferently and without distinction. That is the reason why it can be divinely   334
written both that the Son of Man descended from heaven (3) and that the Lord of
Majesty was crucified on earth (4); and for that reason also, the flesh of the Lord
having been made, the flesh of the Lord having been created, it is said that the very
Word of God was made (5), His wisdom was filled up (6), His knowledge was created
(7), just as in prophecy (8) His hands and His feet are referred to as having been pierced   320
(9). Through this unity of Person, I say, it has also come about, by reason of a
similar mystery, that it is most Catholic to believe and most impious to deny that,
since the flesh of the Word was born of a virginal Mother (10), God Himself, the   311
Word, was born of the Virgin. This being the case, far be it that anyone should
try to defraud Holy Mary of her privileges of divine grace and of her special glory.
For by a certain singular favor of our Lord and God, and of her Son, she must be
confessed to be the most true and most blessed Theotokos; but not Theotokos in the   780
way in which a certain impious heresy claims, which asserts that she is to be called   327
Mother of God merely in name, because, of course, she gave birth to that man who
afterwards was made God, just as we speak of the mother of a presbyter or the mother
of a bishop, not because a woman bore someone who was already presbyter or
bishop, but because she bore a man who afterwards was made a presbyter or bishop.
Not in this way, I say, is Holy Mary the Theotokos, but rather, it was already in her
sacred womb that the sacrosanct mystery was accomplished, that, by reason of a   324
certain singular and unique unity of Person, just as the Word in flesh is flesh, so the
Man in God is God.

2172

[20, 25]
He is a true and genuine Catholic who loves the truth of God, the Church, and the   100
Body of Christ; who puts nothing else before divine religion and the Catholic Faith, neither
the authority nor the love nor the genius nor the eloquence nor the philosophy of any man
whatsoever, but, despising all that and being fixed, stable, and persevering in his faith, is
determined in himself to hold and believe that only which he knows the Catholic Church
has held universally and from ancient times.

2173

[22, 27]
"Guard," he says, "what has been committed (11)." What does it mean, "what   104
has been committed"? It is what has been faithfully entrusted to you, not what has been
discovered by you; what you have received, not what you have thought up; a matter not
of ingenuity, but of doctrine; not of private acquisition, but of public Tradition;
a matter brought to you, not put forth by you, in which you must be not the author
but the guardian, not the founder but the sharer, not the leader, but the follower.
"Guard," he says, "what has been committed." Keep the talent (12) of the Catholic
Faith inviolate and unimpaired. What has been faithfully entrusted, let it remain in
your possession, let it be handed on by you. You have received gold, so give gold.
For my part I do not want you to substitute one thing for another; I do not want you
impudently to put lead in place of gold, or, fraudulently, brass. I do not want the
appearance of gold, but the real thing. O Timothy, O priest, O interpreter, O teacher,   105
if a divine gift has made you suitable in genius, in experience, in doctrine to be the
Beseleel (13) of the spiritual tabernacle, cut out the precious gems of divine dogma, shape
them faithfully, ornament them wisely, add splendor, grace and beauty to them! By your
expounding it, may that now be understood more clearly which formerly was believed even

in its obscurity. May posterity, by means of you, rejoice in understanding what in times past was venerated without understanding. Nevertheless, teach the same that you have learned, so that if you say something anew, it is not something new that you say.

2174

[23, 28]

But perhaps someone is saying: "Will there, then, be no progress of religion in the   105
Church of Christ?" Certainly there is, and the greatest. For who is there so envious
toward men and so exceedingly hateful toward God, that he would try to prohibit
progress? But it is truly progress and not a change of faith. What is meant by progress
is that something is brought to an advancement within itself; by change, something is
transformed from one thing into another. It is necessary, therefore, that understanding,
knowledge, and wisdom grow and advance strongly and mightily as much in individuals
as in the group, as much in one man as in the whole Church, and this gradually
according to age and the times; and this must take place precisely within its own
kind, that is, in the same teaching, in the same meaning, and in the same opinion.
[29] The progress of religion in souls is like the growth of bodies, which, in the
course of years, evolve and develop, but still remain what they were. . . . [30]
For example: Our fathers of old sowed the seeds of the wheat of faith in this field
which is the Church. Certainly it were unjust and incongruous if we, their descendents,
were to gather, instead of the genuine truth of wheat, the noxious error of weeds. On the
contrary, it is right and logically proper that there be no discrepancy between what is first
and what is last and that we reap, in the increment of wheat from the wheat of instruction,
the fruit also of dogma. And thus, although in the course of time something evolved from
those first seeds and has now expanded under careful cultivation, nothing of the
characteristics of the seeds is changed. Granted that appearance, beauty, and distinction has
been added, still, the same nature of each kind remains. May it never happen that the rose
garden of the Catholic sense be turned into thistles and thorns. May it never happen, I say,
that darnel and monk's hood (14) suddenly spring up in the spiritual paradise of shoots of
cinnamon and balsam.

2175

[28, 39]

We must most studiously investigate and follow this ancient agreement of the   106
holy fathers, not in all the lesser questions of the divine Law, but certainly and
especially in the rule of faith. . . . But only those opinions of the fathers are to be
brought forward which were expressed by those who lived, taught, and persevered
wisely and constantly in the holy Catholic faith and communion, and who merited
either to die faithfully in Christ or to be killed gloriously for Christ. Those men,
moreover, are to be believed, in accord with the rule that only that is to be held as
undoubted, certain, and valid, which either all or most of them have confirmed by
receiving, holding, and handing on in one and the same sense, manifestly, frequently,
and persistently, as if by a council of teachers in mutual agreement. But whatever   107
was thought outside of or even against the opinion of all, although it be by a holy and
learned man, or although by a confessor and martyr, must be removed from the authority of
the common and public and general opinion, as being among his personal and peculiar and
private views. In this way we shall not, as is the sacrilegious custom of heretics and
schismatics, reject the ancient truth of universal dogma, to pursue, with great danger to our
eternal salvation, the novel error of one man.

---

1. This is the famous line: *In ipsa item catholica ecclesia magnopere curandum est, ut id teneamus,* **quod ubique, quod**
   semper, quod ab omnibus *creditum est.*

2. *Quod ipsa vis nominis ratioque declarat, quae omnia fere universaliter comprehendit.* The editio princeps read *vere;* but three of the four manuscripts have *fere.* Most translators have read to the effect: ". . . embraces all truly universally." I have no difficulty with what seems to be the better evidenced reading, ". . . almost universally."
3. John 3:13.
4. 1 Cor. 2:8.
5. John 1:14.
6. Sir. 24:35.
7. Sir. 1:4 and 24:12.
8. *in praescientia.*
9. Ps. 21[22]:17.
10. *ex integra matre.*
11. 1 Tim. 6:20.
12. *talentum.* The reference is to the parable talents, *i. e.,* sums of money, entrusted to various servants, in Matt. 25:14-30.
13. See Exod. 31:2. Beseleel was specially called by God to do the goldsmithing and lapidary work on the ark of the covenant.
14. *aconita.* The *aconitum* is a poisonous herb commonly called *monk's hood.* My apologies to the monks.

ST. PETER CHRYSOLOGUS [*ca. A. D.* 405 –*ca. A. D.* 450]

St. Peter Chrysologus, Archbishop of Ravenna and a Doctor of the Church, is, as his surname would indicate, best remembered as a preacher. About the year 830 A. D. the Abbot Agnellus, writing a history of the Church in Ravenna, says of Peter, "The Church has called him Chrysologus, that is, the Golden Preacher, because of his eloquence." It cannot be verified, however, that he was ever called Chrysologus before Agnellus gave him that name.

The Chrysologus was a native of Imola, the ancient Forum Cornelium, in the Emilia. It was in the time of Pope Sixtus III (432-440) that he was made Archbishop of Ravenna, which was then the residence of the Western Emperor, and which was made a metropolitan see sometime between 425 and 440. The probable date of Peter's death is Dec. 3, 450.

Bardenhewer is no doubt justified in saying that Peter is no Western Chrysostom, and that there were other preachers who deserve the title Chrysologus more than he. Nevertheless, there is a simple directness and naive charm to Peter's style which undoubtedly made his preaching very popular in his own time, and which still has a certain power to move a reader today.

SERMONS [*post A. D.* 432]

The Archbishop Felix of Ravenna (*regn.* 709-725) put together a collection of 176 sermons attributed to St. Peter Chrysologus; and it is basically that same collection of 176 sermons that constitutes the corpus of Peter's sermons as we have it today. The so-called Felician collection was first published by Agapitus Vicentinus at Bologna in 1534, and was afterwards several times published again, until Migne reprinted the 1750 edition of Sebastian Pauli in PL 52.

Over the years a number of other sermons have been attributed to Peter Chrysologus, some with his name attaching to them in the manuscripts and some gleaned from the *spuria* of other authors. Something of a guide to developments more recent than Migne can be found in Adalbert Hamman's *Supplementum* to the Migne patrology, Vol. 3, cols. 153-183. Even Hamman, however, is too early to have mentioned the publication of Alexander Olivar's edition of the *Sermons* of St. Peter Chrysologus, Part 1, sermons 1-62 *bis,* in volume 24 (1975) of the *Corpus Christianorum.*

Since I am citing only *Sermons* 94 and 117 I must still rely on Migne's reprint of the text of Sebastian Pauli in PL 52.

2176

[94]

No need to despair, man. Look, there has still remained for you a means to satisfy   912
your Most Pious Creditor. Do you want to be forgiven? Then love! "Love covers   591
over a multitude of sins (1)." What worse crime is there than denial? And yet Peter
was able to wipe away even this by love alone, when the Lord, to test him, says:
"Peter, do you love me (2)?" Among all God's precepts, love takes the first place.

2177

[117]

Where are they who think that the Virgin's conceiving and the Virgin's giving   781
birth are just like those of other women? Theirs is of the earth, hers is of heaven.   782
Hers is by divine power, theirs by human weakness. Theirs is in the passions of the   783
flesh, hers in the tranquillity of the Divine Spirit and in a human body at rest. Blood was
quiet, flesh was still, her members slept, and the Virgin's womb was entirely unmoved in
that heavenly visit, while the Author of flesh was clothing Himself in a garment of flesh
and becoming a Heavenly Man, who would not only restore the earth to man, but would
even give him heaven. A Virgin conceived, a Virgin bore, and a Virgin she remains.

1. 1 Peter 4:8.
2. John 21:15.

LETTER OF PETER CHRYSOLOGUS TO EUTYCHES [A. D. 449]

The Archimandrite Eutyches, in reacting against Nestorianism, which made two
Persons of Christ, became in fact the father of Monophysitism, holding that in Christ
there are not only not two Persons, but not even two natures. In Eutychian
Monophysitism, the human and divine natures are so intermingled and combined as to
become a single nature of some third or intermediate kind, neither human nor divine.

Summoned to appear before a council of bishops at Constantinople in 448 A. D. by
the Patriarch Flavian, Eutyches refused to withdraw from his ill-advised position and the
council excommunicated him. He then wrote letters of appeal to the Emperor
Theodosius II, to the Patriarch Dioscurus of Alexandria, to Peter Chrysologus at
Ravenna, and to Pope Leo I.

Dioscorus promptly absolved Eutyches from the excommunication issued at
Constantinople, and began setting the stage for the Robber Synod of Ephesus, the
latrocinium ephesinum. Pope Leo sent his Dogmatic Epistle to Flavian; but at the
latrocinium it was not allowed even to be read. Barsumas, a Syrian Archimandrite,
arrived with a retinue of monks trained to fight. The Papal legates escaped and were able
to report to Leo. Flavian died of his wounds three days later.

Somewhere in the midst of all this, probably in 449 A. D. and certainly without any
knowledge of what was happening, Peter Chrysologus replied to the appeal of Eutyches.
He cannot at that time have been aware of Pope Leo's intervention, nor of much else in
this matter; but still, he says nothing unworthy or unbecoming. And he urges Eutyches
to be humble, to submit to his superiors, and to be in all things obedient to Rome.

The letter of Peter Chrysologus to Eutyches is preserved in both Latin and in Greek,
and is found as Letter no. 25 in the corpus of the collected Letters of Pope St. Leo I, in
Migne, PL 54, 739-794.

2178

[25, 2]

We exhort you in every respect, honorable brother, to heed obediently what   435
has been written by the Most Blessed Pope of the City of Rome; for Blessed Peter,   436
who lives and presides in his own see, provides the truth of faith to those who   432
seek it. For we, by reason of our pursuit of peace and faith, cannot try cases on the 451
faith without the consent of the Bishop of the City of Rome (1).

1. *Nos enim pro studio pacis et fidei extra consensum romanae civitatis episcopi causas fidei audire non possumus.*

ST. LEO I (THE GREAT), POPE [*regn. A. D. 440-461*]

Pope St. Leo the Great was probably of Tuscan origin, though he calls himself a Roman. Under Popes Sixtus III (432-440) and Celestine before him (422-432), Leo was an Archdeacon of the diocese of Rome, and was on an official mission in Gaul when he learned that Sixtus was dead and that he was himself chosen to succeed to the See of Peter. Hastening back to Rome, he was consecrated on Sept. 29, 440 A. D. The date of his death is uncertain, except that it was rather late in the year 461 A. D. Leo is the first Pope who did not die a martyr's death. In 1754 he was declared a Doctor of the Church by Pope Benedict XIV.

Leo's reign was a burdensome one in which he acquitted himself well, enduring invasions of Vandals and Huns from without, schisms and heresies from within. Chief among the last was Monophysitism, of which we saw something already above (p. 267), in the introduction to the Letter of St. Peter Chrysologus to Eutyches.

After the disgraceful procedure of the Robber Synod of Ephesus, it was Leo who called that meeting a *latrocinium*, a convention of robbers, the name that has clung to it ever since. The Council of Chalcedon in 451 was expected to repair the situation; and it did very clearly condemn both Nestorianism and Monophysitism.

Unfortunately a misapprehension grew in the East, that Chalcedon had contradicted the Council of Ephesus of 431 A. D., and that Leo's Epistle to Flavian (the *Tomus Leonis*) had condemned the Christology of St. Cyril of Alexandria. Neither supposed fact was true, of course; and a little more prudence and circumspection would have made these matters clear. Dioscurus was successfully deposed at Alexandria; but it made no difference to orthodoxy, because Monophysites succeeded him, first Timothy the Cat (Timothy Aelurus), and after him, Peter the Stammerer (Peter Mongo). Moreover, the Monophysites were successful in establishing men of their party in Jerusalem (Theodore) and Antioch (Peter Fullo). Within a hundred years the separation from Rome was consummated, by which nearly the whole of the Coptic, Ethiopian, and Armenian churches, and a considerable portion of the Syrian churches remain monophysite at least in name even today.

Leo's literary remains, that is, his letters and sermons, are better preserved than those of any Pope before him. Apparently, he kept a chancery archives.

LETTERS [*A. D. 442-460*]

The corpus of Leo's letters contains 173 items, of which 143 are of the Pope himself, the other 30 being either letters to him or in which he is in some way concerned. The most famous of the letters is undoubtedly no. 28, which is the *Tomus Leonis ad Flavianum*, which was not allowed to be read at the Robber Synod.

The best general edition of all the letters is still that of the Ballerini brothers, reprinted

in Migne, PL 54, 581-1218. Some of the letters, however, have appeared in more recent and more critical editions: O. Günther's *Epistulae imperatorum pontificum*, CSEL, Vol. 35, part 1, Vienna 1895; E. Schwartz, *Acta conciliorum oecumenicorum*, Vol. 1-4, Berlin 1927-1932; and C. Silva-Tarouca, *S. Leonis Magni epistulae*, in the theological series of the Gregorian University's *Textus et Documenta*, fasc. 9, 15, 20, and 23, Rome 1932-1935.

As the basis for our translations below, Silva-Tarouca's texts are used for letters 28, 35, 114, 119; Schwartz for 124; Migne's Ballerini for the rest. Günther's CSEL volume covers only letters 169-173, which I have no occasion to quote. Neither have I any occasion to cite letters 40-42 and 65-67, the texts of which are edited by Gundlach in Vol. 3 of the *Epistulae* series of the *Monumenta Germaniae historica*, Berlin 1892, pp. 15-22.

LETTER OF POPE LEO I TO THE BISHOPS OF THE PROVINCE OF VIENNE. *July, 445 A. D.* [Divinae cultum]

2178a

[10, 1]
Our Lord Jesus Christ, Savior of the human race, so established the worship of   430
divine religion, which He wanted to shine out by God's grace unto all nations and   432
peoples, that the truth, previously contained in the proclamation of the Law and the   433
Prophets, might go forth through the apostolic trumpet to the salvation of all, as it   435
is written: "Their sound has gone forth to all the earth, and their words to the ends of the earth (1)." But the Lord desired that the sacrament of this gift should pertain to all the Apostles in such a way that it might be found principally in the most blessed Peter, the highest of all the Apostles. And He wanted His gifts to flow into the entire body from Peter himself, as if from the head, in such a way that anyone who had dared to separate himself from the solidarity of Peter would realize that he was himself no longer a sharer in the divine mystery. . . . [2] Your Fraternities must realize with us, of course, that the Apostolic See—out of reverence for it, I mean,—has on countless occasions been reported to in consultation by bishops even of your province. And through the appeal of various cases to this see, decisions already made have been either revoked or confirmed, as dictated by long-standing custom.

LETTER OF POPE LEO I TO THE BISHOPS OF MAURETANIA. *Aug. 10, 446 (?).* [Cum in ordinationibus]

2179

[12, 2]
"Do not impose hands hastily on anyone, and be not a partner in the sins of others   958
(2)." What does it mean to impose hands hastily, except to give the priestly honor to those who have not been tested, before the age of maturity, before the period of trial, before they have merits of obedience, before they have experience of discipline? And what does it mean to be a partner in the sins of others, except that the one ordaining become like the one who did not deserve to be ordained? . . . [3] A man may be found to be of good character and may be adorned with holy works to any degree; but he still must not rise to the rank of the diaconate or to priestly dignity or to the height of the episcopate if it is certain that he has married more than once or that his wife was previously married (3).

LETTER OF POPE LEO I TO ANASTASIUS, BISHOP OF
THESSALONICA. A. D. 446 (?). [Quanta fraternitate]

2179a

[14, 11]
　If in your view, in regard to a matter to be handled and decided jointly with your   410
brothers, their decision was other than you wanted, then let the entire matter, with a   430
record of the proceedings, be referred to us. . . . Although bishops have a common   433
dignity, they are not all of the same rank. Even among the most blessed Apostles,   435
though they were alike in honor, there was a certain distinction of power. All were
equal in being chosen, but it was given to one to be preeminent over the others. From
this formality there arose also a distinction among bishops, and by a great arrangement
(4) it was provided that no one should arrogate everything to himself, but in
individual provinces there should be individual bishops whose opinion among their
brothers should be first; and again, certain others, established in larger cities, were to
accept a greater responsibility. Through them the care of the universal Church would
converge in the one See of Peter, and nothing should ever be at odds with this head.

THE TOME OF LEO: LETTER OF POPE LEO I TO FLAVIAN, BISHOP
OF CONSTANTINOPLE. June 13, 449 A. D. [Lectis dilectionis tuae]

2182

[28, 2]
　This same eternal Only-begotten Son of the eternal Father was born of the Holy   302
Spirit and the Virgin Mary. This birth in time neither added anything nor took
anything away from His divine and eternal birth. He sacrificed Himself entirely in   374
order to redeem man, who had been deceived, so that He might overcome death and so
that He might, by His power, destroy the Devil, who held sway over death. For we
would not be able to overcome the author of sin and death if Christ, whom sin could
not contaminate nor death detain, had not taken up our nature and made it His own.   363
He was conceived of the Holy Spirit within the womb of the Virgin Mother, who   346
gave birth to Him while preserving her virginity just as she had, while preserving   782
her virginity, conceived Him. . . . But that generation, singularly wonderful and   781
wonderfully singular, is not to be understood as being, because of its newness, an   320
entirely different kind. For fruitfulness was given to the Virgin by the Holy Spirit;   311
but the genuinity of the body was taken from her body; and when Wisdom built
Himself a house (5), the Word was made flesh and dwelt among us (6), that is, in
this flesh, which He took from man and which He animated with the spirit of   312
rational life.

2182a

[28, 3]
　While preserving, therefore, the quality proper to each nature and joining both in   322
one Person, lowliness was taken on by majesty, weakness by strength, and mortality   324
by eternity. And in order to pay the debt of our condition, an inviolable nature was   334
united to a nature capable of suffering so that, this being the kind of reparation   347
we needed, one and the same Mediator of God and men, the man Christ Jesus (7), was   387
able to die in one nature and not in the other. In the whole and perfect nature of true
man, therefore, the true God was born, complete in what pertains to His own nature   313
and complete in what pertains to ours. But by what pertains to ours we mean that   343

which the Creator formed in us at the beginning and that which He took upon Himself
in order to redeem it. What the Deceiver added, and man, being deceived, accepted,   344
left no traces in the Savior. He did not share in our sins by the fact that He undertook   345
to share our weaknesses.

2183

[28, 5]

   It is to be understood in the light of this unity of Person in both natures, when we   324
read that the Son of Man came down from heaven when the Son of God took flesh   311
of the Virgin of whom He was born. And again, the Son of God is said to have been   334
crucified and buried, although this pertained not to His divinity itself, in which the
Only-begotten is coeternal and consubstantial with the Father, but in the weakness of His
human nature. In this way, too, we all confess in the creed that the Only-begotten Son of
God was crucified and buried in accord with what the Apostle says: "If they had known,
they never would have crucified the Lord of Majesty (8)."

LETTER OF POPE LEO I TO JULIAN, BISHOP OF KIOS. June 13,
449 A. D. [Licet per nostros]

2184

[35, 3]

   It is true that the birth of the Lord according to the flesh had certain peculiarities   782
by which it transcended the beginnings of the human condition, whether that He alone
was conceived and born without concupiscence from an inviolate Virgin, or that He
came from His Mother's womb in such a way that her fruitfulness bore Him, and her
virginity yet remained; but nevertheless His flesh was not of a nature different from   310
ours, and the soul breathed into Him was not of a source other than in the rest of men,   312
superior not by a difference in kind but in sublimity of power. He had no opposition in   311
His flesh, nor was there any lack of harmony in His desires to cause a conflict of wills (9).   343
His bodily senses were active without the law of sin; and the reality of His emotions   349
was not tempted by allurements nor did it yield to injurious influences, since it was
under the control of His divinity and of His mind. True man was united to true God,
and He was not brought down from heaven in respect to a pre-existing soul, nor was He
created out of nothing in respect to His flesh, bearing the same Person in the divinity
of the Word, and possessing a nature in common with us in body and soul. For He
would not be Mediator between God and men unless He were God and Man both in   387
one genuine Person.

LETTER OF THE FATHERS OF THE ECUMENICAL COUNCIL OF
CHALCEDON TO POPE LEO I. Nov. 451 A. D. [Repletum est gaudio]

2184a

[98, 1]

   For if where two or three are gathered together in His name, He says He is there   433
in the midst of them (10), how much more will He not show His companionship with   435
five hundred and twenty priests, who preferred the spread of knowledge concerning   452
Him to their own home and affairs, when you, as the head to the members, showed
your good will through those who represented you (11)?

LETTER OF POPE LEO I TO THEODORE, BISHOP OF FORUM IULII.
June 11, 452 A. D. [Sollicitudinis quidem tuae]

2184b

[108, 2]

The manifold mercy of God so assists in the event of human lapses, that not only   900
by the grace of Baptism, but even through the medicine of Penance the hope of eternal   836
life is restored, so that those who have violated the gifts of rebirth, when they have
condemned themselves by their own judgment, may obtain the forgiveness of their
crimes, the safeguards of the divine goodness having been so ordained that the
forgiveness of God cannot be obtained except through the prayers of priests. For the   924
Mediator of God and men, the man Christ Jesus (12) gave this power to those placed   925
in charge of the Church, that they might grant a course of penance to those who   387
confess, and admit to the communion of the Sacraments through the gate of reconciliation   916
those who have been cleansed by salutary satisfaction. . . . [5] It behooves each
Christian to pass judgment on his own conscience, and not to defer his conversion to
God from day to day, . . . choosing the narrower limits of a period when there will
scarcely be time for the confession of the penitent or for the reconciliation of the
priest. But, as I said, even such must be assisted in their need, so that neither the action
of Penance nor the grace of Communion may be denied them if, even when the faculty
of speech has been lost, they ask for it by signs clearly understood. But if the violence
of their illness has been so worsened that in the presence of the priest they cannot
even signify what they had asked for only a little while before, then the testimonies
of the faithful standing about must be of service to them, so that they may at the
same time be accorded the benefit of both Penance and reconciliation. The rule
of the canons of the Fathers (13), however, is to be observed in regard to those   902
persons who have sinned against God by abandoning the faith.

LETTER OF POPE LEO I TO THE FATHERS OF THE ECUMENICAL
COUNCIL OF CHALCEDON. March 21, 453 A. D. [Omnem quidem fraternitatem]

2185

[114, 2]

I admonish Your Holiness to be observant also in keeping the statutes which were   452
established by inviolable decrees in the Council of Nicaea, so that the rights of the
Churches, as they were ordained by those three hundred and eighteen divinely
inspired Fathers, may remain.

LETTER OF POPE LEO I TO MAXIMUS, BISHOP OF ANTIOCH.
June 11, 453 A. D. [Quantum dilectioni tuae]

2186

[119, 3]

I have such great reverence for the canons of Nicaea that I have never permitted nor   452
will ever suffer those things which were established by the holy Fathers to be violated
by any sort of innovation. For though prelates may sometimes be of different merits,   433
the rights of sees, nevertheless, are permanent; and although rivalries may sometimes
bring about some disturbance, they cannot impair their dignity.

LETTER OF POPE LEO I TO THE MONKS OF PALESTINE.
June 15, 453 A. D. [Sollicitudini meae quam]

2188

[124, 3]

What reconciliation can there be, by which God might be propitiated for the human   387
race, if the Mediator of God and men had not taken up the cause of all? And by what   386
means could He fulfill the true role of a Mediator, if He that was, in the form of God,
equal to the Father, were not a sharer also of our [nature], in the form of a slave, so   313
that through the new Man there might take place a renewal of the old, and the bond of   376
death contracted by the wrong-doing of one man might be loosed by the death of one
Man, who alone owed no debt to death? For the pouring out of the blood of the   380
Righteous on behalf of the unrighteous was so powerful for the obtaining of privilege,
so rich a ransom, that, if the whole of captive mankind but believed in its Redeemer,
the tyrant's hands could hold no one. . . . [4] What hope, then, do they, who deny   310
the truth of the human substance in the body of our Savior, leave for themselves in
the efficacy of this sacrament (14)? Let them tell by what sacrifice they have been
reconciled; let them tell by what blood they have been redeemed. Who is He that
gave Himself up on our behalf, as an oblation and victim to God in an odor of sweetness   382
(15)? And what sacrifice was there ever that was more sacred than that which the true   381
High Priest placed upon the altar of the cross by the immolation of His own flesh?

LETTER OF POPE LEO I TO RUSTICUS, BISHOP OF NARBONNE.
458 or 459 A. D. [Epistulas fraternitatis]

2188a

[167, 4, 3]

The law of continence is the same for ministers (16) of the altar as it is for bishops   964
and priests, who, when they were laymen or lectors, could lawfully marry and beget
offspring. But when they reached the ministerial ranks what before was lawful ceased
to be such. In order, therefore, that their marriages may become spiritual rather
than carnal, it behooves them not to dismiss their wives, but to "have them as if they
had them not (17);" and in this way, while they retain the affection of their wives,
their marital relations will cease.

LETTER OF POPE LEO I TO THE BISHOPS OF CAMPANIA, SAMNIUM
AND PICENUM. March 6, 459 A. D. [Magna indignatione]

2189a

[168, 2]

I decree also that that presumption contrary to the apostolic regulation, which I   916
recently learned is being committed by some in an illegal usurpation, is by all means to   918
cease. With regard to penance, certainly what is required of the faithful is not that the   919
nature of individual sins be written in a document and recited in a public profession,   920
since it is sufficient that the guilt of consciences be indicated to priests alone in a secret   921
confession. For although that fullness of faith may seem to be praiseworthy which,
for fear of God, is not afraid to blush before men, nevertheless, because the sins of all
are not of such kind that those who seek Penance do not fear to make them public,
such an unapproved custom is to cease (18).

1. Ps. 18[19]:5.
2. 1 Tim. 5:22.
3. This passage provides a good illustration of an extremely important law of hermeneutics: never to suppose more than is actually said. One might easily conclude from the remark which Leo makes, that priest or bishop cannot be twice-married, that Leo does not enjoin celibacy; though, of course, this is not actually stated, and the passage says only that the priest or bishop cannot have been a diagmist. That even according to Leo he must in fact be celibate is clear in his Letter to Rusticus, § 2188a below. The reader may ask, why would Leo say such a thing in his Letter to the Bishops of Mauretania, that priest or bishop can have only one wife, while saying nothing of the fact that such are not allowed to cohabit even with that one? To this we can only answer that digamy and present cohabitation are two very distinct matters, and that in the light of the two letters, it can only be concluded that if he had not need to mention non-cohabitation in the first it can only be because this arrangement was so well-known and so universal that he could assume the recipients of his letter knew of it; he had no need to explain it.
4. *magne ordinatione*.
5. Prov. 9:1.
6. John 1:14.
7. 1 Tim. 2:5.
8. 1 Cor. 2:8.
9. This should not be taken as any sort of condemnation-in-advance of Monothelitism. The problem of two wills had not yet been advanced, and the statement means only that in his flesh there was no concupiscence to bring about a conflict of objects desired. The phrase "conflict of wills" really means "conflict of objects willed." This is the conflict that all other men have, but which Christ did not have, because all other men have concupiscence and he did not.
10. Matt. 18:20.
11. The Ecumenical Council of Chalcedon of 451 A. D. asked in this letter for ratification of their 28th canon, according a primacy of honor, second after Rome, to Constantinople, as had been stated already in the 3rd canon of the Ecumenical Council of Constantinople of 381 A. D. It was refused, in Pope Leo's Letter no. 104 to the Emperor Marcian *(Magno munere)*, and again in his Letter no. 114 to the Fathers of Chalcedon *(Omnem quidem fraternitatem)*. See above, Vol. I, pp. 397-398, 400-401.
12. 1 Tim. 2:5.
13. See, for example, Can. 22 of the First Council of Arles, Mansi, Vol. 2, p. 473.
14. *sacramentum:* which should here be taken in the sense of *mystery*.
15. Eph. 5:2.
16. Ministers here must be taken to mean subdeacons and deacons. It is clear in the same sentence that lectors, representatives of the minor orders, were not required to be celibate.
17. 1 Cor. 7:29.
18. *removeatur tam improbabilis consuetudo*.

SERMONS [*ante A. D.* 461]

Leo is the first Pope a large body of whose sermons or homilies are extant. The edition of the Ballerini brothers contains ninety-six genuine (in their judgment — several of these are now found unauthentic) and twenty spurious or highly suspect sermons. Eight sermons were edited by Armand Caillau and Benjamin Saint-Yves; and these actually duplicate five of the Ballerini brothers' spuria; nor are the other three genuine.

The edition of the Ballerini's was formerly quite highly regarded; and it is, in fact, the best we have. It is now recognized, however, that even the Ballerini edition is hopelessly inadequate in the face of several manuscripts that have come to light since the time of the Ballerini's. The Ballerini brothers relied largely on lectionary collections which were somewhat in the nature of sermon outlines, whereas we now have more complete manuscripts, additional sermons, and two editions prepared by Leo himself. The edition of Antoine Chavasse in the *Corpus Christianorum*, vols. 138 and 138A (1973), with sermons numbered 1-96 but entitled *Tractatus septem et nonaginta* since it has an 84 *bis*, is a vast improvement over that of the Ballerini's, but I doubt that the last word has yet been said on the editing of Leo's sermons. Migne reprinted the Ballerini text in his PL 54, 137-468 with spuria at 477-522. This must now be regarded as superseded by the text of Chavasse.

2190

[3, 1]

Without regard to lineage and inheritance (1), the Church receives those rulers   950
whom the Holy Spirit prepared; thus among the people of God's adoption, the
whole of which is priestly and royal, no prerogative of earthly origin can obtain the
anointing, but a condescension of divine grace begets a bishop.

2191

[4, 2]

From the whole world only one, Peter, is chosen to preside over the calling of all   430
nations, and over all the other Apostles, and over the Fathers of the Church. Thus,   410
although among the people of God there are many priests and many pastors, it is
really Peter who rules them all, of whom, too, it is Christ who is their chief ruler.
Divine condescension, dearly beloved, has granted to this man in a wonderful and
marvellous manner the aggregate of its power; and if there was something that it
wanted to be his in common with other leaders, it never gave whatever it did not
deny to others except through him.

2192

[12, 1]

If, dearly beloved, we want to understand the beginning of our creation faithfully   520
and wisely, we will discover that man was created in the image of God so that he
might be the imitator of his Author. The natural dignity of our race is this: that the
beauty of the divine goodness can shine forth in us as if in a kind of mirror. The grace   376
of the Savior restores us to this beauty daily, since what fell in the first Adam is raised
up again in the Second.

2193

[21, 3]

Let us, therefore, dearly beloved, give thanks to God the Father, through His   752
Son, in the Holy Spirit, who, on account of the great mercy with which He has
loved us, has been merciful to us; and when we were dead in our sins He made us to
live again together in Christ (2), so that in Him we might be a new creation and a new
production. Let us, therefore, put aside the old man with his deeds (3); and, having
obtained a share in the birth of Christ, let us renounce the works of the flesh. O   754
Christian, acknowledge your worth! Having been made a partner of the divine nature
(4) do not return to your old baseness by degenerate conduct. Remember the Head
and the Body of which you are a member. Recall that you have been rescued from
the power of darkness and have been transferred into the light and kingdom of God.

2194

[22, 2]

Christ, however, was begotten in a new kind of nativity, conceived by a Virgin,   781
born of a Virgin, without the concupiscence of paternal flesh, without injury to   782
maternal integrity. . . . His origin is different but His nature is the same. Human   783
usage and custom was lacking, but by divine power it was brought about that a
Virgin conceived, a Virgin bore, and Virgin she remained.

2195

[22, 3]
And, dearly beloved, does not this very fact that Christ chose to be born of a   361
Virgin seem to be part of the deepest design? That the Devil should not be aware, I   313
mean, that Salvation had been born for the human race, and, because that spiritual   374
conception was such a hidden matter, when he saw Him no different than others,
he should believe that He was born in a way no different than others. For when the
Devil would see that His nature was like that of all others, he would suppose that His
origin was the same as that of all others. He would not understand that He was free of
the bonds of transgression, because he would not find Him a stranger to the weakness of
mortality. For the true mercy of God, although it had available an indeclarable number
of ways to restore the human race, chose this way as best of all, in which, for the
destruction of the Devil's work, use would be made not of the strength of power but
of the claims of justice. For the pride of the ancient enemy did not undeservedly make
good its tyrannical rights over all men, nor did it force an undue domination on those
whom it had, volunteers that they were, seduced away from the command of God
to be in the servitude of his will. Thus there would be no justice in his losing the
original servitude of the human race, unless he were conquered by that which he
had subjugated. And so that this might come to be, without male seed Christ was
conceived of the Virgin, whom not human intercourse but the Holy Spirit made   781
fruitful. And if in all mothers conception does not take place without stain of sin, this
Mother drew purification from the Source whence she conceived. For the mildew of   615
sin did not make its entry where the transferal of paternal seed did not obtain. Inviolate
virginity knew no concupiscence when it waited upon the substance. The Lord took
from His Mother our nature, not our fault.

2196

[23, 4]
It was in no new counsel nor by any tardy pity that God took thought of the situation   389
of men; but from the foundation of the world He established one and the same cause
of salvation for all. For the grace of God, by which the whole body of the saints is
ever justified, was augmented, not begun, with the birth of Christ; and this sacrament of
great compassion, wherewith the whole world is now filled, was so effective even in its
significations that those who believed its promise obtained no less than those who
received its fulfillment.

2197

[27, 1]
When we attempt to understand the mystery of Christ's nativity, in which He was   557
born of the Virgin Mother, let the clouds of earthly reasonings be driven far away   558
and the smoke of worldly wisdom be purged from the eyes of illuminated faith. For
the authority in which we believe is divine, and divine is the teaching which we
follow.

2198

[29, 1]
In Christ Jesus, the Son of God, that which was said by the Prophet, "Who shall   320
declare His generation (5)," looks not only to His divine essence but also to His human
nature. For if faith will not believe that both substances are brought together in one   324
Person, speech cannot explain it.

2199

[30, 6]
Because this is the principal assistance of men in need of justification, that the   323
Only-begotten of God deigned even to be a Son of Man, so that the same who was God,   257
homoousios, — that is, of one substance, — with the Father, would become true man   313
and consubstantial with His Mother according to the flesh, we rejoice in both, because
we are not saved except by both, in no way separating the visible from the invisible,
the corporeal from the incorporeal, that which could suffer from that which could not
suffer, the tangible from the intangible, the form of a slave from the form of God.
Although one perdures from eternity and the other begins in time, brought together in a
unity, they are able to have neither separation nor end.

2200

[38, 3]
Without God there is no virtue, nor does a man obtain what is proper to divinity unless   650
he be enlivened by the Spirit of his Author. Since the Lord said to His disciples,
"Without Me you are able to do nothing (6)," there is no doubt that when a man does
good works he has from God both the carrying out of the work and the beginning of   656
his will to do so.

2201

[43, 1]
Without the grace of God there can be no obedience on man's part; nor is man ever   657
abandoned by that Good, without which no good can be done. And if carrying out   712
God's commands proves difficult or impossible for a man, he has no other course but to
return to Him who commands, and who gives His precept so that He may excite desire
and provide help, as the Prophet says: "Turn your thoughts to God and He will nourish
you (7)." Or is anyone so insolently proud, is anyone so unscathed, does anyone   658
presume himself so immaculate, that he has no need of any renewal? Such a conviction   659
were utterly erroneous, and that man has grown old in excessive vanity who believes
that amid the temptations of this life he has been free of every wound.

2202

[45, 3]
What is more fruitful than works of mercy? What is more blessed than humanitarian   651
deeds? Nor is it to be cheated of its own proper praise, if one man assist another with
his help, because of the nature they bear in common. But such does not attain to eternal
rewards because it does not proceed from the font of faith. The status of heavenly works
is one thing, that of earthly another.

2203

[56, 2]
Supplicating the Father, the Lord says: "Father, if it is possible, let this chalice pass   331
from me; yet not as I will, but as You will (8)." The first plea is one of weakness; the
second, of strength. The former He desired by reason of what is ours; the latter, He
chose by reason of what is His own. . . . So that the distinction of the nature   322
receiving and of the nature received might be manifest, what was of man lacked divine
power, what was of God looked to the needs of mankind. The inferior will yielded,
therefore, to the superior will (9); and at the same time an example is given of what
can be prayed for by the anxious, and what must not be granted by the Physician.

2204

[63, 1]

The omnipotence of the Son of God, whereby through the same essence He is equal   361
to the Father, would have been able by the mere command of His will to rescue the   257
human race from the domination of the Devil, if it had not been better suited to the   363
divine operations to conquer the opposition of the enemy's wickedness by that which
had been conquered, and to restore our natural liberty through that very nature
through which a general captivity had come about.

2205

[63, 5]

For all things that, according to the Law, were prior, whether circumcision of the   51
flesh, or the multitude of sacrificial victims, or the observance of the Sabbath,
testified to Christ and foretold Christ's grace. And He is the end of the Law, not by   50
annulling but by fulfilling what is signified. For although He is the Author both of the   52
old ways and of the new, still, He changed the sacraments of the prefigured promises,
because He fulfilled the promises and put an end to announcements by His coming as the
Announced. But in the area of moral precepts, no decrees of the earlier Testament are
rejected; rather, in the Gospel teaching many of them are augmented, so that the things
which give salvation might be more perfect and more lucid than those which promise
a Savior.

2206

[63, 7]

Participation in the Body and Blood of Christ effects nothing else but that we become   878
that which we consume, and we carry Him everywhere both in spirit and in body, in and
with whom we have died, have been buried, and have risen.

2207

[64, 2]

In this indescribable unity of the Trinity, in which works and judgments are in all   283
respects common to the Three Persons, the Person of the Son accepted as proper to
Himself the restoration of the human race; so that, since it is He through whom all things   284
were made and without whom nothing was made (10), and who enlivened man, shaped
from the slime of the earth, with the breath of rational life, the same would restore our   376
nature, fallen at the beginning of time (11), to its lost dignity, and He would be the
Reformer, too, of that of which He was the Creator. And He so directed His counsel
in the project at hand, that for the destruction of the Devil's domination the justice of
reason would be better employed than the power of might. Since, therefore, the whole   614
posterity of the first man was felled by one and the same grievous wound, and no merits
of the saints were able to alleviate the condition of that mortal injury, the one only
Physician came from heaven. Having been frequently announced by many signs and
long promised in prophetic assurances, He remained in the form of God and lost nothing   344
of His own majesty when He came forth in the nature of our flesh and soul, without the   312
contagion of the ancient wrong-doing. For He alone was born son of the Blessed Virgin   311
and without guilt, not outside the human race, but a stranger to sin, . . . when He
became the only one of Adam's progeny in whom the Devil would have nothing to
call his own.

2208

[68, 1]

Our last sermon, dearly beloved, of which we desire now to give you the promised
portion, had reached that point in the argument where we were speaking of the cry
which the crucified Lord uttered to the Father. We cautioned the simple and unthinking
hearer not to understand the words, ''My God, My God, why have You forsaken Me
(12)?'' as if, when Jesus was fixed to the wood of the cross, the omnipotence of the
Father's Godhead had departed from Him; for the nature of God and of man were so
completely joined in Him that the unity thereof could not be impaired by punishment
nor disrupted by death. For each substance remained with its own properties; and God
neither abandoned the suffering of His body, nor did the flesh make God subject to
suffering, because the divinity, though it was in the one who suffered, was not in the
suffering (13).

329

322

2209

[68, 3]

A unique victim was being offered to God for the salvation of the world, and the
killing of Christ, the True Lamb, predicted through so many centuries, was transferring
the sons of promise into the liberty of the Faith. A New Testament was also being
ratified, and the heirs of the eternal kingdom were being enrolled in the Blood of Christ.

380

2210

[71, 2]

The Savior's resurrection did not long keep His soul in the lower regions nor His
flesh in the tomb; and so speedy was the enlivening of His uncorrupted flesh that it bore a
greater resemblance to sleep than to death; because the Divinity, which did not depart
from either portion of the human substance He had assumed, reunited by His power
that which, by His power, He had separated.

390

329

2211

[73, 4]

There was great and indescribable cause for rejoicing when, in the sight of the holy
multitude, above the dignity of all heavenly creatures, the nature of the human race
went up, to surpass the ranks of Angels and to rise beyond the heights of the Archangels,
to have its being uplifted limited by no sublimity until, received to sit with the eternal
Father, it was associated on the throne of His glory, to whose nature it was joined in the
Son. Since, therefore, Christ's Ascension is our uplifting, and the hope also of the Body
is raised to where the glory of the Head has preceded it, let us exult, dearly beloved, with
worthy joy, and be glad in a pious thanksgiving. For today not only have we been
confirmed as possessors of paradise, but in Christ we have penetrated the heights of
heaven, and have gained still greater things through the indescribable grace of Christ
than we had lost through the envy of the Devil. For those whom the virulent enemy
had driven out of the happiness of our first abode, the Son of God has made concorporeal
with Himself and has placed at the right of His Father.

391

385

376

2212

[75, 3]

Let no one suppose that the divine substance of the Holy Spirit appeared in those
things which were seen with bodily eyes. For His nature, invisible and held in common

170

268

with the Father and the Son, showed the character of His gift and work by whatever
outward sign pleased Him, but kept what was proper to His essence within His own
Godhead, because human sight can no more perceive the Holy Spirit than it can the
Father or the Son. For in the divine Trinity there is nothing dissimilar, nothing unequal;   282
and all that can be thought about the Trinity's substance admits of no distinction whether   281
in power, in glory, or in eternity. And while in the properties of the Persons, the Father is
one, the Son another, and the Holy Spirit another, there is no diversity of nature nor
otherness of Godhead. For while the Son is the Only-begotten of the Father, and the   270
Holy Spirit is the Spirit of the Father and of the Son, not as any creature, which also is
of the Father and of the Son, but as living and having power with both, and eternally
subsisting of that which is the Father and the Son.

2212a

[76, 2]
   For the unchangeable Godhead of this Blessed Trinity is one in substance, undivided   282
in operation, harmonious in will, alike in power, equal in glory. In this regard when   283
Holy Scripture speaks in such a way that it can allot something either in deeds or in
words, so that it would seem to belong to the individual Persons, Catholic Faith is not
disturbed but is taught that the truth of the Trinity can be suggested to us through a
peculiarity of word or operation, while the intellect must not divide what the hearing has
distinguished.

2213

[77, 2]
   For if man, made in the image and likeness of God, had remained in the honor of his   360
own nature, and had not been so deceived by the diabolic fraud that through
concupiscence he deviated from the law laid down for him, the Creator of the world
would not have become a creature, the Eternal would not have undergone temporality,
nor would God the Son, equal to God the Father, have taken the form of a slave and the
likeness of sinful flesh. But because by the jealousy of the Devil death entered into the   363
world (14), and human captivity could not otherwise be set free, if He had not taken up
our cause, who without loss of His majesty should become true Man, and alone have no   344
contagion of sin, the mercy of the Trinity divided for Itself the work of our restoration,   345
in such a way that the Father should be propitiated, the Son should propitiate, and
the Holy Spirit enkindle.

2214

[91, 3]
   When the Lord says: "Unless you shall have eaten the flesh of the Son of Man and   850
shall have drunk His blood, you shall not have life in you (15)," you ought to so   851
communicate at the Sacred Table that you have no doubt whatever of the truth of the
Body and Blood of Christ. For that which is taken in the mouth is what is believed in
faith; and in vain do those respond, "Amen," who argue against that which is received.

1. *Cessante privilegio patrum, et familiarum ordine praetermisso.*
2. Eph. 2:5.
3. Col. 3:9.
4. 2 Peter 1:4.
5. Is. 53:8.
6. John 15:5.
7. See Ps. 54[55]:23. Leo's text reads: *lacta in Deum cogitationem tuam, et ipse te enutriet.*

8. Matt. 26:39.
9. *Superiori igitur voluntati voluntas cessit inferior*. As distinct from § 2184 above, which spoke only of a conflict of objects willed, this present passage does in fact speak of two distinct wills in Christ, two faculties of will, the human and the divine.
10. John 1:3.
11. *ab aeternitatis arce deiectam*.
12. Ps. 21[22]:1.
13. *quia divinitas, quae erat in dolente, non erat in dolore*.
14. Wis. 2:24.
15. John 6:54.

VICTOR OF VITA [*fl. ca. A. D.* 485]

Very little is known of Victor, Bishop of Vita in the African province of Byzacena. He is the author of a *Historia persecutionis Africanae provinciae*, which recounts the terrible sufferings of Catholics in Africa in the time of the Vandal kings Geiserich (428-477 A. D.) and Hunerich (477-484 A. D.).

This persecution, as bloody as any under imperial Rome, was not a general persecution of Christianity as such, but of Catholicism as distinct from Arianism. The Vandals were at least nominally Christian; but, like all the barbarian Christians with the later exception of the Franks, their Christianity came to them in its Arian form.

HISTORY OF THE PERSECUTION IN THE PROVINCE OF AFRICA
[*A. D.* 488 / 489]

Victor wrote his *History of the Persecution* while Hunerich was still alive, that is, before December 484 A. D.; for the final chapter of the work, recounting Hunerich's death, is a later and unauthentic addition to the work. The work was not published, however, until 488 or 489 A. D.

Migne (PL 58) reprinted the 1694 edition of the Maurist T. Ruinart, which, like the other early editions, divided the *Historia* into five books. There are two modern critical editions, either of which is vastly superior to Migne's Ruinart; and both divide the work into just three books. C. Halm's Berlin edition of 1879 in the *Monumenta Germaniae historica: Auctores antiquissimi* 3, 1 rejects the final chapter recounting Hunerich's death, but accepts the prologue as authentic. M. Petschenig, much more reasonably, in his Vienna edition of 1881 in the Vienna Corpus, CSEL, Vol. 7, rejects both the final chapter and the prologue. The edition of Petschenig is generally regarded as superior to that of Halm.

2215

[2, 63]

Because we profess that there are two natures in the Son, that is, true God and true Man, having body and soul, whatever the Scriptures ascribe to Him that is of sublimely excellent power we know must be attributed to His wonderful divinity; and whatever is told more humbly of Him and which is below the dignity of heavenly power, we refer not to the Word of God, but to the manhood which He assumed. This then, as we remarked before, is said in regard to His divinity: "The Father and I are one (1)"; and: "Whoever has seen me, has seen the Father (2)." . . . But there are other sayings which are to be referred to Him according to His Humanity: "The Father is greater than I (3)."

322
310
312

2216

[2, 82]

That even until now we may teach very plainly that the Holy Spirit is of one divinity   268
with the Father and the Son is proved by the testimony of John the Evangelist. For   235
he says: ''There are three who bear witness in heaven: the Father, the Word, and the
Holy Spirit; and these three are one (4).'' Does he ever say that there is a qualitative   282
difference in the three that are mutually joined, or that they are divided by any kind
of degrees of difference in a deep gulf of separation? No, what he says is that there
are three, and that these three are one.

1. John 10:30.
2. John 14:9.
3. John 14:28.
4. 1 John 5:7.

ST. CAESAR OF ARLES [ca. A. D. 470 – A. D. 542]

Caesar of Arles was a Burgundian, born at Chalon-sur-Saône; and he was
undoubtedly the most influential Gallic bishop of his time. A monk of the monastery of
Lerins, he held the important archiepiscopal see of Arles from 502 until his death forty
years later.

Caesar was probably the greatest moral preacher of the Western Church between
Augustine of Hippo and Berthold of Regensburg, and was likewise renowned for his
pastoral abilities. Not only did he personally escape the taint of Semi-Pelagianism which
had infected so many of his countrymen and fellow-monks, but he wrote vigorously
against that heresy and presided over the Second Council of Orange in 529 A. D., which
council condemned Semi-Pelagianism while upholding a modified form of
Augustinianism. The proceedings of Orange very shortly received specific papal
approval.

Especially renowned for his works of charity, Caesar himself lived in perfect poverty
while distributing to the poor and using for the ransom of captives all such wealth as
came to him. A valuable life of St. Caesar in two volumes was written by five of his
friends and intimate acquaintances between 542 and 549 A. D.

SERMONS [ante A. D. 542]

There never was a respectable edition of the literary remains of St. Caesar until
modern times, when Germain Morin published his *Sancti Caesarii opera omnia* in two
volumes in 1937 and 1942, the fruit of fifty years of personal labors. Morin's collection
of sermons contains 238 items, gleaned largely from the spuria and dubia once attributed
to other authors, Augustine especially, but containing also a substantial number of
sermons from manuscripts never published before at all. The first printing of the Morin
edition is quite scarce, because shortly after its publication the largest part of the printing
was destroyed in the war, in a fire at Maredsous. A second printing was made after the
war, in 1949.

The two volumes of Morin's edition of the *Sermons* have now been reprinted also in
the series *Corpus Christianorum*, Vols. 103 and 104 (1953), where they are termed the
editio altera. It is expected that further sermons of Caesar of Arles will be edited for the
Corpus Christianorum by Dom Cyril Lambot.

In our selections below the numbering is primarily that of Morin, while the
parenthetical number is that applied to the same sermon where it appears in Migne's PL
39 among the spuria of Augustine. Morin's edition is much superior, and is the basis for
our translations.

2232

[101 (22), 2]

God never deserts a man, unless first He is deserted by that man. For even if a   721
man shall have committed grievous sins once, and twice, and a third time, God still   723
looks for him, just as He says through the Prophet, "So that he may be converted
and live (1)." But if a man begins to continue in his sins, despair is born of the
multitude of those sins, and obduracy is begotten of despair. . . . Obduracy is not
effected by the compelling power of God, but is gotten of the forgiveness and
indulgence of God. And thus, it must be believed that it was not divine power but
divine patience that hardened Pharao.

2233

[179 (104), 2]

Although the Apostle has mentioned many grievous sins (2), we, nevertheless, lest   633
we seem to promote despair, will state briefly what they are. Sacrilege, murder,
adultery, false witness, theft, robbery, pride, envy, avarice, and, if it is of long
standing, anger, drunkenness, if it is persistent, and slander are reckoned in their   904
number. For if anyone knows that any of these sins dominates him, if he does not do
penance worthily and for a long time, if such time is given him, and if he does not give
abundant alms and abstain from those same sins, he cannot be purged in that
transitory fire of which the Apostle spoke, but the eternal flames will torture him   1000
without any remedy. [3] But since the lesser sins (3) are, of course, known to all, and   1030
it would take too long to mention them all, it will be necessary for us only to name
some of them. As often as someone takes more than is necessary in food or in drink,
he knows that this belongs to the lesser sins. As often as he says more than he
should or is silent more than is proper; as often as he rudely exasperates a poor beggar;
as often as he wills to eat when others are fasting, although he is in good physical
health, and rises too late for church because he surrendered himself to sleep; as often
as he knows his wife without a desire for children . . . without a doubt he commits   968
sin. There is no doubt that these and similar deeds belong to the lesser sins which, as
I said before, can scarcely be counted, and from which not only all Christian people,
but even all the saints could not and cannot always be free. We do not, of course,
believe that the soul is killed by these sins; but still, they make it ugly by covering it
as if with some kind of pustules and, as it were, with horrible scabs, which allow
the soul to come only with difficulty to the embrace of the heavenly Spouse, of
whom it is written: "He prepared for Himself a Church having neither spot nor
blemish (4)." [4] . . . If we neither give thanks to God in tribulations nor redeem   929
our own sins by good works, we shall have to remain in that purgatorial fire (5)
as long as it takes for those above-mentioned lesser sins to be consumed like wood
and straw and hay. [5] But someone is saying: "It is nothing to me how long I
stay there, so long as I go on finally to eternal life." Let no one say that, beloved
brethren, because that purgatorial fire itself will be more difficult than any
punishments that can be seen or imagined or felt in this life.

2233a

[67 (261), 1]

As often, beloved brethren, as we see some of our brothers or sisters asking for   904
penance publicly, we can and should, by God's inspiration, stir up great compunction
in ourselves, of divine fear. . . . And certainly he that receives penance publicly   920
could have done it privately. But I think he sees, considering the multitude of his

sins, that he is not strong enough to cope with such great vices alone; and for that reason he desires to solicit the help of all the people.

2233b

[67 (261), 2]

Notice this, brethren, that when someone asks for Penance, he pleads for himself   910
to be excommunicated. For, when he receives his penance, he is covered with a   899
hairshirt and thrown outside. He asks to be excommunicated, because he judges himself unworthy to receive the Eucharist of the Lord; and moreover, he wants to be excluded for some time from that altar so that he may merit to arrive with a clear conscience at the altar in heaven. Moreover, with great reverence he wants to be removed from the Body and Blood of Christ like a guilty and impious person, so that by his humility he may finally one day deserve to come to the Communion of the sacrosanct altar. [3] . . . Unless infirmity permit it, let a penitent not drink wine; or if, because of old age or a stomach disorder, this is not possible, let him heed the Apostle, who says: "Use a little wine for the sake of your stomach (6)." There are some penitents who want to be reconciled immediately, so that they can eat meat. It is certain that a man does not accept his penance with true compunction if he desires or presumes to eat meat without being compelled by infirmity. Therefore, even when a penitent has been reconciled he ought not eat meat whenever, either at his own table or at the table of another, he is able to find potherbs or beans or fish. I mention this because, so much the worse, there are some penitents who eat meat with great eagerness and who drink wine, sometimes perhaps even to excess. Our poor body should be nourished in great prudence lest it be solicited again to commit such sins through drunkenness and gluttony, and then the repentance that seemed to be ours will profit us little or nothing.

2233c

[13 (265), 1]

I beg you, beloved brethren, let us consider more attentively why we are Christians   125
and bear the cross of Christ on our forehead. For we ought to know that it is not   760
enough for us that we have received the name Christian, if we do not do Christian works. . . . If you say a thousand times that you are a Christian and continually sign yourself with the cross of Christ, but do not give alms according to your means, and you do not want to have love and justice and chastity, the name of Christian will profit you nothing. . . . If a man thinks evil thoughts, speaks evil words, or does evil deeds, and does not wish to amend himself, when he signs himself his sin is not lessened but increased. Many men, when they go out to commit robbery or adultery, if they dash their foot against something, they sign themselves; but they do not retreat from their evil deed. . . [2] . . . Flee falsehood, dread perjury as you would perpetual death, speak no false witness, commit no theft. Above all, as I already said before, give alms to the poor according to your means. Present offerings to be consecrated on the altar; a man of means should blush to communicate in the offering of another. Those who are able should give either candles or oil which can be put in lamps. Know the Creed and the Lord's Prayer yourselves and teach them to your children. I do not know how a man can call himself a Christian by signing his forehead when he neglects to learn the few short lines of the Creed or the Lord's Prayer. . . . [3] Go to church every Sunday; for if the unfortunate Jews celebrate the Sabbath with such great devotion that they do no earthly work on that day, how much more should Christians devote themselves to God alone on Sunday and go to church for the salvation of their souls?

2234

[13 (265), 3]

As often as some infirmity overtakes a man, let him who is ill receive the Body   870
and Blood of Christ; let him humbly and in faith ask the presbyters for blessed   940
oil, to anoint his body, so that what was written may be fulfilled in him: "Is anyone
among you sick? Let him bring in the presbyters, and let them pray over him, anointing
him with oil; and the prayer of faith will save the sick man, and the Lord will raise him
up; and if he be in sins, they will be forgiven him (7)." See to it, brethren, that
whoever is ill hasten to the church, both that he may receive health of body and will
merit to obtain the forgiveness of his sins.

2234a

[5 (301), 5]

There are many people who exert greater care for their bodies than they do for   996
their soul. But they should devote a greater solicitude for their souls, where the image
of God is. When the flesh, which they loved so much, begins to be devoured by worms in
the grave, the soul is presented to God by the angels in heaven. Then, if it has been good, it
is crowned; but if evil, it will be cast out into darkness.

1. Ezech. 33:11.
2. *capitalia plura*.
3. *minuta peccata*.
4. See Eph. 5:27.
5. *in illo igne purgatorio*.
6. 1 Tim. 5:23.
7. James 5:14-15.

ST. FULGENCE OF RUSPE [*A. D.* 467 – *A. D.* 527]

St. Fulgence, born in 467 A. D., was the son of a wealthy and influential family, and
was well-educated in both Latin and Greek. At one time a tax-collector in his native
town of Telepte in the African Province of Byzacena, he afterwards became a monk.
About the year 502 A. D. he was made Bishop of Ruspe. A year later, in the
Arian-Vandal persecution, he was exiled with more than sixty other Catholic Bishops to
Sardinia. With the exception of a two-year period when he was at Carthage, sometime
between 510 and 517 A. D., he remained in Sardinia until the death of Trasamund, the
Vandal King, in 523. Fulgence was then able to return to Ruspe, where he remained
until his death on January 1, 527 A. D.

Fulgence is properly regarded as one of the greatest theologians of his age. In his
doctrine on grace he is one with Augustine. He teaches the particular saving will of
God, with unconditional predestination to beatitude or damnation. Unbaptized infants
are excluded from beatitude; and original sin is transmitted because of the concupiscence
of the parents. This latter view very likely leads him to a denial (see § 2242 below) of
the Immaculate Conception of the Blessed Virgin. Yet it must be admitted that this
alleged failing is not nearly so clear in his writing as some would make it; and in
any case, the Immaculate Conception, which seems to be both hinted at and hinted
against in Augustine's writings (§§ 1704 and 1794 above), is a point of doctrine which
had not as yet been formally raised, and to which, as yet, very little thought had been
given.

LETTERS [*post A. D. 512–ante A. D. 527*]

The corpus of St. Fulgence's letters consists of only nineteen items, the last fragmentary. And these nineteen include five addressed to him. The text in Migne PL 65, 303-498 is now superseded by that in I. Fraipont's *opera omnia* of Fulgence in the *Corpus Christianorum*, Vols. 91 and 91A (1968), the letters being in Vol. 91, pp. 187-444 and Vol. 91A 445-629. In the format of the volumes, these are somewhat interlarded with other lengthy treatises.

LETTER OF FULGENCE, BISHOP OF RUSPE, TO SENATOR THEODORE

2235

[6, 12]

Study your heart in the light of the Holy Scriptures, and you will know therein who   692
you were, who you are, and who you ought to be. If you approach the Scriptures in   690
meekness and humility, you will really discover there both the prevenient grace by   691
which it is possible to be inspired to a beginning (1), and the concomitant
grace, by which it is possible to continue a journey on the right path (2), as well as the
subsequent grace, by which one is enabled to achieve the blessedness of the heavenly
kingdom (3).

LETTER OF FULGENCE, BISHOP OF RUSPE, TO DONATUS, A LAYMAN

2236

[8, 10]

True religion consists in the service of the one true God. For it is truth itself   1
that there is one God; and just as, besides the one truth, there is no other truth,   157
so too, besides the one true God there is no other true God. For the one truth itself
is naturally one true divinity. And thus one cannot speak truthfully of two true gods,
because it is not possible for the truth itself, naturally one, to be divided.

LETTER OF FULGENCE, BISHOP OF RUSPE, TO FERRANDUS, A DEACON

2237

[12, 26]

I think, holy brother, that what we have discussed, confirmed by the word of the   871
preeminent teacher Augustine, should leave no room for doubt at all, that anyone of the
faithful becomes a participant in the Body and Blood of the Lord when in Baptism he
has been made a member of the Body of Christ; and, having been brought into the unity
of the Body of Christ, he is not to be alienated from the assembly of that Bread and Cup,
even if before he can eat that Bread and drink that Cup he depart from this world (4).

LETTER OF FULGENCE, BISHOP OF RUSPE, TO FERRANDUS, A DEACON

2238

[14, 26]

When we speak of the soul of Christ we speak of the rational spirit, to which not only   312
did God come through grace, but which received the divinity itself in a unity of Person.   324

For the soul, with the Word, is one Christ; the soul, with the Word, is one, God the
Only-begotten (5). And because God the Only-begotten is equal to the Father, and no   352
one is able to know the whole Son who does not know the whole Father, let us beware
lest, if the soul of Christ is not believed to know the whole Father, knowledge be denied   351
to the one Christ Himself of some part not only of the Father but even of Himself and of
the Holy Spirit. But it is extremely obtuse and utterly foreign to a healthy faith to say
that the soul of Christ did not have full knowledge of His divinity, when with that soul it
is believed that He had naturally one Person.

2239

[14, 31]
   Obviously we are able to say that the soul of Christ had full knowledge of His   352
Godhead; nevertheless, I do not know whether we ought to say that the soul of Christ   188
knew His Godhead in such a way that it knew the very Godhead itself, or whether
this ought rather be said, that it recognized the Godhead, but not with Godhead's full
recognition (6). For the very Godhead so knew itself, that it could naturally discover
itself to be what it knew; but the soul, nevertheless, knew its whole Godhead in such a
way that it knew that it was not the Godhead itself. The Godhead's own knowledge,
therefore, is natural to Godhead itself; but the soul, so that it may know, receives
knowledge from the Godhead itself, which knows fully. Naturally, therefore, the
Godhead of Christ is that which the Godhead knew; but the soul, by the fact that it knows
its Godhead, did not discover itself to be that which it knew. Christ, therefore, according
to His divinity, was not known to His soul in the same way that Father and Son and Holy
Spirit knew themselves; for it certainly does not follow from the fact that His soul has
full knowledge of the Trinity, that it has one nature with the Trinity (7).

LETTER OF THE EXILED AFRICAN BISHOPS, NO. 15 IN THE
CORPUS OF THE LETTERS OF SAINT FULGENCE

See §§ 2276-2278 below.

LETTER OF FULGENCE AND FOURTEEN OTHER AFRICAN BISHOPS
EXILED IN SARDINIA, TO VARIOUS OF THEIR BRETHREN

2240

[17, 5]
   If the Word of God had become flesh in the Virgin in such a way that He had not been   311
of her, without a doubt God would not have had the same substance of flesh from the   314
flesh of the Mother, and His flesh would have been only channeled through the Virgin,   313
and then there would have been no sacrament of a Mediator to assist us unto salvation,   387
for Christ the Son of God would not have united unconfusedly in Himself the full truth   781
of the human and divine substances.

2241

[17, 9]
   The human nature could in no way be sufficient and suitable for taking away the   363
sin of the world, if it had not entered into a union with God the Word, and not in a   321
confusion of natures but only in a unity of Person. For when the Word became flesh, in a   324
wonderful union it made its own the nature which it took from us. But in the deifying

and utterly marvellous union the divinity of the Word was not changed into flesh, and
the true humanity of the Word held forthwith the true nature of our race. The Virgin,   779
therefore,—a matter to which attention must frequently be called,—both conceived   781
and bore God the Word Himself, by the fact that He was made flesh in her.   782

2242

[17, 11]
   For God, not restraining His mercies in anger (8), was made Man to this end, that   376
whatever He had created sound in man, this same creation God might make sound   314
again, assuming it wholly into Himself. [12] This was certainly a wonderful Person,
having the natures of God and of man, but truly conceived and born according to the
flesh, inasmuch as the Virgin, in an indescribable manner, conceived and bore the God
of heaven, and remained inviolate, Virgin and Mother,—she, of course, is truly
designated by the angel "full of grace" and "blessed among women (9),"— because   779
she neither had nor desired any commerce of man but, while retaining a virginity both   782
of mind and of body, she received from Him whom she was about to conceive and bear
the gift of uncorrupted fruitfulness and of fruitful integrity. . . . [13] This is the grace
by which it was brought about that God, who came to take away sins, because in Him   345
there is no sin, was conceived and was born Man in the likeness of the flesh of sin, from
the flesh of sin. For the flesh of Mary, which had been conceived in iniquities in the   786
usual human manner (10), was the flesh of sin which begot the Son of God in the likeness
of the flesh of sin. . . . But when the likeness of the flesh of sin is in the Son of God, or
rather, when the Son of God is said to be in the likeness of the flesh of sin, it does not
mean that the Only-begotten God drew any stain of sin from the mortal flesh of the
Virgin, but that He accepted the full reality of our nature.

2243

[17, 47]
   Just as the flesh does not have life of its very self, but receives it from the soul, so too   656
man cannot have faith unless he receives it as the gift of God, the Donor. And just as   650
for the flesh to live is the work of the soul alone, so too for man to believe is the work of
grace alone; and just as the flesh can do nothing if it lacks a soul to vivify it, so too
man can will nothing good if the assistance of grace is withdrawn from him. So that
the flesh, therefore, may be able to live and operate, it is supported by the enlivening
presence of the soul; man too, so that he may will or do what is good, is helped constantly
by the assistance of vivifying grace.

2244

[17, 51]
   If with some who know God, but do not glorify God (11), that knowledge profits   654
them nothing unto salvation, how should those be able to be righteous before God,
who, though they have some goodness in their moral conduct and actions, have goodness
of such a kind that they cannot refer it to the ends of Christian faith and love? Certainly
such people can possess a certain kind of goodness, which pertains to the justice of   651
human society, but because it is not the product of faith in God and of love of God, it is
not able to assist them.

2245

[17, 52]
   The law which is of creatures, and which is not able to justify a man because no flesh   654

is justified by the works of the law (12), can be found naturally both in the hearts of
the pagans and in the hearts of the unfaithful Jews; but since it is without the faith of
Christ it can in no way justify those who follow it, but keeps them bound with a chain
of impiety (13).

2246

[17, 67]

    The grace of God unto faith and the beginning of a will to do good is given us, and   656
help is accorded the will itself, so that what good it wills, that good may be done;   202
for God, who created man, did Himself will, by His predestination, to give to those   211
whom He prepared, both the gift of illumination for believing and the gift of
perseverance for perfecting and remaining constant, and the gift of glorification for
reigning,—God, who does not bring to perfection of deed anyone whom he has not
prepared beforehand in His eternal and unchangeable will. The Apostle bears witness to
the reality of this predestination, by which we have been predestined in Christ before the
foundation of the world (14).

LETTER OF FULGENCE, BISHOP OF RUSPE, TO COUNT REGINUS

2247

[18, 9]

    Christ bore our corruption only in His flesh, in which truly He bore also our death.   349
In His soul, however, He preserved a perfect incorruptibility, as He had no sin by   344
inheritance nor did He contract any through its contagion. Whence also Christ bore   345
without any corruption the weaknesses of our souls, which He bore in His rational soul.   312
For no deficiency of power could be present where the perfection of love perdured in
the unflagging acceptance of weakness, a perfection of love which brought the Only-
begotten God to march straight to death for us, and, despising shame, to bear the
disgrace of the cross (15). [10] On that account did Christ have the sorrow and grief of
our souls; and if He had the weaknesses of our souls, He had them truly, but voluntarily.
Truly, of course, so that He might manifestly display in Himself the feeling of a rational
soul; and *voluntarily*, so that He could demonstrate that the assistance of His strength
was ready to help our weaknesses.

1. *praevenientem gratiam, qua potest elisus surgere.*
2. *et comitantem, qua viam recti queat itineris currere.*
3. *et subsequentem, qua valeat ad regni caelestis beatitudinem pervenire.*
4. This letter is in reply to a question put by Ferrandus in Letter No. 11. It concerns "the servant of a certain religious man,
   a youth in age and an Ethiopian in color, whom I believe was captured in the most remote parts of the barbarian
   province, where the dry limbs of a man are darkened by the fiery heat of the sun." The young black captive, at any rate,
   was given to a church, and there became a catechumen. Now he is desperately ill, and unconscious. In his unconscious
   state the Baptism that he had desired can be given him; but what if he never receive the Eucharist? For unless a man eat
   the Body of the Lord and drink His Blood he cannot have life in him. Certainly Fulgence shows both good sense and
   ingenuity in his reply.
5. Note that the term God the Only-begotten, frequent in Fulgence, is equivalent to our familiar term God the Son.
6. *quia novit quantum illa, sed non sicut illa.*
7. Notice that Fulgence is not voicing in advance the modern heresy that Christ did not (always) know His divinity.
   Anything but that. He shows only that Christ's soul is human, not divine; that its full knowledge of Christ's divinity
   comes not from knowing itself but is a knowledge imparted to it by His divinity. When Fulgence says in the last
   sentence above: "*Non ergo quemadmodum se noverunt Pater et Filius et Spiritus Sanctus, sic animae suae secundum
   divinitatem notus est Christus,*" the particles *quemadmodum* and *sic* (in the same way that) are of very considerable
   importance. The problems involved here are largely those of the hypostatic union and the communication of idioms.
8. See Ps. 76[77]:10.
9. Luke 1:28.
10. *humana solemnitate.*

11. See Rom. 1:21.
12. Rom. 3:20.
13. Piety is the virtue by which a son accords what is due his father. Those who have an abundant share of what we call "natural goodness" can easily come to trust in so-called natural virtue, bringing with it a false sense of security which can actually lure them away from seeing the need of practicing the religious virtue of piety, that is, so trusting in God that one loves him as a Father. And the "natural virtue", since it is natural, has no supernatural value or merit.
14. See Eph. 1:4.
15. Heb. 12:2.

TO TRASAMUND [post A. D. 510 et ante A. D. 517]

Trasamund was the Arian king of the Vandal nation in Africa who exiled Fulgence, along with more than sixty other Catholic Bishops of the Province of Byzacena, to Sardinia, probably as early as 503. It was probably in 515, and possibly as early as 510, that Trasamund invited Fulgence to Carthage to participate in a theological debate. After Fulgence had remained two years in Carthage he was sent again into exile in Sardinia. Except for the fact of exile itself, incidentally, the life of the bishops in Sardinia was not one of tremendous hardship. They lived in a monastery at Calaris, Lucifer's old diocesan seat, and did pastoral work in the surrounding neighborhood.

It was during his two year sojourn in Carthage, that is, not earlier than 510 and not later than 517, that Fulgence wrote, among else, the three books of his *Ad Trasamundum regem Vandalorum*. The work deals directly with the divinity of Christ, but only in a passing and perfunctory manner with the divinity of the Holy Spirit.

The text in Migne PL 65, 223-304, is superseded by that of I. Fraipont in the *Corpus Christianorum*, Vol. 91 (1968), pp. 97-185.

2248

[3, 16, 1]

From the very beginning of the virginal conception a unity of Person so remained in Christ, and the unconfused reality of both natures so perdured, that neither could the Man be torn asunder from God, nor could God be separated from the Man assumed. Nevertheless, the divinity did not consume the humanity, nor did the humanity change the divinity into something else; and, granted that at the death of Christ the soul would depart from the dying flesh, nevertheless, the divinity of Christ could not be separated from either the soul or the flesh assumed.

322
329

2249

[3, 21, 1]

The wonderful and invincible clemency of the Lord will be better recognized when we have proved that the substance of soul and body with its passions was assumed by God so that, preserving the condition of the divine inaccessibility to passion, it might be made known that our death was killed by the voluntary acceptance of death in His body, just as it is acknowledged that He assumed the rational soul with its passions by the voluntary acceptance of sorrow and fear, as the way in which He might deign to free our souls of all passions (1).

314
349
350

2250

[3, 35, 1]

So that I might suggest some slight reason for this operation, will someone please tell me what the Holy Spirit has that is less than what the Father has and the Son has,

283

since the Holy Spirit, at one with the Father and the Son, both made the beginning of our creation and, at one with the Father and the Son, also perfected the accomplishment of our redemption? God is said to have made the heavens; but the Son is discovered to be the cooperator, and the Holy Spirit too, in the operation of the Father: for, "by the Word of the Lord were the heavens made, and all their powers by the Spirit of His mouth (2)."

1. In the present passage it seemed better to translate *passio* as *passion*, though I usually render it *suffering*; and *impassibilitas* as *inaccessibility to passion* rather than *inability to suffer*. I have the apprehension, however, that the translation does suffer considerably, since the term *passio* herein seems really to have something of both meanings, *passion* (as emotion) and *suffering*.
2. Ps. 32(33):6. St. Fulgence's reading is the same as that of the Vulgate: *Verbo Domini caeli firmati sunt, et Spiritu oris eius omnis virtus eorum*, except that it is obvious that to capture his meaning we must accord an upper case initial to *Verbo* and *Spiritu*, whereas the usual translation would give these terms a lower case initial and read: "by the *word* of the Lord . . . and . . . by the *breath* of His mouth." For Fulgence, the Word of the Lord is not His spoken word, but the Son; and the *spiritus* or *breath* of His mouth is the Third Person, the Holy Spirit, who is breathed out by Father and Son.

THE TRINITY [*post A. D. 510 et ante A. D. 517*]

Like the *To Trasamund*, Fulgence's work on *The Trinity*, or *De Trinitate ad Felicem*, was written in the two year interval at Carthage between his two periods of exile in Sardinia.

The Felix to whom the work is addressed was a public official, a notary, who realized that the Arian Vandals did not have the sound Faith, and asked Fulgence for a written statement on the Faith that is shared by the whole Catholic Church throughout the world. *The Trinity* is St. Fulgence's response.

The text in Migne PL 65, 497-508, is superseded by that of I. Fraipont in the *Corpus Christianorum*, Vol. 91 A (1968), pp. 633-646.

2251

[4, 1]

See, in short you have it that the Father is one, the Son another, and the Holy Spirit another; in Person, each is other, but in nature they are not other. In this regard He says: "The Father and I, we are one (1)." He teaches us that *one* refers to Their nature, and *we are* to Their persons. In like manner it is said: "There are three who bear witness in heaven, the Father, the Word, and the Spirit; and these three are one (2)." Let Sabellius hear *we are*, let him hear *three*; and let him believe that there are three Persons. Let him not blaspheme in his sacrilegious heart by saying that the Father is the same in Himself as the Son is the same in Himself and as the Holy Spirit is the same in Himself, as if in some way He could beget Himself, or in some way proceed from Himself. Even in created natures it is never able to be found that something is able to beget itself. [2] Let also Arius hear *one*; and let him not say that the Son is of a different nature, if *one* cannot be said of that, the nature of which is different.

238

235
293

292

1. John 10:30.
2. 1 John 5:7.

THE FORGIVENESS OF SINS [*post A. D. 512 et ante A. D. 523*]

Fulgence's *Ad Euthymium de remissione peccatorum*, in two books, was written during his second Sardinian exile, that is, not before 512 A. D. and not after 523. The identity of the Euthymius to whom the work is addressed is not known.

The Migne text in PL 65, 527-574, is superseded by that of I. Fraipont in the *Corpus Christianorum*, Vol. 91 A (1968), pp. 649-707.

2251a

[1, 19, 2]

Anyone who is outside this Church, which received the keys of the kingdom of heaven, is walking a path not to heaven but to hell. He is not approaching the home of eternal life; rather, he is hastening to the torment of eternal death. And this is the case not only if he remains a pagan without Baptism, but even if, after having been baptized in the name of the Father and of the Son and of the Holy Spirit, he continue as a heretic. . . . For he is saved by the Sacrament of Baptism, whom the unity of love holds within the Catholic Church up to his passing from this present life.

417
415
831
830
820

2251b

[1, 23, 1]

From this Church even those who are involved in various errors outside the Church can receive the forgiveness of their sins, if, while they are still in this world, they will be converted to this same Church in a correct belief and in contrite and heartfelt humility. Let them hasten, then, while there is yet time, to their legitimate Mother, who diligently sustains and nourishes the sons born of her womb.

900

2252

[1, 23, 2]

Let them abandon heresy and return quickly to the Catholic Church. Let them neither doubt the possession of their inheritance nor despair of the forgiveness of their sins. For anyone who does not believe that within the Catholic Church all sins can be loosed deprives himself of the forgiveness of sins if, persevering in the same hardness of an impenitent heart, he departs from this world alienated from the Church's society.

415
901

TO MONIMUS [*post A. D. 512 et ante A. D. 523*]

The three books of St. Fulgence's *Ad Monimum* were written during his second Sardinian exile. Monimus was a layman who had presented several theological questions to Fulgence for solution. In this, his reply, Fulgence treats in the first book of predestination to beatitude and predestination to damnation; in the second book, of the oblation of the sacrifice, of the mission of the Holy Spirit, and of St. Paul's "counsels" or of works of supererogation. The third book concerns the proper understanding of John 1:1, "And the Word was with God"; and this third book, of course, is directed against the Arians.

The text in Migne PL 65, 151-206, is superseded by that of I. Fraipont in the *Corpus Christianorum*, Vol. 91 (1968), pp. 1-64.

2253

[Prol., 1]

The Blessed Apostle says: "For what have you that you did not receive? But if you   711
received it, why do you glory as if you had not received it (1)?" And in another place
he testifies that "the love of God is poured out in our hearts by the Holy Spirit who has
been given to us (2)." He that, by giving us something, made it necessary for us to
make some return, will give us the means by which we will be able to return what we
owe. He that is the Author of the gift is likewise the Author of our debt; for, by his
bounty, He deigned to make Himself a debtor too, not because, out of any need, He
accepted anything from anyone, but because, out of His abundance, He gave lavishly.

2254

[1, 7, 1]

The evil are not predestined to do evil, drawn away and enticed by their own   215
concupiscence (3); rather, they are predestined to this: that, against their will, they suffer   212
justly. For the term predestination does not express some compulsory necessity (4) of
the human will, but it foretells the eternal disposition, merciful and just, of a future
divine operation. The Church, however, sings to God of mercy and judgment (5),   211
to God, whose predestination is operative in man in such a way that by a hidden though
not unjust resolution of His will, He may either award a gratuitous mercy to the wretched
or weigh out due justice to the unrighteous.

2255

[1, 13, 1]

God was able, as He willed, to predestine some to glory and others to punishment.   211
But those whom He predestined to glory, He predestined to righteousness. Those,   638
however, whom He predestined to punishment, He did not predestine to guilt. It would
be possible for sin to be something of God's predestining only if it were possible for
some men to sin righteously. But no man sins righteously, although God may righteously
permit him to sin. For the man who deserts God is righteously deserted by God.   721

2256

[1, 19, 2]

Man began to sin by the very fact that he separated himself from God. For it is written   630
that "the beginning of pride is to fall away from God (6)"; and in another place:
"Behold, all who go far from You, shall perish; You have destroyed all who fornicated
themselves away from You (7)." Those, therefore, who go away from God and commit
fornication perish forthwith by sinning of their own evil will, which is not God's doing.
But God destroys them by judging them justly, which is God's part. For God would not   215
destroy them by His judgment unless they had themselves perished by their own
iniquities.

2257

[1, 22, 3]

Far be it from us and from all Christians that anyone should dare to assign to divine   638
equity the cause of any sin whatever; for a cause of wickedness or of impiety cannot
exist except in him who is wicked or impious. [4] When evil men become good, and   214
impious men righteous, the mercy of God is to be praised. But when good men become
evil, or righteous men impious, if divine predestination were asserted to be the cause,

then justice, perish the thought, would be to blame. But justice could not at all be called just, if the guilt to be punished were not simply discovered but could be said to have been caused [by predestination]. It would be injustice indeed if God were to mete out punishment to a fallen man who, when he was yet standing, is declared to have been predestined to ruin.

2258

[1, 25, 4]

He foretold and promised a reward for the enjoyment of the righteous; He did not 191
promise, however, but only foretold a torment for the punishment of the unrighteous. 193
But neither did He predestine the wicked to the losing of righteousness as He predestined 638
the saints to the receiving of that same righteousness, because the merciful and just 214
Lord was able gratuitously to free whomever He wished from depravity. He was never 190
the perpetrator of depravity, because no one ever was depraved except insofar as he
withdrew from God. Nor did God predestine any to withdraw from Him, although the
divine knowledge foresaw who would so withdraw.

2259

[3, 7, 2]

The Word is with God, just as a word is in the mind, just as counsel is in the heart; for 265
when the mind has a word with itself, it has it by thinking, because to say "with it" is
nothing other than to think "with it." When, therefore, the mind thinks and, by
thinking, begets a word within itself, it begets the word of its own substance; and it so
begets the word of itself that it has with itself what was begotten. [3] Nor does the word
which is born of the mind have anything less than the mind of which it is born, because
whatever quantity the mind has which begets the word, that quantity too is possessed
by the word itself (8). For just as the word is born of the whole mind, so the word born
perdures within the whole mind.

1. 1 Cor. 4:7.
2. Rom. 5:5.
3. See James 1:14.
4. *coactitia necessitas*. I know no other use of the adjective *coactitus* = *compulsory* prior to the early part of the eighth century. But of course, medieval Latin usages are very poorly indexed and the lack of a truly comprehensive dictionary is a monumental handicap to the obtaining of such knowledge.
5. See Ps. 100[101]:1. *Misericordiam et iudicium* is the Vulgate reading.
6. Sir. 10:14.
7. Ps. 72[73]:27. In many Old Testament passages the term fornication is equivalent to apostasy. The figure was and is an apt one; for Israel was wedded to Yahweh, just as the Church is the Bride of Christ.
8. If quantity here seems a rather odd concept, I can think of no better way to express it. The Latin reads: *quia quanta est mens quae generat verbum, tantum est etiam ipsum verbum*. If we were to translate the *quanta . . . tantum* as *how great . . . . so great*, the reader would think of the greatness of grandeur, whereas clearly what is intended is closer to the concept of greatness of size or extent, that is, quantity. One has the apprehension throughout the whole passage that Fulgence is offering a pitifully inadequate if not utterly nonsensical explanation of an existence so sublime that it defies human conceptualization.

THE RULE OF FAITH [*inter A. D.* 523-526]

St. Fulgence's *De fide ad Petrum seu de regula fidei* was written in the period after his two exiles, between the death of King Trasamund on May 29, 523 A. D. and his own death on Jan. 1, 527 A. D. The otherwise unknown Peter to whom it is addressed was a layman about to undertake a pilgrimage to Jerusalem, and who wanted some sort

of written compendium of Catholic doctrine as a protection in possible encounters with
heretics along the way. The *De fide ad Petrum*, Fulgence's response to the request,
enjoyed a high reputation in the Middle Ages.

The text in Migne, PL 65, 671-706, is superseded by I. Fraipont's edition in his
opera omnia of Fulgence in the *Corpus Christianorum*, Vol. 91 A (1968), pp. 711-760.

2260

[1]

Without faith it is impossible to please God (1). For faith is the basis of all goods.   568
Faith is the beginning of human salvation. Without faith no one can pertain to the number   758
of the sons of God, because without it neither will anyone obtain the grace of justification
in this life nor possess eternal life in the future; and if anyone does not walk now in
faith, he will not arrive at the actuality (2). Without faith every human labor is empty.

2261

[4]

But in the one true God and Trinity it is naturally true not only that God is one but also   238
that He is a Trinity, for the reason that the true God Himself is a Trinity of Persons, and   282
one in nature. Through this natural unity the whole Father is in the Son and in the Holy
Spirit, and the whole Holy Spirit, too, is in the Father and in the Son. None of these
is outside any of the others; because no one of them precedes any other of them in
eternity, or exceeds any other in greatness, or is superior to any other in power.

2262

[11]

On the third day the same God made Man rose again out of hell (3); but in the sepulcher   390
the same God lay only according to the flesh, and He descended into hell only according
to the soul. When on the third day His soul returned from hell to His flesh, the same
God rose from the grave according to the flesh in which He lay in the sepulcher. And on   391
the fortieth day after His resurrection the same God made Man ascended into heaven,   392
sat at the right of God, whence at the end of the world He will come to judge the living
and the dead.

2263

[22]

He it is, therefore, who displayed in Himself alone, one Person, all that He knew was   382
necessary for the accomplishment of our redemption. The same one is Priest and
Sacrifice, the same one is God and Temple: the Priest, *through whom* we are reconciled;
the Sacrifice, *by which* we are reconciled; the Temple, *in which* we are reconciled; and
the God, *to whom* we are reconciled.

2264

[25]

First of all, then, hold that every nature which is not God the Trinity was created out of   461
nothing by the same Holy Trinity which alone is true and eternal God. And thus believe
that all things in heaven and on earth, visible and invisible, whether Thrones, whether   488
Dominations, whether Principalities or whether Powers, are a work and creature of   467
the Holy Trinity, which is one God, Lord and Creator of all things, eternal, almighty   156

and good, of whose nature it is to exist always and never to be able to be changed. This   155
God, who is without beginning, exists always, because He is supreme. He gave to the   468
things He created that they should exist, but not without a beginning, because no creature
is of the same nature of which the Trinity is, one true and good God, by whom all things
have been created.

2265

[32]

    Angels, therefore, and men, because they were created rational, received from God   740
the gift of eternity and beatitude in the very creation of a spiritual nature; in this way, of
course, that if they would cling always to the love of their Creator, they would at the
same time remain eternal and happy. But if they should endeavor to do their own will   486
in the choice of their own freedom against the command of the supreme Creator,   505
happiness would immediately depart from those contumacious ones, and the torment of
a wretched eternity, subject to frustrations and sorrows one after another, would be   371
left them. And that indeed is what God arranged and disposed for the angels, so that if   491
any of them should lose goodness of will, no divine gift should ever restore it.

2266

[33]

    A part of the angels, therefore, which, in a voluntary aversion, withdrew from God its   491
Creator, in whom alone it was happy, by a judgment of supreme justice found the   1031
beginning of its damnation in its own aversion of will, so that the very beginning of its
punishment was in fact its being deprived of the love of that beatific good. God knew
beforehand that this whole part of the angels should remain in eternal punishment, so
He prepared an eternal fire for it. In this eternal fire all those fallen angels can never be   1033
without their evil will nor without their punishment. But just as the wickedness of their
unjust aversion is permanent, so too is the eternal condemnation of just retribution
permanent. The Prince of these wicked angels, the Devil, led the first human beings,   611
when, in his envy, he brought them to a participation (4) in sin, and not them alone
but their whole progeny, to a wickedness of sin deserving of death. But God, merciful
and just, when the Devil and his angels fell by their own volition, confirmed the other   490
angels in His eternal love; and likewise He did not permit the whole lump (5) of the   211
human race to perish eternally, but, those whom He predestined to light, His gratuitous
goodness willed should be drawn back through a turning aside of the darkness by which
every human birth is involved in the condemnation of original sin.

2267

[37]

    There will be a resurrection even of the wicked, but without the change which God is   1012
going to give to the faithful alone and to those who live righteously by faith. For this is   1044
what the Blessed Paul says: "We shall all indeed rise, but we shall not all be changed
(6)." But indicating that the just are to be changed by divine gift (7), he says: "And we
shall be changed (8)." The wicked therefore will have a resurrection of the flesh in
common with the just but they will not have the gratuitous gift (9) of the change that
will be given the just; because from the bodies of the impious, the corruption, shame
and weakness in which they were sown will not be taken away; and for this reason
they will not be extinguished even by death, so that the never-ending torment to body   1034
and soul will be a punishment of eternal death.

2268

[38]
But God gave men a time for acquiring eternal life in this life only, in which He   991
desired there should also be a fruitful repentance. And repentance is fruitful here,
because here man is able to put aside wickedness and live well, and, with a change of
will, to change at the same time his works and deserts and, in the fear of God, to do those
things that are pleasing to God.

2269

[43]
From that time at which our Savior said: "If anyone is not reborn of water and the   831
Spirit, he cannot enter into the kingdom of heaven (10)," no one can, without the
Sacrament of Baptism, except those who, in the Catholic Church, without Baptism pour   833
out their blood for Christ, receive the kingdom of heaven and life eternal. Anyone who
receives the Sacrament of Baptism, whether in the Catholic Church or in a heretical or   830
schismatic one, receives the whole Sacrament; but salvation, which is the strength of   417
the Sacrament, he will not have, if he has had that Sacrament outside the Catholic   799
Church. He must, therefore, return to the Church, not so that he might receive again the   797
Sacrament of Baptism, which no one dare repeat in any baptized person, but so that he
may receive eternal life in Catholic society, for the obtaining of which no one is suited
who, even with the Sacrament of Baptism, remains estranged from the Catholic
Church.

2269a

[53]
Hold most firmly and never doubt in the least (11) that the only God the Son, who is   273
one Person of the Trinity, is the Son of the only God the Father; but the Holy Spirit,
Himself also one Person of the Trinity, is Spirit not of Father only, but of Father and of
Son together.

2269b

[54]
Hold most firmly and never doubt in the least that the same Holy Spirit who is Spirit   273
of the Father and of the Son, proceeds from the Father and the Son.

2270

[62]
Hold most firmly and never doubt in the least that the Only-begotten God the Word   380
Himself become flesh offered Himself in an odor of sweetness as a Sacrifice and Victim
to God on our behalf; to whom, with the Father and the Holy Spirit, in the time of the
Old Testament animals were sacrificed by the patriarchs and prophets and priests; and
to whom now, I mean in the time of the New Testament, with the Father and the Holy   897
Spirit, with whom He has one Godhead, the Holy Catholic Church does not cease in   890
faith and love to offer throughout all the lands of the world a sacrifice of Bread and   892
Wine. . . . In those former sacrifices what would be given us in the future was
signified figuratively; but in this sacrifice which has now been given us, it is shown   891
plainly. In those former sacrifices it was fore-announced that the Son of God would be
killed for the impious; but in this present sacrifice it is announced that He has been
killed for the impious.

2271

[70]

Hold most firmly and never doubt in the least that not only men having the use of　　831
reason but even infants who, whether they begin to live in the wombs of their mothers
and die there, or whether they have been born of their mothers, pass from this world
without the Sacrament of holy Baptism which is given in the name of the Father and of　　826
the Son and of the Holy Spirit, are to be punished in the everlasting torment of eternal
fire.

2272

[75]

Hold most firmly and never doubt in the least that a man who is prevented neither　　651
by illiteracy nor by any imbecillity or disadvantage, can certainly either read the words
of the holy Law and Gospel, or hear them from the mouth of some preacher; but no one　　650
is able to obey the divine commands except one whom God has anticipated with His
grace, so that what such a one hears with his body he may receive also in his heart; and,
good will and power having been divinely received, he is both able and does will to
do God's commands.

2273

[79]

Hold most firmly and never doubt in the least that the Sacrament of Baptism is able to　　830
exist not only within the Catholic Church but also among heretics who are baptizing
in the name of the Father and of the Son and of the Holy Spirit; but outside the Catholic
Church it cannot be of any profit; nay, just as within the Church salvation is conferred　　417
through the Sacrament of Baptism upon those who believe rightly, so too, outside the
Church, if they do not return to the Church, ruin is heaped up for those who were
baptized by the same Baptism. For it is the unity as such of ecclesiastical society that
avails unto salvation, so that a man is not saved by Baptism to whom it was not given in
that place where it is needful that it be given.

2274

[80]

Hold most firmly and never doubt in the least that no person baptized outside the　　417
Catholic Church can become a participant of eternal life if, before the end of this life,
he has not returned and been incorporated in the Catholic Church.

2275

[81]

Hold most firmly and never doubt in the least that not only all pagans but also all Jews　　415
and all heretics and schismatics who end this present life outside the Catholic Church　　417
are about to go into the eternal fire that was prepared for the Devil and his angels (12).

1. Heb. 11:6.
2. *si quis hic non ambulaverit per fidem, non perveniet ad speciem.*
3. *ab inferis.*
4. *participium:* besides which reading, *praecipitium* and *principium* are also found in the manuscripts.
5. *massam . . . totam.* This draws upon the notion of the *massa damnata* as found in Augustine and the Ambrosiaster.
6. 1 Cor. 15:51.
7. *divino munere.*

8. 1 Cor. 15:52.
9. *gratiam*.
10. John 3:5.
11. *Firmissime tene et nullatenus dubites*. This phrase is repeated forty times, introducing each of the forty *capitula* or points of Fulgence's rule of faith, nos. 47 through 86.
12. See Matt. 25:41.

SYNODAL LETTER OF FULGENCE OF RUSPE AND OTHER AFRICAN BISHOPS, TO JOHN AND VENERIUS. [*inter A. D.* 523-526]

This is Letter no. 15 in the corpus of Fulgence's letters, and is generally called the *Letter of the Exiled African Bishops*, or the *Letter of the African Bishops Exiled in Sardinia*. Apparently, however, this usual title is somewhat of a misnomer. The exiled bishops came home to Africa more or less immediately after the death of King Trasamund, in May, 523 A. D. The present synodal letter speaks of Pope Hormisdas "of blessed memory"; and Hormisdas outlived Trasamund by a few months, dying in August, 523, by which time the Sardinian exiles must have been mostly back in Africa.

The letter is addressed to the Priest and Archimandrite John and to the Deacon Venerius, "and to the faithful men whose signatures your letter bore," and is sent by Datian, Fortunatus, Boethos, Victor, Scholasticus, Horontius, Vindician, Victor, January, Victorian, Fontius, and Quodvultdeus. Fulgence's name is not there; but the work has always been associated with him, is preserved among his writings, and bears the undoubted imprint of his Latin style. The omission of his name is difficult or impossible to explain. But however that may be, the work must be reckoned as his.

Closely associated with this letter is a work by Fulgence in three books, *De veritate praedestinationis et gratiae*, the same subject as the letter, and addressed also to John and Venerius. Perhaps this latter work was sent along with the synodal letter.

The edition of Letter no. 15 in Migne, PL 65, 435-442, is superseded by that of I. Fraipont in the *Corpus Christianorum*, Vol. 91A (1968), pp. 447-457.

2276

[15, 5]

Thus man's freedom itself of choice is apart from the gift of grace, just as the eye is without light. For even though the eye is made for seeing, unless it receives some light it will not see. Grace, however, is the true light which enlightens every man who comes into this world (1). It enlightens a man, however, by the giving of itself through grace. Just as the bodily eye needs always to receive light, so that it can perceive the light itself, so too man's free choice can do nothing propitious to grace unless an infusion of spiritual grace itself be given.

650
683

2277

[15, 10]

Grace is not properly esteemed by anyone who supposes that it is given to all men, when not only does the faith not pertain to all, but even at the present time some nations may yet be found to whom the preaching of the faith has not yet come. But the Blessed Apostle says: "How then are they to call upon Him in whom they have not believed? or how shall they believe in Him whom they have not heard? but how are they to hear, without preaching (2)?" Grace, then, is not given to all; for certainly they cannot be participants in that grace, who are not believers; nor can they believe, if it is found that the preaching of the faith has never come to them at all. And grace itself, to whomever it is given, is not given equally, but according to the measure of Christ's bestowal (3),

724

720

and to each one just as God apportioned a measure of faith. He does not respect persons, but all these things are done by one and the same Spirit, who apportions to everyone in whatever measure He wills to do so (4).

2278

[15, 11]

You may perhaps say that a man is saved by God's mercy alone; and others will say   729
that unless a man's own will accompanies and cooperates with that mercy, he will not
be able to be saved. And both views may rightly be held, if a proper order of divine
mercy and human will be observed, so that the one comes before and the other follows
after. The beginning of salvation is conferred by God's mercy alone. With that mercy   656
the human will then becomes the cooperatrix. In this way the mercy of God comes   692
before and directs the course of the human will; and the human will, being obedient,   691
follows after that same mercy, running the course as directed, so as to win the   690
reward (5).

1. See John 1:9.
2. Rom. 10:14.
3. Eph. 4:7.
4. See 1 Cor. 12:11.
5. *secundum intentionem currat ad bravium*. See also 1 Cor. 9:24.

THE PSEUDO-DIONYSIUS AREOPAGITA [*fl. ca. A. D.* 500]

A pseudepigraphal body of writings purporting to have been authored by Dionysius the Areopagite, who was baptized by St. Paul after having heard Paul's discourse in the Areopagus at Athens (Acts 17:34), which writings, were they authentic, would have to belong to the first century of the Christian era, first made its appearance at the beginning of the sixth century. The earliest certain quotations from these writings are to be found in works of Severus of Antioch dating between 518 and 528 A. D. Severus, a Monophysite, quoted Dionysius the Areopagite in support of his own theological stance; and it was quickly pointed out to him that none of the older Christian authors had ever heard of any writings by the Areopagite.

The writings in question consist of four treatises and ten letters. The treatises are on *The Divine Names*, on *Mystical Theology*, on *The Celestial Hierarchy*, and on *The Ecclesiastical Hierarchy*. The ten letters are largely supplementary to the treatises. The terminology of these fourteen writings is similar throughout and is quite foreign to the terminology of their own period and to that of any earlier period of Christianity. There can be no doubt that they are the work of a single author.

These writings, after the lukewarm reception given them by the immediate opponents of Severus, quickly gained a general acceptance and were of very great repute in the High Middle Ages. The question of their authenticity was not seriously raised again until the time of Lorenzo Valla († 1457), who looked upon them with a severely jaundiced eye but suggested no alternative author. From Valla's time almost until our own the authenticity of the Pseudo-Dionysian corpus was periodically questioned or attacked, and just as often was vigorously if somewhat hysterically defended. For about a century past, however, it may be said that the inauthenticity of all writings under the name of Dionysius the Areopagite has been a matter of universal agreement among scholars.

Various attempts have been made to identify the Pseudo-Dionysius as Peter the Fuller of Antioch († 448), Peter the Iberian, Severus of Antioch, Sergius of Resaina, (the above all Monophysites); as Dionysius of Rhinocorura; as the Neoplatonist mystic

Stephen bar-Sudaili, author of the *Book of Hierotheus*; as John of Scythopolis; as Dionysius the Great of Alexandria; and as Ammonius Saccas. After the biography composed and circulated by the Abbot Hilduin the tradition prevailed that identified Paul's Aeropagite disciple with the author of the Pseudo-Dionysian writings and the martyred St. Denys or Dionysius of Paris.

The language and style of the Pseudo-Dionysius is peculiar to himself. Modern scholarship rejects all proposed identifications and the Areopagite remains just what he is: the Pseudo-Dionysius.

Besides the fourteen writings that might be termed as authentic to the Pseudo-Dionysius, there are other writings falsely ascribed to him, so that now we have even one or more Pseudo-Pseudo-Dionysiuses!

The importance of the Pseudo-Dionysian writings is not inconsiderable; but it has by no means been so universal and all-pervasive as was once believed. Otto Bardenhewer remarked more than fifty years ago on how strange it is that so little has been done toward providing a good critical edition of the Pseudo-Dionysius, and his remark is not yet out of date. For the *Letters* and *The Divine Names* we are still dependent upon the text in Migne, PG 3.

LETTERS [*ca. A. D.* 500]

Of the ten *Letters* in the Pseudo-Dionysian corpus, letters one and four are supplementary to the treatise on *Mystical Theology*, and describe the divine darkness and the inaccessible light introduced in that treatise. Letter two supplements the treatise on *The Divine Names*, and deals with the transcendent quality of those names, employing therewith Neoplatonist concepts of Proclus. Letters three and five are concerned with Christology, seven with the phenomena of noonday darkness and earthquake at Christ's death. Letter six is condemnatory of polemics in theology; and letters eight, nine, and ten are in part supplementary to the treatise on *The Ecclesiastical Hierarchy*. The text of the *Letters* is in Migne, PG 3, 1065-1120.

2279

[4]

We may say in summary that [Jesus] was not man, not because He was not man, but   333
because, though born of men, He was beyond men, and though He truly was made Man, He was above man. The result is that He performed divine actions not as God and human actions not as man, but as Incarnate God, introducing to us a certain new theandric operation (1).

1. This formulation was appealed to, as well it might be, by Monophysite and Monothelite alike. The notion of a single theandric operation was rejected by the Third Council (Sixth Ecumenical) of Constantinople in 680-681, which Council formally condemned Monothelitism.

THE DIVINE NAMES [*ca. A. D.* 500]

The treatise on *The Divine Names* in thirteen chapters is fundamental to the rest of the Pseudo-Dionysian corpus. It explains the names applied to God in Sacred Scripture, in attempting to clarify the essence and attributes of God. God is depicted as the Good, the Beautiful, the Deserving of Love, as Being, Life, Wisdom, Power, Justice, Salvation, Redemption, Intelligence, Reason, and as the perfection of other such qualities. Much of this is dependent upon the Neoplatonist Proclus.

The text of The Divine Names is found in Migne, PG 3, 585-996.

2280

[2, 4]

In the divine or superessential union, superessential existence and superdivine　　239
divinity are united and common to the Sole-sovereign Trinity, . . . [as well as]
speechlessness and many-voicedness, obscurity and perfect intelligibility, the
affirmation of all and the abstraction of all, above all affirmation and abstraction, the
unique abiding seat in each other, if it may be so expressed, of the Sole-sovereign
Hypostases, wholly joined in one and never confused in any part; like lights from　　237
lampstands, if I may employ tangible and familiar examples, from lamps which are in
one house; and all are wholly in each other, but not commingled; and existing of
themselves, they are perfectly distinct from each other, unified in distinction and
distinguished in unity. . . . But [with these lamps] even if someone were to remove
[only] one of the lamps from the house the whole light of the house would be
extinguished with it; neither will anything of the other lights continue on in [the light that
is removed], nor will [the light that is removed] leave anything of itself to the others;
for, as I said, all of them were in a total and all .perfect union, wholly unblended and
in no part confused.

2281

[2, 9]

The divine formation of Jesus like unto us (1) is both indescribable by any language　　320
and unknowable by any mind, even by the very first of the most superior angels. That
He assumed the human essence we accept as a mystery (2); but it is not understood　　311
how He was shaped from the blood of the Virgin by some law other than that of nature,　　781
nor how with dry feet, though He had corporeal bulk and material weight, He was able to
walk upon the liquid and fluid substance (3), and the other things which are indicative
of Jesus' supernatural physiology.

2282

[4, 10]

The true word will also be heard saying this: ''He that is the Author of all things, on　　465
account of His goodness loves the excellence of all things, creates all things, perfects
all things, contains all things, converts all things, and is the divine love, Good of Good
for the sake of the good (4).''

1. ἡ καθ' ἡμᾶς Ἰησοῦ θεοπλαστία.
2. καὶ τὸ μὲν ἀνδρικῶς αὐτὸν οὐσιωθῆναι, μυστικῶς παρειλήφαμεν.
3. τὴν ὑγρὰν καὶ ἄστατον οὐσίαν. The reference is to His walking on the water, as recounted in Matt. 14:22-36 and
   parallels.
4. ὁ θεῖος ἔρως ἀγαθὸς ἀγαθοῦ διὰ τὸ ἀγαθόν.

ST. LEONTIUS OF BYZANTIUM [ca. A. D. 500–ca. A. D. 543]

St. Leontius of Byzantium is a man of great obscurity. F. Loofs' attempt to identify
him with others bearing the name Leontius has failed. Leontius is, according to the
investigative conclusions of Berthold Altaner, not to be identified with a Gothic monk
named Leontius, known through the Theopaschite controversy, nor is he the Leontius
who was, as theological adviser of the Emperor Justinian, ultimately responsible for the
condemnation of the Three Chapters. On the contrary he is, according to M. Richard
and B. Altaner, to be identified with Leontius the Hermit, an Origenist.

Leontius of Byzantium or Leontius Eremita is the author of three works judged authentic: *Three Books against the Nestorians and Eutychians*; the *Resolution of the Arguments of Severus*; and the *Thirty Chapters against Severus*. Other works attributed to him are either certainly or probably spurious.

THREE BOOKS AGAINST THE NESTORIANS AND EUTYCHIANS
[*ante A. D.* 543]

The *Lógoi treîs* were probably written as three separate treatises, though joined in their tradition as a single work in three books. The first book shows that Nestorius and Eutyches start from the same false premises to arrive at their mutually opposed doctrines. The second book is against the Eutychians or Monophysites, specifically the Julianists or Aphthartodocetists. The third book is against the Nestorians and is directed especially against errors which Leontius ascribed to Theodore of Mopsuestia.

Monophysitism holds that a nature can subsist only as its own hypostasis, and concludes from the fact of one person in Christ to one nature. Nestorianism likewise holds that a nature can subsist only as its own hypostasis, and concludes from the fact of two natures in Christ to two hypostases. Leontius, however, is able to explain that the notion of hypostasis includes not only individuality but also subsistence or independent existence; but because a nature can have its subsistence in another hypostasis without becoming a mere accident thereof, Leontius can hold that Christ's human nature is not itself a hypostasis (§ 2287a). Such a nature, then, is enhypostate (ἐνυπόστατος) but is not without hypostasis (μὴ ἀνυπόστατος).

In further development, however, Leontius simply translates the heretical Christology of Evagrius of Pontus into Chalcedonian terminology without understanding Chalcedonian thought. Leontius can say with Chalcedon that Jesus Christ has two natures in one hypostasis or person; but for Leontius as also for Evagrius, this Christ is the solitary Spirit or Mind *(nous)* of the intellectual world who did not fall from grace, and so remains united to the Word of God. In the Incarnation this Mind joins Himself to a body in such a way that two natures, the Word and Man, are united in one person.

In spite of such aberrant theology, Leontius' notion of the nature enhypostate is a valid one, and is given further development by Maximus the Confessor and John Damascene.

The standard text of the *Three Books* is in Migne, PG 86/1, 1267-1396.

2287a

[1]

Hypostasis and enhypostate, my dear opponents, are not the same, any more than 324
substance and to be in substance are the same (1); for hypostasis makes individuality
known whereas enhypostate makes the substance known. Hypostasis determines person
(2) in its proprietary characteristics; but enhypostate shows that it is not a mere
accidental quality that something has in another the existence of which is not discernible
in itself. . . . Anyone, therefore, who says that there is no nature that is without
hypostasis speaks the truth; but he will not be making a correct inference if he proceeds
from not being without hypostasis to [being] hypostasis. A nature, therefore,—that is, a
substance,—cannot be without hypostasis. But nature, nevertheless, is not hypostasis,
because [the terms] are not convertible.

2287b

[1]
The Word is perfect and fully supplied with perfection. The soul of man, too, is   324
perfect, according to its own mode of existence. But even though the Word is perfect
God, the Word is not perfect Christ, when humanity has not yet been united to the
Word. Neither is the soul perfect man, even though it has perfect substance (3), when it
is considered apart from the body.

2287c

[1]
Like Sacred Scripture and the speculations handed down to us from the Fathers, we   334
frequently designate the whole from the parts and the part by the name of the whole, as
when we call the Word the Son of Man, and confess that the Lord of Glory was crucified.
But we do not, by this communication of idioms (4), take away the special basis (5) of   324
the propriety of the one or the other in itself. These things are made known to us by
proper names, since we contemplate the communication of idioms in the one Person
(6), and in the difference of natures we acknowledge the propriety that is held in   322
common.

1. οὐ ταὐτόν, ὦ οὗτοι, ὑπόστασις καὶ ἐνυπόστατον, ὥσπερ ἕτερον οὐσία καὶ ἐνούσιον.
2. πρόσωπον.
3. κἂν τελείαν ἔχει οὐσίαν.
4. τῇ ἀντιδόσει τῶν ἰδιωμάτων. This is too familiar a phrase through the corresponding Latin *communicatio idiomatum*
   to allow of any translation except *communication of idioms*. The idea of *communication* in the Greek, however, is more
   one of *exchange*.
5. τὸν ἴδιον λόγον.
6. τὴν μὲν ἀντίδοσιν τῶν ἰδιωμάτων ἐν τῇ μιᾷ ὑποστάσει θεωροῦσι.

ZACHARY OF MITYLENE [† *ante A. D.* 553]

Zachary of Mitylene is known also as Zachary Scholastikos and Zachary the Rhetor.
He was born at Maiuma, the port city of Gaza, and was perhaps a brother of the Sophist
Procopius of Gaza.

About the year 485 A. D. Zachary was a student at Alexandria. In the autumn of 487
A. D. he began his legal studies at Berytus (Beirut); and about 492 A. D. he settled at
Constantinople where, in his pursuit of the legal profession, he acquired the titles
Scholastikos and Rhetor.

In his early years Zachary was a Monophysite and a friend and admirer of Severus of
Antioch, whose biography he wrote. After the year 492 there is a great lacuna in our
knowledge of the man; but in 536 A. D. we find him again, present at a Synod of
Constantinople as Metropolitan Bishop of Mitylene on the Island of Lesbos. He is now a
Chalcedonian and subscribes to the condemnation of Severus of Antioch and others as
Monophysites. Zachary died prior to the Second Council (Fifth Ecumenical) of
Constantinople (553 A. D.).

DISPUTATION THAT THE WORLD IS NOT COETERNAL
WITH GOD [*inter A. D.* 487 / 492]

The disputation on the creation of the world, extant in Greek, is one of the few
writings of Zachary that has survived intact and in its original language. The dialogue
was written during Zachary's years at Berytus. The characters of the dialogue are called

Christian and *Ammonius*. Zachary himself is *Christian*, and he represents himself as a student of the Sophist Ammonius of Alexandria. It is quite possible that he had in fact studied with Ammonius. *Christian* defends the doctrine of the creation of the world, while *Ammonius* holds that the world is coeternal with God.

The standard text is still that of Migne, PG 85, 1011-1144, which is but a reprint of the 1654 Leipzig edition of C. Barth; unless one prefer the 1836 Paris edition of J. F. Boissonade, *Aeneas Gazaeus et Zacharias Mitylenaeus, de immortalitate animae et mundi consummatione*.

2288

[Migne, PG 85, 1113]

Christian: We confess that God is the Creator and Cause of the world.   468
Ammonius: Hear, hear!
Christian: Are you of a mind that the world is coeternal with God?
Ammonius: Very much so.
Christian: Things that are coeternal are ever coexistent.
Ammonius: So what?
Christian: Things that are ever coexistent cannot have their efficient cause (1) in each other, can they?
Ammonius: No.
Christian: If, therefore, the world were coeternal with God as you say it is, it could not have its efficient cause from God. But we agreed that God is the Creator of the world.
Ammonius: Hear, hear!
Christian: The world, therefore, cannot be coeternal with God. For every effect is later in origin and in time than the one effecting it.

1. ποιητικὴν αἰτίαν.

ST. GREGORY OF TOURS [*A. D.* 538–*A. D.* 593 *aut* 594]

Saint Gregory, Bishop of Tours, the son of a respected senatorial family of Gaul, was born on Nov. 30, 538, at Arverna, the modern Clermont-Ferrand. His great-grandfather, grandfather of his mother Armentaria, was Gregory, Bishop of Langres († 539/540). Nicetius, Bishop of Lyons, was Armentaria's great-uncle; and Gallus, Bishop of Clermont († 554), was an uncle of Gregory on his father's side. Gregory's father, Florentius, died young; and it was Gallus, Florentius' brother, who imparted to Gregory his earliest Christian training.

Soon after his ordination to the diaconate Gregory was taken ill, and about the year 563 he made a pilgrimage to the shrine of St. Martin at Tours, where he hoped for a cure. Ten years later, in his middle thirties, he was elected Bishop of Tours to succeed another of his mother's relatives, Euphronius of Tours († 573). It was to celebrate Gregory's accession to the episcopate of Tours that Venantius Fortunatus wrote his poem *Ad cives Turonicos de Gregorio episcopo*.

Gregory was a man of peculiar grace and honor even among his peers and contemporaries, enjoying an enormous respect throughout Gaul, and serving often as an emissary of King Childebert II. The only thing that prevents our styling Gregory the greatest romantic of a most romantic age is the fact that such title belongs already and perpetually to his friend, Venantius Fortunatus. He died on November 17, possibly in 593 but more likely in 594.

As an author Gregory is best remembered for his *Historia Francorum* in ten books. Nevertheless, we shall have occasion to offer citations only from the book *In gloria martyrum* of his *Eight Books of Miracles*.

EIGHT BOOKS OF MIRACLES [*inter ca. A. D.* 575-593]

Gregory's *Octo miraculorum libri* consists of separate writings composed at various times, and finally combined into one work by himself. The first book is *In gloria martyrum*, written about the year 590; the second, *De virtutibus S. Iuliani*, between the years 581-587; books three to six are entitled *De virtutibus S. Martini*, and book three, the earliest of his literary endeavors, was written between 573 and 576, probably in 575. Book four belongs to the year 581, book five to 587; and book six was never completed. The seventh book is *De vita patrum*, completed in its present form soon after 592, and treating of many important and interesting ecclesiastical figures of Gaul, most of them known personally to Gregory, and not a few of them his own relatives. The eighth book, *In gloria confessorum*, was written in 587.

Our citations below are both from the first book, *In gloria martyrum*, written about 590 A. D.

The text in Migne, PL 71, 705-1096, is a reprint of the Maurist T. Ruinart's edition of 1699. The standard edition at present is that of B. Krusch in the *Monumenta Germaniae historica: Scriptores rerum Merovingicarum*, Vol. 1 (1884).

2288a

[1, 4]

The course of this life having been completed by Blessed Mary, when now she would be called from the world, all the Apostles came together from their various regions to her house. And when they had heard that she was about to be taken (1) from the world, they kept watch together with her. And behold, the Lord Jesus came with His angels, and taking her soul, He gave it over to the Angel Michael and withdrew. At daybreak, however, the Apostles took up her body on a bier and placed it in a tomb; and they guarded it, expecting the Lord to come. And behold, again the Lord stood by them; and the holy body having been received, He commanded that it be taken in a cloud into paradise: where now, rejoined to the soul, [Mary] rejoices with the Lord's chosen ones, and is in the enjoyment of the good of an eternity that will never end.

787

2288b

[1, 8 (*al.* 9)]

But Mary, the glorious Mother of Christ, who is believed to be a virgin both before and after she bore Him, has, as we said above, been translated into paradise, amid the singing of the angelic choirs, whither the Lord preceded her.

783
787

1. *esset assumenda.*

ST. SOPHRONIUS OF JERUSALEM [† *A. D.* 638]

Sophronius, Patriarch of Jerusalem, was born at Damascus about the year 560 A. D. and died at Jerusalem in 638 A. D. He is known also as Sophronius the Sophist, the latter term being in no way derogatory, but simply indicating a teacher of rhetoric. Sophronius was a monk in Egypt about the year 580, afterwards at the Jordan monastery, and still later at the Theodosius in Jerusalem. He was a friend and companion of John Moschus on a journey to Rome; and it is to Sophronius that Moschus dedicated his wonderful apophthegmata, *The Spiritual Meadow*.

Sophronius carried on an ardent but not very successful campaign against Monothelitism. His death in 638 was probably hastened by the tragedy of the fall of Jerusalem a few months earlier to the Caliph Omar.

SYNODAL LETTER [*A. D.* 634]

Always an ardent Chalcedonian, Sophronius had traveled already in 633 A. D. to Alexandria to argue against the Monothelite Patriarch there, Cyrus of Phasis. His mission enjoyed no success; but a few months later he undertook a similar mission to Sergius, the Monothelite Patriarch of Constantinople. Upon being made Patriarch of Jerusalem in 634 A. D. Sophronius immediately drew up in synod a letter in which he explained at considerable length his doctrine of the two energies or operations in Christ. Though usually called a *Synodal Letter to Sergius of Constantinople*, it is probably an openly published letter to all who would read it.

The text of the *Synodal Letter* is found in Migne, PG 87/3, 3147-3200.

2289
[Migne, PG 87/3, 3172]

We teach that every word and operation, be it something divine and celestial or be it   332
human and earthly, proceeds from one and the same Christ and Son, and from His one
composite and singular Person (1), in which the Incarnate Word of God was present
and in which the operations of either nature, inseparable but unconfused, were
performed in accord with that nature. . . . His human [words and actions] were   334
above what is human, not that His nature was not human, but because He voluntarily   362
became Man, and having voluntarily become Man, He accepted what belongs to being a
man; nor was this by any kind of tyranny or necessity, so that His becoming like us
were involuntary, but it was when and to the extent that He willed it. . . . At the same
time, however, there were the sublime and preeminent indications of His divinity . . .   781
such as His being conceived without seed, the exultation of John in the womb, the   782
undespoiling birth (2), the immaculate virginity which was unblemished before the   783
birth, during the birth, and after the birth (3), . . . the marvelous and corporeal   391
ascent from earth into heaven, . . . all of which, accomplished on a level above
human reason and nature, were indications proclamatory of the divine essence and
nature of the Word of God (4), and were not done without the flesh animated by a rational   312
soul. . . . For the Word truly was made flesh, and became corporeal in the flesh   310
without deception; and one Son is acknowledged, who performed of Himself every
operation, both divine and human.

2290
[Migne, PG 87/3, 3192]

[Let] Themistius [be anathema], who was the most lawless father and begetter   351
and disseminator of ignorance, who, not knowing that Christ had already declared that He
had been sent forth from God, and not understanding what Christ meant when He spoke of
not knowing, babbled on that Christ, our true God, did not know the day of judgment. For
if Themistius had not been ignorant of the force of his own words, he would not have borne
such deadly ignorance as to hotly defend the pollution of his ignorance, vomiting out his
weakmindedness that Christ did not know the day of consummation and judgment,
[ignorant as he was that Christ was speaking] not as eternal God but as having been truly
made Man.

1. ὑποστάσεως.
2. ὁ τόκος ὁ ἄφθορος.
3. πρὸ τοῦ τόκου καὶ ἐν τῷ τόκῳ καὶ μετὰ τὸν τόκον. This is the classical terminology, *ante partum et in partu et post partum*.
4. τῆς τοῦ θεοῦ λόγου θείας οὐσίας καὶ φύσεως.

ST. GREGORY I THE GREAT, POPE [regn. A. D. 590-604]

Pope Saint Gregory I was born at Rome about the year 540, the son of a celebrated and wealthy family. Early in life he held political office in Rome, and seemed to have a brilliant secular career before him. He had long wrestled inwardly, however, with the problems of the evangelical counsels and of the citizen of the City of God as a resident in the secular city.

Finally he renounced all his worldly aspirations, sold his inherited possessions, the proceeds of which he distributed to the poor and otherwise used for the building of seven monasteries, six on his family's estates in Sicily and the seventh, dedicated to the patronage of Saint Andrew, in his parental home in Rome. Here in his seventh monastery on Mount Celio he himself resided as a monk, practicing the rule of St. Benedict in such austerity that he destroyed his health and endangered his very life. Yet, in his later years he looked back in nostalgic sorrow to his monastic years as the happiest of his life.

Gregory had spent only a comparatively short time in his monastic retreat when he was called upon by Pope Benedict I (574-578) to serve him as regional deacon. Under Benedict's successor, Pope Pelagius II (578-590), Gregory was made, in 579, apocrisarius, an ambassador of sorts, to the Constantinopolitan court of the Emperor Tiberius II. Only in 585 was Gregory able to return to his monastery, where soon he was made abbot.

When Pope Pelagius died of the plague in February 590, Gregory was called to succeed him by the unanimous vote and acclaim of the Roman clergy, senate, and people. He sought to escape so burdensome an office, but was finally consecrated on September 3, 590.

Gregory was Bishop of Rome for fourteen years. Only two Popes are given the title "the great": Leo I, his predecessor of a century and a half, and Gregory himself. It was Gregory who led antiquity into the middle ages, and he who laid the foundations of the medieval papacy that governed the Western world after the calamitous wars and invasions that completed the fall of the Western empire in the sixth century.

It was Gregory who first habitually styled himself, as Pope, the *servus servorum Dei*.

LETTERS [inter A. D. 590-604]

In speaking of the letters of Gregory the Great it is necessary to distinguish the terms *regesta* and *registrum*. A *regesta* is a calendar or catalogue of letters, summarizing their content, such as we have in Philip Jaffé's celebrated work, the *Regesta Pontificum Romanorum*. A *registrum*, however, is an ordered archival copy of letters in full; and Gregory the Great is the first Pope to have kept a *registrum* of his letters.

Of Gregory's letters, the general importance of which can scarcely be overestimated, there are 854 preserved. It is not to be supposed, however, that we have the original registrum which he must have kept at the Lateran, nor even a direct copy of it in its entirety. Extracted collections were made at an early date; and from three such collections now extant, the whole corpus as we have it is compiled. Or to be more exact, 848 of the 854 extant letters derive from three independent collections, the largest being a grouping of 683 letters which Pope Hadrian sent to Charlemagne. To these 683 letters, another 165, totaling 848, are added from a collection of 200 and from a third collection of 51. Another half dozen items are garnered elsewhere, to bring the total to 854.

The text in Migne PL 77, a reprint of J. B. Galliccioli's revision of the Maurist edition, is superseded by the only edition ever used anymore for scholarly purposes, that of P. Ewald and L. M. Hartmann in the *Monumenta Germaniae historica: Epistulae*, Vol.

1-2, Berlin 1891-1899. It was Ewald, likewise, who prepared the *regesta* of Gregory's letters for Wattenbach's edition of Jaffé's *Regesta Pontificum Romanorum*, Vol. 1 (1885), pp. 143-219.

LETTER OF POPE GREGORY I TO JOHN, PATRIARCH OF CONSTANTINOPLE, THE SAME BEING SENT ALSO TO THE OTHER PATRIARCHS, EULOGIUS OF ALEXANDRIA, GREGORY OF ANTIOCH, JOHN OF JERUSALEM, AND ANASTASIUS, EX-PATRIARCH OF ANTIOCH. *February, 591 A. D.*
[Consideranti mihi]

2291

[1, 24 (*al.* 25)]

I confess that I receive and revere, like the four books of the holy Gospel, four   60
Councils, to wit: that of Nicaea, in which the perverse doctrine of Arius is destroyed;   452
that of Constantinople, also, in which the error of Eunomius and Macedonius is
overthrown; the first also at Ephesus, in which the impiety of Nestorius is judged; and that
too of Chalcedon, in which the wickedness of Eutyches and Dioscurus is reproved. These
Councils I embrace with full devotion and I keep to them with fullest approval; for on them
as on a cornerstone rises the structure of the holy faith, and whoever does not hold fast
to their solidarity, whatever else his life and conduct may be, even if he is seen to be a
stone, still, he lies outside the building. The fifth Council too, I equally venerate, in which
a letter said to be of Ibas, full of error, is reproved. . . . But all persons that the aforesaid
Councils reject, I reject; those whom they venerate, I embrace; because, since those
Councils were shaped by universal consent, anyone who presumes either to loose whom
they bind or to bind whom they loose overthrows not them but himself. Whoever,
therefore, deems otherwise, let him be anathema.

LETTER OF POPE GREGORY I TO LEANDER, BISHOP OF SEVILLE.
April, 591 A. D. [Respondere epistulis]

2292

[1, 41 (*al.* 43)]

But in respect to the triple immersion of Baptism, no truer response can be given   825
than what you have already sensed, that where there is one faith a variation in usage does
no harm to Holy Church. . . . It cannot be in any way reprehensible to immerse an infant
in Baptism either thrice or once, since with three immersions the Trinity of persons may be
signified, and in one, the singleness of their Divinity. Yet, inasmuch as it has until now
been the custom of heretics to baptize infants with a triple immersion, I am of the opinion
that this should not be done among you, lest, while the heretics divide the immersions, they
should divide also the Divinity, and while they continue to do as they are accustomed to
do, they should boast of having got the priority of our custom.

LETTER OF POPE GREGORY I TO PETER, A SUBDEACON IN SICILY.
May, 591 A. D. [Quod responsalem]

2293

[1, 42 (*al.* 44)]

Three years ago the subdeacons of all the churches of Sicily were forbidden, in   964
accord with the practice of the Roman Church, all conjugal intercourse with their
wives. To me it seems hard and improper that one who has not been accustomed to

continence and who did not promise chastity beforehand should be compelled to be separated from his wife and thereby, perish the thought, perhaps fall into worse. Hence it seems to me that from the present day all bishops should be told not to presume to make anyone a subdeacon unless he has promised to live chastely. . . . As for those who, since the prohibition, have been unwilling to abstain from intercourse with their wives, we desire that they shall not be advanced to a sacred order; for no one ought to approach the ministry of the altar except one who has proved himself in chastity before undertaking the ministry.

LETTER OF POPE GREGORY I TO JANUARY, BISHOP OF CAGLIARI.
May, 594 A. D. [Fratris et coepiscopi nostri]

2294

[4, 26]

It has come to our attention that some have been scandalized because we forbade   844
presbyters to touch with chrism those who are to be baptized. And we did this, indeed,
in accord with the ancient custom of our Church; but if some are in any way distressed
on this account, we allow that, where bishops are lacking, presbyters may touch
with chrism, even on their foreheads, those who are to be baptized (1).

LETTER OF POPE GREGORY I TO THE EMPRESS CONSTANTINA AUGUSTA.
June, 594 A. D. [Serenitas vestrae]

2294a

[4, 30]

The Serenity of Your Piety, so well-known for religious zeal and love of holiness,   123
has charged me with your commands to send you the head of Saint Paul, or some other part
of his body, for the church which is being built in honor of the same Saint Paul in the
Palace. . . . Let my Most Tranquil Lady know that it is not the custom of the Romans,
when they give relics of the saints, to presume to touch any part of the body. But only a
cloth is put into a box (2) and placed near the most sacred bodies of the saints. When it is
taken up again it is deposited with due reverence in the Church that is to be dedicated, and
effects so powerful are thereby produced, that it is as if their bodies had actually been taken
there. It happened in the time of Pope Leo of blessed memory, as has been handed down
by our forefathers, that, certain Greeks being in doubt about such relics, the aforesaid
Pontiff made a cut with a scissors in this same cloth, and from the very incision blood
flowed forth. In the Roman and in all Western parts it is utterly intolerable and sacrilegious
to touch the bodies of the saints. And if anyone presume to do so, it is certain that this
rashness will in no way remain unpunished. . . . But since so religious a desire of my
most Serene Lady must not be wholly unsatisfied, I will hasten to send you some part of
the chains which the Apostle Saint Peter himself bore on his neck and hands, and from
which many miracles are attested among the people; if, at any rate, I can succeed in
removing something from them with a file (3).

LETTER OF POPE GREGORY TO JOHN, PATRIARCH OF CONSTANTINOPLE.
June 1, 595 A. D. [Eo tempore quo]

2295

[5, 44 (*al.* 18)]

Saints before the law, saints under the law, saints under grace, all these, making   400
up the Body of the Lord, are constituted among the members of the Church.

LETTER OF POPE GREGORY I TO BRUNHILDA, QUEEN OF THE FRANKS.
July, 596 A. D. [Epistolarum vestrarum]

2295a

[6, 55 (*al*. 50)]

The tone of your letter, which shows a religious spirit and the earnestness of a   123
pious mind, causes us not only to commend the purpose of your request, but also to grant
willingly what you demand. . . . Accordingly, greeting Your Excellency with due honor,
we inform you that to Leuparic, the bearer of this letter, through whom also we received
your communication, and whom you described as a presbyter, we have handed over, in
accord with Your Excellency's request, with the honor due them, certain relics of the
Blessed Apostles Peter and Paul.

LETTER OF POPE GREGORY I TO GREGORIA, CHAMBERMAID OF
THE AUGUSTA. *June, 597 A. D.* [Desiderata dulcedinis]

2296

[7, 22 (*al*. 25)]

I have received the treasured letter of Your Sweetness, in which you have been at   762
some pains throughout to accuse yourself of a multitude of sins. But I know that you love
the Almighty Lord fervently, and I trust in His mercy that the sentence pronounced in
regard to a certain holy woman proceeds from the mouth of Truth in your regard also:
"Her sins, though they are many, are forgiven her, because she has loved much (4)." . . .
But when Your Sweetness added in your letter that you will continue to importune me until
I write that it has been revealed to me that your sins have been forgiven, you demanded a
thing both difficult and useless. Difficult certainly, because I am unworthy of having a
revelation made to me; and useless as well, because you must not become secure about
your sins, except when on the last day of your life you shall be able no longer to bewail
those same sins.

LETTER OF POPE GREGORY I TO EULOGIUS, PATRIARCH OF
ALEXANDRIA. *August, 600 A. D.* [Sicut aqua frigida]

2296a

[10, 21 (*al*. 39)]

But concerning what is written, that neither the Son nor the angels know the day   351
and the hour (5), Your Holiness has understood quite rightly; because it is most
certainly to be referred not to the same Son in respect to His being the Head, but in
respect to His body, which we are. . . . Augustine . . . says also . . . that it can
be understood of the same Son, because Almighty God speaks sometimes in a human
manner, as when He says to Abraham: "*Now* I know that you fear God (6)." For
God says this not because it was then that He knew He was feared, but because
it was then that He made Abraham fear Him. For just as we say that it is a happy day,
not because the day itself is happy, but because the day makes us happy, so too the
Almighty Son says He does not know the day which He causes not to be known,
not because He Himself does not know it, but because He does not permit it to be
known at all. Whence also the Father alone is said to know it, because the Son,
consubstantial with Him, has it by reason of His nature, which is above the angels,
that He knows that of which the angels are ignorant. Whence also this can be
understood in a more subtle way, that the Only-begotten, incarnate and made perfect

Man for us, did indeed *in* His human nature know the day and the hour of the
judgment, but nevertheless did not know this *from* His human nature. What
He knew *in* it He did not on that account know *from* it, because God-made-man
knew the day and the hour of the judgment by the power of His Godhead. . . .
Thus the knowledge which He did not have from the nature of His humanity, by
which, like the angels, He was a creature, this knowledge He denied that he,
along with the angels, who are creatures, possessed. Therefore He knows, as   334
God and as Man, the day and the hour of the judgment; but for this reason, that
the Man is God. The fact is certainly plain enough, however, that anyone
who is not a Nestorian cannot possibly be an Agnoite. For how could anyone who   327
confesses that the Wisdom Itself of God is incarnate say that there is anything of
which the Wisdom of God is ignorant? It is written? "In the beginning was the
Word, and the Word was with God, and the Word was God. He was, in the beginning
with God. All things were made through Him (7)." If all things, then without a doubt even
the day and hour of judgment. Who, then, is so foolish as to presume to say that the Word
of the Father made that of which He was ignorant? It is also written: "Jesus, knowing that
the Father had given Him all things into His hands (8)." If all things, certainly the day of
judgment and the hour. Who, then, is so stupid as to say that the Son received into His
hands what He did not know?

LETTER OF POPE GREGORY I TO THEOCTISTA, SISTER OF THE EMPEROR MAURICE. *February, 601 A. D.* [Magnas omnipotenti]

2297

[11, 27 (*al*. 45)]
   If they say that marriages ought to be dissolved for the sake of religion, it must   974
be known that even if human law has allowed this, divine law has nevertheless
forbidden it. For Truth Himself says: "What God has joined together, let man not
put asunder (9)." He says also: "It is not permitted to dismiss a wife, except for
reason of fornication (10)." Who, then, can contradict this heavenly Legislator?

2298

[11, 27 (*al*. 45)]
   Who, therefore, says that sins are not entirely forgiven in Baptism, let him say   751
that the Egyptians did not really die in the Red Sea. But if it is admitted that the
Egyptians were really dead, it must necessarily be admitted that sins die entirely in
Baptism, because the truth surely avails more in our absolution than does the
foreshadowing of the truth.

LETTER OF POPE GREGORY I TO BISHOP QUIRICUS AND OTHER CATHOLIC BISHOPS OF GEORGIA [ASIATIC IBERIA]. *June 22, 601 A. D.* [Quia caritate nihil]

2300a

[11, 52 (*al*. 67)]
   We have learned from the ancient institution of the Fathers that those who, in   797
heresy, are baptized in the name of the Trinity, when they return to the Holy Church,   799
are to be recalled to the bosom of Mother Church either by anointing with chrism,   804
or by the imposition of the hand, or by a profession of faith alone, . . . because the   792
holy Baptism, which they received among heretics, re-engages in them the powers of   826

cleansing at that time when . . . they are united to the faith in the bowels of the Holy and Universal Church. But as to those heretics who are baptized not in the name of the Trinity, . . . when they come to the Holy Church, they are baptized, because that was not Baptism, which, situated in error, they received not in the name of the Trinity. Nor can this be called a repetition of a Baptism, which, as was stated, was not given in the name of the Trinity. Your Holiness may without any hesitation receive into your assembly, their own orders preserved for them, . . . any who return from the perverse error of Nestorius, so that, while . . . through gentleness you make for them no opposition or difficulty about their own orders, you may snatch them from the jaws of the ancient enemy.

2300b

[11, 52 (al. 67)]

The flesh was not conceived before in the womb of the Virgin, with the Divinity   329
coming afterwards into the flesh; rather, just as soon as the Word came into the   781
womb, just then was the Word, the power of His own nature being preserved, made flesh.

1. The better attested reading here is certainly *baptizandos*, and above, *baptizandi*. There are editions and some few manuscripts that read *baptizatos* and *baptizati* in these respective places; and while it is most unlikely that they represent the correct reading, they do undoubtedly better represent what is clearly intended. Presbyters (priests) are forbidden to anoint with chrism, that is, to confirm the *baptizati*, that is, those who have just been baptized. This was the custom of the Roman Church, at least since the days of Hippolytus. Gregory relents, however, to this extent: that in places where there is no bishop, priests may confirm. The term *baptizandi*, while properly it means those about to be baptized, might easily be used in this present context. Baptism and Confirmation were still conferred as two parts of a grander ceremony, the former by priests, the latter by bishops. Those approaching the ceremony are properly called *baptizandi*. And if, technically, midway in the ceremony, as they leave the baptistry to approach the bishop, they should then be called *baptizati*, we can forgive Gregory for calling them baptizands throughout the whole ceremony. We have heard a newly ordained class of priests referred to as "our ordinands" even a few days after their ordination. No one would insist that the ordinands of a few days ago now be called "our ordinates." So much for those who see no evidence of Confirmation in § 2294.
2. *in buxide brandeum mittitur*.
3. After having been lost for centuries the chains of St. Peter were rediscovered in modern times in a church in the Trastevere district of Rome by Louis de Goësbriand, first bishop of Burlington, Vermont. I have before me on my desk an autographed photo of Bishop de Goësbriand, in which he displays in his right hand a reliquary containing a link from that chain, and, draped over his left arm, a reproduction of the entire chain.
4. Luke 7:47.
5. See Mark 13:32.
6. See Gen. 22:12.
7. John 1:1-3.
8. John 13:3.
9. Matt. 19:6.
10. See Matt. 19:9.

MORAL TEACHINGS DRAWN FROM JOB [*inter A. D.* 578-595]

When Gregory, while Apocrisarius in Constantinople, met Bishop Leander of Seville about the year 578, Leander asked him to write a commentary on the Book of Job. Gregory's response was his *Moralia* or *Moralium libri* or *Expositio in librum Iob*, at which he worked intermittently for many years, finally completing the work in thirty-five books about the year 595 A. D.

The *Moral Teachings* is devoted mostly to discussions of questions in moral theology and of practical applications of Gregory's solutions. In a sense it may be regarded as the first manual of moral and ascetic theology.

Galliccioli's text reprinted in Migne PL 75, 509 to PL 76, 782, is still regarded as the standard.

2302

be a vain enterprise to ask who wrote the Book of Job, since   20
nor of the book is believed, in the Faith, to be the Holy Spirit.   21
.e this book, who dictated what was to be written. He wrote it, who is
bc. f him who did the work of writing, and who transmitted to us, by the
word of the c.. vriting, the facts that were to be presented. If we were to read the words
of some great man in a letter we had received, but were to question by what pen the letter
had been set down in writing, it would surely be ridiculous to know the author of the letter
and to recognize its meaning, and at the same time to try to discover by what sort of pen
those words had been inscribed. But when we know the thing itself and hold firmly that the
Holy Spirit is its Author, and yet we inquire after its writer, what else are we doing but
questioning about the pen which inscribed the words we read?

2303

[2, 3, 3]
The angelic nature is distinct from the condition of our nature, because we are   484
both circumscribed in place and confined by blind ignorance, while the spirits of   485
the angels, though certainly circumscribed, are nevertheless incomparably far above
us in respect to their knowledge. Certainly they are more extended interiorly and   172
exteriorly in knowing, because they contemplate the Font Itself of knowledge. For
what about these things that are knowable? Do they not know them, who know Him
who knows all things? Their knowledge, therefore, is very extensive in comparison
to ours; nevertheless, it is very narrow in comparison to divine knowledge. In
the same way, their very spirits, in comparison to our bodies, are spirit indeed;   483
but in comparison to the Supreme and Uncircumscribed Spirit, they are body. And
again, they are sent and they stand by; for, inasmuch as they are circumscribed,   492
they go forth, and inasmuch as they are always interiorly present, they never depart.
Therefore do they always see the face of the Father (1), while at the same time
they do come to us; for they go forth to us externally by their spiritual presence,
while, through internal contemplation they remain in service in the place from whence
they went forth.

2304

[2, 12, 20]
God is within all, without all, over all, under all, is both above with His power   154
and beneath with His support, exterior in respect to magnitude and interior in respect
to subtlety, extending from the heights to the depths (2), encompassing the outside and
penetrating the inside (3); but He is not in one part above, in another beneath, nor in one
part exterior and in another interior. Rather, one and the same wholly and everywhere, He
supports in presiding and presides in supporting, penetrates in encompassing and
encompasses in penetrating.

2305

[3, 14, 26]
If the first man had not sinned, the Second would never have come to the insults of   360
the Passion. . . . If the first Adam had not by his voluntary sin dragged in death
for the soul, the Second Adam would not, without sin, have come to a voluntary   350
death of the flesh. . . . [27] Our Mediator could not be punished on His own account,   387
because He had done no moral wrong (4). But if He had not accepted what He did   345

not deserve, He would never have freed us from a death that was deserved. The
Father, therefore, being just, disposes all things justly when He punishes the Just   383
One; for He justifies all creation by condemning on behalf of sinners Him that is
without sin.

2306

[4, *Pref.*, 3]
 Whoever is not loosed by the waters of rebirth remains bound by the first chains   793
of guilt. But what is accomplished with us by the water of Baptism is achieved among   795
the ancients, either by faith alone in respect to infants, or by the power of sacrifice in
respect to adults, or, in respect to those who were of Abraham's progeny, by the
mystery of circumcision.

2307

[4, 3, 8]
 But He had made two kinds of creatures to know Him, to wit, the angelic and the   466
human. Pride shattered each of them, and each broke away from its state of innate   491
rectitude. But one had a covering of flesh, and the other bore no weakness of flesh.   483
For the angel was spirit alone, while man was both spirit and flesh. The Creator,   370
therefore, was compassionate and redeemed the one He was pledged to lead back   371
to Himself, the one which is sure to have been affected in part by weakness in the
commission of its fault; but He was bound to turn the apostate angel away even
because when this latter fell it was in spite of a constant strength in which it bore
nothing of the weakness of flesh.

2308

[4, 36, 70]
 Since in this life there is with us a distinction of works, in that other life there will   1046
undoubtedly be a distinction of honors, so that, because here one surpasses another in
merit, there one will transcend another in reward. Hence Truth tells us in the Gospel: "In
My Father's house there are many mansions (5)." But in those same many mansions the
very diversity of rewards will be in some way harmonious, because in that peace so great a
strength will unite us that a man will rejoice because another has received even what he did
not himself receive. Whence also those not laboring equally in the vineyard will all be paid
equally a denarius (6). It is true that with the Father there are many mansions; but it is true
also that unequal laborers will receive the same denarius; for joyful beatitude will be one
and the same for all, although the sublimity of their existence (7) will not be one and the
same for all.

2309

[9, 34, 54]
 The Lord certainly does not spare the criminal, because He will not leave the crime   922
unavenged. For either the man repents his crime and punishes himself, or God vindicates it
with the man and strikes him. Never, therefore, is sin spared, because never is it forgiven
without having been avenged.

2310

[16, 37, 45]
 It is one thing to exist, another to exist of one's own nature (8). It is one thing   530

to exist changeably and another to exist unchangeably. For all these things exist,
but they do not exist of their own nature, because they do not at all subsist in themselves,
and unless they were maintained by a governing hand they could not exist at all. . . .   461
For all things were created out of nothing (9), and their being would return again to
nothing (10) if the Author of all did not keep that being in His guiding hand (11).

2311

[17, 30, 46]
    A man filled with that Prophetic Spirit preferred to say that the proud Devil   384
was beaten by the sagacity rather than by the might of God (12). For he does not
say that might but sagacity struck the proud. For although, as we have said,
because of God's simple nature, His might is wisdom, the Lord, nevertheless, on
the face of things (13), overcame the Devil not by strength but by reason (14). For
the Devil himself, tripping us up radically in our first parents, held man bound in his
captivity in a seemingly just way,—man, who, created with a free choice, consented,
under his persuasion, to what was unjust. For man, created unto life in the freedom
of his own will, was, of his own accord, made the debtor of death. This fault, therefore,   363
had to be taken away; but it could not be taken away except through sacrifice. A
sacrifice, then, was to be sought; but what kind of a sacrifice could be discovered
that would suffice for the absolving of men? It would not be just that victims from   383
among brute animals should be slain on behalf of rational man. . . . And if   380
brute animals, therefore, were not worthy victims for a rational animal, that is,
for man, what was needed was a man who would have to be offered for men, so that
a rational victim might be sacrificed for a rational sinner. But what could be done,   344
since no sinless man would be able to be found, and how should a victim offered for us
be able to cleanse us from sin, if the victim himself did not lack the contagion of sin?
Certainly the polluted would not be able to cleanse the polluted. If the victim was to be
rational, a man would have to be offered; and if it was to cleanse men of sin, the
victim must be a man without sin. But how should a man be without sin, if he were
the offspring of a sinful heritage (15)? That is why the Son of God came, for man's
sake, into the womb of the Virgin, where, on our behalf, He was made Man.   781
From mankind He took its nature, but not its fault. He made a sacrifice on our
behalf. For the sake of sinners He delivered up His body as a Victim without sin, a
Victim who would be able both to die in respect to His humanity and to cleanse us in
respect to justice.

2312

[18, 52, 85]
    It was not that a plain man was conceived and brought forth, who afterwards   329
merited to be God. Rather, at the announcement of the angel and at the coming of the   334
Spirit, as soon as the Word came into the womb, just then in the womb did the
Word become flesh; and His unchangeable essence remaining, His coeternal   322
essence in which He is with the Father and with the Holy Spirit, He assumed within
the virginal womb that too by which the Impassible was able to suffer, the Immortal
was able to die, and by which He that was Eternal before the ages was able to be
one who was temporal at the end of the ages, so that through an indescribable
mystery (16), in a holy conception and in an inviolable birth, in accord with the   782
realities of both natures, the same Virgin would be both handmaid of the Lord and   779
His Mother also. . . . And although He is in one way from the Father and in   324
another way from the Virgin, nevertheless, He is not one person from the Father and
another person from the Virgin; rather, He Himself who is eternal from the Father, is

He Himself who is temporal from the Mother; He Himself who made, is He Himself
who was made. . . . He Himself who was before the ages from the Father without
a mother is He Himself who at the end of the ages is from the Mother without a
father. He Himself who is the Temple is He Himself who is the Builder of the Temple.
He Himself who is the Author of the work is He Himself who is the work of the Author.
Remaining from both and in both natures, He is neither the confused product of a   321
coupling of natures (17) nor a twinned product by a distinction of natures (18).

2313

[20, 32, 63]
   God is called jealous, angered, repentant, merciful, and foreknowing. These   189
simply mean that, because He guards the chastity of every soul, He can, in human   177
fashion, be called jealous, although He is not subject to any mental torment. Because
He moves against faults, He is said to be angered, although He is moved by no
disturbance of equanimity. And because He that is immutable changes what He
willed, He is said to repent, although what He changes is a thing and not His counsel.
And when He remedies our misery He is called merciful, although He can remedy
miseries, but can never have a commiserating heart (19). And because He sees
those things that are future to us, but which to Him are always present, He is
called foreknowing, although He in no way foresees a future; for what He sees is
present. Moreover, whatever things are, are not seen in His eternity because they are;
rather, they are, because they are seen.

2314

[25, 11, 28]
   You must know that sin can be committed in three ways. It is done either in   634
ignorance, in weakness, or of set purpose (20). And certainly the sin committed
in weakness is more grave than that done in ignorance; but that done of set purpose
is much more grave than that done in weakness.

2315

[27, 25, 48]
   The wicked hide from human eyes, but certainly they cannot hide from   133
themselves. For they know the evil they do; they have a conscience as witness;
they have their own reason as judge. . . . Certainly they are themselves witnesses in
conscience that they cannot be excused. For by the very fact that God created man as a
rational creature, He puts a stamp on the hands of all men so that individuals know their
own deeds.

2316

[33, 21, 40]
   The good we do is both of God and of ourselves. It is God's through prevenient   690
grace, ours through obedient free will. For if it is not God's, why do we give thanks   692
to Him in eternity? And again, if it is not ours, why do we hope that a reward will   770
be given us? It is not improper that we give thanks; for we know that we were anticipated
by God's gift. And again, it is not improper that we seek a reward, because we know
that by obedient free will we chose to do what is good.

2317

[34, 19, 36]

"But," some may say, "a fault that has a termination ought not be punished   1034
unendingly. Almighty God is undoubtedly just; and if what was committed was not
an eternal sin, it ought not be punished by eternal torment." We hasten to answer that
they would be correct, if the severe and just Judge were coming to weigh men's deeds
and not their hearts. For the sinning of the wicked does have a termination, because
their lives have a termination. They would have wished to live without end so that
they might be able to continue in their iniquities without end. For they seek more to
sin than to live. And they desire to live here always, because if they could continue
to live they would never have to stop sinning. It pertains, therefore, to the justice
of the strict judge that those who were of such a mind in this life, that they willed
never to be without sin, shall never be without torment; and no end of punishment is
given the wicked man, because, so long as it was possible, he did not want there
to be any end to his crime (21).

1. Matt. 18:10.
2. *sursum regens deorsum continens*.
3. *extra circumdans interius penetrans*.
4. *nullum culpae contagium perpetravit*.
5. John 14:2.
6. See Matt. 20:10.
7. *sublimitas vitae*.
8. *Aliud est esse, aliud principaliter esse*.
9. *ex nihilo facta sunt*.
10. *eorumque essentia rursum ad nihilum tenderet*.
11. *nisi eam auctor omnium regiminis manu retineret*.
12. *prudentia Dei potius maluit dicere quam fortitudine esse percussum*.
13. *quantum ad faciem spectat*.
14. *non virtute sed ratione*.
15. *si ex peccati commixtione descenderet*. The term *commixtio* sometimes has sexual overtones; but they are never very
close to the surface, and more often are not present at all. The same term, indeed, can describe the union of the two
natures in Christ, and the mixture of water and wine in the chalice. In the present instance I really do not think that *ex
peccati commixtione* can correctly be translated *of sinful intercourse*. The *commixtio* here is not so much the action of the
parents in begetting a child, but rather a term designating their constant state even from birth, which is described as a
state of sin. The *commixtio peccati*, then, is the heritage of sin which belongs to all offspring. This heritage is implanted
through the *mixtio* of the parents, of course, but not because of that *mixtio*. This, at any rate, is what I have come to
believe is a rather general apprehension among the Fathers; and that is why they sometimes seem almost to be saying
that marital *mixtio* is sinful: not because it is itself a sinful act, but because it is the vehicle by which Adam's sin is
spread, each time conception occurs, to one more human being. A rather gloomy outlook, of course; but a nonetheless
realistic one. Yet, it was only the rare exception and never Catholic that ever suggested that the human race should
abstain *en masse* from *mixtio*, to let God find some other way of getting men, if He still wanted them.
16. *per ineffabile sacramentum*.
17. Contrary to Monophysitism, the God-Man still has both natures.
18. Contrary to Nestorianism, the God-Man is only one person.
19. *misericors vocatur, quamvis miseris subveniat, et cor miserum numquam habeat*.
20. *aut ignorantia, aut infirmitate, aut studio perpetratur*.
21. The usual solution to the problem of eternal punishment in view of man's weak nature is that sin must be measured not
in accord with the worth of the one sinning, but in accord with the worth of the one sinned against. Hence, though the
sinning man is finite, his sin is infinitely heinous because it is an infinite God whom that sin offends; and therefore must
the punishment be infinite. I must confess that I have never found that argument entirely convincing. Gregory's
explanation, it seems to me, is much more satisfactory in respect to elementary logic, involving nothing of the initial
begging of the question that is found in the notion that the gravity of sin must invariably be measured not by the dignity
of the sinner but by the dignity of the one sinned against. If this latter were necessarily true it would be a greater offence
for a dog to bite a man than it is for a man to bite a dog. And actually, of course, the opposite is true: it is a worse thing
for a man to bite a dog than it is for a dog to bite a man. Moreover, it is probably only because of Adam's sin and its
effect on all creation that a dog would bite a man in the first place; whereas, if a man bite a dog, he acts in an entirely
irrational manner and only adds another sin to the one he got from Adam's teeth in the second place.

DIALOGUES [*A. D.* 593 *aut* 594]

The full title of Gregory's *Dialogues* is *Dialogi de vita et miraculis patrum Italicorum*, or *Dialogues of the Lives and Miracles of the Italian Fathers.*

"Some men of the world had one day left me quite depressed with all their noisy wrangling. In their business dealings they generally try to make us pay what we obviously do not owe them." So begins Gregory's *Dialogues*. And the promise it bears of being a charming book of simple faith is perfectly justified by what follows.

The Deacon Peter, a friend of Gregory from childhood, came in to see Gregory just when the latter was so depressed by having to engage in secular affairs; and in their conversation Peter remarked that, in comparison to the East, Italy had produced few men remarkable for asceticism and miracles. In the dialogues which follow, Gregory finds occasion to recount a large volume of anecdotal materials from the lives of numerous saintly ascetics and wonder-workers of Italy.

No doubt the dialogue form is almost entirely literary device; but it is still most probable that Gregory was encouraged to the work by various members of his household staff. The work is not precisely in the genre of the various collections of *Verba seniorum*; yet, it is subsidiary thereto and belongs with any collection of such.

In the Migne edition book two of the four books of *Dialogues*, dealing with Saint Benedict, is given separately in PL 66, 125-204. The other three books are at PL 77, 149-432. The edition presently regarded as standard is that of U. Moricca, Vol. 57 in the series *Fonti per la storia d'Italia*, Rome, 1924. The work is extant also in Old French.

2318

[4, 5]

Gregory: When Paul says, "For faith is the substance of things to be hoped for,   567
the evidence of things not seen (1)," it means that it is what is not able to be seen that
is truly said to be believed. For that which is already able to be seen cannot be said
to be believed.

2319

[4, 12]

Gregory: I must not forget to mention an account related to me by the Abbot   964
Stephen, whom you know very well. He died in Rome not long ago. According to
him there was in the province of Nursia a certain presbyter who ruled the church
entrusted to him in great fear of the Lord. From the time when he received his ordination
he loved his presbyteress as a sister (2), but avoided her like the enemy, and never allowed
her to come near him. Never permitting himself on any occasion to visit her, he cut himself
off absolutely from all familiar communion with her. . . . After a long life in which he
had spent forty years in the priestly ministry he was taken with a severe fever and lay at the
point of death. When his wife saw him lying there half-dead and with all his bodily
strength wasted away she put her ear to his face to catch the least sound of breathing.
Aware of her presence, he gathered all his strength and with the little breath he had left he
rasped out in a hoarse whisper, "Get away from me, woman! The fire is still smoldering!
Take away the tinder!"

2320

[4, 29]

Peter: What reason have we to believe that a corporeal fire can hold fast something   1032
incorporeal? . . . [30] *Gregory:* When we say that a spirit is held fast by fire, we   1033

mean that it is in torment of fire by seeing and by feeling. For it begins to suffer
from the fire when it sees it; and when it sees itself attacked by the flames, it feels
itself burning. That is how a corporeal thing burns an incorporeal one: an invisible
burning and pain is received from a visible fire, and an incorporeal mind is tortured by
the incorporeal flame of a corporeal fire. From the words of Scripture, however,
we are able to gather that the soul suffers not only by seeing but also by   483
experiencing. . . . If the Devil and his angels, although they are incorporeal, are to   996
be tortured by a corporeal fire, what wonder if souls, even before they are reunited
with their bodies, can feel corporeal torments?

2321

[4, 40]
   Peter: I should like to know whether or not we must believe in a purgational fire   991
after death. [41] *Gregory:* . . . Everyone is presented in judgment just as he is when   1000
he departs this life. But nevertheless, it must be believed that there is, for the sake
of certain lesser faults, a purgatorial fire before the judgment, in view of the fact that
Truth does say that if anyone speak blasphemy against the Holy Spirit it will be   903
forgiven him neither in this world nor in that to come (3). In this statement we are
given to understand that some faults can be forgiven in this world and some in the world
to come. For if something is denied to one in particular, the intellect logically infers
that it is granted for some others. But, as I said before, this must be believed to
be a possible disposition for small and lesser sins.

2321a

[4, 43]
   Peter: Can you tell me, then, where hell is located? Is it above or below the surface   1030
of the earth? [44] *Gregory:* I dare not make an offhand statement in this matter. Some
think that hell is in a definite place on the earth, but others suppose that it is under
the earth. It does seem to me, however, that if we call something infernal because it
is situated in a lower position, then hell ought to be infernal to the earth, just as the
earth is infernal to the heavens. Perhaps that is what the Psalmist had in mind when
he said: "You have delivered my soul from the lower infernal regions (4)." The earth,
then, is the upper infernal region; and lying below it is the lower infernal.

2322

[4, 45]
   Peter: Is there one kind of fire in hell, or must we believe that there are many fires,   1035
varying according to the different kinds of sinners? *Gregory:* Certainly the fire of hell   1034
is one; but it does not torment all sinners in the same way. For there each sinner feels
its punishment according to his own degree of guilt. . . . [46] But it remains
unquestionably true that just as there is no end of joy for the good, so too there will
be no end of torment for the wicked.

2323

[4, 60]
   This Victim alone saves the soul from eternal ruin, the sacrificing of which   897
presents to us in a mystical way (5) the death (6) of the Only-begotten, who,—though
He is now risen from the dead and dies no more, and death will no longer have
dominion over Him (7), for He lives immortally and incorruptibly in Himself,—is   895

immolated for us again in this mystery of the sacred oblation. For His body is eaten there, His flesh is distributed among the people unto salvation, His blood is poured out, no longer in the hands of the faithless but in the mouth of the faithful. Let us take thought, therefore, of what this sacrifice means for us, which is in constant   891
representation (8) of the suffering of the Only-begotten Son, for the sake of our forgiveness (9).

1. Heb. 11:1.
2. *Qui ex tempore ordinationis acceptae presbyteram suam ut sororem diligens*. The term priestess or presbyteress is not really so rare as once supposed, and I do not doubt that a dozen or more examples of its use might be adduced in its various forms, whether *sacerdotissa* or *presbyterissa* or *presbytera*. In the present instance it simply designates the priest's wife. For its use as being synonymous with widows or deaconesses, see Canon 11 of the Council of Laodicea, § 745f above in Vol. 1, with the notes thereto.
3. Matt. 12:32.
4. See Ps. 85[86]:13.
5. *per mysterium*.
6. *illam nobis mortem*. The demonstrative pronoun *ille*, having long since become an adjective, is now beginning to serve as the otherwise non-existent Latin article. Eventually it will become the definite article in its several forms in the various Romance languages, *il, el, la, le, lo, lu*, etc.
7. See Rom. 6:9.
8. *semper imitatur*.
9. *pro absolutione nostra*.

HOMILIES ON EZECHIEL [*A. D.* 593]

Gregory began preaching his course of Homilies on Ezechiel to his Roman congregation about the month of September in the year 593 A. D. He had preached the first twelve of these *In Ezechielem homiliae*, up to Ezech. 4:8, when he broke off the cycle about November, 593, in the face of the approach of the Lombard armies of King Agilulf, already beyond the Po. At the entreaties of his zealous audience, however, he consented to treat at least the difficult conclusion of Ezechiel, and then preached the ten homilies on Ez. 40:1-48.

About the year 601 A. D., at the request of the monks at St. Andrew, Gregory presented them with a copy of the twenty-two homilies, the first twelve in one book and the other ten in a second book. Besides the original Latin, the collection of twenty-two *Homilies on Ezechiel* is extant in Old Burgundian and, at least in fragments, in Old Lothringian as well.

The text in Migne PL 76, 785-1072 lacked some fragments that had already been printed by J. B. Galliccioli in his Venice edition of 1769. These fragments were, however, reprinted in Adalbert Hamman's *Supplementum* to Migne, Vol. 4, fasc. 3-4, Paris 1969-1970, cols. 1526-1535. A new edition has now appeared, however, and may be taken as the standard text: Marcus Adriaen's *Homiliae in Hiezechihelem Prophetam*, in Vol. 142 (1971) of the *Corpus Christianorum*.

2324

[1, 5, 11]

In the hearts of the saints the Holy Spirit, in respect to some virtues, remains   541
always; but in respect to others, He comes only to go away again, and He goes away only to come again. For in faith, hope, and love, and in other virtues (1) without which it is not possible to attain the heavenly homeland,—such virtues as humility, chastity, justice, and mercy,—He does not desert the hearts of the perfect. But in the virtue of prophecy, in eloquence of teaching, in the performance of miracles, sometimes He is present with His chosen ones, and sometimes He absents Himself.

2325

[1, 7, 18]

The angelic nature, when it was created, received the free choice of whether it   486
would will to continue in humility and remain within the sight of Almighty God, or
whether it would succumb to pride and fall away from beatitude. . . . But because,   490
though others fell, the holy angels stood firm in their beatitude, they received as a
reward an absolute inability any more to fall, so that in them their own nature,
because it can no longer be directed in any changeable way, has been solidified
as if into a huge crystal (2).

2326

[1, 9, 2]

If whatever good there is in us is a gift of Almighty God, so that in our virtues   690
there is nothing of our own, why do we seek an eternal reward, as if for merits? But if   770
such goodness as we have is not the gift of Almighty God, why do we give thanks for   638
it to Almighty God? It must be understood that our wickednesses are entirely our
own, but our goodnesses pertain both to Almighty God and to ourselves; for He   692
anticipates us with His inspiration so that we may will, and He follows us with His   691
support, so that we do not will in vain, but may be able to carry out what we will (3).
By prevenient grace, therefore, and by subsequent good will, that which is a gift of
Almighty God becomes our merit.

2327

[1, 9, 6]

Neither faith without works nor works without faith is of any avail, except,   758
perhaps, that works may go towards the reception of faith; just as Cornelius (4),   760
before he had become one of the faithful, merited to be heard on account of his good
works. From this it can be gathered that his performance of good works furthered his
reception of faith.

2328

[2, 3, 4]

It is not to be wondered at if there are various degrees of virtue, when each virtue   543
of any sort can be increased as if in varying degrees, and is thus led, through
increasing merits, to the heights. For the beginnings of virtue are one thing,   772
advancement another, and perfection another still. And if faith itself could not be led to
its perfection through various degrees, certainly the Holy Apostles would never have
said: "Increase our faith! (5)"

2329

[2, 4, 12]

We must recognize that the knowledge had by our spiritual fathers increased with   103
the passage of time. For Moses was more learned in the knowledge of Almighty God
than Abraham was, the Prophets more than Moses, and the Apostles more
than the Prophets. If I do not err, the Scripture itself says: "Many shall pass over,
and knowledge shall be manifold (6)."

1. *in bonis aliis.*
2. See Ez. 1:22.

3. *bona autem nostra et omnipotentis Dei sunt et nostra, quia ipse aspirando nos praevenit ut velimus, qui adiuvando subsequitur ne inaniter velimus, sed possimus implere quae volumus.* There is a striking similarity of language between this passage from St. Gregory and the time-honored classroom prayer of Seminary professors: *Actiones nostras, quaesumus Domine, aspirando preveni et adiuvando prosequere: ut cuncta nostra oratio et operatio a te semper incipiat et per te coepta finiatur. Per XDN.*
4. Acts 10:1-48.
5. Luke 17:5.
6. Dan. 12:4.

HOMILIES ON THE GOSPELS [*A. D.* 590-591]

The term Gospels in this title refers not to the Gospel books as such, but to the Gospel pericopes as read at Mass. Gregory's *In evangelia homiliae* consists of forty homilies, each on a different pericope, for forty different Sundays and Feast Days. Apparently they all belong to one ecclesiastical year, 590-591 A. D., and were preached in various churches.

Of the forty homilies, numbers 1 to 20 were dictated by Gregory at home, and were then read in church in Gregory's presence by a notary. Numbers 21 to 40 were delivered by Gregory himself, seated on his papal chair, and were written down by shorthand secretaries who were present in the church.

The text of J. B. Galliccioli (itself a reworking of the Maurist text of 1705) as reprinted by Migne in PL 76, 1075-1312, is still the standard.

2330
[1, 16, 1]

God, who, having been made flesh in the womb of the Virgin, had come into the world without sin, allowed nothing contradictory in Himself. He was able, therefore, to be tempted through suggestion; but the pleasure of sin did not get its teeth into His mind (1); and therefore every diabolic temptation was from without, not from within.

344
343

2331
[2, 26, 1]

We must understand that the divine operation, if comprehended by reason, is not remarkable; nor does that faith which human reason puts to the test have merit. . . . The body of the Lord came into the presence of the disciples through closed doors, which body, in truth, at His birth came forth to human eyes from the closed womb of the Virgin. What wonder, then, if, after His Resurrection and about to reign victorious in eternity, He entered through closed doors, who, coming so that He might die, came forth from the unopened womb of the Virgin?

567

782

2332
[2, 26, 4]

The disciples receive as their lot the preeminence of celestial judgment, so that, in God's stead, they retain sins for some and for some they forgive them. It was fitting that they be so raised up by God, when they had consented to be so grossly humiliated for God's sake. See, they who feared the strict judgment of God have become judges of souls, and they who feared that they would themselves be condemned now either condemn others or release them. [5] Certainly it is now the bishops who hold their place in the Church. They receive the authority of binding and of loosing, who

900

440

have as their lot a degree of governing. It is a magnificent honor, but that honor
carries with it a heavy burden. . . . [6] Reasons, therefore, must be reflected 918
upon; and then the power of binding and of loosing is to be exercised. It must be
seen what fault preceded, or what repentance followed after that fault, so that 911
the sentence of the pastor may absolve those on whom Almighty God bestows
the grace of compunction.

2333
[2, 30, 1]

But see, if any of you is asked whether he loves God, he replies in total 597
confidence and certainty of mind: ''I do love Him.'' But at the very beginning of
the reading you heard what Truth says: ''If anyone loves Me, he will keep My word (2).''
The proof of love, therefore, is the demonstrability of works. Hence the same
John can say in his Epistle: ''Anyone who says, 'I love God,' and does not keep
His commands is a liar (3).'' We truly love God if we subordinate our desires to
His commands. For anyone who has been abandoning himself to his own illicit
desires certainly does not love God, because he gainsays God in his own will.

2334
[2, 30, 2]

Whoever, therefore, truly loves God, whoever keeps His commands, the Lord 597
will come and make His dwelling in his heart, because love of the Divinity so penetrates
that man that he will not draw away from that love in time of temptation. He truly loves,
therefore, whose mind is not, with his own consent, overcome by wicked desire. For to the
extent that anyone is separated from celestial love, to that extent does he take delight in
lesser things. Whence also it is added: ''Anyone who does not love Me does not keep My
words (4).''

2335
[2, 34, 7]

We said there are nine choirs of angels (5) because we know on the witness of 488
Sacred Scripture (6) that there are Angels, Archangels, Virtues, Powers, Principalities,
Dominations, Thrones, Cherubim and Seraphim (7). That there are Angels and
Archangels almost all the pages of Sacred Scripture bear witness. The books of the
Prophets, as is well-known, frequently speak of the Cherubim and Seraphim. . . .
If to the four which Paul mentions in writing to the Ephesians, that is, the Principalities,
Powers, Virtues, and Dominations (8), we add the Thrones (9), there are five choirs
specially designated. And if we add to these the Angels, Archangels, Cherubim
and Seraphim, it will be found that there are beyond a doubt nine choirs of angels.

2336
[2, 34, 15]

We cannot do penance worthily unless we know what penance really is (10). 910
For to do penance is both to weep for wicked deeds done, and not to do anymore
what we would have to weep over. For anyone who deplores some sins but still
commits others either dissimulates in doing penance, or does not know what penance is.

---

1. *sed eius mentem peccati delectatio non momordit.*
2. John 14:23.
3. 1 John 2:4.

4. John 14:24. This "additional" remark in John is subjoined to 14:23, cited immediately before in 2, 30, 1, § 2333 above.
5. *Novem vero angelorum ordines diximus.*
6. *testante sacro eloquio.*
7. *scimus angelos, archangelos, virtutes, potestates, principatus, dominationes, thronos, cherubim atque seraphim.* The number and designations are the same as Cyril of Jerusalem gave us in Greek (§ 849 with its note 121, above in Vol. I); but the order differs slightly. Cyril's Dominations (κυριότητες) are in the place of Gregory's Powers *(Potestates)*, and Cyril's Powers (ἐξουσίαι) are in the place of Gregory's Dominations.
8. See Eph. 1:21.
9. See Col. 1:16.
10. *nisi modum quoque eiusdem paenitentiae cognoscamus.*

ST. ANDREW OF CRETE [*ca. A. D.* 660–*A. D.* 740]

St. Andrew of Crete, called also Andrew of Jerusalem, is reckoned as one of the principal composers of hymns in the Eastern Church. He was born at Damascus about the year 660 A. D., became a monk in Jerusalem at the Monastery of the Holy Sepulchre at the age of fourteen or fifteen, and was ordained a deacon at Constantinople in 685. About the year 692 A. D. he was made Archbishop of Gortyna in Crete.

At a Monothelite synod in Constantinople in 712 he subscribed to the Monothelite repudiation of the two wills in Christ, although the latter doctrine had been defined in the Third Council (Sixth Ecumenical) of Constantinople in 680-681. In 713, perceiving his error, he retracted and presented to the Archdeacon Agathon of Constantinople a profession of faith against Nestorianism, Monophysitism, and Monothelitism. In his later years he was much engaged in the struggle against Iconoclasm and the Iconoclast Emperor Leo the Isaurian (*A. D.* 717-741).

Andrew died at Erissos on July 4, 740. Among his literary remains are a substantial number of homilies or sermons, most of which are judged authentic. He is perhaps best remembered, however, for his numerous metrical compositions in the nature of hymns.

HOMILIES [*ante A. D.* 740]

Of the twenty-four extant homilies of Andrew there are twenty-two in twenty-one in the collection in Migne, PG 97, 805-1302. Migne's No. 19, on the Hermit Patapius, is in fact two sermons: hence the twenty-two in twenty-one. Nos. 1-4 in this collection are on the Nativity of Mary; but no. 3 has been attributed also to St. John Damascene. No. 17 in the Migne collection is on the Martyr St. George. A different encomiastic homily on St. George and attributed to St. Andrew of Crete had been published already at Antwerp in 1675 in the *Acta Sanctorum* of the Bollandists at April 3, but was overlooked by Migne. More recently A. Papadopoulos-Kerameus published a previously unknown sermon of Andrew of Crete on St. James the Brother of the Lord, in the Ἀνάλεκτα ἱεροσολυμιτικῆς σταχυολογίας, Vol. 1, St. Petersburg 1891, pp. 1-14.

Besides the twenty-four complete homilies or sermons, a few fragments also are known to the periodical literature; and some of Andrew's homilies are extant also in a Georgian version still available only in manuscript: see Michael Tarchnisvili's *Geschichte der kirchlichen georgischen Literatur*, vol. 185 in the series *Studi e Testi*, Rome 1955, *passim* from the index. The passage below is translated from the text in Migne, PG 97, 812.

2336a

[1 *(On the Nativity of Mary)*]
Today the pure, noble birth of men receives anew the gift of its first formation by   786

God, and is restored as it was. . . . Today the reformation of our nature begins, and the aging world is transformed anew to the divine likeness and receives the beginnings of a second formation by God.

CANONS

Among the poetical works of St. Andrew of Crete, and besides the profession of faith in 128 iambic trimeters to the Archdeacon Agathon, there are metrical works in two principal forms: canons and idiomela. Idiomela are short hymns with their own melodies. A canon, a form employed also by St. John Damascene, is a poem consisting of nine odes, each with its own structure and melody.

Andrew's so-called *Great Canon*, the length of which is proverbial, is a song of repentance and contrition. It is in four parts and has no less than 250 lines. It still has a place in the Byzantine Liturgy on Thursday of the fifth week in Lent.

The poetical works of St. Andrew are in Migne, PG 97, 1306-1444. The passage below is translated from the text in Migne, PG 97, 1321.

CANON ON THE NATIVITY OF THE BLESSED MOTHER

2336b

[Ode 4]

Today, O Savior, you have given to pious Anne fruitful offspring of her womb,   786
Your Immaculate Mother (1) . . .

[Ode 5]

O Virgin undefiled, undefiled is your birth (2).

1. ἄσπιλον μητέρα τὴν σήν.
2. ἄχραντός σου ἡ γέννησις, παρθένε ἄχραντε.

ST. GERMAIN I OF CONSTANTINOPLE [*ca. A. D.* 634–*A. D.* 733]

Germain or German, the first of that name to be Patriarch of Constantinople, was born there about the year 634 A. D. His father was a nobleman named Justinian, and was a confidant of the Emperor Heraclius (610-641). Justinian gradually lost favor, however, with later emperors, until in 668 he was charged with treasonable conspiracy and executed. Germain was castrated and obliged to join the clergy at the Church of Hagia Sophia. There his fortunes and influence increased, and he was able to persuade the Emperor Constantine IV Pogonatus to convoke the Third Council (Sixth Ecumenical) of Constantinople, which condemned Monothelitism in 681 A. D.

About the year 706 Germain was made Archbishop of Cyzicus. Accusation is made that under pressure from the Emperor Philippicus Bardanes and while still Ordinary of Cyzicus, in 712 at a Synod of Constantinople Germain was weak enough to subscribe to the Monothelitism against which he had earlier fought so well. If that be true, he afterwards quickly reasserted his faith in a Christ of two natures and wills, and in August 715 he was made Patriarch of Constantinople by the orthodox Emperor Anastasius II. Germain immediately convoked the Synod of Constantinople of 715 and issued a formal condemnation of Monothelitism.

Germain was an ardent opponent of Iconoclasm, and on that account was deposed in

730, already a man in his nineties, by the Emperor Leo III the Isaurian. He then retired to his parental estate at Platanion outside Constantinople where he died in 733 A. D. at about the age of ninety-eight.

SERMONS

Among the rather slight literary remains of St. Germain I are nine sermons, seven of which are on the Blessed Mother: nos. 3-4, on the Presentation of Mary; no. 5, on her Annunciation; nos. 6-8, on her Dormition; and no. 9, on the cincture or belt of the Blessed Lady that was kept as a relic in a church in Constantinople.

Unsuccessful attempts have been made to reascribe these sermons to Germain II, the thirteenth century (1222-1240) Patriarch of Constantinople. The seventh sermon, second on the Dormition, which I cite below, is traceable to a period earlier than the time of Germain II, and was accepted as an authentic work of Germain I by Michael Glykas already in the twelfth century.

The text of the nine sermons is in Migne, PG 98, 221-384.

SECOND SERMON ON THE DORMITION OF THE BLESSED VIRGIN MARY

2336c

[Migne, PG 98, 357]

Let death pass you by, O Mother of God, because you have brought life to men.   786
Let the tomb pass you by, because you have been made the foundation stone of inexplicable sublimity. Let dust pass you by; for you are a new kind of formation, so that you may be mistress over those who have been corrupted in the very stuff of their potter's clay (1). . . . Painful though it be for the soul to be drawn away from the body, O Most Immaculate Lady (2), it is far more painful to be deprived of you!

1. ἐν ὕλη πυλοῦ.
2. πανάχραντε.

ST. ISIDORE OF SEVILLE [*ca. A. D. 560–A. D. 636*]

Isidore was born at Seville about the year 560, his family having come there a few years earlier from Carthagena. Isidore was still quite young when his father died, and he was raised by his brother and sister, Leander and Florentina, both much older than he was, and by his brother Fulgentius. Later he was educated in the monastic institutions of Seville, and afterwards entered the religious life there.

Fulgentius became Bishop of Carthagena, and Leander Archbishop of Seville. Leander is known as the Apostle of the Visigoths and was in large measure responsible for their general conversion from Arianism. In 599 or 600 A. D., at Leander's death, Isidore succeeded his own brother as Metropolitan of Seville. From that time until his death thirty-six years later Isidore was one of the most powerful persons in Spain. He presided over numerous councils and synods, including the very important Fourth Council of Toledo in 633 A. D.

This Fourth National Council of Toledo stressed the obligation of clerical celibacy, declared the clergy exempt from taxation and from certain feudal obligations, and decreed the establishment of a college in each diocese for the training of the clergy, thus anticipating the Tridentine establishment of seminaries by nine hundred years. The council gave recognition to King Sisenand over the deposed Suinthila. And while it found King Sisebut's policy of forced conversion of Jews reprehensible it still supported certain anti-Jewish measures of earlier councils and decreed confiscation of possessions as a penalty on converted Jews who afterwards apostatized from Christianity.

In his own time Isidore was of extraordinary importance in his administrative capacity and for his fostering of education. His enormous importance to the Middle Ages was through his writings, and especially by reason of his work entitled *Etymologies* or *Origins*. There is no great originality to Isidore; but he was perhaps the most learned and broadly educated man of his age, and he excelled in synthesizing knowledge and information of the most diverse kinds. He was a true polyhistor; and what he lacked in depth he made up for in breadth. Already in 653 A. D. the Eighth Council of Toledo declared him a Doctor of the Church, and he was so honored in Seville for eleven hundred years before Pope Innocent XIII declared him a Doctor of the Universal Church in 1722.

Isidore's writings are numerous and largely of an encyclopedic nature. In the Middle Ages anyone unfamiliar with Isidore could not be accounted as educated. Today Isidore is almost as thoroughly neglected as he was formerly attended.

Isidore's death in 636 A. D. provides a convenient date at which to close the Patristic Age in the West.

ETYMOLOGIES [*inter A. D.* 627-636]

Isidore's twenty books of *Etymologies* is undoubtedly his best known and most important work. The subject matter of the *Etymologies* is as follows: Book 1, on grammar; 2, on rhetoric and dialectics; 3, on mathematics, including under this heading arithmetic, geometry, music, and astronomy; 4, on medicine; 5, on laws and calculation of time; 6, on books and ecclesiastical offices; 7, on God, angels, and saints; 8, on the Church and the sects; 9, on languages and peoples; 10, on words; 11, on man and portents (physiology and various abnormalities such as hermaphrodites and giants); 12, on animals; 13, on the universe and its parts; 14, on the earth and its parts; 15, on buildings and fields; 16, on stones and metals; 17, on rustic matters (agriculture); 18, on wars and games; 19, on ships, construction, and wardrobe and dress; 20, on food, drink, cooking vessels, and tools. The actual content of most of the books is much broader even than indicated above.

The *Etymologies* is so called because each new subject is usually introduced by an interesting observation on the meaning and origin of the term—the work is also called *Origins* rather than *Etymologies*—and by an often erroneous but no less interesting designation of the etymology of the term of the subject. It is in all a very fascinating work and, as might be guessed from the subject matter or titles listed with each of its individual books and chapters, it contains a wealth of information for historians of every sort, and not the least the social and cultural historians.

The division of the *Etymologies* into twenty books is probably the work of a later hand. St. Braulio of Saragossa and St. Ildephonse of Toledo both state that the work was still incomplete at the time of Isidore's death in 636 A. D. The chronicle of the world at the end of book 5 stops at 627 A. D. Presumably St. Isidore was engaged in writing the *Etymologies* at least intermittently from 627 or earlier until his death in 636 A. D.

The edition in Migne, PL 82, 73-728, reprints the edition of the Jesuit Faustinus Arevalo. It is superseded by the two volume edition of W. M. Lindsay, Oxford 1911.

2336d

[1, 1, 1]

Disciplina (discipline) takes its name from *discendo* (learning); so it might also be said to derive from *scientia* (knowledge). For *scire* (to know) comes from *discere* (to learn), because none of us *scit* (knows) unless he *discit* (learns). *Disciplina* (discipline) may otherwise have its sound as a vocable from *discitur plena* (it is learned in full).

2336e

[1, 2, 1]

The disciplines of the liberal arts are seven in number (1). First there is *grammatica*, that is, skill in speaking. Second, *rhetorica*, which is regarded as a necessity especially in civil proceedings, for the sake of brilliance and fullness of eloquence. Third, there is *dialectica*, surnamed *logica*, which distinguishes the true from the false by means of the most subtle of argumentations. [2] Fourth, there is *arithmetica*, which comprises the rationale and divisions of numbers. Fifth, *musica*, which is made up of lyrics and songs (2). Sixth, *geometria*, which embraces measurements and dimensions. Seventh, *astronomia*, which comprises the laws of the stars.

2336f

[1, 14, 1]

An *interjection* is called such because it is *interjected*, that is, placed between words. It expresses the sentiment of a mind deeply moved, as when someone exulting says *vah* (wow!), or someone in grief says *heu (oy!)*, or somone in anger, *hem (hmmph!)*, or someone fearful, *hei (hey!)*. Every language has such, and they are not easily translatable to another language.

2336g

[4, 7, 31]

Arthritis *(arthriticus morbus)* takes its name from the suffering of joints *(articulorum)*.

2336h

[4, 8, 12]

Elephantiasis *(elephanticus morbus)* is called such because of a resemblance to elephants, the naturally hard and rough skin of which gives a name to this disease in men; for the surface of the body becomes like the skin of an elephant,—or because the suffering part is enormous (3) just like the animal itself from which the name is derived.

2336j

[4, 8, 14]

Cancer, called such because of its likeness in appearance to the sea animals [called crabs] (4), is a disease which, as physicians say, is incurable by any kind of medication. It is customary, therefore, to cut off the part of the body where it arises so that the patient may live a little longer; but then death will only approach more slowly.

2336k

[6, 2, 45]

For many of the Latins it is uncertain that the Epistle to the Hebrews is Paul's, because of the lack of harmony in its vocabulary. Some suspect that it was written by Barnabas, others that it was written by Clement.

1. The trivium and the quadrivium.
2. *quae in carminibus cantibusque consistit.*

3. *sive quia ingens passio est.*
4. The word *cancer* in Latin means a crab; and the same Latin term designates the disease.

ST. JOHN DAMASCENE [*ca. A. D.* 645–*ca. A. D.* 749]

St. John Damascene or John of Damascus is known also as John Chrysorrhoas, the Golden Speaker, and as John Mansur. Mansur is a family name meaning in Arabic the Victorious. The Emperor Constantine V Copronymus (A. D. 741-775), incensed at John's anti-Iconoclastic writings, put a slightly different inflection on the latter name and called him John Mamzer, or Bastard John. One might have expected that a man named Copronymus would have been a bit more careful about playing the fool with people's names, seeing that the Copronymus he bore all his life recalls his own infantile indiscretion of having soiled the font while being baptized.

Although there are several early lives of John, none of them are at all reliable, and for a man of such renown and importance surprisingly little can be said of his career with any great certainty. He died before the year 754 A. D., in which year the acts of a synod refer to him as already dead. The usual date given for his death, which marks the close of the Patristic Age in the East, is 749 A. D.; but even that is by no means certain.

An Arabic *Menologion* says that at his death he was 104 years of age, which would fix his birth at *ca* 645 A. D. Some, however, think that his age is greatly exaggerated and suggest that he was born *ca* 675 A. D. or even closer to the end of the seventh century. Whatever the dates, it does seem certain enough that he was born at Damascus and died in the Monastery of Mar Saba near Jerusalem, where he had long since become a monk.

The Mansurs, John's grandfather and father before him, had occupied ministerial posts at Damascus first under the Byzantine rulers and after 636 A. D. under the Arab rulers of the city. John was educated by a certain Cosmas, probably a ransomed Sicilian captive who was possibly also John's adopted brother. With a thorough knowledge of Arabic and Greek and proficient also in the knowledge of the Moslem religion, John himself served the Caliph's government for a time and enjoyed a position of trust; but the hostility to Christianity displayed by the Caliph Abd-al-Malik (A. D. 685-705) was such that about the year 700 A. D. (or about 720 and for whatever reasons, if one take the shorter view of his life-span) John resigned his civil office and, along with Cosmas, who afterwards was made bishop of Maiuma near Gaza, became a monk at Mar Saba. There John was ordained by the Patriarch John V of Jerusalem (A. D. 705-735) sometime prior to the outbreak of the controversy over Iconoclasm. In that controversy John was decidely anti-Iconoclast, and could safely speak his mind because he was physically removed from the sphere of influence of the emperors and the Byzantine court. John's theology was always orthodox, and in his Christology he was quite Chalcedonian.

The Damascene was a fluent preacher and a prolific writer. Abbot J. M. Hoeck has listed 150 titles as authentic works of John. There is no great originality to John's writings, but he excelled in synthesizing (often in a way that would now be called plagiarism) and in making a presentation of the faith in a style that would appeal to a broad audience.

A great deal of work remains yet to be done in editing the writings of John and in establishing the authenticity or inauthenticity of many that are attributed to him. Certainly he knew Arabic and Syriac; but he seems to have chosen Greek alone for his literary endeavors. For many of his writings there is extant an enormous number of manuscripts, which testifies to his popularity; and again for many of his writings there are versions extant in Syriac, Arabic, Armenian, Old Bulgarian or Old Slavonic, Georgian, and Latin.

The first collected edition of John Damascene's writings is the folio edition in two volumes, Paris 1712, by the Dominican Michael le Quien. It is an excellent edition and was reprinted at Venice in 1748. Migne's edition in PG 94-96 is likewise a reprint of le Quien, but with a supplement drawn from works first printed by Andrew Gallandi and Angelo Cardinal Mai and others. A new critical edition of John's works is presently being prepared by the Byzantine Institute of the Abbeys of Scheyer and Ettal.

THE SOURCE OF KNOWLEDGE [*A. D. 743 aut postea*]

The most celebrated of John's works, *The Source of Knowledge*, cannot have been written before 743 A. D., because it is dedicated to Cosmas and calls him *patér*, indicating that Cosmas is already a bishop; and Cosmas was in fact made Bishop of Maiuma in 743 A. D.

The work is in three parts. Part one opens with a philosophical discussion largely on Aristotelian ontology, and then presents a gleaning of what is best in the Hellenic philosophers, so as "to draw what is useful," John says, "from the enemies."

Part two is a descriptive catalogue of heresies in 103 chapters. The first seventy-nine chapters and part of the eightieth are a summation of *The Medicine Chest* or *Panarion* of St. Epiphanius. Twenty more chapters follow, taken bodily from other authors including Theodoret. Chapters 101-103 on Mohammedanism, Iconoclasm, and the Aposchists (an obscure sect which in general rejected the institutional Church) are original in the sense that they are not summarized or plagiarized from other authors; but on the other hand they are not likely to be authentic to John, and are probably a later addition. They are lacking, in fact, in several of the earlier manuscripts.

Part three, a lengthy treatise on dogmatic theology, is extant in two recensions, both authentic to John. Migne offers the better of the two.

In their Eastern tradition these three very different parts constituted a single work: *The Source of Knowledge*. Western tradition has treated the three parts as separate works: 1) *Dialectica*; 2) *De haeresibus*; and 3) *De fide orthodoxa*. Furthermore, Western tradition, probably in order to make this third part conform at least externally to the design of Peter Lombard's four books of *Sentences*, has broken part three into four books: 1) on God; 2) on Creation and Providence; 3) on Christ; and 4) a continuation of Christology, dealing also with Baptism and Eucharist, veneration of saints and images, the Canon of Scripture, evil, and the last things.

The standard text of *The Source of Knowledge* is still that of M. le Quien, reprinted in Migne, PG 94, 517-1228.

2337

[2, *Epilogue*]

The Father is Father and unbegotten. The Son is Son, begotten and not unbegotten;   238
for He is from the Father. The Holy Spirit is not begotten, but He proceeds; for   269
He is from the Father. There is nothing here of creature, nor a second-first, nor a
servant-master (1). There is, however, Unity and Trinity; and it was and is and   239
will be unto the ages (2): understood and adored by faith; through faith, and not
through inquiry nor investigation nor demonstration. For as much as you seek,
so much the more ignorant will you be; and as much as you pry into it, so much
the more will it be hidden. Let God, therefore, be adored by the faithful without
meddlesome calculation. Believe that God is in three Persons (3). How this is, is
beyond explaining (4); for God is not to be comprehended.

2338

[3, 1, 1]

"No one has ever seen God. The Only-begotten Son who is in the bosom of the   173
Father has made Him known (5)." The Divinity, therefore, is indescribable and
incomprehensible. "For no one knows the Father except the Son, nor the Son except
the Father (6)." . . . Nevertheless, God did not leave us in total ignorance. For   135
the knowledge of God's existence is implanted naturally by Him in everyone. Creation   131
itself and its continuance and its government proclaim the greatness of the Divine
Nature (7).

2339

[3, 1, 3]

Things that are changeable are likewise wholly created. And things that are   137
created are certainly authored by someone. And the one who authors them is necessarily
increate. For if he were created he were certainly created by someone, and so on until we
come to one who is increate. The Author, therefore, since He is increate, is also certainly
unchangeable. And who could this be, except God?

2340

[3, 1, 4]

Concerning God, it is impossible for us to say what He is in His essence (8);   174
it is more fitting, rather, to discuss how He is different from everything else. For   178
He belongs not among things that exist, not because He does not exist, but because   180
He is beyond all existing things, and beyond even existence (9) itself. For if all modes
of knowledge are concerned with what exists, that which is beyond knowledge must
be beyond existence (10) and likewise, what is beyond existence must also be beyond
knowledge.

2341

[3, 1, 5]

The Divinity is perfect and without defect in His goodness, in His wisdom, in   153
His power, without beginning, without end, eternal, infinite, and to put it simply,   157
perfect in every respect. If we were to speak of many gods it would be necessary to
recognize a difference among the many. But if there is no difference among them,
there is but one and not many. And if there were a difference among them, where
then were their perfection?

2342

[3, 1, 8]

[We believe] in one Father, the beginning and cause of all things, begotten of no   250
one, but uncaused and unbegotten, alone subsisting; Creator of all things, but Father
by nature of One only, His Only-begotten Son and our Lord and God and Savior Jesus
Christ, and Emanator (11) of the Holy Spirit. . . . There never was a time when   256
the Father was and the Son was not; but always Father, always Son, who is begotten
of Him; for one cannot be called father apart from a son.

2343

[3, 1, 8]

He is called *Word* and *Reflection* (12) because of His being begotten of the Father   252

without conjugation and without passion and apart from time and without effluence   263
and without separation; *Son* and *Stamp of the Paternal Subsistence* (13), because
of His being perfect and subsistent (14) and like the Father in all things (15) except
[the Father's] unbegottenness; and *Only-begotten* because He alone is solely begotten
of the only Father (16). For no other generation can be likened to the generation of the
Son of God; and neither is there any other Son of God. For even if the Holy Spirit   276
proceeds from the Father, this does not take place generatively but processionally (17).
This is another mode of subsistence, just as incomprehensible and unknown as the
generation of the Son.

On this account all the qualities the Father has are the Son's also, except that the   281
Father is unbegotten.

2344

[3, 1, 8]

The Father and the Son and the Holy Spirit are one in all respects except those   281
of being unbegotten, of begetting, and of proceeding. And it is by thought that the
difference is perceived. For we know that there is but one God. And we but infer
the difference in the singular proprieties (18) of Fatherhood and of Sonship and of
Procession, in respect both to cause and to being caused, and to the perfection of
subsistence (19), that is, of manner of existence. For in reference to the uncircumscribed
we cannot speak of local separation, as we can in respect to ourselves; for their subsistences
(20) are in each other, not as commingled but as coherent, in accord with the word of the
Lord, who says: "I am in the Father and the Father in Me (21)." Nor is there here any
difference of will or of judgment or of operation or of power or of anything else such as
would, in our own case, produce actual and absolute separation. . . . For, if it may be put
briefly, the Godhead is undivided in the face of what is divided; and it is as if there were
three suns cohering in each other and not separated from each other, one in the tempering
and conjoining of their light.

2345

[3, 1, 9]

It seems that the most authoritative of all the names spoken of God is "WHO IS,"   140
as He did Himself say on the mountain in answer to Moses, "Tell the sons of
Israel, 'WHO IS has sent me (22).'" For, since He holds all existence in Himself,
He is like a sea of being (23), boundless and infinite.

2346

[3, 1, 10]

All these other names, therefore, are to be understood as common to the whole   281
Godhead, in the same way and simply, and individually and conjointly. The names
Father, Son, and Holy Spirit, however, and the uncaused and the caused and the
unbegotten and the begotten and the made to proceed, are separately applied; for
these are not indicative of essence (24), but of relationship to each other, and of
manner of subsistence (25).

2349

[3, 2, 2]

Since, therefore, the good and more than good God was not content in the   465
contemplation of Himself, but in His abundant goodness was pleased to produce

such things as might enjoy His benefactions and partake of His goodness, He shaped   461
the universe (26), both the invisible and the visible, and brought it into existence   509
out of the non-existent; and man He combined from the visible and the invisible. He   500
creates by taking thought, and it is thought that is the basis of the work; by the Word
He carries it out, and by the Spirit He perfects it.

2350

[3, 2, 3]
    He Himself is Creator and Artisan of the angels, bringing them into existence   480
out of the non-existent, creating them according to His own image, an incorporeal
race (27), rather like spirit and insubstantial fire (28), as the Divine David says: 483
"He makes His angels spirits, and His ministers a flame of fire (29.)."

2351

[3, 2, 3]
    An angel, then, is an intelligent being (30), ever in motion (31), with free   486
will (32), incorporeal, ministering to God, having by grace obtained immortality in   483
his nature, the form and limitation of whose essence (33) is known to the Creator
alone. But an angel is called incorporeal and without matter only in comparison to
ourselves; for whatever is compared to God, who alone is incomparable, is found   152
to be dense and material. For in fact it is the Divinity alone who is without matter
and bodiless.

2352

[3, 2, 3]
    [Angels are] secondary intelligent lights, having their light from the First Light,   482
who is without beginning. They have no need of speech and hearing, for without   487
uttered word (34) they impart to each other their own thoughts and purposes. Through   284
the Word, then, all the angels were created, and they were perfected through   285
sanctification by the Holy Spirit, each sharing in light and grace in proportion to
his dignity and rank.

2353

[3, 2, 3]
    [The angels] are circumscribed; for when they are in heaven they are not on earth;   484
and when they are sent to earth by God they do not abide in heaven. They are not
inhibited, however, by walls and doors and bolts and seals; for they are not bounded
(35). Not bounded, I say: for it is not as they really are that they appear to the worthies
to whom God wishes them to appear, but in a changed form (36), so that those who see   154
are able to see. For that only which is increate is properly and by nature unbounded.
For every creature is given its limits by God who creates it.   489
    Angels have their sanctification from outside their essence (37), from the Spirit.   285

2354

[3, 2, 3]
    Whether [the angels] are equals in essence (38) or differ one from another, we do   492
not know. . . . They are strong and ready to fulfill the divine will, and they are   493
by nature (39) so swift that they are found immediately everywhere the divine

nod commands them to be. They guard the regions of the earth; they are set over nations and places, as allotted them by their Creator; and they manage all our concerns and assist us.

2355

[3, 2, 3]

As that man, the most holy and most sacred and most learned in theology, Dionysius   488
the Areopagite, says (40), all theology, that is, Sacred Scripture, designates nine (choirs of) heavenly beings (41), which that same divine teacher of sacred matters distinguishes in three triplex groupings. The first group, he says, is of those who are ever in God's presence and are traditionally regarded as being closely and thoroughly associated (42) with Him, the group comprising the six-winged Seraphim, the many-eyed Cherubim, and the most holy Thrones. The second group is that of the Dominations, Virtues, and Powers. The third and last group is of the Principalities, Archangels, and Angels (43).

2356

[3, 2, 3]

Those who say the angels are creators of any kind of beings (44) are the mouth   462
of their father, the devil. For the angels, being creatures, are not creators. He that creates and maintains and provides for all is God, who alone is increate, and who is   530
praised and glorified in Father and Son and Holy Spirit.

2357

[3, 2, 12]

The soul, then, is a living being (45), simple and incorporeal, invisible to the   501
bodily eyes by its very nature (46), immortal, rational and intelligent, shapeless,   502
making use of an organic body, to which body it imparts life, growth, and feeling,   503
and the faculty of generation, mind being its purest part and in no way alien to it; for just as the eye is to the body, so is the mind to the soul. The soul enjoys free choice (47), having the faculty of willing and of acting; and it is changeable, which   505
is to say, it is subject to change, because it is created.

2358

[3, 2, 29]

It is needful to remember that God wills beforehand that all should be saved and   200
come into His kingdom (48). Because He is a good God it was not for punishment that He shaped us, but to participate in His goodness. But because He is a just God, He wills that sinners are to be punished. The first, then, which is from God Himself, is called His antecedent will and good pleasure while the second, having its origin in us, is called His consequent will and permission. . . . . But of actions which are in our   638
hands, the good ones He wills antecedently and in His good pleasure; but the evil ones and the really wicked He neither wills antecedently nor consequently; but He permits them in the exercise of free will (49).

2359

[3, 2, 30]

We must recognize that while God foreknows all things, He does not predestine   191
all things. He foreknows the things that depend upon us, but He does not predestine   193

those things. He does not will the doing of evil, nor does He compel virtue. Thus
predestination is the work of the divine command based on foreknowledge (50).
And He predestines in accord with His foreknowledge those things that are not
dependent upon us. For God in His foreknowledge has already prejudged all things in
accord with His goodness and justice. We must recognize also that virtue is   740
implanted by God in our nature, and that God Himself is the source and cause of all   650
good, and without His cooperation and assistance we are powerless either to will
or to do anything good. We, however, have it in our power either to abide in virtue   700
and to be obedient to God, who calls us to this, or to stray from paths of virtue, which
is to dwell in wickedness, and to follow the devil, who calls to us but cannot compel us.

2360

[3, 2, 30]
   The Creator, therefore, made this man male, imparting to him something of His   523
own divine grace, and thereby bringing him into communion with Himself. And thus man
gave living creatures their names in a prophetic manner, with authority, as if they were to
be his slaves. . . . But since God knew by His foreknowledge that man would transgress
and become liable to destruction, He made from him a female like man himself to be a help
to man; a help, indeed, for the continuance of the race from age to age by generation, after
the transgression.

2361

[3, 3, 3]
   The Word makes the attributes of humanity His own, for whatever pertains to   334
His holy flesh is His. And He imparts to the flesh His own attributes by way of
reciprocating, through the interspreading (51) of parts one into another and through
the hypostatic union (52), and because He was one and the same who was both
divine and human, "in each form, acting in communion with the other (53)." Thus
too is the Lord of Glory said to have been crucified (54), even though His divine
nature (55) endured no suffering; and thus too is the Son of Man confessed to be in
heaven before the suffering, as the Lord Himself says (56). For one and the same is
both Lord of Glory and He who was, in another nature and in truth, Son of Man,
that is, who became Man. We know both His wonders and His sufferings, even if
He worked His miracles according to the one nature, and is the same [Person] who   332
endured suffering according to the other nature.

2362

[3, 3, 5]
   We confess that in the Godhead there is one Nature (57), but say that there are   238
three Persons (58) truly existing, and say that everything pertaining to nature and   281
essence (59) is simple; and we recognize the distinction of the Persons solely in the
three properties (60), that is, in uncausedness and Fatherhood, in causedness and
Sonship, and in causedness and procession; and these Three are indivisible and
inseparable from each other. . . . In the same way, too, in the divine and   320
inexpressible Incarnation (61) which exceeds all thought and comprehension, [the
Incarnation] of the Word of the One God of the Holy Trinity (62) and of our Lord
Jesus Christ, we confess that there are two natures (63), divine and human, holding
intercourse with each other (64) and united in Person (65), one Person brought to
perfection in the compounding of the [two] natures.
   Yet we say that the two natures are preserved, even after their union, in the one   332

compounded Person (66), that is, in the one Christ, and that they truly exist and
have their own natural proprieties (67); for they are united without being confused,
and are distinguished and enumerated without being separated. . . . The natures   321
of Christ, though they are united, are united without being confused; and though
they are interspread in each other, this does not permit of change or transmutation into each
other. . . . For Christ is one, perfect both in divinity and in humanity.

2363

[3, 3, 8]
    Christ is one, perfect God and perfect Man, whom we worship with the Father   342
and the Spirit in one worship, including also His immaculate flesh, not holding that
His flesh is not to be worshiped; for the flesh is worshiped in the Word's one Person (68),
which was made Person with it (69); we do not in this way adore the creature, for
we do not worship Him as mere flesh but as flesh united with divinity, and because
His two natures (70) are brought into the one Person and one Subsistence (71) of
God the Word. I fear to touch a glowing coal because of the fire that is integrated with
the wood. I worship both natures (72) of Christ because of the divinity united to the
flesh. I do not introduce a fourth person into the Trinity. Perish the thought! But I
do confess one Person, of God the Word and of His flesh; and the Trinity remains a
Trinity even after the Incarnation of the Word.

2364

[3, 3, 12]
    We proclaim that the Holy Virgin is properly and truly the Mother of God (73);   780
for since He that was born of her is true God, she that bore the true God, incarnate
of her, is true Mother of God (74). For we hold that God was born of her, not as if the
Divinity of the Word took the beginning of His existence from her, but that God the
Word, who was begotten of the Father timelessly before the ages, and who subsisted
with the Father and with the Spirit eternally and without beginning, in these last
days took His abode in her womb for our salvation, and without change took flesh
of her and was born. For the Holy Virgin did not bear mere man but true God,   311
not naked but incarnate, not with a body brought down from heaven, not passing   313
through her as through a channel, but *homoousios* with us, having taken flesh from her,
though subsisting in Himself. For if the body had come down from heaven and did   314
not share in our nature (75), of what use were His becoming Man? For the purpose
of God the Word in becoming Man was that the very nature (76) which had sinned
and fallen and become corrupted might triumph over the deceiving tyrant and thus
be freed of corruption.

2365

[3, 3, 13]
    We confess that the same Jesus Christ our Lord is both perfect God and perfect   322
Man; and we hold that the same has all the attributes of the Father, except that of   313
unbegottenness; and all the attributes of the first Adam, save only that of sin, which   312
attributes of the first Adam are a body and a soul, both rational and intelligent.   345
Furthermore He has, in accord with the two natures, twofold natural qualities   332
belonging to the two natures (77): two natural wills, the divine and the human, and two   330
natural operations, the divine and the human, and two natural free-wills, the divine
and the human, and [two kinds of] wisdom and knowledge, the divine and the
human (78).

2366

[3, 3, 19]

We hold that the operations are not divided and that the natures (79) do not act   323
separately, but that each acts jointly in communion with the other, in its own   330
proper operation. For that which was human did not operate [merely] humanly,   332
for it was not merely human; nor did the divine operate as God alone, for He was
not naked God, but was at the same time God and Man. For just as with natures
we recognize both their union and their natural difference, so too with the natural
wills and operations.

Note, therefore, that with our Lord Jesus Christ we speak sometimes as about
two natures and sometimes as about one Person (80), and whether the former or
the latter, the idea is the same (81), for the two natures are one Christ and the one
Christ is two natures. . . . Theandric operation (82), therefore, means that when   333
God became Man, that is, when He became incarnate, His human operation was   334
divine, that is, it was deified, and was not without a share in His divine operation; and
His divine operation was not without a share in His human operation, but each was
observed along with the other.

2367

[3, 3, 20]

We confess that Christ took on all the natural and non-reprehensible passions of   342
man. For He took on the whole man and all that pertains to man, except sin. For   345
sin is not natural nor is it implanted in us by the Creator, but it is sown afterwards by the
devil in the voluntary exercise of our free choice, not prevailing upon us by force. The
natural and non-reprehensible passions are those that do not depend upon ourselves, and
which have entered into human life as punishment for the transgression, such as hunger,
thirst, weariness, labor, tears, . . . and other such passions as belong by nature to every
man.

He assumed all so that He might sanctify all.

2368

[3, 3, 22]

[Christ] is said, moreover, to have grown in wisdom and age and grace (83). He   329
did indeed increase in age, and with that increase in age He manifested the wisdom   324
that is in Him. Moreover, He made men's progress in wisdom and grace, and the
fulfillment of the Father's good pleasure, which is to say, men's knowledge of God
and their salvation—this increase, I say, He made His own increase, and in every way
took as His own that which is ours.

Those who say that He progressed in wisdom and grace, as if He received some
addition to these attributes, do not say that the union took place at the very beginning
(84) of the flesh, nor do they give priority to the hypostatic union (85), but paying heed
(86) to the addlepated (87) Nestorius, they talk of such marvels as a relative union (88)   327
and a mere indwelling (89), "understanding neither what they are saying nor anything   341
of what they affirm (90)." For if the flesh was truly united to God the Word   351
from its very beginning, or rather, if it subsisted in Him and He had hypostatic
identity with it, how was it that it was not perfectly endowed with all wisdom
and grace? Not that it might participate in that grace, nor have a share by grace in
what belonged to the Word, but rather, by reason of the hypostatic union, . . .
that He who was at the same time both God and Man should pour out on the world
His grace and wisdom and fullness of every good thing.

2369

[3, 4, 4]

The Son of God became Man in order to bestow again on man that grace for the   376
sake of which He first created him. . . . Since He bestowed on us the better part
and we did not keep it secure, He came to share in the lesser part, I mean our own
nature, so that through Himself and in Himself He might renew that which was made
according to His image and likeness, and might also teach us virtuous conduct,   373
making for us an easier way to it through Himself; that He might by the communication   374
of life deliver us from corruption, becoming Himself the first fruits of our resurrection;
and that He might renew the useless and worn vessel and, while calling us to the
knowledge of God, might redeem us from the tyranny of the devil, and might strengthen
us and teach us how, by patience and humility, to overthrow the tyrant.

2370

[3, 4, 13]

Since the Creator bestowed on us His own image and His own spirit, and we did   376
not keep them secure, He Himself took a share in our poor and weak nature so that
He might cleanse us and make us incorruptible, and reinstate us as participants in
His divinity.

2371

[3, 4, 13]

The Body is truly united to divinity, the Body which was from that of the Holy   856
Virgin; not that the Body which was taken up comes back down from heaven, but
that the bread itself and the wine are made over (91) into the Body and Blood of God.

If you inquire into the way in which this happens, let it suffice for you to hear that
it is through the Holy Spirit, just as it was through the Holy Spirit that the Lord took   320
on Himself from the Holy Mother of God the flesh that subsisted in Himself. More   780
than this we do not know, except that the word of God is true and effective and
all-powerful; but the manner [of the Eucharistic transformation] is inscrutable. It were
not badly put, were one to say this: that just as bread in the natural process of eating,
and wine and water in drinking, are changed into the body and blood of the one eating
and drinking, and do not become another body than his former body, so too the bread
on the credence table (92), as also the wine and water, through the epiclesis and coming   861
of the Holy Spirit, are supernaturally changed (93) into the Body of Christ and into   863
His Blood, and they are not two but one and the same.

For those who partake worthily and with faith, it is for the remission of sins and
for life everlasting, and a safeguard to soul and body. . . . The Bread and the
Wine are not a type (94) of the Body and Blood of Christ,—perish the thought!—but   851
the deified Body Itself of the Lord, since the Lord Himself has said: "This is My   852
Body." He did not say a type of His Body, but His Body; nor a type of His Blood,
but His Blood (95). . . . If some have called the bread and the wine antitypes (96)   853
of the Body and Blood of the Lord, as does the divinely inspired (97) Basil, they   879
said this not after the consecration but before the consecration, giving this name to
the offering itself.

2371a

[3, 4, 14]

[In reference to the Eucharist] participation is spoken of, because through the   881
Eucharist we participate in the divinity of Jesus. Communion is likewise spoken of, and it

is real communion, because through the Eucharist we have communion with Christ and share in His flesh and in His divinity. We do indeed have such communion thereby, that we are united with each other. For since we partake of one Bread we all become one body of Christ and one blood, and members of each other, since we become of one body with Christ. With all our strength, therefore, let us guard against receiving communion from heretics and from giving Communion to them. "Do not give that which is holy to the dogs," the Lord says, "nor cast your pearls before swine (98)," lest we come to share in their dishonor and condemnation. For if this union is truly with Christ and with each other, certainly we are voluntarily united also with all who partake along with us.

2371b

[3, 4, 14]

The incarnate Son of God who was born of [Mary] was not a divinely-inspired (99)   780
man, but God incarnate. . . . Must she not, therefore, be Mother of God (100), who bore God incarnate? Certainly she who performed the role of the Creator's handmaid and Mother is truly and in perfect reality God's Mother, and Lady and Queen over all creation (101).

2372

[3, 4, 14]

And just as He that was conceived kept her that conceived a Virgin still, He that   781
was born kept her virginity intact, only passing through her and keeping her closed.   782
The conception was through the sense of hearing; but the birth was through the usual channel by which children come, even if some do prattle of His birth being through the side of the Mother of God (102). Certainly it was not impossible for Him to come by this gate without injuring its seal in any way. Thus the Ever-Virgin remains after   783
birth a Virgin still, never having consorted with man until death. . . . For how were it possible that she, who had borne God, and had come to know that miracle from her experience of subsequent events, should receive the embrace of a man? Perish the thought!

2373

[3, 4, 17]

Note that in the Old Testament there are twenty-two books, one for each letter of   41
the Hebrew language. For there are twenty-two letters of which five are double, thus totaling twenty-seven. For the letters Kaph, Mem, Nun, Pe and Çadhe are double (103). So too the number of the books is, in similar fashion, twenty-two, but is found to be twenty-seven because of the duplex character of five. For Ruth is joined to Judges, and the Hebrews reckon them as one book; the First and Second Books of Kingdoms are reckoned as one, and so too are the Third and Fourth Books of Kingdoms; and likewise the First and Second Books of Chronicles, and the First and Second of Esdras. In this way, then, the books are collected together in four pentateuchs with two remaining over, to form the canonical books.

Five books are of the Law, namely, Genesis, Exodus, Leviticus, Numbers, Deuteronomy. . . . Then there is another pentateuch, the Writings or, as they are called by some, the Sacred Writings, which are the following: Jesus the Son of Nave; Judges along with Ruth; First and Second Kingdoms, which are one book; Third and Fourth Kingdoms, which are one book; and the two books of Chronicles, which are one book. . . . The third pentateuch is the Poetic Books, namely, Job, Psalms, Proverbs of Solomon, Ecclesiastes of Solomon and the Canticle of Canticles of Solomon. The fourth pentateuch is the Prophetic

Books, namely, the twelve prophets constituting one book, Isaias, Jeremias, Ezechiel, Daniel. Then come the two books of Esdras in one, and Esther.

There is also the Panaretus (104), that is, the Wisdom of Solomon, and the Wisdom of Jesus, which was published in Hebrew by the father of Sirach and was translated into Greek by Jesus, his grandson, the son of Sirach. These are virtuous and elegantly written, but they are not counted [as inspired Scripture], nor are they placed in the ark (105).

The New Testament contains four Gospels, according to Matthew, according   42
to Mark, according to Luke, and according to John; the Acts of the Holy Apostles by the Evangelist Luke; seven Catholic Epistles, namely, one of James, two of Peter, three of John, one of Jude; fourteen Epistles of the Apostle Paul; the Apocalypse of the Evangelist John; and the *Canons of the Holy Apostles*, by Clement (106).

2374

[3, 4, 24]

Virginity, the conduct of the angels, is the property of all incorporeal nature.   983
We do not say this as speaking ill of marriage, perish the thought! For we know   984
that the Lord blessed marriage by His presence (107), and we know the saying,   972
"Marriage is honorable and its bed undefiled (108)." But we say this by way of recognizing that however good marriage may be, virginity is better.

2375

[3, 4, 27]

We believe also in the resurrection of the dead. For it really will be, there   1011
will be a resurrection of the dead. And when we say resurrection, we mean a resurrection of bodies. For resurrection is a second standing erect of what had fallen. For souls being immortal, how should they be raised up? . . . It is this very body, which is   1013
corruptible and subject to dissolution, that will rise again incorruptible.

2376

[3, 4, 27]

We shall rise again, therefore, our souls united again to our bodies, the latter now   1011
made incorruptible and having put corruption aside; and we shall stand before the   1020
awesome tribunal of Christ. And the devil and his demons, and the man that is his, the Antichrist, and the impious and the sinners shall be consigned to everlasting   1034
fire, not material fire such as we know, but such fire as God would know.

And those who have performed good actions will shine like the sun (109) with   1041
the angels in eternal life, with our Lord Jesus Christ, seeing Him forever and being ever in His sight, and deriving increasing joy from Him, praising Him with Father and Holy Spirit in the infinite ages of ages. Amen.

1. οὐδὲν κτιστόν, οὐδὲν πρωτοδεύτερον, οὐδὲν κυριόδουλον.
2. εἰς τοὺς αἰῶνας = forever.
3. ἐν τρισὶν ὑποστάσεσι.
4. πῶς δέ ἐστιν ὑπὲρ τὸ πῶς ἐστι.
5. John 1:18.
6. Matt. 11:27.
7. τῆς θείας . . . φύσεως. See Wis. 13:5.
8. κατ᾽ οὐσίαν.
9. ὑπὲρ αὐτὸ τὸ εἶναι ὤν.
10. ὑπὲρ οὐσίαν.
11. προβολέα. The term ὁ προβολεὺς and its various forms, such as πρόβλημα or προβολὴ = prolatio = emanation is not much used among the Fathers, because of its gnostic overtones, this being the classical gnostic terminology

in reference to the emanations of the aeons. By the Damascene's time gnosticism was not so much a danger as it had been.

12. ἀπαύγασμα might also be translated *splendor* or *effulgence*.

13. χαρακτὴρ τῆς πατρικῆς ὑποστάσεως.

14. ἐνυπόστατον = enhypostate.

15. κατὰ πάντα ὅμοιον τῷ πατρί. This is virtually the old Homoian formula; but Homoianism is dead and the terminology is no longer a danger. Besides, when Arianism long ago reached its logical development in Anomoianism the quasi-legitimacy of Homoian expression gained a quasi-recognition. And John does except unbegottenness from the generality of the formula.

16. μονογενὴς δὲ ὅτι μόνος ἐκ μόνου τοῦ πατρὸς μόνως ἐγεννήθη. This is much the same thing that Gregory of Nazianz expressed in § 983 and § 994 in a much wordier fashion, and where, unwilling to do much paraphrasing, I found it extremely difficult to reproduce his thought in an intelligible fashion,—and perhaps did not entirely succeed. I might also add that while I believe all that the Damascene states in this place about the Only-begotten, I am still not convinced that the term itself expresses so much. The mind of the Byzantine philosopher, however, is not precisely on the same wave-length as that of the rest of humanity. Byzantine philosophy, in fact, is not incapable of trying to play poker with a pinochle deck—and succeeding.

17. Note that in our currently accepted terminology we do not contrast generation and procession. We say that in the Godhead there are two processions: generation and spiration. Thus we make procession a genus, and generation (and spiration) species. The Son's procession is generation, and it embraces the relations of paternity and filiation. The Spirit's procession is spiration, embracing the relations of active and passive spiration. The Father and the Son (*Filioque*) are the Spirator; the Spirit is the Spirated. See also §§ 2344, 2346, and 2362.

18. ἐν μόναις δὲ ταῖς ἰδιότησι.

19. τὸ τέλειον τῆς ὑποστάσεως.

20. αἱ ὑποστάσεις.

21. John 14:11.

22. Ex. 3:14.

23. πέλαγος οὐσίας.

24. οὐσίας.

25. τοῦ τῆς ὑπάρξεως τρόπου.

26. τὰ σύμπαντα.

27. φύσιν ἀσώματον.

28. πῦρ ἄϋλον. Insubstantial is to be taken in the sense of without matter. The term *immaterial* is no longer satisfactory for a technical term in English, having taken on too many other and immaterial connotations, often suggestive of Perry Mason or Agatha Christie.

29. Ps. 103[104]:4.

30. οὐσία νοερά.

31. ἀεικίνητος.

32. αὐτεξούσιος.

33. οὐσίας.

34. ἄνευ λόγου προφορικοῦ.

35. ἀόριστοι.

36. ἐν μετασχηματισμῷ.

37. ἔξωθεν τῆς οὐσίας.

38. κατ᾽ οὐσίαν.

39. φύσεως.

40. *The Celestial Hierarchy* 6, 2.

41. τὰς οὐρανίους οὐσίας ἐννέα.

42. ἡνῶσθαι.

43. Note that the nine choirs are given here in a descending order of dignity.

44. τῆς οἱασδήποτε οὐσίας.

45. οὐσία ζῶσα.

46. κατ᾽ οἰκείαν φύσιν.

47. αὐτεξούσιος.

48. 1 Tim. 2:4.

49. τῷ αὐτεξουσίῳ.

50. τῆς θείας προγνωστικῆς κελεύσεως.

51. περιχώρησιν.

52. τὴν καθ᾽ ὑπόστασιν ἔνωσιν.

53. Pope St. Leo the Great, *Letters* 10, 4.

54. 1 Cor. 2:8.

55. τῆς θείας . . . φύσεως.

56. John 3:13.

57. μίαν μὲν φύσιν.

58. τρεῖς δὲ ὑποστάσεις.

59. καὶ πάντα μὲν τὰ φυσικὰ καὶ οὐσιώδη, ἁπλᾶ φαμέν.
60. ἐν μόναις ταῖς τρισὶν ἰδιότησι.
61. οἰκονομίας.
62. τοῦ ἑνὸς τῆς ἁγίας τριάδος θεοῦ λόγου.
63. δύο μὲν φύσεις.
64. συνεληλυθυίας ἀλλήλαις.
65. καὶ καθ᾽ ὑπόστασιν ἑνωθείσας. This might also be translated: "and hypostatically united."
66. ἐν τῇ μιᾷ συνθέτῳ ὑποστάσει.
67. φυσικὰ ἰδιώματα.
68. ἐν τῇ τοῦ λόγου ὑποστάσει.
69. The Damascene is showing that the Word is one Person, and the incarnate Word is still one Person; and there are not, after the Incarnation, four Persons in the Trinity.
70. δύο . . . φύσεων.
71. εἰς ἓν πρόσωπον καὶ μίαν ὑπόστασιν.
72. τὸ συναμφότερον.
73. θεοτόκον.
74. ἀληθὴς θεοτόκος.
75. οὐ τῆς καθ᾽ ἡμᾶς φύσεως.
76. φύσις.
77. ἔχειν δὲ αὐτὸν καταλλήλως ταῖς δύο φύσεσι, διπλᾶ τὰ τῶν δύο φύσεων φυσικά.
78. δύο θελήσεις φυσικάς, . . . καὶ ἐνεργείας δύο φυσικάς, . . . καὶ αὐτεξούσια δύο φυσικά, . . . καὶ σοφίαν τε καὶ γνῶσιν, θείαν τε καὶ ἀνθρώπινον.
79. τὰς φύσεις.
80. ὡς ἐπὶ δύο φύσεων . . . ὡς ἐφ᾽ ἑνὸς προσώπου.
81. καὶ τοῦτο δὲ κἀκεῖνο εἰς μίαν ἀναφέρεται ἔννοιαν. More literally, "this or that, it goes back to one thought."
82. ἡ θεανδρικὴ ἐνέργεια. The term belongs to the Pseudo-Dionysius. See above, § 2279, note 1.
83. See Luke 2:52.
84. ἐξ ἄκρας ὑπάρξεως = from the point of subsistence.
85. οὐδὲ τὴν καθ᾽ ὑπόστασιν πρεσβεύουσι.
86. Read πειθόμενοι for πείθομαι.
87. ματαιόφρονι.
88. σχετικὴν ἕνωσιν.
89. ψιλὴν ἐνοίκησιν.
90. 1 Tim. 1:7.
91. μεταποιοῦνται.
92. ὁ τῆς προθέσεως ἄρτος. My term *the bread on the credence table* seems fairly apt, though a more literal translation were *the bread of exposition*. πρόθεσις is a *setting forth* or a *display*; and ἄρτοι τῆς προθέσεως is the Old Testament term for the *showbread* of Ex. 25:30. The πρόθεσις, however, is the name given the sideboard in Eastern churches, corresponding to the *credence* in Latin churches (from which also the secular term *credenza*). The point of John's use of the term, at any rate, is to make it clear that he is speaking of the bread prepared and displayed at the ready, but not yet consecrated.
93. ὑπερφυῶς μεταποιοῦνται.
94. οὐκ ἔστι τύπος.
95. Matt. 26:26, 28.
96. ἀντίτυπα.
97. θεοφόρος. See the liturgy of St. Basil at p. 195 in the IEPATIKON published in Rome, 1950. The Damascene, however, does Basil no service with the present explanation of how the term antitype is used. Apparently John Damascene, like so many after him, does not really understand the relationship between type and antitype; or at any rate he does not use these terms in the way that has become standard. See § 853j, note 142, above in Vol. 1, where Cyril of Jerusalem correctly refers to the consecrated Bread and Wine as antitype; and remember that a type is a figure, and an antitype is the reality. An antitype is not as the Damascene supposes, a prefigure or foreshadow. For example, Melchisedech is a type of Christ, and Christ is the antitype of Melchisedech. With the Eucharist there is a special problem in that the type actually becomes sacramentally the antitype. The bread and wine on the credence table is a type of both the Incarnational Body and the Eucharistic Body of Christ. The Body of Christ, whether His Incarnational Body or His Eucharistic Body, is the antitype of that typical bread and wine. The consecrated Bread and Wine on the altar has become and is the real Body of Christ in sacramental manner. That Bread and Wine, therefore, is correctly termed the antitype: it is Christ.
98. Matt. 7:6.
99. θεοφόρος.
100. θεοτόκος.
101. ὄντως κυρίως καὶ ἀληθῶς θεοτόκος καὶ κύρια καὶ πάντων κτισμάτων δεσπόζουσα.
102. τῆς θεομήτορος.
103. In the square Aramaic alphabet employed in writing Hebrew these five letters have each a second form, a final, employed always and only when the letter is in the final position in a word.

104. πανάρετος = all-virtuous.

105. ἐν τῷ κιβωτῷ.

106. St. Clement of Rome was thought by some to be the author of the so-called *Canons of the Apostles*. A variant reading at this point in the Damascene's text has: "and the Canons of the Holy Apostles and two Epistles by Clement." With this latter reading, of course, it is not clear whether Clement is designated as author of the Canons and of the two letters, or only of the two letters, while the Holy Apostles are designated as author of the Canons. For excerpts from the two letters or epistles, see §§ 10a-29a and §§§ 101-106 above. Passages from the *Canons of the Apostles* are at §§ 1237-1239 above.

107. John 2:1.

108. Heb. 13:4.

109. Matt. 13:43.

APOLOGETIC SERMONS AGAINST THOSE WHO REJECT SACRED IMAGES [*post A. D.* 725]

The *Apologetic Sermons against Those Who Reject Sacred Images* are three in number, and are among St. John Damascene's earliest writings.

The first followed quickly upon the first Iconoclastic edict of the Emperor Leo the Isaurian. It was written, therefore, in 726 or 727 A. D.; and it is addressed to the Patriarch Germain of Constantinople and to his people. The second of the *Apologetic Sermons* is in reaction to Leo's second edict, and was written in 730 A. D. The third cannot be dated, except that it is later and probably not much later than the other two. Rather than being a directly anti-Iconoclast statement the third *Apologetic Sermon* so-called is really more of a positive dogmatic treatment of sacred images.

The text in Migne, PG 94, 1231-1420, is still the standard.

2377

[2, 5]

We would certainly be in error if we were making an image of the invisible God; for what is incorporeal and invisible and uncircumscribable and without defined figure is not able to be depicted. And again, if we were making images of men and thought them gods, and adored them as gods, certainly we would be impious. But we do not do any of these things.

1
124

2378

[3, 41]

We worship and adore the Creator and Maker alone, as God who by His nature is to be worshiped (1). We worship also the Holy Mother of God (2), not as God, but as God's Mother according to the flesh. Moreover we worship also the saints, as elect friends of God, and as having gotten ready audience with Him.

1
121
780

1. ὡς φύσει προσκυνητῷ θεῷ.

2. τῇ ἁγίᾳ θεοτόκῳ.

PAMPHLET ON RIGHT-MINDEDNESS

The *Pamphlet on Right-mindedness* is an extended declaration of faith written while John was still residing in Damascus. It was drawn up at the request of a certain Bishop Elias, who had formerly been a Monothelite, and who now wanted the work so that he could present it as his confession of faith to his Metropolitan, Peter of Damascus.

The standard text is still that of Migne, PG 94, 1421-1432.

2379

[2]

And Christ is one, one Lord, one Son of God and Man, the same one being   322
perfect God and perfect Man, one Person composed (1) of divinity and humanity,   324
composed of two natures (2), and the same one Person having two natures and
subsisting in two perfect natures through each of which He has His fitting measure
and rationale (3). Son of God according to His incorporeal generation from the
Father before the ages, the same is Son of Man according to His salvific acceptance
of flesh in these last days. In the first generation, as God, He is from the Father and
without a mother; in the second generation, as Man, the same is from a Mother and
without a father. There are two natures and one Person (4). . . . But I am speaking
of one composite hypostasis. For the animate flesh (5) of the Lord does not subsist
by itself, nor does it have its own hypostasis, nor did it become this particular Man (6)
by itself, but it became such with God the Word, and had Him for hypostasis. I do
therefore confess and proclaim with mind and heart and mouth that the Holy
Virgin Mary is properly and truly Mother of God (7) who truly gave birth to the   780
Only-begotten Son of God who before the ages was by nature God, when He had taken
flesh of her.

1. μία ὑπόστασις σύνθετος.
2. ἐκ δύο φύσεων.
3. ὅρον τε καὶ λόγον.
4. δύο φύσεις καὶ μία ὑπόστασις.
5. ἡ ἔμψυχος σάρξ.
6. ὁ δεῖνα.
7. θεοτόκον.

TO THE JACOBITE BISHOP OF DARAEA

The Greek title of this work has very probably been garbled in the text tradition: Πρὸς
τὸν ἐπίσκοπον δῆθεν Τουδαραίας τὸν Ἰακωβίτην. The import of δῆθεν
Τουδαραίας is not at all clear. δῆθεν seems a very strange particle here. It is a
strengthened form of δή and means *in truth* or *really*; but it is most often used in irony,
its implication then being *supposed but not real*, or *putative*. As to *Toudaraias*: it can
hardly be the bishop's name, which in the present context would require neither a
nominative nor a genitive, but an accusative. Taking the word as being a genitive, it
might well be the name of the bishop's diocese; but who ever heard of a place called
Toudaraia? There was a town called Daras or Daraea about six miles from Damascus,
however, and it seems clear enough to me that Τουδαραίας should be read τοῦ
Δαραίας.

Whatever the precise title, the work is a lengthy letter written by John at the request
of Peter of Damascus to a Jacobite (Monophysite) bishop in regard to conversion.

The text in Migne, PG 94, 1435-1502, is still the standard, except that it should be
supplemented from an article by F. Diekamp. Migne's text and that of his predecessors
has considerable lacunae in it; but in the course of publishing a newly discovered work
of John entitled *On the Faith, against the Nestorians*, F. Diekamp included also
passages to fill out the gaps in the present work: see the *Theologische Quartalschrift*,
Vol. 83 (1901), pp. 555-595.

2380

[52]

Being God beforehand He afterwards became flesh, that is, Man, and is said   324

to be one composite Person (1) of the two natures (2); and in that Person the
two natures are united through the assumption of flesh (3), the divinity and the
humanity, and they are mutually situated within each other (4), the which
circuminsession is initiated by the divine nature (5). For the divinity communicates
to the flesh its own glory and splendor, but does not partake of the passions of the
flesh. Therefore the nature of the flesh is deified (6), but it does not carnalize the   321
nature of the Word (7). [The divine nature] deifies the assumed nature, but is not carnalized
[by the assumed nature]. The lesser is advantaged by the greater, but the greater is not
weakened by the lesser. For just as iron is subjected to the fire, but the fire is not made
iron; and just as the flesh is animated by a soul, but the soul is not carnalized by the flesh;
so too the divine nature deifies the flesh, but is not itself carnalized.

1. μία . . . ὑπόστασις σύνθετος.
2. τῶν δύο φύσεων.
3. διὰ τῆς σαρκώσεως.
4. καὶ περιχωροῦσιν ἐν ἀλλήλαις. This is a rather difficult clause because of its use of a less than standard verb. It might
    be translated quite literally: "and they sit around in each other"; and in any case the notion of circuminsession is quite
    clear.
5. ἡ δὲ περιχώρησις ἐκ τῆς θεότητος γίνεται.
6. ἡ . . . φύσις τῆς σαρκὸς θεοῦται.
7. οὐ σαρκοῖ δὲ τὴν φύσιν τοῦ λόγου.

DIALOGUE AGAINST THE MANICHEANS

The Damascene's *Dialogue against the Manicheans* is a refutation of Manichean
dualism. The work is in the form of a dialogue between a Catholic and a Manichean,
probably directed against the Paulicians, a dualist sect which came to prominence in the
East in the latter half of the seventh century. A work of essentially the same content but
considerably shorter than the *Dialogue*, entitled *Disputation of the Orthodox John with a
Manichean*, was first published by Cardinal Mai in 1847 and is reprinted by Migne in
PG 96, 1319-1336.
    The standard text of the *Dialogue against the Manicheans* is in Migne, PG 94,
1505-1584.

2381

[37]
    A judge justly punishes one who is guilty of wrongdoing; and if he does not   193
punish him he is himself a wrongdoer. In punishing him the judge is not the cause
either of the wrongdoing or of the vengeance taken against the wrongdoer, the cause
being the wrongdoer's freely chosen actions. Thus too God, who saw what was
going to happen as if it had already happened, judged it as if it had taken place;
and if it was evil, that was the cause of its being punished. It was God who created
man, so of course He created him in goodness; but man did evil of his own free
choice, and is himself the cause of the vengeance that overtakes him.

2382

[79]
    God's foreknowledge, as a power, does not have its cause from us; but His   190
foreknowing of what we are certainly going to do, that does have its cause from
us. For if we were not going to do something, He would not foreknow that we were, and

neither would it be done. God's foreknowledge is true and inviolable, but it is not the cause itself, purely and simply, of what is going to be done. It is because we are going to do this or that, that He foreknows it.

THE HOLY TRINITY

The Damascene's work entitled *The Holy Trinity* is a short essay in question and answer form. It deals not only with the doctrine of the Trinity but also with the more important points of Christology.

The text of *The Holy Trinity* is in Migne, PG 95, 9-18.

2383

[1]

In regard to the consubstantial and life-giving Holy Trinity we confess one nature, one will, one operation, one virtue and power and domination, as also one Godhead, three Hypostases or Persons (1), while preserving the propriety (2) of each Person. In the plan of the Incarnation (3) of one Person of the Holy Trinity, that is, our Lord Jesus Christ, there are two natures involved, the divine and the human, two wills likewise and two operations, but one Hypostasis or one Person, because He is one and the same who before the ages was begotten incorporeally and not as effluence, and who in these most recent times was conceived of the Holy Ever-Virgin Mary, Mother of God (4) in an indescribable manner and inviolately. The same Person is whole man and God. In one hypostasis, He is acknowledged, in respect to the divine nature, not to be subject to suffering, but subject to suffering in respect to the assumed nature. And after parturition, of course, the signs of virginity, the seals so to speak, were kept safe.

238

302
330
332
324
780

783

1. ὅτι καὶ μία θεότης τρεῖς ὑποστάσεις ἤτοι τρία πρόσωπα.
2. τῆς ἰδιότητος.
3. ἐπὶ δὲ τῆς ἐνσάρκου οἰκονομίας.
4. τῆς θεοτόκου.

THE TWO WILLS IN CHRIST

Besides the work addressed *To the Jacobite Bishop of Daraea*, which combats Monophysite theology, the Damascene wrote also a work against Monothelitism, entitled *The Two Wills in Christ*. This latter work is very similar in content and argument to writings on the same subject by St. Maximus the Confessor († 662).

The text of *The Two Wills in Christ* is in Migne, PG 95, 127-186.

2384

[8]

Since in Father and Son and Holy Spirit the subsistence of each is distinct (1), there are three Persons (2). And since each does not will and operate in His own peculiar fashion nor separately and apart from the others, but conjointly, there are not three gods but one God.

238

2385

[19]

God Himself has given us the power of doing good. And He made us self-determining   690
(3) so that the good might be produced both from Himself and from us. Whenever a
choice is made that prefers the good, God is cooperating in the good in such a way
that we may do things that are, while consistent with our nature, yet above our
nature.

2386

[27]

In our Lord Jesus Christ there are, in accord with His diversity of nature, two   331
wills; but they are not in opposition to each other. For neither His natural human
will nor His natural faculty of willing nor those things naturally subject to it nor
the natural use of His will are opposed to His divine will. For the divine will is   343
Creator of all things in accord with nature; but whatever things are contrary to nature,
those things alone are contrary to the divine will. Such things are sin, the desire,
in accord with one's selfish purpose, for criminal pleasures. This the Lord did
not take upon Himself. "For He did no sin, nor was deceit found in His mouth (4)."   345
And since the Person of Christ is one, and Christ is one, there is one who wills by both
natures: as God, approving, and as Man, made obedient (5).

1. διάφορος ἡ ἑκάστου ὕπαρξις.
2. τρεῖς ὑποστάσεις εἰσίν.
3. αὐτεξουσίους = self-powered. The noun of this term (here an adjectival usage) is usually translated *free will*.
4. Is. 53:9.
5. ὡς θεός, εὐδοκῶν, καὶ ὡς ἄνθρωπος, ὑπήκοος γενόμενος.

AGAINST THE HERESY OF THE NESTORIANS

Besides the present treatise *Against the Heresy of the Nestorians* the Damascene wrote
also another essay against Nestorianism entitled *On the Faith, against the Nestorians*
(Περὶ πίστεως κατὰ Νεστοριανῶν), the latter first published by F. Diekamp in the
Theologische Quartalschrift, Vol. 83 (1901), pp. 555-595.
The text of the treatise *Against the Heresy of the Nestorians* is in Migne, PG 95,
187-224.

2387

[43]

We proclaim the Holy Virgin the Theotokos (1), because it is she who bore   780
God when the Lord truly became incarnate of her. We know that she is the
Christotokos, because she bore Christ. But since the snake-bit (2) Nestorius abused this
latter term to the detriment of the word Theotokos, we do not call her Christotokos at all,
but look only to the more excellent and call her Theotokos.

1. θεοτόκος = God-bearer = Mother of God.
2. θεήλατος = god-pursued. I think we have no directly corresponding term in English; but the idea is much the same as
   the term *snake-bit* in colloquial usage. No doubt the term *ill-fated* would also satisfy.

HOMILIES

The collected corpus of the Damascene's *Homilies* contains thirteen items. Two others can be found among his lesser dogmatic writings. The thirteen homilies of the collection are: 1) on the Transfiguration of our Lord; 2) on the Withered Fig; 3) for Good Friday; 4) for Holy Saturday; 5-6) on the Annunciation to Mary; 7-8) on the Nativity of the Blessed Virgin Mary; 9-11) on the Dormition of the Blessed Virgin Mary; 12) in Praise of St. John Chrysostom; and 13) in Praise of St. Barbara.

Otto Bardenhewer regarded nos. 5, 6, and 8 as certainly spurious, and no. 7 as probably spurious. More recent scholarship has rescued no. 7; and Franz Dölger recognizes the authenticity of nos. 1-4, 7, 9-13. (See Dölger's *Der griechische Barlaam-Roman ein Werk des H. Johannes von Damaskos*, Ettal 1953, p. [IX].)

The three homilies on the Dormition of the Blessed Virgin Mary were all delivered on the same day, on the Feast of Mary's Assumption into heaven. A later hand has made an insertion into the second of these three homilies. § 2389 is authentic to the Damascene. § 2390 is from the later insertion; but it is interesting enough to be included here anyway. I do not know the Euthymian history; possibly it is to be related in some way to the Armenian St. Euthymius who was the founder of monasteries, including that of St. Sabas or Mar Saba, where the Damascene was a monk. See the note in Migne, PG 96, 747.

The unauthentic first homily on the Annunciation is preserved only in Arabic. The unauthentic second homily on the Nativity of Mary is correctly ascribable to Theodore Studites († 826).

The text of the thirteen *Homilies* is in Migne, PG 96, 545-816.

HOMILY ON THE WITHERED FIG

2388

[2, 3]

If [Adam and Eve] were naked as to the body, they were covered yet by divine grace. They had no physical cloak (1), but they did have the garment of innocence (2). For to the degree that they were, by their obedience, the familiar friends of God, to that same degree they were clothed in the garment of innocence. But when they disobeyed they were immediately stripped of their covering of grace. They were stripped naked, moreover, of their enrapturement in the contemplation of God (3). They saw the nakedness of their own bodies. They yearned for the delights of life; but they were brought down to a poor and impoverished life.

521

612

SECOND HOMILY ON THE DORMITION OF MARY

2389

[10, 8]

We had closed Paradise; you opened again the entryway to the tree of life. We turned joys into sorrow; you turned sorrow back into the greatest of joys for us. And how would you, the Immaculate (4), taste of death? You are the bridge to life, you are the staircase to heaven; and [for you] death will be but a passageway to immortality. O Most Blessed, truly blessed art thou!

786

2390

[10, 18]

In the Euthymian history, book 3, chapter 40, it is written quite eloquently: 787

". . . In answer, Juvenal replied: 'In the Holy and divinely-inspired Scripture no mention   100
is made of anything concerning the end of Mary the Holy Mother of God (5); but   780
we have received from ancient and most truthful tradition that at the time of her
glorious repose (6), all the Holy Apostles, who then were dispersed abroad in the world
for the salvation of the nations, were in but a moment of time transported through
the air to Jerusalem; and when they were there an angelic vision appeared to them,
and the divine chanting of the supernal powers was heard. And thus in divine and
heavenly glory her holy soul was delivered in a way that no word can describe
into the hands of God. And her body, which had been the Tabernacle of God (7),
after the chanting of the angels and of the Apostles was finished and last respects
were paid, was placed in a coffin in Gethsemani (8). In that place the chanting and
choral singing of the angels continued without cease for three days. After the third
day the angelic chanting ceased.

"'The Apostles were present there when Thomas, the only one who had been absent,
arrived after the third day; and since he wanted to worship the body that had been
the Tabernacle of God (9), they opened the coffin. And they were unable anywhere
to find her most lauded body. When they found only her grave wrappings there, and
the indescribable perfume which was borne aloft from them, they sealed the coffin.
Struck by the wonder of the mystery they could only think that He who had been
pleased to become incarnate from her in His own Person and to become Man and to
be born in the flesh, God the Word, the Lord of Glory, who preserved her
virginity intact after her parturition,—He was pleased even after her departure from   783
life to honor her immaculate and undefiled body with incorruption and with
translation prior to the common and universal resurrection.'"   1012

1. σωματικὸν περιβόλαιον.
2. ἔνδυμα ἀφθαρσίας. The term ἀφθαρσία means *incorruption*, from which it acquires also the sense of *immortality*.
   Here, however, and in the next sentence, it seems to mean *innocence*.
3. τῆς πρὸς θεὸν ἐκστάσεως καὶ θεωρίας. They lost their ecstasy and contemplation. In the absence of contemplation, of
   course, ecstasy likewise departed. And it was because of their ecstatic preoccupation with seeing God in their
   contemplation that they had not previously noticed that they were naked. No longer being able to see God they were no
   longer preoccupied; and now they saw themselves and each other, and saw that they were naked.
4. ἡ ἄχραντος.
5. οὐκ ἐμφέρεται τὰ κατὰ τὴν τελευτὴν τῆς ἁγίας θεοτόκου Μαρίας.
6. κοιμήσεως.
7. τὸ δὲ θεοδόκον αὐτῆς σῶμα.
8. ἐν σορῷ τῇ ἐν Γεθσημανῇ κατετέθη.
9. τὸ θεοδόκον σῶμα προσκυνῆσαι.

INDEX OF SCRIPTURAL REFERENCES AND CITATIONS

The reference numbers are to the consecutive numbering of the text passages rather than to pages, whether the Scripture reference be pertinent to the passage itself or to its accompanying notes. Passages which require Septuagint consultation are marked *Sept.*; and in these the numbering is that of the Septuagint. Passages 1-910u are in Vol. 1; 911-1416 are in Vol. 2; and 1417-2390 are in Vol. 3.

DOCTRINAL INDEX

In the following index points of doctrine are numbered consecutively. After each doctrinal statement appear the numbers of the passages of THE FAITH OF THE EARLY FATHERS which have some bearing upon that doctrinal statement. The passage itself will usually be found to be an affirmation of the doctrinal statement; but in some instances it will be found to be in contradiction to it. In the latter case the passage number is enclosed in parentheses. The Fathers and the early Christian Writers do not agree with each other with a precise mathematical unanimity, nor could it be expected that they would. And in any case we must stress that an isolated patristic text is in no instance to be regarded as a ''proof'' of a particular doctrine. Dogmas are not ''proved'' by patristic statements but by the infallible teaching instruments of the Church. The value of the Fathers and Writers is this: that in the aggregate they demonstrate what the Church did and does yet believe and teach. In the aggregate they provide a witness to the content of Tradition, that Tradition which itself is a vehicle of revelation.

Passage numbers 1-910u are to be found in Vol. 1; 911-1416 in Vol. 2; and 1417-2390 in Vol. 3.

NATURAL RELIGION

1. The concept of religion:
     631   635   1603   1743   2236   2377   2378
2. Man has a natural tendency toward religion [see also 130].
     270   275   1841

REVEALED RELIGION

REVELATION

10. Revelation deserves the assent of reason [see also 558].
     173   354a   455   562   818b   1179   1321
11. In the present order revelation is for us a moral necessity.
     334   629   1557   1746
12. Miracles are possible.
     1697   1773
13. Miracles provide an external criterion of revelation [see also 82].
     133b   1784   1819
14. Miracles do not of themselves, however, suffice to confirm the truth of doctrine.
     638
15. Prophecy provides another external criterion of revelation [see also 81].
     57   61   175   276a   530   626   1497   1615
16. There are also internal criteria of revelation: sentiments of the soul.
     1265   1557   1593   1822

SACRED SCRIPTURE

INSPIRATION

20. The Sacred Scriptures, written under the inspiration of the Holy Spirit, have God for their author [see also 50].
     22   26b   122b   123   126   149   185   203   328b   390a   400   404   447a   468a   483   577   976
     1045   1078   1089a   1286   1479   1588   2158   2167   2302
21. Inspiration consists in the action of God's using the intellect and will of the sacred writer after the fashion of an instrument.
     122b   149   162   163   175   179   388   910a   1609   1766   2302
22. The primary object of such inspiration is the things that concern salvation.
     149   818b   1045   1479   1687   1709   2096
23. Nevertheless inspiration extends to all parts of Sacred Scripture and in some sense even to the words themselves.
     483   979   2158
24. But inspiration does not carry with it the revelation of those things to be written which the writer was able, with divine help, to know in a natural way.
     1612   1767
25. No error can be found in the Sacred Scriptures.
     22   138   203   390a   400   480   1106   1347   1417   1421   1597   1612

26. Every assertion made by the sacred writer is true according to the meaning which he wished to express and did express.
    1409 1610a 1611 1804
27. Bearing in mind that every assertion made by the sacred writer is true according to the meaning which he wished to express and did express, the presence of apparent errors in Scripture in regard to history and the sciences can be explained.
    138 1376 1421 1687 2096
28. With the possible exception of the Septuagint the versions of Sacred Scripture are not inspired.
    1347 1421 1597
29. Some of the Fathers believed that the Septuagint version was made under inspiration.
    149a 819
30. In regard to the several senses of Scripture:
    447a 469 480 1588
31. The reading of the Scriptures is recommended also to the laity.
    1159a

CANONICITY

40. The sole criterion of canonicity is Catholic Tradition, which has its basis in Apostolic Tradition.
    341 745s 819 1584 1607 1896
41. The Tridentine canon of the Old Testament is founded in Catholic Tradition.
    190 484 745t 791 819 882 910t 1020 1078 1239 1344 1372 1397 1585 2015b
    2167 2373
42. So also is the Tridentine canon of the New Testament founded in Catholic Tradition.
    94 95 211 268 341 439-440 479a? 503 538 652 652b 653 656 745t 791 819 910t
    1020 1078 1239 1344 1585 2015b 2167 2373

THE OLD LAW

50. God is the Author of the Law, both the Old and the New [see also 20].
    185 230 276a 410a 421a 445 680 1093 1567 1895 2205
51. The purpose of the Old Law was to prepare for the coming of Christ [see also 300].
    61 134b 188 303a 834a 1093 1599 1600 1602 1897 2205
52. The Old Law, therefore, is abrogated by the revelation of the New Law.
    45 46 96 133a 134a 1599 1602 1897 2205

THE GOSPEL

60. Gospel: meaning of the word. The single and fourfold gospel:
    5 7a 9 20 31 57 60 61 81a 112 128 195 208 215 238 288 427 1825 2291
61. The authenticity and historicity of the four Gospels was acknowledged in Christian antiquity.
    129 141 143 199a 208 214 215 268 339 341 439-440 474 503 538 1597 2152
62. The witnesses who affirm the genuinity of the four Gospels are worthy of belief.
    (201) 212 (261) 264
63. The four Gospels contain true histories.
    60 195 264 268 519 619 666 1170 1615 1784
64. The authenticity and historicity of the Gospel of Matthew:
    1 5 7a 10 95 143 167 208 214 339 341 439-440 503 538 1606
65. The authenticity and historicity of the Gospel of Mark:
    13 24 31 95 208 214 268 339 341 439-440 503 538 651bb 652
66. The authenticity and historicity of the Gospel of Luke:
    1 63 143 195 208 214 217 268 339 341 439-440 503 538
67. The Gospel of John is also authentic and historic, although it takes a spiritual approach to history.
    182 208 214 264 268 339 341 439-440 503 538 1825
68. The genuinity of the four Gospels is confirmed from the apocryphal gospels.
    474 1241a-d
69. The genuinity of the four Gospels is confirmed also from the manner in which the heretics of antiquity made use of them.
    195 214 339 340 341 474 2152

DIVINE ORIGIN OF CHRISTIANITY

80. Jesus Christ came into the world as a divine legate [see also 302 and 310].
    47 51 54b 290 405 520 1746 2077

81. The predictions of the Prophets fulfilled in Christ prove His mission divine [*see also* 15 *and* 300].
    61 122 125 127 222 468a 638 1135 1470 1615
82. The divine character of Christ's mission is proved also by His miracles [*see also* 13].
    109 122 189 618 619 1031 1032 1094 1784 1819
83. Christ's predictions of the future, which have been fulfilled, prove his mission divine.
    116 654
84. The Resurrection of Christ is proved by arguments that are certain.
    13 47 51 63 129 665 818a 1156 1471
85. The wonderful spread of Christianity along with its continued endurance serve to prove its divine origin [*see also* 404 *and* 405].
    274 279 282 320a 369 555-556 621 1614 1783 1784
86. The virtues of Christians when compared to the vices of the pagans argue to the divine origin of Christianity and its teachings.
    97 112 186 271 273 274 280 281 283 285 2167a 2167d
87. The change in moral values which comes with conversion argues to the divine origin of Christianity and its teachings.
    118 263 276 369 621 661a
88. Martyrdom is a testimony to the truth of the Christian religion.
    11 63 144 243 285 640 1465
89. The internal character of Christian doctrine argues to its divine origin.
    118 192 276a 405
90. The Church's doctrine is in no way determined by popularity.
    1360a

TRADITION

100. Sacred Tradition is a true source of revelation.
    192 198 242 291 295 371 (818b) 917 954 1098 1213 1358 1419 1419a 1581 1631
    1899 2168 2172 2390
101. Sacred Tradition completes Sacred Scripture through its authentic interpretation thereof.
    242 291 443 1098 1419a 2168
102. Apostolic Tradition has always been acknowledged as the rule of faith.
    74 94 190a 191 192 209 210 211 212 213 257 264 293 296 298 329 341 394
    443 445 785 898 1043 1107 1623 1705 2142
103. There was a progressive revelation until the death of the Apostles.
    239 2329
104. Since the death of the Apostles it has not been possible for the body of revelation either to be augmented or diminished.
    2 213 226 242 288 289 293 785 972 1181 2169 2173
105. Nevertheless the proposition that there is a certain progress in dogma is not in every sense to be rejected.
    226 328a 371 444 1145a 1765 2173 2174
106. Unanimity of the Fathers in matters of faith and morals provides certitude.
    1898 1899 1900 2004 2142 2168 2175
107. As private teachers, however, the Fathers can err.
    190a 1255 1623 2175

RELIGION AND CULT

120. Among the acts of religion there is prayer [*see also* 712].
    26a 55 79 281b 557a 1154 2001
121. The saints in heaven are worthy objects of worship, which worship, however, is not the same as that given to God.
    81 572 1109 1285 1603 2378
122. There is a communion of saints by which the souls of the just dead, knowing us and our needs, pray for us.
    852 1396 1513 1603 1770 1935
123. Christian tradition bears witness to the honoring of relics.
    70 81 1738 2148 2294a 2295a
124. The honoring of sacred images is lawful and pious.
    952 2095 2377
125. The cross of our Lord is to be held in honor, whether it be a question of its actual relics, or images of it, or the sign of the cross made by the motion of the hand.
    367 751a 824 954 1240 1815 1844 2233c

THE ONE GOD
EXISTENCE OF GOD

130. The existence of God is able to be known with certainty by the natural light of reason.
    197 228 269 270 275 287 331 334 416 455 645 662 888 984 1130 1392 1593
    1693

131. Man is able to arrive at a knowledge of God from a consideration of the order in the visible world.
    152 172 198 228 269 332 515 624 662 746 747 959 984 987 1050 1117 1146
    1182 1315 1508 1841 2137 2338

132. Man is able to arrive at a knowledge of God from a consideration of the government of providence.
    110 172 269 987 1032 1557

133. Man is able to arrive at a knowledge of God from the dictates of conscience.
    411 1146 1557 2315

134. Positive revelation is not necessary in order to arrive at a natural knowledge of God.
    (227) 269 1182 1508

135. There is a certain natural knowledge of God's existence innate in men [see also 2].
    130 270 332 403 425 662 987 1182 1841 2093 2137 2338

136. On the direct perception of God in this life:
    1545

137. The existence of God is provable *a posteriori*.
    334 1596 2339

ESSENCE OF GOD

140. The essence of God is existence itself, whence His proper name, Yahweh [see also 174].
    729 786 857 877 993 1015 1046 1262 1367 1489 1493 1591a 1596 1649 1669
    2098 2345

141. God is existence, of Himself and independently.
    754 860 861 932 991 993 1367 1489

ATTRIBUTES OF GOD

150. The divine attributes are really the same as the divine substance (essence).
    192a 199b 229 1481 1664 1666 1669 1670 1676 1748

151. God is utterly simple and admits of no composition whatever.
    199b 321 424 451 754 756 786 822a 911 923 1041 1066 1122 1128 1266 1660
    1669 2066 2067 2081

152. God is spirit.
    111 152 164 277 374 451 452 822b 894 1066 1105 1128 2050 2081 2094 2351

153. God has every perfection in an infinite degree.
    229 423 815 1042 1320 1712 2081 2341

154. God is immeasurable and is present everywhere.
    85 177 234a 424 608 754 815 860 893 894 899 1070 1105 1266 2119 2156
    2304 2353

155. God is completely unchangeable.
    111 132 814 815 1046 1493 1663 1758 2264

156. God is eternal.
    110 152 161 164 206 321 331 608 628 814 822a 860 899 1015 1367 1481 2264

157. God is one and unique.
    45 191 194 196 199a 203 205 274a 275 290 322 328a 331 397 445 515 608
    1089a 1551 2236 2341

158. God is all-powerful.
    111 171 194 205 323 325 402 424 628 651f 815 822a 910a 1089a 1366 1711 1741

KNOWLEDGE ABOUT GOD

170. No creature can of its unaided nature see God.
    236 270 451 452 747 891 986 1075 1106 1123 1125 1126 1127 1128 1161 1398
    1653 2150 2212

171. In regard to seeing God with bodily eyes:
    452 645 1786 1787

172. A creature can be elevated to the sight of God, as in fact is done for the angels and the blessed.
    236 822 988 989 1106 1114 1398 1752 1786 2150 2303
173. God is incomprehensible and inexpressible.
    164 205 234a 270 450 603 668 747 756 786 860 861 900 923 931 984 1015
    1023 1041 1042 1075 1124 1125 1127 1128 1161 1239a 1266 1393 1505 2160 2338
174. We cannot, properly speaking, know the essence of God.
    130 270 416 623 821 923 988 1048 1049 1121 1122 1123 1130 1161 2073 2074
    2340
175. We do arrive at some knowledge of God through various concepts which describe Him.
    192a 199b 331 423 424 455 603 786 821 894 900 908 930 985 1015 1047 1048
    1049 1122 2094
176. The concepts we employ in arriving at a descriptive knowledge of God are at best extremely faulty.
    760a 1047 2073
177. The concepts we employ in arriving at a descriptive knowledge of God are faulty because they cannot be understood of God in the same way in which they are understood of creatures.
    270 623 754 760a 908 1028 1320 1596 2313
178. We attempt to arrive at some knowledge of the perfections of God from a consideration of His creatures, by the *way of negation*.
    110 423 1047 1048 1658 2074 2340
179. We attempt to arrive at some knowledge of the perfections of God from a consideration of His creatures, by the *way of causality*.
    110 455 923 931 1050 1596
180. We attempt to arrive at some knowledge of the perfections of God from a consideration of His creatures, by the *way of eminence*.
    110 450 674 908 1028 1048 1266 1671 2340
181. The names of God are not synonyms.
    930 933 1047 1049

GOD'S OWN KNOWLEDGE

188. God has perfect knowledge of Himself.
    205 270 821 931 1161 2073 2239
189. God knows all things, not only of the present but even of the future, as with a single intuitive act.
    166 177 202 397 429 471 815 822a 1059 1377 1803 2069 2313
190. God's foreknowledge is not the cause of future events.
    471 663 1175 1405 1408 1547 2162 2258 2382
191. God knows all future events, even those which shall come about through man's exercise of free will.
    116 1272 1405 1707 1740 1742 1928 2069 2162 2258 2359
192. God's foreknowledge of events in no way destroys or detracts from man's exercise of free will.
    663 1175 1405 1707 1742 2162
193. In regard to God's foreknowledge of evil [*see also* 469 *and* 638]:
    471 663 1175 1405 1547 1707 1742 2258 2359 2381
194. God knows even the outcome of future conditional events.
    471 1059 1996
195. The providence of God is extended to all His creatures.
    202 1014 1134 1377

PREDESTINATION AND REPROBATION

200. God desires the salvation of all men.
    93b 389 1053 1202 1279 1343 1366 2030 2358
201. St. Augustine's varying interpretations of 1 Tim. 2:4:
    1457 1735 1906 1927 1962 1964 1983 2030
202. In regard to the predestination of the saints:
    28 28a 37a 80a 435 1947 1994 2000 2003 2246
203. According to St. Augustine, God, the merciful dispenser of grace, predestines some to eternal life.
    1882 1951 1985 1988 2002
204. According to St. Augustine, predestination to faith and justification is utterly gratuitous.
    1427 1428 1443 1447 1837 1946 1985 1986 1989 1990 1997 1998 2001
205. For St. Augustine predestination is a mysterious work of God.
    1496 1882 1925 1949 1989 1995 2007
206. St. Augustine's idea of predestination as a call according to purpose and without revocation:
    1570 1948 1949 1959 1987 1988 1990 1991 1999

207. St. Augustine's idea of a specifically determined number of the elect:
  1951 1959 1960
208. St. Augustine's idea that predestination simply does not separate those who are not saved from the *massa perditionis* or "lump of perdition":
  1447 1946 1949 2000
209. St. Augustine knows, however, that none are damned unless they deserve to be damned.
  1496 1735 1901 1998
210. In regard to reprobation or predestination to damnation:
  466 1722 1882
211. For St. Fulgence of Ruspe predestination is a mysterious determination of God.
  2246 2254 2255 2266
212. Predestination, though a mysterious determination of God, does not take away free will.
  1366 2254
213. The idea that predestination is in view of God's foreknowledge of merits, in St. Ambrose and Theodoret:
  1272 2162
214. God reprobates none except those whom He foreknows will sin of their own free will.
  1202 2026 2033 2162 2257 2258
215. Since God reprobates none except those whom He foreknows will sin of their own free will, it may be said that anyone who is damned perishes of his own negligence.
  1053 1279 2030 2113 2254 2256

THE TRIUNE GOD

THE TRINITY

230. That God is triune is clear in the Tradition of the Church even in the pre-Nicene era [*see also* 826].
  20 23 28 40 47a 80 108 112 113 117 126 128 164 165 180 191 235 256 307
  371 376 377 394a 394b 408 445 452 470 479 546 557 596 608 608a 611 681
  701 792a 1650
231. In their struggle against Arianism the later Fathers appeal to the pre-Nicene trinitarian tradition.
  757 782 792a 1107
232. The Fathers believed that they could find in the Old Testament certain hints of the Trinity, the beginnings of a progressive revelation even in this regard.
  180 194 377 405 789 1090 1129 1317a
233. The Fathers did especially find evidence of the progressive revelation of the Trinity in Genesis 1:26.
  31 235 361 1399 1673 1860
234. The Trinity is expressed in the formula of Baptism [*see also* 826].
  784 789 858 910r 917 1246 1682
235. The Johannine comma [1 John 5:7b-8a] cited:
  378 557 1330 2216 2251
236. In regard to the theophanies:
  127 182 290 824 864 937 1400 1653
237. Although Father, Son, and Holy Spirit are one, they are yet distinct.
  (91) 164 179 371 376 596 611 768 778 779 904 907 910o 911 915 1068 1269
  1368 1672 1682 2084 2126 2280
238. Father, Son, and Holy Spirit are distinct in such a way that in the unity of one nature there are three Persons.
  371 376 378 782 898 907 910p 911 915 926 953 997 999 1008 1017 1029 1071
  1269 1650 1668 1752 2082 2090 2132 2251 2261 2337 2362 2383 2384
239. The Most Holy Trinity is a mystery.
  204 668 779 816 834 859 878 915 996 1029 1069 1269 1672 2084 2280 2337

PERSONS OF THE TRINITY

250. Only the Father does not proceed.
  479 608 634 679 814 880 915 917 932 934 936 983 1009 1040 1081 1239a
  1657 1681 2342
251. The Son was not made.
  164 442 470 675 756 761 764 765 866 971 1081 1086 1089a 1239a 2075 2076
252. The Son was truly born of the Father.
  153 373 374 391 540 608 651f 668 674 760 765 816 823 826 866 896 902 910a
  1039 1043 1089a 1271 1325d 2085 2343
253. The generation of the Son from the Father is not free.
  153 775 1102 2106

254. Although the generation of the Son from the Father is not free neither is it forced.
775 879 1102
255. Neither free nor yet forced, the generation of the Son from the Father is voluntary and natural.
470 608 862 879 971 1102 2066 2068 2126
256. The Son is co-eternal with the Father.
130 137? 153 182 189 200 205 391 393 401 442 470 608 611 651f 668 676
679 760 761 813 816 823 877 934 935 936 1009 1014 1040 1089a 1102 1262
1316 1317a 1325d 1460 1518 1656 1816 1859 2076 2126 2342
257. The Son is consubstantial *(homoousios)* with the Father.
153 277 (376) 392 398 409 540 608 651f 755 756 761 765 767 767a 768 769
783 787 792a 826 866 868 880 896 899 907 910a 910r 912 951a 952 970
994 1043 1072 1089a 1157a 1159b 1168 1254 1262 1264 1271 1317a 1656 1677
2015c 2106 2126 2199 2204
258. Between Father and Son there is an identity of nature and distinction of Persons.
374 375 376 409 536 636 862 881 902 952 970 971 1053 1157a 1656 2067
259. In some way the Father is greater than the Son.
256 374 376 608 636 679 896 915 940 1656
260. *Word (Verbum* or *Logos)* is the proper name of the Son.
45 205 290 608 632 632a 770 787 899 910s 969 994 1264 1678 2065 2070
261. The Son is called *Wisdom of the Father*.
137 165 182 373 460 540 674 764b 787 816 826 899 992 1264 1325d 1460
1577 1987 2075
262. The Son is called *Word (Sermo) of the Father*.
371 373 375 379 632 632a
263. The Son is called *Splendor of the Father*.
18 756 768 770 1072 2343
264. The Son is called *Image of the Father*.
536 611 674 746 764b 768 769 787 868 952 969 1006 1072 1317a 2056 2065
2078
265. The Son proceeds from the Father by an intellectual generation.
137 179 182 200 277 373 398 470 610 632 754 825 969 994 1677 1816 2065
2083 2259
266. The Holy Spirit is God.
377 680 779 784a 910a 910k 910m 910q 926 996 999 1089a 1393 1670 2078
2089 2107
267. That the Holy Spirit is God is proved by His operation.
780 1070 1071 1089a 1283 1285 1561 2080 2107 2114
268. The Holy Spirit is consubstantial *(homoousios)* with the Father and the Son.
611 783 784 784a 907 910a 910f 910k 910r 940 951a 996 1040 1069 1081
1082 1089a 1246 1286 1650 1750 2015c 2079 2114 2126 2212 2216
269. The Holy Spirit proceeds from the Father.
164 910a 910s 915 917 983 1009 1038 1039 1082 1089a 1657 2126 2337
270. The Holy Spirit is Spirit also of the Son.
378 388 683 783 784a 834 872 910s 915 951 1082 1099 1459 1650 2132j 2212
271. The Holy Spirit is called *Image of the Son*.
228a 611 2078
272. The Holy Spirit proceeds from the Father through the Son *(a Patre per Filium)*.
372 479 611 878 904 907 953 1040
273. The Holy Spirit proceeds from the Father and the Son *(a Patre Filioque)*.
375? 861a 1067 1068 1086 1099 1284 1662 1678 1681 1681a 1839 2079 2269a
2269b
274. Though the Holy Spirit proceeds from the Father and the Son, He proceeds in a more preëminent way from the Father.
951 1038 1678 1681
275. The Holy Spirit is not a Son [*see also* 237].
778 983 996 1009 1681 1681a
276. Neither is the procession of the Holy Spirit a generation.
(907)? 917 983 996 1009 1068 1081 1681 1681a 2343
277. The Holy Spirit is Holiness itself.
611 914 926 941 950 983 1069 1750
278. The Holy Spirit is the Gift of God.
858 1561 1670 1678
279. The Holy Spirit is the Union in Love between the Father and the Son.
945 1099 1582 1665

RELATIONS AND APPROPRIATIONS

280. St. Augustine, with St. Cyril of Alexandria echoing him, is able to say that each individual Person of the Trinity is not something less than the Trinity Itself.
    1667 1670 2090

281. The Divine Persons are distinguished among themselves only by their relations one to another.
    867 896 907 915 926 983 990 996 1009 1039 1067 1082 1264 1459 1582 1660
    1670 1672 1748 2067 2085 2212 2343 2344 2346 2362

282. Because the Divine Persons are distinguished among themselves only by their relations one to another, they are co-equal as to perfection.
    779 899 903 910p 1582 1677 2212 2212a 2216 2261

283. Their external operations are common to the three Divine Persons [see also 467].
    235 769 779 782 834 910n 949 1037 1039 1071 1169 1186 1661 1662 2132
    2207 2212a 2250

284. Creation is a work appropriated to the Word.
    98 130 153 156 164 179 194 234 235 277 290 371 391 394 398 401 479 608
    651f 748 761 764 764a 767a 814 910a 943 949 1086 1089a 1475a 1816 2066 2207
    2352

285. Sanctification is a work appropriated to the Holy Spirit.
    371 389 449 611 810b 850 853i 907 915 948 949 950 960 1282 2063 2080
    2089 2099 2107 2109 2110 2114 2352 2353

286. The meaning of the word *through (per* or *diá):*
    943 949

THE MISSION OF THE DIVINE PERSONS

290. The Son is sent by the Father.
    182 376 394 398 1239a 1656 1682

291. The Holy Spirit is sent by the Son.
    290 871 1682 2040 2126

292. Arian doctrine in regard to the Son:
    321 608a 648 648a 648b 650 650a 651 651a 777 910h 910i 935 1659 2251

293. Sabellian doctrine:
    371 376 608a 651 768 782 910g 996 2251

THE INCARNATE WORD
TRUE DIVINITY

300. Jesus Christ and His divine mission were predicted in the Old Testament [see also 51 *and* 81]
    31 35 45 57 122 122a 127 133a 141 277 290 390 394 398 445 468a 638 664
    1470 1600

301. That Jesus Christ is true God is witnessed to by pre-Nicene Tradition.
    18 31 35 37a 42 45 52 69 81 98 101 112 113 117 131 136 137 160 189
    191 218 222 248 277 350 377 399 401 405 406 445 468a 596 617 632 634 651a
    692

302. The only Son of God is incarnate, and He is Jesus Christ [see also 80].
    43 45 62 69 (91) 98 112a 117 127 136 141 191 214 218 290 328a 371 377
    393 398 401 632 651f 788 823 875 907 910a 1089a 1518 2048 2059 2060
    2182 2383

TRUE HUMANITY

310. The Son of God took a true human nature, not merely the appearance thereof.
    39 51 62 63 63a 189 217a 343 353 357 394 405 426 445 604 680 767a 794
    817 873 876 928 1076 1083 1086 1089 1110 1160 1254 1288 1400 2184 2188 2215
    2289

311. Christ has a true body, formed of the substance of Mary.
    51 62 112 136 277 290 353 371 389 398 611ii 711 759 817 874a 875 886a
    905 995 1083 1086 1110 1245d 1479a 1518 1578 1578a 1644 2048 2059 2060 2128
    2133 2138 2170 2171 2182 2183 2184 2207 2240 2281 2364

312. Christ has a rational soul.
     394 460 461 874a 875 995 1052 1076 1083 1086 1113g 1245d 1395 1430 1517
     1818 1953 2060 2138 2149 2170 2182 2184 2207 2215 2238 2247 2289 2365
313. Since He is of the race of Adam, Christ is consubstantial *(homoousios)* with ourselves.
     217a 239 353 394 398 604 762 788 794 828 886a 890 995 1006 1052 1159b
     1167 1517 1808 2060 2123 2124 2132e 2182a 2188 2195 2199 2240 2364 2365
314. What were not assumed were not healed: whatever part of human nature the Son had not taken upon Himself would
     not have been affected by His work of salvation.
     221 794 817 827 906 928 1014 1018 1052 1055 1254 1289 1578 1818 2128 2149
     2240 2242 2249 2364

THE UNION OF NATURES, HUMAN AND DIVINE

320. The Incarnation is a mystery.
     1014 1031 1103 1160 1430 1431 1953 2048 2054 2134 2138 2171 2182 2198
     2281 2362 2371
321. The Word was not changed into nor inextricably mixed with a human nature.
     379 394 (634) 905 (1054) 1079 1086 1113k 1160 2048 2061 2124 2128 2138 2170
     2241 2312 2362 2380
322. The Word assumed a human nature, so that now He has two natures, each distinct.
     39 189 353 379 453 482 605 1006 1055 1080 1086 1113c 1113k 1160 1267
     1288 1289 2057b 2064 2071 2088 2132f 2182a 2203 2208 2215 2248 2287c 2312
     2365 2379
323. Though distinct, the two natures of the Word are in some way united.
     221 277 460 759 773 827 874 1001 1113k 1285 2060 2062 2131 2132g 2132h
     2132k 2199 2366
324. The union of the two natures in the Incarnate Word is a personal or hypostatic union.
     379 393 873 1017 1110 1113 1113j 1113k 1288 1354 1431 1518 1680 1842 1859
     1916 1953 2061 2124 2128 2132b 2132c 2132d 2132f 2132g 2132h 2132j 2132k 2132m
     2134 2170 2171 2182a 2183 2198 2238 2241 2287a 2287b 2287c 2312 2362 2368
     2379 2380 2383
326. Theodore of Mopsuestia, in regard to the hypostatic union:
     1113 1113a 1113b 1113c 1113d 1113j 1113k
327. Errors of Nestorius in regard to the hypostatic union.
     2056 2057a 2057c 2057d 2057e 2132a 2132b 2132c 2132d 2132e 2132f 2132g 2132h
     2132j 2132k 2132m 2132n 2171 2296a 2368
329. This union was made in conception and is inseparable.
     218 1017 1055 1079 1113k 1680 1842 2048 2057 2060 2133 2134 2170 2171 2208
     2210 2248 2300b 2312 2368
330. In Christ here are two wills.
     790 1074 (1113c) 1133 1309 2365 2366 2383
331. The two wills in Christ are never contrarily opposed to each other.
     790 2203 2386
332. In Christ there are two operations: one divine, the other human.
     277 379 759 771 773 794 817 1044 1080 1267 1288 1289 1354 2103 2289 2361 2362
     2365 2366 2383
333. In regard to theandric operation:
     771 1651 2279 2366
334. In Christ there is a true communication of idioms.
     460 (482) 759 771 795 830 831 874 889 1044 1055 1089 1267 1651 1859 2056 2060
     2072 2096a 2130 2132d 2132m 2132n 2170 2171 2182a 2183 2289 2296a 2312 2361 2366

CONSEQUENCES OF THE UNION OF NATURES

340. The man Jesus Christ is not the adoptive but the natural Son of God.
     788 863 1433 1777 1811 1836 1916 2049 2077 2106 2132e 2132k
341. Christ is utterly filled with grace and is holy in every respect.
     682 995 1208 1680 1836 1842 2071 2088 2368
342. The Man Christ is to be adored.
     81 762 795 827 1285 2071 2087 2132h 2363 2367
343. Christ was free of concupiscence.
     929 1953 2123 2182a 2184 2330 2386

344. Christ was free of original sin.
611ii 1089a 1808 1872 1899 1916 1929 2010 2182a 2207 2213 2247 2311 2330
345. Christ was free of personal sin.
350 357 394 482 684 929 995 1006 1087 1089a 1198 1224 1342 1406 1654
1916 2031 2132k 2182a 2213 2242 2247 2305 2365 2367 2386
346. Christ was unable to sin.
461 1089a 1721 1916 2141 2182
347. Christ had a body capable of suffering.
31 45 63 66 124 221 371 389 426 445 520 651f 772 773 828 874a 876 889
890 910a 1014 1089a 1859 2182a
348. Christ had a body subject to human infirmities.
379 771 772 817 1462
349. Christ had a body subject to human passions.
131 136 379 (426) 929 1076 1167 1267 2103 2184 2247 2249
350. Christ freely suffered and died.
830 831 889 1224 1275 1595 1654 2039 2103 2249 2305
351. Whether there was any ignorance in Christ:
204 774 992 1178 1348 1389 1410 1555 2049 2072 2238 2290 2296a 2368
352. On the beatific vision of Christ:
2238 2239

NECESSITY OF THE INCARNATION

360. If Adam had not sinned the Incarnation would not have taken place.
254 492 765 1218 1517 1929 2213 2305
·361. God could certainly have effected the redemption of the human race in some other way than through the Incarnation.
767 1577 2149 2195 2204
362. The Incarnation, therefore, is a free gift of God.
99 127 1103 1517 2289
363. Although the Incarnation is a free gift of God, there is yet a certain sense in which it may be said that the Incarnation was necessary.
31 612 751 767 822b 961 1006 1675 1915 1929 2127 2182 2204 2213 2241 2311

PURPOSE OF THE INCARNATION

370. The purpose of the Incarnation and Passion of Christ is the effecting of man's salvation.
12 26 40 45 66 74 75 99 108 112 127 131 389 405a 508 651f 771 822b 901
910a 991 1089 1089a 1245a 1254 1903a 1917 2007 2307
371. The Incarnation and Passion were not intended, however, to effect the salvation of the fallen angels.
356 1369? 1843 1917 2265 2307
372. It was intended, however, that the Incarnation and Passion should serve as a manifestation of God's love of men.
98 248 822b 1103 1589 1595
373. Christ desired to serve as an example for men, to show us how to live.
201 398 401 409a 508 632 634 669 828 910s 995 1589 1715 1929 2369
374. Christ desired to redeem us from sin and from the servitude in which we were held by the devil.
31 69 89 130 133b 221 249 370 399 405 436a 492 498 669 680 684 691 848e
889 928 1007 1014 1052 1077 1085 1103 1198 1201 1218 1252 1257 1401 1527
1655 1675 1715 2031 2063 2149 2182 2195 2369
375. Christ desired to return to men the gifts of grace and immortality.
33 127 345 634 711 751 752 767 828 829 831 1016 1159b 1818 1829a 1929 2069
376. Christ desired to lead men back to the pristine state lost through the sin of Adam.
223 255 394 399 405 563 612 703 767 829 890 928 946 998 1007 1160 1185 1777 18⁵
1857 2038 2115 2141 2188 2192 2207 2211 2242 2369 2370

THE CARRYING THROUGH OF THAT PURPOSE

380. Christ effected redemption by means of a true sacrifice.
18 33 76 80 492 498 664 669 673 751 794 910s 1201 1221 1289 1655 1915 2129
2188 2209 2270 2311
381. Christ offered that true sacrifice on the cross to God.
406 889 901 1103 2188

382. In that true sacrifice, Christ was both Priest and Victim.
    581 910s 1007 1016 1063 1221 1268 1595 1608 1745 2040 2188 2263
383. Christ effected Redemption by means of a true vicarious satisfaction.
    62 140 436a 482 552 565 664 673 691 751 767 831 906 1252 1342 1401 1675
    1903a 1916 2031 2049 2305 2311
384. The true vicarious satisfaction by which Christ effected Redemption was paid out not to the devil but to God.
    (508) (928) 1016 (1257) (1675) 2311?
385. The satisfaction which Christ made is superabundant.
    492 831 1185 2211
386. The satisfaction which Christ made is universal.
    12 224 498 (508) 664 669 751 767 906 927 998 1184 1201 1221 1252 1275 1313
    1527 2031 2149 2188
387. Christ became Mediator between God and man.
    199a 405 691 701 766 769 873 1016 1462 1500 1595 1608 1654 1766 1792 1836
    1857 1884 1891 1929 1930 2038 2182a 2184b 2188 2240 2305
388. Graces are dispensed through Christ and because of the satisfaction He made.
    7 18 61 405 1208 1274 1279 1527.
389. The graces won by Christ were dispensed even to those who found their justification in the period of the Old Law.
    45 57 61 1426 1595 1727 1857 1884 1891 2196
390. The soul of Christ descended into the lower regions.
    238 259 818 1103 1104 1369 2210 2262
391. Christ ascended into heaven in His human nature.
    191 259 371 651f 680 810a 1014 1089a 1784 2040 2211 2262 2289
392. Christ will come again to judge the living and the dead.
    31 33 101 125 191 290 328a 371 552 599a 647 651f 853c 910a 1014 1089a 2167f 2262

THE CHURCH

FOUNDATION

400. In a certain sense the Church may be said to have existed from the beginning of the world.
    82 105 435 1428 1479 1985 2295
401. Jesus Christ founded a society, with Himself its Head, which is to last forever and which is called His Church.
    20 29a 38b 105 217a 289 555-556 571 865 1479 1535
402. This Church which Jesus Christ founded serves to continue His own life on earth.
    62 256 1245d
403. In the Acts of the Apostles, St. Luke recites an authentic history of the primitive Church.
    217 268 538 1358
404. From the earliest times the Church spread thorughout the whole world [see also 85].
    6 7 11 38 77 79 81a 93 97a 112 144 144a 187 191 192 215 257 268 405 652a
405. From the earliest times and even in its initial spread the Church showed that she was a single unified body.
    43 47a 62 77 84 93 188 192 281
406. From earliest times the Church was hierarchically constituted and showed herself as such.
    9 19 20 21 25 38a 43a 44 47a 49 50 56 58a 65 413 427 438 571 599a 1205
    1357 1371

PROPERTIES AND NOTES

410. The Church is a monarchical society.
    546 546a 573 (576b) (599a) 1242 1379 2179a 2191
411. The Church is an independent society.
    759a 1311
412. The Church is a visible society.
    97a 281 1614 2018a
413. As a society the Church consists of twofold elements, visible and invisible, called body and soul.
    97a 982 1523 1523a 1714
414. On earth the Church is mixed in her membership, having both good and wicked within her fold.
    (435) 1714
415. Heretics and schismatics, in the teachings of the Fathers, are not members of the Church.
    213 237 241 257 295a 298 308 587 589 591 593 597 601c 602 602a 1371a 1478
    1492 1523 1562 1974c 1974e 2167c 2251a 2252 2275
416. There is but one true Church of Christ.
    408 435 573 589 680 1428 1479

417. Outside the one true Church of Christ there is no salvation.
    56   226   537   597a   637   1346   1428   1492   1858   2251a   2269   2273   2274   2275

418. The true Church of Christ can be recognized by certain notes.
    587   910a   1089a   1535   1580

419. Sanctity of its leadership and members belongs only to the true Church of Christ.
    226   838   1714

420. Unity of faith and government belongs only to the true Church of Christ.
    1b   6   7   56   93   188   192   213   241   257   292   293   295   296   328a   329   435   555-556   576b   58
    587   588a   589a   865   910u   997a   1239a   1242   1379   1714

421. Catholicity belongs only to the true Church of Christ.
    65   79   80a   81a   435   555-556   575   587   680   838   839   1243   1422   1548   1562   1580

422. Apostolicity belongs only to the true Church of Christ.
    80a   210   213   237   292   293   296   297   298   329   341   589   680   1242   1580

423. In any individual church these notes are discoverable through her union with the successor of Peter.
    574a   587   654a   1261

THE PRIMACY

430. Among the Apostles, Peter received from Christ the primacy of jurisdiction over the Church.
    381   387   436   479a   489   555-556   571   587   592a   693a   706   810   835a   910u   1261   1379
    1526   2178a   2179a   2191

431. Peter came to Rome and died there.
    11   106a   106b   297   341   368a   439-440   611gg   647a   651aa   651cc   651dd   652b   822c   910u   1092

432. Peter established his See at Rome, and made the Bishop of Rome his successor in the primacy.
    54   188   208   210   211   296   575   602a   651aa   702a   897   910u   1092   1242   1418   2178   2178a

433. The Roman Pontiffs have always laid claim to the primacy of jurisdiction.
    10a   21   25   27   28a   29   190a   592a   601a   601b   602a   860a   910u   2014   2015f   2018   2178a
    2179a   2184a   2186

434. From earliest times the Roman Church has been regarded as the center of unity.
    52   53   106c   107   187   210   211   575   580   1242   2015f

435. From earliest times it was acknowledged that supreme power over the whole Church belonged to the Bishop of Rome as successor of Peter.
    82a   107   (190a)   211   265   573   (592a)   (599a)   (601a)   (601b)   (602)   (602a)   702a   702b
    806a   822c   910d   1252a   1346   1346a   1507   1892   2015f   2178   2178a   2179a   2184a

436. The title Pope is of quite early origin, but was not until later restricted in usage to the Bishop of Rome.
    568a   570b   651   1343a   2178

THE EPISCOPATE

440. Bishops are not lsss than the legitimate successors of the Apostles.
    20   21   48   49   56   65   188   209   212   237   242   257   296   341   438   602   1234   1244   2332

441. Although the bishops are the successors of the Apostles, the transmission of jurisdiction was made in various ways in the primitive churches.
    9   575   588   745g   1357   1371   2164   2165

442. In regard to the College of Bishops:
    576b   588a   599b

INFALLIBILITY

450. The Church is infallible in transmitting the teachings of Christ.
    213   295   1581

451. The Roman Pontiff enjoys infallibility when he teaches *ex cathedra*.
    294   580   1507   1892   2178

452. Bishops gathered in an ecumenical council have always been acknowledged as infallible judges of the faith.
    785   792   910b   1250   1419   2141b   2141c   2184a   2185   2186   2291

CREATION
IN GENERAL

460. God created all things.
    13a   14   85   98   110   112   117   152   154   171   178   191   194   199a   205   328a   397   402

409   445   459   608   651r   681   748   814   896a   910u   1014   1089a   1147   1316   1490
1564   1596   2098   2126

461. It was out of nothing (*ex nihilo*) that God created all things.
85   111   114   129   150   171   179   194   199   275   290   323   324   325   326   327   328   363   398
445   628   687   748   750   754   761   1014   1147   1315   1316   1317   1540   1550   1564   1711
2075   2135   2145   2264   2310   2349

462. God alone can create.
178   764   764a   1702   1711   1865   2136   2356

463. God creates freely.
168   196   205   235   391   397   748   1490   1751

464. God creates in accord with divine ideas.
1553   1803

465. God creates because He is good.
168   231   462   884   1005   1751   2282   2349

466. God creates so that His perfections may be manifested and acknowledged.
7   171   179   275   643   2307

467. It is the Trinity who creates [*see also* 283].
235   1317a   1564   1662   1702   2264

468. The material world is not eternal.
154   178   179   206   207   322   391   447   454?   761   1317   1564   1747   1757   2076   2135
2264   2288

469. God is not the author of evil [*see also* 193 *and* 638].
324   398   1366   1974f

470. Some ideas of Augustine on creation and the Genesis account, and his admonitions on hermeneutics:
1541   1683   1684   1685   1686   1687   1689   1690   1692   1695   1865

ANGELS

480. There exist angels created by God.
17   63b   83   113   156   164   165   228a   320   448   643   667   1101   1239a   1315   1316   1479
1782   1805   1865   2350

481. In regard to the time of the creation of the angels:
83   156   448   1101   1316

482. The angels possess by nature a certain excellence.
18   989   1005   1148   1782   1843   2352

483. In regard to the spiritual nature of the angels:
278   354   646   667   895   950   989   1005   1026   1152   1197   1484   1522   1774   2050   2156
2303   2307   2320   2350   2351

484. Angels are not everywhere.
278   781   1070   2156   2303   2353

485. Although angels excel in knowledge they do not know the secrets of men's hearts, nor do they know future events.
2051   2303

486. The angels were created free.
63b   142   156   244   950   1755   1782   1950   2265   2325   2351

487. Angels are able to converse among themselves.
1197   2352

488. The angels are divided into various ranks or choirs.
83'   427   612   822   849   949   989   1125   1127   1148   1239a   1290a   1315   1316   1394   1805
2264   2335   2355

489. The angels are elevated to the supernatural order.
278   941   950   960   1755   2353

490. Many angels, having attained eternal blessedness, are already confirmed in goodness.
853d   989   1755   1950   1955   1971   2266   2325

491. Many angels, having fallen into grave sin, have hastened to eternal damnation.
191   356   446a   567   1708   1753   1843   1950   1955   2013   2265   2266   2307

492. The good angels are ministers of God and assist men in the business of working out their salvation.
83   89   228a   446   448   895   940   1022   1217   1239a   1387   2156   2167e   2303   2354

493. There are guardian angels assigned to individuals, nations, societies, etc.
89   430   475   895   940   1022   1387   2156   2160   2161   2354

494. The devil and the other wicked angels are able to harm men.
69   87   112a   258   278   286   446   475   751a   853h   1022   1488   2161   2167e

MAN

500. Man is composed of body and soul.
  147   159   170   1563   2061   2062   2134   2349
501. The human soul is incorporeal.
  252   346   346a   349   355   1438   1448   1700   (2050)   2357
502. The human soul is immortal.
  (132)?   (133)?   157   168   169   206   249   252   349   355   1100   1700   2357
503. In man there is but one soul only.
  170   467?   1021   1056   2357
504. In regard to the tricotomy:
  133   148   1021   1241   1563
505. Man is free [see also 613].
  123   142   156   184   244   335   446   622   667   1151   1380   2113   2265   2357
506. The human soul is created by God.
  683   1232   1385   1395   1441   1559   1700   1879   1965   2146
507. The soul is not pre-existent to the body.
  (466)   611hh   1004   1058   1395   1456   2105
508. The soul does not spring up through the procreative process.
  (446)?   875   1385   1395   1448
509. Whether God created man immediately:
  250   360   361   611hh   687   1149   1232   1315   1696   2349
510. Woman was made from man.
  1278   1543   1702   2147
511. All men have their origin in Adam and Eve.
  1278   1813   2147
512. Man is created in the image of God.
  156   159   361   746   1673   1732   1806

FIRST MAN

520. Before the fall our first parents were endowed with certain gifts of nature not owed to them: original justice, . . .
  [see also 610].
  225   253   567   612   1318   1698   2192
521. . . . immunity from concupiscence, . . .
  224   1150   1706   1952   2122   2388
522. . . . and immunity from the necessity of dying.
  184   566   749   750   883   1150   1699   1760   1928   1956   2122
523. Adam enjoyed an excellence in knowledge.
  2011   2104   2360
524. On the origin of language:
  1051   1537
525. Our first parents, prior to their sinning, enjoyed a life of the greatest happiness.
  1762   1952   2013   2122

DIVINE WATCHFULNESS

530. God preserves all things.
  171   206   207   458   563   987   1134   1688   1688a   1694   2310   2356
531. God concurs in all the actions of His creatures [see also 690].
  1403

VIRTUES

IN GENERAL

540. The concept of virtue:
  641   1904
541. There are certain infused virtues: faith, hope, and charity.
  72   1424   1425   1469   2324
542. The virtues of faith, hope, and charity are infused with first justification.
  1425   2009

543. The infused virtues of faith, hope, and charity, infused at first justification, are capable of being increased.
    955 2328
544. Furthermore, the infused virtues can be lost.
    1469
545. Faith can subsist without love.
    1469 1679
546. In heaven faith and hope will cease, but love will remain [*see also* 1041].
    1057 1799
547. In regard to the infusion of moral virtues:
    1476 1849
548. In regard to the gifts of the Holy Spirit:
    910s 1332 1337

FAITH

550. The primary object of faith is God Himself.
    923 1739
551. The object of faith embraces the mysteries which exceed human reason.
    1121 1303 1613
552. Faith is intellectual assent.
    62 417 820 1429 1980 2144
553. The intellectual assent of faith is free.
    245 417 1734 1821 2144
554. The free intellectual assent of faith is firm.
    13a 62 418 972 2055 2144
555. Faith is a supernatural act.
    418 419 1204 1486
556. In regard to the *faith of miracles*, which is a charism:
    820 1312
557. The motive of faith is not the rational evidence of the object proposed for belief.
    417 1181 1277 1826 2055 2197
558. The intrinsic motive of faith is the authority of God revealing.
    162 173 175 359a 417 562 1179 1181 1248 1303 1321 1466 2055 2143 2197
559. A sure knowledge of its having been divinely revealed is a prerequisite to faith in any proposed object.
    417 627 629 643a 1486 2144
560. Faith is more certain than any natural knowledge.
    173 417 418 846 1223 1248 1303 1593 1970 2144
561. Faith is not opposed to reason.
    173 1429 1613
562. Faith sometimes precedes reason.
    1321 1429 1486 1499 1554 1826 2111 2144
563. Faith sometimes precedes reason and elevates it to a more perfect mode of knowledge.
    418 433 1429 1486 1746 2111 2144
564. Reason is able to demonstrate the basis of faith.
    344 627 923 924 1551 1613 1980 2143
565. When reason has been illuminated by the light of faith it can perfect our knowledge of divine things.
    433 1486 1672 2111
566. Faith must be universal, extending to every revealed truth.
    298 972 1304 1598
567. There is always some obscurity about faith, precisely because it is those things which are not seen that are believed through faith.
    417 869 1057 1223 1498 1833 2318 2331
568. For those who are of sufficient intellectual maturity faith is of absolute necessity for justification and salvation.
    289 417 886a 1445 1450 1945 2260
569. In regard to the necessity of faith in Christ the Mediator:
    1857 1884

HOPE

580. The object of hope is our future blessedness.
    1057 1187
581. Most especially the object of our hope is our future possession of God Himself.
    1474 1482

582. Hope is founded in faith and for that reason is most certain.
301a 419 864 1057 1187 1223 1913
583. The principal motive of hope is the goodness of God, from whom a reward is expected.
836 1312
584. A secondary motive for hope is our own merits.
836 1312
585. To do good for the sake of the hope of reward is an honorable way of conducting oneself, since the reward hoped for is God Himself.
1025 1312 1474 1491 1933
586. For those who are of sufficient intellectual maturity hope is necessary for justification and salvation.
1292 1512

CHARITY which is LOVE

590. Charity establishes a true friendship between God and man.
26 433 1251
591. Charity is the most excellent of all the virtues.
242 419 1025 1251 1679 1799 1933 2176
592. Charity is the root and perfection of all other virtues.
433 1363 1445 1538 1798 1933 2117
593. Perfect charity is the loving of God above all else for the sake of Himself alone.
1474 1491 1528 1538 1586 1671 1763
594. Secondary to the pure love of God is the love of neighbor because of God.
1528 1583 1586 2117
595. Charity supposes faith and is founded on it.
433 1472 1503
596. The principal motive of charity is the goodness of God.
1589
597. The proof of charity is in the actions it inspires.
1848a 2333 2334
598. Charity is necessary for salvation.
1503 1583 1860a 1943

SIN

ORIGINAL SIN

610. Our first parents, having fallen into grave sin, lost their original justice [see also 520].
225 286 567 1318 1698 2013
611. Death is the effect of Adam's sin.
183 345 395 566 567 612 749 750 829 1150 1184 1245c 1325 1698 1699 1715 1760 2013 2019 2266
612. Through his sin Adam lost other free gifts.
183 225 703 1150 1727 1883 1967 2036 2122 2388
613. But in spite of his fall Adam kept free will [see also 505].
244 349 398 1022 1406 1883 2036 2038
614. The sin of Adam was passed on to all men.
224 224a 255 286 345 486 496 501 586 612 683 684 698 703 763 829 967 1077 1145a 1145b 1184 1185 1245c 1245d 1290 1306a 1341 1715 1725 1728 1791 1871 1872 1876 1877 1899 1951 1984 2007 2013 2019 2122 2123 2207
615. Original sin is transmitted by a father in the natural process of procreation.
586 1077 1290 1456 1715 1728 1870 1871 1918 1960 2007 2195
616. Original sin, as the sin of our first parents, was for them an actual and personal sin, involving free will.
1876 1877 1969 1972 2010
617. The essence of original sin, and its relationship to concupiscence:
1871 1872 1873 1887 1911 1972
618. The lot of infants who die without Baptism:
1012 1441 1456 1525 1878 1882 1901 1908 1924 1946 1997 2019
619. Errors of the Pelagians about original sin and the lot of infants who die without Baptism:
1525 1878 1967 1976 2016 2019 2025

PERSONAL or ACTUAL SIN

630. Sin is a turning away from God and a turning toward creatures.
1546 1565 1586 1605 1753 1761 1763 1904 2256
631. Sin is a negative thing rather than something positive.
1546 1549 1754
632. There are sins which are entirely internal.
119 166 239 273 352 853f 1565 1734 1885
633. Sins are distinguished as mortal and venial.
497 611s (978) 1245a 1300 1382 1536 1733 1846 1918 2233
634. There is a difference in gravity even among mortal sins.
957 1381 1442 1861 1975 2314
635. Whether numerous venial sins can coalesce into mortal sin:
1846
636. Without free consent there can be no sin.
123 244 335 1151 1406 (1454) 1549 1558 1560 1565 1718 1973 2118
637. Ignorance of gravity can be a mitigating factor in regard to the guilt of sin.
611n 611w 611x 611cc
638. God is not the author of sin, but only permits it [see also 193 and 469].
471 1263 1734 1889 2032 2118 2255 2257 2258 2326 2358
639. Sin results in the death of the soul.
184 1030 1828
640. When a sin has been committed something of the sin continues in existence even afterwards.
1873 1912

ACTUAL GRACE

NECESSITY OF GRACE

650. Grace is absolutely necessary for the performance of any good work ordered to salvation.
220 348 558 1003 1153 1219 1302 1455 1456 1569 1572 1719 1733 1791 1821
1832 1835 1855 1883 1890 1902 1903 1914 1936 1937 1938 1954 1966 2004
2200 2243 2272 2276 2359
651. Without grace man can still perform actions that are naturally commendable.
1162 1538 1733 1809 1905 2202 2244 2272
652. God never demands the impossible.
1220 1718 1720 1795
653. In what sense the acts of sinners are sins:
1450 1472 1528 1943 2037
654. In what sense the acts of infidels are sins:
1162 1463 1528 1729 1902 1903 1904 1905 2041 2042 2244 2245
655. Without grace a man cannot very long keep God's law.
1162 1719 1731 1933 1941
656. Grace is necessary even for the beginning of faith and conversion.
114 808 (892) (892a) (1155) 1165 1177 1204 (1207) (1219) 1450 1569 1571 1734
1736 1936 1940 1968 1978 1979 1980 1981 1982 1984 2004 2005 2006 2034 2045
(2052) (2053) 2163 2200 2243 2246 2278
657. Without grace a man cannot for very long resist concupiscence and grave temptation.
436 548 1191 1263 1404 1406 1592 1718 2201
658. Without a special privilege of grace no one can for very long be immune to concupiscence and entirely free even of venial sins.
981 1509 1536 1720 1722 1733 1737 1794 1801 1846 1888 1894 1918 1921 1976
2091 2201
659. Grace is still a necessity even for a man most perfectly justified.
1404a 1792 2159 2201

PERSEVERANCE

670. All the just are able to persevere if they will it.
1177 1945 1955 1956
671. Though the just can persevere if they will it, they cannot persevere for very long without the help of grace.
485 892 1153 1956

672. Final perseverance is a great gift of God.
 79a 557a 1958 1960 1992 1993 1995 1999 2002 2005 2028
673. In what final perseverance does consist:
 1947 1992 1993 1999 2002 2028

NATURE OF GRACE

680. Even if in a less proper sense, creation, free will, and the preaching of the gospel may be termed *graces*.
 114 287 1443 1556 1736 1764 2035 2043
681. Protection from sinning, along with the other external favors of providence directed toward salvation, also pertains to grace.
 59 186 1483 1504 1592
682. Grace is an internal movement.
 833 1443 1556 1736 1764 1853 2043
683. Actual grace consists both in the enlightening of the intellect . . .
 430 548 1483 1485 1720 1722 1724 1852 1853 2034 2091 2276
684. . . . and in the inspiring of the will.
 53 420 548 1159 1458 1485 1568 1572 1576 1720 1722 1724 1736 1821 1822
 1852 1853 1955 2035 2091

NOMENCLATURE

690. Grace so coöperates *(gratia coöperans)* with the human will that a man can do nothing that is good without God's doing it along with him.
 436 465 485 1003 1219 1220 1510 1515 1571 1793 1848 1854 1893 1936 1941
 1999 2235 2278 2316 2326 2385
691. This grace that assists man's salutary actions is called *helping, coöperating*, and *subsequent grace (gratia adiuvans, coöperans, seu subsequens)*.
 1793 1914 1942 2235 2278 2326
692. The grace, however, which precedes and prompts man's salutary actions is called *summoning, arousing*, and *prevenient grace (gratia vocans, exitans, seu praeveniens)*.
 1458 1556 1572 1793 1914 1938 1942 2235 2278 2316 2326
693. The assistance which grace provides is twofold: that by which something is done, and that without which it could not be done.
 1556 1850 1954 1955 1957
694. Grace was necessary to Adam, but not in the same way before his fall as afterwards.
 1949 1952 1954 1955
695. There is a kind of grace called *sufficient grace*, which truly suffices for the producing of its effect, but which does not actually produce it.
 244 247 622 1158 1159 1188 1191 1220 1753 1925 1955 1956
696. There is another kind of grace called *efficacious grace*, which effectively moves the will.
 348 558 1568 1572 1573 1707 1890 1926 1940 1958 1979 1991 1996

GRACE AND FREEDOM

700. Grace does not destroy free will.
 244 436 446 704 1034 1151 1158 1159 1165 1188 1204 1219 1436 1510 1571
 1572 1573 1710 1722 1723 1735 1736 1821 1823 1848 1854 1856 1890 1954 1955
 1961 2359
701. Because grace does not destroy free will, with equal graces one person may succeed while yet another fails.
 247 1159 1753
702. In regard to the *victrix delectatio* or triumphant delight:
 1568 1594 1722 1724 1737 1822 1823
703. God foreknows the use that free will will make of grace.
 1740 1830 1948 1985 2033
704. To some God issues His call of grace in a way that is best suited to them if they are to coöperate with His grace.
 1427 1573 1574

GRACE AS A GIFT

710. Grace can conquer all the demands of nature.
 1939 1982

711. Grace is freely given: *i.e.*, it is gratuitous.
    (808)? (1155) 1355a 1443 1451 1452 1456 1458 1473 1496 1791 1807 1837 1851 1857 1889 1974 1974a 1994a 1999 2005 2034 2044 2045 2253
712. It is proper that we pray for grace.
    507a 1355a 1724 1795 1796 1801 1821 1941 2201
713. It is possible to win the graces of conversion and final perseverance with prayers of supplication.
    699 1456 1827 1940 1993 1994 2001

DISTRIBUTION OF GRACE

720. In a mysterious but just determination God distributes His graces to men unequally.
    1456 1496 1821 1984 1995 2028 2277
721. God never abandons a man unless that man first abandons God.
    1792 1889 1954 1960 2026 2232 2255
722. Hardheartedness is never visited by God upon anyone, except as a punishment for previous sin.
    1830 1907
723. To all sinners, however hardened, sufficient grace is given for them to be converted if they would but will it.
    1220 1405 1830 2097 2232
724. To no one, not even to infidels, does God deny sufficient grace for faith and for salvation.
    12 622 1158 1313 1461 1539 1791 1968 1986 2020 2046 2047 (2277)
725. Pelagian errors on free will:
    1411 1412 1413 1414 1415 1416 1495 1856
726. Pelagian errors on the nature of grace:
    1412 1413 1443 1851 1939 2008 2020
727. Pelagian errors on the necessity of grace:
    1355 1356 1411 1413 1718 1855 1888 1891 1894 1902 1976 2019
728. Pelagian errors on the gratuity of grace:
    1450 1851 1978 1989
729. Semi-Pelagian errors:
    1978 1981 2003 2021 2022 2024 2052 2053 2278

HABITUAL GRACE

THE SUPERNATURAL ORDER

740. Among the gifts which God bestows upon creatures some are natural and some are supernatural.
    253 699 813 941 950 960 1027 1185 1318 1433 1755 2106 2115 2265 2359

JUSTIFICATION

750. In justification the permanent supernatural gift of habitual grace is infused.
    251 253 449 1145a 1282 1319 1698 1701 1715 1730 1732 2063 2080 2099
751. In justification sins are truly blotted out.
    146 407 1256 1886 1910 2009 2298
752. In justification man is renewed internally.
    32 36 219 548 607 835 1011 1144 1203 2080 2089 2106 2109 2193
753. In justification man receives within himself the indwelling Holy Spirit.
    36 158 159 219 251 449 607 683 770 780 813 853a 872 944 1071 1186 2107 2114
754. In justification man becomes a sharer of the divine nature.
    40 412 613 770 780 787 788 944 1171 1283 1468 2063 2079 2106 2107 2193
755. In justification man becomes the adoptive son of God.
    407 766 770 788 813 946 948 1145a 1171 1187 1273 1433 1468 1777 2106
756. In justification man becomes an heir of the heavenly kingdom.
    607 1145a 1187
757. In justification man becomes a friend of God.
    433 1187 1203
758. It is by faith that a man is justified.
    16 48 57 173 245 310a 428 481 910r 1024 1163 1185 1445 1450 2163 2260 2327
759. Man is not justified by works.
    16 (176) 699 2163
760. Although it is by faith and not by works that a man is justified, works too are necessary for his justification.
    15 16 428 481 564 1024 1163 1310 1362 1515 1590 1827 2167a 2233c 2327

761. Habitual or sanctifying grace is lost through mortal sin.
    158   683   770   1701   1944
762. Man can never in this life be certain of his justification.
    1374   1800   2296

MERIT

770. The just man can have true merit.
    68   123   246   311   836   889a   966   1247   1383   (1414)   1449   1452   1477   2316   2326
771. The just can merit eternal life.
    173   176   396   564   1319a   1453   1498   1502   1575   1807   1937
772. The just can merit an increase of grace.
    1446   2027   2328
773. But not even the just can merit justification itself.
    1446   1449   2027   2044
774. Among the conditions for meriting is the promise of God.
    962   1477   1511
775. Besides the promise of God and the state of grace another condition of meriting is free will.
    123   156   1380
776. Besides the promise of God and free will, another condition of meriting is the state of grace.
    1449   1575

MARY

779. Mary is truly the Mother of God, . . .
    42   223   256a   701a   711   (1113d)   1400   2059   2060   2064   2125   2241   2242   2312
780. . . . the *deipara* or *theotokos*.
    680   788   824   1017   1020a   1086   1113b   2054   2058   2060   2125   2132a   2171   2364   2371
    2371b   2378   2379   2383   2387   2390
781. Mary conceived as a virgin (*virgo ante partum*).
    42   112   122a   127   134a   141   191   222   223   224   277   328a   330   358   359   371   380   389
    394   398   408   495   633   634   711   788   817   864   874a   875   886a   910a   910s   995   1017
    1077   1086   1289   1325d   1361   1430   1518   1578a   1610   1614   1680   1808   1899   2054
    2057   2058   2060   2064   2171   2177   2182   2194   2195   2240   2241   2281   2289   2300b
    2311   2372
782. Mary was a virgin during the birth (*in partu*).
    (359)   710a   1014   1289   1327   1430   1518   1808   1975   2177   2182   2194   2241   2242   2289
    2312   2331   2372
783. Mary remained a virgin after the birth of Christ (*virgo post partum*).
    (380)   767a   1020a   1073   1089a   1111   1361   1518   1643   1974d   2048   2133   2177   2194
    2288b   2289   2372   2383   2390
784. Mary is the New Eve, the coöperatrix in the mystery of the Redemption.
    141   224   358   1578   1644
785. The holiness of Mary is entirely unique.
    (927)   1325a   1643   1794
786. Mary was conceived immaculate, *i.e.*, without original sin.
    719   1314   1794   (2242)   2336a   2336b   2336c   2389
787. The body of Mary was assumed into heaven.
    2288a   2288b   2390

SACRAMENTS

IN GENERAL

790. Sacraments are outward signs which confer the grace they signify.
    181   303   590   601b   1179   1423   1424   1432   1475   1524   1601   1647   1744   1847
791. Sacraments are physically constituted of things and words, called respectively the matter and the form.
    1062   1329   1817   1834
792. Among the sacramental rites the imposition of hands signifies in a special way the conferring of grace [*see also* 906, 958 *and* 959].
    304   362   568b   569   595   601b   611v   919   1236   1295   1359   1627   2300a
793. Even before the covenants and under the law of nature there was some remedy, instituted by God, against original sin.
    1909   2306

794. Even under the Old Law there were sacraments, but they did not confer grace of themselves.
1419   1475
795. Circumcision was a sacrament of the Old Law, prefiguring Baptism.
134   1646   1875   2306
796. The Sacraments confer grace more abundantly upon a better disposed recipient.
809   848b
797. If an obstacle is present when the Sacraments are received grace is not conferred; but when the obstacle is removed the Sacraments revivify and grace is then received.
1621   1625   1637   1638   2269   2300a
798. The Sacraments of Baptism, Confirmation and Holy Orders imprint an indelible spiritual character.
712   808   847   968   1011   1233   1240   1282   1332   1337   1620   1642   1713   1867
799. Because Baptism, Confirmation and Holy Orders confer an indelible spiritual character they are never to be repeated.
308   314   592a   593   651n   1617   1621   1623   1627   2269   2300a
800. The Sacraments confer grace from the power, present in the rite, of the Holy Spirit.
303   607   683   835   947   1242a   1282   1329   1423   1834   2110
801. Christ is the author of the Sacraments, each of which He instituted directly.
1301   1338   1419   1638   1814
802. Morally the Sacraments are actions of Christ, who makes use of the ministry of men in performing those actions.
1169   1242a   1280   1339   1638   1810
803. The validity of the Sacraments does not depend upon the faith of their minister [see also 830 and 962].
(308)   (592)   (594)   (596)   (599b)   (601a)   (601c)   (602)   (919)   1242a   (1281)   (1293)   1360   1621
1628   1858
804. The validity of the Sacraments does not depend on the probity of their minister; . . .
1169   1189   1616   1624   1635   1645   1713   1810   2300a
805. . . . but one who administers a Sacrament when he is not himself in the state of grace does so illicitly and is guilty of sacrilege.
1616   1624
806. In adult recipients of the Sacraments the intention of receiving is required for validity.
1632   1639
807. Moreover, for a licit and fruitful reception of the Sacraments on the part of an adult, certain dispositions are necessary
504   1645   1647   1737a   1862
808. The Fathers knew all of our seven Sacraments.
299   362   848a   1419   1635   1844   2100
809. In regard to the washing of feet (lotio pedum):
611y   690   1331   1336   1834
810. The Fathers are witness to the fact that there was, especially in regard to the Sacraments, a rule of secrecy (disciplina arcana or arcani disciplina), the arcane discipline.
274   394i   807   811   834a   954   1084   1166   1199   1239   1520   1815   1838   2151   2157
811. Besides the Sacraments there are certain sacred things or rites called Sacramentals, which also are of value for sanctification.
394i   1241   1536   1888   1921

BAPTISM

820. Baptism is a true Sacrament, instituted by Christ.
4   34   126   299   302   329   362   491   681   690   1242a   1244   1297   1301   1617   1647   2100
2251a
821. The Baptism of John was not a Sacrament.
305   690   1634   1810
822. The remote matter of Baptism is natural water.
4   92   126   302   303   367   394i   810a   954   1330   1395a   1817
823. The proximate matter of Baptism is the washing in water.
4   126   307   394i   810a   1395a
824. There is witness to the washing having been done by immersion, by infusion, and by aspersion.
4   34   92   304   394i   547   590   812   840a   841
825. The triple washing is not of necessity: but it is a usage of greatest antiquity.
4   367   394i   840a   947   954   1368   2292
826. In the form of Baptism it is essential that there be a distinct expression of God as Three and One [see also 234].
4   126   219   307   394i   500   597   601d   647c   651y   745d   840a   858   945   1000   1281   1330   1368
1368   1410   1638   2015c   2271   2300a
827. Baptism conferred in the name of Jesus, lacking the Trinitarian formula, is held to be invalid.
500   597   945

828. In regard to the minister of solemn Baptism:
    65 310 394i 594 601 601c 1108 1120 1236 1244 1359
829. Any man, using the requisite matter and form and having the intention of baptizing, can validly confer Baptism; but he does so licitly only when he does so in a case of necessity.
    310 366 611u 1359 1618 1628 1639
830. Even heretics can baptize validly [*see also* 803].
    (308) (591) (592a) (593) (599b) (600) (601a) 601d (602a) 647c 1360 1492 1621 1623
    1625 1626 1636 1637 1639 2014a 2015c 2251a 2269 2273
831. Baptism is necessary for all in respect to salvation, whether they be infant or adult.
    92 135a 302 306 310 (310a) 496 501 586 601? 752a 810a 811 1206 1323 1324
    1330 1439 1525 1536 1716 1717 1862 1878 1881 1882 2016 2019 2251a 2269 2271
832. In the case of adults the desire for Baptism can take the place of actual Baptism in water.
    (1012) 1328 1629 1630
833. In the case of infants or adults, martyrdom can take the place of actual Baptism in water.
    309 493 597a 598 811 1010 1139 1513 1630 1759 2269
834. A fit subject for Baptism is any person not yet baptized.
    126 201 585 1324 1862
835. The Church has always acknowledged that even infants are capable of receiving Baptism.
    201 394i 496 585 1011a 1012a 1145a 1324 1439 1440 1632 1705 1715 1725 1862
836. The effect of Baptism is spiritual regeneration, which consists in the remission of every sin with the punishment due it, and the infusion of first grace.
    34 87 92 93b 126 181 187a 220 302 304 312 362 394i 407 491 493 501 548
    594 597a 613 683 812 818e 910a 968 1011a 1012a 1089a 1145a 1240 1295 1301
    1331 1335a 1336 1395a 1404a 1536 1622 1715 1725 1726 1768 1864 1874 1918
    2121 2184b

CONFIRMATION

840. Confirmation is a true Sacrament.
    174 304 362 390 547 592 595 698 725 842 1233 1240 1244 1332 1337 1358 1647
    2015d 2100
841. The remote matter of Confirmation is blessed oil (chrism or myron).
    174 304 394i 698 841 954 1062 1240 2015d
842. The proximate matter of Confirmation is the anointing made with chrism on the forehead, in the form of a cross.
    174 299 304 394i 592 745q 842 847 954 1844 1847 2015d
843. In regard to the ordinary minister of Confirmation:
    394i 595 601c 611ee 1244 1359 2015d
844. In regard to the priest as extraordinary minister of Confirmation:
    547 592 611ee 2294
845. There is an obligation, however less strict, of receiving Confirmation.
    547 592 611ee
846. The effect of Confirmation is the more abundant pouring out of the graces and gifts of the Holy Spirit [*see also* 548].
    362 745q 841 842 842a 1240 2100

EUCHARIST

Real Presence

849. The Sacrament of the Eucharist was instituted by Christ in memory of His passion and death.
    135 708 725 1063 1192 1195 1270 1390 1519 1587 1604 1652
850. In the words recounted by John (6:48*ff*), Christ promised that He would give Himself, His own flesh and blood, in a real sense, as food and drink.
    408 491 559 870 916 1270 1365 1480 1587 1824 2116 2131 2214
851. Christ is really present in the Eucharist under the appearances of bread and wine.
    54a 56 64 128 187 187a 234 249 362 367 394i 410 490 707 708 845 846 848
    853j 870 1063 1113f 1179 1192 1194 1195 1207 1333 1334 1479a 1519 1524
    1652 1815 2151 2166 2214 2371
852. The truth of the Real Presence is evident from the words of institution.
    128 232 240 300a 689 707 843 974 1084 1113e 1113f 1179 1239a? 1340 1464 2101
    2371
853. Some Fathers occasionally referred to the Eucharist as a sign or figure of the body of Christ, . . .
    337 343 394i 504 1239a 1424 1566 2371
854. . . . and even of His Mystical Body, the Church.
    589a 1780a

855. The presence of Christ in the Eucharist does not depend upon the faith and dispositions of the recipient.
(504)? (707)? 1633 1820

856. The bread and wine, through the words of consecration, are changed into the Body and Blood of Christ.
128 249 802 840 843 844 850 1035 1062 1113e 1113n 1137 1157 1270 1333 1339 1340 1520 2101 2151 2371

857. In the Eucharist Christ is really present, but in a spiritual manner.
410 1084 1179 1334 1365 1480

858. Christ is present in the Eucharist, entirely in each of the two species.
318

859. Christ is present in the Eucharist, entirely in every particle of each of the two species.
367 490 707 853k 1035 1113h 1222

860. The matter of the Eucharist is bread and wine.
6 128 129 187 249 394i 581 582 671 707 802 840 1062 1113f 1113n 1340 1519 1524 2100

861. A small amount of water is to be added to the wine before the consecration.
128 129 240 249 410 583 1113n 1340 2371

862. The Fathers regarded the form of the Eucharist as consisting either of the words of Christ, . . .
128 1157 1207 1260 1339 1340

863. . . . or of the epiclesis; . . .
234 840 842 850 954 1113f 2151 2371

864. . . . or, less precisely, they refer to it as the *prayer* or *blessing*.
128 504 802 1035 1270 1333 1520 1652 2139

865. The Eucharist is a permanent Sacrament.
301 318 916 2139

866. The minister of the confecting of the Eucharist is a priest.
65 (366) 647e 671 1207 1260 1339 1345 1357

867. In offering the Sacrifice of the Mass the priest functions as another Christ.
584 1260

Communion

868. In regard to the minister of the distribution of the Eucharist:
128 129 394i 552a 916 1236

870. In a broad sense eating of the Eucharist is a necessity for the soul.
845a 1716 1717 1866 2016 2234

871. In the ancient Church it was generally the custom that Communion was taken under both species.
6 7 128 187 436a 552a 845 846 853l 1035 2237

872. Examples of Communion under only one species, however, are not totally lacking.
318

873. It was the practice of the early Church that the faithful received the Eucharist daily.
301 436a 559 916 1519

874. Only the baptized may receive the Eucharist.
6 128 1716

875. For a licit and fruitful reception of the Eucharist it is necessary to be in the state of grace.
7 8 368 504 551 552a 569 853m 974 1180 1532 1536 1633 1780a

876. It was the custom already in the ancient Church to fast before receiving Communion.
1420

877. The Eucharist was so instituted that it might be received in the manner of food, for the refreshment of the soul.
7 187 362 394i 408 410 436a 707 916 1113n 1166 1593 1652 2101 2131

878. Through Communion the just become, in a certain sense, concorporeal and consanguineal with Christ.
249 843 845 853e 853k 870 1035 1137 1166 1180 1194 1524 1593 1824 2116 2206

879. The Eucharist is a pledge of resurrection and of life eternal.
43 234 249 436a 559 1035 2371

880. The Eucharist both signifies and assures the unity of the Church.
6 56 848c 1166 1194 1239a 1519 1824

881. The Fathers did not countenance intercommunion.
6 2371a

The Mass

890. The Mass is a true Sacrifice.
21 232 233 320 382 552a 584 851 1019 1063 1118 1183 1192 1193 1222 1239a 1260 1424 1844 1977 2270

891. The Mass is a re-enactment of the Sacrifice of the cross.
   582   1222   1239a   1604   1745   2270   2323
892. The Sacrifice of the Mass was prefigured in the sacrifices of the Old Law.
   135   233   1193   1222   1600   1604   1744   1866   2270
893. The Sacrifice of the Mass was prefigured in a special way in the sacrifice of Melchisedech.
   581   671   1390   1977
894. The Mass was announced beforehand in the prophecy of Malachias.
   8   135   232   1977
895. Christ is the Victim offered in the sacrifice of the Mass.
   853   1118   1183   1192   1193   1222   1260   1424   2323
896. Christ Himself offers the Mass through the ministry of the priest.
   1157   1207   1260
897. The Mass is a Sacrifice offered for adoration, thanksgiving, propitiation, and supplication.
   232   367   851   853   1173   1206   1239a   1339   1516   1744   1866   1930   1977   2270   2323

Liturgy and Law

898. There were liturgical regulations even in the early Church; . . .
   19   19a   367   394e   651x   651z   671   745k   745l   745r   853k   853l   954   954a   1233
899. . . . and other regulations, seemingly arbitrary, but really prompted by prudence, in view of the necessities of good order.
   611o   611p   611z   647b   647f   647i   651g   651h   651i   651j   651k   651l   651m   651o   651u   651v
   651w   702a   745m   745n   745o   745p   910c   910d   910j   1419a   2015a   2233b

PENANCE

900. The Church has received from Christ the power of remitting or of refusing to remit sins.
   387   584a   602   611e   611f   611i   637   855a   1113p   1119   1234   1244   1287   1293   1297   1345
   1386   1480a   1526   1579   2121   2184b   2251b   2332
901. This power extends to all and every sin committed after Baptism.
   59   385   (386)   561   577   578   1245   1294   1298   1501   1532   1533   1874   1919   2252
902. Adultery, murder, and apostasy or heresy were regarded as more grave than other sins.
   81c   93a   383   385   568   576a   576b   611k   611q   611bb   611cc   611dd   919e   919i   1245a   1501
   1532   1536   2015   2184b
903. In regard to blasphemy against the Holy Spirit:
   1174   1444   1501   2321
904. In the ancient Church public penance was imposed for the more grievous public crimes.
   315   385   568   568b   569   578   611a   611l   611m   651q   651r   651s   651t   745b   922a   1434
   1435   1532   1536   2233   2233a
905. Less grave sins were remitted without public penance.
   485a   497
906. Reconciliation was made through the imposition of hands, ordinarily administered by the bishop.
   386   568b   569   570   611s   647c   651n   745c   752a   1435   1864
907. There are indications that forgiveness through public penitential acts was granted only once to any one penitent; . . .
   81b   86   87   314   315   386a   497   611r   1300   1435
908. . . . but there are indications also, and even clear statements, that the private reception of sacramental forgiveness was repeatable.
   314   317   485e   497   561   637   685   1230   2165b
909. In regard to private absolution, granted in the imminent danger of death:
   570   576   651s   752a
910. Repentance is a true virtue, by which a man detests and grieves for his sin, and intends to repair what was, in a certain sense, an injury done to God.
   27   86a   315   1494   2233b   2336
911. Repentance is necessary in order to obtain forgiveness of sins.
   90   103   315   386   611n   1132   1310   1480a   1919   2332
912. Contrition, which is sorrow for sin motivated by perfect charity, always and immediately by its very nature justifies.
   26   434   493   1846   2176
913. Contrition is able even to take away entirely the punishment due sin.
   1305
914. Attrition, which is sorrow for sin motivated by the fear of punishment, is a good act and suffices, in respect to sorrow, for the obtaining of absolution.
   434   1025   1143   1487   1514
915. For attrition to suffice for the receiving of absolution, it is necessary that a purpose of amendment accompany it.
   1797   1885

916. Some kind of confession, not made to God only, but external, is required for the remission of sins.
    3   8   26a   37   192b   193   315   316   477   485a   493   551   569   570   685   1164   1245a   1298
    1299   1375   1480a   1846   2121   2184b   2189a

917. Some passages in Chrysostom, however, are interpreted by some as indicating that Chrysostom did not require confession to a priest; and there are passages in Socrates and Sozomen that indicate that for a time the practice of confession to a priest was abandoned in some places.
    1131   1132   1136   1145   1164   1196   2165a   2165b

918. For absolution there is required a distinct accusation of sins.
    485a   494   553   1245b   1259   1386   2189a   2332

919. A declaration of sins joined to penance:
    485a   493   1136   1259   1494   2189a

920. Confession was made privately to a priest.
    485a   493   553   685   975   977   1113p   1132   1136   1259   1375   1386   2189a   2233a

921. With confession made privately, the priest was obligated not to make public knowledge the sins confessed.
    685   1113p   1132   2023   2189a

922. Even when guilt is taken away the whole temporal punishment due to sin is not always taken away.
    1845   2309

923. There remains after absolution the necessity of making the satisfaction demanded by God's justice.
    313   315   584a   1305   1434   1494

924. The form of absolution in the ancient Church seems to have been deprecative.
    1287   1627   2184b

925. The minister of the Sacrament of Penance is a priest only; . . .
    73?   315   394a   551   553   578   975   977   1119   1120   1244   1293   1294   1295   1297
    1386   2184b

926. . . . but a deacon might, in case of necessity, be the minister of reconciliation, . . .
    611s

927. . . . and Cyprian of Carthage seems to have allowed in such cases that confession even might be made to a deacon, but whether or not with absolution given by the deacon is not clear.
    570

928. Penance is necessary for all who have fallen into grave sin after Baptism [*see also* 911].
    314   561   1095   1536   1864

929. Venial sins can be remitted by charity, by prayer, and by good works.
    493   563   564   707   1113m   1536   1781   1888   1921   2233

930. Venial sins can be forgiven also in the fruitful reception of the Eucharist.
    1113m

931. Sins forgiven never revive.
    1256   (1622)

Indulgences

935. Something of the canonical penance could be remitted through the intercession of the martyrs.
    387a   570

936. There exists in the Church a treasury of merits from which indulgences can be applied to sinners in respect to the punishments due their sins.
    552   1296

SACRAMENT OF THE ILL

940. Extreme Unction, the Sacrament of the Ill, is a true Sacrament, the effect of which is to blot out the remains of sin and to strengthen both soul and body.
    493   698   1120   1241   1295   2015e   2092   2234

HOLY ORDERS

950. Orders is a true Sacrament.
    919   1062   1617   1642   2190

951. In the Church the clergy constitute a rank distinct from the laity.
    11   48   49   50   300   366   438   477a   611aa   651g   745h   753   919   919b   1062   1236   1345
    1350a

952. Episcopate, priesthood, and diaconate constitute the major orders.
    43a   44   47a   49   50   58a   70a   394c   413   427   546a   611j   611k   745m   1205   1236   1350

953. Bishops are constituted in an order superior to that of priests.
    19   43b   394c   546c   1108   1205   1236   1238   1357?   1359   (1371)   1394   2164   2165

954. Deacons are the helpers of bishops and priests in the sacred functions.
9   19   20   43a   48   84   128   294c   546a   1231   1236   1357
955. Subdeacons were the helpers of deacons; and they were constituted in a rank established by the Church.
70a   394h   546a   745j   745m   1236
956. Besides subdiaconate there were other orders also, called minor orders.
70a   300   394g   546a   570a   745i   745m   1236
957. In the ancient Church women were able to be consecrated to God in a special way as deaconesses or widows; but they received no order in the proper sense, and were not ordained.
70a   300   394f   413   477a   546a   651y   745f   1112   1231   1236   1265b
958. The matter of Orders is the imposition of hands.
394a   394d   588   1108   1205   2179
959. The form of Orders is the prayer which is conjoined to the imposition of hands.
394a   394b   394c
960. The minister of Orders is the bishop only.
394a   394b   394c   601c   753   910e   1108   1234   1236   1237   1357
961. The minister of episcopal consecration is a bishop, and from earliest times three bishops were regularly required.
394a   651j   1205   1235   1237
962. Even heretics can validly ordain; . . .
(592)   651n   (919)   1360
963. . . . but valid Baptism is a necessary prerequisite to a valid reception of Orders.
651y
964. In the Church it was already the custom in antiquity to impose celibacy on clerics in major orders or at least to prohibit their marrying a second time.
299   366   381   611t   647g   919d   919h   1096   1350   2188a   2293   2319
965. The effects of the reception of Orders are the augmenting of grace, the imprinting of a character, and the conferring of spiritual power.
237   394a   1062   1119   1120   1236
966. The Church can establish impediments to the reception of the Sacrament of Orders.
651g   651h   651o   651p

MATRIMONY

968. The ends of Matrimony are the begetting of offspring, the mutual help of the spouses, and the providing of a remedy against concupiscence.
433a   507   818c   818d   1094   1253   1640   1642   1867   1869   2233
969. From earliest times the Church has regarded abortion as a most grievous crime, . . .
1a   396a   919a   919f
970. . . . and contraception, too, as a grievous sin against the ends of marriage.
396a
972. Christian marriage is a true Sacrament.
67   320   384   420a   420b   505   1094   1176   1245d   1249   1253   1342a   1640   1812   1867   1876   2108   2155   2374
973. Marriage is perfected by the mutual consent of the spouses. There was, therefore, a true marriage between Mary and Joseph.
1326   1361   1610   1868
974. Matrimony effects a bond which is completely indissoluble.
86   119   320   420   506   507   611b   611d   642   854   919g   921b   921c   922   1002   1308   1322   1341a   1351   1352   1388   1861   1863   1864   1867   2015   2017   2155   2297
975. The indissoluble bond of Matrimony cannot be broken, not even on account of adultery on the part of one of the spouses.
86   (342)   507   611c   642   854   921a   921c   922   (1341a)   1351   1436a   1737a   1861   1863   1869
976. The Pauline Privilege case:
506?   611d   1190   1307   1341b   1436a
977. The Sacrament of Matrimony effects an exclusive bond.
167   186   271   281a   1097   1176   1322   2017
978. Polygamy was tolerated, however, in the earlier Old Testament history.
1641   1867   2155
979. In regard to second marriages:
88   119   167   366   382   477a   506   611u   651n   745a   818d   919c   1097   1325b   1349   1354a   1354b   1378a   1579   1790
980. The Church is competent to establish matrimonial impediments.
320   384   611g   611h   611i   647d   647h   745e   918   919d   1307
981. The Church establishes matrimonial impediments apart from any consideration of civil law.
1308   1352   1867

982. A vow of chastity is an impediment to subsequent marriage.
     568   1115   1378   1789   2015
983. Matrimony is good and lawful, a holy estate; . . .
     818c   1077   1115   1116   1253   1349   1361   1378   1789   1812   1876   1974b   1974c   2155   2374
984. . . . but it is surpassed in dignity by celibacy and virginity.
     67   433a   516a   818c   1020a   1077   1116   1253   1325c   1327a   1349   1361a   1379   1789   1975
     2167b   2374

ESCHATOLOGY

DEATH

990. Death is the separation of the soul from the body.
     252   345   349a   683   1030   1031   1772
991. After death there is no longer any possibility of meriting or demeriting.
     103   560   561   576   578   693   886   887   966   980   1138   1172   1200   1325   1364   1934a
     2268   2321

PARTICULAR JUDGMENT

995. The soul undergoes the particular judgment as soon as it leaves the body.
     (646)   886   956   1200   1880
996. Even before the general judgment souls are already in blessedness or in torment.
     132   (259)?   (351)?   352   446   (646)   721   886   887   1109   1829   1930   1971   (2140)   2234a
     2320

PURGATORY

1000. A place of purgation exists where those souls of whom further expiation is required undergo temporary punishment.
     352   646?   956   1013?   1061   1467   1544   1737a   1776   1780   1920   1930   2233   2321
1001. The souls of the dead detained in purgatory can be aided by the suffrages of the living.
     187   187a   367   382   852   853   1109   1206   1239a   1513   1516   1780   1930   1934
1002. Purgatory will not continue beyond the day of general judgment.
     1776   1778

END OF THE WORLD

1010. Various signs will precede the end of the world.
     10   832   832a   1771
1011. The dead will rise, . . .
     10   13   13a   51   54   74   112   147   155   157   169   173   190a   249   250   252   272   276
     301a   328a   345   363   364   446   680   681   687   721   836   872   910a   1064   1065   1089a
     1100   1232   1276   1522   1768   1785   2153   2167f   2375   2376
1012. . . . not the just dead only, but all the dead.
     (63)?   (64)?   124   191   290   365   395   646   647   694   837   1232   1829   1922   1922a   2019
     2112   2267   2390
1013. The dead will rise in their same bodies.
     104   120   155   345   365   395   446   468   686   836   837   885   1088   1522   1785   1880
     1923   2375
1014. Origenism, in regard to the final apokatastasis:
     456   457   463   464   467a   468   1013   1033   1353   1373   1384   1402
1015. Origenism, in regard to spiritual fire:
     463   464   1013   1306   1370
1016. Millenarianism or chiliasm was admitted by some Fathers, . . .
     138a   260   261   338   447?   647   658   1407   1521   1769
1017. . . . but was rejected by others.
     138a   263?   658   1769   2154

GENERAL JUDGMENT

1020. After the end of the world there will take place the general judgment.
     74   155   364   396   579   694   1172   1456   1768   1880   2140   2376

HELL AND PUNISHMENT

1030. Those who die in mortal sin are thrust into hell.
    41   317   579   980   1206   2233   2321a

1031. In hell, besides the pain of sense through true corporeal fire, there is also the pain of loss, in the deprivation of God.
    1772   1932   2266

1032. In hell, besides the pain of loss in the deprivation of God, there is also the pain of sense, through true corporeal fire.
    41   78   98a   100   106   115   121   124   166   176   273   276   284   317   346   396   437   560
    646   837   958   1013   1036   1065   1138   1258   1370   1774   2167e   2320

1033. The fire of hell torments both the souls of the damned and the demons.
    124   356   579   646   1013   1370   1402   1525   1774   2266   2320

1034. The punishment of the damned is eternal.
    41   78   100   102   106   115   121   124   176   191   239   273   276   284   290   317   396
    437   446   560   579   646   837   976   1013   1060   1384   (1402)   1525   1772   1775   1779
    1802   1931   1932   2267   2317   2322   2376

1035. Although it is eternal, the punishment of the damned is not of equal severity for all.
    697   976   1778   1860a   1924   1931   2167e   2322

1036. In regard to the mitigation of punishment:
    273   396   560   1036   1932

1037. The notion of limbo reprobated as being of Pelagian origin:
    1878   1976

HEAVEN AND BLESSEDNESS

1040. The object of blessedness is God only.
    53a   1591   1743   1749   1788

1041. Perfect blessedness in heaven consists in seeing and loving God.
    236   301a   579   891   1552   1753   1786   1788   1971   2376

1042. The blessed are not able any more to sin.
    693   1802   1931   1956   2012

1043. Blessedness is eternal and cannot be lost.
    102   176   191   239   276   284   290   396   468   579   693   910a   976   1089a   1552   1674
    1749   1756   1779   1788   1802   1931   1950   2154

1044. The bodies of the blessed will be glorious and immortal.
    166   338   395   468   837   883   885   1520a   1522   1698   1760a   1785   1788   2267

1045. In regard to accidental blessedness:
    78   176   579

1046. There will be various degrees of blessedness, in respect to merits.
    696   1383   1502   1831   1931   2308

GENERAL INDEX

Numbers **1**, **2**, or **3** in boldface refer to the volume of *The Faith of the Early Fathers*; numbers in ordinary face are page references. Numbers followed by an *n* refer to footnotes on the page indicated by the number. Numbers preceded by *DI* are references to propositions so numbered in the Doctrinal Index, which immediately precedes this General Index. Roman numerals following a name (as in Innocent XIII) and the words *a*, *an*, and *the* are ignored in the alphabetic arrangement of this index.

_____ Commentaries on Isaias, introd., **2**: 207–208; texts, **2**: 208–209; notes, **2**: 209

_____ Commentaries on Jeremias, introd., **2**: 212; texts, **2**: 212–213; notes, **2**: 213

_____ Commentaries on Joel, **2**: 197, 205

_____ Commentaries on Jonas, **2**: 205; introd., **2**: 200; texts, **2**: 200–201; notes, **2**: 201

_____ Commentaries on Micheas, **2**: 197, 200, 205; introd., **2**: 197; texts, **2**: 197; notes, **2**: 197

_____ Commentaries on Nahum, **2**: 197, 200, 205

_____ Commentaries on Osee, **2**: 197, 205

_____ Commentaries on Sophonias, **2**: 197, 200, 205

_____ Commentaries on Zacharias, introd., **2**: 205; texts, **2**: 206; notes, **2**: 206

_____ Commentary (-ies) on Ecclesiastes, **2**: 186; introd., **2**: 196; texts, **2**: 196–197; notes, **2**: 197

_____ De viris illustribus, **1**: 392; **2**: 67, 141

_____ Dialogues against the Pelagians, **2**: 216; introd., **2**: 209–210; texts, **2**: 210–212; notes, **2**: 212

_____ Dialogue between a Luciferian and an Orthodox Christian, introd., **2**: 189; texts, **2**: 189–190; notes, **2**: 190

_____ The Galeatic or Helmeted Prologue, introd., **2**: 206–207; texts, **2**: 207; notes, **2**: 207

_____ Homilies on the Canticle of Canticles, translation of Origen's work, **2**: 186, 188n

_____ Letters, introd., **2**: 183; texts, **2**: 183–188; notes, **2**: 188

_____ Letter to Ageruchia (no. 123), texts, **2**: 186–187

_____ Letter to Amandus (no. 55), texts, **2**: 185

_____ Letter to Ctesiphon (no. 133), **2**: 217; texts, **2**: 187

_____ Letter to Damasus (no. 18), **2**: 208; (see also below, Letter(s) to Pope Damasus)

_____ Letter to Demetrias (no. 130), **2**: 210, 214

_____ Letter to Evangelus (no. 146), **2**: 188n; texts, **2**: 187–188

_____ Letter to Hedibia (no. 120), texts, **2**: 186

_____ Letter to Heliodorus (no. 14), texts, **2**: 183

_____ Letter to Marcella (no. 27), texts, **2**: 184

_____ Letter to Nepotian (no. 52), texts, **2**: 185

_____ Letter to Oceanus (no. 77), texts, **2**: 185

_____ Letter to Pammachius (no. 48), texts, **2**: 184–185

_____ Letter to Pammachius and Oceanus (no. 84), texts, **2**: 186

_____ Letter to Pope Damasus (no. 15), texts, **2**: 184–185

_____ Letter to Pope Damasus (no. 16), texts, **2**: 184

_____ Letter to Pope Damasus (no. 18), **2**: 208

_____ Letter to Pope Damasus (no. 36), texts, **2**: 184

_____ Letter to Rufinus, **2**: 179

_____ Letter to Rusticus (no. 125), **2**: 180

_____ Preface to the Three Solomonic Books, introd., **2**: 195; texts, **2**: 195; notes, **2**: 195

_____ Short Commentaries on the Psalms and Treatises or Homilies on the Psalms, introd., **2**: 203–204; texts, **2**: 204; notes, **2**: 204

_____ Treatises or Homilies on the Gospel of Mark, introd., **2**: 213; texts, **2**: 214; notes, **2**: 214

Jerusalem, **1**: 59, 61, 65, 133, 139, 152, 189, 275, 284, 297n, 292, 347, 398; **2**: 1, 182, 201, 206, 212; **3**: 168, 249, 268, 294, 306, 307, 330; synod of J. in 415 A.D., **2**: 209; **3**: 185

Jesus, son of Nave (= Josue, son of Nun), **1**: 15, 61, 63n, 81, 318, 342, 352, 383, 406; **2**: 181, 207; **3**: 53, 180, 340

Jesus, son of (or grandson of) Sirach, **1**: 342n; **2**: 42n, 131, 181, 195, 207; **3**: 52, 54n, 341

Jesus Christ; (see Incarnate Word)

Jews, **1**: 184, 351, 357, 404; **2**: 104, 212; **3**: 17, 33, 35, 114, 117, 168, 171, 205, 247, 284, 289, 327–328

Joannou, P., **2**: 41

Job, **2**: 97; **3**: 22, 92, 93, 313, 314

John, Apostle and Evangelist, **1**: 17, 28, 38, 39n, 76, 82, 91, 102, 106, 107, 122, 124n, 140, 187, 188, 210, 214, 237, 292, 300, 406; **2**: 108, 199; **3**: 103, 107, 111, 119, 143, 180, 181, 211, 221, 222, 226, 323; author of Apocalypse, **1**: 144; (see also in Scripture Index)

John, an archimandrite, **3**: 299

John III, Pope, **3**: 257

John the Baptist, **1**: 122, 127, 129n, 206, 304, 350; **2**: 85, 109n, 134; **3**: 50, 68, 116

John bar Caldun, **2**: 1

John Cassian, abbot, **1**: 372, 373; **2**: 1; **3**: 192, 197; sketch, **3**: 197–198

_____ Conferences, **3**: 192; introd., **3**: 198–199; texts, **3**: 199; notes, **3**: 199–200

_____ De institutis coenobiorum, **3**: 198

_____ The Incarnation of the Lord, a Treatise on Nestorius, **1**: 372; **3**: 198; introd., **3**: 200; texts, **3**: 200–201; notes, **3**: 201

John Chrysorrhoas = John of Damascus = John Mansur = John Mamzer = John Damascene (q. v.)

John Chrysostom, bishop, **1**: 319n; **2**: 3, 67, 77, 213; **3**: 24, 144, 147n, 198, 203, 205, 240, 250, 254, 266, 349; sketch, **2**: 84–86

_____ Baptismal Catecheses, introd., **2**: 99; texts, **2**: 99–101; notes, **2**: 101

_____ Commentary on the Epistle to the Galatians, introd., **2**: 119; texts, **2**: 119; notes, **2**: 119

_____ Explanations of the Psalms, introd., **2**: 123; texts, **2**: 123; notes, **2**: 123

_____ Homilies in Praise of St. Paul, **2**: 97

_____ Homilies on the Acts of the Apostles, **2**: 104

_____ Homilies on the Anomoians and on the Consubstantiality of the Father and the Son, introd., **2**: 95; texts, **2**: 95–96; notes, **2**: 96

_____ Homilies on the Anomoians and on the Incomprehensible Nature of God, **2**: 95; introd., **2**: 90–91; texts, **2**: 91–93; notes, **2**: 93–94

_____ Homilies on the Beginning of the Acts of the Apostles, introd., **2**: 104; texts, **2**: 104

_____ Homilies on the Changing of Names, **2**: 104

_____ Homilies on David and Saul, **2**: 101

_____ Homilies on the Devil, introd., **2**: 88; texts, **2**: 88; notes, **2**: 88

_____ Homilies on the Epistle to the Ephesians, introd., **2**: 120; texts, **2**: 120; notes, **2**: 121

_____ Homilies on the Epistle to the Hebrews, introd., **2**: 124; texts, **2**: 124–126; notes, **2**: 126

_____ Homilies on the Epistle to the Philippians, introd., **2**: 121; texts, **2**: 121–122; notes, **2**: 122

_____ Homilies on the Epistle to the Romans, introd., **2**: 113; texts, **2**: 114–115; notes, **2**: 115–116

_____ Homilies on the First Epistle to the Corinthians, **2**: 87, 119; introd., **2**: 116; texts, **2**: 116–119; notes, **2**: 119

Paul, Abbâ, **3**: 257
Paul, Apostle, **1**: 6, 7, 8, 14, 22, 29, 44, 45, 89, 90, 91, 98,
  100, 107, 122, 127, 137, 138*n*, 140, 141, 142*n*,
  152, 159, 165, 209, 210, 221, 259, 272, 291,
  292, 346, 354, 360, 362, 406; **2**: 45, 54, 62, 72,
  78, 87, 88, 91, 93, 97, 104, 114, 116*n*, 118, 120,
  121, 122, 122*n*, 124, 125, 177, 185, 187, 194,
  199; **3**: 2, 10, 13, 14*n*, 28, 31, 47, 48, 52, 58, 68,
  73, 74, 90, 93, 94, 97, 108, 114, 117, 121, 130,
  131, 133, 135, 139, 149, 152, 153, 155, 169,
  171, 174, 188, 199, 200*n*, 201, 211, 215, 236,
  247, 249, 253, 271, 283, 284, 289, 292, 293,
  296, 299, 300, 301, 310, 311, 319, 329, 341; (*see
  also in Scripture Index at his Epistles*)
Paul, a bishop, correspondent of Augustine, **3**: 112
Paul of Samosata, **1**: 289*n*; **3**: 202
Paula, friend of Jerome, **2**: 182, 191, 196
Pauli, Johannes, **1**: 306*n*
Pauli, Sebastian, **3**: 266
Paulianists, **1**: 286, 289*n*; **3**: 180
Paulicianists, an Eastern dualist sect in the 7th cent., **3**: 346
Paulina, friend of Jerome, **2**: 182
Pauline Privilege, *DI* 976
Paulinian, brother of Jerome, **2**: 201
Paulinus of Antioch = Paulinus of Tyre (early 4th cent.), **1**:
  394
Paulinus of Antioch, bishop (late 4th cent.), **1**: 402; **2**: 182,
  184, 188*n*, 189
Paulinus of Milan, deacon, secretary to Ambrose, **2**: 146; **3**:
  188; *sketch*, **3**: 187
————— *Libellus adversus Caelestium Zosimo papae ob-
  latus*, **3**: 187
————— *Life of Ambrose*, **2**: 146; *introd.*, **3**: 187; *texts*, **3**:
  188; *notes*, **3**: 18b
Paulinus of Nola, bishop, **2**: 206, 214; **3**: 10, 154
Paulinus of Tyre = Paulinus of Antioch (*q. v.*)
Paulus Orosius, disciple of Augustine, **3**: 114; *sketch*, **3**: 185
————— *Apology*, **3**: 114; *introd.*, **3**: 185; *texts*, **3**: 186
————— *Commonitorium de errore Priscillianistarum et
  Origenistarum*, **3**: 185
————— *Historiarum adversum paganos libri septem*, **3**:
  185
Payne Smith, R., **3**: 220
Pectorius, Epitaph of, **1**: 78–79; *introd.*, **1**: 78–79; *text*, **1**: 79;
  notes, **1**: 79
Pelagia, a martyr, **2**: 97
Pelagianism, Pelagians, **2**: 88, 101*n*, 113, 183, 209–210,
  212, 214, 217; **3**: 14*n*, 25, 28, 32, 38, 38*n*, 94,
  110, 113, 127, 128, 134, 138, 139*n*, 139–140,
  141, 145, 153*n*, 154, 163, 164, 167, 168, 171,
  176, 184, 188, 189, 194, 198, 200, 200*n*, 203,
  237; *DI* 619, 725–729
Pelagius, archheretic, **2**: 183, 187, 209, 210, 217; **3**: 9, 38,
  39, 90, 111, 112*n*, 126, 127, 128, 134, 165, 169,
  179, 184, 185, 186, 262; *sketch*, **2**: 214
————— *Commentaries on the Pauline Epistles*, **2**: 191; **3**:
  90
————— *Free Will (De libero arbitrio)*, **3**: 128; *introd.*, **2**:
  215–216; *texts*, **2**: 216; *notes*, **2**: 216
————— *Letter to Demetrias*, *introd.*, **2**: 214; *texts*, **2**: 215;
  notes, **2**: 215
————— *On Nature (De natura)*, **3**: 110, 112*n*
————— *Fragments*, *introd.*, **2**: 216; *texts*, **2**: 216
Pelagius I, Pope, **3**: 257

Pelagius II, Pope, **3**: 308
Pellegrino, M., **1**: 69, 71
Penance, Sacrament of, *DI* 900–931
Penance, (*see under* Ambrose)
Penance, (*see under* Peter of Alexandria)
Penitents, class of, **1**: 252, 285, 288*n*, 316, 318*n*
Pentapolis, **1**: 278, 283, 287*n*
Pentecost, **1**: 151, 286, 289*n*, 381*n*
Peregrinus = Vincent of Lerins (*q. v.*)
The Perfection of Man's Righteousness, (*see under* Augus-
  tine)
Peri archon, (*see under* Origen, *The Fundamental Doctrines*)
Peripatetic(s), **1**: 50
Perpetua, martyr, **1**: 144
Persia, **2**: 134; **3**: 201, 202
Persian language, **1**: 33
Persians, **1**: 296, 307
Peter, Abbâ, **3**: 260
Peter, Apostle, **1**: ix, 6, 7, 17, 22, 24, 38, 39, 44, 45, 73, 89,
  90, 107, 122, 140, 152, 158, 160, 187, 188, 202,
  205, 210, 220–221, 229, 230, 232, 237, 245, 259,
  272, 291, 292, 305, 308, 311, 346, 348, 354,
  358, 361, 362, 390, 406, 407; **2**: 72, 87, 104, 122,
  140, 141*n*, 150, 156, 164, 165, 174, 181, 183,
  194, 199; **3**: 2, 14*n*, 26, 32, 51, 58, 156, 166,
  180, 181, 268, 269, 275, 310, 311, 313*n*;
  pseudepigrapha appropriated to P., **1**: 293; **2**: 181,
  181*n*; (*see also in Scripture Index*)
Peter, deacon, friend of Gregory I the Great, character in
  latter's *Dialogues*, **3**: 319–320
Peter, layman, correspondent of Fulgence of Ruspe, **3**: 294–
  295
Peter, priest of Spain, **3**: 138
Peter, subdeacon in Sicily, **3**: 309
Peter Chrysologus, bishop, *sketch*, **3**: 266
————— *Letter to Eutyches*, *introd.*, **3**: 267; *texts*, **3**: 268;
  notes, **3**: 268
————— *Sermons*, *introd.*, **3**: 266; *texts*, **3**: 267; *notes*, **3**:
  267
Peter Fullo (= the Fuller), bishop, **3**: 268, 300
Peter the Iberian, **3**: 300
Peter Lombard, **3**: 153*n*
Peter Mongo (= the Stammerer), bishop, **3**: 268
Peter of Alexandria, *bishop*, **1**: 275; *sketch*, **1**: 259
————— *The Paschal Feast*, **1**: 259
————— *Penance* or *The Canonical Letter*, *introd.*, **1**: 259;
  texts, **1**: 259
————— *The Soul*, *introd.*, **1**: 259; *texts*, **1**: 259–260
Peter of Damascus, bishop, **3**: 344, 345
Peter of Sebaste, bishop, **2**: 3, 10*n*, 44
Petilian of Cirta, Donatist, **3**: 72
Petschenig, M., **2**: 165; **3**: 65, 72, 89, 130, 199, 200, 281
Pfättisch, J. M., **1**: 50
Pfaff Fragments, **1**: 105
Phaedo, of Plato, **1**: 56*n*, 367*n*
Pharao, at the Exodus, **1**: 328; **2**: 150
Pharisees, **2**: 199; **3**: 72, 124*n*
Philip, Apostle, **1**: 82, 158*n*; **2**: 139; **3**: 23
Philip, deacon in N. T., **3**: 166
Philip, papal legate, **3**: 237
Philippi, **1**: 69, 122, 260; **2**: 194
Philippicus Bardanes, Emperor, **3**: 326
Philippopolis = Plovdiv, **1**: 307
Philocalia, **1**: 200, 203, 209